Understanding Intelligence

Understanding Intelligence

Rolf Pfeifer and Christian Scheier

with figures by Alex Riegler and cartoons by Isabelle Follath

The MIT Press
Cambridge, Massachusetts
London, England

This book was set in Melior and Helvetica by Asco Typesetters, Hong Kong.

Printed and bound in the United States of America.

Library of Congress Cataloging-in-Publication Data

Pfeifer, Rolf, 1947–
  Understanding intelligence / Rolf Pfeifer and Christian Scheier; with figures by Alex Riegler and cartoons by Isabelle Follath.
    p. cm.
  Includes bibliographical references and index.
  ISBN 0-262-16181-8 (hc : alk. paper)
  1. Artificial intelligence. 2. Cognitive science. 3. Expert systems (Computer science)
I. Scheier, Christian. II. Title.
  Q335.P46 1999
  006.3–dc21
                                                                      98-49138
                                                                          CIP

To Beatrice, Serge, and Mischa (R. P.)
To Frank, Lydia, and Walter (C. S.)

Contents

Preface

Intelligence is natural to all of us. We use it with great ease: We can recognize the people around us, walk, read a paper, drive a car and at the same time listen to a silly joke, laugh, go to work, stop at the newsstand to buy a newspaper, count the change, write a memo, order a computer, make a phone call, plan a dinner at a restaurant, play a game of chess, and watch a science fiction movie on TV in the evening. This makes us wonder how all that is possible. How can the mind or the brain manage to make this work? Philosophers for thousands of years have tried their luck on this question with mixed success.

When the digital computer was invented more than half a century ago, many felt that the essence of thinking, the core of intelligence, had been found: not the IQ—computers. Computers were called "electronic brains" in the early days. Soon everybody thought that it was possible to reproduce intelligence with computers. An exciting new methodology emerged: computer simulation. All of a sudden, it became possible to simulate thinking, problem solving, even natural language: Artificial intelligence was born. The human mind was viewed as a computer. Although computers have clearly been one of the biggest technological successes in the history of mankind, at closer inspection they have not fulfilled the expectations of producing intelligence, at least as we normally understand it. Rather than helping clarify the problems involved, computers in fact created considerable confusion. In 1997, when Garry Kasparov played against Deep Blue, IBM's famous chess computer, it became clear that computers could play world champion–level chess. But it is also became clear that this did not imply that Deep Blue was particularly intelligent. Searching many positions does not require much intelligence.

The trouble with computer intelligence became obvious as researchers and engineers were trying to build machines for more commonplace activities like identifying faces in crowds, walking, performing household chores, and talking in natural ways. As it turned out, what is easy for people—recognizing a friend, reading, drinking from a coffee cup, folding a newspaper, preparing a meal—was extremely hard for machines, and what is often hard for people—things like logic, solving puzzles, and playing chess—is easy for computers. The idea that once we have programs that can solve problems and prove theorems, we can simply add a camera and an arm and we have an intelligent robot, turned out to be not only misguided but completely unrealistic.

By the mid-1980s, researchers from artificial intelligence, computer science, brain and cognitive science, and psychology had realized that perhaps the idea of computers as intelligent machines was misguided. The brain does not run "programs": It does something entirely different. But what is it? Evolutionary theory teaches us that the brain has evolved not to do mathematical proofs, but to control behavior, to ensure our survival. The researchers from these various disciplines agreed that intelligence always manifests itself in behavior and that we must understand the behavior. If an organism does not behave, does not do anything in the real world, how would we ever know whether it possesses any kind of intelligence or not? At the very least, the organism, the animal, the person, the machine must make sounds, change the environment in some ways, move, draw something, produce signs that can be interpreted by others.

Toward the end of the 1980s, an exciting new field had appeared: We call it "embodied cognitive science." (It is also called "new artificial intelligence," "behavior-based artificial intelligence," and "nouvelle artificial intelligence.") Rodney Brooks of the MIT Artificial Intelligence Laboratory, one of the founders of this new field, suggested that all this discussion about thinking, logic, and problem solving was based on assumptions that come from our own introspection, from how we tend to see ourselves. He suggested that we drop these assumptions, that we do away with thinking and with what people call high-level cognition and focus on the interaction with the real world. Intelligence must have a body. Brooks called it "embodied intelligence."

What originally seemed nothing more than a cute idea turned out to have profound ramifications and changed the entire research disciplines of artificial intelligence and cognitive science. It is currently beginning to exert its influence on psychology, neurobiology, and ethology as well as engineering. The more deeply people thought about the problems, the more it became obvious that a radical departure from traditional thinking was required; a mere variation on existing methods would simply not do. How can coherent and apparently intelligent behavior come about without thinking? If intelligence isn't thinking, what is it then? This is what the book is all about.

Ten years of research in this new field have generated an enormous number of stunning results and surprising insights. Although it is hard to believe, robots have been built that help each other, even though they have only simple reflexes. Other robots can clean floors, even though they are programmed only to avoid things. Yet others learn to distinguish and collect objects without even knowing about it. How is any of this possible? Even people who have been working in the field of embodied cognitive science for many years are still constantly surprised. The longer one works in the field, the more one marvels at the ingenuity of nature.

The goal of this book is to provide a systematic introduction into this new way of thinking, embodied cognitive science. But before you go on reading, let us issue a warning. We have been using an earlier version of this book to teach interdisciplinary classes in artificial intelligence and cognitive science over the last few years. At the end of the term, students in computer science, psychology, and neurobiology alike have often come up to us, saying that they were very excited about the ideas presented and the potential for new kinds of explanations. However, they found they were having a hard time with some of the other classes they had to take, for example in cognitive psychology. Because of the insights offered by this new approach, they simply could no longer believe the kinds of explanations offered in more traditional fields. So before you start reading, you have to be well aware that you may never again be able to think about humans, animals, computers, and robots in the same, comfortable way as before. On the other hand, you can be assured that you will gain a fascinating new perspective.

We would also like to warn teachers. Because the field is relatively new compared to standard disciplines like theory of computation, mathematics, psychology, the natural sciences, and classical artificial intelligence, it lacks the systematicness and rigor of those disciplines. The book does provide a framework for the study of intelligence, but it does not deliver all the answers. Therefore, it is a book more to stimulate ideas and creativity than to tell students "how things really are." This is why, instead of traditional class-work problems, we have added "Issues to Think About" to each chapter. We hope that you and your students will find pleasure in thinking about them. The book strives to attract your attention to an exciting new field of research, to uncountable fascinating problems, to a whole universe of new experiments to think about and to let your mind wander through. One of its main purposes is to get the reader thinking about old problems in novel ways and to generate new issues for investigation. In this spirit, we are convinced that the book will attract many bright, gifted students and form the basis for highly rewarding course work.

Like traditional artificial intelligence, embodied cognitive science has as its goal understanding intelligence by building artifacts. Because intelligence is "embodied," we need to build physical things: robots. Building robots is not only extremely instructive, it is also fun. And robot building has become much easier in recent years. Moreover, one can now buy relatively cheap robots in the stores that are perfectly suited for the experiments suggested in this book. However, many potentially interested readers may not want to get involved in robot building at all. This presents no problem. If you are such a reader, you can either read the text and simply think about the issues suggested—and you should have no difficulties in getting acquainted with this new field—or, alternatively, you can work with simulation models: It is perfectly possible to do the suggested projects using simulation. Our web page provides a few pointers on simulators that you may want to use (www.ifi.unizh.ch/~pfeifer/mitbook). Both methods, experimenting with real robots and working with simulations, have advantages and disadvantages. In some cases—when doing artificial evolution—simulation is even necessary: Real robots simply won't do, at least not given the current state of the art. We highly recommend experimentation with robots, simulators, or both. The experiences gained through such experimentation are invaluable.

Contents

The book is targeted toward an interdisciplinary audience and requires no prior knowledge or expertise. The first part sets the stage, starting with an introduction of what intelligence is all about. In spite of the wide disagreement on this issue, we try to extract the common denominator underlying all the varying ideas about what constitutes intelligence. We also outline a number of ways intelligence can be investigated. In particular, we introduce the autonomous agents approach, central to embodied cognitive science.

As originally planned, the book was to have two parts, one outlining the traditional view, the other analyzing what is wrong with it, with a small section at the end on alternatives. After discussions with many students, we became convinced that these are not the main things students are looking for: They don't want to know the old way of thinking and why it is wrong, they want to know the new way of thinking and why it is right. This realization entirely changed the book's character. It still contains a chapter, albeit a short one, on the traditional approach: The classical way of thinking about intelligence is still dominant not only in scientific circles, but also in people's everyday thinking (chapter 2). Most of us are comfortable with the idea that the human is an information processing system and that intelligence is located in the brain. What other explanation could there be? Chapter 3 presents the reasons why these kinds of explanations are insufficient and have led to insurmountable problems.

The next part (chapter 4) provides the theoretical groundwork for understanding the terminology and the various approaches discussed in the literature. This part may be difficult reading for some, but it is absolutely essential to appreciating the rest of the book. In it, we discuss the idea of "complete agents," which are the creatures we want to build. You may find that not everything in this chapter becomes clear at the first reading. The best strategy in such cases is to read on and return to this chapter again later. As part of the basics, we have included an introduction to neural networks (chapter 5), which you may choose to skip if you already have a background in neural networks. Even in that case, however, we would recommend that you at least skim the chapter because it is specifically geared toward neural networks for autonomous agents, a type of network not often covered in detail in the standard literature.

The next section reviews the major approaches that have been suggested in the literature, including the Braitenberg vehicles (chapter 6), the subsumption architecture (chapter 7), and the evolutionary approach and artificial life (chapter 8), as well as dynamical systems, behavioral economics, and schema-based approaches (chapter 9).

The section on principles of intelligent systems is one of the core sections. It summarizes the insights of the field, and the consensus —to the extent that it exists—in a compact, general way (chapter 10). Chapters 11 through 14 elaborate the principles governing design of intelligent systems. They contain a lot of detail, and you may want to skip them initially. It should present no problem to the reader to continue with chapter 15 right after chapter 10. Chapter 15 is a case study of how embodied cognitive science, as expressed by the design principles, can be applied to human memory. Memory is clearly one of the most intriguing phenomena in the study of intelligence, which is why we felt it would be an excellent candidate for showing the power of embodied cognitive science for studying what is normally considered a high-level cognitive competence.

The next section is about building and evaluating autonomous agents, both real and simulated. Chapter 16 provides insights into the intertwined and subtle considerations involved in the design process. It turns out that there are no precise recipes for successful design. Actually designing interesting agents, as robots or as simulated creatures, requires a lot of creativity. Chapter 17, on evaluation, is very important; embodied cognitive science is an enormously dynamic field, but there is a definite lack of rigor and scientific method. So do read this chapter carefully and try to apply it to your own experiments.

The last part of the book concerns future and integration. Chapter 18 outlines where the field may go in the coming years. This includes scientific developments, as well as technological developments and applications in industry and society. It has an intentionally speculative character and we hope that this will add to the field's attractiveness. Proposals offered range from such down-to-earth suggestions as building more complex robots to amphibious robots inhabiting the sewage systems of our large cities. Chapter 19, entitled "Intelligence revisited," brings together everything we have said throughout the book in a theoretical framework. Such a framework can be viewed as a first step toward a theory of intelligence. We conclude by outlining some of the more important implications of the insights gained on society at large.

Scope

This book presents all the background knowledge required for understanding the fundamental principles underlying intelligence. It also covers the reasons why the classical approach has failed. Moreover, it provides enough detailed materials on all aspects of physical and simulated agents (robot design, neural networks, control architectures, learning algorithms, programming) so that students can start doing experiments and projects on their own. The entire setup is highly interdisciplinary. Connections between disciplines are woven into the entire text. Thus, the book provides a rich source of associations that will be valuable in particular to the motivated and talented students with interests reaching beyond one discipline. A glossary at the end should also serve as a useful reference.

This book does not cover algorithms of classical artificial intelligence. It is also not a systematic technical introduction into robot vision or other classical topics of robotics such as motion planning. This is due to its complete-agent perspective: its focus is on the agent as a whole, on its behavior, rather than on individual competences. This perspective has been the main organizing principle. It is also the reason some topics that are treated in a single chapter in other textbooks are distributed over several in this one. Learning, for example, is essential to neural networks, categorization, sensory-motor control, and value systems, all of which are principles concerning complete agents and include aspects other than learning.

This book is *not* about robot building; it is not about designing circuit boards and controllers for robots. Though design issues have a prominent place, it is not an engineering text. The book covers a lot of ground from a conceptual perspective. This is unavoidable. It reflects the nature of intelligence, which is multifacated and messy. Also, because it is the first comprehensive book about this field, it includes materials you might disagree with. Although we have tried our best to bring everything together and merge it into a coherent framework, many issues have not yet been settled in the field of embodied cognitive science.

History of This Project

The whole enterprise that has come to fruition with this book started roughly 10 years ago when we began to run into fundamental problems with artificial intelligence. In the mid-1980s we had already been working with expert systems for a number of years. Over time we realized, as did many others, that the technology did not fulfill its promises. Accomplishing what we proposed turned out to be much harder than expected: Only a very few of the projects we undertook ended up with systems that could be used in everyday routine practice. The problems were not simply of practical nature, they were somehow insurmountable. At about that time, Terry Winograd and Fernando Flores's seminal book *Understanding Computers and Cognition* was published. Although we initially did not understand all the issues involved, we realized immediately that there was something important about this book. It tied in smoothly with long-standing criticisms of artificial intelligence by Hubert Dreyfus, and with at least some of the points Gerald Edelman and George Reeke had been making for some time. The main point of criticism for all these critics was artificial intelligence's exclusive information processing perspective. All argued that viewing human intelligence as information processing is misleading and does not provide the best type of explanation for it. We took the Winograd and Flores book seriously and ran a seminar about it. In the meantime, William J. Clancey, an expert systems specialist at Stanford, had also started thinking about the foundations of classical artificial intelligence. His thinking has been very influential for our endeavors.

While on sabbatical leave in 1990–91 at the Free University of Brussels, in Luc Steels' Artificial Intelligence Laboratory, I (Rolf Pfeifer) had plenty of time to think about the fundamental problems in artificial intelligence. This was when I completely changed my whole research program. I had become convinced that we needed an entirely new approach to the study of intelligence, if we wanted to make progress in really understanding it. Since then we have, in our research, been dealing only with embodied cognitive science.

In 1991, a workshop on "emergence" was held in the beautiful monastery of Corsendonk in Belgium, attended by most of the players in the field: Rodney Brooks of MIT; Bill Clancey of the Institute for Research on Learning; John Hallam of the University of Edinburgh; Stevan Harnad of University of Southampton; Leslie Kaelbling of Brown University; Chris Langton of Los Alamos and the Santa Fe Institute; Maja Mataric, now of the University of Sourthern California, Los Angeles; David McFarland of Oxford University; Tim Smithers, now of University of Navara, San Sebastian; Luc Steels of the Free University of Brussels; Chuck Taylor of UCLA; and Francisco Varela of the Ecole Polytechnique in Paris. This meeting can be seen somehow as the founding meeting of the still very young field of embodied cognitive science. Roughly three years later, Lin Chen of the Beijing Open Laboratory for Cognitive Science invited Rolf Pfeifer to deliver a series of lectures on the new approach to cognitive science. He was the first to suggest that these lectures be turned into a book. We would like to thank Lin for this suggestion. Since the Corsendonk meeting, much progress has been made. The field has matured into a scientific discipline. It is time for a comprehensive textbook.

Acknowledgments

Many people have helped make this book possible, starting with Luc Steels, who invited Rolf Pfeifer to fill the Swift AI Chair at the Free University of Brussels, and the members of his group, in particular Jo Decuyper, Bernard Manderick, Philip Rademakers, and Johan Vanwelkenhuyzen, who were very patient in discussing over and over again the same sorts of issues. Rolf Pfeifer would also like to thank Rodney Brooks for inviting him to spend his recent sabbatical at the "Zoo" at the MIT Artificial Intelligence Laboratory. The "Zoo," a creation of Rodney Brooks, is a colorful collection of interesting people who don't fit into any of the established categories. The stay at MIT has greatly contributed to this book. In particular, the many extensive discussions with Yasuo Kuniyoshi of the Electrotechnical Laboratory in Tsukuba, Japan, a member of the "Zoo" at the time, have been highly profitable. Then we would like to thank the members of the AI Lab of the University of Zurich: Andreas Aebi, Nick Almassy, Raja Dravid, Peter Eggenberger, Hansruedi Früh, Bernd Goetz, Charlotte Hemelrijk, Michelle Hoyle, Hiroshi Kobayashi, Dimitri Lambrinos, Lorenz Leumann, Lukas Lichtensteiger, Christopher Lueg, Marinus Maris, Daniel Meier, Ralf Möller, Martin Müller, Alex Riegler, Thomas Rothenfluh, Simona Rusnak, Ralf Salomon, René te Boekhorst, Paul Verschure, Erik Vinkhuyzen, and Thomas Wehrle. Without their contributions, these ideas could not have evolved the way they did. The current members of the lab all invested enormous amounts of work and creativity to make it work.

A big thanks goes to Norman Cook of Kansai University and to Paolo Gaudiano of Boston University, and to three anonymous reviewers for their critical reading and their extremely valuable and constructive remarks. Their suggestions have helped improve the text tremendously. Many students from our classes have also supplied us with valuable suggestions. In particular, we thank Marcel Altherr, Natalie Glaus, and Alex Schröder. Isabelle Follath deserves all the credit for the cartoons, without which the book would not be half as much fun. Alex Riegler did a great job in designing the numerous technical illustrations. And last, but not least, a big thanks goes to Eveline Wittmer for managing all the figures.

Rolf Pfeifer would also like to thank his colleague Kurt Bauknecht, the director of the computer science department, who over the years continuously supported our activities, and Takashi Gomi of Applied AI Systems, who has been extremely supportive and has succeeded in bringing the ideas of embodied cognitive science to the research and engineering communities in Japan. Bob Prior of MIT Press and copy editor Michael Harrup have been exceptionally helpful in providing the right kind of structure for the book. Many thanks also to our Japanese friends for their encourgement. Thanks goes also to our friends at the Swiss Federal Institute of Technology in Lausanne, Jean-Daniel Nicoud and Francesco Mondada, for their support in getting us started on the Khepera robot. We would also like to thank the Swiss National Science Foundation. Without their continuous financial support, we could not have made progress as we did. And last, but not least, we would like to thank our families. Christian Scheier would like to thank his family and friends, in particular his mother and Eveline for their love and patience, and Balz for the many discussions on various topics covered in this book. Rolf Pfeifer would like to thank his family, his wife Beatrice, and his two sons Serge and Mischa for the patience they had with a nervous, overworked husband and father, who had—and still has—too little time for them.

This book's central goal is to allow the reader to acquire a deeper understanding of intelligence. A number of consequences follow from this goal. First, we have to define what we mean by "intelligence." Second a "deeper understanding" implies that our current understanding is insufficient and needs to be improved. Thus, we need to ferret out in what respect it is not satisfactory, which in turn requires analyzing our current view, its underlying assumptions, and its ramifications. Part I is devoted to the elaboration of these points.

Although we all have a good idea of what we mean by "intelligence," there is no general agreement on a particular definition. Moreover, questions like "Are animals intelligent?" "Can animals think?" "Can computers (or robots) be intelligent?" "How can we measure intelligence?" "Is intelligence inherited or can it be acquired?" and "To what extent are emotions involved in intelligence?" provoke a great deal of disagreement. Chapter 1 conveys a flavor of all the aspects and the variety of ideas involved by looking at definitions, commonsense notions, and ways of testing intelligence. Just to illustrate the topic's complexity and controversial nature, the chapter presents the IQ test, "emotional intelligence," and the nature-nurture debate, as well as a test for machine intelligence, the Turing test. Once the parameters of the field "intelligence" have been delineated, the chapter discusses the various ways intelligence can be and has been investigated. Finally, it introduces the main methodology to be used in this book, the synthetic methodology; in particular, the use of so-called autonomous agents to investigate intelligence is considered.

Once we are clear about what we mean by "intelligence" and how it can be investigated, we are in a position to analyze the different theoretical positions. In cognitive science, empirical and theoretical research on intelligence has been dominated by the computer metaphor: intelligence as information processing, as the manipulation of abstract symbols—the essence of the cognitivistic paradigm. The cognitivistic paradigm—elaborated in chapter 2—is intuitively highly appealing and has attracted many of the leading researchers over the last half century or so. As it has turned out, however, the paradigm has a number of undesirable implications that cannot be resolved within the framework it sets up. Very broadly speaking, they all concern the fact that humans, animals, and robots have to interact with the real world, whereas the computer metaphor has focused on abstract virtual or computational worlds and has neglected their relationship to the real world. Chapter 3 discusses the problems and issues this neglect of the real world entails. One very prominent problem, the symbol grounding problem, concerns how the symbols used in a model acquire meaning, that is, how they relate to an organism's experience. Although many solutions to these problems have been suggested, radically different approaches are required if we are to come to grips with them, and this is the crux of the entire book: elaborating these alternative approaches.

Intelligence has always been a controversial topic. Science fiction stories involving intelligent robots abound. Superintelligent machines have, for a long time, been the stuff of nightmares. Computers and, even more so, robots have inspired people's fantasies. Because of the enormous developments in digital electronics and microtechnology in recent years, true artificial intelligence seems to be drawing near. So it is not really surprising that discussions concerning artificial intelligence are often highly emotional. But nightmares and science fiction do not entirely explain the issue's emotional charge. Intelligence was an emotional topic long before computers started to spread. Just think of IQ tests. There has been a long and heated debate about what IQ tests actually measure: Is it really intelligence, or something else? And what about the recent hype about "emotional intelligence"? Is emotional intelligence, rather than IQ, the real intelligence? Another question often asked: Are ants intelligent? Or ant colonies? Are rats intelligent? Maybe not, but they are certainly *more* intelligent that ants. And humans are more intelligent than rats—at least in many respects. Most adults can speak and write and many can play chess—activities no animal can perform. But among humans, talking or playing chess (at least at a basic level) is not considered something exceptional. I, Rolf Pfeifer, know how to play chess, but nobody who has seen my performance in a game would attribute extraordinary intelligence to me. However, if a one-year-old child did exactly the same thing, we would think that the kid was superintelligent. If a dog did it, we would think the dog was a genius. So what we consider intelligent depends also on our expectations. But not only that: Assume you are playing chess against a computer. If you win, you can be happy. But even if you lose, you might still argue that you were playing intelligently, whereas the computer was only testing many alternatives in a completely unintelligent way, as figure 1.1 illustrates.

Well, you might have been able to make that argument, at least, until the May 11, 1997. On that date the world was focusing on a particular room on the 35th floor of 787 Seventh Avenue in New

Figure 1.1 A human playing chess against a computer. Although the human is losing, he still feels he is intelligent, whereas he considers the computer to be stupid. Even after the historic victory of IBM's Deep Blue over world champion Garry Kasparov in 1997, the reaction of the human is still justified. Deep Blue's success is due largely to processing speed.

York City, where, for the first time in history, a chess program won an entire match against the reigning world champion. The hapless champion was Garry Kasparov, the chess program, Deep Blue, developed by a research team at IBM. Kasparov won the first of six games and lost the second. The next three games were draws. At this point, both Kasparov and Deep Blue had 2.5 points, with just one game to go. As we all know, Kasparov lost the final one. What does that mean? Is the person's reaction in figure 1.1 still justified? Or is it indeed the case that now computers have achieved human level intelligence? Deep Blue's victory is certainly a milestone in the history of artificial intelligence. After all, chess was considered the hallmark of intelligence in the old days of artificial intelligence. But we hope to demonstrate in this book that the person in figure 1.1 can relax: Nothing has changed fundamentally. The decisive factor in Deep Blue's victory was the speed of the computer. So this victory was a logical development, to be expected sooner or later. More is required, however, before we can speak of intelligence.

This book is about intelligence. So we should somehow be able to tell what we mean by the term. This is not an easy task, as we have already begun to see. There is very little agreement on what does and does not constitute intelligence. For the most part, the discussion of what intelligence is and isn't seems to concern what people find interesting and what they don't. Some find it interesting that termites can construct enormous buildings and that birds can fly in flocks with marvelous shapes. Others are amazed that humans can speak and recognize a particular face in a large crowd. Still others wonder about dogs catching Frisbees. Almost everybody is impressed with Einstein's achievements in general relativity. And most are still fascinated by grand masters playing a game of chess. To do justice to this variety, we start with a *tour d'horizon* of what many people have said about the phenomenon of intelligence. As we do so, we have to be aware that intelligence is a descriptive term: It describes certain properties of individuals or groups of individuals. Descriptive terms are largely arbitrary, and it is therefore unlikely that descriptive definitions of complex ideas can satisfy everybody. Nevertheless, all definitions of intelligence have a common denominator related to novelty and adaptivity. This forms the starting point of our investigation.

An exact characterization of intelligence is not all that important to understanding it. What does matter is that we work on the relevant issues. Rather than arguing whether a particular behavior should be called intelligent or not—a point that is always debatable—we try to provide answers to the following question: Given some behavior—say of a human, an elephant, an ant, or a robot—that we find interesting in some ways, how does the behavior come about? If we can give good answers to this question for a broad range of behaviors, we can say that we have gained an understanding of the principles underlying intelligence. This is precisely what we are after in this book. Of course, we have to define exactly what we mean by "good answers": Our entire conception depends on this. We do just that, in detail, throughout the book. Thus we are suggesting that we replace the original question of defining intelligence with the more profitable one of how a particular behavior in which we are interested comes about.

Before we start, let us introduce a few terms. By *cognitive science* we mean the interdisciplinary investigation of intelligence, or more generally, the mind. We are mostly interested in that part of cognitive science that applies a synthetic methodology, that is, the methodology of "understanding by building." Cognitive science is also concerned with exploring general principles of intelligence, not only those related to the human mind. It has a large overlap with *artificial intelligence* (*AI*). The difference between the two fields is that cognitive science has closer ties to empirical sciences like psychology, biology, and neurobiology, whereas AI is more closely associated with computer science, algorithms, and logic. But many researchers in AI would consider themselves cognitive scientists. We sometimes use the terms *classical AI* to distinguish the traditional approach from the more recent one described in this book, which we call *embodied cognitive science*. When talking about intelligence, we often do not want to make any distinction among humans, animals, and artificial creatures like robots or simulated organisms. In these cases we normally use the term *agent*.

1.1 Characterizing Intelligence

We start our *tour d'horizon* with a few definitions of intelligence, move on to commonsense notions, then discuss intelligence testing, a particular way of characterizing intelligence. We then turn to a very special kind of intelligence test, the Turing test, and a famous thought experiment, the Chinese Room. From this cursory review, we then define our starting point.

Definitions

As we said, it is hard to define intelligence, and not much agreement has been achieved. The introductory comments on intelligence in the Penguin *Dictionary of Psychology* reflect this lack of consensus: "Few concepts in psychology have received more devoted attention and few have resisted clarification so thoroughly" (Reber 1995, p. 379). Nevertheless, definitions can provide a source of intuition, so let's examine some. In 1921, the *Journal of Educational Psychology* (Vol. 12, pp. 123–147, 195–216) asked fourteen leading experts in the field at the time to provide their definitions of intelligence. As one might expect, the journal got 14 different answers back. Some of the responses received can be summarized as follows: The ability to carry on abstract thinking (L. M. Terman); Having learned or ability to learn to adjust oneself to the environment (S. S. Colvin); The ability to adapt oneself adequately to relatively new situations in life (R. Pintner); A biological mechanism by which the effects of a complexity of stimuli are brought together and given a somewhat unified effect in behavior (J. Peterson); The capacity to acquire capacity (H. Woodrow); The capacity to learn or to profit by experience (W. F. Dearborn). Although the definitions are different, they all make certain points that we find important. Note the very different levels involved. Terman talks about the ability for abstract thinking. By contrast, Peterson refers to biological mechanisms. A crucial point: Some mention the environment, some don't. In many investigations of intelligence, the environment was largely neglected.

The quotations above represented the opinion of experts. Let us now look at what people in general think about intelligence, at commonsense notions of intelligence. You may be surprised at some inclusions in this list.

Commonsense Notions

It is important to understand commonsense notions of intelligence, first because they are a great source of inspiration, and second because, ultimately, the scientific study of intelligence must relate to them: It must provide a better understanding of precisely these concepts. Commonsense notions often specify certain capabilities typical of intelligent beings. They include, among others, thinking and problem solving; the competence to speak, read, and write; intuition and creativity; learning and memory; emotions; surviving in a complex world; and consciousness. They also include the distinction of degrees of intelligence.

A GRADUATED PROPERTY

The first thing to note is that people clearly distinguish levels of intelligence. Albert Einstein (figure 1.2) was certainly extremely intelligent. If you want to go to college, you have to be intelligent. The word is often used in this sense, namely as a synonym for "very intelligent," "more intelligent than others." When we say a person is intelligent, we normally mean that the person has an above average level of intelligence.

Obviously, some people are more intelligent than others. Humans are more intelligent than animals, and among animals, dolphins and apes are considered more intelligent than cows or ants. We have a tendency to order living beings as being more or less intelligent—intelligence is not a characteristic that is either present or not, rather one that is present in degrees. But it is also

Figure 1.2 Portrait of an intelligent person. There is universal agreement that Einstein, an enormously creative thinker, was highly intelligent.

clear that ordering intelligence on a linear scale is not possible. Some students are good at writing essays, others can do math, still others play music, and a fourth group might excel at camping out in the wild: How should we compare their intelligence? It is not obvious how such a comparison can be made in a sensible and profitable way.

THINKING AND PROBLEM SOLVING

The ability to think is often mentioned as an essential characteristic of intelligence. Thinking, in its commonsense meaning, includes problem solving and logical reasoning but also less structured forms of mental activity such as those we use in our everyday lives, when doing household chores or planning a weekend trip. Most people would probably agree with the ordering of the degrees of intelligence of animals mentioned in the previous section. This implies that animals also have a certain level of intelligence. But do animals think? The capacity to think is a characteristic of an intelligent being in commonsense belief. Well, maybe some animals do think, and others don't. We have no way of really knowing. To find out, however, we could conduct an experiment. For example, we could give a horse an arithmetic problem in some form, as is sometimes seen on TV shows, and if it comes up with the right answer, say by knocking on the ground the correct number of times, we might say that it has been thinking. The fact that these demonstrations have been shown to be tricks is beside the point here. What matters is that we never *know* whether another agent is thinking or not: We can only speculate about it.

Problem solving is closely related to thinking. Typical problem solving tasks are finding a bug in a computer program, diagnosing the disease of a patient, finding a solution to a high school physics problem, designing an experiment with animals to test a hypothesis, or compiling a portfolio for a particular customer.

In its everyday meaning, the term "thinking" is often associated with conscious thought. This is compatible with Terman's view of intelligence as abstract thinking. It is also what the philosopher René Descartes had in mind when writing his famous statement "Cogito ergo sum." Abstract thinking is perceived as especially hard by most, and individuals with this ability often command respect and admiration. This ability to think in abstractions is the first one mentioned, almost universally, by most people when asked to define intelligence. Upon further reflection, they come up with all sorts of additional conceptions. Let's look at some of them.

LEARNING AND MEMORY

Good students are usually perceived as the ones that learn easily. We also say that they have a good memory. They study the words once, for example, and they know them and they do not forget them. Many people view learning as the core property of intelligence. That learning per se does not make people intelligent, but the capacity to learn, is also a popular view. So learning to learn appears to be the key point.

Memory is considered equally important, in popular conceptions of intelligence, as capacity to learn. However, rote learning, merely memorizing facts out of context, is generally judged a pointless activity, basically a waste of time, requiring no intelligence. Memory for useful knowledge is what counts. A doctor with extensive experience who can remember all his patients and their diseases and can apply this knowledge to treat new cases is considered intelligent. Transfer of knowledge is the point, not merely storing it.

LANGUAGE

The capacity to communicate in natural language, as we know it from humans, is often considered to be the hallmark of intelligence. Clearly, natural language requires a high level of intelligence. The ability to talk to one another, to read and write, is one of humans' distinguishing features. No animal species has abilities even remotely resembling human natural language. Those who speak multiple languages are often regarded as particularly intelligent. Their ability is a combination of good learning, memory capacity, and talent for languages.

INTUITION AND CREATIVITY

Einstein was creative; so were Beethoven and Picasso. They also had a lot of intuition. Leaders and managers have intuition, too. In fact, all (or most) people do. Intuition is often taken to mean arriving at conclusions without a train of logical thought that can be traced to its origins. Likewise, creativity is a highly complex notion that includes not only the individual but the society as whole. It cannot be defined for an individual in isolation but must be discussed with respect a particular society's value criteria. Many regard creativity as the highest form of human intelligence.

Both intuition and creativity seem in some ways to go beyond thinking. Thinking can be executed in a "cold" manner, independent of emotion, whereas intuition and creativity require the engaging of emotions. Creating something new also has a somewhat mysterious flavor: How does the new thing come about? Can creativity be learned?

CONSCIOUSNESS

Consciousness is often seen as an essential ingredient of intelligence. Like creativity and language, it is a property that we can attribute with certainty only to humans. And like creativity, there is also something mysterious about consciousness: It is hard to grasp, but considered essential for many other abilities. Thinking, language, and creativity are understood as requiring consciousness. Creativity, for example, is seen as the result of a combination between conscious thought and unconscious processes. Because of its subjectivity, consciousness is an elusive concept; it is hard to know what it really is all about. Academic psychology has deliberately tried to avoid dealing with consciousness at all, arguing "that the role of consciousness in mental life is very small, almost frighteningly so. The aspects of mental life that require consciousness have turned out to be a relatively minor fraction of the business of the brain" (Bridgeman 1990, cited in Rosenfield 1992). Although Bridgeman may indeed be right, consciousness is nevertheless seen as important for the study of intelligence by many people.

EMOTIONS

Humans have emotions. Like consciousness, they are something we consider essential for humans. Moreover, most people think that higher mammals, in particular apes and dolphins, but also dogs and cats, have emotions. Whether emotions should be considered an essential feature of intelligent beings, however, is debatable. Recently, so-called emotional intelligence, introduced by Peter Salovey and John Mayer (1990), has been the subject of much discussion. Emotional intelligence refers to the ability to recognize emotions in others, using emotions to support thinking and actions, understanding emotions, and regulating emotions. The general idea is that if you recognize your own emotions, you are better able to perceive the emotions in others and to react appropriately in social situations (Goleman 1995). Apparently this ability can be improved through appropriate practice. Pertinent seminars are already being marketed worldwide.

It is generally agreed that the degree of sophistication of emotions depends to a large degree on intelligence. Humans can be jealous; they can be ashamed or feel guilty. We would normally not attribute such emotions to ants. We would also not, for example, ascribe guilt to a lion that has just killed a deer, whereas we would certainly attribute guilt as a likely emotion for a human who has killed another human.

SURVIVING IN A COMPLEX WORLD

Animals (and humans, for that matter) can survive in highly complex environments, and they sometimes display astounding behaviors. Termites build fantastic towers, and bees dance and communicate, in sophisticated ways, the location of food sources. Other animals use tools in skilled ways. Certain vultures hurl a stone at an ostrich egg to break it, Galapagos woodpecker finches probe for insects in the bark of trees by holding a cactus spine in their beaks, and chimpanzees use twigs to probe for termites. Primates exhibit sophisticated social behavior. We cannot help attributing some kind of intelligence to these creatures and those that engage in similarly sophisticated survival behaviors.

PERCEPTUAL AND MOTOR ABILITIES

Most people don't consider perceptual and motor abilities essential for intelligence. Presumably, seeing the things around us seems so natural and works so automatically that we are not aware of the complexities involved. By contrast, science considers understanding perception one of the most important research issues. Recognizing complex objects in our environment, making out a face in a crowd are amazing abilities to a scientist trying to explain them. Medical doctors, experienced diagnosticians, can sometimes find out what's wrong with a person simply by looking at him. Such perceptual competences are sometimes seen as intelligence. Motor abilities, on the other hand, especially basic ones like walking, are usually thought to require no intelligence. As the complexity of the motor task increases, however, it becomes less and less clear to what extent intelligence is required. Assembling a complex electronic device requires high sensory-motor skills, but does it call for intelligence?

This discussion of commonsense notions of intelligence is, of course, neither complete nor empirically sound. The aim was to provide a sense of the variety of abilities and components involved in what we, scientists and laypeople, think of as intelligence. As we have seen, intelligence is multifaceted and not restricted to one characteristic, like abstract thinking. We have also seen that, in addition to humans, animals often exhibit impressive levels of intelligence. Moreover, there seems to be agreement that intelligence is a gradual rather than an absolute characteristic, though it is not obvious how it should be measured. This is the task of intelligence testing.

Intelligence Testing

Numerous tests for assessing intelligence have been developed. A case in point are IQ tests. The general idea of an IQ test is to measure a capacity that is not dependent on particular knowledge but is, in a sense, a "general intelligence capacity" or "factor g," as it is sometimes called.

The original IQ test was invented in 1905 by French psychologist Alfred Binet, essentially to find out whether children with certain learning deficiencies would be better off in a special school. German psychologist William Stern in 1912 turned the test into a general intelligence test for children, and David Wechsler in 1939 developed it into one for adults. He proposed a Gaussian distribution of test results: two thirds should be between 85 and 115 (100 being the mean), and only 2.3 percent above 130 and below 70. Figure 1.3 depicts a typical item on a modern IQ test.

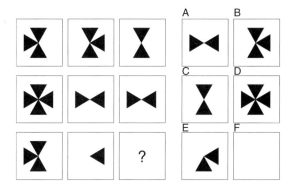

Figure 1.3 Typical problem from an IQ test. One item from the panel on the right (A through F) has to be chosen for the field with the question mark.

In 1904, English psychologist Charles Spearman, in a paper entitled "'General Intelligence' Objectively Determined and Measured" (Spearman 1904), used factor analysis, a method he invented, to support his claim that factor g indeed exists. Spearman based his argument on the finding that there are positive correlations between the different test items on an IQ test. According to Spearman, these results suggest that an underlying factor is responsible for the correlations. Although some psychologists still regard factor g as the most fundamental measure of intelligence, others postulate multiple intelligences, a view supported by recent evidence that more than seventy different abilities can be distinguished by currently available tests (Carroll 1993).

We can conclude that it is problematic to reduce a highly complex phenomenon like intelligence to a single number. This is also the essential point in Howard Gardner's theory of multiple intelligences, or multiple competences. According to Gardner, there is not one intelligence or factor g but multiple ones: linguistic intelligence, musical intelligence, logical-mathematical intelligence, spatial intelligence, bodily-kinesthetic intelligence, and personal intelligences (for perceiving your own and other people's moods, motives, and intentions). Gardner's list of intelligences suggests that there is no simple mapping of intelligence onto one dimension, one number (Gardner 1985). He also argues that some of these competences cannot be measured using standard tests, hence the German translation of Gardner's book has the title *Abschied vom IQ*, which means "Farewell, IQ."

But before we dismiss IQ entirely, let us recall one of the definitions of intelligence provided by the experts in 1921, namely, the

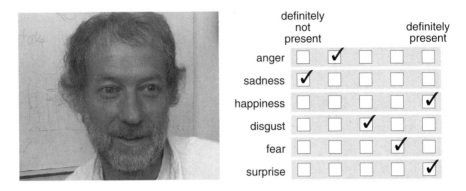

	definitely not present				definitely present
anger	☐	✔	☐	☐	☐
sadness	✔	☐	☐	☐	☐
happiness	☐	☐	☐	☐	✔
disgust	☐	☐	✔	☐	☐
fear	☐	☐	☐	✔	☐
surprise	☐	☐	☐	☐	✔

Figure 1.4 Example of a problem from an EQ test. EQ tests typically consist of four parts, one for identifying emotions, one for using emotions, one for understanding emotions, and one for regulating emotions. The figure shows test items from the test for understanding emotions.

ability to profit from your experience, to be successful in a particular environment. If we take as the environment an industrialized society, it seems that IQ is a good predictor of success in school and in professional life (e.g., Neisser et al. 1996). Recently, some have suggested that emotional intelligence might be equally important for a successful career (e.g., Goleman 1995). Because tests for emotional intelligence (EQ tests) on the one hand are controversial and on the other have only been around for a short period of time (at least compared to IQ tests), it is unclear how exactly they relate to IQ tests. To provide a feel for what these tests are like, we have included an item from an EQ test in figure 1.4.

Testing to measure intelligence has raised the question of whether intelligence is genetically predetermined and to what extent it is influenced by factors other than heredity. This has sparked a heated debate that keeps reemerging periodically: the nature-nurture debate.

The Nature-Nurture Debate

Generally speaking, the nature-nurture debate concerns the origins of knowledge. Those in the nature camp think that development is largely the expression of genetically predetermined factors. For example, it has been suggested that children are born with innate knowledge about basic principles of grammar (e.g., Pinker 1994), physics (Spelke 1994), or mathematics (Wynn 1992). By contrast, people in the nurture camp posit that most abilities are acquired during development and can be learned. The last violent eruption of this debate was in 1994, when Herrnstein and Murrey published their controversial book *The Bell Curve*, in which they claimed that the decisive factor in whether we will be successful in life is not our social environment, but intelligence as measured by IQ. They also maintained that IQ is largely innate, genetically predetermined. This position has, of course, far reaching consequences. For example, it suggests that some social programs are useless because the intended beneficiaries cannot be helped because of their innate limitations in intelligence, as expressed in low IQ scores. This view has a number problems. (See Gould 1996 for an excellent discussion of the main issues.) We mention only two. First, it assumes that intelligence can be captured by a single number, the IQ. Given our discussion of intelligence so far, this is clearly questionable. Second, it is not clear what is meant by the claim that intelligence is innate. Does it mean "coded in the genes"? Genes interact with their environment at all levels, so that "there is virtually no interesting aspect of development that is strictly 'genetic'" (Elman et al. 1996, p. 21). Although there is a certain truth to both extremes in this debate—there are genetic factors in intelligence, and there are strong environmental components—the "solution" presumably lies somewhere in the middle, that is, that the origins of intelligence are to be found in the interaction between nature (genetic factors) and nurture (environmental factors). The problem then becomes determining how development actually works; that is, how precisely genetic and environmental factors interact in the developing organism. Computer simulations of how this interaction might be achieved in very simple organisms are given in chapter 8. These simulation studies lead to additional insights and new ways of thinking about the nature-nurture debate. Meanwhile the nature-nurture war continuous to be waged.

The nature-nurture debate is by no means the only controversy in the study of intelligence. Let us look at another, the intelligence of machines.

The Turing Test and the Chinese Room

So far we have dealt mostly with natural intelligence, because people normally associate intelligence with natural creatures, in particular humans. But what about machines? Can machines be intelligent? This question has led to long, emotionally loaded, and

Figure 1.5 Basic setup of the Turing test. There are three participants, a man (A), a woman (B), and an interrogator (C). The interrogator is in a separate room, connected to the participants only via a computer terminal. His task is to find out who is the man and who the woman. A's goal is to confuse C whereas B tries to help C make the correct identification. The Turing test consists of replacing A by a computer: Can C then find out which is a computer and which a human?

generally nonproductive debates. Frustrated with discussions about the nature of intelligence, in which it is impossible ever to reach consensus because of the strongly subjective components involved, the brilliant English mathematician Alan Turing proposed an operationalization of the question whether machines could be intelligent at all. In 1950, in a seminal paper entitled "Computing Machinery and Intelligence (Turing 1950)" he proposed a procedure now widely known as the Turing test. The refreshing point about the Turing test is that it is an experiment, not speculation. Its results can be assessed objectively, and it does not refer to any kind of thinking or mental processes.

The Turing test consists of an imitation game. Figure 1.5 shows the basic setup. Let us quote Turing himself:

It (the imitation game) is played by three people, a man (A), a woman (B), and an interrogator (C) who may be of either sex. The interrogator stays in a room apart from the other two. The object of the game for the interrogator is to determine which of the other two is the man and which is the woman. He knows them by labels X and Y, and at the end of the game he says either "X is A and Y is B" or "X is B and Y is A." The interrogator is allowed to put questions to A and B thus:

C: Will X please tell me the length of his or her hair?

Now suppose X is actually A, then A must answer. It is A's object in the game to try and cause C to make the wrong identification. His answers might therefore be:

"My hair is shingled, and the longest strands are about nine inches long." (Turing 1950; reprinted in Feigenbaum and Feldman 1963, p. 11)

In order that tones of voice may not help the interrogator, the answers should be written, or better still, typewritten. The ideal arrangement is to have two computer terminals (at the time the test was originated, teleprinters) communicating between the two rooms. Alternatively the questions and answers could be repeated by an intermediary. The object of the game for the third player (B) is to help the interrogator. The best strategy for her is probably to give truthful answers. She can add such things as "I am the woman, don't listen to him!" to her answers, but that will be of no avail, because the man can make similar remarks.

We now ask the question, "What will happen when a machine takes the part of A in this game? Will the interrogator decide wrongly as often when the game is played like this as he does when the game is played between a man and a woman?" These questions replace our original, "Can machines think?" (Turing 1950; reprinted in Feigenbaum and Feldman 1963, pp. 11–12)

The original Turing version of the test involves three parties (the interrogator, one person trying to help the interrogator, and one trying to confuse him), simpler versions have later been proposed in which the interrogator is interacting with a system (human or machine) and has to find out whether the system is a human or a machine.

There has been much discussion about whether the Turing test is a good test of intelligence. Many criticisms have been voiced. One often heard is that the test is constrained to measuring a particular form of natural language communication. One of the prominent critics of the Turing test, philosopher John Searle, has argued, in essence, that observing behavior is not enough, because by merely observing behavior we cannot find out whether a system really understands the questions it is given (Searle 1980). As a thought experiment, he proposed the famous Chinese Room (figure 1.6). In

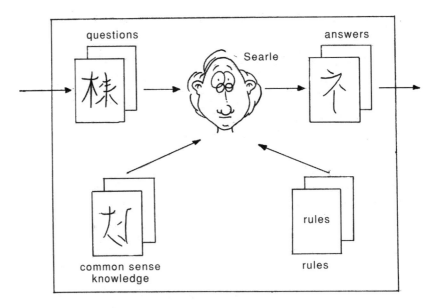

Figure 1.6 Searle's Chinese Room experiment. Using the rules and the commonsense knowledge, Searle is producing an answer to a question that is handed through a window in the room. Even though he does not understand Chinese, he can produce meaningful Chinese sentences.

his original paper, the person locked in the Chinese Room was Searle himself. The argument holds for anyone else, as long as he doesn't speak Chinese. Initially Searle is given two large batches of writing, one with Chinese characters and one written in English. The batch with the Chinese characters represents a data base of commonsense knowledge required to answer questions handed to him through the opening on the left of the room. The second batch consists of rules containing the instructions on how to "process" the questions, that is, they tell Searle how to produce an answer from the questions written with Chinese characters. This is done by comparing the characters of the question to the characters in the commonsense knowledge base and by choosing certain characters that will make up the answer. When this process is finished, the answer is handed through the opening on the right of the room. Note that the comparison of Chinese characters and the choice of characters that make up the answer is done entirely on the basis of their shapes, that is, on a purely formal or syntactic basis. Let us now suppose that Searle keeps playing this game for a while and gets really proficient at following the instructions for manipulating the Chinese symbols. From an external point of view, that is from the point of view of somebody outside the Chinese Room, Searle's answers to the questions are indistinguishable from those of native Chinese speakers. Nobody looking at Searle's answers can tell that he doesn't speak a word of Chinese. He has produced answers by manipulating uninterpreted formal symbols.

Searle, quite in contrast to Turing, is not willing to accept a definition (or a test) of intelligence that relies entirely on behavior. It is not sufficient for him that a system produce the same output as a human. He does not view the Turing test as a good means to judge the intelligence of a system. For true understanding, true intelligence—in his view—something else is required. Many papers have been written about the Chinese Room, and we cannot do justice to the entire discussion. Instead of going into that debate, let us, just for the fun of it, ask the following question: According to Searle, the Chinese Room does not understand Chinese. Now, how do we know Searle understands English? All we can do is say something, observe Searle's behavior and what he says in a particular situation, and if that makes sense, we attribute understanding to him. Just like the Chinese Room! But more probably, we know that Searle is human, we are humans and we understand English, so we simply assume that he also understands.

So far, in our description of the Chinese Room thought experiment, we basically followed Searle's line of reasoning. However, there is a serious problem with the argument. It suggests that there could indeed be a set of rules capable of producing the appropriate outputs based only on manipulation of meaningless characters. Remember that to Searle, the Chinese characters, the symbols, are entirely meaningless. If we interpret the rules as a computer program, then he suggests that there could be a computer program capable of producing the appropriate outputs (the answers) to the inputs (the questions), based on purely syntactic manipulation of some system of characters, the meaningless symbols. From half a century of computer linguistics research, it is well known that this does not work (e.g., Winograd and Flores 1986). At a minimum, this casts doubt on the primary assumption of the thought experiment (Clancey 1997).

To conclude this section on the Turing test, we mention one of its major limitations. If we are willing to attribute at least some level of intelligence to ants, rats, or elephants, the Turing test is obviously out as a tool for assessing intelligence. It can be applied only to systems capable of dealing with "human" natural language.

Whether it is a good test for human intelligence is still subject to debate (e.g., Crockett 1994; Epstein 1992).

The Common Denominator

We have now looked at various ways in which we can characterize intelligence. Our ultimate goal is to understand all of them: abstract thinking, learning and memory, natural language, medical diagnosis, surviving in the wild. But we have to start somewhere. If we look at the various characterizations from an abstract perspective, there seems to be one underlying common theme that involves "coming up with something new." The ability to speak, for example, implies generating new utterances appropriate to the situation. "Appropriate" means that the speaker gets some benefit or value from his utterance—otherwise he wouldn't say it. We would not attribute the ability to speak, for example, to a person who always utters the same five sentences. Nor would we attribute intelligence to a factory robot that only repeats the same movements over and over again. The Turing test becomes interesting only when the interrogator asks new questions, questions that he suspects could not have been preprogrammed. When Terman talks about intelligence as the ability to carry out abstract thinking, what he really means is the ability to come up with something new, a solution to an abstract problem, a mathematical proof, an answer to a hard question, something that did not exist before. Surviving in the wild means coping with novel situations which in turn implies behaving in new ways. Or let us look at Pinter's characterization of intelligence as the ability to adapt oneself adequately to new situations in life. The term "adapt" often suggests something passive, conforming to existing rules. This is exactly what most people do *not* mean by intelligence. But there is another meaning to the term "adapt": to exploit a situation in order to benefit from it. For example, the business world has changed dramatically in recent years. Computer technology, electronic communication systems, in particular the Internet, are by now everywhere. Companies that have adapted to these changes by changing their business practices, by inventing new ways of doing business, have survived; the others have largely disappeared. Note that this innovation requires conforming to the rules of information technology. Both components, conforming and generating are always present. The key point is generation of diversity while complying with the givens. We call this the *diversity-compliance trade-off.*

And now we ask: What are the mechanisms enabling organisms to adapt to, cope with, environmental changes? As we noted, adaptation always contains two components: complying with existing rules and generating new behavior; only if both components are present do we speak of adaptivity. It then makes sense to tie intelligence to adaptive behavior. The term "rule" has been used in a very broad sense. It can refer to the rules of information technology, social rules, the rules of grammar, the laws of nature (e.g., physiology) and physics. This characterization of intelligence as the capacity to adapt is independent of levels. It applies to a mathematician carrying out abstract thinking, to a child talking to his parents (using natural language), and just as much to an animal escaping a predator or searching for food.

These dual meanings of adaptivity, the conservative component, and the innovative component, can be found throughout the literature on intelligence. The famous Swiss psychologist Jean Piaget coined the terms "assimilation" and "accommodation" to designate these two aspects of intelligence (e.g., Piaget 1952). In learning theory, this has been called the stability-flexibility trade-off (e.g., Carpenter and Grossberg 1988). We will encounter these concepts in various guises throughout the book.

Before concluding this section, we should remark that the study of intelligence often does not take interaction with the environment explicitly into account, even though it may be implicitly present. This aspect, which we call *embodiment*, emerges as one of the key factors in understanding intelligence, and embodied cognitive science capitalizes on it. The terms "adaptation," "behavior," and "generation of behavioral diversity" by their very nature imply the existence of a body interacting with an environment.

1.2 Studying Intelligence: The Synthetic Approach

Now that we know what we want to investigate, we have to specify how we are going to proceed. We can distinguish between analytic and synthetic approaches, as shown in figure 1.7. The analytic approach is universally applied in all empirical sciences. Typically, experiments are performed on an existing system, a human, a desert ant, or a brain region, and the results are analyzed in various

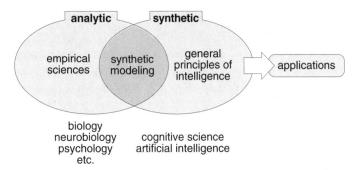

biology
neurobiology   cognitive science
psychology   artificial intelligence
etc.

Figure 1.7   Overview of approaches to the study of intelligence. On the left, we have the empirical sciences like biology, neurobiology, and psychology that mostly follow an analytic approach. On the right, we have the synthetic ones, namely cognitive science and AI, which can either model natural agents (this is called synthetic modeling, the shaded area) or alternatively can simply explore issues in the study of intelligence without necessarily being concerned about natural systems. From this latter activity, industrial applications can be developed.

ways. Often the goal is to develop a model to predict the outcome of future experiments. By contrast, the synthetic approach works by creating an artificial system that reproduces certain aspects of a natural system. This is another important function of models. Rather than focusing on producing the correct experimental results, that is, the correct output, we can try to reproduce the internal mechanisms that have led to the particular results. In a memory experiment, we could predict, say, the number of items recalled, based on a statistical model. Alternatively we could try to model the memory processes themselves. An ethologist may want to predict where an ant path will be formed. Again, he can use statistical modeling, but he can also attempt to model the behavioral rules by which the ants interact with the environment and with each other. Such models are typically computer models that, when run, are expected to reproduce the experimental results. The focus of interest shifts from reproducing the results of an experiment, although that is still an important aspect, to understanding why the results come about. This kind of approach is called *synthetic modeling* and is extremely productive. It is at the core of the discipline central to this book, *embodied cognitive science*. Such an approach can be characterized as "understanding by building." In the study of intelligence, this approach has been championed by AI and cognitive science and it is the approach that we have adopted in this book. The analytic and the synthetic approaches are complementary, however, not contradictory. In many sciences, the computational approach, an instance of the synthetic methodology, has become an integrated part, complementing the experimental method.

Synthetic Modeling: AI and Cognitive Science

Traditional AI and cognitive science proceed by developing computer models of mental functions. As a consequence, intelligence in these disciplines is closely tied to computers. Very roughly, the main idea is that intelligence—thinking—can be understood in terms of computer programs: Input is provided, the input is processed, and finally an output is generated. By analogy, the human brain is viewed in some sense as a very powerful computer. It receives inputs from the outside world through sensors (e.g., eyes, ears, skin). These inputs are processed: for example, stimulation received through the eyes is mapped onto an internal representation or model, and you recognize a cup of coffee standing in front of you. Depending on your internal state, your motivation, this percept generates the intention or plan to drink coffee: the processing phase. Finally, the action is executed: the output. In this view, called the *information processing metaphor*, the brain is seen as the "seat of intelligence," as illustrated in figure 1.8. Input-processing-output in computers corresponds to sensing-thinking-acting in intelligent agents such as humans or robots.

Like no other approach, this view of intelligence, together with the synthetic methodology, has revived the study of the mind and has provided major impulses to the field. It was more than a lucky coincidence that these types of computer models seemed almost perfectly suited to the study of the mind. It has greatly inspired many scientists, in particular psychologists and computer scientists. It has generated a lot of exciting research and applications. Moreover, this approach has strongly influenced psychology and has become known as *information processing psychology*. The focus in this perspective is mostly on thinking, reasoning, and abstract problem solving.

When researchers in AI started applying these ideas to building robots, to developing systems that interact with the real world, however, they found that it was simply not possible to build robots that would do a good job in the real world with this view of intelligence. It proved extremely difficult to get robots to do even simple things like moving around, picking up objects, and bringing them to a designated location. The problems were so serious that many

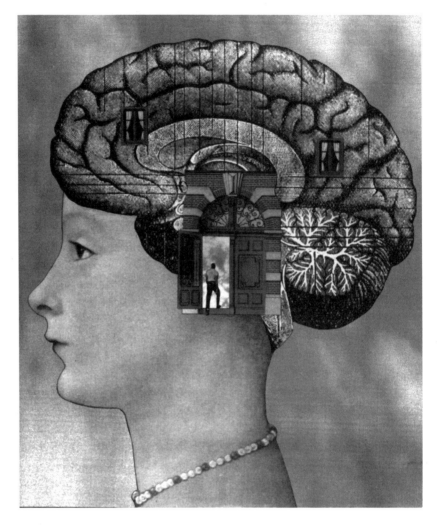

Figure 1.8 The brain as the "seat of intelligence." Sensory stimulation enters the brain, is processed (perception), and is integrated into a model of the environment (modeling). This model is used for planning and task execution, and finally a motor action is performed. This is the "input—processing—output" perspective. (From Uni Magazin 1995, reprinted with permission.)

started looking for alternatives. This resulted in the new field of embodied cognitive science.

Rodney Brooks, the director of the MIT Artificial Intelligence Laboratory and one of the founders of this new field, argued that the traditional approach to AI was fundamentally flawed. He maintained that all of AI's ideas concerning thinking, logic, and problem solving were based on assumptions that come from our own introspection, from how we see ourselves. He suggested that we drop these assumptions, do away with thinking and reasoning, and focus on the interaction with the real world. In a seminal paper in 1986, Brooks proposed the so-called subsumption architecture. He suggested that intelligent behavior could be achieved using a large number of loosely coupled processes that function predominantly in a asynchronous, parallel way. He argued that only minimal internal processing is required and that sensory signals should be mapped relatively directly to motor signals. Such an architecture leads to a tight system-environment coupling. Intelligence, in this view, emerges from the interaction of an organism with its environment, where the organism is equipped with a large number of parallel processes connected only loosely to one another. Such a conception of intelligence contrasts strongly with the information processing view. Note that in this perspective, the agent has a body, sensors, a motor system; in other words, it is embodied. Moreover, it needs to be autonomous. Let us examine this in more detail.

Autonomous Agents

In traditional AI and cognitive science, computer models have been the predominant tools. Synthetic methodology, however, can be extended to include not only simulations, but also physical systems, artificial creatures, behaving in the real world. These systems are called *autonomous agents*. The term "autonomous" designates independence from human control. Typically, autonomous agents have the form of mobile robots and can be used as models of biological systems, humans or animals. We now have a novel situation: The autonomous agents actually behave in the real world without the intervention of a human: They have sensors to perceive the environment, and they perform actions that change the environment. These are the key properties of agents. They are behaving systems in their own right. This is why they are also well suited to explore issues in the study of intelligence in general, not only of biological systems. We can perform experiments with our robots as we like, creating artificially intelligent systems. And because the robots physically interact with the real world, they can also be used for applications, to perform tasks that humans cannot or do not want to do themselves. Thus we can pursue three potential goals with the synthetic methodology: We can model biological systems, we can explore principles of intelligence in general, and we can develop applications.

It is highly instructive and productive to work with physical robots. Depending on what we intend to study, it may even be necessary. But often we can achieve the desired results in simulation. We can simulate the behavior and environment of an animal or robot, or we can produce creatures living in virtual worlds that are not simulations of real systems. The latter is the business of the fields of virtual reality and artificial life. The essential point is to have agents—physical or virtual, because agents interact with their environment on their own. This is why they represent the main tool of embodied cognitive science.

Figure 1.9 provides an overview of different types of agents. *Biological agents* exist in nature—we don't have to build them. Of the two categories of robotic agents, *research agents* and *industrial agents*, we will primarily focus on research agents, because of our focus on cognitive science. But we do believe, and discuss later, that industrial agents have fascinating applications: This is the business of engineering. Among computational agents, we have *simulated agents*, those that simulate an animal or a robot, and

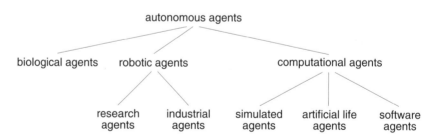

Figure 1.9 Classification of agents. The relevant category of agents for the study of intelligence are the autonomous agents. They can be subdivided into biological agents, robotic agents, and computational agents. Biological agents are naturally occurring. Robotic agents are further divided into research agents and industrial agents. Research agents are used to model natural agents, and to explore general principles of intelligence. Industrial agents are used for practical applications. Computational agents are subdivided into simulated agents (i.e., agents simulating a biological or robotic agent), artificial life agents, and software agents.

artificial life agents that do not necessarily simulate something but are creatures of their own type, digital creatures. There has been considerable hype about the last category of computational agents, called *software agents*. In essence, software agents are computer programs that perform a certain task and interact with real-world software environments and humans by issuing commands and interpreting the environment's feedback. Typical tasks are filtering electronic mail, sending routine messages such as reminders for meetings or announcements of seminars, collecting information on the Internet, scheduling meetings, performing system maintenance tasks like continuous intrusion detection, and assisting in purchasing a car or finding an apartment. Especially with the advent of the Internet, software agents have become enormously popular. They come in many varieties (e.g., Riecken 1994), and it is sometimes hard to distinguish them from other kinds of computer programs. Software agents have a great potential for application, especially in a networked society. However, a detailed treatment would be beyond the scope of this book.

Let us now look at the different ways in which autonomous agents are used.

MODELING

One application of autonomous agents in cognitive science is to model the behavior of biological agents. An example of the modeling approach is shown in figure 1.10, where an autonomous robot is used to model the phonotactic behavior of a cricket (Webb, 1993, 1994). We designate as phonotaxis those processes by which female crickets move towards a particular sound, the calling song of a potential mate. This robot model can be used to generate (biological) hypotheses about cricket behavior; these hypotheses can be tested in experiments with real (biological) crickets.

As a further example, assume that you want to replicate another idea from nature, say, an artificial retina. Once you have developed your conception of how the retina functions, you may very quickly find that your hypothesis about the functioning of the (biological) retina is flawed if you actually build and test it on a robot. Or let's take an example from neurobiology. We know that the control mechanisms of animals are based on neural structures. Biological neural systems have inspired artificial neural network models. Neural architectures, as it turns out, can be understood only in the context of the physical system in which they are embedded. Intro-

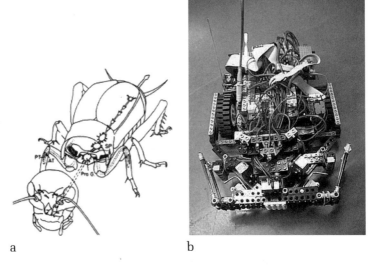

a   b

Figure 1.10 Illustration of the synthetic methodology. The robot cricket (b) can be used to investigate the behavior of the real cricket (a). (Reprinted with permission.)

ducing mobile robots—that is, real, behaving systems—brings a novel perspective to modern neuroscience.

Many researchers have capitalized on this fascinating interaction between biology and autonomous agents research. Lambrinos et al. (1997) have developed a robot that navigates according to the same principles as the desert ant *Cataglyphis*. Ferrell (1994) and others have developed walking robots, applying principles known from insect walking as described by Cruse (1991). And some robots move around using control circuitry just like that of the housefly (Franceschini et al. 1992). Robot modeling has also been successfully employed in the area of psychology. An example is the humanoid robot Cog (Brooks and Stein 1993), used for development studies of how human infants learn to reach for a ball or play with toys, for example. There are also many attractive simulation studies, such as walking insects (Beer 1990), fish learning to swim in simulated water, for example, a shark preying on other fish (Terzopoulos et al. 1994), and a humanoid robot used for developmental and social interaction studies (Kuniyoshi and Nagakubo 1997).

EXPLORING GENERAL PRINCIPLES OF INTELLIGENCE
A second application of autonomous agents in cognitive science is to explore principles of intelligence. This approach draws inspira-

tion from nature, but offers us more freedom than the modeling approach. Experiments can be conducted using any type of sensor, even sensors that do not exist in nature (like laser scanners, or radio emitters-receivers). We can use wheels, magnets, and batteries in our systems; we can exchange pieces of code, place sensors in different positions, add another lens here and there; in short, we can perform experiments. We can build systems that we have invented using artificial devices. Developing systems different from the ones we observe in nature is an extremely productive way of doing research. By doing things differently from nature, we may learn a great deal about how things might, in fact, function in nature.

One of the main motivations to employ autonomous agents is the idea of *emergence*. Autonomous agents, by definition, behave in the real world without human intervention. One of the fascinating features of autonomous agents is that they exhibit so-called *emergent* behaviors, that is, behaviors not programmed into the agents by the designer. Robots programmed only to follow a light start helping each other, or they are cleaning up though programmed only to avoid obstacles. Or a group of simulated birds are flocking, but were programmed only with local rules, that is, rules that make reference only to their immediate neighbors.

In exploring principles of intelligence, the search for emergence is an important motivation. We show many examples of this approach throughout the book. To mention but a few: The famous Braitenberg vehicles are used to explore how very simple mechanisms can lead to truly amazing emergent behaviors; the robot Polly, which used to give tours at the AI Laboratory at MIT, was used to study principles of cheap visual navigation; "boids," a kind of artificial bird, were used to investigate how flocking behavior could emerge from local rules; and fantastic creatures, created by Karl Sims, living in a virtual world of simulated physics were used to explore the evolution of morphology and neural controllers.

The line between exploring principles of intelligence and modeling can be fuzzy. Often agents used for modeling purposes are modified so that they deviate from the model. On the other hand, a robot used to explore general principles might be applied for modeling purposes because it develops interesting related behavior. SMC agents (which we discuss in detail in chapter 12) were originally used to study neural architectures for sensory-motor coordination. Then developmental psychologists became interested in using them to model category learning in human babies. The insights thus gained can then be applied to develop systems that perform useful tasks in the real world.

APPLICATIONS

To date, the enormous potential for applications of autonomous agents technology has hardly been explored. Robots, for example, can be used for marking the mines on a minefield with color, for monitoring sewage systems for leakages, for cleaning up hazardous waste sites, for distributing mail, and for surveilling an industrial plant. Autonomous wheelchairs are another possible application. Computational agents hold tremendous promise for applications, especially in the areas of evolutionary robotics and artificial life. Ideas from natural evolution are employed, for example, for optimization problems and they have also been successfully applied to industrial problems. Simulated agents are used widely in the field of computer graphics and the entertainment industry.

THE DESIGN PERSPECTIVE

The synthetic methodology is closely coupled with the notion of design. Autonomous agents, whether robotic or computational, in order to be built, must be designed. Although we normally think about design as an activity for engineers, the design perspective has proven extremely fruitful in cognitive science for studying natural intelligence. Evolution can be viewed, in a sense, as a designer (e.g., Dawkins 1988), perhaps a blind one, but nevertheless an extremely effective one: Natural systems have truly impressive capabilities. What we are asking is how we would design a system that behaves in a particular way that we find interesting? We devote a great deal of effort in this book to exploring design. In fact, one of our main goals is to elaborate a set of design principles for autonomous agents that, in a sense, constitute our understanding of the nature of intelligence.

Issues to Think About

Issue 1.1: Is IQ Irrelevant for Intelligence?

We have argued, as most people these days do, that IQ is a poor measure of intelligence because it tries to reduce a complex phenomenon to a single number. On the other hand, there is evidence that IQ is a good predictor of some kinds of success. When discussing the nature-nurture debate, we concluded that intelligence originates from a highly complex interaction between genetic and environmental factors, the interaction between nature and nurture. This consideration suggests a generally valid strategy for cognitive science. Experience teaches us that studying an individual's development, rather than the individual in its current appearance, often leads to a better understanding of its behavior, because simply inspecting the organism itself offers us only little insight into the constraints, the history, the personal experiences, the interactions of the individual with the environment. As many developmental studies have shown, concepts, the ability to make distinctions, are a direct consequence of sensory-motor behavior. Thus high intellectual ability resulting in a high IQ score may well be due to a complex mix of sensory-motor abilities that in turn depend on the particular social environment. In other words, before an individual is capable of solving the problems on an IQ test, he has to master many other things including many that do not relate directly to abstract thinking but to other notions of intelligence mentioned above. The reason IQ is a good predictor for certain types of success may eventually be explained on the basis of a developmental perspective, but it remains an open research question.

Issue 1.2:   The Diversity-Compliance Trade-off: The Common Denominator?

We have argued that the common denominator underlying the various notions of intelligence discussed in this chapter is the diversity-compliance trade-off, in particular, that the two core aspects of intelligent behavior are generation of diversity and compliance with rules. In other words, there is always a trade-off between generating new solutions, being flexible and innovative, and complying with the existing rules, exploiting what is already known. This characterization, we have argued, holds for a vast range of agents, from companies that face new challenges in the information age down to ants surviving in the desert. If this view is correct, then it should be applicable to the reader. We would like you, before you continue reading, to reflect for a few moments on whether you feel your own behavior can be described in this way. Think about how you usually solve a problem: Can your approach be described in terms of the diversity-compliance trade-off? Or do you think you behave according to different principles?

Points to Remember

- Intelligence is too complex a notion to be captured by a simple definition. What people in general and even scientists mean by the term varies greatly, and there is little hope that there will ever be agreement. The key aspect, implicitly or explicitly present in many conceptions of intelligence, is generation of behavioral diversity while complying with the rules. This idea is independent of any notion of levels of intelligence. It applies to abstract thinking just as much as to an animal avoiding a predator. An organism that always displays the same behavior is not intelligent.

- IQ tests were originally invented to determine whether certain children would be better off in a special school. Eventually, the IQ test was turned into a general intelligence test, claiming to measure a general intelligence factor g. It is now generally agreed that intelligence is much too complex a phenomenon to be measured by a test yielding one number.

- Emotional intelligence has recently been proposed as being equally relevant for success in life as the kind of abstract intelligence measured by IQ tests. EQ tests measuring emotional intelligence have been suggested to complement IQ tests. It is still open to debate to what extent and in what form the EQ will survive.

- The nature-nurture debate concerns the extent to which knowledge is inborn or can be acquired. The behaviors and capabilities of a human result from a complex interaction of genetic and environmental factors. Thus, the answer to the nature-nurture question can only be that the origins of intelligence come from the interaction between nature and nurture.

- The Turing test was proposed to operationalize the notion of intelligence by means of an empirical test. It is based on the idea whether the (verbal) behavior of a computer can be distinguished from that of a human. If it cannot be distinguished, the computer can be said to have intelligence. Because the Turing test is based on natural language, it is restricted to human intelligence. It is still an open question whether it is a good test for human intelligence.

- The Chinese Room is a thought experiment proposed by Searle. On the basis of a set of rules a person—Searle—locked in a room produces output sentences from input sentences, exclusively on the basis of comparing the shapes of the Chinese characters which, to the person, are just meaningless symbols.

- There are analytic and synthetic approaches to the study of intelligence. The synthetic approach can be characterized as "understanding by building." In traditional AI and cognitive science, the models are computer programs; in embodied cognitive science, they are in the form of autonomous agents, either robotic agents or simulated agents.

- Autonomous agents exhibit emergent behaviors. Such behaviors are not programmed into the agents by the designer but rather are a result of the interaction of the agents with their environment.

- Autonomous agents, robotic or computational, can be used in three ways: as models of natural agents, to explore general principles of intelligence, and for specific tasks and applications. There are large areas of overlap among these three modes, especially between the first two.

- "Synthetic" implies design. The design perspective has turned out to be particularly fruitful for studying natural intelligence. The autonomous agents approach capitalizes on the design perspective.

- Embodied cognitive science designates the research field outlined in this book. It employs a synthetic methodology based on autonomous agents.

Further Reading

Gardner, H. (1987). *The mind's new science. A history of the cognitive revolution.* New York: Basic Books. (Original work published 1985) (An overview of the field of classical cognitive science. Recommended to anyone interested in the field, especially those with a philosophical interest. Does not include issues pertaining to more recent approaches to cognitive science and AI.)

Gould, S. J. (1996). *The mismeasure of man.* New York: W. W. Norton. (Paperback issue published 1996) (Contains, among other things, a treatise on the problems with IQ. Intellectually profound and highly entertaining.)

Kurzweil, R. (1990). *The age of intelligent machines.* Cambridge, MA: MIT Press. (An entertaining book on all aspects of intelligent machines, with many illustrations, photographs, and interviews with people involved in AI and related fields. In particular, topics of computation, Turing machines, and their application to human thought are discussed.)

Searle, J. R. (1980). Minds, brains, and programs. *Behavioral and Brain Sciences, 3,* 417–424. Reprinted in J. Haugeland 1981 (Ed.), *Mind design.* Montgomery, VT: Bradford Books. (The standard reference to the Chinese Room thought experiment. The article is supplemented with various peer comments, including the author's reply.)

In the previous chapter we introduced various ways of looking at intelligence. In this chapter we will briefly review classical AI and cognitive science. It is important to understand the classical view because it is still very popular. For example, if one peruses the literature in cognitive psychology or computational linguistics, we find that, for the most part, classical thinking still dominates. Moreover, the classical perspective has much appeal and is compatible with most people's intuitions about intelligence. Although some critics, most prominently Hubert Dreyfus (1979, 1992) pointed out some of its weaknesses a long time ago, the problems with the classical perspective have started to become clear only during the last ten to fifteen years in the AI community at large. With an understanding of classical AI, the reasons for the embodied cognitive science approach are much easier to see.

This chapter has deliberately been kept short because all that is required here is the general context. For more extended reviews of the field, the reader's attention is directed to any of the many excellent books on this topic, particularly those suggested in the further readings at the end of the chapter. We begin by introducing first cognitive science and the cognitivistic paradigm, Next, we discuss what an architecture based on classical principles might look like, which will also serve as an introduction to some important issues in cognitive science such as perception, memory, and planning. We conclude with an overview of the design principles applied in the cognitivistic paradigm.

2.1 Cognitive Science: Preliminaries

A Short Historical Note

The roots of cognitive science are intimately linked to two scientific meetings in 1956. At the Symposium on Information Theory, held at MIT in September 1956, leading authorities in the information and human sciences presented a number of seminal papers. Allen Newell, a computer scientist, and Herbert A. Simon, a political scientist and later a Nobel laureate in economics, reported on the Logic Theory Machine, a program that could prove mathematical theorems from the *Principia Mathematica*, a classical treatise on logic (e.g., Newell and Simon 1956). Newell and Simon claimed to have developed the first thinking machine. In "Magic Number Seven Plus or Minus Two," psychologist George Miller argued that the storage capacity of human short-term memory is limited to roughly seven items, or "chunks" (e.g., Miller 1956). Linguist Noam Chomsky introduced a new theory of language based on linguistic transformation whose most important contribution was in showing that the essence of language could not be explained by behaviorist concepts, that is, by only focusing on stimulus-response relations (e.g., Chomsky 1959).[1] As a result, linguists started to look for a new language in which to theorize about language. They found it in the theory of computers: the language of information processing.

The other important meeting in 1956 was held at Dartmouth College, New Hampshire. The goal of this meeting, now known as the "Dartmouth Conference," was to think about thinking machines. Programs that could solve problems, recognize patterns, play games, prove theorems, and reason logically were discussed. Among the participants were the founding fathers of artificial intelligence: John McCarthy, Marvin Minsky, Allen Newell, and Herbert Simon. In the preceding decade, a number of important scientists had argued that computers should be able to carry out processes resembling human thinking. Work by Norbert Wiener, John von Neumann, Alan Turing, and Warren McCulloch all pointed toward the development of electronic computers that could simulate functions normally associated with the human brain.

The discussions at both conferences centered on what came to be called artificial intelligence and information processing psychology: the analogy between human thinking and processes taking place in a computer. This early work was the beginning of the

---

[1] Behaviorism was an important orientation in psychology during the first half of this century. It explains behavior in terms of stimulus-response relationships. The most famous example is Pavlov's dog that initially only salivated (response) at the presentation of food (stimulus); it was trained to salivate at the sound of a bell by repeatedly ringing a bell at the presentation of food.

so-called cognitive revolution in psychology: "What began to emerge in the 1950's was a new conception of the human being as machine, and a new language in which to formulate theories about cognitive processes. People could be described, it seemed, as general-purpose computing devices, born with a certain hardware, and programmed by experience and socialization to behave in certain ways. The goal of psychology would be the specification of how human beings process information; the concepts of stimulus and response would be replaced by the concepts of information input and output, and theories about mediating s-r chains[2] would be replaced by theories about internal computations and computational states" (Leahey 1994, p. 282). Broadbent (1957) proposed a mechanical model of attention and memory in which he represented the input to the senses not as stimuli but as information. Simon's claim that within ten years most theories in psychology would take the form of computer programs (Dreyfus 1972, p. 164) represented an extreme manifestation of this general trend. It became natural to think of human beings as information processing systems that receive input from the environment (perception), process that information (thinking), and act upon the decision reached (behavior). This corresponds to the so-called sense-think-act cycle. Psychologists could now talk about "encoding," "search," "retrieval," "matching," and other information processing operations. The hope was to establish a strong theoretical and formal ground for conceptualizing human behavior that would replace behaviorist psychology. It seemed that anything humans do could be viewed in information processing terms: reading, remembering facts, recognizing objects, drawing logical conclusions, solving difficult problems, playing chess, conducting a conversation, and so forth. Moreover, models couched in information processing terms were easy to formalize in terms of computer programs. In 1960, this general trend was summarized in a book of fundamental importance for psychology: *Plans and the Structure of Behavior*, by the already mentioned George Miller, Eugene Galanter, a psychologist with strong roots in mathematics, and Karl Pribram, a neuroscientist. Miller, Galanter, and Pribram argued that the reflex arc of behaviorism—the coupling between stimulus and response—should be replaced by what they called a "TOTE unit" (for "Test-

---

[2] "Mediating s-r chains" are the processes by which sequences of s-r pairs (stimulus-response pairs) are produced.

Operate-Test-Exit"). TOTE units are high-level processes used to establish plans and to control behavior. We describe this approach in chapter 11.

In sum, the core idea that emerged from all this work was the belief that complex processes are required for transforming the stimulus (input) into the response (output). Unlike early behaviorists, such as Watson or Skinner, information processing psychologists were willing to infer central mental processes from observable behavior, and they viewed these central processes as analogous to the processes occurring in a computer: "cognition as computation," where cognition is a vaguely defined term for those processes not directly connected to sensory or motor systems. The information processing metaphor has strongly influenced much of modern (cognitive) psychology. Thus, as they do in classical AI, nearly all cognitive constructs in modern psychology describe information processing mechanisms. In their often-cited book *Cognitive Psychology and Information Processing*, Lachman, Lachman and Butterfield (1979) defined cognitive psychology in terms of the computer metaphor: It is about "how people take in information, how they recode and remember it, how they make decisions, how they transform their internal knowledge states, and how they translate these states into behavioral outputs" (p. 99). The cognitivistic view also spread to other areas of psychology, including social psychology, social learning theory, and even psychoanalysis (e.g., Pfeifer and Leuzinger-Bohleber 1986).

The Interdisciplinary Study of the Mind

As pointed out in chapter 1, cognitive science is the interdisciplinary study of the mind (figure 2.1). Cognitive science has attracted many researchers from different disciplines concerned, in one way or another, with human intelligence, mainly psychologists, neuroscientists, linguists, computer scientists, and philosophers. More recently, engineers and some biologists have also started joining in. Psychology has as its subject of investigation the human being (including the mind, knowledge, and intelligence). Linguistics has focused on particular capacities of the mind—the internal processes by which we understand and produce language. The neurosciences make an essential contribution, since the brain is their substrate. The concept of information processing is central to modern neuroscience, as book titles such as *The Computational*

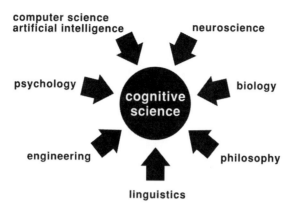

Figure 2.1 The disciplines contributing to cognitive science. Originally, researchers were mostly from psychology, computer science (in particular artificial intelligence), neuroscience, linguistics, and philosophy; more recently, engineers and biologists have joined the endeavor.

Brain (Churchland and Sejnowski 1992) suggest. Computer scientists and AI researchers have traditionally pursued the goal of developing intelligent computer programs. Philosophers have always been strongly involved, especially those from the field of philosophy of mind. More recently, in particular with the advent of robotics, interest has grown among engineers in learning from natural systems, not only humans, but biological systems in general. Biologists, in turn, got interested in interdisciplinary endeavors, in particular ethologists (those working in animal behavior).

One of the true challenges of interdisciplinary research is communication among different disciplines, all of which employ different concepts and languages, different methodologies, different formalisms, and different diagrams. In traditional cognitive science and AI, the language of information processing kept the field together. It is in fact more than a mere language. It endorses basic beliefs about the nature of intelligence. "Computation" and "representation" are the key words that best characterize these beliefs.

2.2 The Cognitivistic Paradigm

The view of cognition as computation, computation as operating on representations, has also been called the "cognitivistic paradigm," or "functionalism." Let us briefly look at some of its basic concepts.

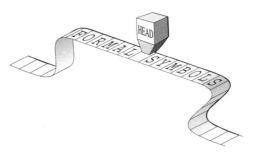

Figure 2.2 The components of a Turing machine. A Turing machine consists of a read-write head and a tape. The head reads a symbol from the tape. Depending on the head's internal state, it then either moves the tape to the left or right and writes a symbol onto the tape, or it stops. (Adapted from Haugeland 1985.)

Computation: Turing Machines and the Church-Turing Thesis

The idea of computation was formalized by Alan Turing (1936), though in fact other mathematicians like Alonzo Church developed similar ideas approximately around the same time. In our presentation we follow Haugeland (1985).

A Turing machine is a theoretical model of a computer. Essentially, it consists of two parts, a head and a tape (figure 2.2). The tape is just a passive storage medium: it is divided along its length into squares, each of which can hold one character from some prespecified alphabet that often consists of 0s and 1s but may contain more characters. The number of tape squares available is unlimited but only a finite segment of them is occupied at any one time; that is, all of the remaining ones are empty or contain only a special blank character. At any given step, the head reads the square that is underneath its reading device. Also, at each step, the head itself is in a particular internal state (from a prespecified, finite repertoire of states). This state typically changes from one step to the next. In a special case, the head enters a "halt" state, in which case the machine stops.

Two factors fully determine what the head does at any step in time: the character it finds in the square it is scanning, and its current internal state. The head's actions determined by these two factors are:

1. what character to write on the square that is currently under the head, replacing whatever was there before
2. whether to move the tape right or left, which determines which square to scan next
3. what internal state is next, or whether the head should halt

Table 2.1 Example of a Turing machine. The character "—" represents a blank square.

	1	2
—	_R2	HALT
A	AL1	BR2
B	BL1	AR2
C	CL1	CR2

The entire functioning of a Turing machine can be specified in a single, two-dimensional chart containing one row for each character and one column for each state. The matrix positions specify the three actions. This is illustrated in table 2.1.

Corresponding to each state and symbol is either a three-character entry in the chart or the word HALT. In the three-character entries, the first character is the character to be written; the second character is an L or an R, for move left or move right; and the third character is the number of the next state. What will this Turing machine do if it is started in state 1, scanning some square in the midst of a string of As, Bs, and Cs? First, no matter which letter it encounters, the head moves to the left and does not change the letter on the tape. (Note that the machine never changes anything if it is in state 1; no matter which letter it encounters, it is instructed to write the same letter.). When it gets to the left end of the string (and encounters, for the first time, a blank) it switches to state 2, and begins moving right, converting all As to Bs and all Bs to As, according to the instructions in state 2. Cs are not changed. At the right of the string, it again encounters a blank square, and it stops, as the instruction it encounters is HALT.

The Turing machine is an abstract machine—its physical realization is irrelevant, as are how much time one step takes and how it is physically performed. What counts is only the steps the machine executes. Turing machines were invented not because they can do particular things, but because they can model or simulate any (abstract) computing machine whatsoever. Thus, Turing machines are universal. This conclusion has inspired Turing to speculate that Turing machines might in fact simulate human intelligence, a hypothesis now known as the Church-Turing thesis. Several versions of the thesis appear in the literature, some

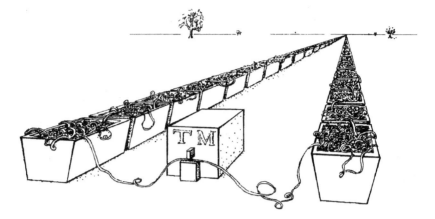

Figure 2.3 Turing machine involving a potentially infinite tape. Managing a tape of indefinite length raises substantial technological problems. Thus there are good reasons why the Turing machine is an abstract concept, rather than something to be physically realized. (From Penrose 1989, p. 36, reprinted with permission.)

stronger, some weaker. It can be broken down into two parts: first, that a problem that cannot be solved through any theoretical means of computation, that is, a Turing machine, cannot be solved by human thought either; second, that if humans can solve a problem or engage in some intelligent activity, then machines can ultimately be constructed to perform in the same way. This latter belief is at the heart of much of AI research (for more detail, see Kurzweil 1990).

If we envision a Turing machine being physically realized and in fact having an infinitely long tape, dealing with this infinitely long tape may turn out to be a formidable engineering problem, possibly even harder than the computational ones that have to be solved by an abstract Turing machine. Consider the cartoon of a Turing machine shown in figure 2.3. It illustrates that what in the abstract sounds unproblematic, such as a potentially infinitely long tape, turns out to be a significant problem when we think about its physical implementation.

Functionalism and Physical Symbol Systems

For our purposes, functionalism and the cognitivistic paradigm are largely synonymous. Functionalism, as proposed by Hillary Putnam (1975), means that thinking and other intelligent functions need not be carried out by means of the same machinery in order to reflect the same kinds of processes; in fact, the machinery could be

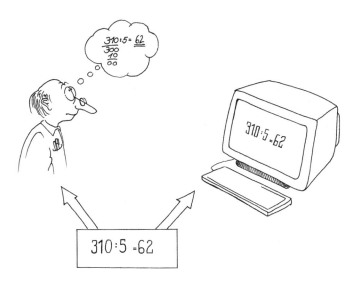

Figure 2.4 Functionalism. Both the human and the computer produce the same result. What matters are the algorithms, not the particular physical instantiation.

made of Emmental cheese, so long as it can perform the functions required. In other words, intelligence or cognition can be studied at the level of algorithms or computational processes without having to consider the underlying structure of the device on which the algorithm is performed. From the functionalist position, it follows that there is a distinction between hardware and software: What we are interested in is the software or the program. If the machine is universal and can carry out any computation, then we are interested not in the hardware but only in the programs that run on it. The brains of Japanese and Swiss people are indistinguishable, but the Japanese and Swiss do speak very different languages and have developed very different social systems. This must be the result of the "software," not the hardware or "wetware." Figure 2.4 illustrates the basic idea of functionalism as precisely the characterization we have given of classical AI: Intelligence as computation. The so-called Physical Symbol Systems Hypothesis, which characterizes the research program of traditional AI, exemplifies the cognitivistic paradigm.

The Physical Symbol Systems Hypothesis, first presented by Newell and Simon in a seminal Turing award lecture entitled "Computer Science as Empirical Inquiry" (Newell and Simon 1976), suggests an empirical rather than a theoretical approach to the study of human intelligence. Intelligence, in Newell and Simon's approach, is viewed as symbol manipulation. The Physical

Symbol Systems Hypothesis states, in essence, that a physical symbol system is a necessary and sufficient condition for general intelligent action. The term "physical" refers to the idea that symbol systems must be realized in some physical medium (paper, computer, brain) but it is irrelevant *how* they are realized. Typical examples of physical symbol systems are production systems (i.e., systems based on if-then rules) or general purpose programming languages like LISP or C. "Necessary" means that any system lacking this property cannot be intelligent, and "sufficient" implies that a system having this property has the potential for intelligent action. In this view, since programming languages are physical symbol systems, computers can potentially be made intelligent. "General intelligent action" means that the system should be able to do not only one thing, like playing chess, but a number of things. This property is extremely important, since agents in the real world always have to do several things. At the very least, agents in the real world, for example, animals, have to eat, drink, avoid being hurt or falling prey to other animals, and reproduce. Although these properties of general intelligence had been recognized early on, in subsequent years they were almost entirely neglected.

Computational processes operate on representations, the *symbol structures*. A (symbolic) "representation" (see figure 2.5) in the sense that Newell and Simon mean it refers to a situation in the outside world and obeys the "law of representation," namely:

```
decode[encode(T)(encode(X₁))] = T(X₁),
```

where X_1 is the original external situation and T is the external transformation (Newell 1990, p. 59). There is an encoding as well as a decoding function for establishing a mapping between the outside world and the internal representation.

It is important to understand the meaning of a representation as used here: Representations are structures that exist within the individual and can be interpreted by the individual itself. This way of looking at representation seems very natural. It is not without problems, however, in particular if applied to humans or animals. The Physical Symbol Systems Hypothesis can be viewed as the research program of classical AI. Note that Newell and Simon did not claim that intelligence equals symbol processing, but they suggested it as a hypothesis to be tested empirically. The goal of AI research is to explore to what extent the Physical Symbol Systems Hypothesis is true.

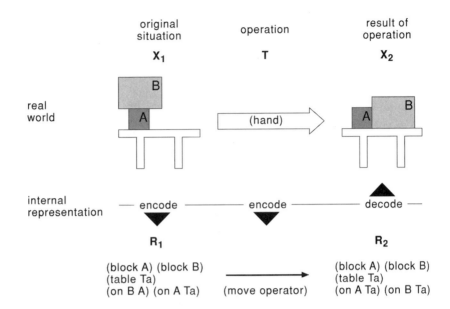

Figure 2.5   The Law of Representation. The situation in the real world (X_1)—a table (Ta), on top of which is a block (A), on top of which is another block (B)—is mapped onto an internal representation (R_1). the operator (T) that puts block B on the table is also mapped onto the internal representation. If the operation (move block B from on top of block A to the table) is performed in the real world and on the internal representation, and the result (R_2) is mapped back from the internal representation onto the real world via the decode function, the two situations—the one generated through the real-world operation T, and the one generated via the internal representation—should be identical. In other words, if R_1 is an internal representation of X_1, operation T should produce the same real-world result (X_2), whether performed in the real world or on the internal representation, then decoded.

Many other researchers adhere, at least in essence, to the cognitivistic paradigm. In psychology, similar views have been expressed by Pylyshyn (1984); in linguistics, by Fodor (e.g., Fodor 1975) (see Gardner 1987 for an overview). The cognitivistic paradigm has strongly influenced psychology, in particular cognitive psychology; The result is known as *information processing psychology.*

The Use of Computers in Cognitive Science
Information processing psychology employs the metaphor of human cognition as computation. The computer's operations (storage, copying, matching, retrieval, logical operations) are taken to be the underlying operations of human cognition. We target precisely this analogy in our criticisms of information processing psychology in the next chapter. We do not disapprove of the use of

Focus 2.1: Topics in Classical AI

> Over the years, AI has split into many different subfields. Topic areas include knowledge representation (how to represent knowledge about the world in the computer), natural language processing (how to get a computer to understand spoken and written human language), problem solving and reasoning (how to have computers solve problems and draw conclusions for us), expert systems (how to make human expertise available to nonexperts by automating expert behavior), qualitative reasoning about physical processes (how to get computers to infer the right things about the physical world), theorem proving (how to have computers automatically prove theorems in logical formalisms), and machine learning (how to get computers to acquire knowledge that has not been programmed into them). Throughout the history of AI there have been efforts in robot building and computer vision. Table 2.2 provides complete overview of topics, taken from Russell and Norvig's (1995) popular textbook in AI. 2.2. it is perhaps interesting to note that the questions being

Table 2.2 Topics in classical AI. (Adapted from Russell and Norvig 1995.)

Topic area	Topic
Problem solving	• Solving problems by searching • Informed search methods • Game playing
Knowledge and reasoning	• Agents that reason logically • First-order logic • Building a knowledge base • Inference in first-order logic • Logical reasoning systems
Acting logically	• Planning • Practical planning • Planning and acting
Uncertain knowledge and reasoning	• Uncertainty • Probabilistic reasoning systems • Making simple decisions • Making complex decisions
Learning	• Learning from observations • Learning in neural and belief networks • Reinforcement learning • Knowledge in learning
Communicating, perceiving, and acting	• Agents that communicate • Practical natural language processing • Perception • Robotics

Focus 2.1 (continued)

> investigated in AI are related to the underlying convictions about the nature of intelligence, with a focus on topics relating to abstract thinking. Topics relating to the real world have a more prominent place, however, in this listing as compared to those of earlier textbooks. (This is also illustrated by the agent perspective that has been adopted in Russell and Norvig's book.)

computers to study human cognition; computers can be used to simulate virtually any natural process, including brain processes, muscle contractions, limb and body movements, and vibrations of the vocal chords. As a simulation device, the computer is not used as a metaphor for intelligence but only as a formal tool—like mathematics. This is not intended to comment about the quality of these simulations, that is, about how closely these simulations reflect the actual physical processes. (As it turns out, even for seemingly simple physical processes, like those of a basic infrared sensor, achieving a realistic level of similarity is highly demanding.) Nor are we, when criticizing information processing psychology, criticizing the mathematical discipline of information theory: Information theoretic concepts may be beneficially applied, for example, to the investigation of brain processes. In fact, in chapter 13, we present complexity measures that capitalize on information theory. What we *do* criticize is the analogy between human thinking and processes running in a computer, that is, information processing as the manipulation of symbols. We leave the actual criticism of this analogy, however, to chapter 3. For now, let us turn to an illustration of the classical AI approach.

2.3 An Architecture for an Intelligent Agent

Now that we have given an overview of the ideas underlying classical AI and cognitive science, let us illustrate some of them. Rather than simply go through the list of topics of AI research presented in the focus 2.1, we look at how an agent might be designed from the classical AI perspective, because we are interested in autonomous agents, rather than in developing AI systems for specialized purposes (like playing chess or proving theorems). We also use this case study to introduce some important conceptual issues in the study of intelligence, for example, on perception and memory. As we mentioned earlier, you will find this way of proceeding very natural. Nonetheless, as we show later, in spite of this approach's apparent naturalness, there are problems that necessitate a different approach, especially if your interest is in autonomous agents.

The most important reason for undertaking such an illustration here is to exemplify the cognitivistic paradigm. Our presentation is inspired by *The Computer and the Mind* by prominent psychologist and linguist Phil Johnson-Laird (1988). Like many others, Johnson-Laird is interested in psychological explanation. In his view, the underlying concept that has the most explanatory power is that of computation or symbol processing.

Johnson-Laird starts from the assumption that the following are the mind's main tasks:

- to perceive the world
- to learn, to remember, and to control actions
- to think and to create new ideas
- to control communication with others
- to create the experience of feelings, intentions, and self-awareness

For each of these tasks, Johnson-Laird's book gives a computational account. Johnson-Laird argues that theories of the mind should be expressed in a form that can be modeled in a computer program, that is, in computational terms, since a working computer program places a minimal reliance on intuition: "the theory it embodies may be false, but at least it is coherent, and does not assume too much" (Johnson-Laird 1988, p. 52). Thus an agent must be equipped with computer programs to perform the tasks listed above. Let us call the robot that we are designing here "JL" (for Johnson-Laird's Robot). JL has never been built—it is a thought experiment that we consider here for the purpose of illustrating design principles from the classical AI perspective. (A famous robot that has actually been built and that implements some of these principles, Shakey, is described in chapter 11.)

Before we start, however, a short note is in order. The topics covered below (vision, learning and memory, control of actions, thinking, etc.) are in themselves entire research areas. We choose to consider only those aspects that we will reconsider later from the perspective of embodied cognitive science.

Perceiving the World: Vision

There are many ways to perceive the world, namely through seeing, hearing, feeling, or smelling. One of the most powerful ways to perceive is seeing. Thus, it is a good idea to equip JL with vision, the only sensory modality that we discuss in this chapter. The history of the investigation of vision shows that it is easy for the brain to do but difficult for us to understand. Normally, things are seen and recognized automatically and without effort. This makes it especially hard for cognitive scientists to understand vision. Rather than delve into the problems associated with vision in detail, we defer to the extensive literature about this field, and here merely outline some of the basic issues. (For more details, see, e.g., Horn 1986), leaving a more extensive treatment of vision for chapter 12.

One of the most influential theories of vision has been developed by David Marr (1982). In Marr's information-processing approach the goal of vision is to reconstruct a three-dimensional representation of the external world from the patterns of light falling on the robot's (or the human's) retina. In other words, the focus of his research is to provide a computational explanation of how people can make sense of what they see in the world. More precisely, he attempts to explain how it is possible to recognize three-dimensional objects from two-dimensional raw images. In essence, he suggests that there are a number of stages in which the original raw image is successively transformed until a three-dimensional representation of the world is found (i.e., the objects have been recognized). Note that in Marr's conception vision is viewed as purely computational and does not take the interaction with the environment into account.

Alternative approaches that take this interaction into account are "animate vision," championed by Dana Ballard and his colleagues (Ballard 1991), or the Gibsonian perspective (e.g., Turvey and Carello 1986).[3] We describe these approaches in chapter 12, where we also present embodied cognitive science's view of perception.

Learning, Memory, and Action

LEARNING
The essence of learning is that the agent can use its own experience to improve its behavior. An important aspect of learning is gener-

---

[3] Both Ballard and Turvey consider motion to be an essential ingredient of vision. In particular, they consider perception and action as one system, not as separate entities.

alization, the transfer of experience to novel situations. Thus, JL has been equipped with a learning system. Learning, in the cognitivistic paradigm, is again a computational process: algorithms operate on certain data structures. For example, a system that often encounters two properties of an object simultaneously might form a new concept: if the properties "apple," "ripe," and "green" frequently co-occur, the learning algorithm might combine them into the concept "G0127," which most people know as "Granny Smith." Other learning algorithms generate rules, decision trees, or logical descriptions from a set of examples. The rich literature on machine learning focuses, almost by definition, on the computational aspects.

MEMORY

Learning is closely tied to the notion of memory. JL is equipped with a memory system consisting essentially of three types of components: sensory buffers (registers) and short-term and long-term memory (figure 2.6). The higher-level cognitive functions like reasoning, planning, and language operate on the short-term memory. The task of a computational theory of memory is to describe how the information transfer among these various systems functions and how such transfers are controlled by the memory system. This clearly corresponds to the metaphor of input-processing-output: Sensory stimulation is transmitted via sensory registers to a short-term store (STS) where the processing—the higher-level cognitive functions—takes place. During this processing, STS interacts with the long-term store (LTS). Finally a response is generated. Figure 2.6 can be seen as a kind of overall architecture of an agent. It is not just any memory model but the landmark model of information processing psychology "from which virtually all later accounts of information processing descend" (Leahey 1994, p. 307).

One of the central questions is in what sort of format the information in the various modules is represented. JL's memory content is represented as stored structures. At some point, these structures are encoded, stored, and later retrieved, depending on the agent's current needs. A well-known example that illustrates this concept is the so-called script (Schank and Abelson 1977; figure 2.7). Natural as it may seem, this conceptualization of memory leads to significant theoretical and practical problems. Chapter 15, devoted entirely to memory, discusses in detail the issues involved.

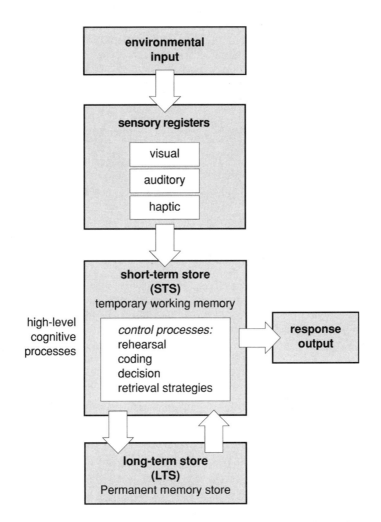

Figure 2.6 The flow of information through memory. Input from the environment passes through the sensory registers and enters the short-term store. Depending on the control processes currently active, the information is stored in the long-term store or results in a response output. Information can also be retrieved from the long-term store. (Adapted from Atkinson and Shiffrin 1968.)

Roles		customer (c), waiter (w), chef (c), owner (o)
Props		tables, chairs, menus, food, bills, money, tip
Preconditions		c has money, c is hungry
Result		c has less money, o has more money, c is less hungry
Scene 1	ENTER	c enters the restaurant
Scene 2	SEATING	c is waiting to be seated, c gets a table, c sits down
Scene 3	ORDERING	c asks w for menu, c studies menu, c orders the meal from w
Scene 4	EATING	w brings the food, c eats the food
Scene 5	PAYING	c asks w for check, g pays check, c leaves tip
Scene 6	LEAVING	c leaves restaurant

Figure 2.7 Illustration of a memory structure. The restaurant script is a representation of what typically happens in a restaurant. "Roles" describes the various participants, "Props" the relevant objects, "Preconditions" the prerequisites for going to a restaurant, and "Result" the effect a visit to a restaurant has on the participants and the situation. A sequence of scenes then represents the events occurring during a restaurant visit.

CONTROLLING ACTIONS—PLANS

According to Miller, Galanter, and Pribram (1960), whom we introduced above in our discussion of cognitive science's early history, a plan is required to control the order in which a sequence of operations is to be performed. Planning is at the core of classical AI. Imagine that JL is trying to get from San Francisco to New York in order to visit the Museum of Modern Art. How does it proceed? As a traditional AI agent, it uses the *goal-directed principle*, according to which behavior results from a comparison of a representation of the goal state (being at the Museum of Modern Art) and the current state (being in San Francisco). Based on this comparison, a plan is constructed for moving the agent from the current to the goal state. A popular planning strategy has been *means-end analysis* (Newell and Simon 1972). Means-end analysis requires a measure of distance between current state and goal state. Operators are then chosen on the basis of an evaluation of how much their application will reduce the distance to the goal state. But before a particular operator can be applied, it has to be tested to see whether certain preconditions attached to that operator are fulfilled. For example, if JL finds an operator that will bring it much closer to its goal, like taking a plane to New York, it must meet a precondition before it can apply that operator: It has to be at the airport first. To fulfill this precondition, the planning system considers this a new subgoal and applies the same procedure again: it looks for an operator that will bring JL close to the airport in San Francisco, tests for preconditions, and so forth. This kind of hierarchical planning has been employed in many AI systems. Examples of well-known early systems are GPS and STRIPS. GPS, the General Problem Solver (e.g., Newell and Simon 1963) is a program intended to solve a large variety of planning problems. STRIPS, the Stanford Research Institute Problem Solver (e.g., Fikes and Nilsson 1971), is a variation on the hierarchial planning principle. It has been used on real robots like Shakey. These planning methods seem intuitively plausible, but they are subject to combinatorial explosion. For example, if there are 10 branching points in a plan and at each branching point there are two possibilities—for example, the choice between taking a car or taking a train to the airport—there will be 2^{10} or roughly 1,000 different plans. Such hierarchical planning systems have therefore not been very successful on real robots. We return to this topic in chapter 11.

Other Tasks

JL is equipped with so-called higher-level functions, with the ability to "think": It can manipulate representations, make logical inferences, draw conclusions, and solve problems as, for example, is done in expert systems. It can also perform induction and develop new concepts like "Granny Smith." JL also has the capacity for creation: Producing diversity is an important aspect of intelligence. We do not discuss how creativity is achieved in computational models; the reader interested in computational issues of creativity is referred to Margaret Boden's *Creative Mind: Myths and Mechanisms* (1996).

If JL is to be intelligent, it must have the capacity to communicate with other agents, that is, with other robots and humans. What comes to mind immediately is that it must be able to speak and hear, since natural language is one of the main means of communication between humans. Thus, JL must be equipped with a facility for natural language. Research in computational linguistics conducted over half a century has shown that this is an extremely demanding task. Although their performance is sometimes impressive, most natural language systems currently still lack flexibility and robustness.

Summary

JL is a representative of how an agent might be conceived in the classical paradigm. The underlying design principles can be summarized as shown in table 2.3. Principle c1 states that the computer metaphor has high explanatory power for psychological phenomena, which is why the models of choice are computer programs. Principle c2 states that agents should be designed with goals and knowledge on how to achieve those goals. Goals are typically organized into hierarchical structures. From these goal structures, plans are derived. This principle is closely related to principle c3, which states that agents should be designed to obey the principle of rationality (further elaborated in chapter 9). Principle c4 asserts that intelligent systems consist of various modules, for perception, learning, memory, language, and so forth, a view championed by Jerry Fodor in *The Modularity of Mind* (1983). The assumption is also made that individual modules can be designed and built separately. Principle c5 states that an agent's actions are based on what it perceives, which is further processed, resulting in a decision as to what action should be taken. Principle c6 suggests that an architecture like the one outlined in figure 2.6 should be used. Principle c7 is derived from Newell's concept of "levels" diagrammed in his seminal paper on the "knowledge level" (Newell 1982). There are three levels: a knowledge level, a logical level, and an implementation level. The knowledge level is a characterization of an agent in terms of goals and knowledge of how these goals can be achieved. For example, JL can be characterized in terms of the goal to visit the Museum of Modern art and the knowledge of how to get there. The logical level is a formalization of how the knowledge level specification is to be achieved (independent of implementation), and the implementation level is the actual program that implements the logical level. Design proceeds from the top down through these stages, from knowledge level, to logical level, to implementation level.

The intention underlying table 2.3 is not so much to provide a comprehensive summary of all ingredients in classical design, but rather to ferret out its essence. In practice, designers, even if they would consider themselves "classical" in the sense discussed in this chapter, would clearly have different views on some of the points. For example, many designers have started to build robots rather than designing computer programs only, with the accompanying need to address the agent-environment interaction. Many

Table 2.3 Overview of design principles in classical cognitive science. The "c" in front of the numbers indicates that they are classical design principles.

Number	Name of design principle	Description
c1	Model as computer program	assumption that good theories are expressed in information processing terms
c2	Goal-based designs	the actions of an agent should be derived from goals and knowledge on how to achieve the goals; from goals, plans are generated that can be executed; goals are organized in hierarchies
c3	Rational agents	if a rational agent has a goal and it knows that a particular action will bring the agent closer to the goal, it will choose that action for execution
c4	Modularity	models should be built in modular ways modules include: • perception (further subdivided into modules for the different modalities, i.e., visual, auditory, olfactory, tactile, taste) • learning • memory • planning • problem solving and reasoning • plan execution (acting) • language • communication
c5	Sense-think-act cycle	the operating principle is as follows: first the environment is sensed and mapped onto an internal representation; this information is processed (e.g., by applying heuristic search), leading to a plan for an action; then the action is executed
c6	Central information processing architecture	information from various sensors must be integrated into a central representational structure in STS; this integration requires information from LTS; memory consists of structures that are stored and later retrieved
c7	Top-down design	design procedure: specify the knowledge level (specification of what the agent should be able to do); derive the logical level (formalization of how the initial specification is to be achieved); implementation level (produce the actual code)

designers therefore no longer adhere to the levels described by Newell (1982), and many have moved to less hierarchical and more reactive approaches. Still, the cognitivistic paradigm has by no means disappeared. On the contrary, as we pointed out at the beginning of the chapter, many cognitive scientists still adhere to it.

Issues to Think About

Issue 2.1: The Sense-Think-Act Cycle

Throughout this book we challenge the idea that intelligent behavior is based on a sense—think—act cycle. Recall that the basic idea is that first, you perceive something (sense), then you process what you have perceived (think) and finally, you execute an action (act). Does this conceptualization of intelligent behavior seem plausible to you? Do you think it might hold more in certain situations, such as math classes, and less in others, such as tennis games? We would like you to think of alternatives to the sense—think—act cycle before we will present the ones developed in embodied cognitive science.

Issue 2.2: Perception and Memory: Computational Phenomena?

As we have seen, in the classical view, perception and memory are two separate modules that interact with one another. For example, during perception, memory structures are consulted. Moreover, the goal of visual perception is taken to be the reconstruction of a three-dimensional representation of the world. Memory is a system consisting of several separate storage devices. Do you think you can accommodate your personal experiences with memory within this framework? For example, assume you meet a friend you haven't seen for a while. You immediately recognize him. What image have you actually "retrieved"? Is it a retrieval process in the first place? What does the image show? Your friend riding a bicycle, or sitting in an easy chair?

Points to Remember

- The cognitive revolution had its beginnings in the 1950s as a new conception of the human being as a machine began to emerge.

The language of information processing was suggested as a suitable means for describing mental phenomena such as language, perception, and thinking. The goal of seeking explanations in terms of information processing replaced the goal of explaining human behavior in terms of stimulus-response relationships (as in behaviorism).

- Cognitive science is the interdisciplinary study of cognition. It involves disciplines such as philosophy, psychology, computer science, AI, linguistics, neuroscience, and more recently, engineering and biology. In the classical paradigm, the "glue" that kept cognitive science together was the notion of information processing.

- According to the cognitivistic paradigm, intelligence can be studied at the level of algorithms. This is also called the functionalist position, which states that the physical substrate on which the algorithms are performed is irrelevant so long as a useable result is achieved.

- Computation—in the sense of Turing machines—and representation are the fundamental ingredients in classical cognitive science and AI. The slogan "cognition as computation" characterizes this position.

- Turing machines are universal in the sense that they can simulate any other Turing machine.

- The Physical Symbol Systems Hypothesis, an empirical hypothesis about the nature of intelligence, states that a physical symbol system is a necessary and sufficient condition for a general intelligent system.

- The notion of information processing has been instrumental in modern cognitive psychology and in the neurosciences. Information processing is an extremely powerful notion. Cognitive psychology is defined by "how people take in information, how they recode and remember it, how they make decisions, how they transform their internal knowledge states, and how they translate these states into behavioral outputs" (Lachman, Lachman, and Butterfield 1979).

- The concept of information processing as used here implies that concepts of computation, such as storage, matching, retrieval, and logical operations, are applied to human thinking. This use of the term is to be distinguished from its use in information theory, and any objections we express to the information processing view are to the former use, not to the latter.

· JL is an agent designed on the basis of the cognitivistic paradigm. It embodies a number of important design principles (summarized in table 2.3).

Further Reading

Johnson-Laird, P. N. (1988). *The computer and the mind. An introduction to cognitive science*. Cambridge, MA: Harvard University Press. (An information processing view of intelligence, presenting an overview of the major topics of cognitive science.)

Lachman, R., Lachman, J. L., and Butterfield, E. C. (1979). *Cognitive psychology and information processing*. Hillsdale, NJ: Erlbaum. (One of the classics of information processing psychology.)

Newell, A. (1990). *Unified theories of cognition*. Cambridge, MA: Harvard University Press. (Even though Newell endorses a symbolic view of intelligence, the book is a rich source of material on anything relating to intelligence, written by someone who has been thinking deeply all his life about intelligence, natural or artificial.)

Newell, A., and Simon, H. A. (1976). Computer science as empirical inquiry: symbols and search. *Communications of the Association for Computing Machinery*, *19*, 113–126. (The classic paper on the Physical Symbol Systems Hypothesis, delivered as an Alan M. Turing Lecture. It outlines the research program of classical artificial intelligence.)

Russell, S. J., and Norvig, P. (1995). *Artificial intelligence: A modern approach*. Upper Saddle River, NJ: Prentice-Hall. (A modern, easy to read introduction to all major topics of AI, including search, problem solving, game playing, logic, knowledge-based systems, planning, machine learning, natural language, and robotics.)

3 The Fundamental Problems of Classical Artificial Intelligence and Cognitive Science

So far we have looked at the nature of intelligence and discussed the cognitivistic paradigm, which still by far dominates scientific and everyday thinking about intelligence. In a number of places, however, we have alluded to potential problems with this paradigm. In this chapter, we inspect more closely what these problems really are and why they have arisen in the first place. As we argue, the cognitivistic paradigm's neglect of the fact that intelligent agents, humans, animals, and robots are embodied agents that live in a real physical world leads to significant shortcomings in explaining intelligence.

Outlining the cognitivistic paradigm's problems and understanding their origins helps us, on the one hand, to avoid making the same mistakes again; on the other hand, it provides us with inspiration about what needs to be done differently. The chapter is relatively short. Most of the issues it raises have been discussed at length in the literature (e.g., Brooks 1991a,b; Clancey 1997; Franklin 1995; Hendriks-Jansen 1996; Winograd and Flores 1986), and an overview of those issues is sufficient here without repeating the details of the arguments. The goal is to outline the main problems that historically have led researchers to reconsider their approach to the study of intelligence.

We proceed as follows in the chapter: first, we work out the main distinctive characteristics of real and virtual worlds. We then present an overview of some of the well-known problems of traditional systems, followed by an inspection of some of the fundamental issues involved. We conclude with a number of suggestions as to what might be to be done in order to overcome these problems.

3.1 Real Worlds versus Virtual Worlds

Classical models, that is, models developed within the cognitivistic paradigm, focus on high-level processes like problem solving, reasoning, making inferences, and playing chess. Much progress has been made, as we have seen, for example, in the case of chess, with computers able to play well enough to defeat world champions. In other areas, progress has been less rapid; for example, in computer vision. It has turned out to be far more involved than expected to extract information from camera images, typically in the form of a pixel array, and map them onto internal representations of the world. The main reason for these difficulties—and the reason for the fundamental problems of AI in general—is that the models do not take the real world sufficiently into account. Much work in classical AI has been devoted to abstract, virtual worlds with precisely defined states and operations, quite unlike the real world.

To illustrate our argument, let us return to the game of chess (figure 3.1a). Chess is a formal game. It represents a virtual world with discrete, clearly defined states, board positions, operations, and legal moves. It is also a game involving complete information: If you know the board position, it is possible to know all you need to know to play the game, because given a certain board position, the possible moves are precisely defined and finite in number. Even though you may not know the particular move your opponent will make, you know that he will make a legal move; if he did not, he would cease to be playing chess any longer. (Breaking the chess board over the opponent's head is not part of the game itself.) Chess is also a static game, in the sense that if no one makes a move, nothing changes. Moreover, the types of possible moves do not change over time.

By contrast, consider soccer (figure 3.1b). Soccer is clearly a nonformal game. It takes place in the real world, where there are no uniquely defined states. The world of soccer—the real world—is continuous. As humans, we can make a model of a soccer game, and that model may have states, but not the soccer game as such. Having no uniquely defined states also implies that two situations in the real world are never identical. Moreover, in contrast to virtual worlds, the available information an agent can acquire about the real world is always incomplete. A soccer player cannot know about the activities of all other players at the same time, and those activities are drawn from a nearly infinite range of possibilities. In fact, it is not even defined what "complete" information means where a game like soccer is concerned. Completeness can be defined only within a closed, formal world. Since completeness is not defined, it is better to talk in terms of limited information. A soccer player has only limited information about the overall situation. In fact, information that can be acquired about the real world

a

b

Figure 3.1   Real worlds and virtual words. (a) Chess is a formal game. It represents a virtual world with precisely defined states, board positions, and operations, that is, the legal moves. (b) Soccer is an example of a nonformal game. There are no precisely defined states and operations. In contrast to chess, two situations in soccer are never exactly identical.

is always limited because of embodiment: the field of view is restricted, the range of the sensors is limited, and the sensory and motor systems take time to operate. Moreover, in the real world there is time pressure: things happen even if we do not do anything, and they happen in real time. If we want to avoid getting hit by cars, we may have to run away quickly. If we are jumping off a wall, the laws of physics act on the body (gravity), and we have to react quickly in order not to get hurt. Other laws of physics are also relevant: Friction is required for locomotion, motion requires energy, and physical organisms all have a certain metabolism that also needs energy. These are physical phenomena. They do not have to be represented somehow in order to function. They are simply there.

In the real world, any physical device is subject to noise, disturbances, and malfunctions. This point holds in principle for any sensory or motor system. In other words, information gathered from the sensors is therefore always subject to errors. Finally, the real world is indefinitely rich: there is always more to be known about it. More precisely, since acquisition of information takes time, one has to restrict oneself to knowledge about a certain part of the real world. This point also holds in principle. It does not depend, say, on the sensory system's sophistication. Given these properties of the real world and the limitations of any kind of physical agent, it follows that the real world is only partially knowable, and this in turn implies that it is predictable only to a limited extent.

Let us conclude our comparison of real and virtual worlds with a note on terminology. We have used the term "virtual" to designate closed, formal worlds such as chess. The term "virtual world" or "simulated world" is often used in a different sense in the areas of artificial life (e.g., Langton 1995) and virtual reality (Kalawsky 1993). Video games are a case in point; another example are Karl Sims's simulated physical worlds, in which artificial creatures evolve under various conditions, for example, on land or in the water (Sims 1994a,b). In these worlds, one can define new physical laws, new laws of nature, which is one of the things that makes them so fascinating. For example, if gravity is simulated in a virtual world, one can adjust g, the constant of gravity, and one can observe the change in the behavior of the (simulated) organisms that inhabit this world. From the perspective of the agents that live in such a virtual world, this virtual world does have some of the characteristics that we pointed out for real worlds. For example, unexpected and novel things happen—from the point of view of the agent! Often, new kinds of enemies emerge who have unknown powers. However, from the point of view of the programmer who created the virtual world, the very same events are neither new nor unexpected: he designed them into the system.

In summary, real worlds differ significantly from virtual ones. The problems of classical AI and cognitive science have their origin largely in a neglect of these differences.

3.2 Some Well-Known Problems with Classical Systems

In what follows we summarize some of the better-known problems with classical AI systems. Throughout the discussion we use the term classical AI systems to denote pure symbolic systems such as expert systems or traditional planning systems like STRIPS. The goal in this section is to describe the issues and problems that historically have motivated researchers to look for alternatives. There seems to be consensus within a large part of the research community in AI that classical systems, lack robustness and generalization capabilities, and cannot perform in real time. This makes them poorly suited for behaving in the real world. Moreover, they are, in essence, sequential; that is, they perform one operation after another. They also run on sequential machines, whereas the human brain is massively parallel in its processing. Let us briefly examine each of these points.

Robustness and Generalization: Traditional AI systems often lack robustness, which means that they lack tolerance of noise and fault tolerance and cannot behave appropriately in new situations. A system has noise tolerance if it functions appropriately when the data contain noise i.e. there are random fluctuations in the data. Sensors are always noisy, because they are physical devices, and motor acts are always imprecise, because they arise from physical devices. A system has fault tolerance if it performs adequately when some of its components break down. Standard symbol processing models are neither noise nor fault tolerant unless their programming explicitly provides for noise and particular types of faults. The most important deficiency of traditional AI systems in terms of robustness, however, is their inability to perform appropriately in novel situations, that is, their lack of generalization capacity. If a situation arises that has not been predefined in its programming, a traditional system breaks down or stops operating. Generalization ability is especially important in the real world, where no two situations are ever exactly the same.

Real-Time Processing: Because the real world has its own dynamics, systems must be able to react quickly in order to survive and perform their tasks. Systems based on the classical paradigm embedded in real robots are typically slow, because they process information centrally. Recall our overview of JL in chapter 2, in which a central information processing module was postulated (see principle c6 in table 2.3), and the discussion in chapter 1 of the view that the brain is the "seat of intelligence". If all sensor signals have to be transmitted to a central device for processing (integration with other sensory signals, mapping onto internal representations, planning of action sequences) and finally generation of motor signals, real-time response can hardly be achieved.

Sequential Nature of Programs: The architecture of today's AI programs is essentially sequential, and they work on a step-by-step basis. By contrast, the human brain's processing is massively parallel, with activity occurring in many parts of the brain at all times. This problem arises from the fact that current computer technology is largely based on architectures of the von Neumann type which are, at the information processing level, sequential machines. As an aside, note that at the physical level a von Neumann machine is also massively parallel, just like any other system in nature.

Other Problems: Additional criticisms have been that classical systems are goal-based, are hierarchically organized, and process information centrally. The problems with goal-based systems are discussed in Montefiore and Noble 1989; the latter two problems are considered in chapter 11.

The criticisms of AI models presented so far are well-known and long-standing. Since the mid-1980s a number of additional ones have been raised pertaining to fundamental issues. Specifically, it has been argued that traditional AI models suffer from the frame problem and the problem of symbol grounding, and that they lack the properties of embodiment and situatedness.

3.3 The Fundamental Problems

In section 3.1 we pointed out that one of the problems with classical AI is that it did not give the real world sufficient consideration. In fact, all the fundamental problems of classical AI concern the relation of an agent and the real world, in particular its interaction with it. Chapter 4 outlines a systematic way of dealing with these relations. In this section, we discuss some specific problems: the frame problem, the symbol-grounding problem, and lack of embodiment and situatedness are treated in detail, and we briefly discuss the homunculus problem and the problem of the substrate required for intelligence.

The Frame Problem

The frame problem was originally pointed out by McCarthy and Hayes (1969) and has more recently attracted a lot of interest (e.g., Pylyshyn 1987). It comes in several variations and lacks one single, overriding interpretation. The central point concerns how to model change (Janlert 1987): How can a model of a continuously changing environment be kept in tune with the real world? Assuming that the model consists of a set of logical propositions (which essentially holds for any representation), any proposition can change at any point in time. Let us explain the frame problem using an example given by Daniel Dennett (1987), who has been working in the field of philosophy of the mind for many years. The initial situation described in Dennett's example is illustrated in figure 3.2, depicting a robot employing a propositional representation. It consists of a set of propositions like INSIDE(R1,ROOM), ON(BATTERY, WAGON), and so forth.

Once upon a time there was a robot, named R1 by its creators. Its only task was to fend for itself. One day its designers arranged for it to learn that its spare battery, its precious energy supply, was locked in a room with a time bomb set to go off soon. R1 located the room, and the key to the door, and formulated a plan to rescue its battery. There was a wagon in the room, and the battery was on the wagon, and R1 hypothesized that a certain action which it called PULLOUT(WAGON, ROOM) would result in the battery removed from the room. Straightaway it acted, and did succeed in getting the battery out of the room before the bomb went off. Unfortunately, however, the bomb was also on the wagon. R1 knew that the bomb was on the wagon in the room, but didn't realize that pulling the wagon would bring the bomb out along with the battery. Poor R1 had missed that obvious implication of its planned act.

Back to the drawing board. "The solution is obvious," said the designers. "Our next robot must be made to recognize not just the intended implications of its acts, but also the implications about their side-effects, by deducing these implications from the descriptions it uses in formulating its plans." They called their next model, the robot-deducer, R1D1. They placed R1D1, in much the same predicament that R1 had succumbed to, and as it too hit upon the idea of PULLOUT(WAGON, ROOM) it began, as designed, to consider the implications of such a course of action. It had just finished deducing that pulling the wagon out of the room would not change the colour of the room's walls, and was embarking on a proof of the further implication that pulling the wagon out would cause its wheels to turn more revolutions than there were wheels on the wagon—when the bomb exploded.

Back to the drawing board. "We must teach it the difference between relevant implications and irrelevant implications," said the designers, "and teach it to ignore the irrelevant ones." So they developed a method of tagging implications as either relevant or irrelevant to the project at hand, and installed the method in their next model, the robot-relevant-deducer, R2D1 for short. When they subjected R2D1 to the test that had so unequivocally selected its ancestors for extinction, they were surprised to see it sitting, Hamlet-like, outside the room containing the ticking bomb, the native hue of its resolution sicklied o'er with the pale case of thought, as Shakespeare (and more recently Fodor) has aptly put it. "Do something!" they yelled at it. "I am," it retorted. "I'm busily ignoring some thousands of implications I have determined to be irrelevant. Just as soon as I find an irrelevant implication, I put it on the list of those I must ignore, and ..." the bomb went off. (pp. 41–42)

Let us briefly summarize the essential points of Dennett's example.

1. Assume that the symbolic description of the situation given in figure 3.2 is stored in R1's memory. It then has the problem of

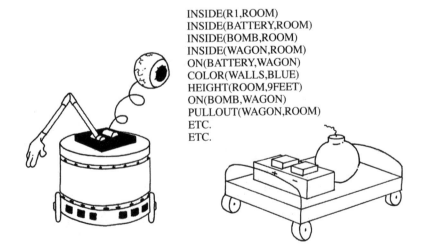

INSIDE(R1,ROOM)
INSIDE(BATTERY,ROOM)
INSIDE(BOMB,ROOM)
INSIDE(WAGON,ROOM)
ON(BATTERY,WAGON)
COLOR(WALLS,BLUE)
HEIGHT(ROOM,9FEET)
ON(BOMB,WAGON)
PULLOUT(WAGON,ROOM)
ETC.
ETC.

Figure 3.2 The frame problem. The robot R1/R1D1/R2D1 (R1 stands for robot, R1D1 for robot-deducer, and R2D1 robot-relevant-deducer) is standing near the wagon with a battery and a bomb. R1/R1D1/R2D1 uses a symbolic representation of the situation to draw inferences and guide its behavior.

determining the implications of an action. In this particular situation, the action of moving the wagon has the side effect that the bomb is also moving, since it is sitting on the wagon. Unfortunately, the robot does not know that this is relevant. What is obvious to a human observer has to be made explicit for R1.

2. R1D1 tries to take a vast number of potential side effects into account. Assessing all of these potential side effects takes a lot of time, and most are entirely irrelevant. For example, the fact that moving the cart does not change the color of the room is totally irrelevant in the current situation.

3. R2D1 tries to distinguish between relevant and irrelevant inferences. But in order to do this it has to consider all of them anyhow, which implies that R2D1 has no significant advantage over R1D1.

There have been a number of proposals for resolving the frame problem. One is the "sleeping dog strategy," in which the robot is programmed to assume that if something is not explicitly changed, it has not changed at all. Physical objects normally do not cease to exist if nothing happens to them, or they do not start to fly without reason, or the color of the room does not change significantly in a short period of time unless it is painted, and so forth. The robot then relies on this assumption in planning its course of action. However, ice cubes can melt, that is, they can cease to exist without an explicit manipulation of them. The bomb on the wagon changes its position if the wagon is moved. Either this fact must be represented explicitly, which would imply that there are very many relations of this kind, requiring significant memory space, collectively, for their representation, or the robot has to infer that the bomb will also move. As we have seen, however, there are typically a very large number of possible inferences that can be drawn and determining the relevance alone does not help (as poor R2D1 found). While the sleeping dog strategy is often useful, it does not completely resolve the frame problem. For example, it does not solve the problem of finding a way for the robot to determine the relevance of relations without having to check all the inferences.

Minsky (1975) and Schank and Abelson (1977) suggested that the robot's attention be focused on the relevant inferences by employing frames (or scripts). (Figure 2.7 offered an example of a script that focuses the attention on things happening in restaurants.) McCarthy (1980) suggested circumscription, which is also a way to restrict the number of inferences. All of these suggested

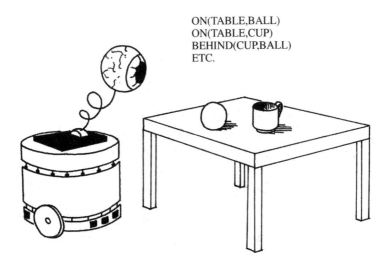

ON(TABLE,BALL)
ON(TABLE,CUP)
BEHIND(CUP,BALL)
ETC.

Figure 3.3   The frame problem and situatedness. R1/R1D1/R2D1 is standing in front of a table. From its current perspective, the cup is behind the ball, and this relationship is reflected in the symbolic description it uses to represent its environment. If R1/R1D1/R2D1 moves to the other side of the table, the symbolic description has to be updated, from the robot's perspective, the ball is now behind the cup. If a robot has a large set of such descriptions, many of them, but not all, may have to be updated as it moves around. Finding the right ones is a fundamental problem. For example, if R1/R1D1/R2D1 moves to the other side of the table, the relative position of the ball and the cup change, but the ball and the cup are still in exactly the same place. In the symbolic approach a way must therefore be found to reflect the change in the position of the objects relative to the robot without altering the robot's representation of their absolute positions. A situated agent can merely "look at" the situation.

solutions try to tackle the problem at the logical level, in a sense, on the inside. The problem, however, is really about the *system-environment* interaction: how models of a changing environment can be kept in tune with the environment. This is not a problem of logic, but rather one of modeling the world.

Another problem arises when modeling the real world that is related to the frame problem. R1D1 represents the situation shown on the right in figure 3.3 by means of a number of propositions. If R1D1 moves around the table, many of the propositions in the model R1D1 uses have to be updated, even though only the position of R1D1 is changing. In the real world it is not necessary for us to build a representation of the situation in the first place: We can simply look at it, which relieves us of the need for cumbersome updating processes. Moreover we can point to things when talking about them. As a robot, R1D1 could also take advantage of these possibilities—if designed properly.

According to Janlert (1987) the frame problem has two aspects. Our robots R1, R1D1, and R2D1 were suffering from one, the *prediction problem*, which has to do with determining what is relevant. The other, called the *qualification problem*, is equally nasty: It involves the preconditions under which an action can be applied. For example, if you are getting into a car, you have to assume that there is no bomb in the car, that nobody put sugar into the gas tank, that nobody has taken out the engine, that no skunk is in the car, that no lion is in the car, that the clutch is still in the same place, and so forth almost infinitely. Another example is that when sitting down on a chair, you do not explicitly assume that it will not break. You do not have to do that because you can be confident that if there were a problem you would recognize it. (But note that this strategy may occasionally fail, and you might indeed land on your behind on the floor.) Humans certainly do not explicitly assume that these preconditions are given. Because we are "grounded" in our environment, we know the things we have to check. To function properly in a changing environment, a robot must somehow be provided with the same capacity.

The frame problem is a fundamental one, and it is intrinsic to any world modeling approach whatsoever. Any model of a changing environment presents a frame problem; the more sophisticated and elaborate the model, the more the frame problem shows up. Thus, we see that the frame problem exists not only for traditional AI models but for models in general. An important goal of intelligent systems design is to minimize the implications of the frame problem. Embodied cognitive science's approach is to minimize the amount of world modeling in the first place.

The Symbol-Grounding Problem

The symbol-grounding problem, which refers to how symbols relate to the real world, was first discussed by Steven Harnad (1990). In traditional AI, symbols are typically defined in a purely syntactic way by how they relate to other symbols and how they are processed by some interpreter (Newell and Simon 1976; Quillian 1968); the relation of the symbols to the outside world is rarely discussed explicitly. In other words, we are dealing with closed systems, not only in AI but in computer science in general. Except in real-time applications, the relation of symbols (e.g., in database applications) to the outside world is never discussed; it is assumed

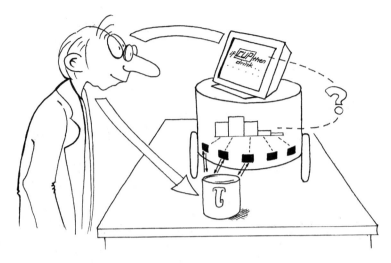

Figure 3.4 The symbol-grounding problem. The scientist has no difficulty associating the cup in the real world with the symbol "cup" on the screen standing on top of the robot. But if the robot is programmed with symbols representing objects and has to interact with its environment on its own, it has to be able to map the sensory stimulation (from the cup itself) onto its internal symbolic representation (the word "cup")— a very hard problem.

as somehow given, with the (typically implicit) assumption that designers and potential users know what the symbols mean (e.g., the price of a product). This idea is also predominant in linguistics: it is taken for granted that the symbols or sentences correspond in some way with the outside world. The study of meaning then relates to the translation of sentences into some kind of logic-based representation whose semantics are clearly defined (Winograd and Flores 1986, p. 18).

Using symbols in a computer system is no problem as long as there is a human interpreter who can be safely expected to be capable of establishing the appropriate relations to some outside world: the mapping is "grounded" in the human's experience of his or her interaction with the real world. However, once we remove the human interpreter from the loop, as in the case of autonomous agents, we have to take into account that the system needs to interact with the environment on its own. Thus, the meaning of the symbols must be *grounded* in the system's own interaction with the real world, as figure 3.4 illustrates. Symbol systems, such as computer programs, in which symbols refer only to other symbols are not grounded because they do not connect the symbols they employ to the outside world. The symbols have meaning only to a designer or a user, not to the system itself. The robot in figure 3.4 is in trouble because it is trying to map a sensory stimulation, a cup, onto an internal symbol, the word "cup." Providing the robot with this capacity is very hard to do, even in simple cases, let alone for more complex ones. But this mapping will always have to be present if there are symbols in the system. (As we argue later, the symbol grounding problem is really an artifact of symbolic systems and "disappears" if a different approach is used. Specifically, in chapter 12 we show how "concepts" can evolve in the interaction of an autonomous agent with its environment, without the need for introducing symbols of any sort within the agent. We put "concepts" in quotes to indicate that we do not mean symbolic concepts.) For a long time, the symbol-grounding problem attracted little attention in AI or cognitive science, and it has never been an issue in computer science in general. Only with the renewed interest in autonomous robots has it reemerged.

The Problems of Embodiment and Situatedness

The problem of embodiment refers to the fact that abstract algorithms do not interact with the real world. Rodney Brooks forcefully argued that intelligence requires a body (Brooks 1991a,b). Only if a system is embodied do we know for sure that it is able to deal with the real world. Moreover, systems that are not embodied all suffer from the symbol-grounding problem. Their connection to the outside world requires a human interpreter in the loop.

Many researchers in AI have recognized this problem. For example, Margaret Boden noted, in *Artificial Intelligence and Natural Man* (1977):

In everyday life you usually remember your "place" largely because the external world is there to remind you what you have or haven't done. For instance, you can check up on whether you have already added the vanilla essence by sniffing or tasting the mixture, or perhaps by referring to the pencil and paper representation of the culinary task that you have drawn up for this mnemonic purpose. A computational system that solves its problems "in its head" rather than by perceiving and acting in the real world, or pencil and paper models of it, has to have all its memory aids in the form of internal representations. (p. 373)

At the time the importance of real-world interaction in controlling behavior was fully recognized, however, the implications—

embodiment—had not been further elaborated; they were fully understood only when people started to use robots for the study of intelligence. As embodied systems, robots have the potential to "solve" the symbol-grounding problem, but this requires them to have "situatedness."

An agent is "situated" if it can acquire information about the current situation through its sensors in interaction with the environment. A situated agent interacts with the world on its own, without an intervening human. To illustrate this point, let us look at an example of a system entirely lacking situatedness. Imagine a remote-controlled device without sensors, such as a remote-controlled toy car. The toy car is controlled only by information from the operator; it has no information about the current situation from its own perspective. A situated agent has the potential to acquire its own history, if equipped with appropriate mechanisms. To understand situatedness and to design situated agents, we have to adopt the agent's perspective, rather than the observer's. For understanding situated agents (e.g., animals), it is important to realize that the world may look very different from the perspective of the animal than from our own. Ants, for example, have completely different eyes so what they see is not what we see. In designing situated agents, adopting the agent's perspective is important because the programs that control the agent's actions are based on the sensor data the robot gets. Since the relation between observer and agent is of fundamental importance, we discuss it in more detail in chapter 4. It turns out that situated agents, that is, agents having the property of situatedness, are much better at performing in real time because they exploit the system-environment interaction and therefore minimize the amount of world modeling required.

Note that embodiment does not automatically imply situatedness. Agents can be equipped with detailed models of their environment to be used in the planning processes. If these plans are employed significantly in controlling the agent's behavior, it will not be situated. Moreover, as we saw in the last chapter when discussing, plan-based systems quickly run into combinatorial problems (cf. also Chapman 1987). If the real world changes, one of the main problems is keeping the models in tune with the environment. Inspection of the problem of behaving in the real world shows that it is neither necessary nor desirable to develop very comprehensive and detailed models (e.g., Brooks 1991a; Suchman

1987; Winograd and Flores 1986): the more comprehensive and the more detailed the models, the more strongly the agent is going to be affected by the frame problem. Typically only a small part of an agent's environment is relevant for its behavior. In addition, instead of performing extensive inference operations on internal models or representations, the situated agent can interact with the current situation: The real world is, in a sense, part of the "knowledge"[1] the agent needs to behave appropriately. It can merely "look at it" through the sensors. In a sense, the world is its own best model. Figure 3.3 illustrates this point.

The concept of situatedness has recently attracted a lot of interest and led to heated debates about the nature of intelligence and the place of symbol-processing systems in studying intelligence. For example, a complete issue of the journal *Cognitive Science* in 1993 was dedicated to the role of situatedness in cognitive science (see also Clancey 1997).

Other Fundamental Problems

A number of other problems with classical systems can be found in the literature, for example, the homunculus problem and the problem of the underlying substrate. "Homunculus" literally means "little man"; as used here, it designates a "little man in the head." The *homunculus problem*, or the *homunculus fallacy*, as it is also called, refers to circular accounts of psychological processes. These processes are circular because they ascribe to some internal mechanism (the homunculus) the very psychological properties being investigated in the first place. For example, a theory of vision might postulate that there is within the brain a mechanism that scans, views, or inspects images on the retina. Such a theory would be vacuous, however, since scanning, viewing, and inspecting are all instances of the very visual processes the theory was supposed to illuminate in the first place (Gregory 1987, p. 313). In other words, the theory has assumed the very things it set out to explain. When used to criticize AI systems, the term "homunculus" designates a subsystem that executes a function specified in purely formal terms (as in the cognitivistic paradigm). In a sense, a homunculus is required to perform the function that the formal system is intended

---

[1] We put "knowledge" within quotation marks to indicate that this is not the standard way of using knowledge in AI. The standard way refers to knowledge structures that are represented internally.

to explain. For example, we saw that the robot R2D1 was lacking a means to determine the relevant inferences. With respect to the homunculus problem, the real problem is that it is not possible to determine the relevance of an inference on a purely formal basis (i.e., by inspecting only its database of symbolic representations and drawing inferences): a link to the environment and thus to the meaning of the representation is required. In other words, the homunculus problem and the symbol grounding problem are closely related: a system containing ungrounded symbols will always require a homunculus giving meaning to them. We do not explore the subtleties of this argument, any further (for a more comprehensive discussion, see, e.g., Edelman 1992 or Bursen 1980).

To bring our review of some fundamental problems to an end let us mention one which is still fairly prominent, the *problem of the underlying substrate.* There is a folklore that true intelligence requires a biological substrate as a basis. Only natural brains can, in this folklore, exhibit "true intelligence." Note that this issue does not only apply to classical AI, but rather concerns any endeavor to build intelligent systems. As far as we can tell there is to date no evidence demonstrating the in-principle impossibility of having intelligence based on substrates other than natural brains. But even if it turned out to be true that a biological substrate were required, we could still use computers and robots to build models.

3.4 Remedies and Alternatives

In this final section, we briefly examine a number of possible ways to deal with the problems we have raised. Again, the overview is very short and the field is very large. Because we want to leave room to present embodied cognitive science, we cannot possibly do justice to all the research that has been done. We have labeled the various positions we present "pessimist," "traditionalist," "pragmatist," and "optimist." These labels are not to be taken too seriously.

The Pessimist: Giving Up. The pessimist knows the fundamental problems of traditional approaches to AI, believes these criticisms to be universally valid, and strongly doubts that there are viable alternatives. For him, the only solution is to give up on the endeavor to build intelligent systems. An example of this position can be seen in the implications of Winograd and Flores' *Understanding Computers and Cognition* (1986), which represents a fundamental criticism of traditional AI and the traditional understanding of intelligence, in particular, natural language. Winograd and Flores' suggestion is to build computer systems that support human activity, in order to support and enhance human intelligence, rather than trying to build computer systems that are themselves intelligent, which is, in their opinion, a futile effort. This view is maintained by a relatively strong group in the area of software engineering that capitalizes on "designing for humans." Greenbaum and Kyng (1991) offer an interesting overview of this field.

The Traditionalist: Improving Classical Methods.   Many researchers in traditional AI and psychology have realized the problems with classical approaches. Clearly, there is a lot of room for improvement. Such researchers have pursued solutions intended to overcome the problems classical approaches present. Problems with generalization and robustness, for example, can largely be overcome with neural networks. Neural networks are also massively parallel and thus less subject to the criticism of being sequential. Then, there is a large field dealing with situated planning where high-level plans are used but they are no longer employed to tightly control behavior, but as resources that can be accessed whenever required (For reviews of this approach, see, e.g., Hasemann 1995; Wolfe and Chun 1992). Methods in computational vision have also been improved significantly. The processors have become so fast that real-time issues become less and less of a problem. This list could still be extended considerably.

The Pragmatist: Working Toward Practical Applications.   The pragmatist is not worried about the foundations: His goal is to get things to work. For him, the ultimate test of whether a solution works is if it can be deployed and routinely used in everyday working environments. Whether a program is labeled "expert system," "decision support system," or "intelligent agent" is entirely irrelevant to the pragmatist—except insofar as it might help sales. The pragmatist is also free to combine various techniques and approaches. For example, neural networks have wonderful properties: They can learn and are adaptive. They are ideal for taking care of low-level sensory-motor control. Rule-based systems have the advantage that they can be quickly built and are easy to understand. Moreover, they can be connected to symbolic planning systems, with the idea that neural networks connect the low-level sensory-motor systems to the high-level symbolic layers. The presence of a symbolic layer has the advantage of facilitating communication between the human and the robot. The pragmatist's point is, Does it work? Do people think they are getting their money's worth? This is a perfectly acceptable position, but not the one adopted in this book. It is our conviction that ultimately, the pragmatist will benefit from the research described here.

The Optimist: Embodied Cognitive Science. In spite of the improvements achieved by the traditionalist we feel that a radically different approach is required. We now embark on this endeavor.

Issues to Think About

Issue 3.1: Prerequisites for Intelligence

In our discussion of the fundamental problems of classical AI, we briefly mentioned the problem of the underlying substrate, the view that a biological substrate is a prerequisite for intelligence. The implication is that there can in principle be no artificial systems that exhibit intelligent behavior. The remainder of this book, however, is for the better part concerned with such synthetic agents. Before reading on, we would like you to reflect for a moment on your own view on this topic. Do you think that, indeed, a biological brain and body is needed for intelligent behavior to emerge, or are you willing to ascribe intelligence to artificial agents? In the latter case, what would agents have to do in order for you to describe their behavior as intelligent?

Issue 3.2: The Symbol-Grounding Problem

Take a concept from your everyday life, for example, "drinking." Now try to make explicit what "drinking" means to you. You may be surprised how tightly concepts are tied to the body, are grounded in sensory-motor experiences. Just to get you started, here are a few points. Drinking relates to liquids; liquids are kept in particular containers like cups or glasses. They can be hot or cold; if they are hot you can get burned. If you grasp the coffee cup, you move it to your mouth slowly. Why? Because you know that liquids spill when you move the cup fast. You then move it close to your lips until it touches them, which you can feel both on your lips and from the feedback from your arm muscles. You then tilt the cup and move your lower lip forward so the liquid can drop into your mouth. You are applying the physical law that the surface of the liquid stays horizontal as the container moves. Then you sense the liquid and its temperature in your mouth, on your lips, and perhaps in your throat and stomach. You also recognize various liquids by their specific reflective properties, viscosity, and so forth. This is what sensory-motor grounding is all about. Now try to do the same thing with an object like a newspaper. How about with more abstract concepts, like "responsibility"?

Points to Remember

- Classical AI systems have been criticized on various grounds: that they lack robustness and generalization capabilities, and cannot perform in real time. Moreover, they are sequential and run on sequential machines. Additional points of criticism have been that they are goal based and organized hierarchically, and that their processing is done centrally.
- Real worlds differ significantly from virtual ones. Virtual worlds have states, there is complete information about them, the possible operators within them are given, and they are static. The real world is quite different. In particular, the real world has its own dynamics, which force the agents to act in real time.
- The frame problem concerns how models of parts of the real world can be kept in tune with the real world as it is changing. It is especially hard to determine which changes in the world are relevant to a given situation without having to test all possible changes. The frame problem has two aspects, a prediction problem and a qualification problem.
- The symbol-grounding problem concerns how symbols relate to the real world. The symbol-grounding problem becomes obvious if the human observer is taken out of the loop and the system must interact on its own with the environment. It is a characteristic of symbolic approaches; nonsymbolic approaches do not have a symbol-grounding problem.
- An agent is situated if it acquires information about its environment only through its sensors in interaction with the environment. A situated agent interacts with the world on its own, without an intervening human. It has the potential to acquire its own history if equipped with appropriate mechanisms.
- Although there have been many suggestions for resolving the fundamental problems with classical systems, we think that the solu-

tion can be achieved only through a new approach that capitalizes on an agent's interaction with the world. This is the major concern of embodied cognitive science.

Further Reading

Brooks, R. A. (1991). Intelligence without reason. *Proceedings of the International Joint Conference on Artificial Intelligence*, 569–595. (An important paper by the founder of the field of behavior-based intelligence. It summarizes the major criticisms of the classical approach by drawing on the vast literature in various fields like robotics, psychology, neurobiology, and computer science.)

Clancey, W. J. (1997). *Situated cognition: On human knowledge and computer representations*. New York: Cambridge University Press. (An elaborate text summarizing 10 years of research trying to come to grips with the large literature on knowledge engineering, knowledge representation, symbolic AI, and subsymbolic approaches, as well as neurobiological theories. Proposes the metaphor of "situated cognition" as an alternative to the classical symbol processing view.)

Harnad, S. (1990). The symbol grounding problem. *Physica D 42*, 335–346. (The standard reference to the symbol-grounding problem. Whereas Harnad is trying to solve the symbol-grounding problem, we think that a different approach—as described in this book—should be used, so that this problem does not occur in the first place.)

Pylyshyn, Z. W. (Ed.). (1987). *The robot's dilemma: The frame problem in artificial intelligence*. Norwood. NJ: Ablex. (An interesting collection of papers about the frame problem.)

Winograd, T., and Flores, F. (1986). *Understanding computers and cognition*. Reading, MA.: Addison-Wesley. (*The* criticism of AI, and more generally the rationalistic view in computer science. A must for any computer scientist, AI researcher, or cognitive scientist.)

In part I, we outlined the general topic area and the methods of investigating intelligence. In addition, we reviewed what we call the classical view of intelligence: the information-processing paradigm. We inspected the implications and underlying problems of this paradigm—recall, for example, the frame problem and the symbol-grounding problem. We also introduced the notion of synthetic modeling and stated that the agents of interest are the so-called autonomous agents. In fact, we are interested in a special breed of autonomous agents, the so-called complete agents. It is our task in part II to characterize complete agents so as to furnish a framework for designing such agents. By doing this, we provide the groundwork for embodied cognitive science.

This characterization requires that the reader understand many theoretical concepts like adaptivity, ecological niche, self-sufficiency, autonomy, situatedness, and embodiment, some of which we introduced briefly in part I. But we do not want only to characterize agents, we want to build them. Building is the essence of a synthetic methodology, and embodied cognitive science is by definition synthetic. Working with a synthetic methodology has important consequences, one being that we have to take the frame-of-reference problem (not to be confused with the frame problem) into account, which in turn implies that we have to design for "emergence", a term that we explain in detail. Designing for emergence in turn requires a "basis" for emergence, which is to be found in the designer's specifications of the agent.

Design efforts are always performed in the context of an overall goal. Goals can be of various types, like understanding biological systems, exploring general principles of intelligence, or developing an application. Depending on the goal, the methodology differs. Also, explanations of natural systems can be given from various perspectives, another topic to be discussed in part II.

But the framework we present is not only theoretical: it also contains concrete suggestions on how to proceed when conducting agent experiments. Moreover, chapter 5 provides an introduction to the appropriate formalism for implementing internal mechanisms: artificial neural networks. In particular, we focus on how to apply neural networks in the context of complete agents, on how to design neural networks for adaptivity. Neural networks, because of their desirable properties, are used widely in the field of embodied cognitive science. This discussion also helps us clarify some issues concerning ontologies and designer commitments; that is, where and at what level designer commitments should be made. Equipped with this background knowledge, we can then embark on a tour of the major lines of thoughts and approaches in the field of embodied cognitive science.

In this chapter, we introduce the concepts that we need later on when exploring the various approaches. Moreover, we need such a framework if we actually want to build agents. One important concept that we discuss is that of the complete agent. Complete agents are inspired by natural agents, animals and humans, which are—quite obviously—capable of surviving in the real world. They are "complete" because they incorporate everything required to perform actual behavior. (Standard computer programs, for example, are not complete because they cannot behave in the real world.) We argue that it is such complete agents that we want study and synthesize. We provide a characterization of what we mean by complete agents, and we show that if we want to model, to synthesize such agents, we must take into account some special considerations relating to the idea of emergence, that is, to the fact that behavior emerges from the agent-environment interaction. Emergence is in turn a consequence of the frame-of-reference problem, which conceptualizes the relationships among those involved in the design process, namely the designer (who is often also the observer), the natural agent (if we are doing modeling work), the agent to be designed, and the environment. One important implication of frame-of-reference considerations is that behavior cannot be reduced to an internal mechanism. This in turn necessitates a new design methodology, which is this chapter's central topic.

We begin the chapter with a characterization of complete agents and discuss a number of basic concepts like adaptivity, autonomy, self-sufficiency, embodiment, and situatedness. We then turn to agents—both simulated and real robots—and discuss how they can be used as modeling tools. We examine the pros and cons of working with real robots and with agent simulations. We also compare this new kind of agent simulation with more traditional forms of simulation. We then outline the framework for design that focuses on emergence, including a description of the frame-of-reference problem. Finally, we discuss what we mean by a good explanation and how we can find explanations of agent behavior by running experiments.

This chapter is difficult and covers a lot of ground. This is unavoidable. At first reading, all the points may not become immediately clear. All the issues raised here, however, will be illustrated in greater detail later on. The reader may find it helpful to return to this chapter after having read through some of the subsequent chapters.

4.1 Complete Autonomous Agents

Biological agents have to perform a number of tasks: searching for food, eating and drinking, grooming, reproducing, and caring for their offspring. The term "task" is normally used in a design context to designate something the agent needs to get done. Typical tasks for autonomous robots, for example, are marking all the mines in a mine field with color, or mowing the lawn of a soccer field. Note that the task of mowing the lawn implies certain desired behaviors on the part of the agent. What is really meant is that the agent's task is to keep the grass short. And because the designer can't think of any other way to accomplish the job, he simply equates the task with the method, that is, with the behavior by which the task is to be achieved, namely mowing. Note that animals don't have tasks. Rather, a task is an observer-based attribution summarizing the effect of certain behaviors of the animals. In the field of embodied cognitive science, researchers often talk about tasks of animals. What they mean is either the behavior involved—collecting food—itself or the effect of the behavior, that is, the fact that if the animals behave in a particular way, the food ends up in the nest. What is important is that we observe the frame-of-reference problem: There need be no internal representation of the task within the agent. Often, the distinction is not so relevant: Both task and desired behaviors can be used to specify what an agent should do.

The ability to survive in complex environments is a given for all biological systems. Achieving this ability in artificial agents turns out to be an extremely hard problem. Complete autonomous agents are physical systems that are able to resolve these issues. For fun and for historical reasons we also call these complete autonomous systems "Fungus Eaters." Let us briefly look at the story of these

"Fungus Eaters." They illustrate the main intuitions underlying the embodied cognitive science framework.

In 1961 the Japanese psychologist Masanao Toda[1] proposed to study "Fungus Eaters" as an alternative to the traditional methods of academic psychology (Toda 1982, chap. 7). Rather than performing ever more restricted and well-controlled experiments on isolated faculties (memory, language, learning, perception, emotion, etc.) and narrow tasks (memorizing lists of nonsense syllables, letter perception on degraded stimuli, etc.), we should study "complete" systems, though perhaps simple ones. "Complete" in this context means that the systems are capable of behaving autonomously in an environment without a human intermediary. Such systems have to incorporate capabilities for classification, for navigation, for object manipulation, and for deciding what to do. The integration of these competences into a system capable of behaving on its own, according to Toda's argument, will yield more insights into the nature of intelligence than looking at fragments of the complex human mind.

The "Solitary Fungus Eater" is a creature—in our terminology, an autonomous agent—sent to a distant planet to collect uranium ore (see figure 4.1). The more ore it collects, the more reward it will get. If feeds on a certain type of fungus that grows on this planet. The "Fungus Eater" has a fungus store, means of locomotion (e.g., legs or wheels), and means for decision making (a brain) and collection (e.g., arms). Any kind of activity, including thinking, requires energy, if the level of fungus in its fungus store drops to zero, the Fungus Eater dies. The Fungus Eater is also equipped with sensors, one for vision and one for detecting uranium ore (e.g., a Geiger counter).

The scenario Toda describes is interesting in a number of respects. Fungus Eaters must be autonomous: They are simply too far away to be controlled remotely. This autonomy in turn implies situatedness: Because they cannot be remote controlled, they have to view the world from their own perspective; that is, the only information the agent has available is acquired through the sensors in interaction with the environment. Fungus Eaters must be self-sufficient, because there are no humans to exchange their batteries and to repair them. They must be embodied, otherwise they would not be able to collect anything in the first place. All this implies

---

[1] This is our own interpretation of his paper; Toda may not agree with it.

Figure 4.1 Toda's Fungus Eater, a complete autonomous agent. The robot is operating on a distant planet. Its task is to collect uranium ore. It feeds on a certain type of fungus. It is autonomous (too far away for remote control), self-sufficient (it must take care of its own energy supply which, in this case, is a particular type of fungus that grows on this planet, thus the name Fungus Eater), embodied (it exists as a physical system), and situated (its knowledge about the environment is acquired through its own sensory system). In the figure, it is in the process of devouring fungus.

that they must be adaptive, because the territory in which they have to function is largely unknown. These concepts are fundamental to embodied cognitive science, and we now discuss each in turn.

Before we do so, however, let us first examine another reason why Fungus Eaters are of particular interest for the study of intelligence, one that relates to evolutionary considerations. Nature has always produced Fungus Eaters, that is, creatures capable of surviving in the real world. There are, for example, the single-cell entities that emerged from the primordial soup 3.5 billion years ago. Only 550 million years ago, the first fish and vertebrates arrived, insects 450 million years ago. Reptiles came 370 million years ago, dinosaurs 330, and mammals 250 million years ago. Primates appeared 120 million years ago, the great apes 18 million years ago, man in its present form only 2.5 million years ago. Writing was invented less than 5,000 years ago. Based on these considerations, Brooks (1991a) argues that the really hard part for nature was to get to the level where creatures could move around and had sensory abilities. Once that was in place, things became much simpler. If we do not understand this sensory-motor basis, we have no chance of ever understanding intelligence. This is another fundamental reason why we must study Fungus Eaters, that is, complete autonomous systems.

Self-Sufficiency

MULTIPLE TASKS AND BEHAVIORS
Self-sufficiency means an agent's ability to sustain itself over extended periods of time. This implies that the agent must maintain its energy supply. A biological agent must eat and drink. Moreover, it has to eat and drink the right combination of foods. A prerequisite of eating and drinking is that the food and drink be there: Humans have to go to the grocery store or a restaurant; an animal typically has to look for food in the environment, an activity called foraging. An agent must also take care of itself; that is, it has to stay sufficiently clean, and it has to try not to get hurt. In other words, it also has to avoid predators. Moreover, it has to get enough sleep. If these conditions are fulfilled, the biological agent can engage in activities leading to reproduction. (Note that this description in terms of tasks is our description as observers. It has nothing to do with what is going on inside the animal.)

Similar considerations apply to artificial systems. A robot, for instance, has to maintain its battery level, or if it is fuel driven, it has to maintain a sufficient fuel supply. To be considered self-sufficient, the robot should be able to maintain its energy supply without external human intervention. Thus, a robot running off a power cable is not self-sufficient. A robot should also maintain a certain operating temperature. If it gets too hot or too cold, it might be damaged. Moreover, it should not bump into things, and it should avoid perils. In addition, robots are always designed for a particular task, or several tasks. They have to clean a factory floor, vacuum a carpet, mow a lawn, deliver mail in an office, collect soda cans, give tours of a university institute, and so on. Hence, agents in the real world, be they animals or robots, always have to engage in multiple behaviors. From an observer's perspective, we can say that they are able to perform multiple tasks.

TRADE-OFFS AND DEFICITS

In the real world, there are always trade-offs. If a robot is collecting soda cans or food or cleaning a park, it always expends energy. So at some point, it must replenish its energy resources; that is, it must go to the charging station and plug itself into an outlet. While doing that, it cannot collect soda cans: It must remain at the charging station until its energy supply is sufficiently high again. So there is a trade-off: Doing one thing implies not being able to do another.

Note that losing energy while collecting soda cans or mowing a lawn is a given, determined by the physics of the agent: It will happen without the agent's knowing about it. If a cleaning robot is recharging, the office space gets cluttered with soda cans or the grass keeps growing without the robot's doing anything about it: Remember, the real world has its own dynamics. If it remains at the charging station for a long time, enough soda cans might have accumulated so that it is no longer possible for the robot ever to collect all of them again. Or, to put it differently, it has incurred an irrecoverable deficit. Another way of defining self-sufficiency, then, is as follows: An agent is self-sufficient if it can avoid irrecoverable deficits. In nature, evolution has "solved" this problem, but robot designers must explicitly deal with it. Figure 4.2 shows a robot that has incurred an irrecoverable deficit.

CIRCADIAN CYCLES

Natural environments have circadian cycles: environmental conditions that change over one day, such as lighting conditions, temperature, or humidity. Similarly artificial environments often have cycles: day-night cycles, or cycles in the frequency of people attending a place (coffee rooms are attended more during day time than at night), and so forth. Conditions for certain types of tasks are usually better during one segment of the cycle than during another. For example, an agent equipped with vision is better off during the day, whereas one with infrared (IR) sensors is better off at night, for the following reason. IR sensors are active sensors: They send out an IR signal and measure the intensity of the reflected IR light, a process that works well in the dark. By contrast, a robot equipped only with IR sensors has trouble during the day. Daylight contains

Figure 4.2 Robot incurring an irrecoverable deficit. Because the robot has been sitting at the charging station for too long, the soda cans have piled up in the meantime to a level where the robot is no longer capable of removing them all, even if it were to spend all of its "spare time," that is, all of the time it has available when not at the charging station, on can collecting. This robot is not self-sufficient.

a certain amount of IR light, which may cause interference with the reflected IR light. For the robot in figure 4.2, soda cans typically accumulate more quickly during the day. The target for a self-sufficient agent is always based on a circadian cycle: It should not incur a deficit over one cycle. If it does, then the deficit is likely to increase indefinitely, because the following day will typically bring an additional deficit. The concept of circadian cycles has not been widely used in embodied cognitive science and will not be further elaborated.

THE PROBLEM OF BEHAVIOR CONTROL

Complete systems always have several behaviors in which they must engage. Some of the behaviors will be compatible, others mutually exclusive. Because not all behaviors are compatible, a decision must be made as to which behaviors to engage in at each point in time. This is the problem of *behavior control*.

The most straightforward solution to this problem is to assume that there is an internal module or representation for each observed behavior category. For example, if we observe that a rat (or a robot) is following a wall, we might postulate that it has an internal module or a representation for wall following. Such a representation is often called an action. Because there are always multiple actions an agent has to engage in, to control behavior under this assumption, you need a mechanism for deciding which action to choose for execution at any given point in time, that is, which internal module to excute. In other words, you have to solve the *action selection problem.*

The problem with this approach to behavior control is that the assumption of a straightforward, one-to-one mapping from a specific behavior to a specific internal action does not reflect what actually occurs in natural systems. (Even the concept of an internal action represents an assumption.) To illustrate this point, let us look at an example. Assume that you are sitting in the cafeteria talking to a friend. Your friend has to attend a class and you are trying to describe his behavior. He gets up and starts moving toward the exit, avoiding chairs, tables, and people who stand around. To describe his behavior, you may want to use terms like "avoiding a chair," "going toward the exit," or "going to class," implying that you somehow carve up your friend's behavior into distinct segments. There are two issues of which to be aware: First, the segmentation of an agent's behavior is observer-based and largely arbitrary. For example, you could also choose a more fine-grained segmentation such as "getting up from chair," "moving left leg forward," "moving right leg forward," and so forth. Not surprisingly, segmentation of behavior is a notorious problem in psychology and ethology. For empirical purposes such a segmentation obviously has to be made, but we need then to make explicit that we are talking about purely observer-based categories. Second, it is not appropriate to conclude that for each of these behavioral segments there is an internal module.

There are mechanisms for behavior control, however, that do not require the existence of internal actions. Chapter 6 discusses an example, Braitenberg vehicles. In fact, we think that the problem of behavior control should be approached differently than described above. This follows from one of our design principles, the principle of loosely coupled, parallel processes (see chapters 10 and 11).

Autonomy and Situatedness

We have been using terms like "autonomous agents" and "autonomous mobile robots." In this context, autonomy generally means freedom from external control. Autonomy is not an all-or-nothing issue, but a matter of degree. Complete, total autonomy does not exist; no agent is totally autonomous. It always depends to some

Figure 4.3 A horseback rider trying to control his horse. He is trying to force his horse to drink, not very successfully. The rider does exert some influence on the horse, and the horse is dependent on the rider for some things, but the horse is also to some degree autonomous. This is why the adage that "you can lead a horse to the water but you can't make him drink" has the ring of truth to it.

degree on external factors, factors beyond the agent's control. There are two aspects of autonomy here: dependence on the environment and dependence on other agents. Organisms depend on the environment for food, drink, oxygen, building materials, and the like. If agents are not capable of acquiring these resources on their own, they depend on other agents—they are less autonomous.

The main difference between dependence on the environment and dependence on other agents is that we do not attribute intentions to an environment, whereas an agent may want another agent to do certain things. Most parents want their children to do their homework and to perform well in school. We know, however, that parents have only a limited influence on their children: The latter have some degree of autonomy. The same holds for animals. We can get horses to do certain things we want them to do. But as the saying goes, "You can lead a horse to the water but you can't make him drink," again implying that the horse does have a certain degree of autonomy. So, in general, agents can be influenced, and they depend on others, but they are not completely controllable, as figure 4.3 illustrates.

From this discussion it becomes clear that when we use the term "autonomous agent," we mean an agent that has a certain degree of autonomy. It is not the case that an agent is either fully autonomous or not at all. From our discussion of self-sufficiency, it should be evident that self-sufficiency increases an agent's degree of autonomy, because a self-sufficient agent does not depend on another agent for its energy supply. The extent to which one agent can control another depends on the controlling agent's knowledge of the state and the internal mechanism of the agent to be controlled. The more precisely parents know what their children feel and think, the better they can influence them toward desired behaviors. One important reason that humans have only a very limited degree of controllability is that they have their own history, which is not, or is only indirectly and to a very limited extent, accessible to others.

Controllability and the capability of acquiring one's own history are correlated: The more an agent can have its own history, the less controllable it will be. The less parents know what their children do and what sorts of experiences they have, the less they know about what they feel and think. If they knew everything about them (including their reaction to all types of events)—which, of course, is impossible—they could easily make them do whatever they wanted, simply by manipulating the consequences of the children's actions according to what they knew the children's reactions would be. Because parents actually have only limited knowledge of their children's reactions, they have only limited control over them. Abstractly speaking, if the controlling agent (A) has access to the controlled agent's (B) internal state, and if he knows the laws by which the state of B can be influenced, A can control B completely, that is, A can get B into whatever state A wants B to be in. The less knowledge A has about B's internal state, the less A can control B. Thus, autonomy is not so much a property of an agent as a property of the relationship between agents (i.e., what one agent knows about the other). Stated differently, B has a certain amount of autonomy relative to A, and the amount of B's autonomy is— qualitatively speaking—inversely proportional to the amount of knowledge A has about B's internal state.

This property can be translated to robots. If a robot is equipped with a learning system, it can have its own experiences; that is, it can acquire its own knowledge over time. Note that this requires the agent to be situated. Recall the notion of situatedness from chapter 3: An agent is situated if it acquires information about its environment only through its sensors in interaction with the environment. A situated agent interacts with the world on its own, without an intervening human. It has the potential to acquire its own history if it is equipped with the appropriate learning mechanisms. Such an agent is potentially more autonomous than its preprogrammed, purely reactive counterpart. One implication of learning is that if the agent, after learning, encounters the same situation it has previously encountered, it will react differently than earlier on. Thus the more the agent has learned in the meantime, the more experiences of its own it has had, the less it will do the same as before, and thus, the less another agent will be able to control it, because its internal state will have changed, and the second agent will now have less knowledge of its internal state than it did previously. From this we can conclude that if we are interested in building autonomous agents, we must design them with learning components, because the capacity to learn increases an agent's autonomy. An agent's degree of autonomy can, in principle, be further increased by applying evolutionary methods (described in chapter 8). If he designs a robot not directly but via an additional evolutionary process, the designer has less control over how the robot will work and how it will behave in a particular situation. Applying evolutionary techniques often makes it difficult for designers—and for other agents in general—to understand why the agent is doing what it is doing; as the agent evolves and acquires its own history, it is progressively more difficult for the designers to understand (and manipulate) its behavior. Evolution makes the agent more independent of designers, and therefore evolved agents have the potential for higher levels of autonomy.

Embodiment

Autonomous agents are real physical agents; in other words, they are embodied. Because we have talked so far exclusively about biological agents (humans or animals) or about robots, it has been implicit that the agents of interest have to be embodied. Embodiment has proven to be an essential characteristic whose importance can hardly be overemphasized. A fundamental consequence of embodiment is that embodied agents must interact with their environments. To understand this interaction, we have to study, for example, how organisms acquire experience: knowledge about the environment obtained by interacting with it. This is one of the hardest problems in the study of intelligence. The vast research field of perception is devoted to elucidating the underlying mechanisms and processes.

Embodiment implies that the agent is continuously subjected to physical forces, to energy dissipation, to damage, in general to any influence in the environment. On the one hand, this complicates matters considerably. On the other, this often leads to substantial simplifications, because advantage can be taken of the physics involved. It has been demonstrated, for example, that walking robots can be built that require no electronic control: They are entirely brainless machines, their actions governed totally by the laws of physics.

The focus on embodied agents often leads to surprising insights, and throughout the book, we provide examples of such insights. We discuss embodied perspectives on learning, categorization, perception, memory, and sensory-motor processing. As the name of the field indicates, embodiment is at the core of embodied cognitive science. It is one of the central constituents in Brooks's (1991a,b) approach, which he called "embodied intelligence." The idea that intelligence can emerge only from embodied agents is one of the fundamental assumptions of embodied cognitive science. (For other perspectives on embodiment see, for example, Lakoff 1987 and Varela, Thompson, and Rosch 1991).

Adaptivity

CHARACTERIZATION AND DEFINITION
Adaptivity is really a consequence of self-sufficiency. If an agent is to sustain itself over extended periods of time in a continuously changing, unpredictable environment, it must be adaptive. Remember that several of the definitions of intelligence given in chapter 1 alluded, in one way or another, to the concept of adaptivity, that is, the ability to adjust oneself to the environment. Thus, adaptivity and intelligence are directly related.

By adaptation, we mean that some structure is maintained in changing environmental conditions. Ashby (1960) used the term "homeostasis," meaning that certain variables, the essential variables, remain within given limits (figure 4.4). Within those limits the organism can function and stay alive. This is called the "viability zone" (Meyer and Guillot 1990).

KINDS OF ADAPTATION
The term "adaptation" has various meanings and is used in different ways by different people. In our discussion, we follow McFarland (1991):

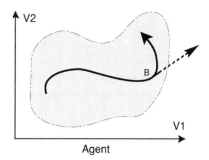

Figure 4.4 Adaptivity. The figure shows the viability zone (enclosed area) between two variables *V1* and *V2* (e.g., level of blood sugar and body fluid). Within this zone, the agent can stay alive and function. The solid arrow marks the agent's trajectory, that is, the development of the two variables over time. At point B, there is a danger that the agent might leave the viability zone (marked by the broken line) if it does not act. The agent is adaptive because it takes corrective action to prevent itself from leaving the viability zone. (Adapted from Meyer and Guillot 1991.)

Biologists usually distinguish between (1) evolutionary adaptation, which concerns the ways in which species adjust genetically to change in environmental conditions in the very long term; (2) physiological adaptation, which has to do with the physiological processes involved in the adjustment by the individual to climatic changes, changes in food quality, etc.; (3) sensory adaptation, by which the sense organs adjust to changes in the strength of the particular stimulation which they are designed to detect; and (4) adaptation by learning, which is the process by which animals are able to adjust to a wide variety of different types of environmental change." (p. 22)

Here are a few illustrations of the types of adaptation McFarland discusses (see also McFarland 1991):

1. *Evolutionary Adaptation:* An illustration of evolutionary adaptation is the peppered moth (*Biston betularia*). Originally these moths were light in color, which made them well camouflaged against lichen-covered, light-colored trunks of trees. In regions that became industrialized, industrial smoke darkened the tree trunks. Gradually the peppered moth population in industrial areas became predominantly composed of a dark variety, which was well camouflaged against the dark trees.

2. *Physiological Adaptation:* Many species can adapt to changes in environmental temperature: sweating, in man, is an example of adapting to heat changes.

3. *Sensory Adaptation:* If we are in a dark room and then the light is turned on, the eye adjusts to the change in a sensory stimulus, light intensity, by changing the diameter of the pupil.

4. *Adaptation by Learning:* This is a very general form of adaptation and is exploited in many ways. Animals can learn which food is most nutritious, where food can be found, which place gives the most shelter, and so forth.

Note that these different kinds of adaptations work on different timescales. Typically, sensory adaptation is the quickest, whereas evolutionary adaptation takes many generations. In this book, we focus mainly on adaptation by learning and through evolution.

Ecological Niches and Universality

DEFINITION

If we look at biological agents—animals—we find that they require a particular kind of environment for survival that is suited to satisfy their needs. Such an environment is called an animal's "ecological niche". Wilson (1975) defines "ecological niche" as follows: "The range of each environmental variable such as temperature, humidity, and food items, within which a species can exist and reproduce" (p. 317). It should be added to this definition that niche occupancy by a particular species usually implies competition. Different occupants of the niche compete for the same resources like food and space.

In nature, there is no such thing as a "universal animal." Animals (and humans) are always "designed" by evolution for a particular niche. (We put the term "designed" between quotation marks to indicate that it is meant metaphorically: Evolution does not have a particular design goal.) Agents behave in the real world. As we pointed out, they always require certain conditions for their survival. A robot always requires some kind of energy source. It must be equipped with sensors and effectors in order to perform its task in a particular environment, or more precisely, in a particular ecological niche. To take the earlier example, if the robot has to work at night, it may be better to equip it with IR devices rather than with vision sensors. So, the idea of an ecological niche holds for robots as well (focus 4.1). It follows that there can be no universal robot, because the robot must perform in the real world, which consists of many varied environments to which a particular

Focus 4.1:   A Market View of Robot Adaptation

David McFarland (1991), a leading ethologist and head of the animal robotics group at Oxford University, proposed an enjoyable analogy between ecological niche in animals and market niche in robots: "Niche occupancy usually implies competition. When animals of different species use the same resources or have certain preferences or tolerance ranges in common, niche overlap occurs. This leads to competition between species, especially when resources are in short supply" (p. 24). Just as animals occupy biological niches, robots occupy market niches: they are toys, cleaning robots, or whatever. A cleaning robot has to compete with human cleaners and other cleaning machines. The customer evaluates the performance of the robots and selects the ones that best fill his or her needs. This induces selective pressures which, in the end, determine whether a robot will "survive" in the marketplace. Table 4.1 provides an overview of the analogy between animals and robots (adapted from McFarland 1991, p. 24).

Table 4.1   Analogies between animal and robotic life cycles (from McFarland, 1991, p. 24).

	Biology (Animal)	Market (Robotic)
Return on investments	Number of offspring	Gross sales income assuming no failures
Reproductive probability	Chance of juvenile surviving to breed	Chance of product reaching the market
Development period	Age at breeding	Development cost
Design success (Rate of return)	Net rate of increase of genes (Fitness)	Net rate of increase of money invested in design (Instantaneous interest rate)

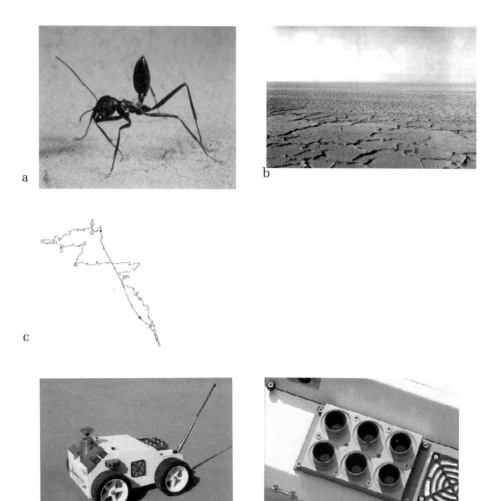

Figure 4.5 A robot designed for a particular ecological niche: (a) The desert ant *Cataglyphis*, (b) its niche, and (c) its navigation behavior—searching for food in a winding path, returning to the nest in a straight line; (d) the entire robot; and (e) the polarized light sensor module it uses for navigation. The Sahabot II (for *Saha*ra Ro*bot* II) has to operate in the Sahara Desert. Because its ecological niche is the desert, this robot is equipped with polarized light sensors and an onmidirectional camera (see figure 16.1). The robot is used for experiments to investigate the navigation behavior of *Cataglyphis*—more specifically, to evaluate different models of acquiring compass information from the polarized light pattern of the sky, and to test different models of visual landmark navigation. (Figures a, b, c by Rüdiger Wehner; reprinted with permission.)

robot may or may not be suited. Figure 4.5d shows an example of a robot, called the Sahabot (for *Saha*ra Ro*bot*) designed for a very special ecological niche, the Sahara desert (figure 4.5b). The Sahabot was developed to investigate the navigation behavior of the desert ant *Cataglyphis* (figures 4.5a and 4.5c).

This nonuniversality is quite in contrast to computation. As discussed earlier, computation is universal: Turing machines are the only machines that need to be studied. This is, of course, only possible because computation, by definition, takes place in a virtual world. And universality holds only in this virtual world. Computers are sometimes said to be universal, universal in the world of computation. If we look at computers as real machines, they depend very much on their environments. They need a continuous supply of electricity, they must be handled by their users with care, they must not be exposed to too much heat, and so forth. In that sense, computers, just like any other artifact, are designed for a particular ecological niche. Of course, some robots can exist in more different types of environments than others, so their niche is broader, but it is still there.

The fact that agents in the real world are not universal but have to function in a particular niche sounds like a severe restriction. But there is a lot of leverage to be gained by it, too. The fact that the ecological niche is restricted and has its own laws and characteristics, its types of objects, its types of agents, its temperature profile (i.e., how temperature changes over time), its lighting conditions, and so forth, can be exploited. Assume, for example, that in a particular niche only large objects are relevant. Then there is no need for a high-resolution sensor for distinguishing really small objects. If the niche is flat, wheels are sufficient. Often, learning problems that seem intractable at the purely computational level converge in real time if the constraints of the ecological niche are exploited. For example, if all objects of interest have a bilateral symmetry, as many living beings, this implies that learning can be restricted to one side, cutting computational costs in half. However, as always, there is a trade-off: The more constraints we exploit in our designs, the less universal the agent is. We return to this issue in chapter 13 when we discuss the principle of cheap design.

CHARACTERIZING NICHES

If we want to exploit the constraints of an ecological niche systematically, we also need a systematic characterization of niches, a kind of taxonomy. Coming up with such a taxonomy, as it turns out, is not nearly the trivial matter it would first appear, because such chacterizations have to be made with respect to a particular agent, to its sensors and its motor system. Only those properties of environments matter that are behaviorally relevant. For example, to an ant, small pebbles, twigs, and puddles are behaviorally relevant —it can sense them and avoid them—whereas to an elephant, they are not—its sensory-motor system is not sufficiently fine-grained. Intuitively, one important distinction is whether the environment is static or contains objects that move on their own, such as other agents. Another concerns the size of objects, the distribution of food, circadian cycles, the roughness of the terrain, and so forth. Although such a taxonomy would clearly be important, it has so far resisted efforts to create it. Only a very few papers have even ventured into this topic area. One approach is to define environments by the constraints they satisfy. Horswill (1992) identified a number of "habitat constraints." One example is what he defined as the "background texture constraint." If the carpets or floors in a building have only fine-scale texture, from a distance, the floor appears uniform. If the illumination is uniform, then the areas of a camera image that correspond to the floor should have uniform brightness. Any deviation from this uniformity must therefore be an object. Horswill also defined the "ground plane constraint." An environment satisfies the ground plane constraint if all objects in the environment, including the agent, rest on a single planar surface. Obviously, exploiting these constraints enormously simplifies vision processing. Office environments usually satisfy both of these constraints, as do some home environments, though some will have more textured grounds. We return to these constraints in chapter 10.

Another approach to classifying niches is to define environments by the predictability of the results of actions within the environment. Certain environments are more predictable than others; the less predictable an environment, the harder it is to design an agent for it. Thus, it would clearly be desirable, from the agent's point of view, to be able to characterize environments in terms of their predictability. (For more detail on this approach, see Wilson 1991.) The important factor in characterizing an environment is that it be done not in isolation, but with respect to an agent's complexity. We have more to say about this topic in chapter 13, where we discuss a particular measure of complexity.

In sum, for our purposes we use the terms "complete agent" and "Fungus Eater" to mean autonomous, self-sufficient, situated, embodied, agents designed for a particular ecological niche.

4.2 Biological and Artificial Agents

From our characterization of complete agents, it should be obvious that biological agents, animals and humans, fulfill all the criteria we set out: They are self-sufficient, autonomous, situated, embodied, and they are designed for a particular ecological niche. This is not surprising: The characterization was developed to explain natural intelligence. If creatures, including humans, had not met these criteria, they would not have survived in the first place.

Every psychologist, every biologist, in fact everyone in cognitive science, recognizes that in the best case, one would investigate complete agents and all their behaviors. However, from a methodological perspective it is not possible to study, for example, humans in all their intricacies. Thus, we must cut the problem down into manageable chunks. So even if we endorse a complete-agent view, we must make simplifications. The question, therefore, is not whether to make simplifications, but how to make them. In contrast to the classical way of modeling, in the embodied approach, the agents are "cut up" in a different way. An excellent illustration is the subsumption architecture that we discuss in chapter 7. The important point to be made here is that whatever aspect of intelligence we investigate, we must keep the entire agent in mind. This is not always easy to do, but it represents an essential design principle. It is summarized as design principle 1, the complete-agent principle, in chapter 10.

Our methodology for studying naturally intelligent systems is synthetic, meaning that we have to build artificial agents to mimic natural ones. The remainder of this chapter develops a basic framework for designing artificial agents.

Artificial Agents

In chapter 1 we mentioned three goals that we may want to pursue when building artificial agents:

1. building an agent for a particular task or a set of tasks
2. studying general principles of intelligence

3. modeling certain aspects of natural systems, that is, humans or animals

Goal (1) is from the engineering perspective, goals (2) and (3) pertain to cognitive science. All three goals are intimately related. In particular, goals (1) and (3) contribute to goal (2). We discuss these goals in more detail in chapters 16 and 17 when we discuss how to design and evaluate the agents we have built. For now we simply provide, as a very cursory review, a few examples illustrating goals (1) and (3), with the intention of providing an idea of what agent models can be used for.

The artificial agents we will design and study are of two types, robotic agents and simulated agents. Both are important tools. Some researchers have a preference for robots, others for simulation. We argue that both are needed, depending on the particular purpose of investigation.

ROBOTIC AGENTS

We now discuss a number of robots developed for various purposes. Let us first look at an example that illustrates the goal (1) above, the Mars Sojourner. Even though it was developed for a particular set of tasks (conducting experiments and collecting data on Mars), it nicely illustrates some of the fundamental issues such as autonomy, self-sufficiency (goal 2). We then turn to a few examples from biology to illustrate goal (3): cricket phonotaxis and human development and cognition.

Mars Sojourner

The Mars Sojourner has recently received a lot of attention in the media. Though today's robotic agents, in contrast to biological agents, do not fulfill all the criteria for complete agents that we set forth in section 4.1, the Sojourner comes relatively close. It is obviously embodied: It is a physical robot equipped with sensors and means of locomontion (wheels). It is self-sufficient, that is, it has to worry about its own energy supply: There is no human to exchange its batteries. It is also situated: The only means it has for acquiring information about its environment is its own sensory system. Further, it has a certain degree of autonomy, at least during real-time operation, though its autonomy is very limited, because most of its decisions are made by the mission control staff in the Jet Propulsion Lab in Pasadena. For instance, the ground staff decides on what task the Sojourner is to execute next, what area it has to explore, what data it has to collect, and what pictures it should take. Focus 4.2 discusses the Mars Sojourner in more detail.

Cricket Phonotaxis

In chapter 1 we mentioned a robot built to model the phonotactic behavior of crickets (figure 1.10). Remember that by phonotaxis we mean those processes by which animals move toward a sound source, in this case the calling song of a potential mate. Our description here is short, just sufficient to make our point. (For details, see Webb 1993, 1994). Male crickets produce a particular sound by rubbing one wing against the other. Females can find a male by this cue over distances of 20 meters through rough vegetation. One would think that the cricket would need mechanisms for distinguishing the sound from the songs of other species and for analyzing the direction from which the sound is coming. It turns out that this is unnecessary because of the way phonotaxis works (Webb 1993). Instead of using a neural mechanism for recognizing the male's calling song, or an information process, the cricket uses a *physical* mechanism. Through this physical mechanism the irrelevant parts of all the sounds present in the environment are filtered out, so that only the ones concerning the calling song of the mate are registered by the cricket. Thus, without "analyzing" the sound, the cricket reacts only to the appropriate songs. This is an example of what biologists call "matched filters."

Webb's robot that models this phonotactic process in crickets has no legs and but two wheels. From this example it becomes clear that however close one tries to mimic a natural system, abstractions will always have to be made. This statement is generally true of models of any sort. Whether one considers Webb's model a valid one is a matter of the criteria to be applied and what one is interested in. Webb was particularly interested in the sensory-motor coupling and the theoretical question of the inseparability of perception from action. (We discuss how to evaluate models in chapter 17.)

Other examples of how robots are used to investigate biological agents are Franceschini's housefly navigation robot (Franceschini et al. 1992), and Lambrinos's ant navigation robot (Lambrinos et al. 1997; figure 4.5). Like Webb, these researchers have also made significant abstractions in constructing their robot models. For example, their robots are wheeled and much bigger than real insects.

Focus 4.2: Sojourner—The Mars Microrover

On December 4, 1996, NASA launched the Mars Pathfinder spacecraft from Kennedy Space Center. The spacecraft landed on Mars on July 4, 1997, and released Sojourner (figure 4.6), the first robotic roving vehicle to be sent to Mars. Sojourner is named after Sojourner Truth, an African-American reformist who lived during the Civil War; the name was chosen because it means "traveler." Sojourner was built at the Jet Propulsion Laboratory of the California Institute of Technology in the southern California city of Pasadena. Sojourner's main function is to demonstrate that small mobile robots can actually operate on Mars. Sojourner is designed to conduct various science and technology experiments. For example, its cameras were used to take images from which a map of the landing site was constructed. Sojourner is unique not only because it is the first robot sent to Mars, but also because its total cost of development was only 25 million, a very low cost compared to that of previous interplanetary spacecraft, and also because its total development time was only three years.

Sojourner weighs 11 kg on earth and is 630 mm long and 480 mm wide. The ecological niche on Mars is a very rocky, uneven surface, and one major task of the NASA engineers was to equip the robot with means to operate in such a difficult environment: The robot therefore has six wheels instead of four: Six-wheeled robots can overcome obstacles three times larger that those that can be crossed by four-wheeled robots. Sojourner moves on its six

JPL-25888AC

Figure 4.6 A picture of the Mars Sojourner (credit: NASA/JPL/CALTECH).

Focus 4.2 (continued)

wheels in a radius of about 10 meters around the spacecraft at speeds up to 0.6 meters per minute. Moreover, Sojourner's wheels and suspension system are built in such a way that the robot can tip up to 45 degrees as it climbs over rocks without falling over. Sojourner is equipped with a large number of sensors for detecting obstacles and hazards. Onboard sensors include simple bumper sensors for collision detection; cameras for imaging, distance calculations, and identification of target objects; accelerometers for hazard detection; and devices for measuring the speeds of the wheels (wheel encoders) that are used for estimating distance traveled.

Communication with the microrover, which is the general name for a robot of Sojourner's type, is accomplished via a radio communications system. The robot operates in a kind of supervised autonomous control. It receives remote commands from engineers on Earth instructing it where to go next. Commands are generated as follows: The camera system on the Pathfinder takes images of the robot. These images, together with additional images from the robot's cameras, are displayed on a computer at the control station on Earth. The engineers can designate goal locations on these displayed images. The robot then receives commands in the form "Go . . . ," which it executes autonomously while simultaneously avoiding obstacles and hazards. Communication with the robot does not occur in real time because it takes about 11 minutes for a signal to travel from Earth to Mars. This means that after the engineers have sent the instructions for the next goal location, the robot navigates there autonomously, that is, without human intervention. But it still has a very limited autonomy.

Like that of every other robot, Sojourner's equipment—computers, motors, communication system, sensors—requires power. The robot generates most of its power by means of a solar array that provides about 16 watts of power at noon on Mars, allowing the robot to perform most of its required tasks. In addition to this solar array, the robot is equipped with batteries that are needed when there is insufficient sunlight for the solar array to provide adequate power. Once depleted, these batteries cannot be recharged. Thus, redundancy has been built into the robot's power system: Should either the batteries or the solar array fail, the robot can still complete its tasks using the other power source. As discussed in Chapters 10 and 13, redundancy in design is very important. More detail on the Mars Sojourner can be found in Matijevic 1996 and Stone 1996.

Human Development and Cognition

Whereas some people would agree that robots can be used to model aspects of insect behavior, there is general skepticism that this can be done for human intelligence. However, a number of recent projects are highly promising. An ambitious approach is the Cog project at the MIT Artificial Intelligence Laboratory (e.g., Brooks and Stein 1993). The main goal of the Cog project is to study developmental processes from the very beginning by focusing on the sensory-motor aspects of intelligence using a complex humanoid robot. (Details of the project are given in chapter 7.) Experiments by Scheier and Pfeifer (Scheier and Pfeifer 1995; Pfeifer and Scheier 1997) demonstrate category-learning capabilities on robots interacting with the real world. Scheier and Pfeifer's working hypothesis is that "high-level cognition" can be achieved by having many, largely peripheral processes working simultaneously without central integrating mechanisms. This strategy is now pursued by a number of research labs around the world. (These experiments will be discussed in greater detail in chapter 12.) Yasuo Kuniyoshi, a leading robotics researcher at the Electrotechnical Laboratory in Tsukuba, Japan, near Tokyo, ventured to build a full-featured humanoid robot to conduct experiments on human development. The project is in its initial stages but holds great promise (e.g., Kuniyoshi and Nagakubo 1997). The point here is that just as it is possible to use robots to model insect behavior, we can use them to model human behavior. But the simplifications and abstractions are of a different nature (see chapters 16 and 17 for more detail).

Conclusions

None of the robots discussed in this section fulfills the criteria of a complete agent as discussed in section 4.1. The Mars Sojourner comes closest, but the Sojourner's autonomy is extremely limited: It is, in fact, deliberately kept within limits to minimize risk. Still, all the robots discussed in this section are, by the very fact that they are robots, embodied. They are also situated, in the sense that they interpret their environments from their own perspective. Some do have a certain level of autonomy: They are equipped with learning mechanisms that enable them to acquire their own history. They are not entirely preprogrammed. Their behavior depends on the situations they have encountered in the past. Finally, they are self-sufficient; only to a very limited extent. We believe that all the robot studies mentioned are highly valuable and provide important insights, but we also see a need to investigate more complete agents.

SIMULATED AGENTS

It is, in principle, possible to simulate any physical process on a computer. As a consequence, it is possible to simulate any physical robot whatsoever: There are no restrictions. Let us look at some examples of such simulated agents.

Insect Walking

Randy Beer, a computer scientist with a strong interest in biology, developed a model of insect walking in simulation (Beer 1995) and used artificial evolution to study what sorts of gaits would evolve. He made many simplifications in his model. For example, the legs he employed were sticks without mass; that is, they had only one joint. Elasticity in the joints, friction, energy dissipation, and the like were ignored. In spite of these simplifications, Beer's simulated insect evolved to the point that it walked with very natural gaits that can be found in biological insects. Other agent simulation studies on insect walking have been conducted by prominent German biologist and neuroethologist Holk Cruse at the Center for Interdisciplinary Research in Bielefeld (e.g., Cruse et al. 1996).

Ant Navigation

Not only insect locomotion has been studied, but also insect navigation: how insects find their way to a food source and back. A famous example of simulation that took into account the situated character of the agent is the "snapshot model" by Cartwright and Collett (1983). The hypothesis to be tested in the models is that the insects, as they leave the nest, take some sort of image, a snapshot of their environment, to be used on their way back. The image is called a snapshot because it is thought to be relatively unprocessed. This idea is currently being vigorously debated.

Locomotion in Fish

Demetri Terzopoulos and his research group of the University of Toronto were interested in complex computer animations that would feature lifelike animals, such as, for example, fish. To achieve natural-looking movement, they decided to simulate not only the movements of the fish itself, but its physical interaction with the environment, the fluid dynamics as the fish is moving its body and its fins (Terzopoulos, Tu, and Grzesczuk 1994). Moreover, they modeled visual perception from an entirely situated perspective. The movements achieved in this way look remarkably natural (see chapter 8). In the field of artificial life, agent simulations are very common.

Humanoid Interaction

The humanoid robot of Kuniyoshi mentioned earlier not only is being built as a physical robot, but is also being tested in simulation before the robot is constructed. This combined philosophy is used in many projects and is highly productive. Kuniyoshi and his colleagues have made a great effort to capture the dynamics (i.e., the physical forces) and not only the geometry (Kuniyoshi and Nagakubo 1997) of movement. Many simulations of robotic systems neglect dynamics or do not take them sufficiently into account.

Artificial Creatures

Simulated agents from the class of artificial life agents are used in studies of goal (2) discussed above, that is, to investigate principles of intelligence. Karl Sims has created a number of fascinating artificial organisms (Sims 1994a, 1994b). Not intended to mimic specific natural organisms. Sims' creatures "live" in a simulated physical environment: There is gravity, so the creatures have a certain weight, and there is friction. Moreover, similar to Terzopoulos's fish, fluid dynamics is modeled for creatures living in water. This environment is independent of the creatures themselves, which gives the simulation the strong flavor of real agent-environment interaction. This kind of simulation is becoming increasingly popular in virtual reality settings. We give a detail account of Sims' creatures in chapter 8, on evolution.

Real-World Robotic Agents and Simulated Agents

Our main interest in building autonomous agents is ultimately to improve our understanding of intelligence. There is an ongoing debate whether in order to achieve this goal, one can work with simulations or whether it is necessary to build real robots. To provide a short answer: Both are needed. The pros and cons are listed in table 4.2. At first sight, it seems best to use simulation because simulation is fast, cheap, and flexible. Closer inspection, however, reveals that a physically realistic simulation, which is often required, for example, when the results are to be tested on a real robot, is extremely hard to develop. Let us illustrate this point with two examples.

Table 4.2 Comparison of real robotic and simulated agents.

Criterion	Robotic agents	Simulated agents
PHYSICAL SYSTEM		
Agent	Must be physically built and run; great potential for breakdowns, slow, cannot be run in the absence of experimenter	Arbitrary number of copies can be produced; well-suited for systems involving many agents and artificial evolution; functions reliably even in the absence of the experimenter
Physical environment	Given; environment has its own dynamics	Everything must be taken into account by programmer; often hard to simulate; realistic simulations computationally expensive
Sensors	Given; no idealizations, no "cheating"; often unanticipated effects occur (interference, reflectory properties of surfaces, drastic changes in intensity)	Sensors hard to simulate realistically; idealized sensors common, e.g., distance, object or agent recognition
Motor system	Dynamics given; complex ones hard to build and hard to control; imprecisions	Dynamics hard to simulate realistically
Dynamics in general	Given; exploitation of dynamics necessary and natural (cf. the passive dynamic walker, chapter 13)	Hard to simulate; often ignored in simulations; dynamics often not exploited
RESEARCH		
Emergent phenomena	Indefinite richness of physical environment offers great potential for emergence	Emergent phenomena frequent, but limited to basic specification present in simulation
Effort required	Can be considerable; experiments take a long time; experimenter must be present; debugging is hard	Effort to develop physically realistic simulations considerable; experiments can be run easily; presence of experimenter not required; changes quickly realizable
Gaining insights (heuristic value)	Highly productive	Highly productive

Table 4.2 (continued)

Criterion	Robotic agents	Simulated agents
Abstractions	Significant and obvious	Significant but less obvious
Scaling to more complex systems	Sensory systems are relatively easily made more complex; motor systems are much harder	Highly complex robotic systems are often not simulated; rather, abstractions are introduced (e.g., a grasp operation as a given elementary action)
Artificial evolution	Only possible for control architecture, not for complete robots	Simulation currently the only possibility; many surprising effects
Agent societies	Currently significant effort to build multiple robots (restricted to small numbers); all sensor processing based on real sensory inputs	Easy to simulate; duplication of agents trivial; idealized sensors (e.g., for object recognition) easily introduced

First, IR sensors are often used to measure proximity (nearness) to an object. But in fact, IR sensors yield an accurate measure of proximity only under unrealistic conditions: IR sensor are active sensors, that is, they send out an IR signal and measure the intensity of the reflected IR light. This creates several problems. First, the amount of light reflected depends on the properties of the materials in the environment. Second, a particular IR sensor cannot distinguish between its own IR signal and those coming from other sensors. And third, sunlight and artificial light contain IR light, which the sensor also measures.

Second, physical robots have mass, and gravity acts on them automatically as it does on any object in the real world (figure 4.7). If we want our simulated robot to have mass and weight (i.e., gravity acting on it), we must explicitly introduce it into the simulator. If a robot has the task of moving around in an office space without getting stuck, one strategy for accomplishing this is to exploit its own inertia to get out of impasses. By rushing into objects with relatively high speed, the robot bounces off, slides around and, very often by chance, faces in a direction in which it can move forward again. This process, which in the real world simply happens, would be extremely hard to capture formally in a simulation.

Figure 4.7 Comparison of real world and simulation. In both cases, gravity has not been pro-grammed into the system. In the real world (a), the robot drops to the ground any-way—gravity is part of the real world and does not have to be programmed. In the virtual world (b), the robot moves off the edge of the table and does not fall, making the simulation a poor representation of real-world events in this case.

Abstractions

Let us stop and summarize what we have said so far in this section. Whenever we are making a model, robot, or simulation, we have to make abstractions. As pointed out above, the insect robots, that is, the cricket and the ant robots, have wheels instead of legs, have electrical motors instead of a carbon-based physiology, and are much bigger and heavier than real insects; the ant robot only has three polarization elements (rather than about 200, as the real ant). Still, the claim is that the robot models reproduce interesting aspects of insect navigation. In building a model, we have to choose a level of abstraction, a level at which we are comparing the bio-logical system and the robot model. Note that the robot model is not only a model, but a behaving system itself that can be studied in its own right. Beer's walking insect, for example, has six massless sticks as legs—a potential source of error.

Implicitly, we are assuming, when we build robot models of insects, that the navigation mechanisms of the insects are not influenced by the means of locomotion, the size, and the body weight, to mention just a few of the assumptions we make. We have to be aware of the fact that these may turn out to be blatantly false. On the other hand, we have fully embodied and situated systems: all the information about the environment is acquired through the models' sensory systems in the interaction with their envi-ronments. The models do have a certain level of autonomy: The Sahabot can acquire some information about the environment, and

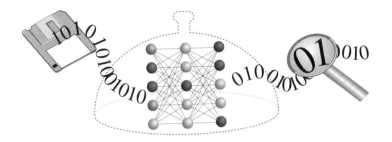

Figure 4.8   The principle of operation of the ALCOVE model. The model receives its input data from a file prepared by an experimenter (illustrated by the diskette). This input is used for learning. The model has no real interaction with the environment. A human (illustrated by the magnifying glass) must interpret the meanings, of the bit strings produced by the network.

its later behavior depends on this information. However, this autonomy is limited. The last property, self-sufficiency, is not characteristic of any of the models. Thus, we are excluding an important consideration from our models.

Another assumption in creating these insect models is that the insects' navigational mechanisms are independent of energy supply. This, once more, may turn out to be false. Although we consider this to be unlikely, we have to keep it in mind and be prepared for it.

Agent Simulation versus Classical Simulation

So far we have been talking about agent simulation, which is concerned with the simulation of a complete agent with as many of its essential characteristics as possible (embodiment, self-sufficiency, situatedness, autonomy). This contrasts with the more classical style of simulation, in which certain aspects of an agent's behavior are simulated in isolation. The differences are best illustrated with an example.

In psychology, connectionist models have become very popular. A prominent example is the ALCOVE model of categorization (Kruschke 1992), explained in more detail in chapter 12. Here we focus on the differences between this model and agent-based models. The point is not to critize this particular model—which in fact explains the results of many psychological experiments—but rather to point out the limitations, from an embodied cognitive science perspective, of connectionist models in general. The schematic overview in figure 4.8 shows the essential differences between connectionist and agent models.

In the ALCOVE model, there is an input, an intermediate, and an output layer (the category layer). The data are provided by the model designer: the model reads one input vector after another and processes it. In contrast to agent simulations, the model has no direct interaction with its environment. One important implication is that the model's output has to be interpreted by the designer and does not lead automatically to the next input. In agent-based models, the loop from input to output to input is closed; so there is no human intermediary in the loop. This characteristic is highly constraining—errors in the output lead to subsequent erroneous input patterns; the model has to be consistent with respect to its own outputs—and can be exploited in various ways. (In fact, we devote chapter 12 to mechanisms that allow an agent to structure its own input by interacting appropriately with the world.) Finally, the ALCOVE model processes all data it receives; it does not have to determine which of the data are relevant. In agent models, one of the hard tasks is to determine which of the continously changing input data should be considered relevant by the agent, for example, for learning. This book focuses on agent simulation and, of course, real-world physical agents.

We have looked at the kinds of agents that we want to build. Let us now look at how to go about designing agents and how to conduct experiments using the synthetic methodology.

4.3 Designing for Emergence—Logic-Based and Embodied Systems

This entire book is about design. In this chapter, we lay out some of the groundwork for design. The considerations outlined in this section are fundamental to every design effort, and getting them right from the beginning can help you avoid a lot of confusion and fundamental problems later on. The kinds of considerations relevant for agent design and design of classical systems are very different, as we will see shortly. In this section we use examples from two areas, medical diagnosis and agent design, to illustrate both so-called domain ontologies and low-level specifications. We also use the term "high-level ontologies" to clearly distinguish these from low-level designer commitments.

The section proceeds as follows. We first discuss classical design, starting with high-level concepts. We then introduce agents and show that the commitments involved in designing agents must be made at a different, lower level: What we are really interested in is adaptivity, which requires diversity and emergence. The art of agent design is design for emergence, as Luc Steels (1991) has called it: Make design commitments that leave room for emergence of behaviors as the agent interacts with its environment. Throughout the book, we refer to emergence, a concept that we have already introduced and briefly discuss again below.

The Frame-of-Reference Problem in Autonomous Agent Design

Whenever we are involved in designing an intelligent system, we have to be aware of the frame-of-reference problem. As we discussed in chapter 3, the frame-of-reference problem concerns the relation between the observer, the designer (or the modeler), the artifact, the environment, and the observed agent. The artifacts that we study in embodied cognitive science are autonomous agents, but the argument holds for computer programs as well. Again we emphasize, because we can hardly overstress it, the importance of getting this problem straight from the very start. Our outline of the problem is based on Clancey's (1991a) extensive treatment. The frame-of-reference problem has three main aspects:

1. *Perspective issue:* We have to distinguish between the perspective of an observer looking at an agent and the perspective of the agent itself. In particular, descriptions of behavior from an observer's perspective must not be taken as the internal mechanisms underlying the described behavior.

2. *Behavior-versus-mechanism issue:* The behavior of an agent is always the result of a system-environment interaction. It cannot be explained on the basis of internal mechanisms only.

3. *Complexity issue:* The complexity we observe in a particular behavior does not always indicate accurately the complexity of the underlying mechanisms.

Let us briefly illustrate these points with a famous example, Simon's ant on the beach.

SIMON'S ANT ON THE BEACH

Simon (1969) has used the metaphor of an ant to illustrate some basic principles of behavior; here we use his metaphor to illustrate the three aspects of the frame-of-reference problem. Let us assume that an ant starts on the right and its nest is somewhere on the left. So it travels roughly from right to left. Figure 4.9 shows a typical path the ant might take. From the perspective of the observer, the path is seen as a trajectory on the beach between pebbles, rocks,

Figure 4.9 Simon's ant on the beach. Herbert A. Simon suggested that an ant walking on the beach illustrates that behavior that looks complex to an outside observer may in fact come about by very simple mechanisms.

puddles, and other obstacles. From the perspective of the ant, the world looks completely different because of its entirely different embodiment (different sensors, different brain, different body): To the ant, there are no pebbles, rocks, and puddles as we see them. This illustrates the perspective issue.

What the observer sees as a complex path is the result of the ant's behavior, that is, of the interaction of the ant with its environment. How does this behavior come about? It would be a mistake to assume that the entire path of the ant is stored in the ant's brain and then used to guide its behavior. More likely, the mechanisms driving the ant's behavior are actually very simple, implementing "rules" that we could describe as follows: "if obstacle sensor on left is activated, turn right (and vice versa)." (These rules are, of course, implemented in the ant's neural structures). This illustrates the behavior-versus-mechanism issue: behavior must be clearly distinguish from internal mechanism.

The behavior-versus-mechanism issue is directly related to the complexity issue: The trajectory, the result of the ant's behavior, looks complex to an outside observer, but in fact it came about by applying simple rules.

The point is that the complexity of the ant's trajectory emerges from the interaction of the ant with its environment, not from the internal mechanisms alone. Therefore, the complexity of the environment is a prerequisite for the complexity of the ant's behavior. To further illustrate this point, let us assume that we increase the size of the ant, say, by a factor of 100, and let it start in the same location with exactly the same behavioral rules as before, it would go more or less in a straight line! What appeared to the normal ant as obstacles would no longer be obstacles for the giant ant, whose sensors would not be sufficiently fine grained even to detect the irregularities of the beach. Thus in order to fully explain the ant's behavior, we need to take the internal mechanisms, the environment *and* their interaction into account. Behavior cannot be reduced to internal mechanisms, i.e. it cannot be explained on the basis of internal rules alone. We must take the agent's body into account; Changing the body leads to different behavior.

An example from robotics that also demonstrates the dependence of the behavior on the embodiment concerns the position of the sensors. Figure 4.10a shows a Didabot, a very simple kind of robot used for classwork exercises. In this experiment, only two IR sensors are used. The position of the sensors is shown in figure 4.10b. The control architecture consists of a very simple neural network that implements the rules of Simon's ant on the beach: If sensory stimulation on left, turn right; if sensory stimulation on right, turn left. This leads to obstacle avoidance behavior. However, if the robot encounters an object head-on, it pushes it, because it gets no stimulation from its sensors. If we now change the position of one of the sensors by moving it to the front (figure 4.10c), the pushing behavior disappears, (the robot will either turn left or right) even though exactly the same neural network was used. This illustrates the general point that the neural substrate of any agent can be understood only in the context of its embodiment.

BUILDING A MODEL OF THE ANT'S BEHAVIOR
Let us further illustrate the frame-of-reference problem by looking at how a biologist might go about understanding the behavior of Simon's ant on the beach. Assume the biologist employs a synthetic approach; that is, he tries to understand the ant's behavior by building a model capable of reproducing certain aspects of its behavior.

The most straightforward approach he could take would be to suppose that the trajectory of the ant is stored in its head, represented, for example, as some kind of network structure (figure 4.11a). This trajectory can be used as a plan for generating behavior: To find its nest, the ant simply replays the trajectory. Note that the biologist is making a category error: He is confounding a description of behavior (the trajectory) with the internal mechanism. To test the model, he now wants to use it to control a robot.

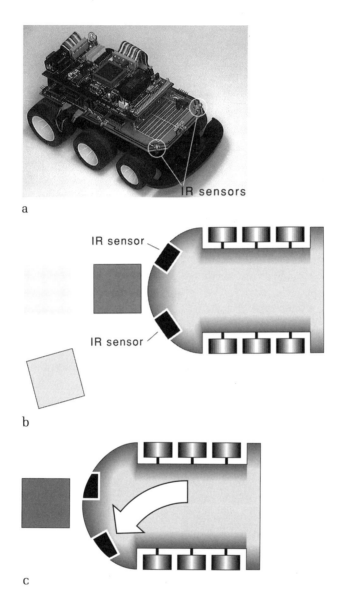

a

IR sensor

IR sensor

b

c

Figure 4.10 Illustration of embodiment. (a) The Didabot. (b) Sensor configuration 1. (c) Sensor configuration 2. Sensor configuration 1 leads to pushing and obstacle avoidance behavior, whereas sensor configuration 2 leads to obstacle avoidance only. Both configurations use the same internal neural control mechanism.

Figure 4.11 A biologist trying to understand the behavior of an ant. (a) First, he develops a model that directly maps the behavior onto an internal model. This illustrates the perspective issue. (b) Then he tries to use this model to control a walking robot. He discovers that it does not work well—the robot does not move. In other words, the model he hypothesized in (a) does not lead to the desired behavior. This illustrates the behavior-versus-mechanism issue. (c) Next, he realizes that a much simpler network will lead to the desired behavior. This illustrates the complexity issue.

This does not work very well (figure 4.11b) because of the category error. Because behavior is the result of a system-environment interaction, it is of little use to record past behavior and employ it to generate future behavior. If there is even the slightest of changes in the environment, the plan no longer works. This illustrates the behavior versus mechanism issue and the perspective issue. Behavior is something different from internal mechanism; it can be observed by an outside observer, whereas the mechanism is internal to the agent. Because of these considerations, the biologist realizes that a different kind of mechanism is required, and to his delight he finds that it is much simpler than the previous one (figure 4.11c).

We have deliberately chosen to illustrate the frame-of-reference problem with two somewhat whimsical examples, the ant on the beach, and the hypothetical biologist building a model of the ant's behavior. Here we only wanted to provide an intuition of the issues involved; the application of the problem to the scientific study of intelligence follows later.

High-Level Domain Ontologies and Low-Level Specifications

The title of this section may sound a bit cryptic but the basic idea is actually very simple. Whenever we design a system, we have to define the basic concepts or components, the *primitives*, that the system will use. For classical systems, databases, or AI systems, a *high-level ontology* or domain ontology has to be designed. It contains items such as, for a database system, a personnel record (with fields for name, age, sex, salary, department, projects, address, etc.), or for a medical system, symptoms and diseases. When designing an agent that has to interact with the real world, however, this no longer works. Designer commitments can no longer be made at this level—otherwise the designer runs into all sorts of problems, such as the symbol-grounding problem, to mention only one particularly thorny one. For an agent in the real world, design commitments have to be at a lower level, concerned with the agent's physical setup, its body, sensory, and motor systems. Whatever the agent learns about its environment should then result from the agent's interaction with the environment. We call these designer commitments a *low-level specification*.[2]

---

[2] We prefer the term "low-level specification" to "low-level ontology" because ontology triggers associations with logic-based systems.

HIGH-LEVEL ONTOLOGIES

Let us now be a bit more precise with some definitions. We use the term *ontology* very simply, in the standard way of the artificial intelligence literature (e.g., Russell and Norvig 1995, p. 222). A *domain* (or *high-level*) *ontology* has three essential characteristics:

1. It designates the basic vocabulary, the primitives, that are going to be used in designing the system. These are the only components that can be used: Everything in the system is built on top of these basic elements.
2. The meaning of these primitives is assumed to be given and shared by those involved, that is, the designers and the users.
3. The domain ontology remains constant for an extended period of time, often for the entire life of the system.

Thus, a domain ontology is a systematic account—a list—of all the basic concepts (i.e., the objects, relations, and operations) that are needed in a particular domain. The primitives have to be defined for any system whatsoever, be it a database system, a communication system, an expert system, a system for understanding natural language, or a robot. However, the kinds of primitives employed for computational systems and robots differ considerably. In a medical expert system—a computational system—they might include symptoms (red spots on skin, fever, diarrhea), patient characteristics (age, race, history), diagnoses (organisms, diseases), medical procedures to be applied (tests, treatments, therapeutic programs), and medical knowledge combining the concepts (bacterial meningitis is a subclass of meningitis). For each of the attributes within the primitives, all possible values have to be given. For example, for the attribute "red spots," the values could be "absent," "present," "strongly present." Table 4.3 offers a highly simplified sample domain ontology for a medical system.

All that the system to be designed will be able to do springs from and depends on this set of primitives initially specified by the designer. A state is a description of the current situation in terms of the primitives of the domain ontology. By means of the rules of inference, states are transformed into other states. For example, the state described by high fever, muscle pain, and high sensitivity to light, might be transformed into a new state called "flu." In this perspective, learning—that is, the formation of new concepts—consists only of combining basic components or compound concepts in different ways. As an example, recall the robot JL that we designed in chapter 2. It combined the basic concepts "green,"

Table 4.3 A simplified high-level domain ontology for a medical expert system. (To keep the example simple, the ontology here is based entirely on intuition and should not be taken seriously from a medical point of view.) Realistic medical systems can contain hundreds and even thousands of components in their domain ontologies.

Category	Attributes
Symptoms	• Red spots on skin (absent, weakly present, strongly present) • Fever (none, weak, strong; alternatively: °C) • Diarrhea (absent, present, strongly present)
Characteristics of patient	• Age (a number) • Race (Caucasian, Indo-European, Pan-Asian, Semitic, etc.) • Weight (a number) • History (medical history)
Diagnoses	• Organisms (bacteria, viruses) • Diseases (influenza, pneumonia)
Medical procedures	• Tests (blood tests, growing cultures, urine tests) • Treatments and therapeutic programs (cures, diets, operations, physical therapy, psychotherapy, medication, radiation, etc.)
Relations, medical knowledge, problem solving methods	• Bacterial meningitis is a subclass of meningitis • Heuristic classification • Hypothesize and test

"ripe," and "apple" to form the compound concept "Granny Smith." Here is another example: If we want to develop a natural language processing system that understands stories about restaurants (e.g., Schank and Abelson 1977), we must have an ontology that includes, for example, the components used in the restaurant script shown in figure 2.7, either as part of the ontology itself, or as concepts accessible by combining more basic parts. An ontology for a restaurant would have to contain elements like glasses, cups, tea, coffee, beer, serving, checks, eating, and so forth, again either as elements, or as compound concepts made up of more basic components.

Ontologies at the computational level are well defined because they have their origin in logic. The situation is much messier in the case of robots, in which we have to define low-level specifications.

LOW-LEVEL SPECIFICATIONS

Above we defined a domain ontology as the vocabulary, the primitives that will be used in the design of the actual system. For clas-

a   b

Figure 4.12 Comparison of high-level ontologies and low-level specifications. For the robot (a), there is no ambuiguity about the amount of stimulation at the sensory level, whereas the doctor (b) has a lot of room for interpreting whether red spots are present in the patient.

sical systems, it is fairly easy to decide at what level to designate the domain ontology. It is much less clear, however, at what level these primitives should be designated in the case of a robot. Obviously the robot's body, its sensory system, and its motor system have to be designed. Moreover, the individual components have to be connected in appropriate ways. Table 4.4 provides an overview of the components for a low-level specification of robots. The table's second column provides an abstract characterization in terms of states; the third suggests possible implementations.

As an example of a component in a low-level specification, let us take a standard vision sensor which is normally realized as a camera. What are its basic characteristics? It contains a number of light-sensitive cells. These cells can be in various states that are determined by physical processes, that is, the intensity of light registered at the cell. The output of the cell, that is, the signal produced by it (to be further processed), is roughly proportional to the light intensity. In other words, the interpretation of the signals from the light-sensitive cells is straightforward.

By contrast, attributes of high-level ontologies are often open to a great deal of interpretation. For example, what does "red spots (weakly present)" really mean? When do we talk about red spots? How red do they have to be? How big do they have to be? How dense is "weakly present"? As a consequence of the great room

Table 4.4 A simplified low-level specification for a robot. The second column provides an abstract characterization in terms of states; the third suggests possible implementations.

System	Component	Characterization	Typical implementations
Body	body (without sensor and motor system components)	shape, weight, size, rigidity points of attachment for sensory and motor components	rigid frames (wheeled robots) multisegment flexible (humanoid robots)
Sensory system	visual sensors	light-sensitive cells (states: on-off, grayscale, color)	camera
	proximity/distance	sensor readings related to distance (states: number of different readings)	IR, ultrasound, or laser range-finder sensor
	touch	requires physical contact (states: on-off)	microswitch; saturation of IR sensor; skin sensors
	speed sensors	sensor stimulation related to speed (states: number of different readings)	wheel encoders (wheel turns); optical flow
Motor system	wheel drive system	speed and direction of wheels (states: speeds, steering angles)	wheels driven individually by electrical motors
	leg locomotion system	(states: joint angles, forces)	forces supplied by electrical motors
	arm	(states: joint angles, forces)	forces supplied by electrical motors
	body motion system	(states: joint angles, forces)	forces supplied by electrical motors
Interactions among components	mechanical	type of connection between mechanical parts	mechanical connections always (implicitly) given
	electrical	types of signals that can be exchanged within the robot	bus system connected via a microprocessor; separate physical connnections possible
	electromagnetic	components interact without a wire connection	given by physical system; not deliberately designed
	thermal	interactions through materials surrounding a component	given by physical system; not deliberately designed
	environment	not explicit	given by system-environment interaction

for interpretation, such systems always require a human for their operation; in fact, they require a human expert, as figure 4.12 illustrates.

Many more sensors could be added to table 4.4 (torque sensors in the joints, position sensors, flow sensors, temperature sensors, etc.). The particular choice of sensors depends on what the designer intends to use. The position of the sensors on the robot is also an essential part of the low-level specification.

Let us now look at the motor system for a moment. Just as on the sensory side, the ways in which motor systems can be designed are virtually unlimited. Take a legged robot. Its legs have joints that can assume different angles, and various forces can be applied to them. Depending on the angles and the forces, the robot will be in different positions and behave in different ways. Further, the legs have connections to one another and to other elements. The details of how the various elements are connected are not important for here, but it is important to note that these connections are often not made explicit in the specification, though they are essential for the robot's performance. If a six-legged robot lifts one of its legs, this changes the forces on all the other legs instantaneously, even though no explicit connection needs to be specified. The connections are implicit: They are enforced through the environment, because of the robot's weight, the stiffness of its body, and the surface on which in stands. Although these connections are elementary—and the robot's behavior builds on them—they are not explicit in the low-level specifications, although they could be made explicit and included if the designer wished. Connections may exist between elementary components that we don't even realize. Electronic components may interact via electromagnetic fields that the designer is not aware of. What is normally explicitly designed are wire or data bus connections. So we see once again that because robots, bodies, sensor systems, and motor systems are real physical entities, it is not possible to define neatly what belongs into a low-level specification, certainly not as neatly as we can define the components of a high-level ontology. Moreover, the agent has a body with a particular shape, and it is not clear how shapes should be generally described.

We mentioned that the communication between the legs of a robot can be implicit. As a general rule, much more is implicit in a low-level specification than in a high-level ontology, simply because the physical world is always a given and it has its own properties, irrespective of whether a designer is fully aware of them. Here we are encountering a fundamental implication of simulated agents versus real agents: In simulated agents, only what is made explicit exists, whereas in the real world, many forces exist and properties obtain, even if the designer does not explicitly represent them.

The Sensory Space, the Motor Space, and the Sensory-Motor Space

The notion of *sensory space* denotes all possible configurations of the sensory states. If we have a black-and-white camera with only two intensity levels (activation or no activation) and a 100×100 image, that yields a sensory space with 2^{10000} possible states. (There are 10,000 sensors, each having two possible states.) Remember that 2^{10} is roughly 1,000, so we have approximately 10^{30} different states. If instead of just these two intensity levels, we have 256 different gray levels, this yields an incredibly large number of states. We do not discuss the implications of this here, but simply point out that this very large number of possible states is a prerequisite for the generation of diversity (in other words, for adaptivity). Similarly to the sensory space, the *motor space* can be defined as the ensemble of possible states the motor system can assume, given a particular low-level specification. In this book we rarely look at sensory and motor systems in isolation: we normally consider the entire sensory-motor space, which denotes the entire range of possible configurations of sensory and motor states together. Logic-based systems, such as expert systems or natural language processing systems for written text (in electronic form), have no sensory space in the same sense robotic systems do, simply because they lack sensors. Nevertheless, we can define the sensory space for logic-based systems as the set of potentially different inputs the system can accept. This is precisely given by the domain ontology. Anything not predefined in the ontology (or not combinable from the elements of the ontology) cannot be presented as input to the system. Defined in this way, the sensory space (or better, the *input space*) is typically much smaller for an expert system: there are only the predefined concepts, and the values they can assume are restricted (e.g., the concept "red spots" can have the values "absent," "weak," "clearly present," or "strongly present"). Moreover, the number of basic concepts in such an input space is comparatively small, on the order of a few hundred. The input space can still be of considerable size, leading sometimes to combinatorial problems, but it is normally considerably less than 2^{10000} (and that's a very simple case). Complexity in expert systems (and logic-based systems in general) is therefore computationally manageable.

From this discussion it follows that a system always communicates with its environment—including other agents—through its primitives. If we want to put a request to a database system, we can do this only by using terms that are already defined in the system, that is, terms either contained in the basic domain ontology or combinations of the latter. The same holds for the output of the system. If we want to interact with a robot, it has to be via components of the low-level specification.

Emergence

Our goal is to design agents that display emergent behaviors. The term *emergent* is used mainly in three different ways. First, it is often applied to situations, agent behaviors, that are surprising and not fully understood. Second, it refers to a property of a system that is not contained in any one of its parts. This is the typical usage in the field of artificial life, dynamical systems, and neural networks for phenomena of self-organization. Third, it concerns behavior resulting from the agent-environment interaction whenever the behavior is not preprogrammed. It is thus not common to use the term if the behavior is entirely prespecified like a trajectory of a hand that has been precalculated by a planner. Agents designed using high-level ontologies have no room for emergence, for novel behaviors. High-level ontologies are therefore used whenever we know precisely in what environments the systems will be used, as for traditional computational systems (like an accounts payable–accounts receivable program) as well as for factory robot systems. In unknown environments, a better strategy is to define the low-level ontology, introduce redundancy—and there is a lot in the sensory systems, for example—and leave room for self-organization. The following question immediately arises: Given a set of desired behaviors, how do we design the agent so that these behaviors will be emergent? How does design for emergence work? Chapter 16 discusses these topics; in chapters 11 through 13, we show concrete examples of how we can actually design for emergence.

Novel Situations and Novel Actions

In chapter 1, we saw that one of the important aspects of intelligent systems is adaptivity, that is, the ability to perform in novel situations. This implies on the one hand recognizing that a situation or environment is novel, and on the other generating new behavior appropriate to the now-changed situation. Let's investigate this point a little further.

"Computers can act only in situations that have been predefined by humans!" computer skeptics often assert, "and this is why computers cannot be used in environments in which there may be potentially novel situations." Computer enthusiasts reply: "No problem. If a situation is encountered that has not been predefined, the computer simply displays a message on the screen saying something like 'no information available,' in which case the human operator can handle the situation." We can use the idea of domain ontologies to define more precisely what is meant by "predefined" and "novel."

Take our medical expert system. If the system encounters a patient with a combination of symptoms, say red spots, fever, liver pain, and a broken leg, and there is no rule that covers that particular symptom pattern, the system might display the message "no information available," and the physician could take over. Such a case presents no problem. All the symptoms involved have been predefined; certain combinations have not been foreseen, but such cases are covered by the domain ontology: In these cases, a pertinent message can be displayed. However, if a symptom is not predefined, the system does not even recognize that it is faced with something new, and that does present a problem. Another example is a system for some type of process control: If there is no temperature sensor, the system—quite obviously—cannot sense temperature. So if the temperature rises above an unacceptable level (a novel situation), the system does not even know that it is a new situation because it does not "know" anything about temperature. Note that precisely the same point holds for robots, and for animals and humans, for that matter. Anything they can learn is constrained by the basic primitives, the low-level specifications. The reason humans can recognize truly novel situations is because of the large redundancy contained in their sensory systems. This point is of fundamental importance, and is incorporated as a design principle, the redundancy principle (see chapters 10 and 13).

A Hybrid Specification

We have discussed high-level ontologies and low-level specifications. We have also said that agents should first be designed by

Figure 4.13 A Japanese robot serving tea (from Kurzweil 1990, p. 319). The robot has to know about tea, teacups, saucers, the properties of liquids, and serving. But it also has to recognize and manipulate them through its sensory-motor system, its hardware. (Picture by Georg Fischer; reprinted with permission.)

defining the low-level specifications and then use mechanisms of self-organization. But why not have both a low-level specification and a high-level ontology on top?

Assume that you have the task of developing a robot to serve tea in a restaurant, like the Japanese robot in figure 4.13. Because you have to design a robot, you need a low-level specification that lists your commitments about the robot's physical setup and the potential connections between the components. Moreover, the robot needs to know about tea, teacups, saucers, properties of liquids, and serving, so you may want to include those concepts in its domain ontology. If you do this, you are defining a high-level ontology that implies a designer-based categorization of the real world. So there are now two levels at which you, as a designer, are making commitments. This introduces a new problem: the two levels have to be compatible. Achieving this compatibility has turned out to be extremely difficult, as the problems with model-based computer vision show (e.g., Tistarelli 1995). Moreover, defining a high-level ontology on top of a low-level one entails the symbol-grounding problem that we discussed in chapter 3. Thus, if the agent is to be situated and adaptive, it must learn about the environment as it is interacting with it, thus it is nonstatic. This nonstatic bottom-up component must then match the high-level concepts. This is a notoriously hard problem to solve, because if implies solving the symbol grounding problem. But what should we do then, if we want to design a tea-serving robot? This is a fundamental research issue, and the interested reader is referred to issue 4.1 at the end of the chapter.

To conclude, the idea of this section has not been so much to map out a general low-level specification for robot design. From what we have said so far, it should be clear that it is not possible to define low-level specifications as clearly as high-level ontologies. Instead, the section has stressed the distinction between high-level and low-level design decisions. Low-level specifications make no mention of high-level categories corresponding to what we, as observers, would call objects (coffee cup, saucer, tea, beer, etc.). As we argue later, if concepts are going to be grounded, they have to emerge from this low-level specification, and the way of proceeding that we suggest does not work with high-level ontologies.

What we have said about design of agents so far must be embedded into the context of conducting agent experiments. We discuss this topic next.

4.4 Explaining Behavior

In placing our discussion of design of agents into the context of conducting agent experiments, we must first ask ourselves what the goal of these experiments is. The main goal of doing experiments within a synthetic approach is explaining behavior, as we have said. This can be the behavior of a natural agent, or of an artificial one. Before describing the experimental steps that need to be followed, let us highlight some core aspects of explaining behavior.

Time Perspectives for Explanations

Given that our stated goal in conducing agent experiments is to find mechanisms that underlie behavior, we can examine in more detail the kinds of explanations we are looking for. Again, what we regard as good or interesting explanations strongly depends on our research goals. Our general goal is to understand the phenomena reviewed in chapter 1. To do so, we must discuss intelligence at three different levels or time perspectives: short-term, ontogenetic, and phylogenetic. One might add a fourth perspective concerned with what purpose a behavior serves.

1. The *short-term* perspective explains why a particular behavior is displayed by an agent based on its current internal and sensory-motor state. It is concerned with the immediate causes of behavior. We used the short-term perspective when we explained the behavior of Simon's ant on the beach. In that case, we referred to the ant's current sensory states: If stimulation on right, then turn left, and vice versa. Figure 4.14 shows how short-term explanations can be found in a robotic setup. The robot's behavior is shown in the lower right corner. Its internal state is displayed (sensors, activation levels, and weights of the neural network) in the other windows, and we can use this information to explain the behavior we are seeing. For example, we can explain why the robot has turned away from an obstacle based on its internal state, that is, the values of sensor signals, activation levels, and perhaps motor speeds. This setup has the advantage of enabling us to record anything we would like about the robot's internal state, an option we do not have for living beings like animals and humans. Clearly, if we do not have a short-term explanation of an agent's behavior, we simply do not understand how it works.

2. The *ontogenetic* perspective resorts not only to current internal and sensory-motor state but also to some events in the more distant past in order to explain current behavior. The ontogenetic perspective is also called the learning and development perspective. Explanations from the ontogenic perspective are almost universally used in the study of intelligence. The entire field of instructional sciences is based on it. When we say a student has done well on a test because he studied a lot, we reference a sequence of events in the past: the student reviewing the materials for the test repeatedly. If a robot initially crashes into obstacles but over time starts avoiding them, it has learned a behavior. Both of these explanations of the student's and the robot's behavior are framed in an ontogenic perspective.

3. The *phylogenetic* perspective asks how the behavior evolved during the history of the species. Finally, this perspective puts the agent into the context of an evolutionary process, a timescale in the very long term. An illustration of this has already been discussed: The "peppered moth" that changed its color from light to dark because the tree trunks had changed from light to dark as a result of industrialization.

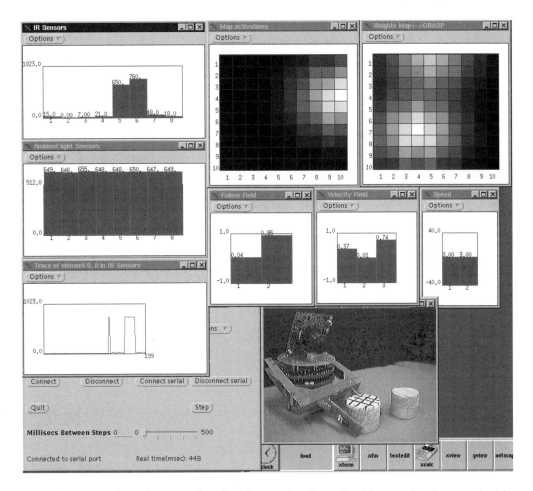

Figure 4.14 Setup for generating short-term explanations. Short-term explanations can best be made by displaying both the robot's internal state and its behavior on the screen. The robot's behavior is recorded via a video camera mounted over the experimental area. From this video information, the trajectory and other behavioral data (like the direction the robot is facing, its speed, and its direction of motion, which does not have to coincide with its direction of movement) can be extracted. The information extracted from the videotape is synchronized with the data about internal state (such as battery level, activation levels, and weights of neural networks—see chapter 5) and a time series file containing all this information is created. If this recording is performed over extended periods, behavior changes over time—that is, learning behavior—can be studied.

Throughout this book, different theoretical positions we examine attribute different weights to the three perspectives: dynamical systems place emphasis on the short-term perspective (chapter 9), connectionism and neural networks place it on the ontogenic, specifically learning (and partly development—chapter 5), and evolutionary approaches place it on the phylogenetic (chapter 8). All three kinds of explanations contribute in important ways to our understanding of intelligence. None can replace all the others.

4. One could add a fourth perspective that is not a temporal one: One can ask what a particular behavior is for; that is, how it contributes to the agent's overall fitness, a concept we elaborate on in chapter 8. In biology, this is called the *ultimate* or *functional* perspective. This question can only be answered if fitness has been defined. Except in the field of artificial evolution, this is generally not the case for autonomous agents. Moreover, in many cases, it is not obvious how a particular behavior contributes to fitness. We return to this point in chapter 8. In this book, we focus on perspectives (1), (2), and (3).

These perspectives can perhaps be best illustrated with an example. Suppose we ask why drivers stop their cars at red traffic lights. One answer would be that a specific visual stimulus, the red light, reliably leads to specific behaviors like changing gear and applying the brakes: This would be an explanation in the short term. A different answer is that individual drivers learn this rule from books, television, and driving instructors: This would be an explanation in terms of ontogenesis, learning, or development. An evolutionary explanation would deal with the historical process whereby a red light came to be used in many countries as a way of stopping traffic at road junctions. A functional explanation would be that drivers who do not stop at traffic lights are liable to have an accident, or at least be stopped by the police. (Example adapted from Martin and Bateson 1993.)

These perspectives closely resemble what is called "the four whys" in biology (e.g., Huxley 1942; Tinbergen 1963). What we have called the short-term perspective is also called a proximate explanation by biologists. What we have called the ontogenetic perspective is similar to its use in biology, but we have a stronger focus on learning. Our use of the phylogenetic perspective is identical to that in biology.

Table 4.5 Guidelines for conducting agent experiments. Note that this is the basic scheme and is more like a checklist rather than a step-by-step procedure.

Step	Description	Chapters
0.	Decide on research goal.	16
1.	Define the tasks/desired behaviors and the ecological niche, i.e., the task environment.	16
2.	Define the low-level specifications.	5, 16
3.	Choose a platform.	16
4.	Define the control architecture.	11–14, 16
5.	Define the concrete experimental setup and the experiments to be run.	17
6.	Before running the experiments, formulate predictions and hypotheses and provide the rationale for them. Think about how the agent's performance is to be evaluated.	17
7.	Perform the experiments; collect data about • agent behavior • internal state of the agent • sensory-motor state.	17
8.	Describe the agent's behavior and perform various kinds of statistical analyses.	4, 17
9.	Formulate explanations of the agent's behavior. Analyze the model's limitations. Report on failures.	4, 17

Conducting Experiments with Complete Agents

We have pointed out three main purposes for which one might pursue building complete agents: modeling certain aspects of natural agents, studying general principles of intelligence, and building agents for a particular task (or tasks). We have also described and compared two types of artificial, complete agents: simulated and robotic agents. In this section we summarize the guidelines to conduct scientific experiments with complete agents. An overview is provided in table 4.5. We give only a short description here; details are left for chapter 16.

Before we start conducting experiments, we have to know what *research issues* we want to investigate. Normally this should be fairly obvious: navigation behavior of desert ants, for example, or phonotactic behavior of crickets, category learning in human infants, cooperation in primate societies, or data collection on Mars. The next things to decide upon are the *tasks* or the *desired behaviors* of the agent and its *ecological niche*. Because behavior always takes place in a particular environment, we use the term *task environment* to designate the two together. The task of the Sojourner, for example, is to collect data on the planet Mars, and its ecological niche is the surface of Mars. We have also discussed the robot cricket built by Webb (e.g., 1993). The desired behaviors of Webb's robot cricket (e.g., 1993), which we discussed earlier, are to approach a sound source from various initial positions according to principles observed in the real cricket. Then, the low-level specification needs to be defined. In other words, a decision must be made—given the agent's task and ecological niche—as to what the agent should be able to sense, what its body should look like, how it should interact with its environment, and so on. The Sojourner, for example, has to navigate on the surface of Mars while avoiding obstacles. Thus, it needs an appropriate set of sensors. On the Sojourner, cameras, bumper sensors, and proximity sensors were used to provide this ability. Its body and motor system had to be built to enable it to overcome obstacles of considerable height, which is why six wheels were incorporated, rather than four. Similar considerations apply for the robot cricket, which needs means of detecting sounds of particular wavelengths and of navigating toward the sound source.

Then, a *platform* has to be chosen; that is, how should the low-level specification be realized (implemented)? Among other things, a decision must be made whether to use simulation or a real robot. For the Soujorner, this choice was obvious: A simulation on Earth cannot produce measurements on Mars. It may not have been so obvious in the case of the robot cricket. If the designer opts for a robot, the choice is between buying a platform off the shelf or building one. The decision strongly depends on resources and know-how already available (see also chapter 16).

The next step involves defining the *control architecture*, which essentially specifies how the various parts of the low-level specification, the primitives, should be connected to produce the desired behavior. In the case of the robot cricket, this was in fact the main research issue: How can the robot cricket be "wired up" or programmed so that it produces a behavior comparable to the one observed in the real cricket? The control architecture—appropriately embedded in the robot cricket—thus implements hypotheses about the mechanisms underlying the real cricket's behavior. The Sojourner robot's purpose was not to understand natural intelligence, but rather to achieve a particular task: Biological or psychological considerations were irrelevant. The particular control architecture chosen for an agent crucially depends on the purpose for which the robot is being designed. If the goal in building the robot is to model natural intelligence, the main considerations are biological or psychological plausibility, whereas if it is to fulfill some task, the control architecture must be chosen to implement efficient task-related behaviors.

The final step before the actual experiments can be run entails formulating *predictions (hypotheses)* about what is going to happen, given the agent's platform, control architecture, low-level specification, ecological niche, and task. In addition, decisions about the *evaluation* of the robot's performance have to be made. It is not effective research design simply to run a large number of experiments, collect data, then think about evaluation at the very end. One should be clear before any experiments are run about what types of data one wants to collect and how one wants to analyze that data, for example, in terms of statistical analyses. Of course, this can be an iterative process whereby preliminary experiments reveal what kinds of data are most relevant, but as a general rule of thumb, it is good practice thinking about these issues beforehand. The case of the Sojourner robot makes the point very clearly: Imagine what would have happened if evaluation criteria had been derived only after the robot had been sent to Mars! The same case could be made about the robot cricket. In any case, from a purely scientific perspective, hypotheses always have to be formulated before the experiments are actually performed.

When running the actual experiments you need to *collect data* about all relevant aspects of the robot's behavior. This includes the behavior as seen by an outside observer and the robot's internal state, for example, the sensor data and data on the neural network dynamics and motor states. The setup from figure 4.14 can be used to record behavior and internal states automatically. Finally, once you have all the data you need, you can start describing the robot's behavior and analyzing these data. There are many ways to describe behavior, and the descriptions can be made on very different levels. For example, we can give verbal descriptions, or we can draw the trajectories exhibited, preferably automatically. We can approach this more quantitatively and do various kinds of statistical analyses. Statistics often lend themselves most readily to interpretation if they are represented graphically. We can also describe agent behavior in terms of mathematical models (e.g., differential equations). Additional methods can be found in any textbook on general experimental methodology. Note that a description of behavior implies a segmentation of behavior: The behavior has to be cut up into meaningful pieces, the segments, to be described effectively. For example, saying that someone is eating, drinking, getting up, and leaving the table represents a segmentation of the behavior "eating dinner." In the robotic domain, examples of behavior segments would be turning toward a light source, picking up a peg, following a wall, or recharging its batteries. In addition to a description of its behavior, the robot's performance needs to be evaluated. Experiments can be evaluated in many ways. We leave providing a detailed overview to chapter 17 but present examples of experiment evaluation as we go along.

Issues to Think About

Issue 4.1: Hybrid Specifications—Choice of Tasks

Earlier in the chapter, we made a preliminary try at designing a robot to serve tea in a restaurant. On the one hand, such a robot has to know about its environment: about restaurants, objects, and procedures in the restaurant. On the other, it has to act physically in the restaurant: It must actually bring the tea to customers. We argued that if you start by designing the high-level ontology and the low-level specification using a design in which concepts emerge through agent-environment interaction, there will be incompatibilities between the two. If that is so, how *do* we design a tea-serving robot in a principled way? We honestly don't know. You will find, as you read through this book, that the kinds of behaviors we can engender through emergent designs are, though interesting, not sufficient to produce such complex behaviors as those required in a restaurant. The object recognition problems are enormous, the object manipulation skills, considerable. Just think of preparing a cup of tea, putting it on a small tray, and carrying it to the—right—customer. It is also implied that the robot would need some way of communicating with the customers. We could probably produce a "hack": We could try to introduce physical constraints in the environment: For example, we could specify that the cups are always found in exactly the same location, we could put identifiers on the tables and the different kinds of tea, and we could arrange for smooth grounds so the robot could use wheels. We could also scale down the robot's task by not having it manipulate the tea cups themselves: Personnel could put them on the robot, and the customers could pick them up themselves once the robot has arrived at their tables. But what would we then learn about the principles of intelligence? Presumably not too much. So the conclusion seems to be that it may be premature to actually try to build a tea serving robot. But we might be able to make a compromise. We could make some simplifications, changes to the environment, and try to cause at least some of the behaviors to emerge. If these changes were done right, the robot might actually be able to learn to look out for cluttered tables with no customers, for example, and recharge its battery on its own, if required. Alas, this kind of study has not been widely attempted. One project that moves in this direction, however, is the sewage system robot project that we outline in chapter 18. As we see later on, the choice of appropriate tasks is crucial to the success of an agent experiment. Try to apply these considerations to an application of your choice.

Issue 4.2:   Limitation by Low-Level Specification

We have stressed the limitations imposed by high-level ontologies. But robots, and humans for that matter, are also constrained. Anything for which our sensory system makes no provision, we can simply not sense. Our visual system can detect electromagnetic waves only within a certain limited range. Anything outside is simply not accessible to the visual system. (We function as well as we do because of the redundancy built into our sensory system that enables us to detect events beyond the capacity of a sensor. For example, although our eyes can't measure temperature, we can often "see" whether objects are really hot or really cold.) Try to think of other limitations of our sensory system to get an idea of what our own "low-level specification" is and how it constrains our potential interactions with the real world.

Points to Remember

- The agents of highest interest for our purposes are complete agents. They are autonomous, self-sufficient, embodied, and situated. They have been given the name "Fungus Eaters."

- Self-sufficient agents can perform multiple tasks, can exhibit multiple behaviors in the real world over extended periods of time; that is, they do not incur an irrecoverable deficit in any of their resources. Self-sufficiency implies adaptivity.
- Self-sufficiency always pertains to a particular ecological niche. An ecological niche is the range of environmental variables within which a species, or an autonomous agent, can exist. Agents are always designed (by an engineer or by evolution) for a particular ecological niche: There is no universal agent in the real world. If the specific properties of the ecological niche are exploited, scalability of learning algorithms can often be achieved.
- Because self-sufficient agents always have many tasks, they have to solve the problem of behavior control: loosely speaking, the problem of doing the right thing at the right time. Action selection designates the problem of choosing an action in a particular situation from a given set of actions. The problem with the action-selection approach is that in general there is no straightforward mapping of desired behaviors to internal actions.
- Autonomy means independence of control. This characterization implies that autonomy is a property of the relation between two agents, in the case of robotics, of the relations between the designer and the autonomous robot. Self-sufficiency, situatedness, learning or development, and evolution increase an agent's degree of autonomy.
- A situated agent acquires all information about the environment from its own perspective through its sensory system.
- Embodiment means existing as a physical entity in the real world, that is, as a robot. Embodied agents can also be simulated, as is often done in virtual reality environments. The positioning of the sensors on the agent must be specified because where the sensors are positioned affects system-environment interaction. Moreover, how the control architecture is embedded in the agent must also be defined.
- There are four kinds of adaptation: evolutionary, physiological, sensory, and adaptation by learning. All operate on different timescales.
- There are three potential goals when building an artificial agent: (1) building an agent for a particular task or a set of tasks, (2) studying general principles of intelligence, and (3) modeling certain aspects of natural systems, that is, humans or animals.

- Standard simulations differ from agent simulations in that a simulated agent interacts with a simulated environment through its own sensory-motor system, whereas in a standard simulation, the agent does not interact with the environment at all.
- The frame-of-reference problem conceptualizes the relation between the designer, the observed agent, the artifact to be designed, and the environment. There are three issues: perspective, behavior-versus-mechanism, and complexity.
- A high-level domain ontology is a systematic account of the basic components, the primitives, that will be used in the system. Anything the system will be able to do builds on this ontology. This holds also for the communication with the environment.
- A low-level specification is the equivalent of a domain ontology for a robot: It includes the body, the sensory and motor systems, and potential connections. Robots should be specified in terms of low-level specifications rather than high-level ontologies. Hybrid specifications should be avoided.
- Sensor spaces typically have very large numbers of states. To make them manageable, we need to exploit constraints that we get from interaction with the environment.
- The term "emergence" is used primarily in three different ways: (1) something surprising and not fully understood, (2) a property of a system not contained in any one of its parts, and (3) behavior that is not preprogrammed that arises from agent-environment interaction. Definition (2) is the meaning intended in the self-organization and artificial life communities, and (3) is the one in the autonomous agents field. Our goal in building autonomous agents is to design for emergence.
- When conducting agent experiments, the following steps must be taken (though not necessarily in this order): decide on research goal; define tasks or desired behaviors and ecological niche; define low-level specifications; define control architecture; choose a platform; define concrete experimental setup and experiments to be run; formulate predictions; run experiments and collect data; describe agent's behavior; and formulate explanations.

Further Reading

Hendriks-Jansen, H. (1996). *Catching ourselves in the act: Situated activity, interactive emergence, evolution, and human thought*. Cambridge, MA: MIT Press (A Bradford Book). (A philosophical treatment of the entire field of embodied cognitive science. The idea of emergence is given extensive treatment. Contains many examples described in great detail. Also discusses the major criticisms not only of classical approaches in AI but also in ethology and psychology.)

McFarland, D. (1995). Autonomy and self-sufficiency in robots. In L. Steels and R. Brooks (Eds.), *The artificial life route to artificial intelligence: Building embodied, situated agents* (pp. 287–309). Hillsdale, NJ: Lawrence Erlbaum. (A comprehensive discussion of the concepts of autonomy and self-sufficiency in the context of the behavioral economics approach.)

Toda, M. (1982). *Man, robot, and society.* The Hague The Netherlands: Nijhoff. (An entertaining and intelligent discussion of many fundamental problems in cognitive psychology and the psychology of emotion. Masanao Toda is one of the leading psychologists in Japan who for many years has been working on developing a comprehesive theory of emotions.)

In this chapter we discuss some tools for building agents and examples of specific classes of agents. We start with neural networks, which we work with throughout the book, so it is important that we develop an intuitive understanding of how they function. There are various reasons for using neural networks. First, they have a number of wonderful properties: They are fault and noise tolerant, they are intrinsically learning systems, and they can generalize; in short, they are robust. Second, because they are inspired by natural brains, it is relatively straightforward to implement in them ideas from neurobiology. One such idea is the parallel nature of the neural systems. Neural systems typically consist of a very large number of neurons that can be active and process information simultaneously. A significant advantage of parallelism is that it makes a great deal of processing possible even if individual components are relatively slow, as natural neurons are. Parallelism also implies robustness: If, for example, a few neurons cease to operate, there are still enough others to perform the desired function. Parallelism has another—somewhat surprising—implication: It requires learning. If there are, say, a million connections between units in a network, we can no longer by analysis or by trial and error find out what the connection strengths have to be. They must be adjusted through a learning process. Modeling some of the properties of natural brains is an important factor in understanding and constructing intelligent systems. Thus, even if it were possible to build more efficient agents using other formalisms such as fuzzy logic or control theory, it is more sensible to employ neural networks from the perspective of understanding natural intelligence.

A third reason for using neural networks is that they can be embedded into physical robots in natural ways. Using neural networks for robot control has an interesting theoretical implication. As we have seen, the brain is normally considered to be the "seat of intelligence." Modern neuroscience has focused on the brain's information-processing capacity (e.g., Churchland and Sejnowski 1992). When using neural networks in robots, we are immediately alerted to the fact that we can understand the functioning of the network only if we know how it is connected to the sensors and effectors (electrical motors in robots, muscles in animals and humans), how they work, and where they are physically located on the robot. These considerations imply that if we are to understand the functioning of a neural substrate, we must extend our investigation beyond its information processing (or algorithmic) properties and focus on its embodiment. For the study of intelligence, this implies that the seat of intelligence is not the brain but rather the organism as a whole.

We start our investigation by motivating neural networks from biological neurons. We show how we can arrive at abstract, mathematically describable models of the messy world of real biological neurons. This leads us to generally known and widely used neural networks, sometimes called artificial neural networks (ANNs) to distinguish them from biological ones. We then introduce the basics of neural networks and illustrate them with an example of an autonomous agent. Readers already familiar with neural networks may skip the basics and move directly to this example (section 5.3). At the end of the chapter, we present a somewhat polemic argument for the need to work with physically embodied systems. In the course of this argument, we also demonstrate that using neural networks alone is not sufficient to build genuine intelligence, because neural networks in isolation, like any other computational model, only process information.

Before we begin, a short note on terminology: we use the term *connectionism* synonymously with neural networks in the context of embodied cognitive science. Neural network researchers focusing on modeling cognitive science–related phenomena are called *connectionists*. We find many connectionists in psychology and natural language processing. The field of neural networks is much wider, however, and includes applications in physics, optimization, control, time series analysis, finance, signal processing, and pattern recognition. A short historical review of connectionism is provided in focus box 5.1.

5.1 From Biological to Artificial Neural Networks

There are literally hundreds of textbooks on neural networks, and we have no intention whatsoever of reproducing another such textbook here. What we would like to do is point out those types of

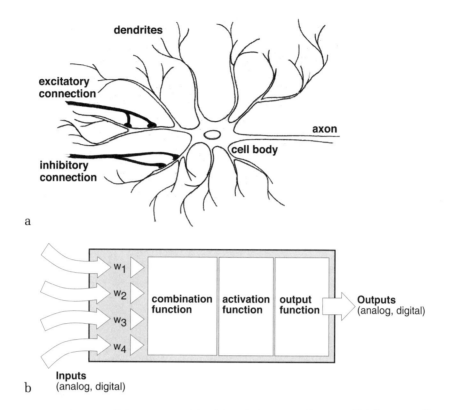

Figure 5.1 Natural and artificial neurons: (a) a biological neuron, (b) an artificial neuron. The dendrites in the natural neuron correspond to the connections between the cells in the artificial one, the synapses to the weights, the axons to the outputs. Computation is done in the cell body.

neural networks that are essential for modeling intelligent behavior, in particular those relevant for autonomous agents. The goal of this chapter is to provide an intuition about neural networks rather than develop them in a lot of technical detail.

The human brain consists of roughly 10^{11} neurons. They are highly interconnected, each neuron making up to 10,000 connections, or synapses, with other neurons. This yields roughly 10^{14} synapses. These specifics are not the focus here; we would simply like to communicate a sense of the brain's awesome complexity. The human brain is, in fact, the most complex known structure in the universe.

Figure 5.1a shows a model of a biological neuron in the brain. (For our purposes here, we can ignore the details of the physiological processes involved. The interested reader is referred to the excellent textbooks in the field, such as Churchland and Sejnowski

1992 and Kandell, Schwartz, and Jessell 1991.) The main components of a biological neuron are the dendrites, the cell body, the axon, and the synapses. The *dendrites* have the task of transmitting activation from other neurons to the *cell body* of the neuron, which in turn has the task of summing incoming activation; there is also the *axon*, which transmits information, depending on the state of the cell body, to other neurons by means of a *spike*, that is, an action potential that quickly propagates along an axon. The axon thus makes connections to other neurons via *synapses*. Synapses can be excitatory, which means that they increase the activation level of a neuron, or they can be inhibitory, in which case they potentially decrease a neuron's activity. The impulses reaching the cell body (*soma*) from the dendrites arrive asynchronously at any point in time. If enough excitatory impulses arrive within a certain small time interval, the axon sends out signals in the form of spikes.

Of course, this description of neuron structure and function is drastically simplified; individual neurons are highly complex in themselves, and additional properties are discovered almost every day. If we want to develop models of even some small part of the brain, however, we have to make significant abstractions. We now discuss some of these abstractions (figure 5.1b). One abstraction typically made is that there is some kind of a clock that synchronizes all the activity in the network which means that the entire neural network is updated at each time step. In this abstraction, inputs to an (artificial) neuron can simply be summed (the combination function) and passed through an activation function to yield a level of activation. The output of an artificial neuron is normally taken to be its activation level (or it is passed through an output function). By contrast, to model a real biological system, one would have to take the precise arrival times of the incoming signals into account or assume a statistical distribution of arrival times. Moreover, the spikes are not modeled individually in the artificial neuron, only their average firing rate. The firing rate is the number of spikes per second the neuron produces. It is given by one simple output value. An important aspect that many ANN models neglect is the amount of time it takes for a signal to travel along the axon. Some architectures consider such delays explicitly (e.g., Ritz, Gerstner, and van Hemmen 1994; Rieke, Warland, de Ruyter van Steveninck, and Bialek 1997). Nevertheless, it is amazing how much can be achieved by employing the very abstract model. Table 5.1

Table 5.1 Comparison of natural and artificial neurons.

Nervous system	Artificial neural network
Neuron	Processing element, node, model neuron, abstract neuron
Dendrites	Incoming connections
Cell body	Activation level, activation function, transfer function, output function
Spike	Output of a node
Axon	Connection to other neurons
Synapses	Connection strengths and weights
Spike propagation	Propagation rule

shows the correspondences between the respective properties of real biological neurons in the nervous system and abstract neural networks.

Given these properties of real biological neural networks we have to ask ourselves, how the brain achieves its impressive levels of performance on so many different types of tasks. How can we achieve *anything* using such models as a basis for our endeavors? Since we are used to traditional sequential programming this is by no means obvious. In what follows we demonstrate how one might want to proceed.

Before going into the details of neural network models, let us make just one point concerning the level of abstraction. There are a large number of different types of neurons and many different ways for neuron-to-neuron communication. (e.g., Kandell, Schwartz, and Jessell 1991; Reeke et al. 1989). Figure 5.2 shows, different types of neurons in the human brain. Moreover, the spike is only one way in which information is transmitted from one neuron to the next, although it is a very important one. Just as natural systems employ many different kinds of neurons and ways of communicating, there are a great variety of abstract neurons in the neural network literature.

5.2 The Four or Five Basics

For every artificial neural network we create, we have to specify the following four—or five, if we are designing an autonomous agent—elements:

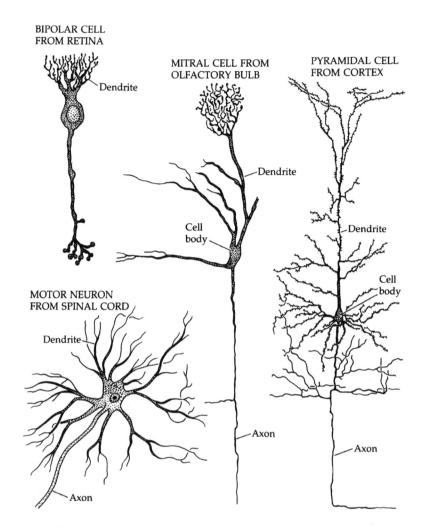

BIPOLAR CELL
FROM RETINA

Dendrite

MITRAL CELL FROM
OLFACTORY BULB

PYRAMIDAL CELL
FROM CORTEX

Dendrite

Cell
body

Dendrite

Cell
body

MOTOR NEURON
FROM SPINAL CORD

Dendrite

Axon

Axon

Axon

Figure 5.2 Different types of neurons. Natural brains, especially the human brain, contain many different types of neurons (from Churchland and Sejnowski 1992, p. 42). The great number of different types of networks in the neural modeling literature reflects the great variety of neurons in natural systems. (From Kuffler, Nicholls, and Martin (1984), *From neuron to brain.* Second Edition. Sunderland, MA: Sinaur Associates. Reprinted with permission.)

Focus 5.1: The History of Connectionism

During the 1980s, a new kind of modeling technique or modeling paradigm emerged, connectionism. We already mentioned that the term "connectionism" is used to designate the field that applies neural networks to modeling phenomena from cognitive science. By neural networks, we mean a particular type of computational model consisting of many relatively simple, interconnected units working in parallel. Because of the problems inherent in classical approaches to AI and cognitive science, many researchers warmly welcomed connectionism. It soon had a profound impact on cognitive psychology and large portions of the AI community. Actually, connectionism was not really new at the time; it would be better to speak of a renaissance. Connectionist models have been around since the 1950s, when Rosenblatt (1958) published his seminal paper on the perceptron, illustrated in figure 5.3.

Even though all the basic ideas were there, perceptron research never really took off. One reason was the publication of Minsky and Papert's seminal book *Perceptrons* in 1969, in which they proved mathematically some intrinsic limitations of certain types of neural networks. These limitations seemed so restrictive that, as a result, the symbolic approach began to look much more attractive. Many researchers then chose to pursue the symbolic route, and the symbolic approach dominated the scene until the early 1980s; then problems with the symbolic approach started to emerge.

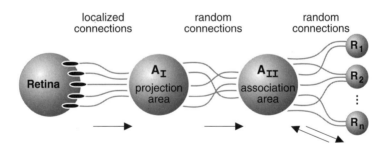

Figure 5.3 Rosenblatt's perceptron. Stimuli impinge on a retina of sensory units (left). Impulses are then transmitted (from the retina to a set of association cells, also called the projection area. (This projection area may be omitted in some models.) The cells in the projection area each receive a number of connections from the sensory units. These cells are binary threshold units. Between the projection area and the association area, connections are assumed to be random. The responses R_i are cells that receive input typically from a large number of cells in the association area. Whereas the previous connections were feedforward only, the ones between the association area and the response cells work in both directions. They are either excitatory, feeding back to the cells from which they originated, or inhibitory to the complementary cells (the ones from which they do not receive signals). Although there are clear similarities to what is called a perceptron in today's neural network literature, the feedback connections between the response cells and the association area are normally missing (see section 5.4).

Focus 5.1 (continued)

> The period between 1985 and 1990 was really the heyday of connectionism. There was an enormous excitment and a general belief that through connectionism enormous progress in our understanding of intelligence had been made. What the researchers and the public at large seemed most fascinated with were essentially two properties: First, neural networks are learning systems, and second they have emergent properties. Recall the three conceptions of emergence we introduced in the previous chapter. In this context, the notion of emergent properties refers to behaviors a neural network (or any system) exhibits that have not been programmed into the system. These behaviors result from an interaction among various components (and of the system into which the neural network is embedded with the environment, as we show later). A famous example of an emergent phenomenon has been found in the NETTalk model, a neural network that learns to pronounce English text. (NETTalk is discussed in more detail below). After some learning, the network starts to behave as if it had learned the rules of English pronunciation, even though there were no rules in the network. So for the first time, computer models were available that could do things the programmer had not directly programmed into them. The models had acquired their own history! This is why connectionism, that is, neural network modeling in cognitive science, is still surrounded by a somewhat mystical aura.
>
> Neural networks are now widely used beyond the field of cognitive science. Applications abound in areas like physics, optimization, control, time series analysis, finance, signal processing, pattern recognition, and of course neurobiology. Moreover, since the mid 1980s when they started becoming popular, many of their properties have been proven mathematically. An important one is their computational universality (Hornik, Stinchcombe, and White 1989). Another is their close link to statistical models (e.g., Poggio and Girosi 1990). These results perhaps make neural networks somewhat less mystical and less exotic, but no less useful and fascinating.

1. *The characteristics of the node:* We use the terms *nodes, units, processing elements, neurons,* and *model neurons* synonymously. We have to define the way in which the node sums the inputs, how they are transformed into a level of activation, how this level of activation is updated, and how it is transformed into an output that is transmitted along the axon.

2. *The connectivity:* We must specify which nodes are connected to which and in what direction.

3. *The propagation rule:* We must specify how a given activation traveling along an axon is transmitted to the neurons to which the axon is connected.

4. *The learning rule:* We must specify how the strengths of the connections between the neurons change over time.

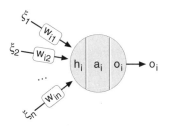

Figure 5.4 Node characteristics: h_i: summed weighted input into the node (from other nodes or from sensors, indicated by ξ_1), a_i: activation level, o_i: output of node (often identical with a_i), w_{ij}: weights connecting nodes j to node i. Moreover, the following items are associated with each node: an activation function g, transforming the summed input h_i into the activation level, and a threshold, indicating the level of summed input required for the neuron to become active.

5. *Embedding the network in the agent:* If we are interested in neural networks for autonomous agents, we must always specify, in addition to the first four elements, how the network is embedded in the agent.

The neural network literature depicts thousands of different kinds of network types and algorithms. All, in essence, are variations on these basic properties.

The First Basic: Node Characteristics

We have to specify in an ANN how the incoming activation is summed and processed to yield level of activation and how output is generated: that is, we must specify the node characteristics (see figure 5.1b and 5.4). The standard way of calculating a neuron's level of activation is

$$a_i = g\left(\sum_{j=1}^{n} w_{ij}o_j\right) = g(h_i), \tag{5.1}$$

where a_i is the level of activation of neuron i, o_j the output of other neurons, g the activation function, and h_i the summed activation. Normally we have $o_i = f(a_i) = a_i$, that is, the output is taken to be the level of activation. In this case, o_i can be replaced by a_i in equation (5.1). The activation is updated at each time step. If we want to make this explicit, we can rewrite equation (5.1) as:

$$a_i(t+1) = g\left(\sum_{j=1}^{n} w_{ij}a_j(t)\right). \tag{5.2}$$

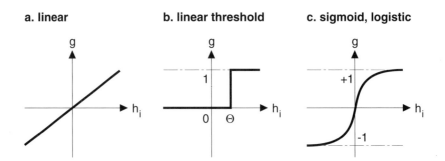

a. linear   **b. linear threshold**   **c. sigmoid, logistic**

Figure 5.5 Most widely used activation functions: (a) linear function, (b) step function, (c) sigmoid function. The variable h_i is the summed input, g, the activation function. The sigmoid function varies between -1 and $+1$ or between 0 and 1.

The explicit reference to the time steps is frequently omitted because it is evident.

Figure 5.5 shows the most widely used activation functions. The linear function simply sums the inputs (figure 5.5a). The step function sums the inputs and the neuron is silent until the threshold θ is reached, at which point the neuron becomes active (figure 5.5b). Units employing the step function are often called *linear threshold* units. The third activation function to be discussed here is the *sigmoid* or *logistic* function (figure 5.5c). The sigmoid function is, in essence, a smooth version of a step function. Its value is zero (or -1) for low input. At some point, it starts rising rapidly and then, at even higher levels of input, it saturates. This saturation property can be observed in nature, where, for example, biological factors limit the firing rates of neurons. The slope (also called gain) of the sigmoid function can be changed.

The Second Basic: Connectivity

The second property to be specified for any neural network is its connectivity, that is, how the individual nodes are connected to one another. This can be shown by means of a directed graph with nodes and arcs (arrows). Connections are assumed to be in only one direction; if they are bidirectional, this must be explicitly indicated by two arrows. Figure 5.6 shows a simple neural net. Nodes 1 and 2 are input nodes; they receive activation from outside the network. Node 1 is connected to nodes 3, 4, and 5, whereas node 3 is connected to node 1. Nodes 3, 4, and 5 are output nodes. They could be connected, for example, to a motor system, where node 3 might

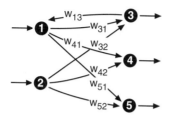

Figure 5.6 Graph representation of a neural network. The connections are denoted w_{ij}, meaning that a particular connection links node j to node i with weight w_{ij}. Table 5.2 shows the matrix representation for this network.

stand for "turn left," node 4 for "straight," and node 5 for "turn right." Note that nodes 1 and 3 are connected in both directions, whereas between nodes 1 and 4 the connection runs only one way. Connections in both directions can be used to implement some kind of memory. Networks having connections in both directions are also called recurrent networks. Nodes that have similar characteristics and are connected to other nodes in similar ways are called a *layer*. Nodes 1 and 2 receive input from outside the network; they are called the *input layer*, whereas nodes 3, 4, and 5 form the *output layer*.

For larger networks, graph notation gets cumbersome, and it is better to use matrices. The idea is to list all the nodes horizontally and vertically. The matrix elements represent the connection strengths. They are denoted w_{ij}, meaning that node j is connected to node i with a particular connection strength, or weight, w. (note that this is intuitively the "wrong" direction, but it is just a notational convention.) Such a matrix is called the *connectivity matrix*. It represents, in a sense, the "knowledge" of the network. In virtually all types of neural networks, the learning algorithms work through modifying the weight matrix. Matrix notation, illustrated in table 5.2, is used throughout the field of neural networks. Node 1 is not connected to itself ($w_{11} = 0$), but it is connected to nodes 3, 4, and 5 (with different strengths w_{31}, w_{41}, w_{51}). The connection strength determines how much activation is transferred from one node to the next. Positive connections are excitatory, negative ones inhibitory. (The numbers in this example are chosen arbitrarily.) Zeroes mean that there is no connection between two nodes. By analogy to biological neural networks, the connection strengths are sometimes also called *synaptic* strengths. The weights are typically adjusted gradually by means of a learning rule until the network is capable of performing a particular task (see below). As in linear

Table 5.2 Connectivity matrix.

	Node 1	Node 2	Node 3	Node 4	Node 5
Node 1	0	0	0.8	0	0
Node 2	0	0	0	0	0
Node 3	0.7	0.4	0	0	0
Node 4	1.0	−0.5	0	0	0
Node 5	0.6	0.9	0	0	0

algebra, the term *vector* is often used in neural network jargon. The values of the input nodes are called the *input vector*. In the current example, the input vector might be (0.6 0.2) (the numbers have again been arbitrarily chosen). Similarly, the list of activation values of the output layer is called the *output vector*.

Neural networks are often classified with respect to their connectivity. If the connectivity matrix has all 0s in and above the diagonal, we have a *feedforward* network, since in this case there are only forward connections, that is, connections in one direction (no loops). A network with several layers connected in a forward way is called a *multilayer feedforward network* or *multilayer perceptron*. The network in figure 5.6 is mostly feedforward (connections only in one direction), but it contains one *loop* (between nodes 1 and 3), that is, two nodes both connected to one another in both directions. Loops are important for the network's dynamic properties. If all the nodes from one layer are connected to all the nodes of another layer, we say that the two layers are *fully connected*. Networks in which all nodes are connected to each other in both directions are called *Hopfield* nets.

The Third Basic: The Propagation Rule

The propagation rule determines how activation is propagated through the network. Normally, a weighted sum is assumed in determining propagation. For example, if we call the summed imput to node 4 h_4, we have $h_4 = a_1 \cdot w_{41} + a_2 \cdot w_{42}$, or generally

$$h_i = \sum_{j=1}^{n} w_{ij} a_j, \tag{5.3}$$

where n is the number of nodes in the network, h_i the summed input to node i. The variable h_i is sometimes also called the *local field* of node i. To be precise, we would have to use o_j instead of a_j, but because a node's output is nearly always taken to be its level of activation, this amounts to the same thing. This propagation rule is in fact so common and taken so for granted that it is often not even mentioned. (Note that there is an underlying assumption here, that activation transfer across the links takes exactly one unit of time). We want to make the propagation rule explicit because if—at some point—we intend to model neurons more realistically, we have to take the temporal properties of the propagation process, such as delays, into account.

The Fourth Basic: The Learning Rule

Learning rules are required in neural networks to modify the weights. Let us consider an example that we use again later on. In 1949 physiologist Donald Hebb proposed that if two neurons are active at the same time, the connection between them is strengthened. Hebb's own formulation is somewhat different, a bit more precise, but states essentially the same fact: "When an axon of cell A is near enough to excite a cell B and repeatedly or persistently takes part in firing it, some growth process or metabolic change takes place in one or both cells such that A's efficiency, as one of the cells firing B, is increased" (Hebb, 1949, p. 50). Mathematically we can write

$$\Delta w_{ij} = \eta \cdot o_j \cdot a_i, \tag{5.4}$$

where η is the so-called learning rate, o_j the output of node j, and a_i the activation of node i. If we again assume that $o_i = a_i$, we have

$$\Delta w_{ij} = \eta \cdot a_j \cdot a_i. \tag{5.5}$$

The learning rate η determines how quickly the weight changes. It should be neither too small, because then learning would be too slow, nor too large, because in that case the network would react too strongly to fluctuations in the environment and would not stabilize easily. The weights are changed (updated) as follows:

$$w_{ij}(t + 1) = w_{ij}(t) + \Delta w_{ij}, \tag{5.6}$$

where t represents time. As in the case of activation update, we have now introduced time explicitly to indicate that the weight at time $t + 1$ is calculated from the weight at time t.

Hebbian learning comes in many variations. The representation here is just one very simple form. One problem that must be resolved is that with this simple rule, the weights can only increase: Mechanisms must also be defined for reducing the weights (e.g., Hertz, Krogh, and Palmer 1991). An example of how this can be done is shown in section 5.3.

There are many other learning rules, and we will discuss some of them as we go along. Hebbian learning has the advantage of being simple and based only on local communication between neurons: No central control is required.

The Fifth Basic: Embedding the Network in the Agent

If we want to use a neural network for controlling an autonomous agent, it is quite obvious that we have to connect it to the robot. We have to specify how the sensory signals are going to influence the network and how the computations of the network are going to influence the robot's behavior. In other words, we must know about the physics of the sensors and the motor system. Signals originating from a video camera have a completely different meaning than those coming from a touch sensor. Similarly, motor signals for a speech generator have an entirely different impact on the robot's behavior than signals going to a wheel motor. Thus if we want to understand the network's behavior, we must know how it is embedded in the robot, and we must know about the physics of the sensory and motor systems. To make matters more concrete, let us look at an example from the field of autonomous agents.

5.3   Distributed Adaptive Control

We want to develop a neural network architecture for an autonomous agent that should be able to move about in an environment without hitting obstacles (Pfeifer and Verschure 1992; Verschure, Kröse, and Pfeifer 1992). The specific network architecture has been derived from a general model of conditioning (Verschure and Coolen 1991), but that is not of much importance here. What does matter is that we have to find a solution to the hard problem of processing continuously changing sensory stimulation: As the agent moves, the stimulation changes, depending on the agent's behavior. What patterns should the agent react to? Surely, not everything—that would make no sense. What patterns should be

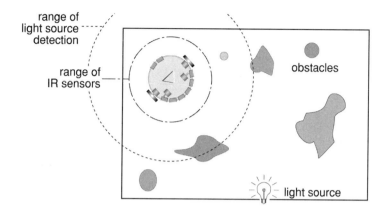

Figure 5.7   Basic setup for the experiments with Distributed Adaptive Control. The ecological niche is very simple: a closed environment with obstacles and light sources (only one light source shown). The light sources are placed along the walls. The direction of the robot's motion is indicated with a triangular arrow in the center of the robot. The large circle depicts the range at which the robot can detect light sources. In the situation shown, the robot does not sense the light source because it is outside the robot's range. The small circle indicates the range of the proximity sensors. (Outside of this range, the sensors deliver no activation.)

learned? In standard neural network applications the network designer carefully prepares the data to train and test the network. In contrast, if neural networks are used to control mobile robots, there are no neatly prepared training and test sets. Thus out of this continuous stream of sensory stimulation, the agent must select the relevant patterns itself. Distributed Adaptive Control provides such a selection mechanism.

Task and Ecological Niche

The first thing we have to do in developing our neural network is define the task and the ecological niche (see table 4.5). The robot's ecological niche will be a simple closed environment with obstacles and light sources. We call the light sources "targets," because the robot will have a tendency, because of its light-triggered reflexes, to move towards targets: If there is stimulation of the light sensor on the right, it will turn toward the right (and vice versa for the left light sensor). The robot's "task" is to move toward targets while avoiding obstacles. We put "task" within quotation marks because there is no representation of the "task" inside the robot. Figure 5.7 shows a schematic representation of the setup.

A Generic Agent Architecture

Throughout the book, we present various examples of autonomous agents implemented on different types of robots. Figure 5.8 shows examples of such robots. These robots all implement—in one way or another—the following generic scheme (figure 5.9): They all have a left-right symmetry, a number of proximity or distance sensors (e.g., IR sensors, ultrasound sensors), collision sensors, and two wheels that can be individually driven. This scheme in its essence is used in all the examples presented throughout this book. Proximity sensors ringing the robot (medium shading in the figure) yield a measure of "nearness" to an obstacle: the nearer to the obstacle the robot is the higher the activation level. If the obstacle is far away, activation will be 0 (except for noise). A number of collision sensors (darkest shading) transmit a signal when the robot hits an obstacle. In addition, the robot has light sensors (lightest shading). The robot's two wheels are individually driven by electrical motors. If both motors turn at equal speeds, the robot moves straight; if the right wheel is stopped and only the left one moves, the robot turns right; and if the left wheel moves forward and the right one backward with equal speed, the robot turns on the spot. This architecture represents a generic low-level specification for a particular simple class of robots and is used to implement the Distributed Adaptive Control architecture.

Network Architecture and Agent Behavior

In the Distributed Adaptive Control example, only the following sensors from the generic setup are used: The collision and proximity sensors on the front half of the robot and the leftmost and rightmost light sensors. The sensors on the back of the robot are not used.

We now define the control architecture. The robot has a number of built-in reflexes. If it hits an obstacle, activating a collision sensor on the right, it backs up a little and turns to the left (and vice versa). Whenever it is sensing light on one side, it turns toward that side. If it senses no obstacles and no lights, it simply moves forward. How can we control this robot with a neural network? Figure 5.10 shows how a neural network can be embedded in the robot. (For reasons of simplicity, we omit the light sensors for the moment.) Each sensor on the robot is connected to a node in the neural network: the collision sensors to nodes in the collision layer, the

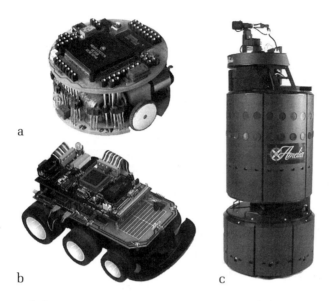

a

b   c

Figure 5.8 Different types of robots: (a) Khepera, (b) Didabot, (c) B21 from Real-World Interface. The Khepera robot is a widely used robot platform in the field of autonomous
agents. It is especially convenient because of its small size. Khepera can be used by
people who have only a superficial knowledge of robots. The Didabot is similar to the
Khepera robot in basic functionality, but it is bigger, which makes it easier for the
designer to add his or her own sensors. It can be built by students under
supervision in a few days. B21 is, in a sense, the Rolls Royce of mobile robots. It
comes equipped with, among many other things, sensory systems, including a
stereo vision system. There are considerable differences in cost between the different
platforms.

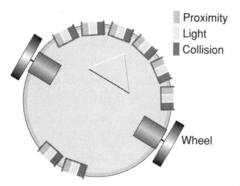

Proximity
Light
Collision

Wheel

Figure 5.9 Generic agent scheme. The triangular arrow indicates the direction the robot is facing. The sensors (proximity, light, collision) are distributed along the front half of the
robot, and two are in the back. There are two wheels, each with one motor. This is
the generic agent scheme that we employ most of the time in this book. There are
many variations, for example, cameras and arms or grippers can be added.

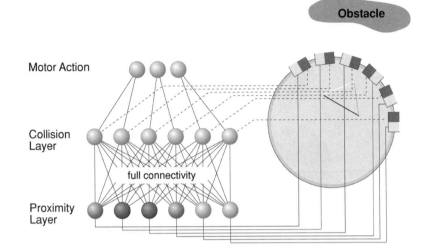

Figure 5.10   Neural network embedded in a robot. There are three layers of nodes, a proximity layer, a collision layer, and a motor action layer. Each proximity sensor is connected to a node in the proximity layer. Similarly, each collision sensor is connected to a node in the collision layer. Proximity nodes have continuous activation levels and sigmoid activation functions; collision nodes are binary threshold. The proximity layer is fully connected in one direction (feedforward) by modifiable connections to the collision layer. Modification is achieved by a certain type of Hebbian learning. The collision layer is hard-wired to the motor action layer to implement the basic reflexes that don't change over time. The levels of gray in the proximity layer indicate the strength of the activation: the darker the shade of gray, the higher the level of activation.

proximity sensors to nodes in the proximity layer. The collision nodes are binary threshold; that is, if their summed input h_i is above a certain threshold, their activation value is set to 1, otherwise it is 0. Proximity nodes are continuous. Their value depends on the strength of the signal they get from the sensor. In figure 5.10, the nodes in the proximity layer show varying levels of activation (the darker the shading of a circle, the stronger its activation), whereas the nodes in the collision layer are inactive (0 activation) because the robot is not hitting anything (i.e., none of the collision sensors is turned on).

The proximity layer is fully connected to the collision layer in one direction. (The arrows are omitted here because the figure would be overloaded otherwise.) If the proximity layer has six nodes and the collision layer six, as in figure 5.10, there are 6 connections. The nodes in the collision layer are in turn connected to a motor output layer; these connections implement the basic reflexes. The arrangement is exactly analogous for the light sensors, so there

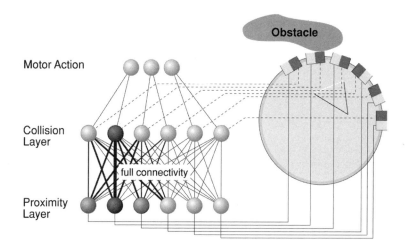

Figure 5.11 The robot making a collision. Because of the collision, the corresponding node in the collision layer is turned on. At the same time, there is an activation pattern in the proximity layer. The connections between the active nodes in the proximity layer and the active nodes in the collision layer are reinforced by Hebbian learning.

is also a layer of nodes (in this case only two), one for each light sensor (because we are only using the leftmost and rightmost light sensors).

In figure 5.10, the robot is moving straight and nothing happens. If it keeps moving, it will eventually hit an obstacle. When it does so, (figure 5.11), the corresponding node in the collision layer is turned on (i.e., its activation is set to 1). As there now is activation in a collision node and simultaneously in several proximity nodes, the corresponding connections between the proximity nodes and the active collision node are strengthened through Hebbian learning. Figure 5.12 shows in more detail how this works. The proximity sensor starts becoming active at around step 14 (figure 5.12b); at step 24 there is a collision (figure 5.12a), at which point Hebbian learning sets in and the weights are strengthened (figure 5.12c).

This strengthening of the connections means that next time around, in a similar situation more activation from the proximity layer will be propagated to the collision layer. Assume now that the robot hits obstacles on the left several times. Every time it hits, the corresponding node in the collision layer becomes active and there is a pattern of activation in the proximity layer. The latter will be similar every time, thus the same connections will be reinforced each time. Because the collision nodes are binary threshold, the activation originating from the proximity layer will at some point be strong enough to raise the activation level in the collision node

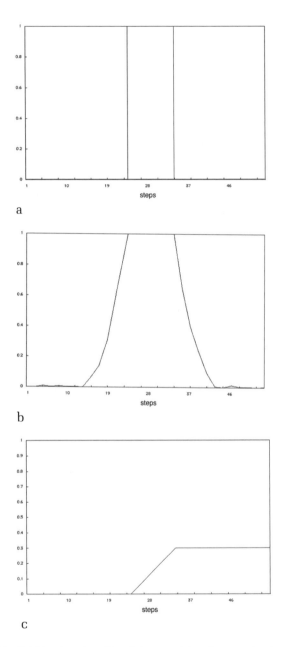

Figure 5.12 Hebbian learning. The data were taken from an implementation of the Distributive Adaptive Control architecture in a Khepera robot. (a) Activation of a collision node. Around time step 24, the robot collides with an obstacle. (b) Activation of a proximity node connected to the collision node shown in (a). The collision is reflected in the proximity node's activation pattern. (c) Weight of the connection between the proximity node and the collision node. The weight increases because both nodes are active (Hebbian learning).

above threshold without an actual collision. When this happens, the robot has learned to avoid obstacles: In the future it should no longer hit obstacles but take corrective action before hitting them, as figure 5.13 illustrates.

The robot continues to learn. Over time, it starts turning away from the object earlier and earlier. This is because two activation patterns in the proximity sensor, taken within a short time interval, are similar when the robot is moving toward an obstacle. Therefore, as the robot encounters more and more obstacles as it moves around, it continues to learn, even if it no longer hits anything. Figure 5.14a illustrates this behavior change.

We can now look at the weight patterns underlying this behavior. Figure 5.15 shows the evolution of the connection weights between the collision and the proximity layer as the robot interacts with the environment. Dark areas indicate large, and light areas indicate small weights. At the beginning of the experiment (figure 5.15a), the weights are randomly distributed: There is no clear structure in the connectivity between the proximity and the collision layer. After the robot has collided 10 times, this randomness has disappeared, and we begin to see a structured connectivity pattern (figure 5.15b). This pattern already makes the robot avoid walls. We said earlier that learning does not stop even when the robot successfully avoids the walls. Figure 5.15c shows this: The connectivity pattern now has a clear diagonal structure reflecting the fact that the proximity and collision nodes are simultaneously active. This structure emerged because the collision and the proximity sensors are based on different physical processes but are located next to each other on the robot's body, thus yielding correlated signals. For example, whenever the robot has had a collision on the left, the proximity nodes on the left have been highly active. Similarily, whenever the robot has had a collision in the front, the corresponding collision and proximity sensors have been activated. This correlation has then been picked up by the Hebbian learning mechanism, resulting in the diagonal weight pattern shown in figure 5.15c. Finally, note that the correlation implies a certain amount of redundancy: the information the agent gets from one sensor overlaps to a certain degree with the information it gets from the other. This overlap, that is, the correlations between proximity and collision sensors, is the basis for learning in the Distribute Adaptive Control architecture. This is a fundamental point in the study of intelligence. It is an instance of the redundancy principle,

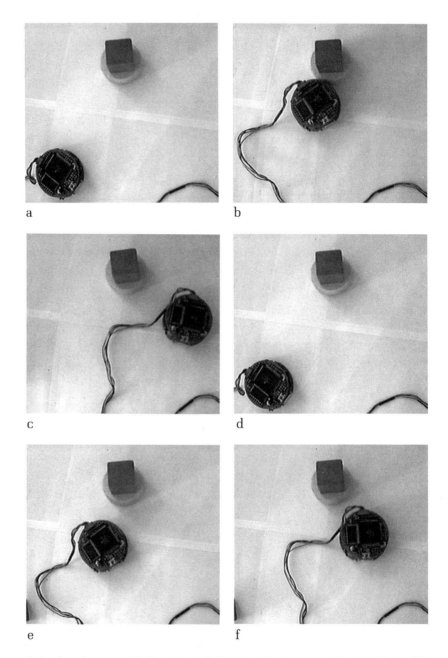

Figure 5.13 Robot learning to avoid obstacles. Initially, the robot is approaching (a), hitting (b), and moving away from the obstacle (c). After a number of collisions, the robot approaches the obstacle (d) and turns away from it without hitting (e) and (f).

a.　　　　　　　　　　　　　**b.**

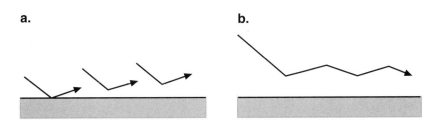

Figure 5.14　Development of robot behavior over time. (a) Obstacle avoidance behavior. Initially, the robot hits obstacles. Over time, it starts turning away before hitting. (b) Wall-following behavior. When light sources are found along walls, wall-following behavior emerges over time.

one of the design principles of embodied cognitive science we discuss later (chapters 10 and 13). Let us now look more closely at how the various activations are calculated, and how the Hebbian learning mechanism is implemented.

Mathematically, the input to the node i in the collision layer can be written as

$$h_i = c_i + \sum_{j=1}^{N} w_{ij} \cdot p_j, \tag{5.7}$$

where p_j is the activation of node j in the proximity layer, c_i the activation resulting from the collision sensor, w_{ij} the weight between node j in the proximity layer and node i in the collision layer, and h_i the summed activation at collision node i. The value of c_i is either 1 or 0, depending on whether there is a collision; p_j has a value between 0 and 1, depending on the stimulation of the proximity sensor j (high stimulation entails a high value, and vice versa). N is the number of nodes in the proximity layer. Let us call a_i the activation of node i in the collision layer. Node i is, among others, responsible for the motor control of the agent. a_i is calculated from h_i by means of a threshold function g:

$$a_i = g(h_i) = \begin{cases} 0: & h_i < \Theta \\ 1: & h_i \geq \Theta \end{cases}. \tag{5.8}$$

The weight change is

$$\Delta w_{ij} = \frac{1}{N}(\eta \cdot a_i \cdot p_j - \varepsilon \cdot \bar{a} \cdot w_{ij}), \tag{5.9}$$

where η is the learning rate, N the number of units in the proximity layer as above, $\bar{a}$ the average activation in the collision layer, and ε the forgetting rate. (Forgetting is required because otherwise the

Before

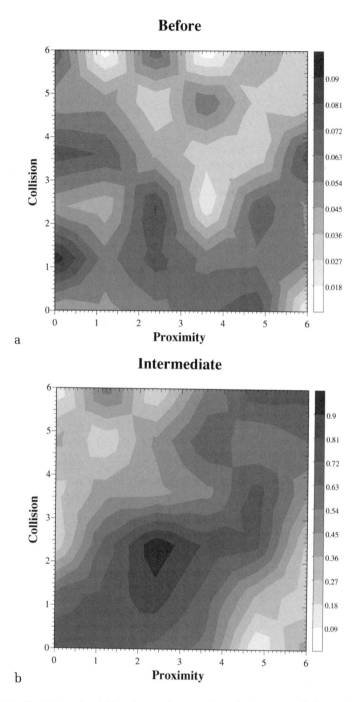

a

Intermediate

b

Figure 5.15 Evolution of weight patterns of connections between proximity and collision layers. The data were taken from the run described in figure 5.12. Dark areas indicate strong weights, light areas indicate weak weights. There are six collision and proximity sensors, corresponding to the IR sensors of the Khepera robot. (a) Weight pattern at the beginning of the trial. There is no apparent structure; the weights are randomly

After

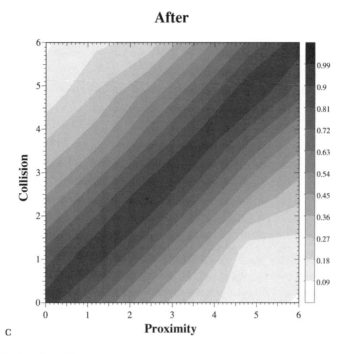

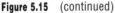

C

Figure 5.15 (continued)
distributed. (b) Weight pattern after the robot has collided 10 times. A diagonal
pattern begins to emerge. (c) Weight pattern after the robot has encountered (not
necessarily collided with) a wall another 10 times. The diagonal structure is now very
clear and robust. The robot no longer collides with walls. (To get a better intuition of
the changes in the weight matrix, the resolution has been increased and the gray-
level values have been calculated by interpolation.)

weights would become too large over time.) Note that in the forgetting term we have $\bar{a}$, the average activation in the collision layer.
This implies that forgetting takes place only when something is
learned, that is, when there is activation in the collision layer (see
figure 5.12). This is also called *active forgetting*. The factor 1/N is
used to normalize the weight change.

Figure 5.16 shows the complete Distributed Adaptive Control
architecture. A target layer (T) associated with light sensors has
been added whose operation is analogous to that of the collision
layer (C). Assume that there are a number of light sources near
the wall. As a result of its built-in reflex, the robot turns toward a
light source. As it gets close to the wall, it turns away from the wall
(because it has learned to avoid obstacles). Now the turn-toward-
target reflex becomes active again, and the robot wiggles its way
along the wall, as figure 5.14b illustrates. Whenever the robot is
near the wall, its proximity layer receives stimulation. Over time, it

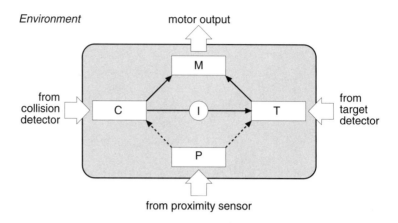

Figure 5.16 Complete Distributed Adaptive Control architecture. In addition to the collision layer (C) there is a target layer (T). The network processes operating between the proximity layer and the target layer are entirely analogous to the ones between the proximity layer and the collision layer. The connections shown by solid arrows are hardwired (they don't change over time), whereas those shown by broken arrows are modified by Hebbian learning. There is also an inhibitory element (I) whose purpose is to inhibit the output of the target layer if the agent hits obstacles too often. This happens if the robot is, for example, attracted to a light source in a corner. It hits the walls frequently, which activates the inhibitory element. If I is sufficiently active, it inhibits the output of the target layer, which implies that the robot is—for a short time—no longer attracted to the light. I is not essential, but it often helps the robot get out of impasses.

comes to associate light with lateral stimulation in the proximity sensor (lateral meaning "on the side"). In other words, it begins to display the behavior in figure 5.14b even if there is no longer a light source near the wall.

Let us, for the sake of the argument, assume that light represents food. We could say that the robot has learned that food is normally located along walls. Because it has this knowledge, it follows the walls: It hopes to find food, even if it currently does not sense any. This is another instantiation of the perspectives issue in the frame-of-reference problem. We have given our interpretation of the robot's behavior as observers. All that has happened within the robot is a change of weights in the neural network.

Finally, the Distributive Control Architecture includes an inhibitory element (I). Roughly speaking, it is a sluggish element designed to inhibit the target layer's output if the agent hits obstacles too often. With this element, the robot can get itself out of impasses.

So far we have described our planned neural network's ecological niche and task as well as its low-level specification. We have also introduced the control architecture that will govern it. We have formulated some hypotheses about our robot's behavior. If we go back to table 4.5 we see that we are still missing a number of elements. For example, we have yet to choose a robot platform (or a simulator), we have to define the actual experiments (number, shape, and position of obstacles and light sources, starting position of the robot, duration of experiment, evaluation criteria). Then we actually have to run the experiments. During the runs, if possible, data should be collected about the robot's behavior and internal state. Then, various ways of describing the behavior should be applied. In our formulation of the hypotheses about the robot behavior, we have used mostly verbal descriptions, interspersed with a few graphic ones (e.g., figure 5.14). Finally, we need to generate explanations, which the next section does. Often, these explanations correspond to the rationale underlying the predictions. (For those interested in acquiring practical experience with these matters, we suggest doing the programming example "Distributed Adaptive Control," on our web page).

Conclusions

Here are some important points illustrated by this example of a neural network:

1. Distributed Adaptive Control provides a solution to the problem of selecting the relevant data for learning. Whenever a motor signal is generated that is associated with a basic reflex, Hebbian learning automatically takes place. The intuition behind this mechanism is that something should be learned when something relevant happens. This is the case when the robot's motor system is activated.

2. The agent learns to generalize. It starts avoiding obstacles and finally ends up "anticipating" them as a result of an appropriate process of generalization. (We put "anticipating" in quotation marks to indicate that this is an attribution by an observer.) As pointed out above, the activation patterns in the proximity layer are very similar, because the agent is facing the same obstacle, if the distance to the obstacle differs only by a small amount. The everyday meaning of anticipation implies that the agent has an explicit expectation about a future situation that may or may not materialize. As observers, we could argue that the agent anticipates that it will hit the obstacle if it continues in a straight line, which is why it

is turning away. In this example, we know that there is no internal representation of a future situation: This "anticipation" comes about through simple associative learning. The range of "anticipation," that is, how far away from an object the robot starts turning, is limited by two factors: First, the range of the proximity sensors is restricted. Second, the forgetting term in equation 5.9 prevents overgeneralization; that is, it prevents the network from reacting to weak stimulation.

3. Collision sensors and proximity sensors operate on different physical processes. The patterns of activation in these sensors are correlated, implying that there is a certain amount of redundancy: The information the agent gets from one type of sensor overlaps to a certain degree with the information it gets from the other. For example, whenever there is a collision, there is high activation in the corresponding region of the proximity sensor. Note that the correlation between the patterns comes about as a result of the agent's physical interaction with the environment. This correlation cannot be explained by looking at the neural network alone. Correlations thus generated are the basis for learning (see figure 5.15). This is an instance of the redundancy principle.

4. Learning is completely integrated and takes place continuously. There is no distinction between a learning and a performance phase, in contrast to many standard neural network paradigms.

5. The agent not only learns, but also forgets. One problem of (algorithmic) Hebbian learning is that the weights can potentially get very large. The model here corrects for this by active forgetting: Whenever the robot learns something, it forgets a little bit of what it "knew" before. The idea behind this mechanism is that the current situation is a bit more important than the earlier ones. The forgetting mechanism keeps the weights low, and learning can go on forever. If the environment does not change, the weight matrix converges to an equilibrium state.

6. Because of the way the network is embedded in the agent, its behavior is robust. If one of the sensors does not work properly, as often happens, the network still functions. This is because there is redundancy in the system: On the one hand, nodes associated with neighboring sensors have learned similar associations (e.g., figure 5.11), and on the other, neighboring sensors are likely to have similar levels of activation. Thus if one sensor is broken, signals from adjacent sensors are sufficient to perform the function (such as obstacle avoidance).

In the neural network literature there is a classification of the different types of networks. The kind of network presented here belongs to the category of nonsupervised models. The classification scheme is based on the kind of learning that is incorporated in the network. Let us briefly examine the various types.

5.4   Types of Neural Networks

Nonsupervised Networks

Neural networks that require no teacher are said to be *non-supervised*. The Distributed Adaptive Control architecture employs a nonsupervised network based on Hebbian learning: learning simply takes place when the nodes on both sides of the connection are simultaneously active (or both active within a given time interval). In neural network terminology, the activation of the node from which the connection originates is said to be *presynaptic* and the activation of the node into which the connection leads (or projects), *postsynaptic* (see figure 5.1). Thus, Hebbian learning reinforces the synaptic strength between two neurons if presynaptic and post-synaptic activation occur simultaneously, or within some small time interval. Hebbian learning comes in many variations and is used widely in the field of embodied cognitive science for several reasons: First, Hebbian learning is unsupervised (as already mentioned). Second, it is simple and thus requires little computation. Third, it is purely local, meaning that for learning, only the neuron itself and its neighbors need to be considered: There is no need for some kind of global control structure. And fourth, Hebbian learning is biologically plausible. The neuroscience literature describes variations on Hebbian learning (e.g., Churchland and Sejnowski 1992; Edelman 1987).

Another important category of nonsupervised networks is the so-called topology-preserving feature maps, or simply Kohonen maps (named after their inventor, Kohonen, 1988a). Kohonen maps are widely used in many application areas. In the field of robotics, they are often used for motor control (e.g., arm control) and for navigation purposes. Like most of the common neural network schemes, they come in many variations. Figure 5.17 shows their basic architecture. The input layer is fully connected to the map layer. In the map layer, lateral connections are excitatory for close

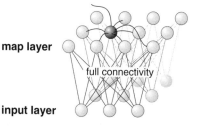

map layer

full connectivity

input layer

Figure 5.17 Basic architecture of a Kohonen network. The input layer is fully connected to the map layer. The map layer has lateral connections that are excitatory for close neighbors, inhibitory for those further away, and neutral for the ones still further away. In the map layer, clustering of input patterns takes place.

neighbors, inhibitory for those further away, and neutral for the ones still further out. (Connections are called *lateral* if they link nodes within a layer, rather than between layers.) Patterns are presented to the model at the input layer, and depending on the particular architecture and choice of parameters, the system will eventually learn a particular categorization of the input space. The details of the algorithm are of little significance here; what does matter is the basic principle that there is no need for the system to be given a classification of input patterns by the designer (which is why this is called nonsupervised).

An example of a Kohonen map is the "neural phonetic typewriter" (Kohonen 1988b). Inputs to the typewriter are spectral patterns corresponding to preprocessed speech signals, and the classes which are formed in the map layer can be interpreted as phonemes. More precisely, they are "pseudophonemes," which are like phonemes but have a shorter duration (10 ms rather than 40 to 400 ms). But this detail is not essential to the points to be made here.

The popularity of Kohonen maps derives from several factors. First, the Kohonen algorithm can be used if the categories in a data set are unknown: the algorithm finds categories (clusters) by itself. In the phonetic typewriter example, the algorithm finds the phonemes by itself, given the spectral speech data as input. Second, the Kohonen algorithm can be used to map high-dimensional spaces onto low-dimensional ones while preserving the topology; that is, neighboring points in the input space are mapped onto neighboring points in the output space. In the typewriter example, close points in frequencey space (from the speech spectrum) are mapped onto neighboring phonemes (which sound similar to humans). And

third, as does Hebbian learning, Kohonen maps have certain neurobiological plausibility (e.g., Kohonen 1988a).

Supervised Networks

Another large and important class of neural networks are the
so-called supervised networks. The term *supervised* is used both in
a very general and a narrow technical sense. In the narrow technical sense, supervised means that if, for a certain input, the corresponding output is known, the network is to learn the mapping
from inputs to outputs. In supervised learning applications, the
correct output must be known and provided to the learning algorithm. The task of the network is to find the mapping. The weights
change depending on the magnitude of the error that the network
produces at the output layer: the larger the error, that is, the larger
the discrepancy between the output that the network produces and
the correct output value, the more the weights change. The most
frequently used algorithm is back-propagation. It is extremely
powerful. There are literally hundreds of variations of backpropa-
gation, and the potential for applications is enormous.

Supervised networks have been used in many different areas.
A prominent example is in the recognition of handwritten zip
codes, which can be applied to sorting mail automatically in a
post office. In chapter 4, we discussed the ALCOVE model, which
captures psychological data from category learning experiments.
Other application areas include optimization, control, time series
analysis, finance (e.g., stock market prediction), signal processing,
and pattern recognition.

To illustrate the main ideas involved in supervised networks,
let us look at a famous example, NETTalk. NETTalk, now mostly
of historical interest, is a connectionist model that translates
English text into speech. It uses a multilayer, feedforward, back-
propagation network model (Sejnowski and Rosenberg 1987).
Figure 5.18 illustrates the architecture involved, which consists of
an input layer, an intermediate layer, called hidden layer, and an
output layer. Whereas the function of the input and output layers is
clear, a hidden layer is frequently added because it significantly
augments the learning capacity of the neural network by introducing many additional weights. Text is presented at the input layer,
which has a window of seven slots representing seven letters. This
window is needed because the pronunciation of a letter in English

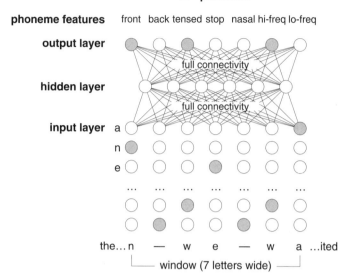

Figure 5.18 Architecture of the NETTalk model. The text shown in the window is contained in the phrase "then we waited." The input layer contains about 200 nodes (seven slots of 29 symbols each, consisting of the letters of the alphabet, space, and punctuation). The input layer is fully connected to the hidden layer (containing 80 notes), which is in turn fully connected to the output layer (26 nodes). At the input layer a letter is encoded by setting the activation of 1 of the 29 nodes representing the slot in the window to 1 and all the others to 0. Each position encodes one letter. At the output layer, the phonemes are encoded in terms of phoneme features.

depends strongly on the context in which it occurs. In each slot, one letter is encoded. For each letter of the alphabet (including space and punctuation) there is one node in each slot, which means that the input layer has 7×29 nodes. Input nodes are binary on-off nodes. Therefore, an input pattern, or input vector, consists of seven active nodes (all others are off). The nodes in the hidden layer have continuous activation levels. The output nodes are similar to the nodes in the hidden layer; they encode the phonemes by means of a set of phoneme features. Phonemes are encoded in terms of phoneme features that can be fed into a speech generator, which can then produce the actual sounds. For each letter presented at the center of the input window—"e" in the example shown in figure 5.18—the correct phoneme is encoded. By "correct," we mean the one that linguists have encoded earlier.[1]

[1]In one experiment, a tape recording from a child was transcribed into English text, and for each letter the linguists worked out the phoneme encoding as pronounced by the child. In a different experiment, the prescribed pronunciation was taken from a dictionary.

The model starts with small random connection weights. It propagates each input pattern to the output layer, compares the pattern in the output layer with the correct one, and adjusts the weights according to the back-propagation learning algorithm. After presentation of many patterns (thousands), the weights converge, that is, the network picks up the correct pronunciation.

NETTalk is robust: that is, superimposing random distortions on the weights, removing certain connections in the architecture, and making errors in the encodings do not significantly influence the network's behavior. Moreover, NETTalk can handle—that is, pronounce correctly—words it has not encountered before: It can generalize. The network behaves "as if" it had acquired the rules of English pronunciation. We say "as if" because there are no rules in the network, yet its behavior is rulelike. Learning is an intrinsic property of the model. One of the model's most exciting properties is that at the hidden layer, certain nodes start distinguishing between vowels and consonants. In other words, they are on when there is a vowel at the input, otherwise they are off. Because this consonant-vowel distinction has not been preprogrammed, it is emergent.

At the beginning of this section we mentioned that there is both a technical and a nontechnical use of the word "supervised." So far we have described its technical use. In a nontechnical sense, supervised means that the learning, say of children, is done under the supervision of a teacher who provides them with some guidance. This use of the term is very vague and hard to translate into concrete neural network algorithms.

Neural Networks with Reinforcement Learning

We now introduce a third large class of neural network: reinforcement neural networks. If a teacher tells a student only whether her answer is correct or not, but leaves the task of determining why the answer is correct or incorrect to the student, what occurs is an instance of *reinforcement learning*. The problem of attributing the error (or the success) to the right cause is called the credit assignment or blame assignment problem, and it is fundamental to many learning theories. The term "reinforcement learning" also has a more technical meaning as it is used in the neural network literature: It is used to designate learning in which a particular behavior is to be reinforced. Typically, the robot receives a positive reinforcement signal if the result it has produced was successful, no reinforcement or a negative reinforcement signal if it was unsuccessful. If the robot has managed to pick up an object, has found its way through a maze, or has managed to shoot the ball into the goal, it gets a positive reinforcement. Chapter 14 provides an overview of reinforcement learning. From a cognitive science perspective, we are mostly interested in unsupervised and reinforcement schemes. Reinforcement learning is not tied to neural networks: There are many reinforcement learning algorithms in the field of machine learning in general.

5.5 Beyond Information Processing: A Polemic Digression

We now digress a bit to make a point. We start with an example of supervised learning and show that the supervised-learning model is almost as symbolic as the traditional ones and that it can thus not solve the symbol-grounding problem. We also show that what seems to be novel in the behavior of the model, that is, what the model has actually learned, is in fact built into the model by the designer. We then look at nonsupervised learning.

Let us examine NETTalk, the example of supervised learning we discussed above. We are interested in whether NETTalk actually resolves the symbol-grounding problem. We inspect the frame-of-reference issue first. Each input node in the NETTalk model corresponds to a letter. Letters are symbols; that is, the encoding at the input layer is in terms of symbolic categories. Phoneme features are designer-defined categories, and thus the respective sound encodings are also symbolic. Therefore, even though the model processes patterns of activation rather than symbols, it still has a strongly symbolic character. This leads us to two points. First, the system is not coupled to the environment. The interpretation of input and output is entirely determined by humans, who have to interpret the symbols at both the input and the output. That the output is fed into a speech generator is irrelevant, since this has no effect on the model. The purpose of the speech generator is only to make intuitively accessible to an observer how effectively the network does what it is set up to do. Therefore, NETTalk, just like any traditional model in AI, suffers from the symbol-grounding problem. Second, the consonant-vowel distinction that the hidden layer acquires the ability to make is not really emergent, but—in a sense—precoded. Of those phoneme features used to encode vowels, only about 5 percent are also used to encode consonants, and vice versa (Verschure 1992). In other words, the ability to distinguish vowels from consonants is not really acquired by the system but rather (indirectly) preprogrammed by the way the examples are encoded in a symbolic way. Again, this distinction acquired is not grounded in the model's experience but is based implicitly on designer knowledge.

From this discussion, we can conclude that supervised learning does not solve a certain class of problems. The problems it solves are, in a sense, internal and pertain mostly to algorithmic aspects. For example, NETTalk does learn a mapping from inputs to outputs; that is, over time, it does learn to produce the correct pronunciation. But because the interaction with the environment is mediated by a designer-based, high-level domain ontology, the symbol-grounding issue remains.

Although many would probably agree that supervised models in essence pick up the ontology predefined by the designer and therefore do not resolve the symbol-grounding problem, there is likely disagreement about nonsupervised models. In other words, some researchers would claim that by applying nonsupervised learning methods, meanings of symbols can indeed be acquired. We find that this, again, is not automatically the case.

As an example of nonsupervised learning, let us examine the neural phonetic typewriter mentioned in the last section. Just as in the case of supervised networks, the designer has carefully preselected the patterns presented to this model. This does not imply that the designer determines the individual patterns to be presented, but he does determine the types of patterns that the system should be able to process. In other words, the designer, as in NETTalk, makes a preclassification of the world in terms of what is meaningful to the system. In the phonetic typewriter model, speech samples have been selected to cover the space of possible phonemes and then appropriately preprocessed. The neural network generates a classification of the input patterns at the map layer. This classification, again, has to be interpreted by a human. Interpreting the output of the neural network as phonemes is a function of the observer: The network itself knows nothing about phonemes; it simply processes the input patterns and forms clusters. Moreover, the output has no effect whatsoever on the behavior of the network itself. Nonsupervised learning is clearly an important step toward a solution because, within the preselected set of patterns, the system finds its own categories. Because the human designer is still mediating the interaction with the environment, however, it still does not resolve the symbol-grounding problem.

So far we have argued that neither supervised networks nor unsupervised ones are the solution to the symbol-grounding problem. What *is* the solution, then? To approach this issue, let us return to the Distributed Adaptive Control architecture. In contrast to what was done with NETTalk, we defined only a low-level specification for the robot in which we placed this architecture. Thus we avoided having to define a high-level ontology, which then would have to be mapped onto the input space. Because NETTalk is not directly connected to the outside world, there are many problems it does not have to solve; they have already been solved by the network designer. These problems include interpreting sensory data, determining relevance of input patterns, continuous learning, and effect of the model's behavior (the output) on the environment and on its input, among others. In contrast to NETTalk, the Distributed Adaptive Control architecture is embedded in a physical robot. The sensory stimulation, and thus the input to the system, are the results of physical processes occurring in the robot's interaction with its environment. The robot's own movements have a strong effect on the sensory stimulation to which it is exposed. The outputs correspond to the robot's movements. In this sense, the outputs have meaning directly to the robot: They affect its behavior. The robot selects the meaningful patterns from its own perspective. Meaningful patterns are the ones that cause the robot to change its behavior; examples are activation patterns that get the robot to turn. Note that in order to learn something new the robot has to move—it has to interact physically with its environment. Physical processes are required, not only informational ones, as in NETTalk and the neural phonetic typewriter. In other words, if we want to make progress in resolving the fundamental issues, we have to move beyond pure information processing. Neural networks are information processors, but if they are embedded in physical robots they can—at least potentially—turn robots into intelligent autonomous agents (see Pfeifer 1996a).

Issues to Think About

Issue 5.1:   Neural Networks as Modeling Tools

We have argued that we are interested in the biological plausibility of neural networks because we want to incorporate insights from biology into our designs. We also noted that neural networks, as we use them in our robots, are highly simplified and therefore not very good models of biological neurons. There is a trade-off between biological veracity and algorithmic simplicity: The more biologically plausible the models, the more computational resources are required for their simulation. What is open to debate is whether we are making the right kinds of abstractions. It is possible that in simplifying, we are losing the very properties that account for the incredible intelligence of natural systems, the properties that we wish to study in the first place. We have no final answer to this question. We must make compromises if we are interested in building complete agents that function in real time in the real world. Why then use neural networks in the first place, and not other formalisms like production rules, fuzzy logic, or direct programming? Why the "detour" through neural networks? We have seen that even if artificial neural networks represent significant abstractions from biological neurons, they nevertheless possess important properties that resemble those of biological systems: capability for generalization, robustness, and parallelism. Moreover, it is relatively straightforward to include biological consideration in these networks: no central control, no external supervision by a teacher, connections in one direction only, and incremental algorithms (i.e., algorithms that function continuously).

Issue 5.2: Understanding Neural Networks

One of the fundamental advantages of the synthetic methodology is that we build the systems ourselves; thus, we know exactly what is inside them. One of our main modeling tools is artificial neural networks. It turns out that it is a nontrivial enterprise to determine how neural networks really function, what is really happening, why they produce a certain output, and so forth. This is especially true if the networks learn. We can look at activation patterns given a certain input, or we can analyze the weight matrices. Feedforward networks have simple dynamics—inputs are simply propagated to the outputs. Recurrent networks are much harder to understand. There are currently no systematic ways of analyzing large, complex, recurrent neural networks. Nevertheless, compared to natural neural systems and the difficulties in understanding them, artificial neural networks have the advantage of allowing one repeatedly to manipulate and analyze every single component.

Points to Remember

- Neural networks have proven extremely useful for control architectures of autonomous agents because they are robust and are excellent learning and generalization models. They are inspired by natural neural systems, but they are abstract modeling tools, and do not mimic biology very closely.

- For each neural network, we have to specify (a) the node characteristics, (b) the propagation rule, (c) the connectivity, (d) the learning rule, and, in the case of autonomous agents, (e) the embedding into the agent. Different types of neural networks all incorporate variations of these basic properties.

- The function of a neural network (natural or artificial) can be appropriately understood only if it is also understood how they are embedded in a physical agent, how the sensors and effectors work, and how they are positioned on the robot. This goes beyond the pure information-processing capabilities of neural networks.

- There is a distinction between supervised, nonsupervised, and reinforcement learning. From a cognitive science perspective, only nonsupervised and reinforcement schemes are of interest. Supervised systems (in the technical neural network sense of the term) do not exist in nature: They are neither biologically nor psychologically plausible.

- The correlation between sensory patterns generated as the agent interacts with the environment (originating from different sensors based on distinct physical processes) is a fundamental requirement for learning to take place.

- The fact that autonomous agents move around in the real world defines completely new requirements for neural network models employed in these agents: They must be able to process a continuously changing stream of signals delivered to the network. Among other things, this implies determining the relevance of a particular set of signals. In traditional applications, whether supervised or unsupervised, the designer who determines the training and the test sets also determines the relevance.

- If a robot has to remain adaptive over time, learning must be continuous. There must be no distinction between a training and a performance phase.

- Neural networks by themselves do not resolve the symbol-grounding problem. Most neural network approaches start from designer-defined, high-level ontologies. What is important in terms of resolving the symbol-grounding problem is the appropriate embedding of the neural network in an agent architecture.

Further Reading

Anderson, J. A. (1995). *An introduction to neural networks.* Cambridge, MA: MIT Press (a Bradford Book). (A well-written introduction to the field of neural networks by one of the leading experts in the field; especially geared toward the biologically interested reader.)

Hertz, J., Krogh, A., and Palmer, R. G. (1991). *Introduction to the theory of neural computation.* Redwood City, CA: Addison-Wesley. (A mathematically sound introduction to neural networks. Useful as a reference book, it covers most of the relevant aspects of the field. Reinforcement learning is discussed very briefly, and temporal difference learning and Q-learning are missing. Recommended to anyone involved in neural networks—although it has a bias towards physics.)

Rumelhart, D. E., and McClelland, J. L. (1986). *Parallel distributed processing: Explorations in the microstructure of cognition.* Volume 1: Foundations. McClelland, J. L., and Rumelhart, D. E. (1986) Volume 2: Psychological and biological models. Volume 3: Explorations in parallel distributed processing. Cambridge, MA: MIT Press (a Bradford Book). (An excellent, easy-to-read introduction to neural networks. Accessible even to people with very little mathematical background. Focuses very much on intuitions. Contains an introduction to linear algebra for neural networks, again, understandable to everyone. Many application examples in psychology, language processing, and biology are given. Because the book is already more than 10 years old, it does not contain the more recent developments.)

Sejnowski, T. J., and Rosenberg, C. R. (1987). Parallel networks that learn to pronounce English text. *Complex Systems, 1,* 145–168. (The classic paper on NETTalk, one of the best known early neural network models.)

Verschure, P. F. M. J., Kröse, B. J. A., and Pfeifer, R. (1992). Distributed adaptive control: The self-organization of structured behavior. *Robotics and Autonomous Systems, 9,* 181–196. (A detailed technical description of the Distributed Adaptive Control architecture, including experimental results.)

So far we have been constructing the foundations of embodied cognitive science. In part III, we review a number of important approaches to the study of intelligence. All contribute in interesting ways to our understanding of intelligence. A wide gamut of approaches and agent architectures have been proposed in the past. The goal of part III is first to provide an intuitive understanding of autonomous agents by means of examples and case studies, second to illustrate some of the theoretical concepts introduced in chapters 4 and 5, and third to derive principles that characterize designs resulting in intelligent behavior. We discuss agent types that include Braitenberg vehicles (chapter 6), impressive in how well they illustrate that intelligent behavior can be seen very differently, subsumption-based agents (chapter 7), which, so to speak, got the entire field started, and agents designed using evolutionary methods (chapter 8), which hold great promise, especially for generating diversity of behavior. Closely related to artificial evolution is the field of artificial life, from which we can also draw a lot of inspiration; the two are discussed alongside one another. We might also want to call "collective behavior" an approach: The philosophy is to solve problems by having many agents—perhaps simple ones—work on the same problem. This approach shows up in a number of places in the book. We round up our tour by summarizing a number of additional approaches to agent design in chapter 9, in particular dynamical systems, behavioral economics, and schema-based approaches. We think that the selection of approaches presented here is representative of the field of embodied cognitive science. But others, of course, could have been included.

Table III.1 Overview of approaches and agent examples.

Approach	Main characteristics	Examples	Chapters
Braitenberg	Bottom-up: starting with simple sensory-motor couplings; getting increasingly complex	fourteen vehicles	6
Subsumption	Layered architecture of sensory-motor couplings with little internal processing; layers largely autonomous;	Brooks's Ghengis; Horswill's Polly; Myrmix	7, 11
Artificial evolution	Inspired by natural evolution: simulation of development, selection, and reproduction	Evolutionary DAC; Beer's walking insect; Eggenberger's AES; Sims's virtual creatures	8
Artificial life	Local rules; bottom up; emergent behaviors	Didabots; Sims's virtual creatures; Terzopoulos's fish; Hemelrijk's emergent hierarchies	8, 14
Dynamical systems	Unifying nature; attractive metaphors; mostly analytic; synthesis hard	Beer's walking insect (analysis); Steinhage and Schöner (design)	8, 9
Behavioral economics	Applies principles of micro-economics to animal/robot behavior	MacFarland and Bösser's approach	9
Schema-based	Focus on the organization of sensory-motor behaviors	Arbib; Arkin	9
Collective behavior	Focus on emergence; local interactions	Craig Reynolds's Boids, Didabots; Mataric's flocking robots	6, 8, 11, 14

6 Braitenberg Vehicles

In this chapter we look at a famous kind of agent, the Braitenberg vehicles, named after their inventor, neuroscientist Valentino Braitenberg. Braitenberg vehicles are ideally suited for illustrating some fundamental theoretical points, such as the frame-of-reference problem. They also provide an interesting perspective on the problems of behavior segmentation and action selection. Moreover, the principles employed by Braitenberg vehicles have been extended to address the design of autonomous agents in general. Not surprisingly, this approach is called Extended Braitenberg Architecture (EBA). Braitenberg vehicles are instantiations of a synthetic methodology. Braitenberg proposed studying principles of intelligence by building successively more complex agents. The original Braitenberg vehicles were meant to be thought experiments. However, some of them can easily be implemented in physical robots, and we will discussed one such example, the "timid" vehicle, in this chapter. After a short discussion of Braitenberg's motivation, his vehicles are introduced along with an additional example. We conclude with a note on segmentation of behavior and extensions of Braitenberg's approach.

6.1 Motivation

Michael Arbib, one of the inventors of computational neuro-ethology—the discipline studying the neural systems underlying behavior—wrote in his preface to Valentino Braitenberg's seminal book *Vehicles: Experiments in Synthetic Psychology* (1984): "[The book] is serious fun and will help many people, specialists and layman alike, gain broad insights into the ways in which intelligence evolved to guide interaction with a complex world" (p. x). Particularly relevant for our purposes is Arbib's reference to interaction with a complex world. We have seen in chapter 5 that focusing on brain structures alone is insufficient for really understanding their operations—they must be looked at within a behavioral context. Although this is a very hard thing to do in real brains, it is both possible and important in artificial ones. Braitenberg vehicles demonstrate that often even extremely simple brains can show behaviors that look remarkably sophisticated to outside observers. The field of autonomous agents draws a lot of inspiration from the study of these vehicles: Everyone interested in intelligence, natural or artificial, should know about them. Braitenberg vehicles can teach us much about the interplay between brain and behavior, or in embodied cognitive science terms, between mechanism and behavior.

Braitenberg is a well-known brain researcher. Rather than explaining a lot of technical detail on neuroanatomy and neurophysiology, though, he discusses a series of thought experiments, conducted not on real brains but on toy brains. Many of the important ideas on autonomous agents have been discussed by Braitenberg in a highly entertaining way.

The design of Braitenberg vehicles has a strong biological motivation based on many years of in-depth brain research. It is interesting to see at what level a connection is made between neurobiology and vehicles or, in our terminology, autonomous agents. Clearly, no biological creatures have wheels. Nevertheless, even though equipped with wheels, Braitenberg vehicles have a definite biological appeal.

6.2 The Fourteen Vehicles

Braitenberg vehicles represent a series of agents of increasing complexity. Although some are purely reactive, others include learning mechanisms, and thus have their own history.

In the simplest vehicles, it is quite obvious what they do. As matters get slightly more involved, predicting their behavior turns out to be very difficult, even in purely reactive systems, because the mechanisms generating the vehicles' behavior interact in interesting ways. Even if we have complete knowledge of the vehicle's insides, it still proves difficult to control it. Its interaction with its environment adds complexity, which leads to some degree of unpredictability, even if the driving mechanisms are entirely deterministic—in physics, there are always fluctuations. Taking up on our discussion of autonomy in chapter 4, we can conclude that even the simplest vehicles have a certain degree of autonomy.

Let us examine the Braitenberg vehicles one by one. As always, we pay attention to the frame-of-reference problem. In examining

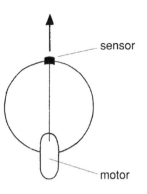

Figure 6.1 Braitenberg vehicle 1. A sensor controls the speed of the motor. Motion is always forward, in the direction of the arrow, except in the presence of perturbations, like friction.

this series of vehicles, it is always a good idea to imagine how they move around under various conditions. This process of imagination is best complemented with computer simulations or with experiments on real robots.

Vehicle 1: Getting Around

As shown in figure 6.1, the first Braitenberg vehicle has one sensor, for one particular quality, and one motor. The sensor and the motor are connected very simply: The more there is of the quality to which the sensor is tuned, the faster the motor goes. If this quality is temperature, it will move fast in hot regions and slow down in cold regions. An observer might get the impression that such a vehicle likes cold and tries to avoid heat. The precise nature of this quality does not matter; it can be concentration of chemicals, temperature, light, noise level, or any other of a number of qualities. The vehicle always moves in the direction in which it happens to be pointing.

If we introduce friction into the vehicle's environment, its behavior gets interesting, because friction is always a bit asymmetric. The vehicle eventually deviates from its straight course, and in the long run, is seen to move in a complicated trajectory, curving one way or another without apparent (to the observer!) good reason. Perturbations other than friction that will force the vehicle from its straight course are, for example in water, streams, waves, fish, and other obstacles.

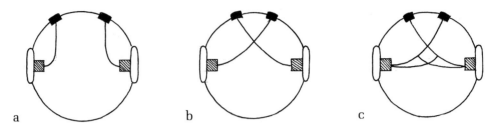

Figure 6.2   Vehicle 2. This vehicle has two motors and two sensors; otherwise it is like vehicle 1. Only the connections differ in (a), (b), and (c). 7.8

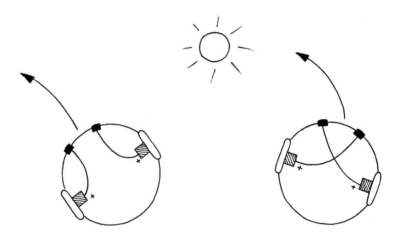

Figure 6.3   Vehicle 2a and 2b in the vicinity of a light source. Vehicle 2b orients itself toward the source, vehicle 2a away from it.

Vehicle 2:   Approach and Avoidance

Vehicle 2 is very similar to vehicle 1, except that it has two sensors, one on each side, and two motors, right and left (figure 6.2). There are three possibilities for connecting the sensors to the motors, as the figure shows. Case (c) in which both sensors are connected in the same way to the motors, is essentially the same as vehicle 1, so we consider only (a) and (b). The resulting behaviors are shown in Figure 6.3, in which the sensors are tuned to a light source. Because the right sensor of vehicle 2a is closer to the light source than the left, it gets more stimulation and thus the right motor turns faster than the left. As outside observers, we might characterize the vehicles as follows: Vehicle (a) is a coward, whereas vehicle (b) is aggressive: Vehicle (a) avoids the source, whereas (b) moves towards it and will hit it, possibly even destroying it.

Focus 6.1: Helping Behavior

> Let us look at an experiment involving a group of robots, each a Braitenberg vehicle 2b, which turns toward a light source. For this particular experiment, the generic robot scheme as introduced in chapter 4 was extended with a light mounted on top of the robot. The experiments have also been performed with the Didabot platform. Two Didabots are frequently observed to get stuck along a wall because they follow each other and because a white wall reflects the light very well. This following behavior is also generated by the Braitenberg architecture: One vehicle following another squeezes the one in front of it toward the wall (figure 6.4). A third robot comes from quite a distance and hits one of the robots in an effort to free it from being stuck. If it does not succeed in doing so, it turns back and hits the other agent again until all can get away from the wall. Of course, describing the robots' behavior in these terms attributes to them "motivations" they could not possibly possess. We can go to any level of anthropomorphization, actually, and there is nothing wrong with such descriptions, as long as we make no claims about the

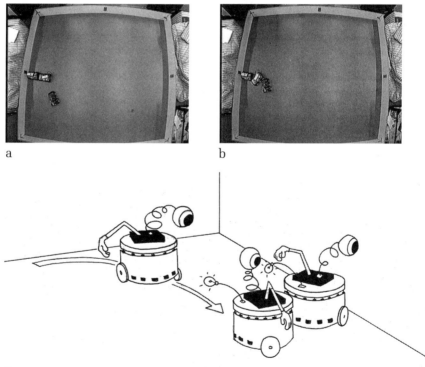

a   b

c

Figure 6.4 Helping behavior. (a) Two vehicles are stuck along the wall. A third vehicle is approaching. (b) The third vehicle hits the one pushing the other against the wall. Observers say "it comes to the rescue" of the two that are stuck. (c) Cartoon illustration of the same phenomenon.

Focus 6.1:   (continued)

internal mechanisms based on such descriptions. In this case, we know that the internal mechanism is a simple Braitenberg architecture, in fact almost the simplest one. Nevertheless, the behavior looks surprisingly intelligent to an observer.

We have reproduced this phenomenon a number of times, so it is more than purely accidental. Why does it happen? One explanation is as follows: The robots are very sensitive to light. They move toward the brightest light source within their "visual" range. Two robots stuck along the wall have two lights relatively close together. Two lights are brighter than one. The "helper" is thus attracted to this double light source. Because it is simple Braitenberg, it runs into the other two vehicles. If it is "successful," that is, if it breaks their deadlock, the two robots get away from the wall. If not, they stay there, and they continue to be the brightest light source in the "helper's" environment, so it returns and hit them again, repeating this pattern until they are freed. But nowhere is there any intention to "help" represented in the vehicle; it is simply acting as it has been programmed to do.

The "brains" of these vehicles are very simple. They consist merely of two neurons connecting the sensors to the motors. Note, however, that seemingly complex interactions among these vehicles can emerge. Focus 6.1 describes one example, "helping" behavior.

Vehicle 3:   Attraction

The first two Braitenberg vehicles have only excitation: the more stimulation at the sensors, the more the motors are powered. Let us now introduce inhibition: the more stimulation, the less power is delivered to the motors. This principle is incorporated in Braitenberg vehicle 3 (figure 6.5).

The behaviors involved are fairly obvious. Vehicle 3a ends up facing, say, a light source, whereas vehicle 3b turns away from it but also remains near the source, unless there is a disturbance, like another source. Additional sensors can also be introduced, and each stimulus can be connected either to the motor on the same or the opposite side, and can be excitatory or inhibitory (see figure 6.6). Stimuli to which the sensors are attuned could be light, oxygen concentration, temperature, concentration of organic molecules (food), or similar things. The vehicle has a tendency to stay longer in certain areas than in others because when its sensors are

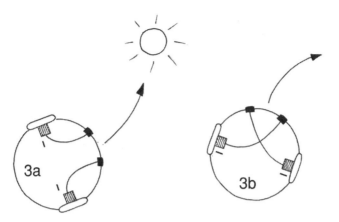

Figure 6.5 Vehicle 3. The vehicle's sensors exert an inhibitory influence on the motors. Vehicle 3a, turns toward the light source and stops, when it is close enough to the light source, i.e. as soon as the light stimulation is large enough to exert sufficient inhibitory activation. Vehicle 3b is similarly inhibited, but it moves away from the source.

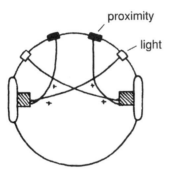

Figure 6.6 A multisensorial vehicle of type 3c. Sensors for various qualities have either positive or negative connections to the motors.

activated by the presence of a stimulus, its motors and thus its movement are inhibited. We cannot help admitting that the vehicle appears to have a set of "values" and that it incorporates them in some way that we would want to call "knowledge." "Knowledge" in this context does not mean "stored representations;" that is, it is not—as in the classical AI view—stored in an explicit form to be manipulated by the agent (the vehicle) itself. Rather, it is attributed to the vehicle as a whole by an outside observer. Attributing "knowledge" to an agent is a way of describing its behavior—it has nothing to do with the agent's internal structure.

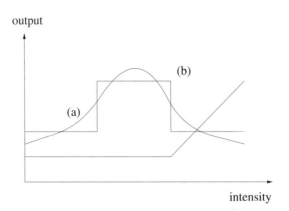

output

(b)

(a)

intensity

Figure 6.7 Nonlinear dependencies of motor output on intensity of sensory stimulation. Graph (a) shows a curve for a type 4a vehicle, graph (b) for a type 4b vehicle.

Vehicle 4: Values and Special Tastes

We can introduce a further complication by making the motors' dependency on the sensors nonlinear. Figure 6.7 depicts a few alternatives. Sensory stimulation may first increase, and then, at higher levels of stimulation, decrease the motor speed, for example. This would cause a vehicle to approach a distant source first slowly, then faster as it draws closer, and, as it gets still closer, it would slow down again. A vehicle of this sort is said to be of Braitenberg type 4a. If we allow thresholds, for example, a motor gets powered only if the stimulation of the corresponding sensor exceeds a certain threshold, we then have a vehicle of Braitenberg type 4b. The variety of such vehicles is enormous, and their behavior is very exciting. For example, a vehicle may sit still and, at some point, all of a sudden, start moving again. Or it may start describing patterns as shown in figure 6.8. As an observer, we might be tempted to say that these agents in fact "ponder" their decisions. Their behavior can be quite involved and difficult to understand.

Vehicle 4 is a purely reactive system: it does not have its own history; that is, it does not change over time. Nevertheless, it looks very much like an autonomous agent. If it has many sensors and they are connected in complex ways to the motors, it would in fact be very difficult to control the agent's behavior.

In chapter 4, we pointed out that neural networks are ideally suited to building agents capable of learning. We equated learning with changes of the weights in the connections within the neural network. As an aside, note that changes in the network are not

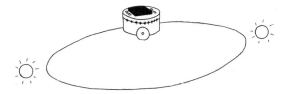

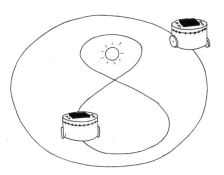

Figure 6.8 Trajectories of vehicles of type 4a around or between sources.

the only "experiences" a vehicle can have. It can also be damaged in some ways, receive a dent in the fender, suffer from a drained battery, or incur a broken sensor or motor. When experiencing these changes, the vehicle may behave quite differently, even if the internal control architecture remains the same. Thus, changes can occur without learning. This is another illustration of the implications of embodiment.

Vehicle 5: Adding "Brain Power"

We can now add arbitrary complexity by introducing threshold devices. In chapter 5 we called these "devices" nodes or model neurons. The kinds of nodes suggested here are of the linear threshold variety, but they could also be of the sigmoid type. They can either be interposed between sensors and motors or connected to each other in various ways. A vehicle possessing these devices is of Braitenberg type 5.

Threshold units can also be used to implement some kind of memory by introducing recurrent connections or loops. Imagine a threshold node connected to a sensor for red light. When activated by a red light, the sensor activates the threshold node, which then activates another threshold node connected to the first. Thus, once one of the nodes is turned on by a red light, the two nodes will keep activating themselves forever through mutual feedback. If a wire is attached to one of the two nodes and connected to a bell, the ringing of the bell signals that at some point in the past, this particular vehicle encountered a red light.

Vehicle 6: Evolution

Suppose we put a number of vehicles that we have built on a table containing light sources, sounds, smells, and so forth and let them move around. We pick out one vehicle, the model, make a copy of it, and put both the model and the copy back on the table. We pick out another, and repeat the process indefinitely. Of course, we do not choose vehicles that have fallen on the floor, because they are obviously incapable of coping with this particular environment. We produce vehicles at a pace that roughly matches the rate at which vehicles fall off the table.

If we play this game in a hurry, we are likely to make mistakes now and then. A well-tested vehicle might still fall off the table. Particularly shrewd variations might also be introduced unwittingly into the pattern of connections with the result that our copy survives, whereas the original may turn out to be unfit for survival after all. If the imperfect copying results simply from sloppiness, the chances that something interesting will emerge because of the mistakes in copying are small. However, a "better" sort of error would involve creating new combinations of partial mechanisms, and structures such as IR sensors, cameras, motors, or wheels, each of which has not been disrupted in its own well-tested functionality. Such errors have a much greater chance of transcending the intelligence of the original plan. If these "lucky" incidents live forever, they will have many descendants, because they and their descendants will frequently be chosen for copying simply because they stay on the table all the time.

This is, of course, a model of Darwinian evolution. It reminds us of the metaphor of the blind watchmaker, created by Richard Dawkins (1988) to describe evolution. Vehicles created in such a scenario are said to be Braitenberg type 6. We may, by accident, create vehicles whose behavior is extraordinary without understanding why they behave as they do, because building something that works is typically much easier than analysis: Braitenberg called this the "law of uphill analysis and downhill invention." Indeed in evolutionary approaches you can quite often get the agents to do what they should do, but it is usually hard to understand why they do what they do. (Evolutionary methods are discussed in detail in chapter 8.)

Other Vehicles

We discuss the remaining vehicles 7 to 14 only briefly, because for our purposes, the simple vehicles are more interesting: They illustrate the sensory-motor couplings and how they lead to remarkable behavior. The later ones, especially vehicles 7 and above, have a cognitivistic flavor and are therefore bound to run into the problems discussed in chapter 3.

For the sake of completeness, let us briefly summarize the remaining vehicles. The general idea is to augment existing vehicles by more sophisticated types of neural networks. For example, a vehicle of type 5 can be turned into one of type 7 by adding more network nodes, connecting them and using Hebbian learning to form associations between the nodes whenever they are simultaneously active. As we discussed in the previous chapter, associations can be formed in this way. In the Distributed Adaptive Control architecture, the presence of light has been associated with stimulation of IR sensors on the side of the robot. We could say, from our perspective of observers, that the robot has learned the concept "light along walls." Such concepts can be used to guide the agents' behavior: if light corresponds to food, then it is a good idea to follow walls to find food. These associations can become more complicated if more sensors and larger neural networks are involved.

Further improvements of the vehicles include mechanisms for shape detection (e.g., for squares and circles), for detection of temporal order (strong stimulation in proximity sensor, activation of collision sensor), for prediction (strong sensory stimulation in the proximity sensors is a predictor for an impending impact), and for something like short-term memory (it is important to keep track of what has happened in the recent past in order to decide what to do next).

Let us now turn to a final example of a Braitenberg type vehicle: the timid vehicle.

The Timid Vehicle

The "timid" vehicle is one of a number of vehicles that Hogg, Martin, and Resnik (1991) have introduced. They describe 12 vehicles they have built with electronic bricks. Electronic bricks are specially modified LEGO bricks with simple electronic circuits inside. Braitenberg vehicles of various types can be constructed using these bricks. Among others, one can build "paranoid," "dogged," "insecure," or "frantic" vehicles with these bricks. We focus on the "timid" vehicle, which is an instantiation of vehicle 2a discussed earlier: The more sensor stimulation it receives, the faster it moves. When it receives no stimulation, it does not move at all. We have implemented this vehicle in a Khepera robot. Figure 6.9 shows its basic behavior. The vehicle seems to be "timid": Whenever an object comes in its vicinity, it avoids contact with the object by powering its motors appropriately. In the implementation shown in the figure, all IR sensors of the Khepera robot were connected to the motors, so the vehicle avoids obstacles coming from any direction.

More interesting is an experiment that shows how even such simple vehicles can show rather complex behavior. Let us add a bias toward moving forward to the "timid" vehicle just described. By adding, at each time step, a small constant to both motors. Now in addition to turning away from objects it approaches, the vehicle also moves forward a specified, constant distance for each unit of time (say, a second). Figure 6.10 shows the resulting behavior: The "timid" vehicle can drive through mazes without hitting the walls! This occurs because the vehicle is "timid"—it avoids all walls— and because it also has a bias to move forward. As a result, it avoids the walls, but still drives through the maze. If a biologist showed us such a trajectory that he recorded from, say, a rat, we might be inclined to postulate some kind of sequence generator in the animal. We therefore have to be careful with such speculations about internal mechanisms that generate a given trajectory. The maze-following behavior of the "timid" vehicle illustrates beautifully that coherent, sequential behavior can emerge out of a number

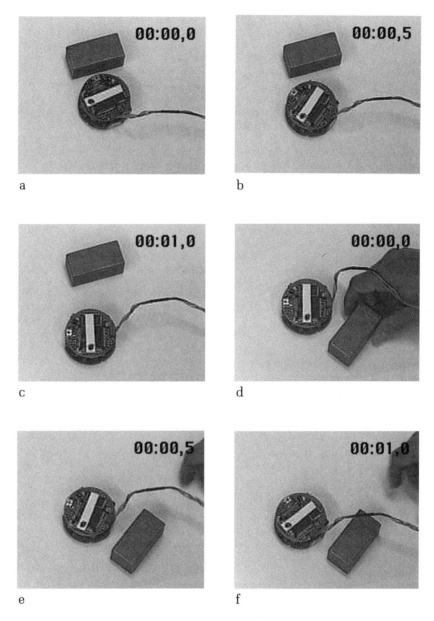

Figure 6.9 Basic behavior of the timid vehicle. When an object approaches the vehicle from the right (panels a, b, c) or left (panels d, e, f), it moves away.

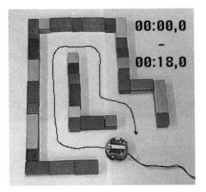

Figure 6.10 Maze-following behavior of the "timid" vehicle. When a simple default speed is added to the motors, the "timid" vehicle can be made to drive through mazes.

of simple processes that operate in parallel. Similar to Simon's ant on the beach, the complexity arises from the interaction with the environment (beach, maze) and not from the agent alone.

Conclusions

Braitenberg vehicles are great fun to work with. They also provide deep insights into the nature of intelligence. For example, they beautifully illustrate the "frame-of-reference" problem: Even very simple designs can lead to surprisingly interesting kinds of behavior, especially if several vehicles are involved. They also demonstrate nicely that the neural substrate is by no means the only thing that governs the vehicles' behavior. It is just as important what sorts of sensors are on the vehicle, how they function, and where they are positioned.

An interesting point relates to the vehicles' autonomy. Braitenberg vehicles are hard to control. Although fairly accurate predictions can be made about the general quality of the behavior of certain vehicles, it is next to impossible to make more precise forecasts. In other words, Braitenberg vehicles have a certain degree of autonomy: Getting them to do exactly what you want is difficult. This is true even for vehicles with no learning.

For our purposes in this book, the simple Braitenberg vehicles are the most interesting, because they illustrate sensory-motor couplings and how they lead to remarkable behavior. In vehicles 7 through 14, in essence, the sophistication of the "brain" is progressively increased with each subsequent vehicle built. Although this is useful to some extent, it cannot be continued indefinitely, unless the sensory-motor complexity is also increased. Take, for example, vehicle 1. If we increase the complexity of the vehicle's brain, not much will change in the behavior of the agent, because its sensory-motor system is so simple: Increasing its brain power doesn't have any real effect on the simple behaviors it is set up to perform, because the original brain power was already more than sufficient for the simple tasks. However, if we add additional sensors and motor capabilities, we get more interesting behaviors very easily.

These vehicles illustrate an additional fundamental point: the segmentation of behavior. From these considerations, we can derive important principles for control architectures. This requires some elaboration.

6.3 Segmentation of Behavior and the Extended Braitenberg Architecture

Assume that you have a Braitenberg vehicle of type 3. It has no internal "actions," in the sense of separate internal modules, only internal processes connecting sensors, via some intermediate mechanisms, to effectors. So it is not possible to list the actions in which the agent is involved. It is obvious that in this case any segmentation of behavior is purely observer based, and it is very difficult to come up with a consistent rating between different observers. Consider now a vehicle of type 3c, as shown in figure 6.11. There is a light process with a positive connection, meaning that the vehicle is attracted to the light. There is a proximity process (high proximity means high activation) that makes the vehicle turn away from close objects. If we consider the potential trajectory, the vehicle will initially turn toward the light source (because of the light process), then slowly begin to turn away as it approaches it (because of the proximity process). What action is it involved in, "turning toward the light" or "turning away from the obstacle"? We cannot say, because there are no internal actions, only processes feeding onto the two state variables, namely the speeds of the motors.

How could we then sensibly segment the agent's behavior? What the agent really does is engage in behavior that is emergent from the dynamics of its internal variables (the intensity of the sensor stimulation and the motor speeds) in the interaction with the environment. We can extend this architecture to any number of internal variables, some of which, like the speed variables, will directly

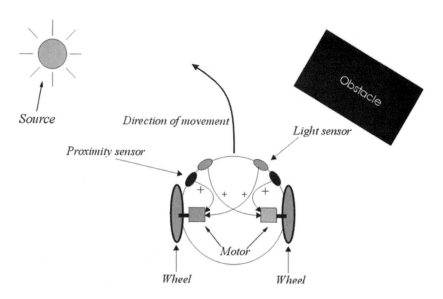

Figure 6.11 A vehicle of type 3c. The vehicle has two light sensors and two proximity sensors. The closer to an object the agent comes, the higher its activation. Because of its wiring, this vehicle turns towards a light source, but if the weights are chosen appropriately, it will turn away from the light source, when it is close enough.

influence the vehicle's behavior. Such an architecture is called an *Extended Braitenberg Architecture*. For natural systems, this kind of architecture has high explanatory power, and it demonstrates nicely why the segmentation of behavior is notoriously difficult. The Extended Braitenberg Architecture is illustrated with a number of examples in chapter 11.

Issues to Think About

Issue 6.1: Sensory-Motor Coupling and Brains

Braitenberg vehicles 1 through 6 capitalize on system-environment interaction. Their behavior control is based largely on direct sensory-motor couplings with relatively little internal processing. In this sense, they represent the epitome of embodied cognitive science. As we mentioned above, vehicles 7 through 14 have a strongly cognitivistic flavor. Remember the thought experiment we suggested with vehicle 1: We simply increased its brain power. Now, what on earth is this more powerful brain going to do? What functions could it have? As it turns out, it is hard to think of any sensible task for this brain. Thus, it becomes obvious that increasing brain power alone does not make sense: The sensory and the motor systems have to be improved as well. This is an important design principle that we will discuss more later. As we said in chapter 1, we feel that AI and psychology have focused too much on the brain itself (see figure 1.4: the brain as the "seat of intelligence"). From this perspective, vehicles 7 to 14 are less attractive. In vehicle 10, for example, the idea of a coin with two faces should evolve through the observation of someone repeatedly turning a coin. However, from the mechanisms described, it is not clear how that could come about. Just think of the awesome complexity a perceptual system would have to have to make sense of a coin-flipping situation. Neglecting the coupling to the real world in this way is typical of approaches focusing on so-called higher-level processes and on brains. A better approach is to start from the working hypothesis that we have simple sensory-motor processes with little intermediate processing that form the substrate of intelligence. How far we can get with this assumption is an open question. Because of the fundamental importance, this issue is discussed in a number of places throughout the book. Think of other examples of tasks that look very simple in the abstract but get enormously complex as you add the interaction with the environment.

Issue 6.2: Uphill Analysis and Downhill Invention

Intuitively, we would think that it is easier to analyze something that already exists than to build something new. The law of uphill analysis and downhill invention suggests the exact opposite. Indeed, experience shows that it is surprisingly simple to build Braitenberg-style vehicles and to increase their complexity step by step. Even for relatively simple vehicles, however, it is very hard to understand what precisely is going on as they exhibit various behaviors. Their interaction with the environment is largely unpredictable in detail. This is somewhat counterintuitive, because we built the systems ourselves—but we still have a hard time understanding their behavior. This holds in particular for neural networks, and Braitenberg architectures are specific instances of neural networks. In spite of these difficulties, they are highly productive tools. We consider the synthetic approach to cognitive science to be the most successful one currently.

Points to Remember

- Braitenberg vehicles are a set of fourteen types of vehicles designed to explore, in a bottom-up fashion, principles of intelligence. They are ideally suited to studying the relationship between behavior and mechanism.

- Often, even very simple Braitenberg vehicles display, because of their interaction with the environment, surprisingly sophisticated kinds of behavior. This is especially true if other vehicles are present in their environment.

- Braitenberg vehicles consist of parallel processes connecting sensory stimulation to actuators via some intermediate mechanisms. The values of the motor variables determine what the agent does. There are no internal actions.

- The Braitenberg approach can be extended to agent design in general. This is called the Extended Braitenberg Architecture.

- Braitenberg vehicles explain why the problem of segmentation of behavior is notoriously hard to solve. The vehicles have no internal actions corresponding to specific observer-based behavioral categories.

- The mechanisms implemented in Braitenberg vehicles are entirely deterministic. Nevertheless, it is virtually impossible to predict the vehicles' behavior.

- The Braitenberg approach is appealing, since it is biologically motivated and has high explanatory power.

Further Reading

Braitenberg, V. (1984). *Vehicles: Experiments in synthetic psychology*. Cambridge, MA: MIT Press. (A must for anyone interested in cognitive science and autonomous agents. Beautifully written, simply a seminal book.)

Hogg, D. W., Martin, F. M., and Resnick, M. (1991). *Braitenberg creatures*. MIT Media Laboratory, Cambridge, MA. (Available online at http://les.www.media.mit.edu/people/fredm/papers/vehicles/). (Describes how various Braitenberg vehicles can be constructed using simple electronic bricks. Strongly suggested for those interested in actually building Braitenberg vehicles.)

In the last chapter, we focused on the cognitive science aspects of autonomous agents—the synthetic methodology was very explicit. In this chapter, we continue in our series of important types of agents. We now discuss an approach that, in contrast to the cognitive science–oriented Braitenberg vehicles, has more of an engineering flavor; the subsumption architecture, first introduced by Rodney Brooks of the MIT Artificial Intelligence Laboratory in 1986. Brooks's intention was to create a methodology that would make it easy to design robots that pursue multiple goals and respond to multiple sensors, that perform robustly, and that are incrementally extendable. This last factor, incremental extendability, has largely been responsible for the subsumption architecture's popularity. You start by building a basic module or layer, say for obstacle avoidance. Once you finish that module, you can build the other modules on top of it—you do not need to change what you have already built.

Although the subsumption architecture has a definite engineering bias, it also has a number of important cognitive science aspects. First, it is conceived to reflect aspects of natural evolutionary theory. The idea of having layers that need not be changed once they have been created is a case in point. To make a parallel with nature, once the eye had been "invented" by evolution, it would not be changed any more (at least not in fundamental ways), but reused. Second, the subsumption architecture is based on the same notion of simple, sensor-action couplings with little internal processing that we encountered in the last chapter. Having relatively direct couplings from sensors to actuators leads to better real-time behavior, because it makes time-consuming modeling operations and higher-level processes such as planning activities largely unnecessary. (We deal with potential objections to this design philosophy at the end of the chapter.) Third, the subsumption architecture does not consider intelligence to be something centralized in a brainlike entity; rather, behaviors that we consider interesting or requiring intelligence emerge in the subsumption architecture from a large number of loosely coupled processes. This is, of course, an empirical hypothesis, but it has a lot of appeal, and we take it up again when discussing the design principles for autonomous agents in chapter 10.

Before discussing the subsumption architecture in greater detail, a few remarks about terminology are in order. The first comment is about the term "behavior." Behavior, as we introduced the concept earlier, is by definition the result of a system-environment interaction. The subsumption architecture literature uses the term in two ways, an informal use and a more technical one. The informal sense corresponds to our own usage, that is, behavior as the result of a system-environment interaction. In the technical sense, "behavior" refers to internal structures, namely the particular layers or modules designed to generate particular behaviors (in the everyday sense). We point this out to avoid confusion later. It is unfortunate that Brooks uses the term "behavior" or "task-achieving behavior" for internal structures. We use the terms "layer" and "module" instead whenever referring to an internal structure. The term "subsumption" is also used in logic to designate a particular relation between two clauses, namely that one clause has no more literals than the other. Quite obviously, there is no relation between these two notions of subsumption. A final point about terminology pertains to the use of the terms "behavior-based approach" or "behavior-based robotics" (see section 7.1). In the narrow sense, these terms refer to subsumption-based approaches. But it has become customary to simply use these terms to refer to the whole field of embodied cognitive science, not all of which depends on the use of the subsumption architecture. "Behavior-based" in this latter sense is to be seen as meaning "non-information-processing-based": It is used in contradistinction to classical "knowledge-based" approaches.

The discussion in this chapter picks up from our discussion in chapter 1 of the transition from classical AI, that is, physical-symbol systems, to embodied cognitive science. In addition, it provides some technical detail and introduces the subsumption terminology. We begin by outlining the behavior-based approach, of which subsumption is the most important representative. We then outline a couple of design principles we need later on. Next, we show how to develop subsumption-based systems with two examples: Myrmix and Ghengis. We end the chapter with a few reflections on the subsumption architecture.

7.1 Behavior-Based Robotics

Brooks's subsumption architecture was the first approach toward a new paradigm in the study of intelligence which he called "behavior-based robotics" (see also Arkin 1998); we refer to the field as it presents itself today as "embodied cognitive science." Subsumption is a method of decomposing a robot's control architecture of a robot into a set of task-achieving behaviors or *competences*. The usual approach to building control architectures for mobile robots is functional decomposition: First, there is sensing and perception. In this step, information from different sensory systems (vision, auditory, tactile) is integrated into a central representation. Then internal processing takes place. This includes building or updating a model of the environment (often called a "world model"), planning the next actions, and deciding which action plans to actually execute (decision making). Finally some actions are executed in the real world (e.g., moving forward, grasping an object). Functional decomposition of a robot's task thus leads to the sense-think-act cycle of the traditional information processing approach. Because the cycle involves modeling and planning, it is sometimes called the sense-model-plan-action (SPMA) cycle (Brooks 1991a,b). The "thinking" is split into a modeling and a planning activity. Figure 7.1a depicts this way of conecptualizing an agent.

In contrast to the traditional approach, the subsumption architecture builds control architectures by incrementally adding task-achieving behaviors on top of each other (figure 7.1b). Implementations of such behaviors are called *layers*. Higher-level layers (e.g., `explore`) build and rely on lower-level ones (e.g., `avoid objects`). `Explore` means that the robot is moving around in the environment in order, for example, to find food or the location of light sources or of other robots. Higher layers can *subsume* lower layers (see section 7.2). Instead of having a single sequence-of-information flow—from perception to world modeling to action—there are multiple paths, the layers, that are active in parallel. Each of these paths is concerned only with a small subtask of the robot's overall task, such as avoiding walls, circling around targets, or moving to a charging station. Each of these layers can function relatively independently. They do not have to await instructions or results produced by other layers. Thus control is not hierarchical in the traditional sense of the term. In short, the subsumption approach realizes the direct couplings between sensors and actuators,

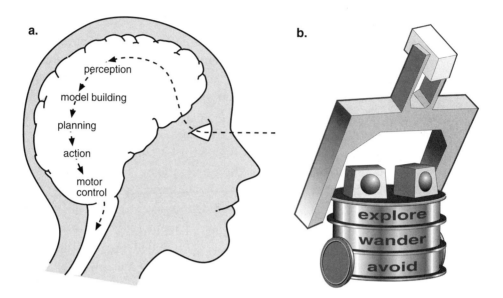

Figure 7.1   Different ways of decomposing an agent. (a) Traditional (functional) decomposition: In the traditional view, the control architecture is decomposed into a sequence of functional modules, all of which have to be activated in order to generate behavior. (b) Modern (subsumption-based) decomposition: In the subsumption perspective, the control architecture is decomposed into modules called ''task-achieving behaviors'' (adapted from Brooks 1986, p. 14).

with only limited internal processing, that we mentioned in the introduction to the chapter.

The subsumption architecture comes in several varieties (e.g., Brooks 1986; Connell 1990; Ferrell 1994). The differences among the various approaches are not of central relevance to our discussion here. In essence, we follow the outline of Brooks. The terminology in the literature is not consistent. We have taken care to take into account the frame-of-reference problem, always distinguishing behavior from internal mechanism.

7.2   Designing a Subsumption-Based Robot

Levels of Competence

The starting point of the subsumption approach is defining levels of competence (see figure 7.2). A *level of competence* is the informal specification of a class of desired (external) behaviors that the robot should be able to perform in the environments in which it will have

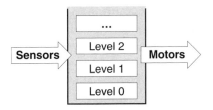

Figure 7.2 Levels of competence. This kind of conceptual diagram represents an informal specification of the robot's desired behaviors: It specifies what the to-be-designed robot should be able to do.

to operate. Implementations of the behaviors that are grouped into levels of competence are sometimes called *task-achieving* (internal) behaviors, because they are designed to achieve some small task on their own. We have added the qualifications (external, internal) in order to do justice to the frame-of-reference problem.

One of the elementary things a mobile robot should be able to do is not to bump into objects, or stated a little differently, to avoid objects. Hence, it should be equipped with the *competence* to avoid obstacles. Therefore, we first need an `avoid obstacle` competence. It is designated level 0 because it is the most basic one. Next there could be a `wander around` (level 1) competence, an `explore` (level 2) competence, or any sort of more complex competence like `collect objects`.

The key point of having levels of competence is as follows: Each level of competence is implemented as a layer of the control architecture. These layers can be built incrementally. This naturally leads to extendable designs in which new competences can simply be added to the already existing and functioning control system. There is another essential element in this organization: At each level, there are sensory inputs and motor outputs. In other words, higher levels, just like lower ones, can directly interact with the environment, without the need to go through lower levels.

Layers of Control

In designing a subsumption-based robot, we first have to design a layer that implements the level 0 competence. Proceeding in this way has the advantage of making the robot functional solely with this level 0 competence: We do not have to wait until all the layers have been designed and can be put together to deploy the robot. Moreover, this layer does not have to await instructions from a higher layer or from a central controller (because there is no central controller). In a sense, we already have a functioning robot, but the minimal things it can do are perhaps not yet so interesting. The robot's functionality strictly within level 0 also makes it easy to debug the layer for the level 0 competence on its own. Even if there are higher-level layers of control above this one, the lower-level layers continue to function independently. Thus if not inhibited, the robot will avoid obstacles, whatever else it may be involved in doing: searching for the charging station, mowing a lawn, or collecting soda cans.

Once each layer has been built and debugged, it never has to be changed again. Higher-level layers build and rely on lower-level layers (the evolutionary idea). They are able to examine data from lower levels. Moreover, they are permitted to send data to the lower levels, suppressing the normal data flow. This may be necessary, for example, if the robot is to push chairs into a corner. Obviously, in this case, it should not avoid the chairs but move up to them and touch them. The lower levels continue to run, but in a sense are "unaware" of the higher ones. As we see, the statement that the layers, once tested, never have to be changed is not quite true: We sometimes have to add links between layers to inhibit certain behaviors. A chair-pushing robot has to stop avoiding obstacles when it has to push a chair.

Structure of Layers: Modules

Once they have been defined, how are the layers implemented? Each layer consists of a set of modules that asynchronously send messages to each other over connecting wires (see figure 7.3). Each module is an augmented finite state machine (see below). Input to modules can be *suppressed* and outputs can be *inhibited* by wires from other modules. Metaphorically speaking, we can say that through this mechanism, higher-level layers can *subsume* lower-level ones—thus the term *subsumption*. This implies a certain amount of interaction between the modules. The idea is that this interaction should be minimized to facilitate the design process, to achieve maximum "incrementality" and emergence.

In summary, designing a subsumption architecture involves the following steps: First, the designer decides which behaviors the robot should be able to perform. These behaviors are then organized into levels of competences (e.g., level 0 for obstacle

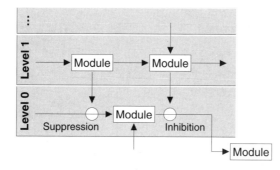

Figure 7.3 Structure of layers. Each layer contains several modules connected by wires. Modules can suppress inputs to or inhibit outputs of other modules through suppression and inhibition links. The modules are implemented as augmented finite state machines.

avoidance, level 1 for exploration, level 2 for collecting objects). Note that at this stage of the design process, we can draw conceptual diagrams like the one in figure 7.2. These conceptual diagrams usually show which and how many levels of competences a particular control architecture contains. Conceptual diagrams specify behavior; they have to be distinguished from the *technical diagrams*, like figure 7.3, which illustrate the result of the next design step, the actual implementations of each level of competence in terms of augmented finite state machines. We now examine in greater detail the techniques used in this step. Note that the literature offers several different approaches toward the implementation of the subsumption architecture. In what follows, we present the original proposal by Brooks (1986, 1990a).

Layers are implemented as collections of modules, as mentioned above. Each module is implemented as an augmented finite state machine. A finite state machine (FSM) is a simple computational device that changes its state depending on the current state and input. A finite state machine can assume a finite number of different states, and it changes from one state to another according to predefined rules. An example is a turnstile (figure 7.4). If the turnstile is locked (state 1) and a token is inserted, the machine changes to state 2 (corresponding to unlocked). Then, if the input is "person," that is, someone is turning the turnstile, the machine changes back to state 1, meaning that the turnstile is now locked again. If it is unlocked, and a token is inserted, the machine remains in state 2. If it is locked (state 1) and the input is "person," it remains locked. Augmented finite state machines (AFSMs) are,

a.

b.

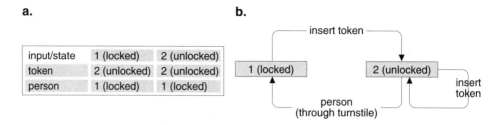

input/state	1 (locked)	2 (unlocked)
token	2 (unlocked)	2 (unlocked)
person	1 (locked)	1 (locked)

Figure 7.4 A finite state machine: a turnstile. (a) Representation as a transition table. (b) Representation as a transition graph. Adding a register for maintaining a state for a particular period of time would turn this into an augmented finite state machine.

as the name implies, finite state machines to which some sort of mechanism or facility has been added. The augmented finite state machines are relatively simple finite state machines to which a number of facilities have been added (like registers for program code and timing mechanisms that enable state changes after a certain period of time, for example, when hitting an obstacle on the left, the robot should turn right for a second or so). A programming language, the Behavioral Language, has been developed specifically to implement these augmented finite state machines (Brooks 1990b).

The details of the internal structure of modules need not concern us here too much. (The interested reader is referred to the literature on this topic: Brooks 1986; Connell 1990; Ferrell 1994.) Augmented finite state machines represent one particular formalism Brooks has chosen to use, but the specific formalism used is not essential to the idea of the subsumption architecture. Often, the modules are simply implemented as computer programs. The next section presents several examples of control architectures that have been built with the subsumption architecture.

7.3 Examples of Subsumption-Based Architectures

Many robots have been built using variations on the subsumption architecture. Examples are Myrmix, Ghengis, Herbert (Connell 1990), and Hannibal (Ferrell 1994).

Myrmix

Following the outline of table 4.5, we first have to specify the agent's ecological niche and the task. In the case of the robot

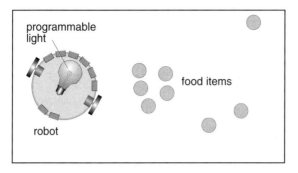

Figure 7.5 Setup for Myrmix experiments: Myrmix's ecological niche consists of a closed environment with a number of objects representing "food" for the robot. The robot is to find food items and "eat" them. Eating means turning toward an object, switching a light on for a few moments, and switching the light off again. A schema of the robot used in the experiments, a variation on the generic robot introduced earlier, is shown on the left. The robot has no light sensors, but there is a programmable light on top of the robot.

Myrmix, its task is to find objects and to collect them. In the particular example presented here, the robot collects objects by grasping, "eating," and "digesting" them, rather than by bringing them to a home base. Of course, robots don't really eat, so we have to specify what we mean by "eating." Whenever Myrmix detects a target, it turns toward the target, stops in front of it, and turns on its light: It is "eating" the object. After a certain amount of time, the robot turns away and starts moving straight ahead again. It takes Myrmix a certain time to "digest" its food items, and during the "digestion period" it simply avoids all objects it encounters. (The light remains on to indicate this.) As soon as the target has been entirely "digested," it switches off the light and engages in "eating" behavior again. Figure 7.5 provides an overview of the situation; Myrmix's low-level specification is a variation on the generic robot introduced earlier. It has no light sensors, but a light on top of the robot can be controlled by the robot itself.

The next step, according to the outline, is to specify the control architecture. This is subsumption's main focus. Myrmix has three basic competences: `safe-forward`, `avoid-obstacle`, and `collect`. Figure 7.6a diagrams these levels of competences conceptually, and figure 7.6b shows Myrmix's layers, which consist of modules, connected by wires, and inhibition and suppression links. The modules are implemented as augmented finite state machines. Let us examine the robot's three layers in more detail.

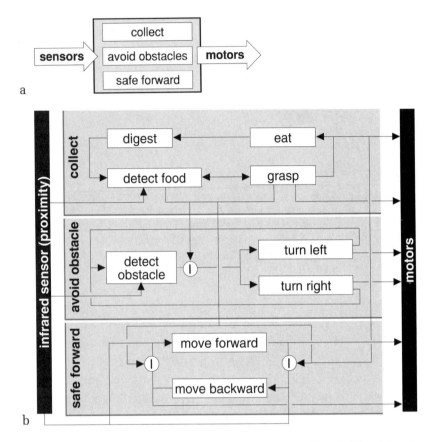

Figure 7.6 Control architecture of Myrmix. (a) Conceptual diagram of Myrmix: Myrmix has three levels of competence: safe-forward, avoid-obstacle, and collect. (b) The layers of Myrmix: Myrmix's layers consist of modules, connected by wires, and inhibition and suppression links. The modules are implemented as augmented finite state machines. The safe-forward layer consists of two AFSMs: "Move_Forward" and "Move_Backward." The avoid-obstacle layer consists of three AFSMs: "Detect_Obstacle," "Turn_Left," and "Turn_Right." The collect layer consists of four AFSMs: "Detect_Food," "Grasp," "Eat," and "Digest."

THE safe-forward LAYER

The lowest layer of control, safe-forward, causes the robot to move straight ahead and, at the same time, makes sure that the robot does not collide with obstacles. It contains two modules: "Move_Forward" and "Move_Backward." Myrmix usually starts an experiment in the "Move_Forward" state. The "Move_Forward" module first sets the two motor speeds to a predefined value, which causes the robot to move forward at that speed. Before the robot actually starts moving forward, however, a number of other steps have to be performed involving potential obstacles in the robot's path. First, the front IR sensor is read to check whether there is an obstacle in the robot's way. If this is indeed the case—indicated by an IR sensor value larger than some threshold, the system switches to "Move_Backward," otherwise it remains in the same mode ("Move_Forward"). If the system switches to "Move_Backward," that module first sets the motor speeds to some negative value causing the robot to move backward for a certain amount of time. Next, the back IR sensor is read to test for collisions. If there is a collision in the back or the time period for moving back has expired, the system switches to the "Move_Forward" module. The main result is that the robot can move forward but does not crash into objects: whenever it detects an obstacle in the front, it moves backward, thereby testing whether it collides with an object in the back. Once it has moved backward for a sufficient amount of time, it starts moving forward again. It becomes clear that we need an additional layer that makes the robot not only move backward, but actually turn away from the object. This is the task of the next layer, the `avoid-obstacle` layer.

THE `avoid-obstacle` LAYER

The `avoid-obstacle` layer consists of three modules, "Detect_ Obstacle," "Turn_Left," and "Turn_Right." The principles are similar to the ones used in the `safe-forward` layer. "Detect_ Obstacle" first calculates the sensor input on the right and the left side of the robot by summing over the respective IR sensor activations. If an obstacle is detected—that is, if at least one of the summed sensor activations has a larger value than a predefined threshold—the robot turns left if the total sensor activations was larger on the right side than on the left side, and turns right if the total sensor activation was larger on the left side than on the right side of the robot. By the output of the "Detect-Obstacle" module, either the "Turn_Left" or the "Turn_Right" module is activated. Depending on the sensor activations. The "Turn_Left" and "Turn_ Right" modules first set the speed of the robot to values that cause the robot to turn in the respective direction (left or right). The robot turns in the respective direction for a predefined amount of time and then the "Detect_Obstacle" module checks if there are still any obstacles present. The `safe-forward` and the `avoid-obstacles` layers enable the robot to move around in its environment without crashing into objects. The next layer we have to implement to make Myrmix actually collect objects is the `collect` layer.

THE collect LAYER

There are four modules in the collect layer: "Detect_Food," "Grasp," "Eat," and "Digest." The "Detect_Food" module first reads each of the frontmost three IR sensors and determines whether its activation value is larger than a predefined threshold. "Food" items are small objects, so if the adjacent sensors on both sides of the active sensor are below some (smaller) threshold, the robot is likely to be detecting a potential "food" item. In this case, the "Detect_Food" module inhibits the sensory input of the safe-forward layer as well as the inputs to the "Turn_Left" and "Turn_Right" modules in the avoid-obstacle layer by setting them to 0. If the potential "food" was detected not directly in front but somewhat to the side, it also sets the variable grasping to some positive or negative value, according to the side on which the "food" was detected, and the "Grasp" module becomes active. In the "Grasp" module, the safe-forward layer as well as the avoid-obstacle layer are still inhibited while the robot is turning left or right, depending on the sign of the variable grasping, thereby decrementing it (or incrementing it, if it is negative). If the variable grasping equals 0, the robot checks again whether there is something now exactly in the front that could be "food." If so, the "Eat" module becomes active; but if the object in front does not look like "food," the "Detect_Food" module becomes active again. When the "Eat" module is active, the system turns on the light, indicating that the robot is actually eating, stops the motors, and inhibits the avoid-obstacle layer (otherwise the robot would back away from the "food" item). The "Eat" module stays active for a predefined amount of time and then the "Digest" module becomes active. The "Digest" module no longer inhibits the avoid-obstacle layer, that is, the robot now moves away from the "food," at the same time avoiding all other objects including other potential "food" items, since the "Detect_Food" module is not active. After a predefined amount of time has elapsed, the "Detect_Food" module becomes active again and the whole cycle restarts.

Our description of this process suggests that its implementation is straightforward, and in general it is. One problem needs to be dealt with, however: recognizing objects in the environment, as illustrated in figure 7.7. "Detect_Food" and "Grasp" check whether there is a target in front of the robot. If the targets consist of small isolated objects, as in our example, only one IR sensor has high

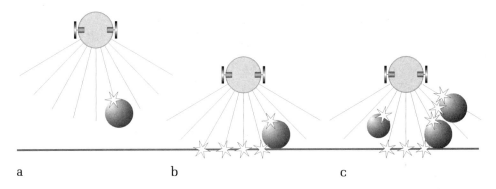

a   b   c

Figure 7.7 Problems in recognizing targets. (a) A small target. Small targets in isolated positions can easily be recognized. (b) A small target near a wall. A small target near a wall activates several sensors and thus cannot be recognized. (c) Several targets close to each other. Clusters of targets also activate several sensors and can thus not be recognized.

activation (figure 7.7a). But if the modules assume that targets correspond to high IR activation in one sensor and lower activities in the neighboring sensors, the robot will not recognize targets near a wall, because the wall will activate several sensors (figure 7.7b). If there are several small targets close to each other, the robot will no longer be able to distinguish them from obstacles (figure 7.7c), because the "Detect_Obstacle" module will detect sufficient activation in the robot's various sensors (those detecting the numerous small targets the robot is simultaneously encountering) to arrive at a summed value larger than the threshold value that indicates an obstacle in the robot's path. There are no perfect universal solutions to this problem, but good compromises have to be found in each case. We will return to this important problem in chapter 12.

According to table 4.5, we now have to define the concrete experiments to be run, choose a robot platform, make predictions about the robot's behavior, then run the experiments. The predictions in this case are fairly obvious. The robot should behave as it was designed: It should find targets, turn toward them, switch the light on, and so forth through the sequence. Once the experiments have been run, the robot's actual behavior should be described. Examples of how this might be done are drawing the trajectories it follows, generating simple statistics (number of targets "eaten" per minute), or writing verbal descriptions. Figure 7.8 provides an example description of Myrmix's behavior. Figure 7.8a offers a bird's-eye view on parts of the robot's environment (recorded by a camera mounted on the top of the environment). The robot's tra-

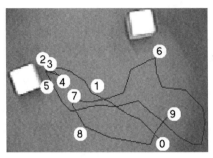

Positions of robot	0 - 1	1 - 2	2	3	3 - 4	4 - 5	5 - 6	6 - 7	7 - 8	8 - 9
Move_Forward	+	+	s	s	-	+	+	+	+	+
Move_Backward	-	-	s	s	+	-	-	-	-	-
Detect_Obstacle	+	s	s	s	+	-	-	-	-	+
Turn_Left	-	s	s	s	-	+	+	+	+	-
Turn_Right	-	s	s	s	-	-	-	-	-	-
Detect_Food	+	+	-	-	-	-	-	-	-	+
Grasp	-	-	+	-	-	-	-	-	-	-
Eat	-	-	-	+	-	-	-	-	-	-
Digest	-	-	-	-	+	+	+	+	+	-

Figure 7.8 Results for a typical run of Myrmix. (a) Bird's-eye view of Myrmix's environment. There are two objects, indicated as white cubes. The black line indicates the robot's trajectory. The numbers in the white circles are pointers to the table shown in (b); they indicate different time steps in the robot's trajectory. (b) Table indicating the states of the nine different modules between the nine different time steps in the run. The first two, "Move_Forward" and Move_Backward," belong to the safe-forward layer; "Detect_Obstacle," "Turn_Left," and "Turn_Right" belong to the avoid-obstacle layer, and "Detect_Food," "Grasp," "Eat," and "Digest" belong to the collect layer. Each row indicates whether it was active ($+$), inactive ($-$), or surpressed (s) between each of the 10 different positions. For example, "Move_Forward" was active between positions 0 and 1 (0–1), and 1 and 2 (1–2), then was supressed at positions 2 and 3, and was inactive between positions 3 and 4 (3–4), and so forth.

jectory is shown, together with numbers indicating different time steps during the robot's run; the same numbers are used in the table in figure 7.8b, which shows which modules were active, which inactive, and which supressed at various points during the recorded time period. Let us briefly reconstruct the robot's behavior, using the data of figure 7.8. Between time steps 0 and 1 (column "0–1" in figure 7.8b), the robot was moving forward, and, as it approached the object on the left, it detected an obstacle and food. In the next interval (1–2), the robot continued to move forward, but since is had detected food, the output of the "Detect_Obstacle" module, as well as the outputs of the "Turn_Left" and "Turn_ Right" modules, were supressed (indicated by an "s"). At time step 2, the robot grasped the object. During grasping, the outputs of "Move_Forward," "Move_Backward," "Detect_Obstacle," "Turn_ Left," and "Turn_Right" were suppressed. The output of the "Move_Forward" module was still suppressed at time step 3, because the robot was eating the food item it had just grasped. After it had eaten the food item, the robot "digested," and at the same time detected an obstacle and started to move backward until, in the interval between time steps 4 and 5, it started to move forward again because it no longer detected any obstacles. The robot kept moving forward at time step 6, moving to the other object in the environment, which it avoided by turning left. It did not grasp and "eat" this object because it was still "digesting." The same states were active as the robot approached the object it had first encountered. It also avoided this object by turning left: It was still "digesting," and thus did not grasp and "eat" the object. Finally, between time steps 8 and 9, it had finished "digesting" and started to look for food again; that is, the "Detect_Food" module was activated.

To gain more insights about Myrmix and to learn about it in greater detail, the interested reader is encouraged to work through programming example "Myrmix," on the internet page.

Ghengis

We now turn to a different robot, Ghengis (figure 7.9). Ghengis is challenging, because it has many sensors and motors to control and to coordinate. Ghengis is a hexapod (six-legged) robot built at MIT (Brooks 1989). It is a by-now classic example of how the subsumption architecture can be used to control a robot's behavior.

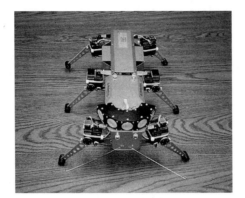

Figure 7.9   The six-legged walking robot Ghengis, built at the MIT AI Lab. Each of Ghengis's 6 legs has two degrees of freedom (up-down, forward-backward). It has 12 model airplane servo motors, 12 force sensors (2 for each leg), 6 pyroelectric infrared sensors (to measure heat), 2 inclinometers (to measure the angle between the body and the horizontal plane), and 2 front whiskers (to measure touch). It is about 35 cm long, has a leg span of 25 cm, and weighs about 1 kg. Four onboard micro-processors are linked by a 62.5K-baud token ring. The robot has 1 Kbyte of RAM and 10 Kbytes of EPROM. It is powered by three batteries (from Brooks 1989, p. 257, reprinted with permission).

An important goal of the Ghengis project was to demonstrate that coherent behavior can be achieved using a distributed architecture without central control. Moreover, Ghengis is an example of how an architecture can be built *incrementally* by designing one layer of competence, testing and debugging it, and then adding new layers on top of those already functioning. Each of the robot's six legs has two degrees of freedom (lift and shoulder, that is, up-down and forward-backward). It has 12 motors, 12 force sensors (to measure forces on the joints of the legs), 6 pyroelectric sensors (to measure heat), an inclinometer (to measure the angle between the robot's body and the horizontal plane) and 2 whiskers (to measure touch).

Ghengis was designed to walk over rough terrain and to follow people. Its control architecture has been implemented using the subsumption approach. It has 8 layers of competence, with a total of 57 augmented finite state machines controlling its walking behavior. We restrict our discussion here of the control architecture underlying Ghengis to the two layers that together make the robot walk in a simple way. The remaining six layers essentially improve the robustness of this walking behavior. (For a discussion of the complete architecture, the reader is referred to Brooks 1989.) Here

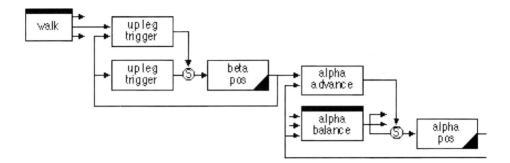

Figure 7.10 Part of Ghengis's control layers. The figure shows the network of AFSMs that together produce the robot's walking behavior. Only two—standup and simple-
walk—out of the eight layers of competence underlying the complete control architecture are shown. There are a total of 32 AFSMs, 30 of which implement 6
identical copies, 1 for each leg, of a network of 5 AFSMs. The remaining 2 state
machines implement the global coordination enabling the robot to walk: the "Alpha-
Balance" machine tries to keep the sum of the leg swing angles (angles of the *alpha*
motors) to zero, and the 'Walk" machine sequences the lifting of the individual legs.
Note that there are different types of AFSMs, indicated by boxes without a band on
top, with a solid band, and with a filled triangle in their bottom right corner. The
AFSMs without bands are used for each leg, that is, they are repeated six times. The
AFSMs with solid bands are unique, and the AFSMs with a filled triangle in their
bottom right corner control the actuators (*alpha* and *beta* motors) of the robot
(adapted from Brooks 1989, p. 259).

we focus on the main principles underlying the subsumption
approach. Figure 7.10 shows the network of AFSMs that implement the first two layers, standup and simple-walk. We refer to
the motors on each of Ghengis's legs as either an *alpha* motor (for
*a*dvance) or an *beta* motor (for *b*alance). Alpha motors swing the
legs back and forth; beta motors lift the legs up and down. In other
words, the alpha and beta motors implement the two degrees of
freedom of each leg referred to above.

Two layers of competence enable the robot to walk: the standup
layer and the simple-walk layer.

THE standup LAYER
The standup layer is implemented with two AFSMs per leg,
"Alpha_Pos" and "Beta_Pos." These two machines store the
desired positions for the *alpha* and *beta* motors, respectively, and
ensure that the motors actually receive instructions to assume those
positions. When the robot is started up, the values stored in the
"Alpha_Pos" and "Beta_Pos" AFSMs make the robot assume a
stance position.

THE `simple-walk` LAYER

Simple walking behavior is achieved by adding additional AFSMs to the already functioning `standup` layer. Together, this additional network of machines constitutes the second layer of competence, the `simple-walk` layer. This layer is implemented by means a number of state machines: Six "Leg_Down" machines, one for each leg, read the up-down position of the legs. Whenever a leg is not in the down position, the respective "Leg_Down" machine tries to set the leg down by writing the appropriate commands to the "Beta_Pos" machine. Next, a global "Alpha_Balance" machine is added that notices the *alpha* position (forward swing) of each of the six legs. It sums the six position values, treating a straight-out position of a leg as 0, a forward position as positive, and a backward position as negative. "Alpha_Balance" then sends the same message to all six "Alpha_Pos" machines that increments, decrements, or leaves unchanged each leg's current *alpha* position, depending on the sum "Alpha_Balance" computes. The main result is that if one leg moves forward, all other legs are instructed to move backward slightly.

Then six "Alpha_Advance" machines are added, one for each leg, to monitor the output of the "Beta_Pos" machine. Each time an "Alpha_Advance" machine notices that the corresponding leg is raised, it makes that leg move forward by supressing the signal coming from the global "Alpha_Balance" machine. This effectively means that if a leg is raised, that leg moves forward, while all other legs swing backward slightly to compensate. This illustrates the subsumption mechanism: The forward-swinging leg does not receive the instruction to move backward issued by the "Alpha_Balance" machine, because the "Alpha_Advance" machine suppresses it. Next an "Up_Leg_Trigger" machine is added, again one each for all six legs. An "Up_Leg_Trigger" machine lifts the corresponding leg by suppressing the messages from the "Leg_Down" machine and writing the appropriate commands to the "Beta_Pos" machine.

Finally, a "walk" machine is added. This global machine coordinates the robot's walking behavior by sending appropriate trigger messages to each of the six "Up_Leg_Trigger" machines. If an "Up_Leg_Trigger" machine receives such a trigger message, it lifts its associated leg. This in turn triggers a reflex to swing the leg forward (via the "Alpha_Advance" machine), and then the appropriate "Leg_Down" machine forces the leg to move to the down position. At the same time all other legs currently not moving forward, that is, all legs still on the ground, move backward, thus moving the robot forward. The "walk" machine can be used to implement different walking patterns, also called *gaits*. Brooks himself has experimented with two types of gaits. One gait, the alternating, tripod gait, is implemented by simultaneously instructing three out of the six legs to lift. This is achieved by sending the appropriate trigger messages to the "Up_Leg_Trigger" machine of each of the legs to be lifted. The other gait produces a back to front ripple gait by sending a trigger message to a different leg every 0.4 seconds.

In sum, the `standup` and `simple-walk` layers enable Ghengis to walk. Note, however, the architecture that drives Ghengis makes no provision for feedback. The robot is thus insensitive to the particular terrain over which it walks, resulting in significant roll-and-pitch behavior as the robot walks over obstacles. To compensate for this effect, Brooks has added additional layers that compensate for rough terrain. In essence, these layers use sensory feedback from the legs to adjust the gait (walking) pattern. For example, the `force-balancing` layer (not shown in figure 7.10) monitors the force on each leg and causes a leg to back off if that force rises beyond a predetermined threshold. Finally, layers have been added that enable the robot to walk only when something is moving nearby (the `prowling` layer), and to follow moving objects such as a slow-walking person (the `steered-prowling` layer). It is important to note that these additional behaviors have been implemented by adding only a very few AFSMs to the original architecture described above. For example, the `steered-prowling` layer was implemented by means of one single AFSM. The important point is that there is no need to represent different behaviors explicitly in the robot: Rather, coherent behavior such as following can emerge from many independent microbehaviors. Moreover, there is very little centralized control; the greater part of the walking behavior is implemented by means of local asynchronous state machines. As chapter 11 shows, the subsumption approach is an instantiation of the principle of parallel, loosely coupled processes.

One of the fascinating results to emerge from experiments involving the subsumption-equipped robot Ghengis is that coherent, robust real-time behavior can be achieved by having relatively independent layers working in parallel. Ghengis and Myrmix are very simple robots. The question that immediately arises is whether the subsumption approach also works for more complex robots. Toward this end, let us examine a highly complex robot, Cog.

Cog: Subsumption and Beyond

Cog is a humanoid robot developed over the last few years at the MIT Artificial Intelligence Laboratory, again by Rodney Brooks and his collaborators (Brooks 1994, in press; Brooks and Stein 1993). "Humanoid" simply means anthropomorphic, "like a human." The goal of the Cog project is to study human-level intelligence. Two important hypotheses underlie the Cog philosophy. First, human-like intelligence requires humanlike interactions with the world. A large part of what it means to be human is to have interactions with other humans. Such interactions require a humanlike body. Second, high levels of intelligence can be achieved with the principles outlined in the subsumption architecture. This amounts to saying that intelligence is emergent from many, relatively independent processes, and moreover, that these processes are based on sensory-motor couplings with only little internal processing. We discuss this important design principle in more detail in chapters 10 and 11. For now, let us point out the reason for the project's name: Obviously, "Cog" stands for "Cognition," but it also stands for the little cogs on a cog wheel such as those you find in watches and transmission boxes. Translated, this means that intelligence can be achieved by many very simple processes. How far Brooks and his colleagues will get with this approach is an empirical question. We return to this issue in various places throughout the book.

Let us now scrutinize the Cog project to allow us to inspect the subsumption architecture further. As originally proposed, the subsumption architecture did not include learning. It was applied mainly to comparatively simple robots. As a consequence, some of the hard problems of building autonomous agents had not really emerged in working with this architecture, including complex sensor and actuator processing, extending the architecture by building on top of many already existing layers, and behavior control. Because it had been applied only to relatively simple robots, there was always the question of whether it would scale to more complex robots and ultimately to human-level intelligence. Cog is an attempt at answering at least some of these problems. Let us look at each in turn.

Cog has many degrees of freedom. Figure 7.11 depicts the robot and provides a short description of these degrees of freedom. It has arms and hands capable of complex motor behavior. Moreover, it has a complex visual system. The eyes, consisting of two cameras each, can move in ways and at speeds comparable to those of human eyes. Thus, the question arises of whether simple sensor-motor couplings will be sufficient to control the robot or whether more complex internal processing will be required in order to achieve high levels of intelligence. As it turns out, if physics is exploited in the right way, often simple sensory-motor couplings can achieve surprisingly sophisticated behaviors (see also chapter 13). Marjanovic, Scassellati, and Williamson (1996), three of Brooks's collaborators, have successfully applied simple neural networks for sensory-motor control. In complex systems like Cog, and even in simpler ones like Ghengis, it has become clear that when additional layers have to be added on top of existing ones, the latter may have to be modified with additional suppression and inhibition links. Thus, the principle that once in place, layers do not need to be changed, cannot be strictly maintained.

Despite the surprisingly sophisticated behaviors achieved through sensory-motor couplings, it has turned out to be necessary to include learning in Cog to achieve coherent behavior. According to Brooks and Stein (1993), behavior control is achieved by "... many pathways between sensors and actuators ... each one contributing to some aspect of the resulting behavior of the system" (p. 126). Note that this view contrasts sharply with existing centralized notions of behavior control. The jury is still out on whether this principle can be maintained for highly complex systems. More work on complex robots like Cog will shed light on this issue.

7.4 Conclusions: The Subsumption Approach to Designing Intelligent Systems

Let us now summarize what we can learn about the subsumption architecture from our three examples.

Engineering and Cognitive Science

The subsumption architecture encompasses a set of engineering principles, outlined in section 7.2, about how to build robots. They

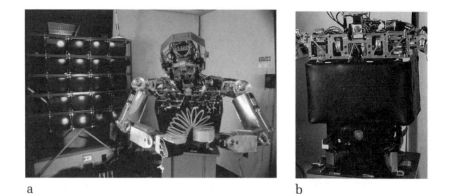

a   b

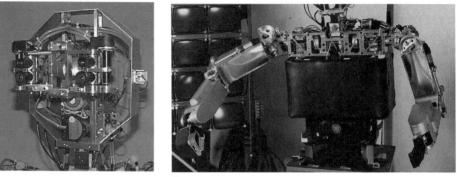

c   d

Figure 7.11 The humanoid robot Cog. It is designed as an anthropomorph, that is, it should be similar to a human in shape and size. Cog has many degrees of freedom that make it difficult to achieve coherent behavior. (a) Overview of the robot. (b) Cog's torso has six degrees of freedom: the waist bends side to side and front to back, the "spine" can twist, and the neck tilts side to side and front to back and twists left to right. (c) Cog's visual system consists of four cameras, two for each eye: one for peripheral vision, the other for foveal vision in the center of the visual field. Each eye can rotate up, down, and sideways at speeds comparable to those of humans. (d) Cog's arms and shoulders move with six degrees of freedom, two each at the shoulder, the elbow, and the wrist. Cog also has many sensors, for example, for measuring the forces at the joints. In addition, it has an auditory system, and there are plans to cover the robot with skin sensors. For those interested in technical detail, Cog is controlled by an offboard computer, that is, the computer does not sit in Cog's head. It is an MIMD computer consisting of up to 239 processor nodes (only a small portion of which are currently in operation). The nodes, consisting of Motorola 68332 microprocessors, are connected to one another in a network. The distributed nature of Cog's computer system is conducive to distributed implementation of the layers of control in the manner of subsumption architecture (reprinted with permission).

include specifying levels of competence and designing layers of control using augmented finite state machines. All the layers in a subsumption architecture receive signals from the sensors and can directly influence the motor system without passing through other layers. Each layer has a certain autonomy and functions independently (except for suppression and inhibition links). The lower levels are designed first, leading to a fully functioning robot. Higher layers are built on top of the lower ones incrementally. The layers implement direct sensor-motor couplings with relatively little internal processing. This philosophy leads to robust real-time behavior in the real world.

Subsumption is sometimes criticized as being an engineering principle that bears little relationship to designing intelligent systems. However, if we look at the underlying principles more closely, we find that they implement important cognitive science principles. First and most important, subsumption represents a radical departure from functional decomposition as depicted in figure 7.1. This new way of thinking leads to different questions being asked. Rather than asking how to integrate and process sensory information centrally, the questions are about the sensory-motor couplings. There is a change in focus from the brain, from thinking and high-level processes, to the interaction with the environment. We have argued this point all along. The subsumption architecture was the starting point for this change in focus, and it is therefore of historical importance for the field of embodied cognitive science. Second, the subsumption architecture is strongly coupled with the notion of embodiment. As we saw in chapter 4, when we have an embodied system, we must concern ourselves with how to embed the control architecture into the agent.

Whenever there is a physical system, we can potentially exploit its physics. For example, in a real, walking robot, we can exploit the friction generated because gravity is acting on the robot automatically. Third, subsumption outlines a different way to achieve behavior control, a fundamental issue in the study of intelligence. Having many independent processes is very different from having centralized control processes (see chapter 11). Fourth and finally, subsumption combines robot design with evolutionary principles. The idea that once a particular competence is in place it should no longer be changed is motivated from evolutionary considerations.

Design Method or Design Philosophy

One way of looking at subsumption is as a particular design methodology (as described in a number of examples in this chapter). The other is as a synonym for the whole field of behavior-based robotics. Whereas in very simple cases, subsumption can be applied very much in its "pure," original form, in more complex cases, its rather rigid principles give way to more flexible ideas. For example, in Cog, neural networks have been used for motor control. Thus, the formalism of augmented finite state machines in not really essential to the subsumption architecture. The concept of an "augmented" finite state machine implies that one does not have to adhere very strictly to a particular formalism. It is an interesting observation that the farther away we move from 1986, when the original paper on the subsumption architecture was published, the less the papers employ the term "subsumption." From this we should not conclude that the general design philosophy of subsumption has become obsolete, but rather that we should not adhere to literally to the technical details of the design method. In this sense, the design principles that we introduce in chapter 10 are all compatible with the subsumption architecture.

One of the main problems in the literature on subsumption is a terminological rather than a conceptual one. As we already indicated, the term "behavior" should be used to describe system-environment interaction; it is inappropriate to use it for an internal structure, for a module. An additional problem pointed out in the literature is that the suppression and inhibition links must be prewired at design time. This is how behavior control is implemented. If the agent has the task of pushing chairs into a corner, appropriate suppression and inhibition links have to account for this: The robot sometimes has to avoid obstacles, but when those obstacles happen to be chairs, it has to push them. But even the restriction that suppression and inhibition links have to be prewired can be relaxed without sacrificing the basic philosophy.

Issues to Think About

Issue 7.1: From Earwigs to Humans?

Rodney Brooks's (1986) seminal paper on the subsumption architecture is probably the most quoted paper in embodied cognitive science. It is, in a sense, the idea with which the field embodied cognitive science started. When a scientific field undergoes a paradigm shift, critics will always try to salvage the existing positions. Most often, researchers endorsing the old paradigm acknowledge that the new ideas have interesting aspects, but also have some intrinsic limitations that will prevent them from replacing the existing ones entirely. This is precisely what David Kirsh (1991) tried to do in "Today the Earwig, Tomorrow Man?" His reply to Brooks's 1986 paper. Kirsh acknowledges that, indeed, Brooks points to serious problems in traditional thinking and suggests an interesting alternative. He then argues that this approach is viable only for simple systems: For human-level intelligence, concepts and symbolic computation will be required. We might summarize his conclusion as follows: "Today the earwig?"—yes, no problem; "tomorrow man?"—no, never. In a later paper (1997), Brooks indirectly replied to Kirsh by proposing a route by which we might eventually indeed achieve human-level intelligence without the need to introduce symbolic concepts explicitly. We used the term "explicitly" to indicate that Brooks would not exclude the possibility that Cog might eventually exhibit behavior that we might want to describe by resorting to the notion "concept." (See also chapter 4 on the frame-or-reference problem). As we might expect, Brooks is referring to the Cog project. We might summarize Brooks's position as follows: "Earwigs?"—of course, we did that a long time ago; "Humans?"—we don't know, but we have good ideas about how to make progress toward higher levels of intelligence in artificial systems.

Issue 7.2: Subsumption—Engineering or Cognitive Science

"Subsumption is an engineering approach—it does not relate to cognitive science" is what we often hear in informal discussions. The subsumption architecture postulates modules. Once these modules have been developed, they are not changed. They can be used as building blocks in a more complex system. Viewed in this way, subsumption indeed has a strong engineering flavor. However, the whole motivation for subsumption has its origins in cognitive science. Brooks made a strong point about AI, about building artificially intelligent systems (Brooks 1991b). He carefully analyzed the characteristics of classical systems and argued why it is not possible with the classical approach to achieve realistic levels of intelligence. Having direct sensory-motor couplings with little internal processing in order to achieve intelligent behavior was a new idea in the study of intelligence at the time subsumption architecture was proposed. Moreover, there is an evolutionary motivation for the architecture: Capacities, once evolved, are carried on to future generations without—or without significant—modification. We believe that, in spite of the approach's engineering flavor, it has important messages for cognitive science.

Points to Remember

- The subsumption architecture was originally proposed as an alternative to traditional symbol-processing approaches to intelligence. In subsumption architecture, the robot's specifications, that is, the desired behaviors, are given as levels of competence that are then implemented as layers, consisting of modules connected by wires. The modules, in turn, are implemented as augmented finite state machines, that is, finite state machines with additional registers to store program code and for timing the duration of states.

- Although the subsumption architecture is ideal from an engineering perspective, it also contributes a number of highly relevant ideas from a cognitive science view. It is based on evolutionary considerations, it realizes sensor-actuator couplings with relatively little internal processing, and it conceptualizes intelligence emergent from a large number of loosely coupled parallel processes.

- The subsumption literature uses the term "behavior" for real behavior resulting from a system-environment interaction as well as for internal modules (the task-achieving behaviors). The term "behavior-based robotics" is sometimes used as a synonym for subsumption, and sometimes more broadly to mean the field of embodied cognitive science.

- The ability, in the subsumption approach, to develop robot architectures incrementally has contributed greatly to its popularity. Layers of control can function independently and need not await signals from higher-level layers (although there can be some interaction).

- In spite of their simplicity, subsumption-based robots are surprisingly robust.

- The subsumption approach has been used in a number of robots performing behaviors of varying complexity, from insect walking

(Ghengis), to food collection (Myrmix), to humanlike interactions (Cog).

- The "philosophy" underlying subsumption is one of cheap robots that have to perform in a real world rather than in an artificial one.

Further Reading

Brooks, R. A. (1986). A robust layered control system for a mobile robot. *IEEE Journal of Robotics and Automation, RA-2* (April), 14–23; also published as *MIT AI Memo 864*, September 1985. (The first publication concerning the subsumption architecture.)

Ferrell, C. (1994). Robust adaptive locomotion of an autonomous hexapod. In P. Gaussier and J.-D. Nicoud (Eds.), *Proceedings of the From Perception to Action Conference* (pp. 66–77). Los Alamitos, CA: IEEE Computer Society Press. (A description of the robot Hannibal.)

Gat, E., Rajiv, D., Ivlev, R., Loch L., and Miller, D. P. (1994). Behavior control for exploration of planetary surfaces. *IEEE Transactions on Robotics and Automation 10*, 78–95. (A description of the control architecture of a protoype of the robot which has been sent to Mars.)

Mahadevan, S., and Connell, J. (1992). Automatic programming of behavior-based robots using reinforcement learning. *Artificial Intelligence, 55*, 311–365. (A paper applying reinforcement learning to a real robot (also to a simulated one). Interesting results can be achieved with modifications of Q-learning (see chapter 14) by using a clustering procedure.)

In chapter 4, we introduced the term "emergence." This chapter is about emergence to the maximum degree. The study of artificial evolution and artificial life has shown that many of the phenomena we observe in nature, from the organization of the brain to the stripes on the fur of the tiger, are not preprogrammed in the genes —at least not directly—but emerge in an organism's interaction with the environment as it develops. Also, behavior, as we have seen, can often be produced in simple, cheap, and elegant ways by exploiting emergence. The field of artificial life capitalizes on evolution and emergence, and in this lies its fascination. In this chapter, we would like to convey at least the essence of this fascination.

We have already encountered a number of different types of agents. All have involved a great deal of work on the part of the designer. There is an ongoing debate as to how much should or can be hand designed, and what should be done otherwise. Humans have strong biases in their thinking because of the way they are built and interact with their environments. Thus, their designs are always biased and perhaps they miss some important ideas. For example, the means of locomotion that evolved in the creatures of Karl Sims (e.g., 1994a)—as we will see—are often truly surprising, are sometimes even funny, and do not directly relate to anything known in biological or artificial systems. The pertinent knowledge that constrains our thinking is largely implicit: We are not even aware of it. Given these biases, it might be better to let evolution do the work for us. If we could put evolution into algorithmic form, we could let evolution come up with agent architectures or even entire agents. These algorithms would not suffer from constraints by implicit knowledge—in an algorithm everything is explicit—so this might result in designs that we would not have thought of. But of course, even in artificial evolution the designer always has to make decisions that bias the result.

We have already encountered evolution in a number of places. Remember that Braitenberg type 6 vehicles were chosen from a set of vehicles running around on a table and copied, and both the vehicle chosen and the copy put back on the table. Errors could occur during copying. Some vehicles dropped to the floor. We saw that, in some sense, this is a model of Darwinian evolution. We also mentioned evolutionary approaches when discussing autonomy: Evolved agents are potentially more autonomous because after a number of generations, it is difficult to know "what is going on" inside the agents. It is therefore difficult to control them, to get them to do what we want them to do. We have encountered another example of evolution in the subsumption architecture, which was explicitly motivated by evolutionary considerations. For example, once a particular layer has been built and works well, it is changed no more, but rather is used as it is.

The field of artificial evolution started in the 1960s with developments by John Holland and L. J. Fogel in the United States, and by Ingo Rechenberg in Germany. Holland's breed of evolutionary algorithms are called *genetic algorithms*, or GAs (DeJong 1975; Goldberg 1989, Holland 1975); Fogel's *evolutionary programming*, or EP (Fogel 1962; Fogel 1995); and Rechenberg's *evolution strategies* or ESs (Rechenberg 1973; Schwefel 1977). Holland was interested in adaptation in natural systems, Fogel and Rechenberg more in exploiting evolutionary algorithms for optimization. All share a strong belief in the power of evolution. Although from an algorithmic perspective these three types of procedures have important differences, for our purposes these differences are not important. (For a comparison of the three approaches, the interested reader is referred to Bäck and Schwefel 1993.)

Artificial evolution is closely related to the field of artificial life, or ALife. Biologists have long been interested in applying evolutionary techniques to study the nature and the origins of life. Similarly they have been interested in the nature of evolution. These interests, together with autonomous agents and aspects of nonlinear dynamics and chaos, form the not-well-defined discipline of artificial life. Christopher Langton of the Santa Fe Institute for nonlinear dynamics, who organized the first conference on artificial life, defined as follows:

Artificial Life is the study of man-made systems that exhibit behaviors characteristic of natural living systems. It complements the traditional biological sciences concerned with the analysis of living organisms by attempting to synthesize life-like behaviors within computer and other artificial media. By extending the empirical foundation upon which biology is based beyond the carbon-

chain life that has evolved on Earth, Artificial Life can contribute to theoretical biology by locating life-as-we-know-it within the larger picture of life-as-it-could-be. (Langton 1989, p. 1)

Autonomous agents are considered part of this endeavor because they represent an attempt to create systems, namely intelligent creatures, that indeed show characteristics of natural living systems. Given an appropriate level of abstraction, we have indeed seen behaviors of autonomous agents that are in some sense "lifelike." Artificial life is mostly concerned with computer simulations, with virtual creatures inhabiting virtual worlds (the artificial life agents introduced in chapter 1). Figure 8.9 shows a typical application. In contrast, we have been concerned so far with real-world agents. We have seen that computer simulations can support the design of real-world agents. Evolutionary approaches are a case in point. The simulation studies of artificial life in general can be expected to make interesting contributions to autonomous agents and to the field of embodied cognitive science.

In this chapter, we show that artificial evolution can be put to work for autonomous agent design. This approach is also called "evolutionary robotics." (e.g., Harvey et al. 1997) We start by discussing some of the fundamental concepts of evolutionary theory, namely random selection and cumulative selection, genotype, phenotype, and reproduction. We then outline various ways in which evolution can be—and has been—employed to design agents. The first example concerns the evolution of a control architecture for the Distributed Adaptive Control agent that we encountered in chapter 5. We then introduce some variations on the basic algorithms frequently used in the literature. Next an example of the evolution of a controller for walking in a simulated insect is shown next. In nature the neural system quite obviously never evolves after the body is full grown; rather, as the organism grows, the neural substrate develops also, or to put it differently: There is always coevolution of morphology (shape) and control. Karl Sims' approach takes this into account. Sims succeeds, as we show, in evolving fascinating creatures with surprising behaviors. We then move on to the Artificial Evolutionary System, an attempt to model actual developmental processes as they occur in natural systems. The section following concerns evolution on robot hardware. Using an example of a robot that learns to recharge its batteries at the right point in time, we discuss the pros and cons of this approach. We then look at some additional examples of ALife agents, starting with the artificial fish created by Demetri Terzopoulos. These fish are especially interesting because, like Sims' creatures, these fish behave in a simulated physical environment. Moreover, they also exhibit interesting group behaviors, which is subsequently discussed. We close the chapter with some methodological considerations.

8.1 Basic Principles

Cumulative Selection

In our presentation here, we largely follow Richard Dawkins' excellent and entertaining book, *The Blind Watchmaker* (1988). As the title suggests, evolution is seen as a watchmaker, a designer of sorts that builds wonderful things, but has no particular goal: There are no specifications or requirements to be fulfilled. Dawkins points out the fundamental distinction between random selection and cumulative selection. Let us look at random selection first.

Assume that a monkey sits in front of a computer and types letters randomly. Even though his key strokes are entirely random, there is a certain—though extremely small—probability that at some point he will have typed Shakespeare's *Hamlet*. To make things a bit easier, let us look at one simple sentence from *Hamlet*, in which the title character discusses with Polonius the shape of a cloud. Remember the dialogue in which Hamlet points out various shapes of animals and Polonius always goes along with whatever Hamlet suggests? The final shape Hamlet proposes is a weasel: "Methinks it is like a weasel." Including the blank spaces between the words, the sentence has 28 characters. There are 27 possible letters, again including the blank space. This yields 27^{28} possible arrangements of the letters, a very large number indeed. The chance that the target sentence will be reproduced during the monkey's lifetime is virtually nil. Even if we let a computer program, which can generate thousands of random alternatives a second, do the work, it would have almost no chance of producing the right sentence during the computer's lifetime. Thus, if the sentences are simply produced at random without further considerations, the goal cannot be achieved. In other words, *random selection* in this case is an entirely useless strategy. Something more is needed.

generation	winner sentence	distance to target
0	WDLDMNLT DTJBKWIRZREZLMQVOP .	25
10	WDLDMNLT DTJBSWIRZREZLMQVOP .	24
20	MDLDMNLS ITJISWHRZREZ MECS P.	20
30	MELDINLS IT ISWPRKE Z WECSEL.	8
40	METHINGS IT ISWLIKE B WECSEL.	4
43	METHINKS IT IS LIKE A WEASEL.	0

Figure 8.1 Cumulative selection. The original sentence typed by the monkey is given at the top (generation 0). On the right, the distance to the target sentence is given (that is, the number of incorrect letters out of the target 28). Then a number of new sentences are generated by randomly changing one of the letters in the previously generated sentence. From these, the best one—the one closest to the target—is chosen. The procedure is repeated until, after 43 generations, the target sentence has been obtained.

Let us now change the procedure. Instead of simply generating random sequences of letters, we start from a given, randomly generated sentence, say WDLDMNLT DTJBKWIRZREZLMQVOP. We now generate a number of sentences by copying this sentence and randomly changing, say one letter in the string. Out of these newly generated sentences we select the one that is closest to the target sentence METHINKS IT IS LIKE A WEASEL. We can assess this by simply counting the number of correct letters in the correct positions. The winner might be WDLDMNLT DTJBSWIRZREZLMQVOP. Figure 8.1 continues the development. After 43 generations, we arrive at the target sentence. Note the difference: 43 generations as opposed to 27^{28}!

This example demonstrates the power of *cumulative selection* in contrast to random selection. The alternatives were generated starting from a particular sentence by making random changes in individual positions. These changes are also called *mutations*. Because only the best among the newly generated sentences is selected for further evolution, its "good properties," that is, the correct letters in the right position, are generally retained generation to generation (with the exception of small mutations). Thus, the term "cumulative selection": good properties accumulate rather than get lost in a random process. Of course, this is not a realistic model of natural evolution. In nature there is no "target sentence"—nature has no goal in mind. In nature, those individuals that survive long enough in the competition for resources will reproduce. Depending on their ecological niche, various properties

a.

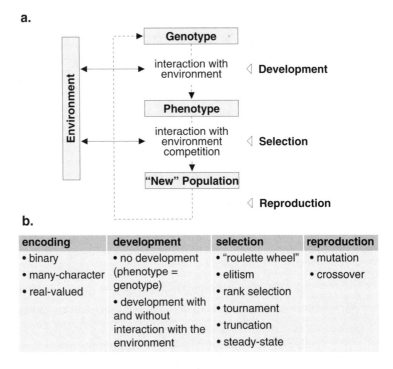

b.

encoding	development	selection	reproduction
• binary	• no development (phenotype = genotype)	• "roulette wheel"	• mutation
• many-character		• elitism	• crossover
• real-valued		• rank selection	
	• development with and without interaction with the environment	• tournament	
		• truncation	
		• steady-state	

Figure 8.2 Overview of the process of evolution. (a) The main components. The genotype is translated into a phenotype through a process of development. The phenotypes compete with one another in their ecological niche, and the winners are selected (selection) to reproduce (reproduction), leading to new genotypes. (b) Genetic algorithms can be classified according to a number of dimensions: encoding scheme, nature of developmental process, selection method, and reproduction (genetic operators). Mitchell (1997, pp. 166–175) discusses the pros and cons of these various methods in detail. We point out some of these pros and cons in our examples.

will be important for survival (eyes, limbs, body, size, speed). These properties are encoded in the individual's genes. The set of all genes is called the organism's *genotype*.

The Evolutionary Process

Figure 8.2 offers an overview of the evolutionary process. Evolution always works within populations of individuals. In nature these are creatures; in artificial evolution, they are often solutions to problems. Each individual agent carries a description of some of its features (color of its hair, eyes, and skin; body size; limb size; shape of nose, head, etc.). This description is called its *genome*. The term "genotype" refers to the set of genes contained in the genome. It is used to express the difference between the genetic setup and the final organism, the *phenotype*. The genome consists of a number of genes, in the simplest case of which one gene describes one feature. Genes are identified by their position within the genome. If the individual members of the population to be investigated are of the same species, they all have the same numbers of genes, and the genes are at the same location in the genome. But the values of the genes can differ. The values of all genes of an individual are determined before it starts to live and never change during its life.

Through a process of *development*, the genotype is translated into a phenotype. In this process, genes are expressed, that is, they exert their influence on the phenotype, in various ways. The growing organism's interaction with its environment determines the precise ways in which the genes are expressed. In the example from *Hamlet*, the genotype is simply the string of letters. There is no process of development. So, for this specific case, the phenotype is the same as the genotype. In terms of natural evolution, this is unrealistic. There is always development: The egg has to mature into an organism. But in artificial evolution, the phenotype and the genotype are indeed often the same. If we remain aware that we are dealing with algorithms, rather than with a model of natural evolution, there is absolutely nothing wrong with this. Then the phenotype competes in its ecological niche for resources with other individuals of the same or other species. The competition in the *Hamlet* example consists of measuring the distance to the target sentence: the smaller the distance, the fitter the individual. The winners of this competition are selected (*selection* process), which leads to a new population. Because of how they were selected, the members of this new population have higher average fitness than the one before. The individuals in this new population can now reproduce. Evolutionary approaches characteristically work with populations of individuals rather than individuals only. There are many variations of how selection can be done (see below).

So far we have discussed only asexual reproduction, in which an individual duplicates only its own genotype, possibly with some small random mutation. In the *Hamlet* example, only one sentence was involved in reproduction, so the reproduction was asexual. There is also sexual reproduction, in which two individuals exchange parts of their genotype to produce new genotypes for their offspring. The most common type of sexual reproduction is called crossover (see below); it is often used in combination with mutation. Finally, there is a *reproduction* process. Reproduction, like selection, comes in many variations.

Development, selection, and reproduction are closed processes in themselves: They receive a certain input and deliver some output. For example, the development process receives a genotype as input and eventually produces a phenotype as output. But the phenotype cannot influence the genotype. Because we are dealing with algorithms, it would be no problem to have the phenotype influence the genotype. But that has not been systematically explored, presumably because that would correspond to a so-called Lamarckian position. According to Lamarck, an organism's learned properties can be passed on genetically to the offspring.

The scheme in figure 8.2b can be used to classify different evolutionary approaches to autonomous agent design: Some approaches comprise all these components in nontrivial ways, some lack development—in fact, most evolutionary algorithms lack development, and some have it, but without interaction with the environment. Additional classification can be made according to the way the features are encoded in the genome, the type of selection, and the kind of reproduction performed. We provide only a short review and give examples of the most common kinds of evolutionary approaches (Many excellent textbooks include systematic reviews of the various types of algorithms, such as Goldberg 1989; and Mitchell 1997.)

8.2 An Introduction to Genetic Algorithms: Evolving a Neural Controller for an Autonomous Agent

To make matters more concrete, let us look at an example (also available as a programming example on our Internet page). For the sake of simplicity, let us assume that we have a scheme in which all members of the population are always involved in the same kind of activity: developing and competing in the ecological niche, or reproducing. This is called a *generational* scheme (in contrast to a *steady-state* scheme, in which individuals are, asynchronously, involved in different kinds of activities). Moreover, let us assume that the size of the population is held constant over time.

We are already familiar with the Distributed Adaptive Control architecture, having discussed it in chapter 5. There, the obstacle avoidance reflexes based on collision detectors were given in the system design. Through an associative neural network, the agent learned, over time, to avoid collisions altogether using the IR sen-

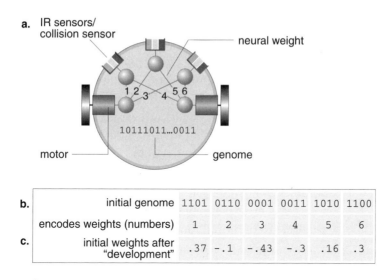

b.

initial genome	1101	0110	0001	0011	1010	1100
encodes weights (numbers)	1	2	3	4	5	6
c. initial weights after "development"	.37	−.1	−.43	−.3	.16	.3

Figure 8.3   Setup of the agent and the genome encoding in the GA experiment. (a) Agent with the sensor-to-motor connections: The weights in the neural network are numbered 1 through 6. The IR sensors and the collision sensors are in the same location. (b) initial genome: It consists of six genes, each having a size of four bits. The position of the gene in the genome determines which weight of the neural network it encodes. (c) Initial weights after "development": There is a trivial "development" process; the weights are calculated as follows: $(v/15) − .5$, where v is the value of the bit string of the gene. This yields values between $−.5$ and $+.5$.

sors. In the example in this chapter, we work differently. Rather than use reflexes based on the collision sensors, we only work with IR sensors and we do not provide any reflexes: we expect them to be evolved, starting from random weights. Figure 8.3a shows the basic setup, which is a variation on the generic robot architecture.

Let us work through the various steps involved in creating the agent. First we have to decide what properties to encode in its genome. In this example, only the sensor-to-motor weights are encoded. Thus, the genome has six genes. The initial values of the genes are chosen randomly (figure 8.3b). These genes are then *expressed*, that is, transformed into traits of the organisms, in this case, the connection weights. This is done by normalization to 1 (dividing by 15) and subtraction of .5 to get weights between −.5 and +.5 (figure 8.3c). Again, to make matters as simple as possible, all individuals live for the same period of time. Two values are associated with each individual, its lifetime and its fitness. Both are initialized to 0. Whenever a collision occurs, the fitness value is reduced by 1. After the lifetime is over, selection takes place, based on the individuals' final fitness values.

Figure 8.4 illustrates selection and reproduction. As always in the field of genetic algorithms, there are many variations, with their advantages and disadvantages. The following selection process was performed here: The individual with the highest fitness was chosen and mated with a randomly chosen individual from the rest of the population (figure 8.4a). The reproduction itself consisted of crossover and mutation, as shown in figure 8.4b. The crossover point was chosen randomly and the corresponding parts of the genome were exchanged to produce two offspring, A and B. The new population is then subjected to a mutation process. Typically, the mutation rates are relatively small; they serve the purpose of keeping variation in the population. It is important that the mutation rates be small to preserve the benefit of cumulative selection, or to put it another way, to keep the good gene combinations around while still exploring new ones. The goal of crossover is to combine partial solutions into complete ones with high fitness. Once a new population of genomes has been generated, the genes can be expressed; that is, the weights can be calculated. Figure 8.5 illustrates the progress in the behavior of these agents over time. In every application of evolutionary methods, we have to specify the size of the population and the number of generations the algorithm was run. The results in figure 8.5 were achieved using a population size of 10, and the simulation was run for 21 generations.

Variations on Evolutionary Methods: Theoretical Issues

As we have already mentioned, there are many variations on evolutionary methods. Like neural networks, evolutionary algorithms are fascinating and seem to exert an inescapable attraction urging the user to play around and tinker with them. Here we present a few variations; for systematic reviews, see, for example, Mitchell 1997.

Encoding Scheme

The most widely used encoding scheme is what we have seem in our earlier example, binary encoding in terms of bit strings. A few others appear elsewhere in this book, such as many-character encodings, as in Eggenberger's Artificial Evolutionary System, or the graph structures used by Karl Sims. The rule here is to use whatever is best suited. Choice of encoding scheme is not a matter of religious devotion to one scheme over all others.

a. selection

1. take the individual with the highest fitness
2. choose another individual from the population at random, irrespective of fitness, for sexual reproduction
3. add the fittest individual to the new population

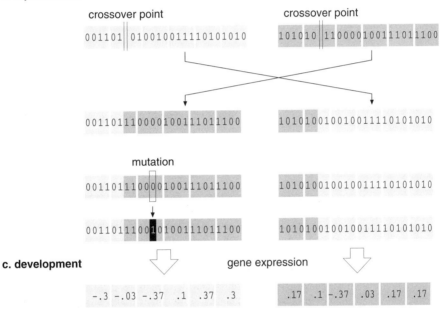

b. reproduction

c. development

Figure 8.4 Selection and reproduction. (a) Selection: After their final fitness values have been determined, individuals are selected for reproduction. The strategy chosen here for selection is as follows: take the highest-ranking individual (highest fitness) and mate it with a randomly chosen individual in the population. This can be viewed as a variation of rank-based selection. (b) Reproduction: The crossover point is chosen at random, and then the corresponding parts of the genome are exchanged to produce two offspring, A and B. Then the entire new population is subjected to a small mutation. In the example, 10 percent of the population was subjected to a mutation of 1 bit. The bit position was determined randomly, and the bit was then flipped. (c) Development: After reproduction, the new genome is expressed to become the new individual.

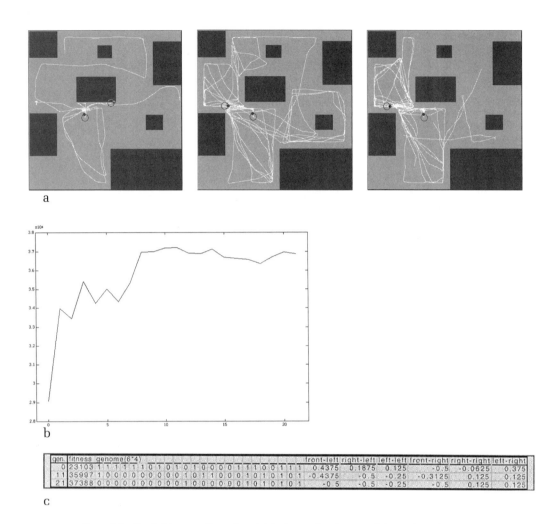

Figure 8.5 Evolution over time. Panel (a) shows the change of the trajectories of generations 0, 11, and 21, panel (b) shows the increase in the average fitness of the population, and panel (c) shows the changes in the genome and the weights of an individual from generations 0, 11, and 21.

Development

As we mentioned, development is often entirely neglected—it may not be necessary at all. In its absence, selection is performed directly on the genotype. There are also trivial forms of development in which the representation in the genome is directly mapped onto the organism's features without interaction with the environment. We have seen this in the example above. More complex, but still lacking interaction with the environment, is Sims' approach. One model that capitalizes on ontogenetic development is Eggenberger's Artificial Evolutionary System.

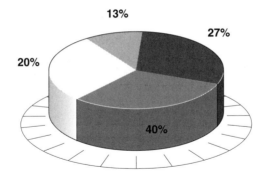

Figure 8.6 Roulette wheel selection. Individuals are selected with a probability that corresponds to their relative fitness within the population. This is represented as the size of their slices of the "fitness pie."

Selection

One gets the impression that researchers in the field have tried virtually any method of selection that even remotely promised to improve their algorithms' performance. All methods have their pros and cons—discussing them in any depth is well beyond the scope of this chapter. One might be tempted simply to take the best individuals and ignore the others. However, that would lead to a quick loss of diversity. Those individuals currently not doing as well as the others may have properties that will prove superior in the long run. Thus, a great deal of attention has been devoted to getting just the right mix of individuals. The problem is sometimes called the exploration-exploitation trade-off. It is related to the diversity-compliance trade-off discussed in chapter 1. The goal is to search the space in the region of the good individuals but still to explore other regions, because the one currently the best may turn out to be only locally optimal.

Holland (1975) proposed using a method in which an individual's probability of being selected is proportional to its fitness. This is also called *roulette wheel sampling*: Spin the roulette wheel and select the individual where it stops. The size of the segment of the roulette wheel for an individual is proportional to its fitness. *Elitism* is often added to various schemes, meaning that the best individuals are copied automatically to the next generation. Figure 8.6 illustrates roulette wheel selection. In rank selection, individuals are chosen with a probability corresponding to their rank (in terms of fitness), rather than their actual fitness value. Tournament selection is based on a series of comparisons of two individuals: through some random procedure that takes their fitness into account, one individual "wins" and is selected for reproduction. Finally, there is a distinction between generational and steady-state selection. As we mentioned above, rather than producing an entirely new population at the same time, in steady-state selection, only a small part of the population changes at any particular time, while the rest is preserved.

Reproduction

The most-often-used genetic operators are mutation and crossover. We have seen both in the example above. Although evolutionary methods are easy to program and play around with, their behavior is difficult to understand. It is still subject to debate how they work and what the best strategies within them are for reproduction and selection. Let us turn to natural evolution for a moment. Once good partial solutions have been found for certain problems, they are kept around and are combined with other good solutions. An example is eyes and visual systems: Once they had been "invented," they were kept around and perhaps slightly improved. In evolutionary algorithms, there is an analogical idea of good "building blocks" that are combined to increasingly better solutions.

Crossover is designed to combine partial solutions into complete ones with high fitness. There are a number of conjectures about why crossover leads to fast convergence while maintaining a high chance of reaching the global optimum. One is the *schema theorem* and, related to it, the *building block hypothesis* (e.g., Goldberg 1989). Schemas are particular patterns of genes that, depending on the algorithm chosen, proliferate in the population. The details need not concern us here; there is an ongoing debate as to the relevance of this theorem to evolutionary methods. The related topic of how useful crossover really is and how it contributes to resolving this trade-off is also still subject to debate (e.g., Srinivas and Patnaik 1994).

The preceding discussion can best be summarized as follows: There is no one best encoding scheme, selection strategy, or genetic operator. It is all a question of having the right balance suited for the particular issues one intends to investigate.

8.3 Examples of Artificially Evolved Agents

The ultimate goal of evolutionary approaches toward autonomous agents is the automated synthesis of an entire agent. This goal clearly has not yet been achieved. What researchers have mostly done thus far is to evolve neural network controllers for a given robot. In this case, the low-level specification is given; that is, the morphology, the types of sensors and their position on the robot, and the types of motor components are fixed. The agent's genotype codes for (i.e., represents) the properties of the neural network, that is, the connectivity, the number and types of neurons, and so forth. Typically, both the control network and the agent are simulated. But experiments have been conducted in which a controller has evolved on a physical robot. This work ranges from experiments in which real robots are used to test controllers evolved in simulation (e.g., Nolfi and Parisi 1995; Salomon 1996) to the evolution of robot control hardware (e.g., Thompson 1995). A more advanced approach would be to evolve both the control networks and the morphology. In this case, the agent's genotype would have to code not only for the details of the control network but also for the robot's body and the physical positioning of the sensors and motor components on its body (limbs, wheels, motors, etc.). A particularly interesting example of this approach is the work by Sims (e.g., 1994a, 1994b), which is summarized below. (For reviews of evolution of agents, see Kodjabachian and Meyer 1995 and; Mataric and Cliff 1996.) In what follows, we describe two examples in more detail. The first illustrates the standard methodology for evolving neural network controllers for a given simulated robot (Beer 1995). The second illustrates how morphology and neural controllers can be evolved (Sims 1994a).

Evolving a Neural Controller for a Simulated Walking Insect

The agent under discussion is a simulated walking insect, also called a hexapod (see figure 8.7a). It has six legs, each of which may be either up or down. There are thus two phases for the legs: first, the stance phase, in which the foot is down, the leg provides support to the body, and the forces it generates contribute to the body's movement; second, the swing phase, in which the foot is up and any forces generated by the leg cause it to swing. Each leg is controlled by an effector (a subsystem for moving a mechanical part) that governs the state of the foot (i.e., whether the foot is up or down) and two effectors that determine the forward and backward torques about the leg's single joint. If there is backward torque, the body moves forward (if it is in balance). "In balance" means that the

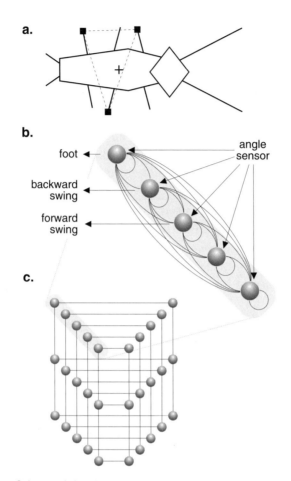

Figure 8.7 Schema of the simulated insect. (a) Body and legs: There are six legs, each with a foot that may be positioned up or down. Horizontally, the legs can move back and forth. The insect shown in this figure is standing on three feet (marked with black squares). The insect must always be in a static balance; in other words, its center of gravity must be within the triangle (or the polygon) formed by the supporting feet (dashed line). The center of gravity is marked with a cross. The insect's antennas are not used in this experiment. (b) Neural controller for legs: Each leg is controlled by a fully connected recurrent network that receives external input from the angle sensors. (c) The coupling between the leg controllers: The marked region corresponds to a leg controller as shown in (b); the recurrent connections are not drawn here. Note that nodes are connected only to neighboring nodes—there is no global, central control (adapted from Beer 1995).

insect stands on at least three legs and its body's center of gravity falls within the triangle (or polygon) spanned by the feet on the ground. Note that this kind of nondynamic walking can be practiced only by creatures having four or more legs: at least three are always needed to keep the balance. See focus 13.1 for an example of dynamic walking.) Each leg is also equipped with a sensor that measures its angle relative to the body axis. This angle sensor enables the agent, loosely speaking, to "know" where its legs are.

Curious about what evolution would come up with, Beer (1995) used genetic algorithms to evolve neural networks for controlling the agent. Thus the agent's morphology, its limbs and how they can be moved were given, as well as the sensors. Figure 8.7b shows the architecture of the neural network Beer used. Each leg employed a network of five nodes with full connectivity. All the nodes were of the continuous, sigmoidal type. Each node received input from its angle sensor. Three of five nodes were associated with the effectors, that is, the muscles—corresponding to the electrical motors in robots; one controlled whether the foot was up or down (if the activation level was 0.5 or greater, the foot was considered to be up, otherwise down), one was for forward swing, and one was for backward swing (the level of activation corresponded to the force applied to the movement). The remaining two nodes were not further connected—the designer left their function unspecified. Thus, each module had 40 parameters: 25 connection weights, 5 weights for the connections from the angle sensor, 5 thresholds (determining the location of the sigmoid), and 5 time constants (determining the slope of the sigmoid). The complete architecture consisted of six leg controllers assumed to be identical and connected to each other as shown in figure 8.7c. It was further assumed that the ipsilateral connections (the connections along one side) were the same on both sides, and that the contralateral connections (connecting the two sides) were also identical for the three left-right pairs. If we now further assume that we have an additional 10 parameters, we get a total of 50 parameters—50 parameters to be optimized using an evolutionary algorithm.

For every evolutionary algorithm, we have to specify the encoding of the parameters, the selection method, and the reproduction operators. In Beer's example, encoding was in terms of bit strings, four bits per parameter; selection was by roulette wheel; the genetic operators were crossover and mutation. The mutation rate was 0.0001. Individuals were subjected to crossover only 60 percent of the time. There was no development process; selection was performed directly on the genotype. Simulations were run for 100 generations with population sizes of 500. The fitness function was defined as the distance the agent moved forward in a fixed amount of time.

Note that the problems the evolutionary algorithm had to solve were far from trivial. For one thing, it had to generate the appropriate motor signals to get the agent to walk. But in addition, it had to maintain the agent's stability, that is, its center of gravity had to be kept within a specified triangle (or polygon, see figure 8.7), otherwise the agent would not be balanced and could not move forward. Let us now look at some results. Eventually, the networks Beer employed evolved a so-called *tripod gait*, in which the front and back legs on each side of the body swing in unison with the middle leg on the opposite side. The tripod gait is found commonly in nature among fast-walking insects. During the evolutionary process, different types of controllers appeared. At the beginning, agents emerged that stood on all six feet (instead of only three) and pushed until they fell. Other agents could swing their legs, but the legs' movements were not coordinated; these agents were able to move forward, but they fell quite often because evolution had not yet solved the balance problem. Finally, there were agents capable of moving forward and keeping stability. They slowly improved over further generations.

In this experiment, no neural network learning occurred. An evolutionary process determined the weights of the connections in the network, just as in the Distributed Adaptive Control experiments described in this chapter. What comes to mind immediately is the idea of combining the two: Some traits would be encoded genetically, others acquired through learning. Indeed, in recent years, there has been work in the autonomous agents field trying to combine the two approaches. In biology, how evolution and learning work together and the combined effects they produce have been the subject of many investigations at least since James Baldwin's seminal publication more than 100 years ago, "A New Factor in Evolution." (Baldwin 1896). Baldwin suggested ways in which learning might benefit evolution, an idea that later became known as the "Baldwin effect."

What can we learn from this example? First, setting up an experiment in artificial evolution is easy. Second, evolution can indeed be used to solve nontrivial design problems. Third, evolution is computationally expensive: Just think of the 50 parameters, the 500 individuals, and the 100 generations involved in Beer's work, then consider all the processing that has to be done for every generation in terms of selection and genetic operators. And fourth, note how much design still has to be done manually to make evolution work: the shape of the agent, its sensors, and its limbs, as well as the structure of the neural networks and how they are embedded in the agent. The only thing evolution does is determine the weights of the connections in the neural network. Let there be no misunderstanding, however: Setting the weights of the connections in a fully recurrent neural network is a very hard task, and evolution does an excellent job of it.

Evolving Morphology and Control: Incorporating a Simulation of a Physical Environment

Let us now look at a more complex example, Karl Sims' virtual creatures (1994a, 1994b). These creatures hold an inescapable fascination—and they are a lot of fun. A number of factors underlie this fascination: First, Sims evolves morphology *and* neural control. This relieves the human designer of having to come up with a fixed design for the entire low-level specification: The designer commitments are pushed one step further back. We examine these below. And second, Sims was one of the first to use a 3-D world of simulated physics in the context of virtual reality applications. Simulating physics includes considerations of gravity, friction, collision detection, collision response, and viscous fluid effects (e.g., in simulated water).

The details of such simulations are not essential for our purposes; what is essential is that the creatures must perform and compete against each other in this virtual world. As we will see, evolution generates some fascinating morphologies for agents that occupy these virtual worlds, and because of the simulated physics, these agents interact in many unexpected ways with the environment.

In developing his agents, Sims needed to specify the representation of the genotype, the process of development, the selection process, and the reproduction strategy.

Representation of the Genotype
Again, we apply the scheme of figure 8.2 to describe Sims' approach. The genotype specifies a directed graph, which is considerably more complex than the bit strings used in the standard

evolutionary algorithm. The genotype specifies how the phenotype is to be generated. This requires an interpreter for the genotype that knows what the specifications mean and how the various parts are to be expressed in the phenotype. Figure 8.8 gives an idea of what this might look like.

Development
In contrast to Beer, Sims uses a procedure development. The phenotype consists of a structure of three-dimensional rigid parts described by a directed graph (see figure 8.8). The developmental process requires an interpreter for these graph structures, depicted on the left side of each panel in the figure. The graph in figure 8.8a, for example, states that two segments are to be simultaneously attached to the existing segment. The shape, length, joint types, angles at which the joints are attached, and various other parameters are all subject to variation by the genetic algorithm; that is, they are subject to mutation and crossover. One of these parameters is the number of times a particular schema is to be applied. In this case, as can be seen on the right of figure 8.8a, this number is four, which leads to the standard, treelike structures shown. The examples in figures 8.8b and 8.8c are somewhat more complicated, but the principle is the same. The developmental procedure always maps the same genotype onto the same phenotype: There is no interaction with the environment during development. The genotype also encodes information about sensors, effectors, and neurons that connect the senors and effectors. The tactile sensors can be put onto all the structures's faces. Light sensors can also be defined in the genotype. Each different morphology (body, limbs, position of sensors) requires a different neural controller to match the morphology's requirements.

Fitness and Selection
Once the phenotypes have been generated, they have to perform in the simulated world of physics. Swimming, walking, jumping, following, and getting control over a cube have been used to evaluate the creatures' fitness. The creature that can swim the longest distance within a given period of time is selected, and similarly for walking and jumping. Figure 8.9a shows creatures that have been evolved for swimming. Figures 8.9b and 8.9c show creatures evolved for walking and jumping, respectively. In the case of following, the average speed at which a creature moves toward a light source is taken as the fitness criterion. In another set of experiments, inspired by nature, the creatures must compete directly for a

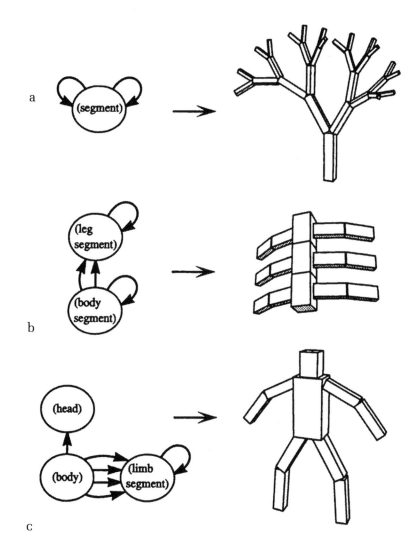

Figure 8.8 Generating a phenotype from the genotype. The genotype specifies a graph structure, the phenotype a (simulated) structure of 3-D parts. In each panel, the graph structure on the left is used to generate the (simulated) physical structure on the right. (a) A tree-structure: The graph indicates that each segment spawns two other segments. Parameters are physical shape of part (this normally comprises several parameters, e.g., shape type, length, height, or diameter), joint type (rigid, revolute, twist, universal, bend-twist, twist-bend, or spherical), joint limits (amount of movement allowed for each degree of freedom, e.g., maximum angle), and number of iterations to be applied. Moreover, a set of neurons is included in each node to be used to connect the neural controller. The connections contain information on where and at what angle to connect the spawned parts. (b) A body and a six-legged creature. The body segment has an iteration maximum of three; the segments of legs, a maximum of two. (c) A humanlike body. (From Sims, 1994a, p. 16, Figure 1, reprinted with permission.)

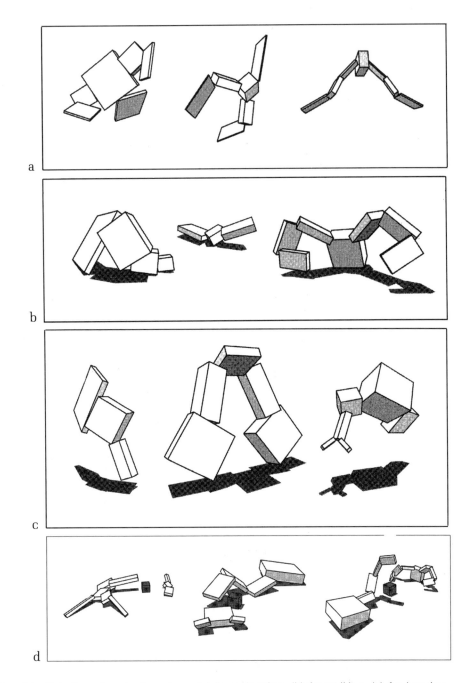

Figure 8.9 Selection of evolved creatures (a) for swimming, (b) for walking, (c) for jumping, and (d) for getting control over a cube. The fitness functions for (a) and (b) were distance traveled, for (c) how high the creature could jump, and for (d) how close the creature was to the cube. Because of the different physical conditions involved— water versus solid ground—strikingly different morphologies evolved in the two environments. Moreover, the ways in which the segments are moved also differ (though this cannot be seen in the figure). In the water, flapping and smooth snakelike or fishlike movements are predominant, whereas on land, walking, crawling, or dragging emerge most often. The creatures that had to compete for a cube (d) were evolved on land. Again, because of the different task environment, as specified by the fitness function, their shapes are noticeably different from those of the other creatures (reprinted with permission).

particular resource. In nature, creatures always have to compete in their ecological niche. In Sims' experiments, they have to try to get control over a cube. The creatures' final distances from the cube were used to calculate their fitness scores (the closer to the cube, the higher the score). Again, the details are not essential for our purposes. Figure 8.9d shows examples of creatures evolved by direct competition. The simulations typically use a population size of 300. Selection is by truncation, meaning that the populaton is "truncated," so that only the agents in the upper, say, 20 percent survive for reproduction. Furthermore, each surviving individual generates a number of offspring proportional to its fitness.

Reproduction
The creatures are then subjected to a reproduction process that includes mutation and crossover. Both operations are more complicated than in the case of simple GAs in which the genotype is simply a bit string. Here, graph structures have to be manipulated appropriately to yield structures that the developmental process can interpret. (For details on the reproduction process, the reader is referred to Sims' original papers 1994a, 1994b).

What can we learn from this example? First, the example shows that it is indeed possible to evolve creatures even if the morphology is not given a priori. Second, the creatures that evolved were surprising and funny. Especially if we look at their ways of locomotion, we find that they can be truly innovative. For example, one creature in figure 8.9b moves by continuously flipping over. Such unexpected things can happen because the search space, that is, the space of possible creatures, is enormous, and the more possibilities there are, the more chances that among them are creatures that can adapt to the demands of the environment. The third lesson follows directly from this point: The larger the search space, the more computation is required. Computation required to evolve these creatures is immense. Not only must we consider the space of connection weights in the neural network, which is bad enough, as we saw in the case of Beer's walking insect: We must also consider the space required by possible morphologies. We know that by introducing constraints, we can cut down computation by orders of magnitude. However, and this is the fourth lesson to be gleaned from the example, the more constraints, the fewer the degrees of freedom, and the less surprise. This is similar to the exploration-exploitation trade-off. If everything is entirely unconstrained, we are certain not to get any convergence, that is, no creatures with good fitness values. Note that in spite of the fact that morphology is not given, those that result are still very constrained. The possible morphologies are composed of particular types of segments joined in a limited number of ways. This certainly helps evolution to converge, but it also forces it in a particular direction. The final lesson that we would like to take from the example is that certain kinds of locomotion that can be evolved are not found in natural systems. One example is a creature that sort of rolls over. We see that evolution, at least artificial evolution, is by no means confined to the organisms we find in nature: It potentially exploits anything that is possible. And this is, among many other things, what makes it so fascinating.

8.4   Toward Biological Plausibility: Cell Growth form Genome-Based Cell-to-Cell Communication

Although vaguely inspired by nature, Sims is not trying to imitate specific natural systems. Natural systems always include a process of development. Although Sims has to translate genotype into phenotype, this process is entirely deterministic: If the genotype is given, the phenotype is determined. Peter Eggenberger, a medical doctor and theoretical physicist, is interested in modeling development from a biological perspective. He wants to create a computer simulation starting from what is currently known about the mechanisms of cell growth. His ultimate goal is to evolve an entire organism: its morphology, its neural substrate, its sensors, and its motor system. In particular, he wants to study the interaction of genetic and environmental factors in development. Remember that this precisely echoes the conclusion drawn from the nature-nurture debate that we raised in chapter 1. Of course, it will be a while before this can be achieved. As a first test, Eggenberger's Artificial Evolutionary System was used to grow simple shapes and controllers for existing robots (Eggenberger 1996, 1997). Because many authors have tackled the latter task, we focus on the first, the evolution of shapes.

The Artificial Evolutionary System is based on the notion of genome-based cell-to-cell communication. What is encoded in the genome in this system is not the organism's structure, but rather the growth processes. Here is how it works: All the cells are placed on the points of a 3-D grid, which is then immersed in a solution of transcription factors: proteins produced by different cells. The

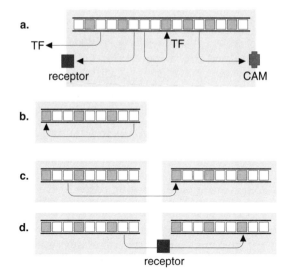

Figure 8.10 Basic mechanisms of the Artificial Evolutionary System. (a) Some basic functions of a gene: production of a transcription factor, formation of receptor cell, creation of a CAM, used by other cells to make connections. This is required to build neural networks. (b) A transcription factor influences a regulatory gene within the same cell. (c) a transcription factor diffusing into another cell. (d) a transcription factor with affinity to a receptor.

concentrations of these transcription factors determine what a cell is going to do next. So let us briefly look at how individual cells "work."

Every cell contains a genome consisting of so-called regulatory genes and structural genes. The regulatory genes determine whether a particular structural gene is turned on. If turned on, the structural genes each perform their predefined functions, namely

- producing a transcription factor (dumping a transcription factor into the environment)
- forming a receptor (forming a receptor on the surface of the cell)
- forming a so-called cell adhesion molecule (CAM) on the surface of a cell
- cell division
- cell death
- searching for partner (searching for matching CAM in the cell environment)

Figure 8.10 illustrates some of these functions. When a transcription factor is produced, its concentration is highest at the location of the cell where it was produced. Further away on the grid, the concentration of this particular factor is lower because of diffusion. Regulatory genes are activated whenever the concentration of a transcription factor at a particular cell's location is high enough. Whether activation occurs depends on concentration and affinity. Affinity is calculated on the basis of geometric properties: The geometric properties of the transcription factors are compared to the geometric properties of the regulatory gene or the receptor protein on the surface of the cell. These geometric properties are represented in the genotype as sequences of four digits—1, 2, 3, and 4—meant to model the four bases of DNA: adenine, thymine, guanine, and cytosine. Figure 8.11 shows the encoding scheme. The typical length of a genome as used in the simulations was eight units. Each unit consisted of two regulatory and two structural genes, for a total of 32 genes (or one regulatory unit and two structural genes, as shown in figure 8.11).

Encoding of the Genotype
At the beginning of a simulation run, a sequence of the four bases is generated at random (figure 8.11a). At each cycle, the cells "read" the concentrations of the transcription factors on the 3-D grid where they are located. Depending on the affinity of these transcription factors with the regulatory genes of the cell and their concentration, the regulatory genes are activated and the structural genes turned on. Figure 8.11b shows how a structural gene is activated. Activation in turn causes the structural genes to perform their function. We have discussed the production of a transcription factor and the formation of a receptor cell. CAMs are used to form connections between cells, connections needed to grow neural networks. CAMs are used together with the function "searching for partner." If a cell "searches for a partner," it looks in the cell environment for a matching CAM. The search radius is encoded in the genome (see figure 8.11c). If a match is found, a connection is established. If the gene for cell division is turned on, the neighboring grid points are searched for an empty space. If all are occupied, the cell does not divide. In other words, cells inside the organism can no longer divide. If the gene for cell death is on, the cell is removed from the grid.

Development, Fitness, and Selection
In this setup, development results from highly complex dynamics. The organism's structure is not predefined in the genome. Figure 8.12 illustrates some of the shapes that have been grown. The goal

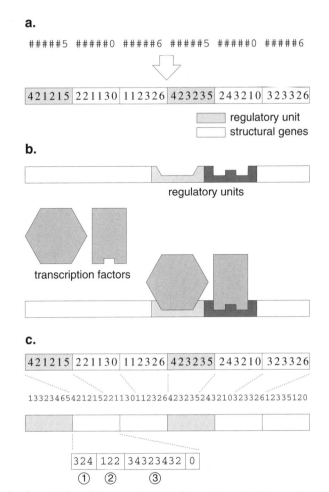

Figure 8.11 Implementation of the genotype. (a) Generation of initial genotype. Initially, a genome
is generated at random. The structure of the gene is given: the position of the genes
in the genome determine their function. "0" is an end-of-gene marker; "6" marks the
end of a structural region, "5" the end of a regulatory one. The positions marked
with "#" are filled with random digits 1 through 4, corresponding to the four bases
of DNA: adenine, thymine, guanine, and cytosine. Panel (b) depicts the matching
process. (c) Details of the encoding. The first three digits (1) in the structural gene
encode the class of substance the gene produces (transcription factor, receptor, or
CAM. The next three digits (2) indicate the range within which a search for a partner
is performed and the diffusion coefficient of the transcription factor. The following
eight digits (3) encode geometric properties of the gene. These digits are used to
generate the geometric properties of the transcription factor the gene produces. The
regulatory gene also contains a region for geometric properties. Affinity is calculated
by comparing the geometric properties of the transcription factor and this region in
the regulatory gene.

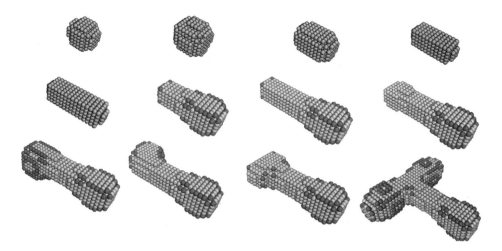

Figure 8.12 Philogenetic development of an organism using the Artificial Evolutionary System. The goal was to evolve T-shapes. A population of 40 individuals was used. The shapes of the best individuals are shown after every six generations. The final shape had emerged after 72 generations. The size of the final organism is about 1,400 cells.

in these examples was to grow organisms of a fixed size with a T-shape. The fitness function in these examples therefore has two components: (1) the number of cells in the final organism, and (2) a measure of "T-shapeness." The fitness function was set to 0 if the number of cells in the organism was more than 4,000. The "T-shapeness" measure was implemented as follows: A 3-D model of a T-shape was defined in Cartesian coordinates, and whenever a cell happened to be placed within this shape, the organism's fitness value was increased, otherwise it was decreased. Each generation consisted of 40 individuals. The final organism emerged after 72 generations.

The procedure, in general, works as follows. Start with a population of 3-D grids; these will eventually host a population of organisms. In each of these grids, put one cell on a grid point. The genome for this cell is initialized to a random sequence of letters, as shown in figure 8.11a. Depending on the initial concentrations of transcription factors, certain genes will be activated. Let the cells do their work, that is, divide, producing transcription factors, a receptor, a CAM, and so forth. Calculate the new concentrations of the transcription factor for each grid point according to the laws of diffusion. This leads to a changed organism and changed levels of transcription factors. Repeat this cycle for all organisms a preset number of times. (We have to be careful not to confuse an organism, that is, collection of cells, with the population of organisms.)

What can we learn from this example? First, it demonstrates a fascinating way of growing entire organisms without predefining their final structure in the genome. This makes the length of the genome independent of the organism's size. Second, the example shows a way biological insights can be translated into a simulation model in a natural way. For example, having the same genome for all the organism's cells and having cell differentiation as the result of which genes are active is a biologically motivated assumption. Any resulting organism has emerged because of a complex dynamic process. If this process is influenced, for example, by introducing additional transcription factors, the organism's shape changes. Third, the process of development in this example is more realistic than in the other models discussed so far. The designer does not precode the organism's shape. Fourth, as always, computation is expensive. The search space is very large. It is a real challenge to find appropriate constraints. And fifth, at the moment, the organisms have only shape. It would be more realistic if they also displayed interesting behavior. After all, behavior is the business we are interested in.

In summary, although this model is only a beginning, it opens up the possibility of experimenting with shapes. As we show later, shapes are crucial for intelligence, but this point has largely been neglected in the study of intelligence.

8.5 Real Robots, Evolution of Hardware, and Simulation

In the research we have described so far, evolution has always been performed in simulation. Throughout the book we have stressed the importance of embodiment. As we have pointed out in a number of places, embodiment can, at least to some extent, be simulated on a computer: The work of Karl Sims provides a nice illustration. In chapter 4 we summarized the pros and cons of simulated and robotic agents. Dario Floreano and Francesco Mondada, two researchers at the Swiss Federal Institute of Technology, in Lausanne, were convinced that evolution had to be modeled on hardware. Let us look at an example where the robot Khepera, which closely resembles our generic agent, was used.

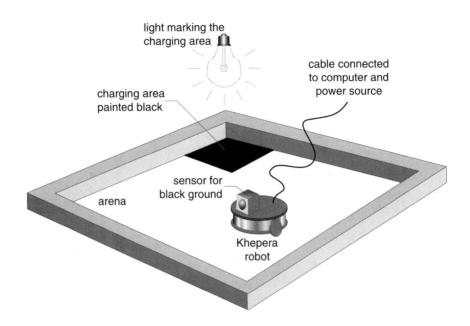

Figure 8.13 Evolution on a real robot. In this experiment, a controller for the robot Khepera was evolved. The robot's task was to move around as much as possible while maintaining its battery charge. A recharging area, painted black and marked with a light, was located within the robot's environment. The robot could exploit this by means of its light sensors. As soon as the robot entered the recharging area, its battery was fully charged instantaneously. The robot had a special sensor to detect the black areas.

A Robot That Learns to Run and Recharge Its Batteries

Floreano and Mondada's goal was to see if they could evolve a self-sufficient robot (figure 8.13) (Floreano and Mondada 1994). The robot's task was defined as follows: It had to move around in an arena, covering as much distance as possible while staying away from obstacles and walls. Its fitness value was increased if the motors moved forward a lot; it was decreased when it was near obstacles (including walls), as measured by activation of IR sensors.

Because the robot was supposed to be self-sufficient, there was one additional very hard constraint: The robot had to maintain its battery charge. For this purpose, there was a charging area in the arena, painted black and marked by a light source. An additional sensor was mounted on the bottom of the robot for detection of black areas. The robot's battery was simulated: It lasted for 20 seconds of motion and was charged instantaneously as the robot sensed the black area. Note that this instantaneous recharging process can, of course, only work in simulation; in the real world everything, including charging a battery, takes time.

The robot's controller was also specified: a multilayer feedforward neural network with one hidden layer. The input layer was for the sensor signals, the output layer for the motor signals. The hidden layer had recurrent connections, that is, the nodes in the hidden layer were connected to one another. They can be used to implement memory about the agent's recent past. Here, just as in the case of Beer's walking insect, it is up to evolution to determine what it will do with these connections. The fitness function was defined as follows:

$$f = V(1 - IR), \qquad 0 \le V \le 1, \qquad 0 \le IR \le 1, \tag{8.1}$$

where V is the average rotation speed of the two wheels and IR is the activation value of the proximity sensor. V is maximized by speed, $1 - IR$ by obstacle avoidance: The larger the distance to an obstacle, the smaller IR, and so the higher the second term. The results were pretty amazing. After about 240 generations, the best individuals moved around in the arena, and immediately before the battery ran out, they managed to return to the black area and get their batteries recharged.

Once more, let us see what we can learn from this experiment. First, if we want to evolve controllers for existing robots, it can be done on the actual physical robots. A real robot is programmable, and therefore we can evolve its controller. We cannot change anything on the physical setup of the robot—it is given. Second, evolution has once again produced a surprising result: The robot acquired a completely nontrivial behavior. The robot learned to do exactly the right things, and it stared exploiting its sensors, the IR sensors for obstacle avoidance, the light sensors to move quickly to the charging area if need be. Finally, evolution on hardware takes a very long time. Moreover, the experiments reported could be simulated without too much effort.

While Floreano and Mondada's experiments demonstrate the in-principle feasibility of evolving robot controllers in hardware, their experiments definitely raise the question of cost versus performance. Do the results really make it worth going through all the trouble of using real robots? We strongly feel that this is not a matter of principle but rather an entirely pragmatic issue. We are interested in the study of intelligence, in revealing the mechanisms underlying behavior. Thus, the goal is to employ the method best suited for our purposes.

Nick Jakobi of the University of Sussex in Brighton, England, an expert in the field of evolutionary robotics, argued very strongly for the use of simulation. He demonstrated convincingly that at least one particular aspect of agent evolution, the evolution of controllers, can be studied in simulation. Given enough variation and enough noise, controllers evolved in simulation produce reliable behavior if translated to real robots (Jakobi, in press). But if our robots grow more complex, they will become much harder to simulate, and computation will become an extreme draw on resources. Using real robots would not help in this case because of the many alternatives that would have to be tested: the more complex the robot, the larger the search space—the space of possible controllers. Because of the laws of physics, the speed of real robots cannot be increased indefinitely, whereas there seem to be virtually no limits to speed of computation—at least for the time being.

The Evolution of Hardware

The next logical step, then, would be to evolve not only controllers for robot hardware but the hardware itself. This approach, however, has an obvious fundamental problem. Simulation's great advantage is that millions of alternatives can be explored in a very short period of time. How can this be done with real robots at the same speed? The technology is certainly not yet at a stage that would permit this. However, an exciting recent development has great potential: the Field Programmable Gate Array, or FPGA. An FPGA is a VLSI (Very Large Scale Integration) silicon chip containing a large array of components and wires (figure 8.14a). Switches distributed throughout the chip determine how each component behaves and how the components are connected to the wires. The specific arrangement is defined in a configuration memory. According to this specification, a *physically real electronic circuit* is configured. So the FPGA is not programmed to follow a sequence of instructions; it is configured, then allowed to behave in real time according to the laws of physics governing electronic circuits. A host computer can be used to specify the contents of the configuration memory. In other words, it can be used to determine the electronic circuit the FPGA will embody. We use the term "embody" to stress that it is a physical circuit, not a simulation.

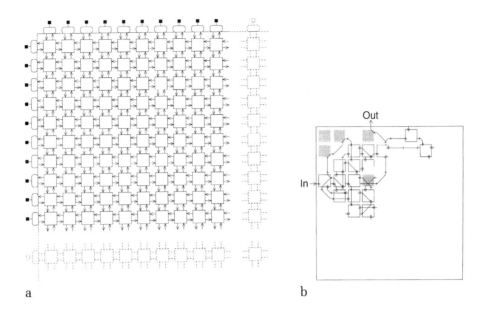

a   b

Figure 8.14 Hardware evolution. (a) Schema of a field programmable gate array. Thompson's experiments use only the 10 × 10 array of components in the upper left corner. (b) A circuit evolved for distinguishing low- and high-frequency signals (1 Khz and 10 KHz). Note in particular the shaded areas: They are not connected by wires to the rest of the circuit. Nevertheless, they are needed for the circuit to function properly. Evolution has exploited this subtle interaction (reprinted by permission of Adrian Thompson).

Adrian Thompson, also of the University of Sussex, an expert in artificial evolution, had the idea of using this arrangement to evolve electronic circuits on hardware (Thompson 1996, 1997). The task was to distinguish between tones of 1kHz and 10KHz. The fitness function involved maximizing the difference in the average output voltage for the two input signals. The genome encoded the possible FPGA configurations. FPGAs are designed to perform digital logic, which requires them to use a synchronizing clock, but Thompson's experiment did not use the clock. The goal was to see in what ways evolution would exploit the rich natural unconstrained dynamics of the silicon chip to achieve the task. The FPGA was used in a way its designers had not thought about. In Thompson's experiment, out of the 64 × 64 array, only the 10 × 10 square in the upper left corner was used. There were 50 individuals per generation (i.e. 50 circuits for the tone separation task). After 3,500 generations, the response of the circuit was perfect. Figure 8.14b shows the chip resulting from the experiment. Note in particular the cells shaded in gray: If the values of these cells are kept fixed (clamped), the circuit no longer works. But the gray cells are not connected by wires. Thus, they must be interacting with the rest of the circuit by some other means, for example, by electromagnetic coupling. Evolution has been exploiting these couplings in clever ways.

Although this is an extraordinary development with enormous potential, it is, at least for the time being, limited to electronic circuits. So it seems that entire robots cannot currently be evolved in hardware. But some researchers argue that simulation is just as good, or almost as good. With the exception of a few hard-liners, most researchers in the field of artificial evolution would agree that simulation is a very good substitute for evolution in the actual hardware.

8.6 Artificial Life: Additional Examples

All the examples introduced in this chapter are basically part of the (ill-defined) field of artificial life. Sometimes, the field of autonomous agents is considered part of artificial life because these creatures, mobile robots and simulated agents, indeed do exhibit lifelike behaviors. We don't really like the term; it carries a somewhat negative connotation: people playing God by creating lifelike artificial organisms. For our purposes, we have a somewhat more sober attitude. We are interested in exploring intelligence, and for this purpose, artificial life provides us with a lot of fascinating case studies, examples of emergence. For us, the term simply refers to the combination of complex dynamic systems, chaos, virtual reality, multiagent systems, and autonomous agents. Artificial life is mostly concerned with computer simulations, with virtual creatures inhabiting virtual worlds, like Karl Sims' creatures.

Virtual Creatures and Collective Behavior

From virtual creatures we can learn to think differently about intelligence. New morphologies may emanate or new ways of locomotion might appear, as we have seen in Karl Sims' virtual creatures, or we may discover that sophsticated group behavior emerges from simple rules. We now review a few famous examples.

"BOIDS" AND FLOCKING ROBOTS

The boids are among the most famous creatures in artificial life. They were invented by Craig Reynolds who was at the time, in the mid-1980s, working as a computer animator. In Culver City, California, where he lived, Reynolds would observe flocks of blackbirds. He wondered how he could get virtual creatures, "boids," to flock in similar ways. He hypothesized that simple rules would account for this behavior. It was clear to him that the boids would have to be agents: They would have to be situated, viewing the world from their own perspective rather than from a global one. Their behavior would then be controlled by a number of local rules. Reynolds (1987) came up with the following set:

1. Collision avoidance: Avoid collision with nearby flockmates
2. Velocity matching: Attempt to match velocity with nearby flockmates
3. Flock centering: Attempt to stay close to nearby flockmates

Collision avoidance is the tendency to steer away from imminent impact with an object. Static collision avoidance is based on the relative position of the flockmates and ignores their velocity. Conversely, velocity matching is based only on speed. The third rule engenders flock centering: It makes a boid want to be near the center of the flock. Because of the boid's situated perspective, "center of the flock" means the perceived center of gravity of the nearby flockmates. If the boid is already well within the flock, the perceived center of gravity is already at the boid's position, so there is no further pull toward the center. However, if the boid is on the flock's periphery, flock centering causes the boid to deflect its path somewhat toward the center. Together, these three rules lead to surprisingly realistic flocking behavior.

Reynolds was interested in what would happen when the flock encountered obstacles (figure 8.15). Would the boids continue to flock? Would they all move past the obstacle on one side? Or would they split? The last is exactly what happened. Note that splitting was nowhere programmed into the boids. Both the flocking behavior and the splitting behavior they exhibited are truly emergent. A number of internal processes, functioning in parallel (obstacle avoidance, velocity matching, and flock centering), account for these behaviors. These processes are based on the boids' situated view of their environment. The boids' flocking behavior is very robust because of the mechanism's local distributed nature. It is another wonderful example of sophisticated behavior emerging from simple rules.

Figure 8.15 Craig Reynolds' "boids" engaged in flocking behavior. The boids encounter a cluster of pillars. Amazingly, the flock simply splits and rejoins after it has passed the pillars. Note that "splitting" is not contained in the set of rules. It is truly emergent: the result of several parallel processes as the boids interact with the environment. Reynolds' himself was surprised: He did not know what was going to happen. The boids' behavior can be fully explained; although remarkable and beautiful, there is nothing mystical about it (reprinted with permission).

One last point: In chapter 1 we argued that robots are behaving systems in their own right. Researchers in artificial life claim very much the same for their science. Boids are digital creatures as such, not just models of real birds. "Flocking in boids is true flocking, and may be counted as another empirical data point in the study of flocking behavior in general, right up there with flocks of geese and flocks of starlings" (Langton 1989, p. 33).

Rodney Brooks, Pattie Maes, Maja Mataric, and Grinell Moore used rules almost exactly like Reynolds' to achieve flocking behavior in real robots. At an IROS (International Conference on Intelligent Robots and Systems), conference in 1990, they suggested using a swarm of robots to prepare the lunar surface for a manned mission. Mataric produced flocking in her robots using a variation on Reynolds's rules. Her model was based on the subsumption architecture. Her robots, like the boids, exhibit robust flocking behavior. Again, flocking is emergent from local rules. According to Mataric, "The robots are flocking, but that's not what they think they are doing" (quoted in Dennett 1997, p. 251). What they think they are doing is applying Reynolds' rules: Another example of the notorious frame-of-reference issue. (For those interested in collective robotics, Mataric has investigated the field for many years. A thorough review would be beyond the scope of this book, so the interested reader is referred to some of the review papers, such as Mataric 1995, 1997.)

ARTIFICIAL FISH

Locomotion in boids is rather primitive. It works only in simulation; it was designed for the simulation. Demetri Terzopoulos of the University of Toronto in Ontario, Canada, a computer graphics researcher, was interested in generating realistic behavior in artificial fish (Terzopoulos, Tu, and Grzesczuk 1994). It turned out that the best way to produce realistic animations was to model not just 3-D form and appearance, but also the basic physics of the animal and its environment. This was Terzopoulos's ingenious idea. His fish are modeled as full-featured autonomous agents with sensory, motor, and control systems. Just like Sims' creatures, they interact with a simulated environment of realistic physics. In this case, the hydrodynamics required for locomotion are modeled. In contrast to Sims who used evolution, Terzoupoulos hand-designed his creatures because he wanted to model real fish, not some arbitrary creature. Figure 8.16a shows the model developed for the fish's

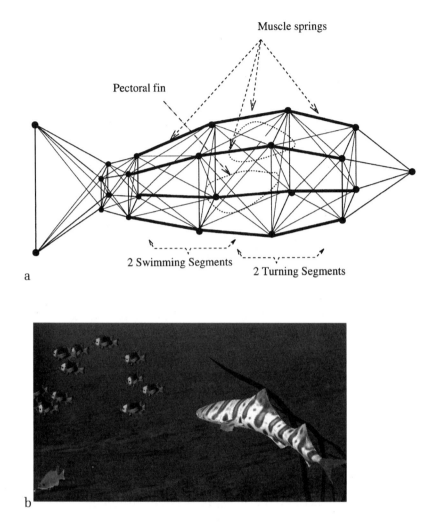

Muscle springs

Pectoral fin

2 Swimming Segments

2 Turning Segments

a

b

Figure 8.16 Artificial fish. (a) Model for physical motion. The tail fin and the rear part of the fish are used for swimming, the front part for turning. To achieve realistic appearance, a technique from computer graphics (nonuniform rational B-spline surfaces) has been used. (b) A number of fish created using this technique. The figure shows a predator shark stalking a school of prey fish (reprinted with permission).

physical motion. The tail fin and the rear part of the fish are used for swimming, the front part for turning. To achieve realistic appearance, a technique from computer graphics (nonuniform rational B-spline surfaces) has been used. Figure 8.16b shows a number of fish created using this technique. To achieve naturalistic movement, a variation of reinforcement learning was used (see chapter 14). After a short learning period, the movements of these fishes are surprisingly natural and realistic. Terzopoulos and his coworkers have also modeled schooling, mating, escaping, preying, and courting behavior among fish.

This example shows that highly sophosticated agent models, models of biological systems, can be constructed in simulation. Let us summarize some of the interesting results. First, the importance of modeling the actual physical interaction for agent behavior has again been demonstrated. Embodiment is the key word here. We see that embodiment can be simulated realistically. With increases in computer power, we can expect to be able to model even more complicated (embodied) agents and behaviors in the near future. Rodney Brooks at IS Robotics in Somerville, Massachusetts, has started building artificial fish as real, physical robots. Their behavior is also surprisingly natural and lifelike. The race between computer modeling and robot building is still open. As pointed out earlier, we do not think this is a matter of dogma. Rather, it is a pragmatic decision that depends on the issues we intend to investigate. Second, relating more to computer animation, this study makes it evident that often, the best way to achieve realistic, lifelike animations may be to model the underlying physical processes, rather than only modeling visual appearance.

This case study leads us directly into biology, in which artificial life studies have already started having a significant impact. We summarize very briefly a few examples.

ETHOLOGY
A wide variety of studies that pertain to ethology are of interest. Rather than discussing them in detail, we would simply like to insert a "bookmark" here for the interested reader. Ant societies are popular in the field of artificial life. Ants are comparatively simple animals, and they live in large societies; there are always many of them, a typical prerequisite for artificial life studies. Jean-Louis Deneubourg at the Free University of Brussels, Belgium, was convinced that ant societies obey principles of self-organization. Of

course, he was influenced by his next-door colleague, Nobel Prize winner Ilya Prigogine, who pioneered work in self-organization. Let us briefly inspect the latter topic.

The term "cooperation" is problematic. It somehow suggests that agents have the goal of cooperating with the others, and that they have the necessary cognitive structures to enable them to communicate with other agents in order to cooperate on the task at hand. Studies on social ants demonstrate that cooperation is often emergent (e.g., Deneubourg, Theraulaz, and Beckers 1992; Goss and Deneubourg 1992). Emergent cooperation behavior has also been demonstrated in robots (Maris and te Boekhorst 1996; see also chapter 14 for discussion of an example). Let us illustrate the point with an example of collective sorting (Deneubourg et al. 1991). Examination of an ant nest yields the observation that brood and food are not randomly distributed throughout the nest, but that there are piles of eggs, larvae, cocoons, and so forth. How can ants do this? If the contents of the nest, the brood, are distributed onto a surface, very rapidly the workers gather the brood into a place of shelter and then sort it into different piles as before. Deneubourg and his colleagues show that this sorting behavior can be achieved without explicit communication between the ants.

The model works as follows. Ants can recognize objects only if they are immediately in front of them. If an object is far from other objects, the ant has a high probability of picking it up. If other objects are present, the probability is low. If the ant is carrying an object, its probability of putting it down increases if there are similar objects in its environment. Here are the formulas. The probability of picking up an object is

$$p(pick\ up) = (k^+/(k^+ + f))^2,$$

where f estimates the fraction of nearby points occupied by objects of the same type and k^+ is a constant. If $f = 0$, that is, if there are no similar objects nearby, the object will be picked up with certainty $(k^+/k^+ = 1)$. If $f = k^+$, then $p(pick\ up) = 1/4$, and $p(pick\ up)$ gets smaller as f approaches 1. The probability of putting down an object is

$$p(put\ down) = (f/(k^- + f))^2,$$

where f is as before and k^- a different constant. The probability p is 0 as f is 0; that is, if there are no similar objects nearby, the probability of putting the object down approaches 0. The more objects of the same type there are nearby, the larger is *p(put down)*. Figure 8.17 shows the development of the clusters for real ants and for a simulation. Sorting is achieved by the simple probabilistic rules given. There is no direct communication between the ants: The sorting behavior is an emergent property.

Although many people would agree that artificial life models have explanatory power for ant societies, they would be skeptical of such models' ability to say much of interest about higher animals or humans. Charlotte Hemelrijk and Rene te Boekhorst, two primatologists at the University of Zurich, Switzerland, had become interested in artificial life and autonomous agents. They were convinced that the kind of modeling technique described above for the ants could also be applied to societies of of very high–level mammals like chimpanzees or orangutans. They started a campaign against cognitivistic thinking in primatology. Hemelrijk used computer simulation models to study emergent phenomena in societies of artificial creatures that for her were abstract simulations of orangutans. In an instructive paper entitled "Cooperation Without Genes, Games, or Cognition," Hemelrijk (1997) demonstrated that cooperation in the sense of helping behavior is entirely emergent from interactive factors. Often what seems to be a tit-for-tat strategy, as game theorists term it, turns out to be a side effect of interactions. (A tit-for-tat strategy is one in which individuals keep track of what has happened and give back only as much as they have previously received.) More parsimonious explanations of primate behavior based on local rules of interaction also obviate explanations resorting to high-level cognition. For example, participants in a conflict are thought to keep track of the number of acts in which a particular individual has helped them and in which they have helped the individual. (For more detail, the reader is referred to Hemelrijk 1997.) Along similar lines, te Boekhorst did a simulation of artificial "orangutans," demonstrating that travel band formation in orangutans can be explained in very simple terms (te Boekhorst and Hogeweg 1994). This kind of research is predominantly conducted at the simulation level, since it often uses high-level operators like "recognize dominance rank" that cannot be translated to real robots in a straightforward manner.

SOCIAL SCIENCE
So far, we have seen that artificial life techniques can be applied to the study of ants and primates. Surprisingly, these techniques have also been applied to the social sciences; to economics, to the study

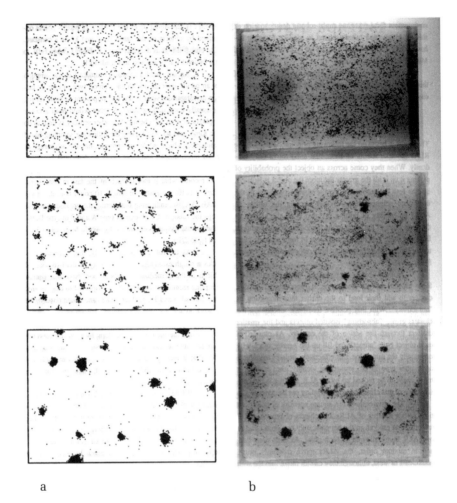

a b

Figure 8.17 Development of clusters of objects in a society of ants: (a) simulation, (b) real ants. The simulation is based on local rules only. The simulated ants can recognize objects only if they are immediately in front of them. If an object is far from other objects, the probability that the ant will pick it up is high. If other objects are present, the probability is low. If the ant is carrying an object, the probability of putting it down increases as there are similar objects in its environment. This leads to the clustering behavior shown (reprinted with permission).

of migration patterns, and to cultural phenomena. This field is called "artificial societies." It has been championed by Josh Epstein and Robert Axtell (1996), both associated with the Santa Fe Institute in New Mexico, where all the artificial life activities started. Convinced of the explanatory power of simple rules, Epstein and Axtell launched a new research program in the social sciences. It is a synthetic approach, that is, an approach based on the idea of "understanding by building." They wanted to create a "laboratory for social science." Their ambitious goal was to develop a better understanding of the complex dynamics of society and culture in general. Societies are strange and highly intricate mixtures of biological, psychological, economical, and legal factors (among many others).

To illustrate the power of Epstein and Axtell's approach, let us discuss just one example. Epstein and Axtell asked a question that had never really been asked before, or at least a question that could not be investigated before: How does the legal system influence evolution? This seems a strange question, for how can a man-made law influence the course of biological evolution?

Epstein and Axtell developed a model, called "sugarscape." In the model, there is a distribution of sugar on a landscape. Creatures, the autonomous agents that inhabit this sugarscape, constantly collect and consume sugar. One of their "traits" is vision, that is, how far they can see. Of course, the further they can see, the better. Simulations show that selection pressure favors those individuals that can see further. If a law is assumed that offspring can inherit sugar from their parents, sugar that the parents had collected, vision turns out to be no longer the decisive factor in evolution. The inheritance law, in a sense, "buffers" the power of vision, a comforting thought to all who are nearsighted (like Rolf Pfeifer). Note that here we have a fascinating interaction of social rules (inheritance) and biological selection. The implications of this "laboratory for social science" are enormous. Already a new field, agent-based economics, is forming. Many surprises can be expected, because in contrast to those in most classical economic theories, the phenomena in agent-based worlds are highly nonlinear and therefore hard to understand intuitively.

Other Work

The field of artificial life is diverse and extremely rich. Researchers from many fields—computer science; biology, in particular evolutionary theory; developmental biology; ethology; biochemistry; genetics; robotics; engineering; economics; social sciences in general; and, of course, embodied cognitive science—have been attracted to it. All share an interest in complex dynamic systems, self-organization, and emergent phenomena. Because of the enormous diversity of research, we have focused up to this point on those aspects that relate to the embodied cognition approach by focusing on autonomous agents of sorts. But there is an enormous amount of appealing work based on cellular automata, which are among the key computational devices for local rules. There is work on pattern formation in plants and animals, for example, of patterns of sea shells (e.g., Meinhardt 1995). There is research on growing shapes in natural systems, on the origins of life. The research spans everything from protein folding to economics—a vast field indeed, and way too much to cover in a single book, let alone one chapter.

8.7 Methodological Issues and Conclusions

Let us now summarize what we can learn about agent design from artificial evolution and artificial life.

Emergence in Agent Design

The synthetic approach now fully starts showing its value. Artificial evolution and ALife are synthetic disciplines par excellence. We have remarked, in this chapter, on the fascination with artificial evolution. We have also seen how truly surprising designs, strange but efficient creatures, emerged. As always, the value of the methods depends on the goals: Are we interested in engineering, designing useful artifacts that perform tasks for us, or are we interested in understanding principles of intelligence? Let us look at the former for a moment. "Design is out, evolution is in" is a slogan sometimes heard in evolutionary circles. Artificial creatures like those of Karl Sims stimulate our fantasy and boost our hopes that, at least potentially, entirely new forms of intelligent creatures might emerge that will do wonderful things for us. There is an enormous potential for applications of evolution.

There are two questions to be addressed here. One is about the power of the evolutionary approach, and the second is whether we want to eliminate design completely. Let us first look at the former.

It is often argued that artificial evolution can be beneficially applied whenever the behaviors we want to achieve are too complex to be hand designed. One major implication of this claim is that evolutionary robotics is capable of automatically synthesizing more complex behaviors than those that can be designed by hand. As far as we can tell this has not been demonstrated so far. Mataric and Cliff (1996), in a recent review of the state of the art in evolutionary robotics, argue "a survey of the results in the field to date does not show any demonstrations that have reached that goal.... none of the evolved behaviors have been particularly difficult to implement by hand" (p. 17). If Mataric and Cliff are referring to designing robots for practical purposes, they are certainly right. Viewed from this perspective, Sims' creatures basically move forward, jump, or get control over a cube, all behaviors for which better robots could easily be designed by hand. But designing robots for practical applications is not our main interest: We want to understand behavior. Before we look at that, let us discuss the second question.

The real question is not "to design or not to design," but rather what to design and how to design. This is almost a trivial point. Since the methodology is synthetic, there must be design. In chapter 4, we argued that the designer should focus on low-level commitments and leave room for emergence. The same holds here. When employing evolutionary methods, we are pushing the designer commitments, in a sense, further "back" in time; we leave more up to self-organization. Thus, in the design process, we must include the agent's autonomous interaction with its environment. Once we are finished with the design, we still do not know the final product, because that product strongly depends on the agent's interaction with the environment. This makes it particularly hard to predict the outcomes of our designs. Note that such an agent has potentially more autonomy than one that is completely hand-designed. There is currently no systematic, top-down methodology for designing for emergence. The field is largely exploratory and because our main goal is to understand intelligence, this is not a problem, but a virtue.

Here, the principles and ideas shown in this chapter are highly revealing. Remember that a comprehensive understanding of intelligence always requires three perspectives: short term, ontogenetic, and phylogenetic. We can ask ourselves what we have actually learned about behavior from the examples of evolutionary and artificial life systems that we have discussed. One of the main insights we have gained is the importance of morphology, development, and physical interaction with the environment. Moreover, if we want to study morphology, we must not encode the structure directly in the genome: we don't want to design the morphology directly, but to let it emerge! Even in a relatively simple developmental process like the one proposed by Sims, surprising things happen.

We can order our examples according to how far the designer commitments have been pushed back. The Eggenberger model has pushed them farthest back, followed by Sims, then Beer, and finally Florano and Mondada. But there are always trade-offs. If the designer commitments are pushed too far back, convergence becomes a problem (i.e., we don't get agents with high fitness), especially if we are interested in complex behaviors. If the agents and their ecological niches get too complex, the fitness function, a very global performance measure, does not exert sufficient influence on specific properties of the individual. This is the reason why Harvey and his colleagues use a kind of "staged development" in which they manually chose "interesting" candidates as "seeds" for further generations (e.g., Harvey, Husbands, and Cliff 1994).

There is another problem, if designers let evolution do a lot of their work: The more evolution does for the designer, the more difficult it will be to understand what the resulting agents are finally able to do. We feel that if we are to understand intelligence, we not only need to model the evolutionary process, but we must also understand why the product of evolution, the agent itself, works. We should not only be able to give explanations from a phylogenetic perspective, but from a short-term one as well. This is especially necessary if at some point parts of the agent start malfunctioning and it has to be repaired.

Challenges

What are the major challenges faced by the fields of artificial evolution and artificial life? We focus on those aspects that concern autonomous agents.

- *Evolving physical robots:* Two issues here concern us. First, evolving controllers on physical robots, and evolving physical robots themselves. One problem is the amount of time required. For example, Floreano and Mondada (1994) reported that it took them 65 hours to evolve obstacle avoidance behavior in a real robot. Moreover, robots have batteries that need to be recharged. This further slows down the evolutionary process. Finally, hardware needs to be maintained and repaired and might not survive the continuous testing, yet we do not want to evolve controllers only for existing robots. So the more challenging issue is how to test enough hardware configurations in a short period of time. FPGAs are a start, but they are circuits, not entire robots.

- *Evolving in simulation:* Simulations are currently the only means of evolving artificial agents if morphology is not predetermined. But we know that especially complex robots are hard to simulate accurately (e.g., Brooks 1991a,b; Mataric and Cliff 1996). Simulation techniques need to be improved. Artificial life and virtual reality will be extremely helpful here. Remember, for example, the sophisticated simulation of Terzopoulos's artificial fish.

- *Coevolving morphology and neural controllers:* Normally, only controllers, typically in the form of neural networks, are evolved. However, in natural systems, morphology and neural systems always coevolve. Work on this problem is only in its initial stages but has a lot of potential (e.g., Sims 1994a; Eggenberger 1997). Obviously, given the current state of technology, it is as yet confined to simulation.

- *Evaluation:* One fundamental problem in evaluating evolved behaviors is that determining when a desired behavior has been achieved on a robot is very difficult. Typically, this judgment is qualitative, subjective, and based on face validity (i.e., by merely looking at the agent's behavior). As a result, quantitative analysis is the exception in the field. We return to the problems of evaluation in chapter 17.

- *Fitness function design:* Designing a fitness function is notoriously difficult, mainly because in essence, anything the robot should or should not do has to be couched in one single formula. Natural systems have no fitness function; the individuals that survive long enough simply reproduce. In robots, it is not obvious what "surviving long enough" means.

- *Understanding emergence and designing for emergence:* Although there are many exciting examples of emergence, it is still not a well-understood phenomenon. If we are to design for emergence, we badly need a better understanding of it.

Issues to Think About

Issue 8.1: Generating Diversity and Unexpected Behavior

Evolutionary approaches are praised for being ideally suited to designing autonomous agents. The argument is that humans' experience biases them and makes them unable to discover designs that evolutionary algorithms, which have no such bias, can. Although this may be true to an extent, it does not hold generally. The search spaces involved in evolutionary approaches are much too large to be searched without significant constraints imposed. Constraining the search imposes a priori design knowledge, whether explicitly or implicitly. For example, in one of their experiments, Harvey et al. (1997) used a process of staged evolution, which involves nothing less than introducing designer knowledge: the designer knows that it is better for the agent to learn one thing (in this case, moving forward) before another (recognizing triangles and circles); it can then learn to move towards triangles and circles, combining the two. As always, there are trade-offs. The more the evolutionary process is constrained, the smaller the potential for unexpected things to happen, but the higher the chance that the procedure will converge and the agent will do something sensible. The slogan "Design is out, evolution is in" is only part of the truth.

Issue 8.2: Simulation and Real Robots

Throughout the text we have stressed the importance of using real, physical robots. Theoretically, these considerations also apply to evolutionary techniques. But the reproduction in hardware is clearly not feasible with today's technology. Perhaps with the advancement of the new field of nanotechnology (e.g., Drexler 1992) this may eventually change, but not in the near future. So we are stuck with simulations. Some people have used real robots to test systems evolved. The disadvantage of using real robots in evolutionary studies is that their sensory-motor setup is predetermined. Thus, only their control architecture can be evolved. To bring about interesting evolution, the sensory systems, the motor system, and the neural substrate must coevolve. This is currently possible only in simulations. Unfortunately, most approaches to date have been geared toward evolving control architectures only (typically neural networks). We hope that this changes in the future. If morphology is included as well, this research could shed interesting light on the relationship between sensory-motor systems and neural substrate. Will the agents generated by such research evolve gigantic brains, or will they also augment the degree of sophistication of sensory-motor systems if environmental pressures increase? Our current thinking suggests that the latter will happen. Evolving complete agents requires better systems for simulating the real physical world than are currently available. Karl Sims has made an important step in this direction.

Points to Remember

- Implicit knowledge constrains human designers in their thinking. Thus, their designs will always be biased, and they may miss interesting and truly novel design ideas. Evolutionary methods have been suggested, in part, to overcome these biases.
- The evolutionary process can roughly be depicted as a cycle: genotype—*development*, phenotype—*selection*, new population of individuals—*reproduction*. This scheme can be used to classify the various evolutionary approaches.
- Selection is the process by which individuals are chosen for reproduction. Random selection means that the genotypes of new individuals are generated from scratch, whereas in cumulative selection, existing genotypes of individuals with high fitness are chosen for modification, thus keeping their "good" properties.
- The two most common operators used in evolutionary methods are mutation (asexual reproduction, requiring only one individual) and crossover (sexual reproduction, requiring two individuals).
- The genetic algorithm is a commonly used optimization procedure. In the field of autonomous agents, it is often used to optimize parameters of a control architecture. In classical GAs, the genotype represents a solution and the selection is performed directly on the genotype. There is no development.
- Evolutionary methods can also be used to evolve control architectures and morphology. If evolutionary methods are used in a strong sense to evolve the architecture or even the morphology of a complete agent, that is, if the search space is very large, there is a significant danger that the algorithms will not converge, because the only "guidance" provided comes from the global fitness function.
- While it has been demonstrated that artificial evolution can be performed in hardware, these experiments have, for the better part,

been restricted to evolving the control architectures. Evolution of entire robots in hardware is, given the current technology, not feasible. Thus studies involving the coevolution of morphology and control architecture have to be performed in simulation. If this is to be done realistically, it requires the simulation of physical environments independent of the agent's own dynamics.

- The design and evolution of virtual creatures and collective behavior are important subfields of artificial life. Often, sophisticated behaviors can be achieved by designing systems with many individuals and applying local rules only. Examples are Craig Reynolds's flocking "Boids" and Maja Matarics's flocking robots.

- Often, more natural animations can be achieved by modeling the physics of the underlying processes responsible for the locomotion of an agent (e.g., a fish) than by merely trying to reproduce the shape changes.

- Artificial life studies can shed light on behavior of animal societies (ants, primates) where often simple explanations of behavior in terms of local rules can be found.

- It is an open question how much hand-design should be done and how much work the designer should leave to evolutionary methods. This decision strongly depends on the purpose of the investigation and cannot be answered in general. All evolutionary methods currently in use still require many designer decisions.

- The evolutionary perspective contributes in interesting ways to the explanation of intelligence. It complements the short-term and the ontogenetic perspectives, but does not replace them.

Further Reading

Goldberg, D. E. (1989). *Genetic algorithms in search, optimization and machine learning.* Reading, MA: Addison-Wesley. (The classical introduction to genetic algorithms. Does not relate specifically to autonomous agents.)

Langton, C. (Ed.). (1995). *Artificial Life: An overview.* Cambridge, MA: MIT Press (a Bradford Book). (A collection of papers of active researchers in the field of artificial life. The book's editor, Christopher Langton of the Santa Fe Institute and Los Alamos. started the field of artificial life and coined the name for it.)

Levy, S. (1992). *Artificial life: A report from the frontier where computers meet biology.* New York: Vintage Books (a division of Random House). (An entertaining, novel-like tour through the turbulent history of artificial life. Not scientific, but highly instructive and mostly accurate.)

Mitchell, M. (1997). *An introduction to genetic algorithms.* Cambridge, MA: MIT Press (a Bradford Book). (A modern introduction to genetic algorithms by one of the leading researchers in the field. It contains thought excercises and computer excercises and offers a good amount of theoretical background for those interested in a mathematical analysis.)

In previous chapters, we discussed some of the main approaches to designing autonomous agents. In this chapter we outline additional ones. Given that the field is still relatively young, "evolution" has not had enough time to select the "fittest" of these approaches, and many are still in competition. The selection so far represents something of a bias on the part of the authors. The jury is still out on which ones will become established and which will fall out of favor. We look in this chapter, at dynamical systems, behavioral economics, and schema-based approaches. We keep our overview deliberately short, because our main goal is to provide a general idea of each of these approaches: A detailed discussion would fill an additional book.

9.1 The Dynamical Systems Approach

A review of the approaches discussed in the last few chapters, gives the impression that what is lacking in the field of embodied cognitive science is a unifying framework as we find it in other sciences. In physics, quantum mechanics and the general theory of relativity fill this function, and in biology, the theory of evolution. In classical cognitive science, as well as neuroscience, the information processing framework plays a central role. A number of researchers have suggested that the theory of dynamical systems might provide just that framework for autonomous agents and what we now call embodied cognitive science (Beer 1997; Steinhage and Schöner 1997; Thelen and Smith 1994; van Gelder 1998).

The dynamical systems approach has become increasingly popular in recent years in many sciences. Artificial evolution and artificial life are building strongly on the theory of nonlinear dynamical systems. But it has also spread to many other disciplines, such as physics, immunology, biology, brain sciences, psychology, management science, and business economics, mainly because nonlinear systems have attracted a lot of interest over the last one or two decades as computer power has become more and more widely available. Computing power is a necessity for non-linear systems, because in general they have no closed solutions. The dynamical systems field provides highly appealing and intuitively plausible metaphors for characterizing the behavior of a system. It should be noted, however, that the dynamical systems perspective is not really new. What used to be called "systems theory" had exactly the same goals, but its focus was more on linear, rather than nonlinear systems.

Before we begin our discussion, we need to define some terminology. The term *dynamics* is used in at least three different ways. First, it is used for anything that changes, in contrast to something static. In this sense, any equation containing time, or any neural network that changes in certain ways over time, has dynamics. Second, it is used to designate a mathematical discipline that studies the properties of certain types of systems of differential equations. Third, it is used to distinguish geometrical or kinematic aspects from physical ones. This distinction is made by roboticists. The shortest path for a hand to follow in grasping a particular object can be found on a purely geometric basis by knowing the coordinates of the target position, the degrees of freedom of the arm, the spatial constraints given by the arm's geometry, and the hand's initial position. Dynamics then refers to the physics of the process, namely the forces, gravity, inertia, friction, and stiffness of the springs or muscles.

Dynamical systems are a particular mathematical formalism. In this sense, like any other formalism, such as logic or computation, the formalism does not provide the content. Thus, it is not a theory of a particular field. It does not tell us how to apply it to a particular problem domain. Its main use in the field of autonomous agents is as a descriptive tool, that is, to describe and analyze an agent's behavior and internal dynamics.

We start with a very short introduction to the basic concepts of dynamical systems theory. We include an example to convey the essence of the approach. No prior knowledge of the theory of dynamical systems is required to understand the discussion presented here. The field of dynamical systems is vast, and it has produced an enormous amount of literature. A comprehensive review is clearly beyond the scope of this book. (For those interested in more details of the dynamical systems approach, there are many excellent textbooks, such as Arrowsmith and Place 1990; Baker and Gollup 1990; and Jackson 1991).

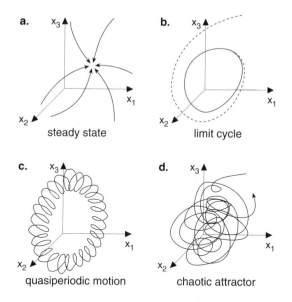

Figure 9.1 Different types of attractors in a three-dimensional phase space. The state of the entire system is exactly characterized by a point in phase space. A point in an *n*-dimensional phase space is characterized simply by the values of all variables, that is, by a vector. (a) point attractor (steady state), (b) limit cycle, (c) quasi-periodic motion, (d) chaotic attractor.

The *phase space* of a dynamical system is a mathematical space with each dimension representing a variable needed to specify the system's state. For example, the state of a particle moving in one direction is specified by its position (*x*) and velocity (*v*); hence its phase space is two-dimensional. Assume now that the "particle" is a robot moving on a flat surface. In this case there are two dimensions for its position and two for its velocity vector: the phase space is therefore four-dimensional. Essentially, two types of equations can be used to describe trajectories of dynamical systems in phase space. One operates with discrete time using *difference equations*; in the other, time is a continuous quantity, thus *differential equations* are used. In essence, there are four possible characteristics of bounded development in phase space, bounded meaning that none of the variables gets indefinitely large (see figure 9.1):

1. motion toward a stable steady state or point attractor (figure 9.1a).
2. motion toward a stable periodic orbit or limit cycle (figure 9.1b).
3. quasiperiodic motion, in which events never repeat exactly, but neighboring trajectories remain neighbors (figure 9.1c).
4. motion in a chaotic attractor. The region in phase space in which the system moves around is bounded but the trajectory cannot be

predicted (figure 9.1d). Such motion is characterized by sensitive dependence on initial conditions, which means that even the smallest change in the starting point can lead to an entirely different trajectory.

The first three types have been well known for a long time, but chaotic dynamics have become a major research topic only relatively recently. Although the great French mathematician Poincaré already knew about the chaotic properties of some dynamical systems in the last century, investigating them systematically really requires today's high-speed computers.

Dynamical systems terminology is applied in two ways, metaphorical and formal. In its metaphorical use, one essentially applies the dynamical systems vocabulary to better characterize what a robot is doing. For example, if an agent's behavior stabilizes in a particular environment and the agent starts going in circles or oscillates to the left and to the right in a corner, this is said to constitute a limit cycle.

When using dynamical systems formally, we first need to specify what system we intend to model and then we have to establish the differential (or difference) equations. One approach would be to model the agent and the environment separately and then to model the agent-environment interaction by making their state variables mutually dependent. The dynamical laws of the agent (A) and of the environment (E) can be described by the following differential equations:

$$(dx_a/dt) = A(x_a; u_a), \qquad \text{and} \qquad (dx_e/dt) = E(x_e; u_e), \tag{9.1}$$

where x represents the state variables, such as angles of joints, body temperature, or location in space, and u the respective parameters describing thresholds, learning rates, and fuel efficiency, all of which are subject to change.

As stated in equation (9.1), the agent and the environment are independent. We can couple them by defining a "sensory function" S and a "motor function" M. The environment influences the agent through S; the agent influences its environment through M. S and M constitute the agent-environment coupling. Formally, we can write

$$(dx_a/dt) = A(x_a; S(x_e); u_a), \qquad \text{and} \qquad (dx_e/dt) = E(x_e; M(x_a); u_e), \tag{9.2}$$

where u_a and u_e are those parameters not involved in the coupling. It is assumed that the behavior of this system is always bounded; that is, the variables do not diverge to infinity.

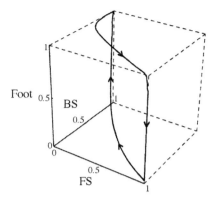

Figure 9.2 The limit cycle behavior of a central pattern generator. The three axes graph output of the foot (*Foot*), backward swing (*BS*), and forward swing (*FS*) motor neurons. The foot is considered to be down when the output of the foot motor neuron is larger than 0.5 and up otherwise. Two main regions in the phase space correspond to the two phases of the leg: In the region near the back, upper left-hand corner, the stance phase is located where the foot and backward swing motor neurons are active. The region near the front, lower-right-hand corner of the phase space corresponds to the swing phase in which the forward swing motor neuron is active and the foot and backward swing motor neurons are inactive. The system's state moves in a limit cycle between these two points in phase space (after Beer 1995, p. 195).

To make matters a bit more concrete, let us look at the example of the evolved controller for a walking insect by Beer (1995) that we described in chapter 8. Here we summarize Beer's analysis of the agent's behavior in dynamical systems terms. Beer states the basic analysis problem as follows: Given an environment dynamics E, an agent dynamics A, and sensory and motor functions S and M, explain how the agent's observed behavior is generated.

To see how Beer uses dynamical system concepts to address this analysis problem, let us now examine his analysis of one of the controllers, the central pattern generator. Central pattern generators evolved when the agent's angle sensors were turned off, that is, when it could not sense the position of its legs. In this case, the activation levels of the neurons exhibit a limit cycle that causes the agent's single leg to stand and swing rhythmically; that is, it causes the insect to walk, as figure 9.2 illustrates. The system's state repeatedly changes from the stance phase (foot on the ground; upper left-hand corner in the figure) to the swing phase (foot in the air; lower right-hand corner in the figure) and back.

This example illustrates how the notion of a phase space can be applied to an agent's behavior. In essence, it allows us to visualize a system's dynamical variables. Even though this example of a central pattern generator is relatively simple, it nicely illustrates the basic idea of how dynamical systems tools can be applied to behavior analysis. The interested reader can find more complex examples in Beer 1995.

In spite of its popularity, the dynamical systems approach has not been widely adopted by the autonomous agents community for several reasons. First, equations (9.1) and (9.2) are readily written in their general form but much less easily worked out for concrete situations. For example, establishing the environment function $E(x_e, u_e)$ implies modeling those aspects of the environment that are relevant to the agent-environment interaction. If this entails modeling the (physical) effects of an agent's motor system on the environment as well as the environment's physical influences on the agent (as the agent is hitting an obstacle, is being heated by sunlight, or affected by sensory stimulation), it is feasible only for very limited aspects of the agent (as in our example above). Second, the approach is often used in an analytic rather than synthetic way: It starts from a given agent-environment interaction, which is formalized in terms of differential equations. These equations *describe* the behavior: They do not provide the mechanisms. (We discuss an exception just below.) In general, if we want to *build* agents, as in the synthetic approach, we need the mechanisms. Finally, if systems of differential equations are indeed used as the mechanisms, the approach turns out to be computationally very expensive (e.g., Schöner, Dose, and Engels 1995).

Let us conclude with an example of how the dynamical systems approach can be used not for describing and analyzing, but rather to actually design agents. The latter is the focus of the work by Gregor Schöner and his group (e.g., Schöner, Dose, and Engels 1995; Steinhage and Schöner 1997), whose main focus is robot navigation. Central to their approach is the notion of "behavioral variables" which characterize behaviors of the agent. These variables define the state of the system. Such variables have to fulfill two important requirements. First, they must be capable of expressing the agent's task environment—as points in the state space spanned by the behavioral variables. Second, the variables must be linked to the agent's sensory-motor apparatus. In other words, there must be sensory signals that specify the variable's level of activation, which is used to set the agent's motor variables. An example of such a variable is an agent's heading direction ϕ in the environment. For example, if the agent's task is to move to a lamp located in direction ϕ_t, the agent can determine that direction using a set of light sensors.

The most important aspect of this approach concerns the generation of behavior, which is achieved by defining a differential equation—a dynamical system—that governs the behavioral variables. Behavior is generated by integrating the differential equation, then using the solutions to steer the agent. We do not further elaborate on these considerations here but rather point out that one key advantage of this approach is that much of the agent's behavior can be designed by means of analytical tools from the theory of dynamical systems. Most of the work so far has been conducted in simulation, and it remains to be seen how this approach scales to physical robots, but first attempts seem promising (Bicho and Schöner 1997).

9.2 Behavioral Economics

In this section we introduce an approach that emerged from a theory in the field of animal behavior, namely David McFarland's "behavioral economics" (McFarland and Bösser 1993). It is inspired by economic theories of decision making based on the ideas of costs, utilities, and rational man, ideas which lead to interesting conclusions about how to design robots. Over the last few years McFarland, an ethologist at Oxford University, has become increasingly interested in autonomous agents. He has also championed an approach called "animal robotics" that is of particular interest because of its strong theoretical foundation and consistency. Our discussion implies a number of simplifications; we report only the essential of McFarland's approach. (The interested reader should consult McFarland and Bösser 1993, which explains the approach in detail.)

Before we continue, we must introduce an important distinction that takes us back to chapter 2, where we introduced the cognitivistic paradigm. Simon defined the principle of rationality as follows: If an agent has a goal and the knowledge that an action will get him closer to the goal, he will in fact perform that action (Simon 1969). Thus, the agent needs a representation of a goal, knowledge, and a way of deciding whether a particular action will bring it closer to the goal. As is so often the case, there is a frame-of-reference issue involved here: We must make a distinction between *rational thought*, which concerns the mechanisms within the agent, and *rational behavior*, which pertains to the agent's interaction with the environment. Rational behavior is, of course, behavior and can thus be perceived by an observer. It is not necessary, in order for rational behavior to take place, to postulate goals and knowledge as being explicitly represented within the agent. In other words, rational thought is not a prerequisite for rational behavior. This requires a bit of elaboration.

According to McFarland and Bösser (1993), rational behavior has four basic requirements:

- *Incompatibility:* An agent cannot perform certain activities simultaneously, such as moving forward and moving backward. If it could, it would not have to make choices, and the notion of rationality would not make sense. More generally speaking, this is why we need behavior control in the first place.

- *Common currency:* If different (incompatible) activities compete for expression, they must somehow be made comparable, otherwise it is not possible to choose between them; that is, there must be a common currency to enable decision making. Typically, the potential consequences in terms of costs and benefits of taking a particular action are translated into this common currency. For example, if a choice must be made between drinking a beer and going to a concert, the very different consequences of these alternatives must be made comparable by a common currency: They must be put in terms that allow a comparison for a decision to be made.

- *Consistency:* An agent's behavior must have consistency; that is, any time the agent is in a particular state, it must make the same choice as it did the last time it was in that state and as it will when it is in the same state again. If it makes an apparently different decision, the agent must be in a different state; otherwise, it would not be acting rationally. For example, if an agent capable of learning encounters an environmental situation similar to a situation it has previously encountered, it normally acts differently than before, because it is now in a different state. Recall the agent equipped with the Distributed Adaptive Control architecture. Initially, when receiving sensory stimulation from its proximity sensors, it kept moving straight. After a number of collisions, given the same sensory stimulation as before, it turned away because through Hebbian learning some of the weights had been strengthened so that the same sensory stimulation led to a different internal state (one in which a collision node was active as well) and thus to a

Figure 9.3 Distinction between (a) rational behavior and (b) rational thought. The boy in (a) is exhibiting rational behavior; we can make no valid inferences as to whether his thoughts are rational, because we do not know what they are. He may have swerved deliberately to avoid the snail, or he may have swerved for some other reason entirely (or for no reason at all). So rational behavior does not necessarily imply rational thought. Note that the converse is also true: The professor in (b) is shown having an (apparently) rational thought, but his behavior can hardly be considered rational.

different behavior (turning away, rather than moving straight). Such an agent is still behaving consistently.

- *Transitivity of choice:* If the agent chooses among potential behaviors on the basis of some common currency, then if it chooses A over B and B over C, it must choose A over C to behave rationally.

If the agent acts consistently, its choices are transitive, and if it always chooses the top-ranking alternative available to it, then it maximizes a quantity normally called *utility* (see below). In doing so, it engages in rational behavior, but we must be careful not to infer rational thought from this. Figure 9.3 illustrates the difference between rational thought and rational behavior. According to this definition of rational behavior, animals behave rationally. Note that they do not have to be aware of it to behave rationally: There need be no explicit internal representation of utility. Utility in this sense is an observer-defined quantity: The agent behaves as if it were maximizing utility, even though it has no internal representation of "utility." As always, we come back to the frame-of-reference problem.

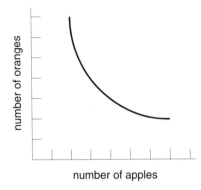

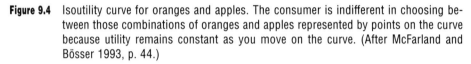

number of apples

Figure 9.4 Isoutility curve for oranges and apples. The consumer is indifferent in choosing between those combinations of oranges and apples represented by points on the curve because utility remains constant as you move on the curve. (After McFarland and Bösser 1993, p. 44.)

So we see that we can define rationality without resorting to any kind of internal representation. The idea here is that biological agents, animals and humans, obey the laws of microeconomics, that they behave rationally. Quite obviously, if we want to design a robot, it has to behave rationally, because we expect rational behavior from an intelligent agent. Consider the requirement of consistency. Who would want to buy a robot whose behavior is not consistent? For example, when a lawn-mowing robot is in a particular idle state and the grass is high, we always want the robot to mow the lawn, not just sometimes.

In microeconomic thinking, the individual spends his money in a way that maximizes utility. In this context, isoutility curves can be used to determine what choices are neutral (that is, they do not change the utility). For example if you derive the same utility from two apples and six oranges as from two oranges and six apples, you will be indifferent with regard to these two selections of fruit. Figure 9.4 shows this idea graphically. The point here is, stated broadly, that rational agents maximize utility or, put differently, they minimize cost. As we explain below, three kinds of costs can be identified: the cost of being in a state, the cost of a particular behavior, and the cost of changing between behaviors. The agent has no information about the real costs involved, which is why the term *notional costs* is sometimes applied. This does not mean that costs have to be explicitly represented internally. The decision mechanisms can simply be wired into the agent's neural substrate. Real cost is what matters in terms of Darwinian fitness, whereas

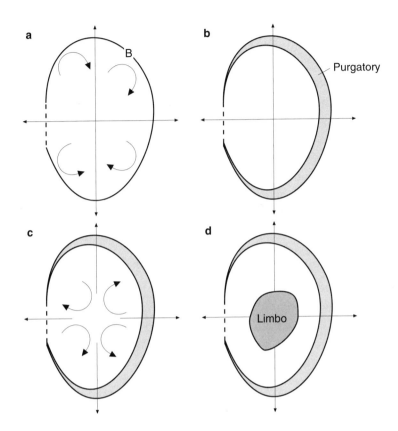

Figure 9.5 State space for an agent. The axes represent any two physiological variables. B is the lethal boundary. Trajectories are repelled at the boundary (a) by physiological emergency mechanisms. The region in which these mechanisms are active is called purgatory (b) Trajectories are repelled at the center (c), leading to a region called limbo (d). (After McFarland 1989; quoted in McFarland and Bösser 1993, p. 75.)

notional cost is what an animal has been "equipped" by evolution to perceive. For example, real cost is the amount of energy required to climb a tree or the amount of fuel used to travel a particular distance. Notional cost refers to the apparent costs, that is, the costs used by an animal's decision mechanism or a car's driver in making a decision whether to climb the tree or to travel to a particular place. The closer the match between notional costs and real costs, the better an animal's behavior contributes to its fitness.

As we noted, three factors are involved in cost, namely the cost of being in a particular state, the cost of performing a behavior, and the cost of changing between behaviors. Consider the diagram in figure 9.5. For the sake of simplicity, it only shows two state variables of an agent, say temperature and energy supply. Both are physiological variables. The dashed vertical line indicates the minimum possible value for the variable on the horizontal axis (e.g., the contents of a fuel tank can be no less than empty). The oval labeled B indicates the lethal boundary; for values of the two variables outside this boundary, the animal dies. If the animal approaches this boundary, automatic mechanisms (e.g., shivering) are triggered that attempt to move it away from the boundary toward the center. As it goes closer and closer to the center, there is less and less for the animal to do in terms of physiological survival, and normally it will then engage in activities that will bring it away again from the center (e.g., reproductive activities). The region near the lethal boundary is called *purgatory*, and the inner region near the center, *limbo*.

Let us return to the idea of costs and first look at the cost of being in a particular state. This cost is taken to be the risk of reaching a lethal boundary. Thus, near B, the costs of being in this particular state are high, and near the center they are low. If you are driving in a car and the fuel gauge indicates low gas (approaching a lethal boundary), the risk of running out of gas is high, whereas it is low if the tank is nearly full (nearing the center of the space). The cost curve can be expected to rise steeply as a state approaches the lethal boundary. In our car example, an empty fuel tank is considered to be "lethal." Thus, if your fuel gauge displays a nearly empty tank, you are on the alert for a gas station, even if this implies having to drive off the highway. Driving off the highway for refueling illustrates the costs involved in changing from one behavior to another. Changing from one behavior to another always involves costs. This is why, if you have an almost full tank, you are less likely to drive off the highway to get gas. The costs in terms of say, lost time, outweigh any potential benefit—when your tank is nearly full. However, if the gas station happens to be on the highway and you want to eat something anyhow, you might as well get some gas at the same time. You incur no extra costs by getting the gas—you are already stopped for food—so the cost for changing from one behavior to another does not come into play in the decision.

The cost of performing a behavior has to do with energy expenditure and the fact that the agent cannot engage in other behaviors at the same time. Driving fast consumes more fuel for the same distance than driving slowly. Often the cost of performing a behavior is assumed, based on empirical evidence to be the square of the rate at which it is performed (in our car example, the speed). In the car example, the first idea that comes to mind on how to implement a decision mechanism on when to refuel is a (fixed) threshold model: Whenever the fuel level drops below the threshold, go to the next gas station. A moment's reflection tells us that this cannot work. First, the density of gas stations can vary greatly. If the density is high, we can comfortably drive until the tank is almost empty (low threshold), whereas when it is low, the threshold has to be set higher. However, an equally disturbing problem with this model is that at high speeds the car consumes more fuel for the same distance, and there is an "optimal" speed at which the car consumes the least fuel per unit distance traveled. We put "optimal" in quotation marks because there might be additional constraints to comply with, such as maximum driving time. Thus depending on the speed chosen, the threshold for refueling would have to be adjusted. This is the reason why instead of a fixed threshold model, it is better to have a model based on the consequences of behavior in terms of cost or utility.

The Robot Ecosystem

Based on these ideas about cost and utility, David McFarland, together with Luc Steels, the director of the AI Laboratory at the Free University of Brussels, developed a so-called robot ecosystem (McFarland 1994; Steels 1997). McFarland, as an ethologist, was interested in using robots to investigate biologically realistic issues. Moreover, both wanted to investigate emergence, a phenomenon that we have identified as crucial in the study of intelligence. The topic area they chose was cooperation. How could something like cooperation emerge among robots? The setup of an experiment to explore this question would have to be such that the robots would benefit from cooperation in some way. Otherwise, there would be no incentive for them to learn to cooperate.

In this robot ecosystem (figure 9.6), there are a few robots and a few boxes with infrared lamps. The lamps are called "competitors" because they—like the robots—consume energy from the ecosystem, and because the overall amount of electricity is limited, the robots have to compete with the lamps for the electricity. A constant but restricted influx of energy into the system limits the amount of electricity available. The robots have to push against the competitors to reduce the competitors' energy consumption.

Figure 9.6 The robot ecosystem. Two robots and one competitor (the black box behind the robot on the left) are shown. The charging station is on the right in the back (marked with a light) (reprinted with permission).

Reducing the infrared lamps' energy consumption dims their lights. The darker the boxes, the more current there is in the charging station. The robots are equipped with sensors whose activation levels can be coupled to motivations. If the environment is made more taxing, for example, by increasing the number of energy-consuming boxes, the robots have to exploit these sensors to produce beneficial sensor-to-motor couplings. "Beneficial" in this case means "leading to higher energy levels." For example, the robots have a sensor for internal energy level. If this sensor is coupled directly with the motivation for forward movement, the robot moves more slowly when the energy is low, which makes the robot take longer to move through the charging station. The robots also have a sensor for detecting the charging station. If this sensor is inversely coupled to the motivation for forward movement, this keeps the robot in the charging station even longer. In addition, the robots have light sensors, and the charging station is marked with a light, so they can potentially use phototaxis to approach the charging station. If the robots exploit the various sensory modalities in appropriate ways, they get an advantage in terms of energy management (value). This implies increasing the complexity of their behavioral repertoire: among other things, better exploitation of the motor system. When an ontogenetic perspective is applied, we need a value system. In the robots' case, it is related to energy supply: Increase in energy level is of value. The task of energy management is difficult, because the beneficial effects of certain actions manifest themselves only much later. (As we will see in chapter 14 this is a fundamental issue in reinforcement learning). The entire experiment can also be put into an evolutionary context. It would be interesting to study what sorts of value systems would evolve.

Another issue can be studied: cooperation. The energy influx into the charging station increases if another robot pushes against the energy-consuming boxes. In a sense, the robot that pushes against the boxes works for the one in the charging station. If the robots cooperate in this way they can potentially draw more current from the charging station. Thus, they may be able to support more robots, because they manage to divert electricity from the competitors. This entire procedure can also be embedded into an evolutionary cycle, and we can see what sensors will be exploited given a particular environmental pressure. The fitness criterion in this case would be how long the agents can survive (maintain energy level above 0).

The "behavioral economics" approach to autonomous agents is refreshing and brings in important ideas, one of which is a precise characterization of self-sufficiency: Thinking in terms of utilities rather than specific quantities leads to plausible models of rational behavior. McFarland's framework is highly useful in understanding animal behavior and behavior of autonomous agents in general. For example, the idea that rational behavior can occur without rational thinking or that the notorious problems of thresholds can be avoided by using utilities is highly appealing. However, the behavioral economics approach is not without problems. As in the case of dynamical systems, the main drawback of behavioral economics is that the approach is more analytic than synthetic. It does not provide heuristics on how to derive the mechanisms that lead to the desired behaviors. Another difficulty is that the approach is top-down and suggests that careful prior analysis of the problem can produce optimal designs. Experience from 40 years of software engineering suggests that a top-down approach may not work well in an unstructured domain. Moreover, from a cognitive science perspective, a bottom-up approach seems more promising. These may be among the reasons why the behavioral economics approach has not been widely recognized in the autonomous agents community.

9.3 Schema-Based Approaches

The term "schema" has been used in many different ways in the literature and is somewhat controversial. It has been used to refer to structures stored in memory (records, objects, scripts, and the like). This is the typical way of employing the term in cognitive psychology and traditional AI. It has also been used to designate certain "modules" in robotic systems. Arkin (1993) focuses in particular on motor schemas, which he defines as follows: "A motor schema is the basic unit of motor behavior from which complex actions can be constructed. It consists of both the knowledge of how to act and the computational process by which it is enacted" (Arkin 1993, p. 385). In this sense, the subsumption architecture can also be viewed as "schema based." Note, incidentally, the inconsistency about the frame-of-reference problem. A schema, in Arkin's definition, clearly refers to some extant structure within the system. But it is defined as a unit of motor *behavior*. As we know, the latter is emergent from the system-environment interaction; it is not to be taken as a mechanism. The term is used in yet another way: to designate some kind of organization. Let us quote Bartlett (1932), who is often cited, along with Piaget, as being responsible for the introduction of the concept of a schema to psychology: "'Schema' refers to an active organization of past reactions, or of past experiences, which must always be supposed to be operating in any well-adapted organic response" (p. 201). A more comprehensive review of the various notions of the terms in psychology, neuroscience, AI, and robotics can be found in Arbib 1995.

The main purpose of schema-based theories is to find an intermediate level of abstraction, a level that is neurologically plausible and at the same time permits abstraction from too much detail. In neurobiologically oriented studies (e.g., Arbib 1981) "schema" refers to a distributed organization of perceptual and motor systems. Arkin (1989, 1993) has successfully applied the notion to robotic systems. As we pointed out above, the schema-based approach, as used in these studies, has similarities to the subsumption approach. Motor schemas operate as concurrent, asynchronous processes each of which instantiates a behavioral "intention" such as `avoid-static-obstacle`, `avoid-robot`, or `move-to-goal`. In this approach, sensory signals are translated into an output for each active schema. The resulting outputs are summed and normalized and then written onto the motor variables (see Arkin 1989 for more details). Thus, as in subsumption, a number of parallel processes are each connected to the agent's sensory-motor apparatus. In contrast to the subsumption approach, however, there is no explicit arbitration in the schema-based approach between the different schemas: There is only summation and normalization of schema outputs. We will see in chapter 11 that this is an instantiation of so-called cooperative process coordination, whereas the subsumption architecture is an example of so-called competitive process coordination.

Arkin has used the schema approach in multiagent systems. In a typical setup, a number of agents (e.g., four) have to build various formations (e.g., line, column, diamond, wedge) and keep that formation while traveling through an obstacle field. Arkin showed that this behavior can be achieved with four schemas: avoid-static-obstacle, avoid-robot, maintain-formation, and move-to-goal. Each of these schemas generates an output representing the desired behavior—direction and magnitude of the movement—for the agent given the current sensory stimulation. Together, they consistently lead to the aforementioned formation patterns.

Another exponent of schema theory in robotics is Michael Arbib, who has based his ideas on extensive studies of biological systems, in particular the frog (Arbib 1981, 1992, 1995). Arbib has built a set of models of visuomotor coordination in the frog and toad called *Rana computatrix*. Both animals snap at small moving objects and jump away from large moving objects. A simple schema-based model of the frog brain consists of four schemas, two perceptual (for recognizing objects and situations) and two motor (for controlling the two behaviors). One perceptual schema recognizes small moving objects and activates the motor schema for approaching prey; the other recognizes large moving objects and activates the motor schema for avoiding a predator. (For details, see Arbib 1981, 1995.)

In summary, it is difficult to identify definitively the central characteristics of the schema-based approach because the term "schema" is so variously defined. Thus, many schema-based approaches share, one way or another, some major assumptions. Perhaps the most characteristic commonality of the various schema-based approaches is that, based on neurobiological or psychological evidence, they are trying to abstract chunks of structure or organization located at an intermediate level of abstraction and therefore suited not only for analysis but also for synthesizing robotic systems.

Issues to Think About

Issue 9.1: Driving Cars

In the section on the behavioral economics approach, we discussed the problem of how to decide when to refuel. We argued that a simple threshold model—whenever the fuel level drops below the threshold, go to the next gas station—does not work because the density of gas stations can vary greatly and because at high speeds the car consumes more fuel for the same distance; further, there is an "optimal' speed at which the car consumes the least fuel per unit distance traveled. Thus, depending on the speed chosen, the threshold for refueling would have to be adjusted, so a threshold model is inadequate. What other mechanism can you think of that might be more satisfactory? What variables does such a decision mechanism need to take into account, except the obvious one of the current fuel level? Chapter 11 offers an example of how the problem can be addressed in a robot, but we would like you to reflect on this important problem before reading that case study.

Issue 9.2: Why So Many Different Approaches?

We have seen many approaches to autonomous agents: Braitenberg vehicles, subsumption, artificial evolution, artificial life, collective agents, dynamical systems, behavioral economics, and schema-based. We could ask ourselves why there are so many different ones. We have seen that all have their merits and their problems. Which ones will survive, which will come out as leaders, and which will eventually die out is an entirely open question at this point. But would it really be desirable to have only one or two paradigms? This too is an open question. Recall that in artificial evolution diversity is one key factor. On the other hand, diversity with no structure would be just as bad as no diversity at all. Intelligence is multifaceted, and multiple methods will presumably always be required. From your perspective, where do you see the advantages and disadvantages of having this diversity in approaches?

Points to Remember

- So far we have discussed the following approaches to autonomous agents: neural networks, Braitenberg vehicles, subsumption architecture, evolutionary robotics, dynamical systems, behavioral economics, schema-based approaches, collective behavior, and artificial life. Each of these approaches focuses on different aspects of intelligence. Thus it is currently not possible to evaluate them against one another. All are needed for the progress of the field. Nevertheless, a coherent framework would be desirable. The design principles introduced in the chapter 10 are a step in this direction.

- The dynamical systems approach to autonomous agents is used mainly to describe and assess behavior in a qualitative, metaphorical sense. Among its major advantages are its formal character, its intuitive appeal, and its potential as a unifying framework. Among its major disadvantages are its analytic nature (it is difficult to employ it for design) and the difficulties in applying the framework to problems of even moderate complexity.

- The behavioral economics approach is based on the idea of a rational agent, which is in turn based on utility and cost, as in traditional economic theory. This approach posits four basic requirements for rational behavior: incompatibility of activities, common currency, consistency, and transitivity of choice. Animals have been shown to behave rationally according to this definition. The robots that we want to design must behave rationally, otherwise they would not be of much use or interest.

- Schema-based approaches are hard to delineate. Many approaches could—depending on the perspective adopted—be classified as schema-based. A case in point is the subsumption architecture. In general, the common denominator of these approaches is that they try to abstract chunks of structure or organization located at an intermediate level of abstraction. Typically, they are based on neurobiological or psychological evidence.

Further Reading

Dynamical Systems

Beer, R. D. (1997). The dynamics of adaptive behavior: A research program. *Robotics and autonomous systems*. R. Pfeifer and R. A. Brooks (Eds.), *20*, 257–289, [Special issue: Practice and Future of Autonomous Agents.] (Provides an overview of how to employ dynamical systems in the field of autonomous agents. Includes an introduction to dynamical systems.)

Steinhage, A., and Schöner, G. (1997). Self-calibration based on invariant view recognition: Dynamic approach to navigation. In R. Pfeifer and R. Brooks (Eds.), *Robotics and Autonomous Systems*. [Special issue: Practice and Future of Autonomous Agents.] (One of the few papers in which the theory of dynamical systems is actually used to design robots.)

Behavioral Economics

McFarland, D., and Bösser, M. (1993). *Intelligent behavior in animals and robots*. Cambridge, MA: MIT Press. (McFarland is one of today's leading ethologists. The book is full of highly interesting ideas. It represents a style of thinking completely different from what computer scientists or psychologists are used to.)

Schema-Based Approaches

Arbib, M. A. (1992). Schema theory. In S. C. Shapiro (Ed.), *Encyclopedia of Artificial Intelligence*, 2nd ed (pp. 1427–1443). New York: John Wiley. (A comprehensive review of schema theory by one of the champions in the field.)

Part IV is an attempt to integrate insights in the field of embodied cognitive science into a coherent theoretical framework. It complements the design framework outlined in part II. The "design principles of autonomous agents" represent a compact way of characterizing the essence of what we mean by an intelligent system. We have to keep in mind that the field has been around only for a little more than 10 years. Thus, we cannot expect it to have a well-established set of principles that most researchers in the field would accept as basically correct. As a consequence, it is not so much a matter of whether the design principles set forth are right or wrong. Rather, they should be taken as a first pass, a set of working hypotheses to be explored in more detail in the future: They point to the important issues on which research could focus. Although chapter 10 is entitled "design principles of autonomous agents," we should not look at agents in isolation: the triad "agent–task/desired behavior–ecological niche" must always be specified and continuously taken into account in all considerations. Generally speaking, intelligence should not be considered in isolation, as a property of an agent only; we must consider the ecological niche—the environment—in which the agent is to operate as well, since behavior is emergent from the system-environment interaction.

Because these design principles are at the core of our new understanding of intelligence, after we summarize them in chapter 10, we elaborate on them in separate chapters. The reader who wants to get an overview of the field of embodied cognitive science may wish to continue with the case study on memory (chapter 15) right after this chapter—he or she can skip the significant amount of detail provided in chapters 11 through 14 without losing the argument and consult these chapters only later.

The principle of parallel, loosely coupled processes is in essence a statement of the core belief of the field as outlined in Brooks's subsumption architecture (chapter 11). To ferret out the essential features of this principle, we contrast it with more classical views.

The principle of sensory-motor coordination elaborates the nature of an agent's interaction with its environment such that it can structure its own input, which often vastly simplifies learning or enables it in the first place (chapter 12). The principles of cheap design, redundancy, and ecological balance are closely related and are discussed in one chapter (chapter 13). These principles deal with the complex relationships among embodiment, morphology, dynamics, internal mechanisms, and environment. The value principle deals with the driving forces behind agent behavior, in particular the control of learning and of how processes of self-organization can be influenced in certain ways (chapter 14). Finally, chapter 15 presents a case study of human memory. The field of embodied cognitive science has a bit of an "insect flavor": Many people believe that the approach is valid for understanding simple creatures like insects or worms but not higher mammals and humans. This case study demonstrates how this approach, and the design principles we have formulated can be productively applied to a phenomenon normally classified as a "high-level cognitive" one.

In the last few chapters, we have looked at a number of different approaches, types of agents, frameworks, and models. As we have seen, all have their particular merits and problems. In this chapter, we map out the territory of embodied cognitive science. On the one hand, this enables us to locate the various approaches on the map; on the other, it provides direction for further explorations undertaken in the remainder of the book. The basic infrastructure was provided in chapter 4, which introduced a framework for describing, understanding, and designing autonomous agents. In this chapter, we want to establish the landmarks that further delineate the basic territory of embodied cognitive science. This territory is still rough, and navigating on it is still a challenging endeavor. The design principles provide a conceptual framework, a first step toward a theory of intelligence. Because we are still at the beginning, it is not so much a matter of whether these principles are right or wrong: Rather, they point to the core issues that need to be researched in this field.

In this chapter we give a short overview of all the design principles. This overview provides enough intuition to understand their intention and the general idea. We proceed as follows. First, we discuss the nature and status of the design principles. Second, we elaborate the design principles themselves. Then we discuss the design principles in context: We outline how they are interrelated, and how they compare with the principles underlying other approaches in the field as well as the principles of traditional AI.

10.1 The Nature of the Design Principles

We have established the landmarks of the territory of embodied cognitive science in the form of design principles (see figure 10.1). There are several reasons for doing so. First, the design perspective is highly productive. Embodied cognitive science is by definition synthetic: Its goal is understanding by building. The way we design our agents is a manifestation of our views of intelligence.

Figure 10.1 Scientist wondering how to proceed. The design principles provide guidance on how to build autonomous agents. They incorporate the insights gained in this new research field in a compact and coherent form. Design principles guide us in asking the right questions when investigating issues concerning intelligence.

Experienced designers often rely on their intuitions, and these intuitions are implicit. One purpose of the design principles is to make this knowledge explicit. Alternatively, scientific papers contain descriptions of architectures, and it is shown that they work. But often the rationale for the designs is left implicit. Second, and related to the first point, design can offer a beneficial perspective from which to view natural systems, animals and humans: that of evolution as a designer. One of the goals of embodied cognitive science is to include ideas from biology for designing artificial systems. Viewing biological systems from a design perspective is a good strategy for making this transfer possible. Third, because we are still at an early stage in the field of embodied cognitive science, it is neither desirable nor possible to have a fully formalized "theory" of intelligence. A less formal description in terms of a set of principles is more appropriate. These principles capture compactly the better part of insights contained in the very rich and diverse literature the field has produced. And fourth, the principles can be seen as a set of design heuristics for autonomous agents. They are good heuristics only if you are interested in issues

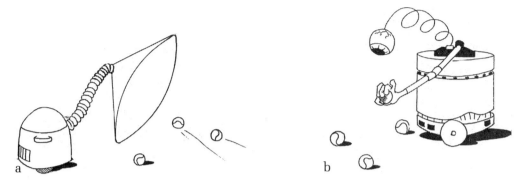

Figure 10.2 Collecting ping-pong balls. (a) engineering solution, (b) cognitive science solution. The solution in (a) requires no behavioral diversity, whereas the one in (b) does. The design principles discussed in this chapter are not very helpful for designing solution (a), whereas they can sensibly be applied to solution (b).

relating to cognitive science. If your main goal is to develop applications, other principles have to be applied (see chapter 16).

Chapter 4 elaborated on the distinction between a cognitive science and an engineering approach to design of autonomous agents. In figure 10.2, we see two designs for the same task: collecting ping-pong balls. The design principles for autonomous agents give a good characterization of the agent in figure 10.2b, but they are not very helpful for agents like the one shown in figure 10.2a. The agent in figure 10.2a sucks in the balls with great speed, the one in 10.2b searches for the balls, picks them up, and puts them into a bin. The latter has been built based on the design principles explained in this chapter, the former has not. The design principles we set forth here can be used for engineering, but only when the solution of the tasks requires behavioral diversity. Most designs, like revolving doors, paper clips, zippers, or drinking glasses do not require diversity. Even most of today's computer or robot applications rely on the fact that the computer or the robot always executes exactly the same programmed sequence of actions. The robot in figure 10.2a is of this type. The one in figure 10.2b is expected to exhibit behavioral diversity. For example, it should be able to explore the environment, search for balls, move up to them, avoid obstacles and people standing around, pick the balls up, go to a bin, and deposit the balls.

The principles of design we are advancing should enable the generation of empirical hypotheses. If these principles indeed do characterize intelligence appropriately, they have to apply to natural systems, to animals and humans, as well as to artificial ones. Currently, they must be considered as working hypotheses. A considerable amount of empirical support bolsters them, but it remains to be seen whether they can stand up to hard empirical testing. Although such testing is an important scientific criterion, it is not—given the current state of the field—the major focus here. However, as we go along, we discuss the relation of the design principles to empirical findings.

10.2 Design Principles for Autonomous Agents

The set of design principles consists of two parts: a metaprinciple (principle 1) that tells us the essential constituents of the design process, and a number of principles that concern the agent itself, its morphology, its sensors and effectors, and its control architecture, that is, its internal mechanisms (principles 2 to 8). Table 10.1 provides an overview of these principles. The design process itself is discussed in chapter 16.

A Metaprinciple

We call the first principle a "meta" principle because, in contrast to the other principles that characterize the agent itself, it is about the context in which the other principles have to be embedded.

PRINCIPLE 1: THE THREE-CONSTITUENTS PRINCIPLE

Designing autonomous agents always involves three constituents: (1) definition of ecological niche, (2) definition of desired behaviors and tasks, and (3) design of the agent. Constituents (1) and (2) together are referred to as the task environment. They are discussed in this section. Constituent (3), agent design, has been split into design principles 2 through 8. They are discussed in later sections. The design problem can be stated as follows: Given the intended ecological niche and the desired behaviors, how do we design the agent? If we are interested in explaining the behavior of natural systems, we start from a particular set of behaviors and ask how they come about and what the mechanisms are. Behavior is always tied to a particular niche; it cannot be considered in the abstract.

Alternatively we could proceed as follows. Assume that you already have an agent with a particular architecture. Assume also that you have a particular ecological niche. You can now ask what

Table 10.1 Overview of design principles of autonomous agents.

Principle	Name	Summary	Chapter(s)
Constituents of design			
1	The three-constituents principle	Designing autonomous agents always involves three constituents: (1) definition of ecological niche, (2) definition of desired behaviors and tasks, and (3) design of the agent.	4, 16
Morphology, architecture, mechanism			
2	The complete-agent principle	The agents of interest are the complete agents, i.e., agents that are autonomous, self-sufficient, embodied, and situated.	4, 10
3	The principle of parallel, loosely coupled processes	Intelligence is emergent from an agent-environment interaction based on a large number of parallel, loosely coupled processes that run asynchronously and are connected to the agent's sensory-motor apparatus.	11
4	The principle of sensory-motor coordination	All intelligent behavior (e.g., perception, categorization, memory) is to be conceived as a sensory-motor coordination that serves to structure the sensory input.	12
5	The principle of cheap designs	Designs must be parsimonious and exploit the physics and constraints of the ecological niche.	13
6	The redundancy principle	Sensory systems must be designed based on different sensory channels with potential information overlap.	13
7	The principle of ecological balance	The "complexity" of the agent has to match the complexity of the task environment. In particular, given a certain task environment, there has to be a match among the complexity of sensors, motor system, and neural substrate.	13
8	The value principle	The agent has to be equipped with a value system and with mechanisms for self-supervised learning employing principles of self-organization.	14

behaviors will emerge as the agent functions in its ecological niche. An example of this strategy involving self-organizing robots is given in chapter 14. A third possibility would be to start with an existing agent and a set of desired behaviors. The question then becomes in what environments the agent will exhibit the desired behaviors. This strategy might be important for a robot manufacturer interested in selling existing robots to operate in many different environments. From a scientific perspective, the first strategy, detailed in this chapter, is the most frequently used, although, it is often mixed with the others.

Definition of the Ecological Niche
Recall our discussion of ecological niches in chapter 4. We pointed out that there is no universality in the real world. Agents are always "designed" for a particular niche (by either evolution or engineers). The ecological niche, the environment in which the agent has to operate, must be defined. For example, if the goal is to investigate the navigation behavior of the desert ant *Cataglyphis*, it has to be decided what aspects of the animal's niche are relevant and should be taken into account in the investigation. One has to decide, for example, whether indoor experiments are feasible or whether one has to work outside. One may even decide to go to the desert.

Clearly specifying the agent's ecological niche is important for several reasons. First, the design of the agent depends crucially on its niche. If a robot for collecting ping-pong balls has to operate in several rooms, it has to be mobile. If it has to operate only in one room, it might be stationary, and its design would then be much simpler. Second, specifying the ecological niche makes it explicit that there is no universality in the real world, that the agent is designed for a specific environment. If it is designed for an office environment, it will likely look very different than if designed for the surface of Mars. Third, the definition of the ecological niche significantly constrains the agent's design. An illustrative example is Ian Horswill's robot Polly, based on a vision system that exploits the fact that office floors are flat (remember the "ground plane constraint" from chapter 4). This has several advantages: If floors are flat, wheels can be used. Moreover, a higher y-coordinate in the image supplied by this vision system—a camera pointed at the ground in front of Polly—implies that the object is further away (given that the object is standing on the ground; e.g., Horswill 1993), as figure 10.3 illustrates.

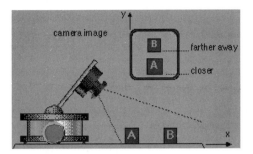

Figure 10.3   An illustration of Ian Horswill's robot Polly. It is designed to give tours to visitors at the MIT Artificial Intelligence Laboratory. Offices are its ecological niche. Polly exploits the fact that office floors are flat. If an object is standing on the ground, whatever is higher on the *y*-axis of the image it obtains through a camera that points at the ground in front of it is further away.

Definition of Task and Desired Behaviors

In chapter 4, we distinguished between task and desired behaviors. Both robots in figure 10.2 achieve the task of collecting the ping-pong balls, but they do so using behaviors that are very different. So the task is concerned with the effect of behaviors rather than the behaviors themselves. Often the separation is not so clear. Recall the example from chapter 4: the robot's task was to mow the lawn. Mowing is in fact the desired behavior to achieve the task of keeping the grass short. We also know from chapter 4 that complete agents must always engage in a number of different behaviors. A garbage-collecting robot obviously has the task of collecting garbage, or rather of eliminating garbage from the streets. Its designer has to map this task onto desired behaviors like searching for garbage, picking it up, bringing it back to a garbage truck, and so forth. Alternatively the garbage could be burned on the spot, requiring no collecting. If the robot is to be self-sufficient, it has the additional task of charging its batteries. Note that, strictly speaking, the definition of the task is independent of the agent itself. The designer decides what the tasks of the agent are to be and designs the agent in such a way that it can accomplish them. This does not mean that there must be an explicit representation of the task within the agent. One of Maja Mataric's remarks about the behavior of her robots illustrates this point nicely: "They're flocking, but that's not what they think they are doing" (quoted in Dennett 1997). As we know from the discussion in chapter 8 of flocking in Craig Reynolds's boids, flocking can be achieved by a few local behavioral rules. If all the agents follow these rules, their behavior looks like flocking. It is an emergent phenomenon. The flocking is in the head of the observer rather than in the head of the robots.

Morphology, Architecture, Mechanism

Once we have defined its ecological niche and desired behaviors, we can design the agent itself. We now look at the principles that characterize the designs of intelligent agents.

PRINCIPLE 2: THE COMPLETE-AGENT PRINCIPLE

The complete-agent principle states that intelligent agents are complete. Recall from chapter 4 that complete agents are capable of exhibiting a set of behaviors in the real world independently and without human intervention. More precisely, they are (a) autonomous, (b) self-sufficient, (c) embodied, and (d) situated. Chapter 4 elaborated on all of these characteristics; we only summarize them here. Autonomous agents have to be able to function without human intervention, supervision, or instruction. Self-sufficient agents have to be able to sustain themselves over extended periods of time. Embodied agents must be realized as physical systems capable of acting in the real world. Finally, situated agents view the world from their own perspective; information about the environment is acquired through their own sensory system. An example of a complete agent is the Fungus Eater shown in figure 4.1. Natural agents, animals and humans, are true complete agents by definition: They fulfill all the criteria of principle 1. Artificial agents that fulfill all those criteria to the same extent as natural agents do still do not exist. As we have seen, the Mars Sojourner, for example, has very limited autonomy.

In summary, the complete-agent principle states that we should aim for a particular class of agents, those that have characteristics (a)–(d) above. These kinds of agents have the potential for what we would intuitively call intelligence. In chapter 1, we said that one may choose whatever behavior one finds interesting and then ask the question of how it comes about. Here we are specifying instead which agents are the most interesting agents.

PRINCIPLE 3: THE PRINCIPLE OF PARALLEL, LOOSELY COUPLED PROCESSES

Intelligence emerges from an agent-environment interaction based on a large number of parallel, loosely coupled processes that run asynchronously and are connected to the agent's sensory-motor apparatus. The motivation for this principle comes from Brooks's (1986) subsumption architecture that we discussed in chapter 7. We also introduced, in chapter 2, the sense-think-act cycle. During sensing, information from various sensors is collected and integrated into a central representation of the environment, the world model that forms the basis for planning. A number of plans are generated and one of them is chosen for execution and finally executed. This requires a great deal of central processing. One of principal 3's main claims is that coherent behavior can be achieved largely without hierarchical control as we will argue in detail in chapter 11. This principle is at the core of most control architectures in embodied cognitive science. Its essence is that the individual processes can independently lead to behavior—they do not have to await instructions from other processes. Moreover, these control architectures can be built incrementally by adding processes on top of already existing ones. We have already encountered this evolutionary idea in the subsumption architecture. Processes can be implemented through a number of different formalisms, from finite state machines to immune system algorithms to neural networks. One of the main questions that arises concerning this principle is how the independent processes are coordinated. Such coordination is achieved both within the agent and from the interaction with the environment as well. Within the agent, competitive or cooperative mechanisms coordinate the processes. Since these processes are coupled to the sensory-motor apparatus, their activation and thus their coordination depends on the environmental context.

One of the main advantages of the approach implied in principle 3 is that it offers room for emergent behaviors, and emergence is required because (according to the frame-of-reference problem) behavior cannot be reduced to internal mechanism only. For example, if we want to achieve wall-following behavior, we should design not a module for wall-following within the agent, but instead basic processes that together, interacting with the environment, engender this desired behavior. We have already encountered two examples of emergence of wall-following in agents: in Distributed Adaptive Control (chapter 5) and in the timid vehicle of chapter 6.

PRINCIPLE 4: THE PRINCIPLE OF SENSORY-MOTOR
COORDINATION
The principle of sensory-motor coordination states that all intelligent behavior (e.g., perception, categorization, memory) is to be

conceived as a sensory-motor coordination. Note that sensory-motor coordination does not mean simply "behavior." The behavior must be directly guided by the sensory input; a robot that is simply turning about its own body axis is not engaged in a sensory-motor coordination. The principle has two main aspects. The first relates to embodiment. Perception, categorization, and memory, processes that up to this point have been viewed from an information-processing perspective only, must now be interpreted from a perspective that includes sensory *and* motor processes. Principle 4 thus provides a heuristic for analyzing and designing behavioral systems. Whatever behavior we are analyzing or whatever behavior we want to design for a robot, principle 4 suggests that we focus on how sensory and motor systems are coordinated. Embodiment plays an important role in this coordination. Let us examine categorization for a moment. Categorization is often viewed as a mapping of a stimulus onto an internal category representation. According to this principle, however, categorization and in particular, category learning, also includes motor processes. Similarly, perception does mean the passive reception of information but crucially involves, for example, the oculomotor system as well. More generally, perception and action cannot be separated, as chapter 12 explains in detail.

The second, more specific point of this principle is that through sensory-motor coordination embodied agents can structure their input and thereby induce regularities that significantly simplify learning. "Structuring the input" means that through the interaction with the environment, sensory data are *generated*, they are not simply given. Moreover, the sensory data thus generated are "good" data, that is, correlated data (for details, see chapter 12).

The principle of sensory-motor coordination has a number of implications. Let us briefly look at an example: category learning in human infants. According to the principle category learning is a consequence of sensory-motor coordination, a prediction recent evidence from developmental psychology supports (Thelen and Smith 1994; Smith and Thelen 1993). Figure 10.4 shows an infant engaged in category learning through sensory-motor coordination. One implication of the view that category learning is based on sensory-motor coordination is that the categories humans employ are automatically "grounded." (Recall the symbol-grounding problem discussed in chapter 3). Similarly, if this principle is applied to artificial agents, the implication is that they will form only fully

Figure 10.4 Infant categorizing objects and building up concepts while engaged in sensory-motor coordination. Infants never just sit there and watch an object; rather, they manipulate and continuously interact with it.

grounded categories. Stated differently, the symbol-grounding problem is really not an issue, according to principle 4: Anything the agent learns is based on—grounded in—its sensory-motor coordination, which by definition connects any learning to the real world.

Another approach closely relates to this principle, namely active vision (e.g., Ballard 1991). In this approach, vision is not seen as something that concerns not just input: Movement is also considered to be an integral aspect of the perceptual process. Chapter 12 discusses active vision further.

PRINCIPLE 5: THE PRINCIPLE OF CHEAP DESIGN
The principle of cheap design states that good designs are "cheap," with the word "cheap" not to be taken too literally. We use it here to mean essentially three things. First, "cheap" design implies exploiting the physics of the system-environment interaction. Second, it means exploiting the constraints of the ecological niche. And third, it means designing parsimoniously. Designs that embrace all three aspects seem intuitively cheap, which is why this is called the principle of cheap design. This requires some explanation.

Let us start with the idea of exploiting the physics of the system-environment interaction. Insect walking illustrates this point nicely. Leg coordination in insects requires no central controller. Insects have no internal process corresponding to global communication among the legs; they communicate only locally with each other (e.g., Cruse 1991). In other words, the legs have direct neural connections only with neighboring legs (ipsilateral (i.e., along the side) and contralateral (i.e., from one side to the other)). Global communication among all the legs does occur, but the neural system does not mediate such communication. Rather, the communication is achieved through interaction with the environment. If the insect lifts one leg, its weight changes instantaneously the force exerted on all other legs. This communication is exploited for the purpose of coordination.

Ian Horswill's robot Polly, which we introduced earlier in this chapter, illustrates the second aspect of cheap design, exploitation of the constraints of the ecological niche. To implement vision-based obstacle avoidance (figure 10.3), Polly's design exploits the fact that office floors are flat and that the objects relevant for Polly's navigation are standing on the ground.

The use of matched filters in biological systems offers an example of the third aspect, parsimonious design. Recall our case study on cricket phonotaxis in chapter 4, as illustrated by Barbara Webb's phonotactic robots. In phonotaxis, the females turn toward the males' calling song. They do not "perceive" the full spectrum of sounds and then "decide" on the one originating from male crickets. Rather, they have a "matched filter." Matched filters are systems that react only to a very narrow frequency range. The other frequencies simply do not register on the animal's sensory equipment, and therefore it cannot hear them. On the one hand, matched filters exploit the constraints of the agent's niche because agents "expect" to hear a sound of the right frequency. On the other, this design qualifies as parsimonious. It is, for example, much simpler, much "cheaper," than a system that analyzes the whole spectrum and then chooses a particular sound. The requirement that designs be parsimonious is a generally accepted principle in the philosophy of science called Occam's razor. However, there are no generally agreed upon ways of measuring parsimony. We treat this issue extensively in chapters 13 and 17.

The principle of cheap design has an interesting relationship to societies of animals. Often, tasks can be accomplished much more cheaply by having a society of less sophisticated agents, rather than having one or only a few highly complex individuals (e.g., Mataric 1995). It is also interesting to analyze social insects from this perspective. What these comparatively simple creatures achieve collectively, like constructing a termite's tower, has astonished scientists and laypeople alike. Chapter 14 elaborates this principle further.

PRINCIPLE 6: THE REDUNDANCY PRINCIPLE

The redundancy principle states that redundancy must be incorporated into an agent's design. More specifically, it states that the agent's sensors have to be positioned on the agent in such a way that there is potential overlap in the information acquired from the different sensory channels. Introducing redundancy is a well-known engineering principle normally applied to make systems more secure. Systems with built-in redundancy should continue to function satisfactorily even in unforeseen situations; such systems are said to be *robust*. Because robustness in aviation is extremely important, airplanes incorporate a lot of redundancy: They are equipped with several computers for the same function have two pilots, and employ several braking systems (through the jets, through the wheels, through parachutes). Although robustness itself is also an important issue in an autonomous agents context, what we are even more interested in here is *generation of diversity*: How can we design agents so that new behaviors can emerge? As pointed out in chapter 1, truly adaptive systems have the capacity to come up with new kinds of behaviors. As it turns out diversity can be achieved only be having redundancy: Low-level specification and neural control should include resources that are currently not required. At a very abstract level, generation of diversity can be viewed as an elegant way of achieving robust behavior in the sense that it enables the agent to continue to function even though significant environmental changes have occurred. Note that this goal is very different from that of achieving robustness by duplicating computers and power supply systems in an airplane.

Let us now look at the more specific part of the principle governing the positioning of the sensors. An agent's sensors should be positioned in such a way that the information acquired from different sensory channels in the interaction with the environment overlaps. The Distributed Adaptive Control architecture described in chapter 5 is designed with an overlap of spatial information: Whenever the agent bumps into an obstacle, the collision sensors report that the distance to the object is 0, and at the same time, the proximity sensors, the IRs, show high activation. Thus, there is redundancy in the sensory stimulation: Whenever the collision sensors are activated, IR sensors are likely to be stimulated also. The overlap occurs because the sensors have been positioned in the right places. While in the case of Distributed Adaptive Control, hitting an obstacle was sufficient to achieve the correlations in the different sensory channels, a sensory-motor coordination (i.e., the active manipulation of the environment like grasping and turning an object) is often required for learning to take place: there is a close interdependency between the redundancy principle and the principle of sensory-motor coordination.

The term "redundancy" is used in a number of different ways. So far we have been applying it in an informal way to mean something in addition to what is minimally required to make a particular system work. This is the term's most widespread use, and it is the meaning we intended when we talked about redundancy in sensory channels. The term also has a more precise characterization in the field of information theory, which has its origin in Shannon and Weaver's famous mathematical theory of communication. Shannon and Weaver define redundancy as "the fraction of the structure of the message which is determined not by the choice of the sender, but rather by the accepted statistical rules governing the choice of the symbols in question" (1948, p. 13). For example, if an English text is transmitted, there are constraints on the sequences of letters, because on the one hand only certain letter combinations are possible in English, and on the other certain letter sequences are more frequent than others. The fact that there are these constraints implies that a sentence, for example, can still be understood even if certain letters are missing. In other words, the redundancy contained in language results from the constraints on the letter combinations (Ashby 1956). Whereas in Shannon and Weaver's theory, the focus was on transmission of messages over noisy channels, we focus on (physical) agent-environment interaction, in particular, on exploiting the constraints from this interaction. Recall the robot Polly. The constraints of Polly's ecological niche (flat office floors, objects standing on the floor) enormously reduce the amount of information required for Polly to determine the relative distance of objects. Ashby made this point more than 40 years ago: "When a constraint exists advantage can usually be taken of it." (1956, p. 130).

PRINCIPLE 7: THE PRINCIPLE OF ECOLOGICAL BALANCE
The principle of ecological balance brings together the ecological niche, the desired behaviors, and the agent itself. It states that the agent's "complexity" has to match that of the ecological niche and the desired behaviors. In particular, given a certain task environment, there has to be a match in the complexity of sensors, motor

system, and neural substrate.[1] The way the term "complexity" is used here appeals to our everyday understanding: A human hand is more complex than a simple gripper, and a standard camera more complex than an IR sensor. We have also deliberately used the term "match" to relate the complexities of the sensory system and the motor system, because we do not mean "equal". Rather, we mean that these systems cannot be chosen arbitrarily, but each must be selected with the others in mind. For example, given a particular task environment, the motor system has to be taken into account when designing the sensory system and vice versa.

It seems of interest also to apply this principle when studying natural agents. In this case, the principle of ecological balance tells us that we should never look at the agent's sensory side, perception, in isolation, but always, instead, in the context of its motor system and physical setup. Many examples from nature illustrate ecological balance; let us mention just two. According to the principle of ecological balance, redundancy in sensory systems that is normally not used can be exploited if other sensory modalities fail, as illustrated by people who become blind and then start exploiting their auditory channels to a higher extent. In child development, acuity of visual distinction has been shown to coevolve with certain motor capabilities (e.g., Bushnell and Boudreau 1993).

Even though this principle in its current formulation is relatively vague and general, we can get considerable leverage from it. For example, when we are augmenting an agent's capacities, the principle draws our attention to the fact that we have to maintain some balance in our designs between the various systems and components: There must still be a rough correspondence in complexity among these systems and components once we make our design change. Take the Cog project (or other projects on humanoid robots, e.g., Kuniyoshi and Nagakubo 1997). The approach employed in the Cog project is fully compatible with the principle of ecological balance. As discussed in chapter 7, Cog has been designed to study developmental processes, to investigate how intelligence might emerge from sophisticated sensory-motor coordination, and for that purpose the agent has to be ecologically balanced. An easy way to augment the complexity of an agent is to add additional

---

[1] In an earlier publication (Pfeifer 1996b) we focused too much on the agent itself, rather than viewing the agent vis-à-vis its task environment. We would like to thank the many commentators for pointing this out to us.

sensory capabilities like sophisticated cameras. It is much harder to increase the complexity of the motor system. Because the developers of Cog were aware that sensory-motor coordination is required for interesting developmental processes to take place, they invested a great deal of effort into the design of Cog's motor system: Explicitly or implicitly, they were applying the principle of ecological balance. Because Cog's task environment is the same as that of humans (except that it cannot walk), that is, a standard office environment, humans, with their sensory and motor systems, can be taken as "models" of ecologically balanced designs (see figure 7.11). Generally speaking, by mimicking natural systems, one automatically takes the principle of ecological balance into account: Natural agents are by definition ecologically balanced: They have survived the evolutionary process.

As with all the principles, we have to ask how good a principle this one is. One way to go about finding the answer is to use artificial evolution for this purpose. Assume that we were able to evolve entire agents including their bodies, sensors, motor systems, and neural systems. Assume further that we choose a particular task environment such as collecting garbage while maintaining sufficient battery supply in which the agents are evolved. It will be interesting to see to what extent the evolved agents will be "ecologically balanced." We have used the hypothetical form because we know from our discussion of artificial evolution that evolving a complete agent is not only difficult but involves an entire research program. So, it will be a good while before we can test this principle synthetically in evolution.

Before going on to the next principle, we should state explicitly one point that we have glossed over. We have used the term "complexity" in its everyday sense. It would be desirable and would make the principle more powerful if we had a more quantitative description of this concept. The difficult part of finding such a measure is that we cannot look at the agent in isolation, we have to assess the agent's complexity vis-à-vis a particular task environment. Chapter 13 presents preliminary considerations concerning such a measure. The redundancy principle is tightly interconnected with the principle of cheap design and the principle of ecological balance; these relations are also discussed in section 10.3 and in chapter 13.

Let us conclude the presentation of the principle of ecological balance with a quote from the 19th century. Hering (1868!) said: "It is obvious that the motor apparatus of the visual organ has to fit the sensory apparatus as the shell does an egg. For, whether one assumes that they were set up according to a wise plan, or that they developed with each other and through each other in an inevitable way as the evolutionary series is traversed, in any case: the capabilities of the one have to correspond to the needs of the other" (cf. Wechsler 1990, p. 252).

PRINCIPLE 8: THE VALUE PRINCIPLE

The value principle states that the agent has to be equipped with a value system and with mechanisms for self-supervised, incremental learning employing principles of self-organization. If the agent is to be autonomous and situated, it has to have a means of "judging" what is good for it and what is not. Such a means is provided by an agent's value system. A value system modulates an agent's learning process, either explicitly or implicitly. In an explicit value system, value signals are generated within the agent. These signals can be neural or hormonal. In neural network–based architectures, this modulation concerns the learning rules, that is, how fast the change in synaptic strength occurs. Implicit modulation is achieved by mechanisms that increase the probability that an agent gets into a situation in which it can learn something useful, useful here being defined as leading to increased adaptivity. An example of an implicit modulation mechanism is the capacity to distinguish between food and nonfood items based on visual cues rather than taste. This capacity enables the agent to search for food more quickly: It can simply look at something and make a determination rather than having to put it into its mouth to find out. Reflexes are examples of implicit value mechanisms: They increase the probability of getting explicit value, as the following illustration shows.

Assume that a garbage-collecting robot has the task of collecting small objects only and not large ones. Further assume that the robot is equipped with two reflexes: one for turning toward an object and one for grasping and for picking up. Sensory stimulation on the side triggers the first, proximity to an object for a certain period of time the second. Together these reflexes increase the probability of an interesting interaction with the environment, such as the agent's picking up an object. In other words, the agent's reflexes introduce a bias toward interactions that are beneficial for learning. If the agent were to make only random movements, the probability for

Figure 10.5 Garbage collecting robot successfully grasping a small object. An explicit reinforcement signal is generated that enables the robot eventually to learn the distinction between small (graspable) objects and large (nongraspable) objects. Because it is internal to the robot, the value signal is not visible.

interesting interactions would be much lower, and learning would be much slower. If the grasping behavior is successful, for example, if the agent manages to pick up an object, a value signal has to be generated. In this case, an *explicit* value system is required that generates the appropriate signals whenever the agent has performed a useful behavior. In this way, the intuition that grasping is considered rewarding in itself can be modeled. Figure 10.5 shows a learning robot that has successfully grasped a small object, thus generating an explict value signal via its neural system to reinforce the behavior.

According to the value principle, an agent's learning mechanisms have to be based on principles of self-organization, because the environment is unknown and the categories to be formed are not known to the agent beforehand. The value system is the "teacher," telling the agent what actions to repeat, that is, what actions are good for it. ("Teacher" is put in quotation marks here, because the value system is built into the agent itself.) Moreover, learning has to be incremental: If the agent is to survive and adapt to novel situations over extended periods of time, learning must always be active. This is an important requirement for autonomous agents, and one that is often not considered in the neural networks community at large.

Additional Principles

We have referred to evolution in a number of places, arguing that evolutionary considerations are important in agent design. In chapter 8, we saw that principles of evolution—artificial evolution—can be used for design. The designer commitments are in that case made at a different level: The design decisions pertain not to the agent itself, but rather to the level of the genes, selection strategies, and fitness criteria. The design criteria for evolutionary approaches could also be couched as design principles, similar in spirit to the ones presented so far. One example might be that all cells in an organism must have the same genome. Cell differentiation then comes about as a result of different genes within the same genome being expressed in different cells. Another example could be that the organism's final structure is not be predetermined in the genome, but must be conceived as emergent, that is, as the result of an interaction of genetic and environmental factors during development. There could then be principles concerning good selection strategies for particular types of problems, good genetic operators, and so forth. Elaborating on such principles would fill another book; moreover, it has not been our central focus. Coming up with a neat set of principles would also require a lot more additional research. We hope that researchers will develop design principles for the field of artificial evolution, in particular for autonomous agents, so that these principles can be applied to the study of intelligence.

Another area discussed in chapter 8, albeit briefly, that requires additional design principles is group behavior, or collective robotics. Many of the principles presented here for individual agents can be translated directly to groups of agents. The ecological niche and the desired behaviors must be defined. Then the agents must be designed. Of course, principles 2 through 8 can be applied to designing the individual agents in a group, but often simpler ones can be used. Some of the design principles described in this chapter can also be applied at the level of group behavior. The principle of parallel, loosely coupled processes, for example, can apply to systems with many agents. The individual agents within the system can be viewed as representing individual processes that run in parallel. Communication, the loose coupling, can be effected using local rules. Reynolds's boids and their flocking behavior illustrate this idea. The principle of cheap design is also fully compatible with collective behavior because many tasks can be achieved more cheaply and robustly by having many simple agents working in parallel rather than a single, sophisticated one. We have yet to elaborate these principles systematically. (For a review of some of

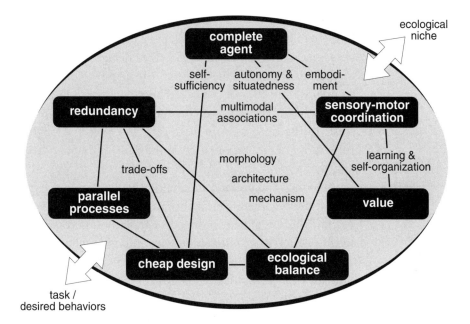

Figure 10.6 The design principles and their interdependencies. All the principles presented in this chapter are, in fact, connected because they all concern agents embedded in their task environments (ecological niches, desired behaviors, and tasks). Some principles are more closely related than others, however. The various dependencies are discussed in the text.

the design principles for the field of collective robotics, see, for example, Mataric 1995.)

10.3 Design Principles in Context

Interdependencies among Principles

We have examined one by one the principles governing design of autonomous agents. Figure 10.6 provides an overview of these principles. In various places, we have also discussed the interdependence of these principles. Let us just briefly point out the most important of these dependencies.

The complete-agent principle states, among other things, that the agents of interest must be embodied and self-sufficient. Self-sufficiency in turn implies that the designs must be cheap: The more an agent takes advantage of the physics of its environment, the more likely it is to consume less energy. Moreover, agents tend to be cheaper if they are designed in an ecologically balanced way.

The complete-agent perspective implies sensory-motor coordination: To act adaptively in the real world, the agent has to have adequate sensory-motor coordination. Sensory-motor coordination is implied by the embodiment requirement. Interesting kinds of sensory-motor coordination require appropriate design of the sensory-motor system, which can be achieved through observing the redundancy principle. If the agent is to be autonomous, it must have the capacity to learn on its own about the environment; that is, it must have the capacity for self-organized learning. Moreover, the complete agent has to receive value from the behaviors in which it engages in order to be motivated to engage in more complex behaviors over time, and value is required in turn for sensory-motor coordination. The redundancy principle and the principle of cheap design are related to one another by the task environment: The task environment for which the agent is designed, will require more or less redundancy. Exploiting the constraints of the ecological niche leads to cheap designs and the amount of redundancy necessary may be reduced in this way. Cheap designs can often be created by having many simple parallel processes rather than only a few complex ones. Finally, redundancy can be achieved by having many loosely coupled, parallel processes. When we discuss the individual principles in detail in the next several chapters, we provide additional illustrations of these interdependencies.

It is essential that the design principles we have formulated not be looked at in isolation. Their real power comes from their connections. Together, they form a coherent story—a tentative building block of a "theory of intelligence." They obviously do not represent the final answer. However, they do capture, in a very compact form, a significant proportion of the insights of the very rich literature in the field. They are not only enormously effective as design heuristics, but they also lead us to ask interesting questions. The principles have been deliberately stated in a general way, to help us keep the grand scheme in mind and not get bogged down in details. Each of the principles can of course be spelled out more explicitly, which we in fact do in chapters 11 through 14.

Other Principles for Agent Design

The design principles established by Brooks (1991a,b) overlap significantly with those presented here. (This is not surprising given that we have drawn a lot of inspiration from Brooks's work) Here are a few examples of Brooks's principles:

- The goal is to study complete, integrated, intelligent autonomous agents.
- The agents should be embodied as mobile robots, situated in unmodified worlds found around the laboratory. This confronts the embodiment issue.
- The robots should operate equally well when visitors or cleaners walk through their work space, when furniture is rearranged, when lighting or other environmental conditions change, and when their sensors and actuators drift in calibration. This confronts the situatedness issue.
- The robots should operate on timescales commensurate with those used by humans. This too confronts the situatedness issue. (Brooks 1991b, p. 571).

Quite obviously, these principles relate to the complete-agent principle (for embodiment and situatedness). They also pertain to the specification of the ecological niche (that it should not be modified, people should be moving around, lighting conditions can change, and so forth). One of Brooks's overarching principles is the following:

- The overall organizing principle is the subsumption architecture.

As we discussed in chapter 7, this principle can be viewed at both the conceptual and implementation levels. For our arguments, the conceptual level is more relevant; Implementation is secondary. Implications of applying these principles have already been pointed out: No central model of the world is maintained; all data are distributed over many computational elements; there is no central locus of control (no central program calling other programs) and no separation of perceptual system, central system, and actuation system; layers can be incrementally added; run in parallel, and are often coupled through the environment (Brooks 1991b). As we discuss in chapter 11, most of these points are covered by the principle of parallel, loosely coupled processes.

Maes (1993) has established two important abstract design principles:

- Looking at complete systems changes the problems, often in a favorable way.
- Interaction dynamics can lead to emergent complexity.

Table 10.2 Comparison of design principles of autonomous agents and traditional AI.

Principles for autonomous agent design	Related/contrasting classical design principles
The three-constituents principle	Model as computer program (c1)
The complete-agent principle	Model as computer program (c1) Rational agents (c3)
The principle of parallel, loosely coupled processes	Modularity (c4) Sense-think-act cycle (c5) Central information processing architecture (c6) Goal-based designs (c2)
The principle of sensory-motor coordination	Sense-think-act cycle (c5) Central information processing architecture (c6)
The principle of cheap design	No related/contrasting principle
The redundancy principle	No related/contrasting principle
The principle of ecological balance	No related/contrasting principle
The value principle	Goal-based designs (c2)

Note: Numbers in parentheses at right refer to table 2.3.

We can keep the discussion of these principles short, because they echo some of ours. The first closely matches the complete-agent principle, for example, though Maes also includes the ecological niche in this principle. In addition, she points out that agents are always part of society. The main point in the second principle concerns emergence, and it is a point that we have already made in various places throughout the book.

Relating to Classical Thinking

Let us close this review of design principles for autonomous agents by relating them to classical thinking, as outlined in chapter 2 and summarized in table 2.3. Table 10.2 provides an overview of the design principles underlying the two approaches. We first discuss the case of traditional AI and cognitive science, the better part of whose output is still in the form of computer programs (principle c1). Then we briefly discuss robot models employing a classical AI approach.

The three-constituents principle has no equivalent in the classical domain: A computer program has a very limited ecological niche, since its communication with the environment is restricted to the high-level ontology and it cannot interact with its environment in a nontrivial sense. The same holds for the complete-agent principle: It does not apply to classical models because the issues of autonomy, self-sufficiency, embodiment, and situatedness simply are not relevant for computer programs. In classical design, agents obey the principle of rational agents (principle c3), which pertains to rational *thinking* (see chapter 9). Complete agents exhibit rational *behavior*, but the rational behavior is not the result of rational thinking. The principle of parallel, loosely coupled processes contrasts with the modularity principle in classical AI: Rather than defining components for categorization, learning, memory, and so forth, embodied cognitive science considers these capacities to be emergent. The processes in the principle of parallel, loosely coupled processes correspond to nonhierarchical sensory-motor couplings with comparatively little internal processing, thus contrasting with principles c5 (sense-think-act cycle) and c6 (central information processing architecture) in the classical paradigm and c2 (goal-based designs). The principle of sensory-motor coordination contrasts with the traditional view of categorization as a process of mapping a sensory stimulus onto an internal representation, as suggested by principles c5 and c6. The principle of cheap design has no analog in classical AI and cognitive science. There is no embodiment in classical AI, the notion of an ecological niche does not exist, there are no physics to be exploited, and there are no interesting interactions with the environment. By analogy, one might view the application of heuristics to limit large search spaces in classical AI as an instance of the principle of cheap design, because in a sense this exploits constraints present in the data. But then, input data don't constitute a real environment: They are still part of the computational framework. The only real overlap between the two approaches' design principles is Occam's razor. The redundancy principle and the principle of ecological balance are not applicable in a classical framework; there is no physical system outside the computer, so redundancy is not crucial, and there can be no question of "ecological balance" for systems that do not interact with the real world. The value principle, that is, the view that learning is to be conceived as a process of self-organization guided by a value system, contrasts markedly with classical thinking. The value principle can be seen as providing the motivation for autonomous agents which, in classical thinking, is achieved instead by goal-based designs (principle c2). The agent's goals in classical AI result from a designer-based high-level ontology. The value principle for embodied agents advocates specification of only the basic values to guide a process of self-organization.

Because most classical models take the form of computer programs, we have been focusing on them in our review. We could now make the same kind of comparison for classical robotic agents. Most considerations would still apply. Of course, in this case the agent from classical AI is embodied, but that does not automatically imply that the agent is designed according to the design principles introduced in this chapter. The same holds for redundancy: As soon as there is a physical system, redundancy becomes potentially relevant. Again, compliance with the redundancy principle is not automatically entailed by the choice of an embodied agent.

As we pointed out in chapter 2, our intention has been to ferret out the essence, the gist of what constitutes classical thinking because it still dominates a large part of the literature in cognitive science. In this section, our intention was to contrast classical thinking with the new principles of embodied cognitive science. Some of our contrasts, of course, imply criticism of the classical position: If we agreed with classical thinking, we would not have written this book. But we should keep in mind, having said that, that it is always easy to criticize in hindsight. We have the definite advantage of having all the knowledge and experience acquired in embodied cognitive science at our disposal that classical AI researchers at the time of its predominance obviously did not have.

Issues to Think About

Issue 10.1:   Motivation, a Missing Principle?

Complete systems have many things to do. To determine when they should do which task is a difficult problem. Some people view it as one of action selection. Seen from a broader perspective, we are really talking about *motivation*. Why have we set forth no design principles concerned with motivation? This question is entirely justified, and the answer is not straightforward. The lack in our scheme of principles concerning motivation relates to, among other things, the frame-of-reference problem. The agents that we build do things. They learn certain things but not others. They pick up certain objects and not others. In some situations, they go to the charging station, in others they search for objects. They behave as we expect motivated agents to behave. That does not necessarily imply that there is an internal representation of motivation, a module, that accounts for it. Rather, what the observer interprets as motivation is emergent from the interaction of many different kinds of processes. An example are the Braitenberg vehicles, for example, the ones of type 4: They sit there, doing nothing, and then all of a sudden start moving. We as designers know that there is no explicit motivational system in the vehicles but simply a number of parallel processes influencing the motor variables. Stated differently, the type 4 vehicles illustrate that motivation does not need to be engineered explicitly into the system. The principle of parallel, loosely coupled processes touches on motivation, as does the value principle. It is interesting to ponder at what point we will have to design an explicit motivational drive for our agents. Motivation is often related to emotion. Do we need to engineer emotions into our models to achieve appropriate motivational behavior? This is another open research topic. Don Norman's paper entitled "Twelve Issues for Cognitive Science" (Norman 1980) remarks on motivation in a way analogous to our remarks here on whether a thirteenth issue was missing. That thirteenth issue was motivation. Norman also suggested that motivation should be seen as emergent from the other issues (which we do not list here). We suspect that the same holds for emotion (e.g., Pfeifer 1994).

Issue 10.2: Empirical Testability of Design Principles

In the empirical sciences, the experimental testing of hypotheses is one of the most fundamental scientific principles. We have said that the design principles are to be seen as working hypotheses on the nature of intelligent systems. Thus, they should, in principle, be subjected to empirical tests. We have argued that, given the state of the field, this is currently not our main focus. In the synthetic sciences, empirical testing, though important, is not the only evaluation criterion (see chapter 17). Pick out one of the design principles discussed in this chapter and try to think about how you would go about testing it. For example, take the principle of parallel, loosely coupled processes. What would constitute evidence and what counterevidence? Note that in embodied cognitive science, an agent constitutes an organism that can be empirically investigated. If the agent exhibits the desired behaviors robustly, would you consider this as evidence supporting the principle, or would you accept only evidence from natural systems?

Points to Remember

- Design principles of autonomous agents concisely summarize and make explicit the insights gained from the field of embodied cognitive science. These principles represent only a first step toward a more comprehensive theory of intelligence. It is currently entirely an open question what such a "theory" might look like if it is ever developed.
- The design perspective is productive for the following reasons: (a) It captures insights in compact ways; (b) It enables natural systems to be viewed beneficially from a design perspective; (c) Given the current state of the field, the framework of design principles is preferable to a formal system, and (d) The principles are heuristics for agent design. They should also enable the generation of empirical hypotheses.
- The design principles set forth here apply to a cognitive science perspective. Engineering design is not covered here (but see chapter 16 for some pertinent ideas).
- A single metaprinciple, the three-constituents principle, structures the entire design process. There are three components in agent design, ecological niche, task and desired behaviors, and the agent itself. Most design principles currently formulated apply to the agent's morphology, architecture, and mechanism.
- This chapter discusses the following principles: complete agent; parallel, loosely coupled processes; sensory-motor coordination; cheap design; redundancy; ecological balance; and value. The reader is encouraged to consult table 10.1 for a summary.
- Artificial evolution will eventually require a separate set of design principles, as will collective robotics. This work remains to be done.
- The interdependencies among the design principles set forth here demonstrate the principles' overall coherence. They have been discussed throughout this chapter.
- The design principles for autonomous agents presented here overlap significantly with those suggested by Rodney Brooks. This is not surprising, because we have drawn a great deal of inspiration from Brooks's work.

Further Reading

Brooks, R. A. (1991). Intelligence without reason. *Proceedings of the International Joint Conference on Artificial Intelligence-91*, 569–595. (An instructive and entertaining introduction to behavior-based robotics. Provides a lot of the background for the ideas and the scientific and intellectual environment in which they evolved. Also presents a number of design principles.)

Additional readings are provided in subsequent chapters that discuss the design principles in detail.

The principle of parallel, loosely coupled processes introduced in the previous chapter states that intelligence is emergent from a large number of parallel, loosely coupled processes as the agent interacts with the environment. These processes run asynchronously and are coupled to the agent's sensory-motor apparatus, requiring little or no centralized resources. This principle has been pointed out in various places throughout this book, in particular in chapters 6 and 7. It is at the core of the embodied approach to cognitive science. Figure 11.1 illustrates how it relates to the other design principles. The principle of parallel, loosely coupled processes is closely linked with the redundancy principle and the principle of cheap design. We discuss these connections in more detail as we go along. Let us first elaborate on the principle's main focus: behavior control. The claim underlying this principle is that a number of loosely coupled processes running in parallel can control behavior. It postulates that an explicit process that controls all the others is unnecessary. At first thought, coherent behavior seems impossible without such a controlling process. How can a human being, who has an enormous number of different sensory-motor systems (eyes, ears, neck, arms, fingers, legs, and mouth, to mention but a few), function at all if there is no central agent interpreting all sensory inputs, making sense of it all, then generating the next output? How can a rat with many different needs like eating, sleeping, drinking, reproduction, and curiosity do at the right time what it must do to survive? Indeed, many traditional behavioral control models assume a hierarchy in which higher levels control lower ones. Hierarchical models are popular because it is clear how they can be employed to generate coherent behavior. Let us briefly look at an example of hierarchical control. For drinking a beer in a pub (top-level goal), you first have to get to the pub (subgoal), which implies that you have to find a means of transportation (sub-subgoal), for example, a car, you have to go the garage, and so forth. Once all the subgoals have been achieved, the top-level goal has been achieved. A clear goal hierarchy controls

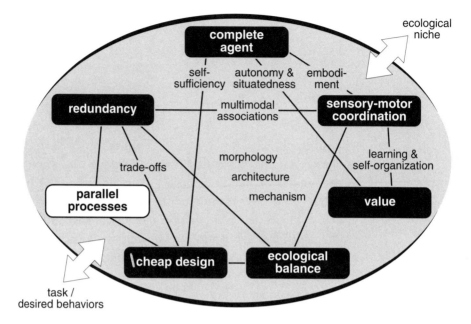

Figure 11.1   Overview of the design principles for autonomous agents. This chapter discusses the principle of parallel, loosely coupled processes. This principle relates directly to the redundancy principle and to the principle of cheap design: The redundancy principle requires parallel processes, and observing the principle of parallel, loosely coupled processes can lead to cheap designs.

the agent's behavior. This is an important design principle in classical cognitive science (cf. table 2.3, principle c2).

In order to avoid confusion, a note on terminology is in order. Throughout the literature, the term "hierarchical" is used in very different ways. Of course, everyone knows about hierarchies in companies, in political systems, or in armies. Sometimes the term "hierarchy" is used to characterize static structures. In this sense, object hierarchies, as they are known from object-oriented programming, are hierarchical. Objects lower in the hierarchy inherit properties from those higher up. Another view of hierarchy is also employed in computer science: A program calls a subprogram. The subprogram is executed, and control is returned to the calling program, which is higher up in the program's hierarchy. This leads to what is known as a subroutine-call hierarchy. In a strict hierarchy, the calling program typically has to wait until the subroutine has done its work. The term "hierarchy" has still other aspects. Sometimes it means feedforward organization as we find it in the human visual system, which has about 14 layers connected in a forward way. Related to this view is the one common to neural networks, in which, especially in pattern recognition tasks, local features are successively integrated: lower-level features such as corners, T-junctions, arcs, and the like are combined into higher-level ones, like letters, which are combined to form words. Simultaneously, there is top-down activation (from hierarchically higher levels) guiding the process of feature integration. But it gets even worse. The term "hierarchical" has also been used to characterize the subsumption architecture: One layer is on top of the other; there are lower levels and higher levels. "Hierarchical" is also used to mean that certain functions are automated and don't need centralized, high-level resources. For example, when learning to drive beginners typically have to concentrate, which requires high-level centralized resources. They are hardly able to lead a conversation while driving. Over time, high-level resources are less and less necessary: Hierarchically lower levels of organization take over. Similarly, the term sometimes means that there are hierarchically lower sensory-motor processes on the one hand and cognitive processes higher up in the hierarchy on the other. This notion is implied when one talks about "high-level intelligence." Finally, in a view often adopted in psychology and everyday thinking, the term hierarchical is used to designate systems with a central resource that gives orders to lower levels, just as in the army model, or in the computer subroutine-call model. The lower levels execute their tasks and deliver the required information to the central resource.

It is precisely this latter view of hierarchy that we want to challenge: It is this view of intelligence that is inappropriate. It is also this conceptualization that Rodney Brooks had in mind when he suggested the subsumption architecture as an alternative. The principle of parallel, loosely coupled processes is meant to contrast with this particular view of hierarchical organization. One of the key problems with this view, as we argue in this chapter, is that it is an eternal conundrum what that central resource should be. In any case, this notion of hierarchical processing also implies *centralization* and *sequentiality*. The central resource (whatever it is) decides what is to be done next, and everything is done sequentially. It should not be surprising, then, that the notion of parallel, loosely coupled processes implies decentralized, *distributed* control.

Many people would agree that intelligence involves some sort of parallelism. For example, the brain is a massively parallel system; this is also reflected in the connectionist paradigm, in which many cognitive functions (e.g., perception, memory, categorization) are often modeled by means of distributed, parallel neural networks: "In psychology, continued failings of the symbolic paradigm made parallel, connectionist processing an attractive alternative to the old game" (Leahey 1994, p. 343). Psychologists were and are attracted to connectionism because it provides an alternative view to sequential symbol processing, an alternative that capitalizes on parallel, loosely coupled processes. As we argue repeatedly throughout this chapter, the concept of parallelism underlying the principle of parallel, loosely coupled processes has a precise meaning in embodied cognitive science. It goes beyond and extends in important ways this general notion of parallel processing. The crucial point is that the different processes, for example, in the Extended Braitenberg Architectures discussed below, can, in parallel, create *sensory-motor couplings*. In such couplings, the higher levels do not have to wait for preprocessed signals from lower levels: All the processes have relatively direct sensory-motor couplings—in parallel. In addition, the processes are relatively independent of one another, each being an implementation of a mechanism that can control the agent on its own. Recall, for example, that one of the hallmarks of the subsumption architecture is that each layer implements a particular behavior and, once debugged, is left unchanged while other layers are added. In other words, the principle of parallel, loosely coupled processes encompasses a class of problems that goes beyond the tasks studied by connectionist models such as associative recall or pattern recognition.

We will proceed as follows. First, we discuss general issues in the design of control architectures. We outline some well-known hierarchical models of behavior control and point out their major problems. Then we introduce the alternative approaches. The details of one approach, the Extended Braitenberg Architecture, are presented via a case study of a garbage-collecting robot.

11.1 Control Architectures for Autonomous Agents

The general issue underlying the problem of behavior control is how an agent's sensory input should be mapped onto motor output in order for the robot to be able to fulfill its tasks. In other words, a control architecture has to be designed and implemented. The subsumption architecture is by far the best-known control architecture in embodied cognitive science. This section discusses some

Table 11.1 Overview of agent architectures in embodied cognitive science.

Architecture	Process definition	Implementation	Coordination
PDL	Parallel processes with direct connections to sensory-motor system	Functions to change the rate of change of motor variables	Cooperative (process output summation)
Subsumption	Layers of competences	Augmented finite state machines	Competitive (supression, inhibition)
Action selection dynamics	Parallel processes with direct connections to sensory-motor system	Behavior rules with precondition and postcondition lists	Competitive (winner-take-all)
EBA	Parallel processes with direct connections to sensory-motor system	Neural networks	Cooperative (process output summation)
Immunoid	Parallel processes with direct connections to sensory-motor system	Sensory inputs as antigens; internal processes as antibodies	Competitive (winner-take-all)
Schema-based approach (chapter 9)	Parallel, asynchronous schemas	Perceptual and motor schemas	Cooperative (process output summation)
Collective approach	Group of robots (parallel processes)	Individual robots, simple and local rules	Cooperative and/or competitive

additional ones. Table 11.1 provides an overview of some control architectures for autonomous agents.

Characterization of Control Architectures

In chapter 4 we listed a number of steps to be followed when conducting experiments with complete agents (see table 4.5). In this section and the remainder of this chapter, we focus on the third step on this list: The design and implementation of a control architecture. We have said that a control architecture essentially specifies how the various parts of the low-level specifications should be connected to produce a desired behavior. Consider the following problem. As you might know, one of the authors of this book, Rolf Pfeifer, is Swiss. The Swiss like to have things neat and clean. This does not necessarily imply that they like to actually clean things themselves. If they had robots to do the work, things might even be cleaner than before. So it is a sensible task for a laboratory to try to build a garbage-collecting robot that operates on a university campus. Such a robot would have to explore the given environment, locate and categorize the relevant objects, grasp them, put them into a container onboard, and take them to some predefined location in the environment. In addition, it would have to avoid obstacles such as other people walking on the campus and maybe go to a charging station when its battery was getting low. In other words, the robot would have to engage in multiple behaviors. How can we design a robot to perform such a complex series of behaviors? In other words, how can we design a control architecture for a particular problem such as collecting garbage?

Intuitively, we perceive that the problem has to be broken down somehow into a number of simpler problems. The classical approach employs the modularity principle (cf. table 2.3, principle c4) which was applied in designing the agent JL. Earlier we said that this approach runs into the action selection problem, in which at each point in time an internally represented action module has to be selected. Moreover, we argued for a more general term, behavior control, which does not imply any particular architecture. Behavior control denotes the problem of how to coordinate the processes running within the agent—however they might be represented—in order to achieve coherent behavior. This coordination is not just an internal activity, but strongly depends on the agent's interaction with its environment.

The design and implementation of a control architecture encompasses three main aspects:

1. *Process definition:* A methodology that allows us to define the basic processes, that is, to decompose the overall problem into smaller subproblems according to established principles. In the field of embodied cognitive science, this typically means that the desired behavior (e.g., garbage collecting) is broken down into a set of basic processes. Note that the main focus is to define processes for system-environment interaction (e.g., processes for approach, avoidance, or object exploration behavior) rather than internal modules (e.g., object recognition, memory, or planning).

2. *Implementation:* Formalisms and methods for implementing solutions for these subproblems. We call the result of such an implementation an *internal process.*

3. *Coordination:* Mechanisms to coordinate these internal processes in such a way that the desired behavior results. There are both competitive and cooperative coordination mechanisms. Particular

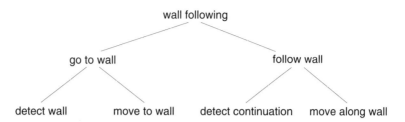

Figure 11.2 Hierarchical decomposition of wall following. The global functionality, wall following, is decomposed into a number of modules, each responsible for a particular subfunction involved in wall following. The modules are organized hierarchically. Each subfunction is either directly realized by a particular module (e.g., "detect_wall," "move_to_wall") or further decomposed (e.g., "go_to_wall," "follow_wall"). (Adapted from Steels 1991, p. 452.)

examples of each are discussed in more detail below. A core aspect of the coordination mechanisms advocated in the field of embodied cognitive science is that coordination is seen as an *interactive* process, including the agent *and* the environment. There is no module within the agent that decides which process should be active at a given point in time. Rather, all processes run in parallel, and the interaction of the agent with the environment leads to the emergence of a particular behavior. The environment can in fact be exploited to simplify the coordination problem. For example, when an insect lifts up one leg, the forces on all other legs are changed, which in turn has an impact on their coordination, as the following quote from Cruse et al. (1996) illustrates: "Let us assume that only one of the joints is moved actively. Then, because of the mechanical connections, all other joints begin to move passively, but exactly in the proper way. Thus, the movement direction and speed of each joint does not have to be computed because this information is already provided by the physics" (p. 453).

The traditional and the embodied approach lead to different ways of implementing a particular function. Assume that you want to build a robot that is capable of following walls. If you build this agent along classical principles, you start by decomposing the global functionality (wall following) into different subfunctions (figure 11.2). In the specific example the figure presents, you might decompose the wall-following module into two modules, "Go to wall" and "Follow wall." Both modules might be further decomposed into still more modules, each implementing a particular subfunction such as detecting a wall or moving to a wall. Note that each subfunction is either directly realized by a particular component (e.g., "move_to_wall" and "move_along_wall" in figure 11.2) or further decomposed into lower level-modules (e.g., "go_to_ wall" might be decomposed into "detect_wall" and "move_to_ wall"). An agent's functionality thus arises directly from its particular components, each of which is designed with a particular function in mind. The alternative approach advocated here, that is, the embodied cognitive science approach, is that a function such as wall following can emerge from the joint dynamics of a number of basic processes, each of which contributes to the overall function, as the agent interacts with the environment. We said in chapter 4 that the art of agent design is design for emergence. Emergent functionality arises through interaction among processes not themselves designed with that particular function in mind. Take again the wall-following robot. Mataric (1991) has developed a wall-following robot along the principle of parallel, loosely coupled processes. Wall following results from the joint processing of four processes called stroll, avoid, align, and correct, each of which is closely coupled with the agent's environment. It is an emergent behavior: the robot has no internal instructions that tell it to follow walls, nor is there an internal representation for wall following inside the agent. This is one of the core ideas underlying the principle of parallel, loosely coupled processes: Intelligent behavior emerges from an ensemble of parallel processes. It is important to note that one and the same process can contribute to several functions. For example, a process implementing a sensor- stimulation-left-turn-right behavior can be used for obstacle avoidance, for picking up an object with a wire loop (see the case study in section 11.4), or as a part of a moving-along- object behavior (see the SMC I agent, described in chapter 12). This is a type of resource sharing, in which different functions share overlapping processes.

The Coordination Problem

We now look at how these processes can be coordinated. What do we mean by "loosely coupled"? This is obviously a description of how various processes are coordinated. We cannot overstress the point that this coordination is always a result of system-environment interaction. Of course, there have to be ways to couple the processes within the agent, especially if they influence the same motor variables. However, a particular behavior is always emergent from interaction between the internal processes running within the agent and the current environmental situation. Hendriks-Jansen (1996) makes this point forcefully in his discussion of a robot incorporating the principle of parallel, loosely coupled processes:

It is possible to classify the decision-making process as decentralized and dynamically reconfigurable, but this does not describe its most important features. Each of the robot's sensory-feedback loops (internal processes in our terminology) is in continuous operation. The effect they have on its drive motors depends on contingencies in the environment. If it makes any sense to talk about a decision-making process that activates one reflex rather than another, that process clearly cannot be located inside the robot. To a large extent, it is the particular environment for which the robot was designed that serves as the choice mechanism between the various low-level reflexes. (p. 190)

Hendriks-Jansen further argues that the robot itself plays an active role in this process, because its own behavior is equally responsible for the particular behavioral "choices": the environmental circumstances themselves change only because the robot moves. Thus "the agent does not choose, nor does the environment; the agent is constructed so that the right choices will emerge from the interactions between its movements and the environment" (Hendriks-Jansen 1996, p. 191). Consider the following example. Assume you want to build a soccer-playing robot. One way to proceed would be to implement processes that make the robot kick the ball and processes that make the robot "fight" with its opponent if the latter is at a very close distance. If your robot and its opponent are in the middle of the field, the robot should try to fight its opponent. On the other hand, if the two robots are near the goal and everything else is the same as in the situation in the middle of the field, then the robot should try to kick the ball instead of attacking its opponent. In other words, the environment strongly influences the coordination of the robot's processes. We might be tempted to simply define logical conditions such as "if near opponent and near goal, then kick ball," or "if near opponent and near center of field, then attack opponent." But then we would have to predefine all possible situations, and we would loose the potential for emergence. Moreover, the goal here is to coordinate the processes such that they are continuously active. Let us look at how this coordination can be achieved.

The first question that arises is what should be coordinated? We have said that most (if not all) control architectures within embodied cognitive science encompass a number of parallel processes, most of which are coupled to the robot's sensors and motors. The main issue with respect to coordinating these processes is that typically, a large number of such processes try to control the same motor. For example, assume a particular robot has a process for avoiding obstacles and one for moving to a charging station. Both processes write their outputs to the motors controlling the robot's wheels. These outputs have to be coordinated somehow before they are allowed to change the motor speeds, because otherwise the robot would be likely to hit obstacles or never get to the charging station. Clearly, it is mainly the outputs of the processes that have to be coordinated to avoid inconsistent motor activations.

The literature has suggested two main approaches to process (output) coordination: competition and cooperation. In *competitive coordination* of process, only one process writes its output to the motor[1] at any point in time; the others are deactivated or inhibited while that process is active. Such a competitive coordination mechanism is used in the subsumption architecture, for example, in which a higher behavior, if it has something to contribute, overwrites or supresses any outputs generated by lower behaviors. For example, if the agent is to pick up a soda can on the campus, it should obviously not avoid it, but approach, touch, and grasp it. So in the agent's design, a competitive coordination mechanism ensures that the process for obstacle avoidance is inhibited when the process for can retrieval comes into play. A popular criterion employed in many ethological approaches is time: The probability that a given behavior will win the competition decreases the longer it goes on (and vice versa). For example, in Lorenz's (e.g., 1981) famous "psycho-hydraulic" model, each behavior exerts a constant pressure to get activated that increases over time. The longer a behavior has been activated, therefore, the higher its probability of being executed. Another example of competitive coordination is *sequencing*, in which process outputs are written to the motors in a fixed temporal sequence. For example, assume that an agent first uses a process to reach for an object, then uses another process to grasp that object. Both processes control the same effector (the

---

[1] It would be more precise to say: The process writes its output to the motor speed variables, but if no confusion can arise we use the shorthand: The process writes to the motor.

arm), but at different time steps in the sequence of actions necessary to pick up an object. A final example is *winner-take-all* strategies, in which processes compete against each other for access to the motor, and one process wins the competition and gets exclusive control over the motors.

Cooperative coordination means that the output of two or more processes that involve the same motor is combined into a single output that is then sent to the motor. The most popular mechanism for combining process outputs is summation. In addition, the outputs are often individually weighted before the sum is computed. With this kind of cooperation mechanism we can specify how much a process should contribute to the overall output. Using weights to modulate a process's influence on the overall output also has the advantage of enabling the system to learn such weights as the agent performs a task using standard learning rules. In some cases, the weights can be evolved by using genetic algorithms. This type of cooperation is used in many architectures. We discuss representative examples below. Finally, it should be noted that the coordination mechanism itself can be evolved. We addressed in chapter 8 the question of what aspects of a control architecture should be designed and what parts should be evolved. We do not discuss evolutionary approaches further in this chapter, because our main interest here is how agents can be designed by employing the principle of parallel, loosely coupled processes.

11.2 Traditional Views on Control Architectures

The general idea of goal-based, hierarchical behavior control has its roots in an influential paper by Rosenblueth, Wiener, and Bigelow (1943), in which goal-directed behavior was conceptualized in terms of the cybernetic concept of negative feedback: The difference between the present state of the agent and the goal controls intelligent behavior. The idea that behavior is controlled by its desired results has been very influential in such diverse areas as artificial intelligence, cognitive psychology, ethology, psychopathology, and neuroscience. In all of these fields, a tremendous amount of work has been undertaken to extend this basic idea. In most of this work, the major conceptual step has been to postulate mental operations that increase an agent's ability to achieve the goal state. The most prominent such mental operation suggested in traditional cognitive science is planning. To be able to plan a

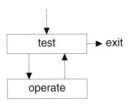

Figure 11.3 Example of a simple TOTE unit. There is a `test` module that continuously checks the output of the `operate` module until the difference between the test outcome and a given criterion, the goal, is zero.

sequence of actions, an agent must have (a) an internal model, to be able to estimate the outcome of an action without waiting for the sensory feedback, or even without performing the action and (b) a notion of distance between goal and current state. Let us look at a classical and very influential instantiation of the traditional way of thinking about behavior control: the Test-Operate-Test-Exit (TOTE) model (that was introduced in chapter 2) (Miller, Galanter, and Pribram 1960).

Psychology

The action selection problem in psychology has a long history of research. The most popular approach is called *action theory* (e.g., Heckhausen and Kuhl 1985). Within the action theoretic framework, the term "action" has a specific meaning: an action is always related to an anticipated result—a goal—and to an intention to reach this result. In other words, in the context of action theory action always refers to *goal-directed* action. TOTE systems illustrate this idea. As noted in chapter 2, the TOTE model has become a landmark in psychology. It nicely summarizes the main ideas underlying the traditional approaches to behavior control. Its basic idea is that behavior control can be conceptualized as involving a sequence of testing, then operating, then testing again, and finally exiting, as illustrated in figure 11.3. This is the TOTE model, which is based on the concept of negative feedback. In essence, the difference between the system's current state and its goal state controls behavior. A continuous evaluation of this difference guides the system's actions. The `test` module in figure 11.3 continuously compares the output of the `operate` module until the difference between the test outcome and a given criterion is 0. This criterion is derived from the goal. The TOTE model can be illustrated with the

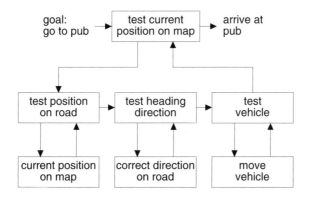

Figure 11.4 A hierarchy of TOTE units for going to a pub. A top-level goal (go to pub) translates into three subgoals (test position on road, test heading direction, and test vehicle, which tests whether the vehicle makes the right kind of movement). When the top-level goal (being at the pub) has been reached, the TOTE system is exited. (Adapted from McFarland and Bösser 1993, p. 182.)

example of going to a pub. Going to the pub is your goal. According to the TOTE model, your behavior is controlled as follows. You have to represent the goal mentally (being in the pub). As you drive toward the pub (`operate`), you continuously compare this mental representation to your current position; that is, the `test` subsystem continuously evaluates the degree of incongruity between the goal and the current state. As soon as the goal state is achieved, that is, as soon as you enter the pub, the TOTE system is exited. Note that behavior control is accounted for in purely cognitive terms.

TOTE units can be arranged hierarchically into larger TOTE systems, as figure 11.4 illustrates. Assume again that you want to go to a pub. This is the goal. To achieve the goal, you need to know how to get to the pub. If you don't know where the pub is, you can use a street map to determine a route to the pub before you start driving there. As you drive along the route you have planned, you continuously compare your current position on the map to the position of the pub. The main idea of the TOTE model is that this comparison is the main variable controlling your behavior. The behavior (going to the pub) only comes to an end when your current position coincides with the goal position, that is, when you are actually in the pub. More specifically, you start by pinpointing your current position on the map. (Note that the map could be a mental map instead of a real one.) If you realize that you are not yet in the pub (your goal), you check your position on the road (e.g., by reading the street names). If your current position does not correspond to where you thought you were on the map, you adjust your position on the map. Next you check where you are currently heading. If you are currently heading in a direction that is not in the direction of the pub, you adjust your direction on the road. Finally, you test the car (e.g., by making a U-turn) until the car points in the desired direction. This closes the loop, and your next step is again to check your position on the map. Miller, Galanter, and Pribram (1960) suggested that such a hierarchy of TOTE systems is at the core of behavior control: "the underlying structure that organizes and coordinates behavior is ... hierarchical" (p. 34). It is hierarchical in the narrow sense of the word as we have used it to characterize the traditional view: Lower levels in the control hierarchy are activated from higher levels and the higher levels have to wait for the results from the lower levels before they can go on. The TOTE model was developed almost 40 years ago. We have summarized it here because, as McFarland and Bösser (1993) have pointed out, "this basic principle ... has persisted in artificial intelligence and in robotics up to the present day" (p. vii). The incorporation of plans essentially extends the basic idea underlying the TOTE model—the comparison between the goal state and the current state—by means of more sophisticated internal processes that serve to enable the agent to better achieve the goal state.

Artificial Intelligence

The literature in artificial intelligence abounds with examples of hierarchical, goal-based control. One of the earliest robots used to study intelligent behavior was Shakey (figure 11.5), developed at the Stanford Research Institute in the early 1970s. Shakey implements aspects of the JL agent discussed in chapter 2. Shakey's task was to navigate autonomously from one room to another, to avoid obstacles, and to push boxes from one room to another. The primitive actions available to the robot were precoded in a set of "action routines." For example, execution of the action routine "Go_Thru (D1, R1, R2)" caused the robot to go through the doorway D1 from room R1 to room R2. The robot was equipped with a world model that contained representations of the different rooms, doorways, and boxes. Tasks were given to the robot by specifying the goal state the robot was supposed to achieve. For example, to direct the robot to room R2, the designers gave the robot the instruction "In_Room (Robot, R2)." To reach this goal, Shakey used the

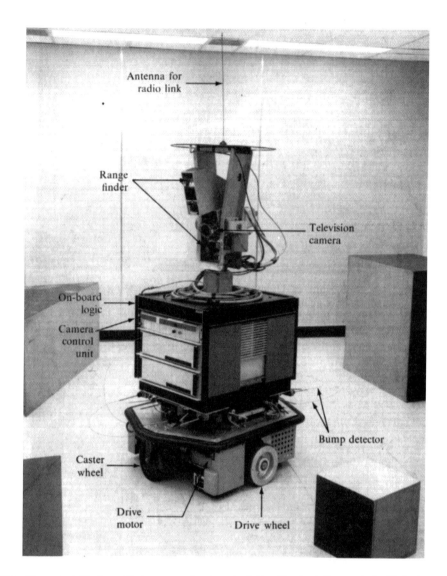

Figure 11.5 The robot Shakey. Shakey was developed at the Stanford Research Institute to explore in particular the relation between problem-solving systems and plan execution. It was equipped with the STRIPS planning system. (From Raphael 1976, p. 252, reprinted with permission.)

STRIPS planner (introduced in chapter 2). STRIPS's main purpose was to come up with a plan that solved the task, that is, a sequence of actions that would change the world in such a way that the goal would be reached. To do this, STRIPS had a model of each action—the operators mentioned above—that allowed it to predict an action's effects. Moreover, operators were invested with certain preconditions that had to be met before they could be applied. For example, the operator "Go_Thru" could be applied only if the robot was at the door. By applying a sequence of operators to the initial world model, STRIPS searched for the sequence of actions, a plan, whose execution would result in the agent's achieving desired goal state.

One of the important insights gained in the Shakey project was that one cannot simply transfer to a robot algorithms that work well in other areas: "You could not, for example, take a graph-searching algorithm from a chess program and a hand-printed-character-recognizing algorithm from a vision program and, having attached them together, expect the robot to understand the world" (McCorduck 1979, p. 232). STRIPS was developed nearly 30 years ago, and considerable effort has been expended to improve planning systems in the meantime. (For a review, see Fikes and Nilsson 1971, 1993.) For example, the classic scheme described here has been improved to include *partially ordered* (also called *nonlinear*) *planning techniques*, in which the initial plan represents only the start and the finish (goal) steps, and on each iteration one more step is added. Partially ordered plans were first introduced by the NOAH planner (Sacerdoti 1974). More recently, *situated planners* have been developed capable of refining a plan in light of additional information obtained during execution or of unexpected changes in the environment. Situated planners are hybrid systems that combine traditional planning methods with methods from embodied cognitive science. Typically, they implement low-level behaviors using, for example, the subsumption approach. On top of this, a planner is implemented. The idea is that the reactive system handles the real-time issues of having to interact with the real world, whereas a traditional planner controls planning of behavior. In chapter 3, we characterized this approach to planning as the "traditionalist" alternative to the problems of classical planners.

We conclude this section with a critical remark from Brooks (1991b), who suggests that such hybrid approaches suffer from the horizon effect: They may be a little more robust and fault tolerant, but "they have simply pushed the limitations of the reasoning system a bit further into the future" (p. 571). The future will tell how far this hybrid approach can be pushed.

Ethology

The last field we consider in our discussion of traditional views on behavior control is ethology. Again, only a very brief summary of the best-known ideas is presented here. (For a detailed review of most important ethological approaches and their relation to autonomous agents research, the reader is referred to the discussion in Hendriks-Jansen 1996, chaps. 11 and 12.) Consider the following situation. A lion starts its prey-catching behavior by following its prey from a distance. It then attacks by increasing its speed and chasing the prey. Finally, it goes in for the kill, for which it uses yet another behavior. There seems to be an underlying plan to this behavior, because there is a clear serial organization: The lion does not attack before having followed its prey. This type of structured behavior can be found in many species. It led Tinbergen (1951) to postulate a hierarchy of "behavior centers." At the top level of such a hierarchy are very general behaviors such as "reproduce" or "look for food." At lower levels of the hierarchy, we find more-specific behaviors like "fighting" or "nesting," and at lowest levels, motor units that move the effectors. Tinbergen's notion of hierarchies differs from that instantiated by the TOTE approach and AI planners discussed previously in two important ways. First, Tinbergen rejected the idea that animals have explicit knowledge of their goals, that is, the idea, that behavior is governed by the goal-directed principle: "There has been, and still is, a certain tendency to answer the causal question by merely pointing to the goal, end or purpose of behavior, or of any life process. This tendency is, in my opinion, seriously hampering the progress of ethology." (Tinbergen 1951, p. 4). Tinbergen believed that natural selection imposed the apparent goal-directed behavior he observed in animals and that it did not result from the animal's knowledge of that goal. Second, Tinbergen postulated that there exists an energy that flows down the hierarchy to motivate behaviors below. The idea was that behaviors must be "motivated" by a form of energy. Although there have been many advances since Tinbergen's original proposals, his notion of hierarchies, behavior centers, and energy can be found in a number of recent autonomous agent architectures (e.g., Blumberg Todd, and Maes 1996).

More recent ethological approaches have replaced Tinbergen's notion of energy with concepts from control theory and AI, resulting in hierarchical systems very much like the ones formulated in the TOTE approach and traditional AI. One of the key papers in establishing this direction was written by Richard Dawkins (1976), whose ideas on cumulative selection we summarized in chapter 8. Dawkins argued that behavior control in animals is achieved through a hierarchical architecture. In essence, he suggested that these hierarchies are organized like computer programs in which high-level programs call subroutines whenever the situation at hand indicates that they are needed.

This completes our far from complete summary of the main ideas on how to approach the behavior control problem in psychology, AI, and ethology. One of the main reasons that the hierarchical view of behavior control has been (and still is) so popular is that it is straightforward and easy to understand. Moreover, it has a strong basis in folk psychology: It seems compatible with what we do in our everyday activities.

Problems and Issues

In this section, we briefly summarize the main problems underlying traditional views on behavior control. We discuss two types of problems. First, we talk about theoretical or conceptual problems with hierarchical thinking that relate, in essence, to the frame-of-reference problem. Second, we elaborate on practical problems, such as brittleness, and real-time issues.

PRACTICAL PROBLEMS

We listed the most important practical problems of classical architectures in chapter 3. These problems also apply to hierarchical systems of the type described in this section. They are well known (see, e.g., Steels 1991), so we do not discuss them in great detail. The first problem with classical architectures is that hierarchical AI systems are not fault tolerant and not robust with respect to noise. When a module is removed or breaks down, the whole system's functionality is affected. For example, when the "Go_to_wall" module in figure 11.2 is removed, the robot can no longer follow walls. Another problem relates to real-time issues. We have seen that in hierarchical systems, only a small proportion of modules are devoted to receiving input from the environment. For example, the "Move_to_wall" module in figure 11.2 receives input only through the "Detect_wall" module. This leads to limited means of interacting with the environment and thus to a significant amount of internal processing, which can make the system rather slow, so that it may not be able to react to the demands from the environment in real-time. Yet another problem relates to dependence on prior analysis. For example, if a module is assumed for detecting walls, a prior analysis needs to be made about what counts as a wall. As we discuss extensively in the chapter 12, this is very difficult, particularly in realistic environments.

THEORETICAL PROBLEMS

Let us now turn to problems that are more of a theoretical nature. Hierarchical systems, such as TOTE systems, consist of a set of modules arranged in a hierarchy. Each of these modules implements a subfunction of the system's global functionality. This approach presents a problem in that it leaves no room for emergence: Everything is prespecified. We provide examples of this point in the remainder of this chapter. Our discussion of the frame-of-reference problem in chapter 4 revealed that we have to be careful about the relationship between our description of an agent's behavior, which might employ concepts such as hierarchy, module, or goal, and the mechanisms underlying that same behavior. Finally, hierarchical, modular approaches suffer from the fundamental problems of classical architectures that we discussed in chapter 3. For example, systems employing plans suffer from the frame problem. We do not repeat the arguments here but encourage the reader to go back to chapter 3 and apply the arguments presented there to the approaches summarized above.

11.3 Parallel, Decentralized Approaches

Let us now discuss alternative approaches to the behavior control problem. (see table 11.1) The hallmark of all of these approaches is that they decompose the problem, in one way or another, into a number of parallel, loosely coupled processes. They differ in the particular ways they implement these processes and in how they coordinate them. We discuss here all the approaches listed in the table except the schema-based approaches, which we discussed in chapter 9.

Process Description Language

Process Description Language (PDL) was introduced by Steels (e.g., 1992). Its main idea is many processes operating in parallel. All processes are active all the time. No behavior control mechanism gives one behavior precedence over another. Instead, each process has a certain influence on some variables, typically the motor speeds. Let us look at an example. Assume we want a robot to move forward. This seems to be a trivial problem, because one can simply set the translation speeds of the left and right motors to a positive value. PDL, however, approaches the matter differently: The forward movement process influences the translation *(forward)* speed to move toward a desired default value. Moreover, the rotation (turning) should become 0 so that the agent moves in a straight direction. In PDL, to get the robot to move forward, one writes:

```
add_value(Translation, (DefaultTranslation -
value(Translation))/MovementChange);
```

The `add_value` function increases or decreases the variable `Translation` (i.e., the forward or backward speed). The change to this variable is calculated by taking the difference between the default translational speed and the current translational speed. The default speed is stored in the variable `DefaultTranslation`, and the function `value(Translation)` returns the current value of the variable `Translation`. Finally, the difference between the desired and actual translation is divided with (or normalized by) the value stored in the variable `MovementChange`. For example, suppose we want the robot to move forward at a speed of 40 units (e.g., cm per second). Further assume that the robot is currently running at 25 units. Calling the `add_value` function would yield `add_value(25, 40−25)`. Thus, it would increase the current translational speed (25) to the default speed (40) by adding the desired value (15), assuming that the `MovementChange` variable is set to 1. In order to keep the robot moving straight, the rotational speed needs to be 0. This can be achieved by calling the following PDL function:

```
add_value(Rotation, DefaultRotation -
value(Rotation)/MovementChange);
```

Here, the variable `Rotation` is increased or decreased based on the difference between it and the default rotation, which is 0 in our example. In sum, then, PDL consists of a set of calls to the function `add_value(q, v)`, which adds the value v (e.g., the difference between actual and desired translational speed) to a quantity q (e.g., `Translation`).

The PDL architecture is based on parallel processes: Many different processes can add to the same quantity. For example, a move forward process as described above might add 20 units to the quantity `Translation`, whereas an avoid obstacle process might subtract 10 units from the quantity `Translation`. At each time step, all these additions and subtractions are simply summed, and the resulting value of the quantity determines what the robot does, for example, how fast it moves forward. In other words, PDL is based on a cooperative coordination mechanism. Note that in PDL only changes are added to the quantities. In other words, PDL works by manipulating derivatives of the various variables. This implies that a very fast control loop must be used, because otherwise the system might become unstable (e.g., oscillatory behavior or dithering).

Subsumption Architecture

We discussed the subsumption architecture in detail in chapter 7. Here we discuss only briefly how it relates to the issues of process definition, implementation, and process coordination. The subsumption architecture was the first architecture to exploit fully the principle of parallel, loosely coupled processes. Recall the Cog project described in chapter 7. We said that "Cog" stands for "Cognition" but also for the little cogs on a cog wheel as they can be found in watches and transmission boxes. We suspect that by this, Brooks means that intelligence can be achieved by many very simple processes. This is why, in general, the principle of parallel processes is linked to the principle of cheap design: Each process is very simple, requiring very little internal computation. In the subsumption approach, the problem is decomposed by defining layers of competence such as `safe-forward`, `avoid`, or `collect`. These layers are implemented by means of augmented finite state machines. The coordination of the various processes is competitive via suppression and inhibition links.

Action Selection Dynamics

Action selection dynamics was developed to achieve robust and flexible behavior in a complex dynamic world. Its design was guided by the conviction that such behavior could be achieved only in a bottom-up way (Maes 1991). In the action selection dynamics approach, a creature is viewed as having a set of behaviors in which it can engage. (In earlier papers, these behaviors were called "actions," thus the phrase "action selection dynamics.") The terminology used here is similar to that in the subsumption architecture (i.e., behavior refers to an internal structure). Behaviors are represented as nodes in a network. They have a level of activation, a set of preconditions that must be fulfilled for the behavior to be "executable," and a threshold above which the behavior can be selected for execution. The preconditions are expressed in terms of what the agent perceives in the environment. A precondition for the eating behavior, for example, is that the food must be within reach. Other examples of behaviors in which the agent can engage are obstacle avoidance, exploring, fighting with another creature, going toward another creature, fleeing from another creature, going toward food, drinking, and sleeping. It also has a set of motivations, like curiosity, laziness, hunger, thirst, aggression, fear, and the desire for safety. These motivations are connected to behaviors. As hunger increases, the activation of the eating behavior increases; if aggression increases, the activation of the fighting behavior increases. Conversely, eating reduces the activation of the hunger motivation.

The behaviors in action selection dynamics are integrated into a behavior network that functions on the basis of a spreading activation mechanism (figure 11.6). They are connected to one another via "predecessor," "successor," and "conflicter" links. A behavior is connected to another behavior via a predecessor link if the execution of the latter leads to the fulfillment of a precondition of the former. Another way of expressing the same relationship is to say that the latter behavior is connected to the former via a successor link. For example, the execution of the go-to-food behavior leads to food being within reach, which is the precondition for the eating behavior. Thus, the eating behavior is connected to the

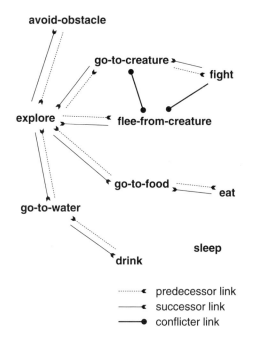

avoid-obstacle

go-to-creature

fight

explore

flee-from-creature

go-to-food

eat

go-to-water

sleep

drink

········◄ predecessor link

——————◄ successor link

——————● conflicter link

Figure 11.6 Action selection dynamics. Individual behaviors are connected via predecessor, successor, and conflicter links through which activation is transmitted. They also receive activation both from internal motivations and through perception. Behaviors whose preconditions are fulfilled and have a level of activation above threshold can be selected for execution.

go-to-food behavior via a predecessor link, whereas the go-to-food behavior is connected to the eating behavior via a successor link. "Conflicter" links are employed whenever the execution of a behavior precludes the fulfillment of a precondition of another: fleeing, for example, by definition makes the precondition for fighting unfulfilled because in order to execute the fighting behavior, the agent has to be near the other agent, which is impossible if it is fleeing from it. Figure 11.6 shows an example of a behavior network. Here is how such a network works. Assume, for example, that the hunger motivation is increasing: The agent is getting hungry. This increases the activation level of the eating behavior. Eating has as a precondition that food must be within reach. Through the predecessor link, the go-to-food behavior is activated. The latter, in turn, has as a precondition that food must be perceived. This precondition can, in turn be satisfied by the explore behavior. In other words, the go-to-food behavior has a predecessor link to the explore behavior. On the other hand, the explore behavior is connected to the go-to-food behavior via a successor link. The intuition is that if the explore behavior is executed, the go-to-food behavior is "almost executable," since its preconditions will be fulfilled after the explore behavior has been completed. The last important point is that behaviors can also be activated through the perceptual system. The presence of food increases the activation level of the eating behavior, even if the hunger motivation is low.

The activation levels of the behaviors in the network are changing continuously and in parallel. The implementation is distributed: The behaviors watch the environment and interact with the other behaviors in the network without central control. The agent is driven by internal motivations on the one hand, but the behaviors can also be activated through the environment on the other, which enables the agent to take advantage of a given situation. If several behaviors are above threshold, one is chosen for execution. There is a certain similarity between this concept of behaviors and the operators in the STRIPS model: A number of preconditions have to be fulfilled, and if executed, the behaviors have a certain effect on the agent or the real world. Although in simulations the satisfaction of these preconditions is easily recognized, in robotic agents it has to be extracted from sensory readings.

Action selection dynamics has been tested on both simulated and robotic agents. For an evaluation and comparison with other mechanisms for action selection (or behavior selection), the reader is referred to Tyrell 1993.

Extended Braitenberg Architectures

In chapter 6 we discussed Braitenberg vehicles. Instead of modules or behavioral layers, Braitenberg vehicles have a number of simple processes all of which run in parallel and continuously influence the agent's internal state. We have seen that in this way coherent and sometimes surprisingly sophisticated behavior can be generated. We mentioned that these ideas can be extended to agent architectures in general (Lambrinos and Scheier 1995; Scheier and Pfeifer 1995). The approach is called Extended Braitenberg Architecture (EBA) and is illustrated with an example in the next section. Here we summarize the main principles, which figure 11.7 depicts graphically. The agent is equipped with a number of sensors ("sensor 1," "sensor 2", and "sensor 3"). Sensors can be anything from infrared sensors to wheel encoders that measure the

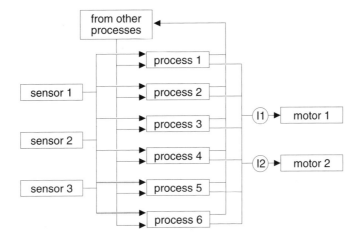

Figure 11.7 Basic EBA scheme. Sensors provide input to processes. Processes compute an output that is integrated for each motor separately ("I1" and "I2"). In the simplest case, integration is computed by summing over all process outputs. Processes can also give input to other processes, as indicated by the arrows going back from the output to the input side of the processes ("from other processes"). This allows processes to influence (e.g., modulate) other processes.

robot's speed. Each sensor is connected to a number of processes ("process 1" to "process 6"), and this connection can be weighted to modulate a particular sensor's influence on a process. A small weight means that the sensor contributes only weak input to the process, even if the sensor is fully activated. The designer has to decide which sensor has to be connected to which process. Typically, a sensor is connected to only a subset of the existing processes. Processes are usually implemented as neural networks. (There are, however, other possible implementations of a process.) A process for controlling the motion of a camera upon input from that camera, for example, could be implemented using standard active vision techniques (see chapter 12). The next section presents an example of an architecture in which all processes are implemented as neural networks.

Processes provide output to other processes (see arrow pointing to "from other processes" in figure 11.7) as well as to the motors ("motor 1" and "motor 2" in the figure). Let us first look at the former, i.e., process outputs that give input to other processes. This type of connection between processes allows one process to modulate the activation of another. Processes also send output to the motors. For example, the output of a `move-forward` and an `avoid` process might be fed into a robot's left and right motor.

For this to work, the outputs have to be integrated ("I1" and "I2" in figure 11.7). The most straightforward way to integrate process outputs is simply to sum the individual outputs and set the motor variable equal to this sum (which might be normalized in some way, e.g., using the number of processes over which the sum has been taken). Even though this integration scheme is simple, it can lead to surprising and complex behavior, as the next section shows. Nevertheless, it is clear that eventually more complex integration schemes have to be used, especially if the number of processes involved exceeds a critical number.

Finally, it is important to note that all the processes run in parallel and all the time. They exert a varying influence on the agent's behavior depending on the circumstances. So under certain conditions, they have no influence on the agent, and in others, they constitute its major influence; but they are not "on" or "off." What the agent does at any point is the result of all the processes. This is an important point, because it effectively means that it will not be trivial to infer from observing the agent's behavior what the underlying mechanisms are, since the behavior is the result of the compound activity of many processes running in parallel. Given this architecture, the agent's behavior is emergent from the joint activation of the processes and not determined by some sort of selection mechanism. In contrast to the action selection dynamics model, EBA has no selection process: Processes are not behaviors that can be chosen for execution.

Interestingly, Kien and Altman (1992) have made a proposal very similar to EBA for behavioral control in animals, particularly in the insect motor system. Figure 11.8 depicts their model, which considers the motor system as a set of several loops acting in parallel. The authors suggest that it is the "consensus of the activity in these loops that regulates behavior and provides the basis for decision making" (p. 164). Note the striking similarity to the EBA (and the other approaches discussed in this section): there are several parallel, loosely coupled processes that together lead to coherent behavior. Interestingly, Kien and Altman stress that in their model, "decisions are an emergent property of the whole system; they are the outcome of the total activity in all the loops at any time, where each loop regulates different aspects of motor output and hence of behavior" (1992, p. 165). This is precisely what we claimed for the behavior control problem in robots, too: Behavior is

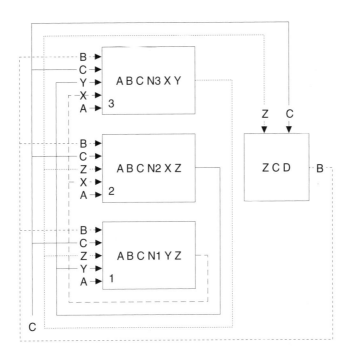

Figure 11.8 Behavior control model of Kien and Altman (1992). The model is composed of several parts (1–3) representing different systems of functional organization. The output of each system (X,Y,Z) provides one component of the input to the other systems, so that all parts are kept informed about the state of the others. Each part also receives sensory stimulation (A,B), and the internal state of the animal (C). The model operates as several loops, each of which makes a different contribution to the selection of the final motor output. (Adapted from Kien and Altman 1992.)

an emergent property of the whole system of processes running in parallel.

Kien and Altman's model summarizes data on insect behavior. The question arises whether the same, or at least similar, principles hold in so-called higher animals like primates or humans as well. Kien and Altman explicitly address this issue: "The principles we propose here are generally applicable to the study of motor systems in a wide range of animals from mollusks to mammals, and perhaps to sensory processing as well" (1992, p. 166). Additional evidence that this might indeed be the case comes from a recent book by Milner and Goodale (1995) on the human visual system. In essence, Miller and Goodale show that there are many sets of parallel pathways in the visual systems of many species, including humans. For example, in a large group of animals (both amphibian and mammalian), separate pathways from the retina right through the motor system mediate several behaviors triggered by visual stimulation such as escape or obstacle avoidance. Moreover, the cerebral cortex has many interacting visuomotor systems, and these systems support a range of skilled behaviors, such as visually guided reaching and grasping. How are these visuomotor loops integrated? According to Milner and Goodale, there is no need "to suppose that the different actions controlled by these networks are guided by a single visual representation of the world residing somewhere in the animal's brain. There is clearly no single representation or comparator to which all the animal's action are referred" (1995, p. 12). This suggests that much of the skilled behavior we observe in humans might be based on the principle of parallel, loosely coupled processes as well, implemented by many visuomotor loops running in parallel.

The Immunoid Approach

Ishiguro and his coworkers (e.g., Ishiguro et al. 1997; Watanabe et al. 1998) have introduced the immunoid approach to the behavior control problem. The main idea of this innovative approach is that insights and concepts from immunology can be used to solve the behavior control problem, because both the immune system and the behavior control system have to solve similar problems: They deal with various sensory inputs through the interaction among a number of parallel processes. Naturally, the immunoid approach draws heavily on concepts from immunology, which is why we only give a brief summary here; a detailed discussion would require the introduction of the necessary terms from immunology and is beyond the scope of this book.

The human body's immune system consists, among other things, of so-called antibodies. An antibody recognizes specific foreign substances such as viruses or cancer cells that invade the human body. These substances are called antigens. The so-called immune network hypothesis suggests mechanisms of how antibodies (and other components of the immune system) act together to generate appropriate responses to invading antigens. The main idea underlying this hypothesis is that antibodies are not isolated structures, but rather communicate with each other, leading to a large-scale network (figure 11.9a).

The application of this hypothesis to the behavior control problem is as follows. The robot is equipped with a number of sensors. The sensory readings act like antigens invading the robot's control

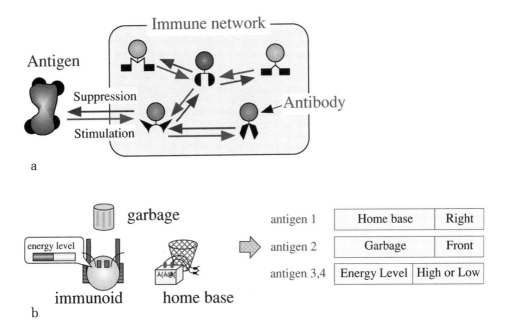

Figure 11.9 The immunoid approach. (a) The main idea. Sensory input is conceptualized in terms of antigens, and internal processes are viewed as antibodies that neutralize the invading antigens. The antibodies form a distributed, decentralized network. (b) Application to a garbage collecting robot. An antigen indicates that energy is low and an appropriate internal process (in the form of antibodies) is selected. The selection depends on the concentration of the antibody as determined by the goodness of match to the antigen. The situation shown on the left is represented in terms of antigens on the right (reprinted with permission).

architecture, which consists of a number of processes each of which implements a simple behavior such as obstacle avoidance, grasping, or exploring. The key idea is to conceptualize these processes as antibodies, and their interaction as a stimulation and suppression between antibodies. The main result is that such an architecture selects processes (antibodies) appropriate for the current situation as indicated by the sensory readings (antigens).

When an antigen enters the architecture, an appropriate antibody must be selected. In other words, a process suitable for the current situation has to be identified. This is of course the core issue in behavior control. Antibodies are activated whenever they match with an antigen. For example, if an antigen indicates that the energy level is low (figure 11.9b), the antibody corresponding to this situation (low energy level) will be selected. More specifically, each antibody has an associated variable that indicates the concentration of the antibody. This concentration is high when the antibody matches perfectly with the incoming antigen. The antibody with the highest concentration is selected and the corresponding behavior is executed (e.g., going to the home base). In other words, there is a competitive coordination among the different antibodies. This approach has similarities both with the subsumption architecture, as well as with the EBA approach. Similar to the subsumption architecture, there is only one behavior that is selected at each point in time. All other behaviors (antibodies) are suppressed. Unlike subsumption-based architectures, and similar to the EBA, there is no layering of processes.

There are several interesting extensions to the basic setup just described. First, the connectivity between antibodies can be learned using reinforcement learning techniques. In other words, the coupling of the parallel processes can be learned and does not, as in the case of, for example, the subsumption architecture, have to be specified a priori. A second, very interesting extension concerns the question of what kinds and how many antibodies should be used for a particular task. In other words, what type of behaviors, and how many of them should be implemented by the designer? This is a fundamental question for which there currently exists no decisive methodology. The core problem is that once the basic set of processes is defined, the robot will not be able to go beyond these behaviors. How can we make a robot produce behaviors that we, as designers, have not implemented beforehand? Within the immunology framework there is a natural way to approach this basic problem, called metadynamics. In essence, metadynamics refers to a process whereby antibodies are removed or created. Since each antibody corresponds to a particular behavior, this is equivalent to having certain behaviors removed, and new ones added. Ishiguro and his colleagues are currently implementing such a metadynamics in the setup just described. This work is an important step toward resolving one fundamental issue of intelligence: the generation of diversity.

Collective Approaches

So far we have discussed approaches in which the principle of parallel, loosely coupled processes is used to control the behavior of one agent. The principle is not restricted to single agents, however, but also holds for the control of a group of society of agents. The idea, introduced in the previous chapter, is to view each agent as a process (which might itself consist of a number of processes). Collective behavior among these agents can then be viewed as resulting from a number of parallel, loosely coupled processes. The coupling here can often be achieved through changing and perceiving or changing the environment in some way (e.g., pheromone trails) or some other simple form of communication between the agents. We emphasized in chapter 8 that studies on social ants demonstrate that often cooperation between such agents is emergent. For example, experiments by Deneubourg and his colleagues show that sorting behavior in ants can be achieved without explicit communication between the ants (Deneubourg et al. 1991). Other examples of emergent collective behavior we have mentioned in chapter 8 are Reynolds' boids and Mataric's flocking robots, as well as the artificial societies of Epstein and Axtell.

From this discussion we can see that the principle of parallel, loosely coupled processes is compatible with ideas of self-organization theory. Self-organization is found in systems (a) that are distributed and (b) whose individual components interact only locally with each other. Moreover, from this interaction, coherent patterns emerge. Examples of emergent patterns include heap building in ants (Deneubourg et al. 1991) or robots (Maris and te Boekhorst 1996), insect walking (Cruse et al. 1996), or even human behavior (Kelso 1995).

Finally, it is important to note that analogous to the coordination problem in the control of single agents, the cooperation between a group of agents results from the agents interacting with their environment. We can see again that the core idea of coordinating a number of processes, either internal or implemented in various agents, is to exploit the system-environment interaction.

This completes our overview on some of the better known behavior control architectures. We have discussed a variety of different approaches employing the principle of parallel, loosely coupled, processes. We now take a very close look at an example. It is time to explore some experiments that further illustrate how behavior can be controlled according to this principle.

11.4   Case Study: A Self-Sufficient Garbage Collector

In this section, we use the EBA discussed earlier in this chapter to build a garbage-collecting robot that has to maintain its battery charge. The case study illustrates how the concepts of the EBA, and

Figure 11.10   Task environment of garbage-collecting robot: collecting objects while maintaining a sufficient level of battery charge. The home base is marked as a shaded area, the charging station is equipped with a light source.

more generally the principle of parallel, loosely coupled processes, can be used to actually design and implement a control architecture for an autonomous agent. The overall structure of this section follows the steps in designing agent experiments we have described in chapter 4 (table 4.5). The first question to be answered is what research goal we are pursuing. In the case study presented here, we are interested in testing the principle of parallel, loosely coupled processes, as instantiated in the EBA. In other words, we focus on general principles of intelligence, rather than modeling a particular natural agent or solving a task from an engineering perspective.

Desired Behavior and Ecological Niche

Table 4.5 tells us that whenever designing an agent, we have to specify the ecological niche and the agent's desired behaviors or tasks. The ecological niche for the robot in this example is a flat environment with a recharging station and a home base to which the agent has to bring the garbage it collects (figure 11.10). The home base is marked with a shaded area so that the agent can detect it with its floor sensor. It is located on the opposite side of the charging station. The task of the agent is to collect the objects in its environment and bring them to the home base. At the same time, it has to sustain itself by regularly visiting the charging station, which is equipped with a light source. The agent uses this light to find the charging station and the home base with its ambient light sensors, that is, by performing phototaxis (i.e., moving toward a

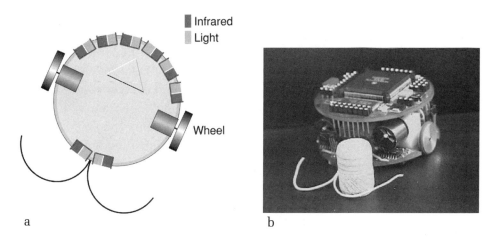

Figure 11.11 Robot platform used in the experiments. A two-sided wire loop has been attached to the rear of the robot, enabling the robot to grasp small objects. (a) Schematic of robot, which is the generic robot introduced in chapter 5 (figure 5.8). (b) Real robot.

light source) and antiphototaxis (moving away from the light source), respectively. Whenever the light values exceed a certain threshold, the agent receives energy according to the equation

$$\Delta E = E_c(1 - E(t)^2), \tag{11.1}$$

where E_c is a constant. Thus, the energy inflow, ΔE, depends on the current battery level, $E(t)$. It is larger when $E(t)$ is low and vice versa. Objects for the experiment are small, wooden cylinders. In all experiments conducted, 30 objects were randomly distributed over the whole arena.

Low-Level Specifications and Platform

How we define our agent's task environment largely determines its low-level specifications. An agent with small wheels has been used in this instance, the miniature robot Khepera, because its intended ecological niche consisted of a flat and clean surface. A "gripper" made out of two bent wires was attached to the back of the agent, forming a kind of a two-sided hook. With this "gripper" the agent could grasp objects distributed in the environment (see figure 11.11b). We did not have to use a more sophisticated gripper because we knew in advance that there would be only objects of a particular diameter in the task environment. The hook was adjusted to match this diameter, which amounted to creating a kind of object recognizer: Only those objects would be "recognized" that fit into the wire loop, that is, that had the appropriate diameter. This provides an example of how constraints in the morphology can be exploited to simplify a problem that would otherwise be more difficult to solve. Rutkowska (1997) has made a similar point. In her theoretical analysis of the agent discussed here, she pointed out that this "constrained grasping" is a kind of "embodied knowledge," provided through physical-morphological constraints: "Different environmental objects permit different activities of the *Khepera* agent, and the diameter of its collection wire [its wire loop] contributes to determining what are graspable and non-graspable things, providing the agent with a 'body-scaled' notion of object size" (p. 292). Note that even in this simple setup, the agent is—from an observer's perspective—making distinctions between walls and garbage. Walls simply don't fit into the wire loop, so they belong to a different category than garbage.

Now that we have described the low-level specification of the agent's motor system, let us look at its sensors. The agent was equipped with nine IR sensors, six in the front, two in the back and one on the bottom of the agent. Objects inside the wire loop could be detected by one of the rear IR sensors. The sensor on the bottom of the agent formed a kind of "floor sensor" that could detect black markers in the environment, such as the one at the home base (see figure 11.10). Except for this floor sensor, the agent is an instantiation of the generic agent architecture introduced in chapter 5 (see figure 11.11a).

In addition to being able to detect objects, walls, and its home base, the agent had to maintain its battery level, and thus had to be able to sense the current level of energy contained in its battery. We added a sensor for the battery level, E. In the present implementation, the agent could not sense its actual, physical battery level; rather the battery level was simulated (as was the recharging process).

Control Architecture

The next step in designing our garbage collector involves the definition of the control architecture. The control architecture used here is based on the EBA. A number of simple, prewired processes all run in parallel and continuously influence the agent's effectors: move-forward, avoid-obstacle, home, deposit, go-to-charging-station, and recharge. We have chosen names for

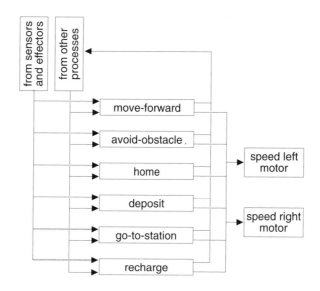

Figure 11.12 Control architecture of the garbage-collecting robot. The architecture is based on the EBA. Six processes run in parallel: `mode-forward`, `avoid-obstacle`, `home`, `deposit`, `go-to-charging-station`, and `recharge`. They receive input from the robot's sensors and contribute activity to the robot's motors. Each process is implemented as a Braitenberg-style process, that is, a simple neural network that couples the robot's sensors and motors. The processes are coordinated by a cooperative cooperation scheme: linear summation of process outputs.

the processes that relate to behaviors in order to provide some intuitions as to the effect a process has on the agent's behavior when none of the other processes is active (which is, strictly speaking, never the case). However, it might have been better to name them differently, for example, the move-forward process might be called "send same amount of activation to both motors." Again, strictly speaking, from the agent's perspective, it is not executing a move-forward process but sending activiation to the motors. The processes are implemented as Braitenberg-style processes: In other words, they receive inputs from the sensors and contribute their activation to the motors. Figure 11.12 shows the architecture. Two variables are associated with the two motors, corresponding to their respective speed. The processes continuously change these speed variables by adding or subtracting particular values. A sum of the output values from all processes determines the speed variables. Formally, this can be written as

$$\mathbf{s}(t) = (s_l(t), s_r(t)) = \left(\sum_{i=1}^{N} o_i^l(t), \sum_{i=1}^{N} o_i^r(t) \right), \tag{11.2}$$

where $s_l(t)$ and $s_r(t)$ are the left and the right motor speed, $o_i^l(t)$ and $o_i^r(t)$ the contributions of process i to the motor speeds, and N is the total number of processes. This is the most simple form of cooperative coordination. The speed variables determine what the agent does, since the two wheel motors are the only ways it can control its motor system.

The complete source code for all the processes listed in figure 11.12 can be downloaded from the internet page. The reader is encouraged to have a look at (or even run) the complete source code to get an idea of the workings of the complete architecture. Here we focus on four of the six processes: `move-forward`, `avoid-obstacle`, `go-to-charging-station`, and `recharge`. Together, the processes make the agent avoid and grasp objects and keep the energy level above critical values. We show how this functionality can be achieved by incrementally adding processes to the architecture.

The first thing with which a mobile agent has to be equipped is a process for moving forward. The activity of the `move-forward` process is extremely simple: A constant value is written to the motors (figure 11.13b), making the agent move forward at a fixed speed (figure 11.13a). Note that, as expected, all the agent did was move forward. At some point, however, it crashed against the wall after about five seconds (figure 11.13c). This is obviously not very wise and potentially harmful. So, in addition to the `move-forward` process, we needed to define a process by means of which the agent could avoid obstacles and walls. Moreover, we needed a process that caused the agent to grasp the objects it was supposed to collect. In the set-up used here, only one process was needed to accomplish both tasks. We called this process `avoid-obstacle` because avoiding was all it could make the agent do. The grasping behavior came free from the interaction with the `move-forward` process, because as the agent turned away from the object, the object would end up in the hook on the agent's rear, as figure 11.14 shows.

The agent successfully avoided the object. The two processes, `move-forward` and `avoid-obstacle`, were running in parallel, and their output was summed to yield the motor speeds (figure 11.14a). Note that the agent was moving forward and avoiding the object, using the only two behaviors available to it at that point, but from an observer's point of view, it seemed to grasp the object. Grasping was not explicitly represented in the agent's processes. Rather, it was emergent from the parallel activity of the two pro-

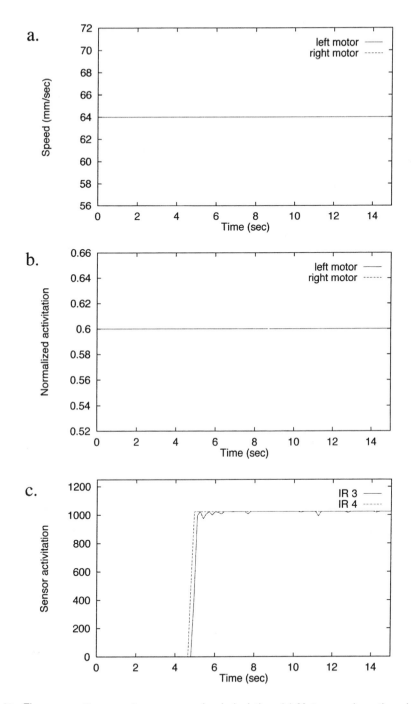

Figure 11.13 The move-forward process running in isolation. (a) Motor speeds as the robot moves in the environment. (b) Contribution of move-forward. It is a simple constant added to the motor speed variables. (c) Activation in the two front IR sensors. The sharp increase after about five seconds indicates that the robot crashed into a wall because at this point it had only the move-forward process and therefore lacked means of avoiding obstacles.

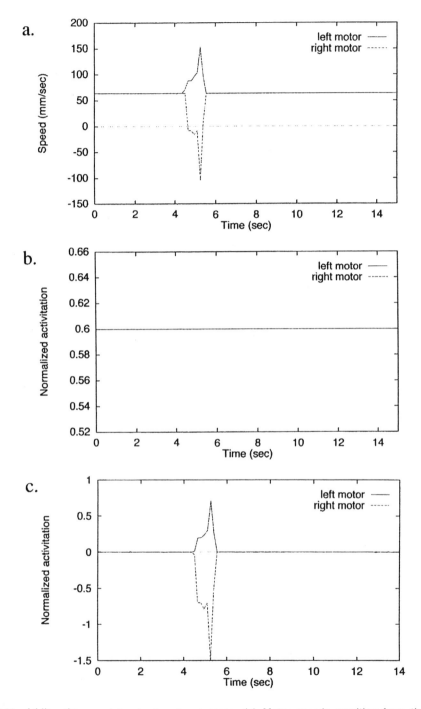

Figure 11.14 Adding the `avoid-obstacle` process. (a) Motor speeds resulting from the parallel processing (the thin line indicates 0 speed). (b) Output of the `move-forward` process. It is the same constant as in figure 11.13. (c) Output of the `avoid-obstacle` process. The robot encountered an object after moving forward for about 5 seconds and avoided it by turning to the right. A strong negative

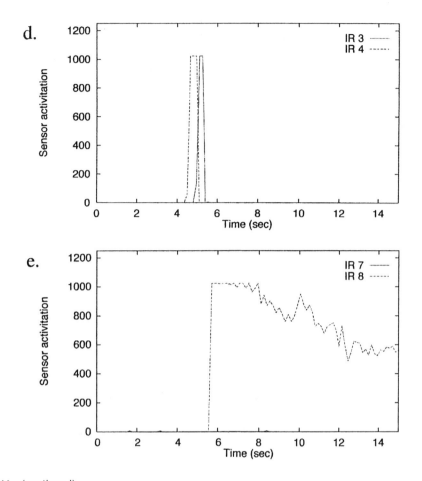

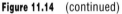

Figure 11.14 (continued)
output of the `avoid-obstacle` process to the right motor and a positive output to the left motor generated the turning behavior. (d) Activation in the two front IR sensors. There is only very brief activation in the two front IR sensors; that is, the robot hits the obstacle very shortly and then avoids the obstacle successfully. (e) Activation in the back two IR sensors. IR8 is activated because the robot now has a cylinder in the wire hook. Note that both processes are active during this "grasping" behavior. The robot is moving forward and avoiding—the only two behaviors it has at this point—but to an observer it seems to grasp objects.

cesses controlling the agent's behavior and its interaction with the object. It is clear that this emergent grasping occurred only because of the particular positioning and shape of the hook. Although this might seem like cheating, it was, as mentioned earlier, an instantiation of the principle of cheap design in that we exploited constraints of the niche (e.g., size and shape of objects) to simplify certain otherwise difficult problems (e.g., identifying objects to collect, mechanisms of grasping).

Let us briefly look at how the `avoid-obstacle` process is implemented. The process increases its influence on the speed variables as the agent gets close to an obstacle. Its output is a weighted sum of the activation of all front IR sensors:

$$o_l^{(ao)}(t) = \sum_{i=1}^{6} w_{il}^{(ao)} IR_i(t),$$ (11.3)

$$o_r^{(ao)}(t) = \sum_{i=1}^{6} w_{ir}^{(ao)} IR_i(t),$$ (11.4)

where $w_{ij}^{(ao)}$ are weights determining the influence of each corresponding IR sensor $IR_i(t)$ on the activation of the process. These weights are chosen such that obstacles on the right lead to high activity in $o_r^{(ao)}(t)$ and low activity in $o_l^{(ao)}(t)$ and vice versa. As a result, the agent turns in the opposite direction of the high IR sensor activation (figure 11.14a) and thus avoids the obstacle (figure 11.14d).

So far, we have discussed two processes, `move-forward` and `avoid-obstacle`. These processes enabled the agent to explore its environment (by moving straight forward), avoid obstacles, and, via an emergent behavior, grasp objects. In addition, the agent needed to be equipped with processes that would make it bring the objects it had grasped to a home base and visit the recharging station whenever its battery level reached critical values. Let us first discuss the latter, the `go-to-charging-station` process. Whenever the battery level was low, the `go-to-charging-station` process needed to be highly active so that the agent visited the charging station and recharged. The tendency to go to the charging station depended on the battery level and the agent's distance from the charging station. The agent found the charging station using its light sensors, that is, by phototaxis, as figure 11.15 shows.

Because of the joint processing of the `move-forward`, `avoid-obstacle`, and `go-to-charging-station` processes, the agent

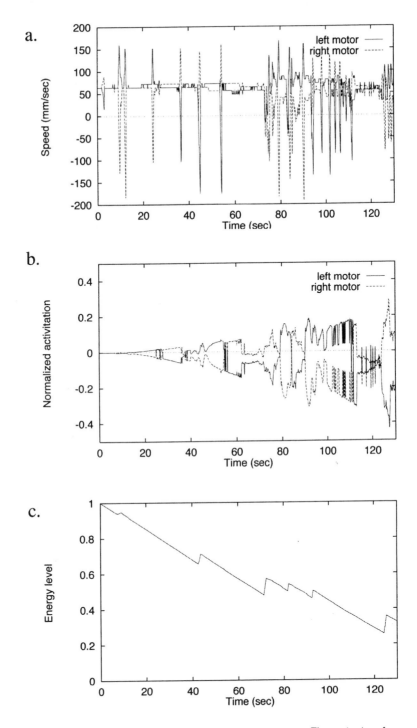

Figure 11.15 Adding the go-to-charging-station process. The outputs of move-forward and the avoid-obstacle are similar to those in figure 11.14. (a) Motor speeds from the joint processing of the three processes. (b) Output of the go-to-charging-station process. The output of the process increases as the overall energy level decreases and drops to 0 when the robot receives energy. (c) Time series of energy level. The agent visits the charging station regularly, but only small increases in the energy level result, because the robot does not stop at the charging station: It lacks, at this point, a recharge process.

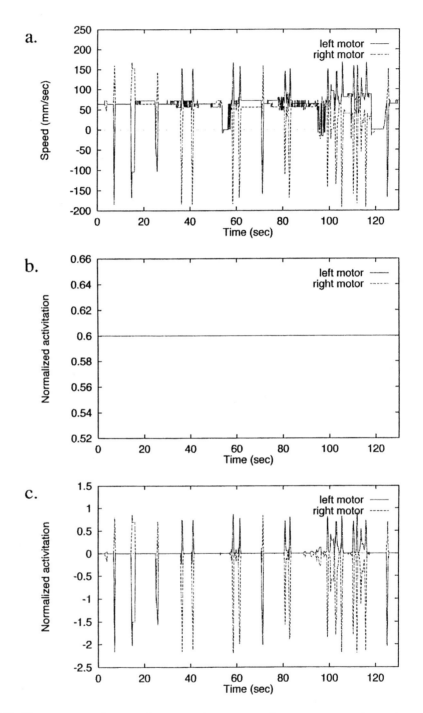

Figure 11.16 The move-forward, avoid-obstacle, go-to-charging-station, and recharge processes running in parallel. (a) Motor speeds resulting from the parallel processing. (b) Output of the move-forward process. (c) Output of the avoid-obstacle process. (d) Output of the go-to-charging-station process. (e) Output of the recharge process. This

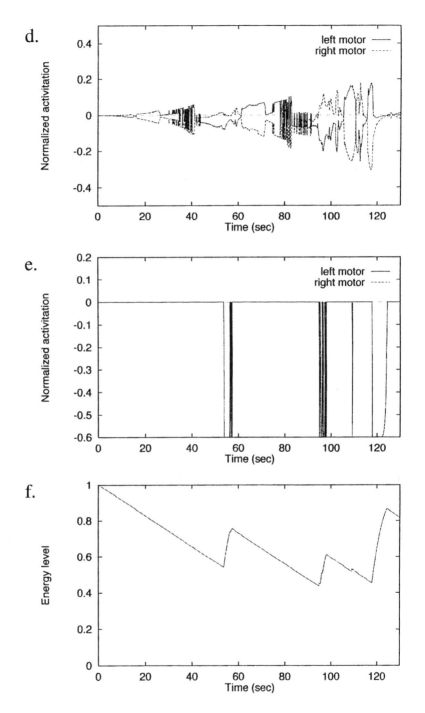

Figure 11.16 (continued)
process tries to stop the robot (the motor speeds become 0; see panel a) by producing an output (−0.6) that "neutralizes" the output of the move-forward process (0.6). This can be seen clearly at around 120 seconds. (f) Time series of energy level. In contrast to figure 11.15c, the energy level is now kept in a safe range because of the activity of recharge.

moved to the charging station. It received small amounts of energy from the charging station (figure 11.15c), but it couldn't really recharge, because it didn't stay in the charging station long enough. Given its setup at the time, the agent did not really stop at the charging station: It had no process to generate such a stopping behavior. This can be seen in figure 11.15c: Whenever the agent entered the charging station, it received small amounts of energy, resulting in small increases in its energy level. Overall, however, the absolute energy level decreased from its initial value of 1 to 0.3 after about 120 seconds. This was undesirable: We needed an additional process to make the agent stop at the charging station. This is the task of the recharge process, which causes the agent to slow down once inside the charging station. The activity of this process is a function of the energy inflow. The energy inflow is large when the battery level is low and vice versa, as discussed above. Thus when the agent enters the charging station with a low battery level, the inflow is large, and as a consequence, the recharge process tries to stop the agent. Figure 11.16 shows the dynamics of the complete system discussed so far. The agent was at this point self-sufficient: Its energy level did not drop below critical levels (figure 11.16f), because the agent, due to the activity of the recharge process, stopped at the charging station (figure 11.16a) and received much more energy than before, when it only passed by the energy station (figure 11.15d).

The parallel architecture just discussed has several side effects. Let us look at two in more detail, illustrated in figure 11.17. The figure shows that the agent can behave "rationally": Whenever its energy level was low, it stopped grasping objects it encountered on its way to the charging station (figure 11.17c), because the go-to-charging-station process "drove" the agent toward the charging station; its influence on the motor speeds was stronger than usual (figure 11.17b) and caused the agent to avoid objects, but not grasp them. This behavior had not been explicitly programmed. Rather, it emerged because all the agent's processes run in parallel: the avoid-obstacle process was still running, but its influence on the motor speeds was at that point now smaller because of the large output of the go-to-charging-station process. As soon as the energy level was within safe ranges again, the agent returned to grasping objects (figure 11.17c).

The parallel processing had another interesting side effect. In some situations, the agent got stuck and could no longer move. For example, it sometimes got stuck in a corner of the environment: There were a number of objects in the corner, and the agent tried to avoid them, which resulted in a 0 motor speed when there was an object on the left, on the right, in the back and in the front of the agent. In this situation, the energy level kept decreasing because the robot was still trying to move. This energy decrease increased the activation of the `go-to-charging-station` process; that is, its influence on the motor speeds increased. As a result, the agent was "pulled" in a different direction—the charging station—and started to move again. Initially, it made only small wiggling movements, but since this did increase its energy use, the activation of the `go-to-charging-station` process further increased. At some point, the agent's wiggling behavior became strong enough for it to get out of the impasse and reach the charging station. This illustrates an advantage of having parallel processes that operate autonomously: The agent could get out of the impasse only because the `go-to-charging-station` process was continuously contributing activity to the motor variables.

Once the agent has grasped an object, it should bring it to the home base. High activity in the `home` process, which generates such behavior, causes the agent to go to the home base. The agent estimates direction of the home base via antiphototaxis, that is, by going in the opposite direction of the light gradient emitted from the charging station. Antiphototaxis is used because the home base is located at the corner opposite the charging station, where the lamp is mounted. The tendency to go to the home base is proportional to the number of objects the agent is carrying. Note that the agent cannot count the number of objects it is carrying. It can only sense whether it is carrying something in its left or right wire loop by using the two IR sensors on its back (see figure 11.14e). Both sensors are active when the agent is carrying two or more objects, leading to a strong tendency to visit the home base. Similarly, when only one sensor is active, the agent is carrying one object only, and there is a weaker tendency to go to the home base. Finally, when the agent reaches the home base, the floor sensor sends strong activation to the `deposit` process.

Our discussion so far illustrates the incremental nature of designing and evaluating control architectures. We started with one process only, the `move-forward` process. We then ran experiments (figure 11.13) and realized the need for an `avoid-obstacle` process. After having added means for avoiding obstacles, we again

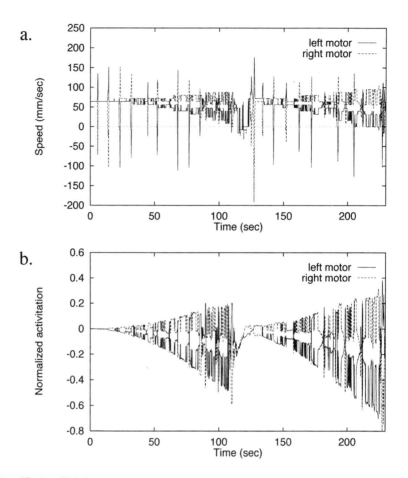

Figure 11.17 "Rational" behavior of the garbage-collecting robot: Whenever its energy is low, it does not grasp objects it encounters on its way to the charging station. (a) Motor speeds resulting from the parallel processing. (b) Output of the `go-to-charging-station` process. The output increases as the energy decreases and vice versa. (c) Activation of the rear IR sensors. (d) Time series of energy level. After about 80 seconds, the agent no longer grasps objects (indicated by 0 activation of the rear IR sensors; see panel c). The output of the `go-to-charging-station` process increases significantly (panel b). This output influences the motor speeds in such a way that the robot avoids objects but does not grasp them. This is "rational" because if the robot had grasped the object, it would not have made it to the charging station.

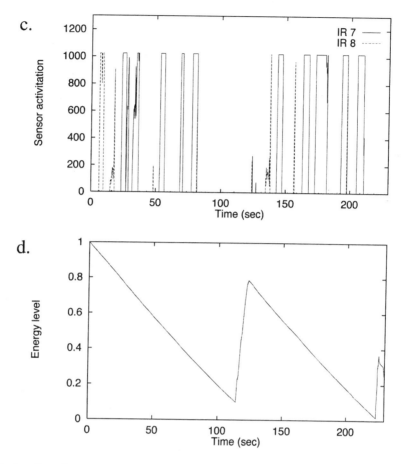

Figure 11.17 (continued)

ran experiments (figure 11.14), after which we decided to add the `go-to-charging-station` process. Experiments with this three-process architecture (figure 11.15) revealed the need for an additional process to make the agent stop sufficiently long at the charging station for its energy level to increase significantly. This was accomplished by adding the `recharge` process (figure 11.16). Running this architecture in turn showed interesting side effects (figure 11.17). Throughout the discussion, we have illustrated the experiments by plotting the relevant internal data: the motor speeds, the contribution of the individual processes to the motor speeds, the activation levels of the sensors, and the energy level. We have chosen to represent the results in terms of internal data in order to illustrate the parallel dynamics underlying the agent's behavior. We said in chapter 4 that there are many ways to describe an agent's behavior; only one was shown here. For example, we could have added summary statistics of the agent's performance: We could have recorded, among other things, the number of objects the agent had grasped per unit time (or before the energy level dropped to 0), the distance it had traveled until the energy level dropped below some threshold, or the number of objects the agent did not collect. We could have also varied the number of objects in the environment to assess how this affected the agent's performance. Moreover, we could have systematically changed critical parameters (e.g., the weights connecting the processes to the motors) in order to evaluate how the agent's performance was affected by these changes. Clearly, the presentation of all these results would be beyond the scope of this chapter. In general, however, we should always collect summary statistics in addition to data showing the dynamics within a single trial.

Issues to Think About

Issues 11.1: Coherent Behavior and Sequencing

The main question researchers have asked is how one can obtain coherent behavior from an agent in the form of sequences of actions if there are merely a number of parallel processes and if the information generated from the various processes is not integrated in a central process or representation. One of the essential points here is that sequences of behavior can occur even if there is no internal representation of these sequences. Simon's ant on the beach walks, turns, walks, turns, picks up food, and so forth, and we strongly suspect that the sequence of these behaviors is not represented as a plan. It is often surprising how far we can get in terms of generating sequences of behavior without representing them internally. Sequences can arise simply because the loop between output and input is closed: An agent's action leads to the next input, which in turn triggers the next action. One should first exploit these interactions before explicitly designing sequencing mechanisms into the agent. Think about potential sequencing mechanisms that one might consider necessary to get the agent to do its job in the right sequence (but that turn out to be unnecessary). An example of such a mechanism might be one that prevents the agent from grasping pegs if it is on the way to the charging station.

Issue 11.2:   Free Will?

The principle discussed in this chapter makes a strong claim: Intelligence is emergent from a large number of parallel, loosely coupled processes. In other words, there is no need for a controlling agent that manages the dynamics of these processes; rather, they are coordinated by means of competitive or cooperative coordination mechanisms as the agent interacts with the environment. With this focus on emergence, you may start to wonder about your own actions. If behavior is emergent, how do you control it? We usually have the feeling of being in control of our own actions, of knowing what we want to do and how we want to do it. The principle presented in this chapter claims that a large part of your actions are emergent: Is this a contradiction? How can you reconcile your own feeling of possessing free will with the notion of parallel, loosely coupled processes that are *not* controlled by some internal or external agent?

Points to Remember

- The principle of parallel, loosely coupled processes states that intelligence is emergent from a large number of parallel processes loosely coupled to the sensory-motor system. These processes run asynchronously and are largely peripheral, requiring little or no centralized resources. The principle is fundamental to most control architectures in embodied cognitive science. It addresses the behavior control problem.

- The design and implementation of control architectures for autonomous agents encompasses three main aspects: process definition, implementation, and coordination. First, the basic processes need to be defined. The implementation of these processes requires appropriate formalisms and methods. The resulting processes have to be coordinated. There are competitive and cooperative coordination mechanisms; the environment can be exploited to simplify process coordination.

- Traditional approaches design control architectures by means of functional decomposition, which leads to a sense-think-act cycle. Embodied approaches employ a different strategy in which instead of a number of functional modules, parallel processes with direct connections to the sensory-motor apparatus are designed. These processes lead to emergent functionality: Each function emerges out of their concurrent activity.

- Many approaches to behavior control are based on the notion of hierarchies. They employ the goal-directed principle, according to which behavior results from a comparison between a representation of a goal state and the actual (usually current) situation. The following models fall into this category: TOTE (psychology), STRIPS (artificial intelligence), and Tinbergen's model (ethology).

- We have discussed alternative approaches based on the notion of parallel, loosely coupled processes: Process Description Language, subsumption, action selection dynamics, EBA, and the immunoid and collective approaches. All but the last are control architectures for autonomous agents that fully exploit the principle of parallel, loosely coupled processes.

- The case study of the self-sufficient garbage collector illustrates how coherent behavior can be incrementally designed by means of parallel processes. We have looked in detail at how one such agent behaved in the various stages of its design. It turned out that the avoid-obstacle process, in addition to preventing collisions, made the agent grasp objects; there was no need to explicitly design grasping behavior.

- Behavior control based on parallel processes can lead to interesting side effects. For example, the garbage collector stopped grasping objects when it was low on energy because of the increased activity of the go-to-charging-station process. In other words, it displayed rational beheavior.

Further Reading

Jeannerod, M. (1997). *The cognitive neuroscience of action.* Oxford, UK: Blackwell. (A recent monograph by one of the leading researchers in the neuroscience of behavior control. The book presents a large amount of empirical data about behavior control, together with an overview of the most important ideas and concepts of (traditional) approaches to behavior control, including Jeannerod's own model.)

Kien, J., and Altman, J. S. (Eds.). (1992). *Neuroethology of action selection.* Cambridge, MA: MIT Press. (This book summarizes the major findings on behavior control in invertebrates.)

Miller, G. A., Galanter, E., and Pribram, K. (1960). *Plans and the structure of behavior.* New York: Holt, Rinehart and Winston. (A seminal book outlining the classical cognitivistic view of behavior control.)

One core assumption of the embodied cognitive science approach is that intelligence must be studied in the context of system-environment interaction. In chapter 10 we introduced the principle of sensory-motor coordination, which states that all intelligent behavior (e.g., perception, categorization, memory) is to be conceived as a sensory-motor coordination that serves to structure the input. This principle has two main aspects. First, whatever behavior we are analyzing, or whatever behavior we want to design for a robot, the principle suggests that we focus on how sensory and motor systems are coordinated. Second, embodied agents can structure their own sensory input, and thereby induce regularities that significantly simplify learning. Figure 12.1 shows how this principle relates to the other principles.

In the present chapter, we use the principle of sensory-motor coordination to study categorization, a fundamental concept of cognitive science. Any agent in the real world has to be able to make distinctions between different types of objects; that is, it must have the competence of categorization, a prerequisite for intelligence. Making distinctions in the real world comes very naturally to all of us: we recognize objects and find our way around with great ease. However, getting machines—robots—to do the same thing has turned out to be an enormously hard problem, one of the hardest in the study of intelligence. We discuss the question of why this is so hard and we show that the problem of categorization in the real world is significantly simplified if it is viewed as one of sensory-motor coordination, rather than one of information processing. A series of agents is presented to illustrate the ideas. We start by outlining the information processing approach to categorization, and we point out its problems. We then introduce theoretical aspects of viewing categorization in terms of sensory-motor coordination, followed by a number of examples that instantiate, in one way or another, the principle of sensory-motor coordination we then illustrate the theoretical concepts with a case study.

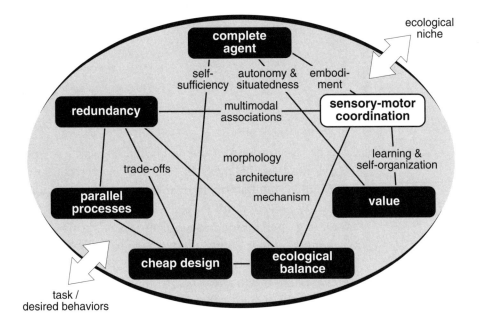

Figure 12.1 The relationship of the principle of sensory-motor coordination (highlighted) to the other design principles. This principle is directly related to the complete agent principle, the value principle, the redundancy principle, and the ecological balance principle. The agent's overall adaptivity is increased if it exploits sensory-motor co-ordination. The value principle is required for sensory-motor coordination because the agent has to have a means of assessing in what sorts of sensory-motor coordinations to engage. A prerequisite of sensory-motor coordination is the appropriate positioning of the sensors on the agent providing the required redundancy for concept learning. Finally, only if the design is ecologically balanced will there be interesting kinds of sensory-motor coordination.

12.1 Categorization: Traditional Approaches

For the most part, research on categorization has been conducted within the information processing framework. In this section, we summarize work from cognitive psychology and machine vision. Our goal is to elucidate the main ideas rather than to give a comprehensive review. Later (section 12.2), we contrast the information processing view on categorization with the one derived from embodied cognitive science.

Cognitive Psychology

Cognitive psychology has a long history of research on categorization, which is not surprising, since categorization is a fundamental act of human cognition. How can we account for the amazingly sophisticated categorization behavior of humans? Cog-

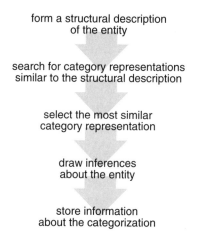

form a structural description
of the entity

search for category representations
similar to the structural description

select the most similar
category representation

draw inferences
about the entity

store information
about the categorization

Figure 12.2 The information processing approach to categorization. According to this view, categorization proceeds through the following steps: First, a structural description of the entity to be categorized is formed. Next, category representations with similar structural descriptions are searched, and the most similar category representation is selected. Based on the selected representation, inferences about the entity are drawn, and finally information about the categorization is stored in memory. (Adapted from Barsalou 1992, p. 48.)

nitive psychology has addressed this question from an information processing perspective (figure 12.2). According to this view, categorization in humans and higher animals involves the following steps (Barsalou 1992): First, a structural description of the object to be categorized is formed. This description provides information about the object's primitive perceptual features, such as horizontal and vertical lines and the relations between these basic features. Next, category representations with similar structural descriptions are searched in memory, and the category representation most similar to the structural description is selected. Based on the selected representation, inferences about the object are drawn, and finally information about the categorization is stored in memory. If the object is a chair, for example, the categories chair, sofa, stool, or table might be considered, given their structural similarity. The selection process would then choose the category "chair" because it is the most similar. Inferences about the chosen category, "chair," would then be drawn—for instance, that it can be sat upon.

Psychological theories of categorization fall into three families; classical, prototype, and exemplar, depending on how categories are assumed to be represented in memory. The modern view on categorization was initiated by Rosch, who showed in a seminal work (1973) that people judge some instances of a category to be better members of that category than other instances. For example, for most people a robin is a better instance of the category "bird" than a penguin. Similarly, when humans are asked to judge typicality of fruits, the most typical fruits are apples and oranges, and less typical fruits are mangos or coconuts (Rosch 1975). These results contradicted the *classical* view that an object is a member of a particular category if and only if it possesses a set of defining features. A category was defined in the classical view to be a description that specified the necessary and sufficient features to be a member of that category. Rosch's main discovery was that people organize categories according to prototypes and that a particular object could be judged to be a good or bad instance of a category, depending on its similarity to the prototype. Thus, categorization turned out to be a matter of degree, and not an all-or-nothing judgment. In this view, categories are defined by a set of features none of which is critical. An object is then an instance of a category to the degree that it possesses a number of characteristic features.

An alternative approach to the prototype view is the *exemplar* approach. According to the exemplar-based approach, the learner stores mental representations of exemplars, grouped by category, then categorizes new instances on the basis of their similarity to the stored ensembles. That is, according to the exemplar view, people do not form abstract category knowledge, such as prototypes, but instead store collections of exemplars. We have already encountered one of the most popular exemplar-based models, ALCOVE, in chapter 4, where we contrasted it with agent-based models. We said this model can account for a wide range of empirical phenomena. Let us look more closely at how exactly it works.

Most connectionist models of categorization consist of an input layer that codes object features and an output layer that represents the categories (e.g., Gluck and Bower, 1988). Typically, the goal is to learn, via supervised learning schemes such as the delta rule, an association or mapping between activations in the input layer and the corresponding activations in the output or category layer. More elaborated models, of which ALCOVE is the best-known example, use a hidden layer in addition to an input and an output layer. Figure 12.3 illustrates this basic scheme. ALCOVE is a feedforward network with three layers of nodes. We encountered a similar network in chapter 5: NETTalk, the network that learns to pronounce English. Both networks have an input layer, a hidden layer, and an

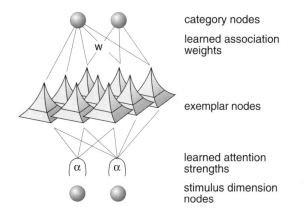

category nodes

learned association
weights

exemplar nodes

learned attention
strengths

stimulus dimension
nodes

Figure 12.3 Overview of the ALCOVE network. ALCOVE is a feedforward network that has input, hidden, and output layers. The weights between the input and the hidden layer are called attentional strengths. The hidden neurons represent the exemplars the network has learned. The output nodes represent the categories.

output layer. The input nodes encode the stimulus, one node per feature dimension or feature. Each input node of ALCOVE is connected to the hidden layer via weights called "attention strengths." These weights change to reflect the relevance of a dimension for the categorical distinction being learned. The larger the weight between an input and a hidden node the more attention the network pays to the feature encoded by that input node. The hidden layer consists of nodes that represent training exemplars. A hidden node is activated when a particular stimulus is similar to the exemplar represented by that node. The larger the resemblance of the input to the stored exemplar, the stronger the activation of the exemplar node. Finally, the output layer consists of one node per category, with each node's activation level computed as a sum of weighted activations from the exemplar nodes. Category activation levels are converted to choice probabilities that is, the activation values in the output nodes are interpreted as indicating the probability with which the network chooses a particular category. Large activation values lead to a high probability and vice versa.

Learning is supervised and involves a learning phase and a test phase. In the learning phase, input vectors (typically binary feature vectors) are presented to the network. The network processes this input and activates one or several category nodes. The difference between the network's output and the correct output (the "categorization error") is then propagated back to the hidden layer, where the weights are adjusted in order to minimize the error. Note that this is, in essence, the standard back-propagation algorithm. (For a discussion of the similarities and differences between ALCOVE and standard back-propagation, see Kruschke 1992.)

In sum, the ALCOVE network instantiates the view that category learning is supervised and that categorization consists in finding a mapping from stimuli onto category representations. Let us now look at how machine vision has addressed categorization.

Machine Vision: Object Recognition

We summarized some of the basic ideas of machine vision in chapter 2 in our discussion of the robot JL. Here we focus on one particular aspect of machine vision: object recognition. In our discussion, we largely follow Ullman's (1996) review of the state of the art in object recognition.

A typical object recognition system consists of a camera attached to a computer. The generic problem artificial object recognition systems address is how to determine which out of a number of individual objects has generated the image currently registered by the sensor (camera). In order words, the system must, based on the camera image, identify the corresponding object, The problem is that objects can change their appearance because of viewing positions, photometric effects (e.g., light conditions), object setting (e.g., different backgrounds), and changes in shape (e.g., animals). The core problem in object recognition is to somehow relate the many views that one and the same object can generate. For example, a car can look very different depending on the viewing position, but it is always the same car. This is also called the object constancy problem. We return to this problem below, because it concerns not only the traditional approaches but categorization models in general.

The core idea in most machine vision approaches to object recognition is similar to the one underlying the psychological approaches summarized above: An input—an image of an object— has to the mapped onto an internal representation—in this case stored templates or views of images. Ullman (1996) distinguishes three major approaches to object recognition, all of which are based on the idea that in order for the agent to match an image of an object to the stored internal representation, regularities across different views of one object have to be exploited. These approaches differ in their specific ways and assumptions of how these regularities can be extracted. The *invariant properties method* assumes that certain basic properties remain invariant under the transformations of changes an object is allowed to make. This has for a long time been the most popular approach. The *parts decomposition method* relies on the decomposition of an object into its constituent parts or generic components. For example, a face might be decomposed into the eyes, nose, and mouth, each of which can often be recognized on their own. The task then is to first locate such a part (e.g., a view on a mouth), then find the corresponding generic component (e.g., mouth), and finally describe the object in terms of its constituent parts. The parts decomposition approach has become more popular in recent years, both in cognitive psychology and machine vision. A third approach, also receiving increasing attention, is called the *alignment method*, described in great detail in Ullman (1996). The core idea in this method is to align the image of the object and the corresponding stored model. For example, if the image of an object and the stored model are very similar except for a difference in size, then aligning the two involves scaling either image or model, thereby reducing the discrepancy and improving the match. More generally, the idea is to store not only a model of an object but also a set of "allowed transformations" that the object may undergo (e.g., changes in size, position, orientation). Object recognition then becomes a matter of searching for a particular model *and* a particular transformation that increase the match between model and image.

Let us look at an example that is based on the alignment approach; the invariant properties and the part decomposition method will not be further elaborated. The particular example summarized here (Basri 1996) is instructive because it combines the alignment approach with the prototype approach to categorize images. We have seen that according to the information processing framework, categorization involves finding a mapping of an input, the image to some internal representation, the stored category representations. The first step in such a scheme is to store a library of object representations (also called object models) in memory. In the example discussed here, a library of 3-D object models was divided by the designer into categories, and 3-D prototype objects were selected to represent the category. A category representation thus consisted of the prototype object and the corresponding set of object models belonging to the category. More specifically, the library of object models consisted of two categories. The first included two chairs, and the second contained two car models (see figure 12.4).

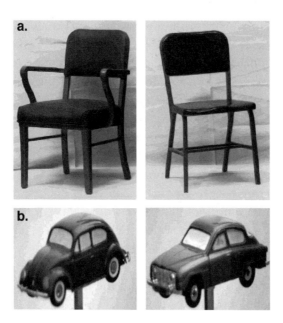

Figure 12.4 The categories used in Basri's (1996) study on object recognition. (a) Pictures of two chairs used as models. The chair on the left was used as prototype and was matched to an image of the chair on the right. (b) Pictures of two cars as models (a VW model, and a Saab model). The task of the object recognition system is to map an image from a model (e.g., an image from the VW model) onto the correct category (a car). (From Basri 1996, p. 21, reprinted with permission.)

Once the object models and the category representations have been established, the system can be used for object recognition. It works in two stages. In the first stage, the *categorization stage*, the image is compared to the prototype objects previously stored in memory. For example, an image of a chair (see figure 12.4) was compared to the chair and the car prototype: This was done by (a) determining the transformation that best aligns the prototype with the image, (b) applying this transformation to the prototype and (c) determining the degree of similarity between the transformed prototype and the image. If the degree of similarity is better than a predefined *categorization threshold*, i.e., the prototype is sufficiently similar to the image, the category of the object has been found. The system has correctly categorized the image as belonging to the category "chair." Figure 12.5 shows a typical result of a good match.

In the second stage, the *identification stage*, the image is compared to the individual object models in its category, which involves searching for an object model that matches the image. In

Figure 12.5 The categorization stage: matching a prototype chair to an image of another chair. (left) The image to be recognized (an image of the chair on the right in figure 12.4); (center) appearance of the prototype (the chair on the left in figure 12.4) following the transformation; (right) overlay of the image (left) and the transformed prototype (center). The match is good despite the differences in shape. (From Basri 1996, p. 22, reprinted with permission.)

Figure 12.6 The identification stage: matching a model of one chair (center) to an image of the same chair (left). The match is nearly perfect (overlay on the right), so the system has "identified' the particular chair. (From Basri 1996, p. 22, reprinted with permission.)

the example, it involved searching through the models of chairs until a match with the image of the chair (figure 12.5a) was found. Again, the system tries to find the transformation that aligns the model with the image. If such a matching model is found, the object's specific identity is determined, and the object recognition process stops (figure 12.6).

This scheme illustrated the core ideas underlying the information processing framework of categorization. Above all, categorization is viewed as a process of matching an image to a library of stored object representations. According to this view, categorization has two main objectives: First, it enables a vision system to derive properties of unfamiliar objects on the basis of their resemblance to familiar ones. Second, for familiar object, categorization helps finding a particular object in a library of object models. Several things should be noted. The recognition problem is solved by means of internal processing only, for example, by aligning a stored model of a chair with the current image using a predefined transformation scheme. As we show below, one of the underlying reasons for neglecting system-environment interaction in this way is the belief that "recognition is the ultimate goal of any visual system" (Wechsler 1990, p. 303). However, from an evolutionary perspective the ultimate goal of vision is not recognition per se, but rather enabling an agent to behave efficiently in the real world. The main idea that we will elucidate throughout this chapter is that recognition can be drastically simplified by allowing an agent to manipulate the object it is supposed to recognize, or, in other words, when the system-environment interaction is exploited. Another issue relates to the system's domain ontology. The object models and thus the categories in the information processing framework are fixed a priori. This means that the ontology—a high-level ontology—of the system is fixed. In the particular example used above, the system knows only about chairs and cars and is unable to deal with other categories, such as airplanes or houses. Note that there is in fact no need for the system to do so, since it does not have to rely on the categories to recharge its batteries, for example. If that were the case, then the system would be in trouble, because its categories are not grounded in its own experience with the objects. Rather, the designer has defined the categories for the system.

Problems and Issues

We have seen that the information processing framework defines categorization in terms of mappings of sensory stimulation onto internal representation. In the ALCOVE model, this involves the mapping of an input pattern to a category node, and in machine vision it involves the mapping of an image onto an internal object model. We see again and again that the main problem with these models from an embodied cognitive science perspective is their neglect of the system-environment interaction. Before discussing this in more detail, however, we have to address two issues. The first relates to the frame-of-reference problem, and the second concerns the question of why categorization is such a hard problem in the first place. Let us start with the frame-of-reference problem.

THE FRAME-OF-REFERENCE PROBLEM

We are interested in how agents (as complete, embodied systems) perform categorization tasks in the real world. Our main question is the following: What are the underlying mechanisms of a particular behavior that we term "categorization" or "category learning"? When looking for these mechanisms, we have to take the frame-of-reference problem into account. The description of a behavior in terms of categories that an agent "has" does not imply that the mechanisms that generate this behavior actually employ explicit category representations (such as category nodes or prototype models).

Let us take an example. We observe an infant picking apples from a table while leaving the newspapers. We say that his behavior is based on a category that we might want to call "apple." Note that this is an attribution made to the infant by an observer. Moreover, it is an attribution to the infant as a whole, not of one part of the infant, say its brain. We do not have to postulate any kind of representation in order to describe its behavior. Thus, if an agent consistently displays one kind of behavior when it encounters one type of object but not when it encounters other objects, it is reasonable to say that the agent somehow has means of categorizing that object type. If an infant initially picks different kinds of things off the table and over time only chooses apples, we say that it has learned the category that we call "apples."

How this change comes about is an entirely different issue. In this chapter, mechanisms are introduced that lead to categorization behavior. It is then of interest to correlate behavior and internal mechanism to deepen our understanding of how this behavior comes about. In sum, we have to be very careful in distinguishing our description of an agent showing categorization behavior from and our hypothesis about the underlying mechanisms.

THE OBJECT CONSTANCY PROBLEM

One of the main reasons why categorization in the real world is hard is the *object constancy* problem, that is, the problem of determining what parts of the input belong to one and the same object. The problem is hard because the same object can lead to a very large number of different input patterns depending on the viewing angle relative to the object, the lighting conditions, noise in the sensors and so forth. Let us briefly illustrate the problem with an example. In an experiment by Moses et al. (1994) human subjects had to recognize face images from different individuals, different views (five per individual), and different illumination conditions (four per individual). The conditions were such that when compared (using various similarity measures) the differences in the images of one individual induced by changes in the viewing conditions were larger than the differences between different individuals. Humans, who had to recognize those same images, nevertheless had a very high (97 percent) recognition rate when trained with a single image of each one of the individuals and tested on all other images.

The object constancy problem makes the categorization of real-world objects a very difficult task for robots or any other artificial recognition system. Humans, however, have no problem whatsoever in solving these problems. In fact, we are hardly aware of them because we categorize seemingly without effort even such complex patterns as faces, houses, animals, and the like. So why do agents in the approaches summarized above have such difficulties in categorizing even the simplest stimuli?

At the beginning of this section we suggested that the main problem from an embodied cognitive science perspective is the neglect of system-environment interaction in the traditional approaches to object recognition and categorization. Let us look at an example that supports this idea.

Nolfi (1996) studied a robot whose task was to distinguish between walls and target objects (small cylinders). In other words, the robot faced a category-learning problem: It had to learn to distinguish between walls and targets, a seemingly trivial task. Sensory data from walls and target objects were collected by placing the robot (reflecting our generic robot architecture) in front of them and storing the activations of the IR sensors for 180 different orientations and for 20 different distances. These data were then used to train a back-propagation network to categorize the two types of objects. Three types of network architectures were used: a two-layer network with six input neurons (one for each IR sensor) and one output neuron (coding walls by responding with a 0 and targets by responding with a 1), and two architectures in which an additional layer of four and eight hidden neurons, respectively, were added. The networks received the collected sensory data at their input layer, and were to learn to respond appropriately by activating the output node for sensory data originating from targets, and by being silent when data from the walls were presented. Note that this essentially corresponds to the approach taken by most connectionist models of categorization, according to which categorization involves mapping sensory patterns onto category representations (the output node). There is no motor component, and thus no sensory-motor coordination.

The results of these experiments in spite of the apparent simplicity of the problem, showed a very poor categorization performance. Networks with no hidden units correctly categorized 22 percent of the patterns, and networks with hidden units, on average, were correct in 35 percent of the cases. Adding four extra hidden units did not improve performance. The main reason for this poor performance is the ambiguity in the sensory data, as can be seen in figure 12.7, which depicts positions from which the networks categorized correctly the sensory patterns as a function of the distance and the angle of the robot relative to the objects.

Two important points need to be noted with respect to the data shown in figure 12.7. First, because only the front sensors were used, categorization could not be achieved beyond an angle of $\pm 120°$: there were simply no sensors. Also, at a distance greater than about 35 mm, categorization was not possible because of the limited range of the IR sensors. In all other cases, the sensory data were ambiguous, and the network could not categorize them appropriately. Second, note that the two "wings," representing correct categorizations, are not symmetrical, implying that the sensors on the left and on the right of the robot, despite being physically and electronically identical, responded differently. Such a result would not have occurred in a simulation study.

In sum, back-propagation networks similar to the ALCOVE model performed very poorly for the two categories. We return to this study below where we discuss the alternative solution to this categorization task that Nolfi describes, which involves the evolution of the control architecture by means of genetic algorithms.

TYPE-1 AND TYPE-2 PROBLEMS
So why is it so difficult for an agent to learn about categories in the real world by trying to learn a mapping from sensory patterns to an internal representation (e.g., a category node)? In essence, it is difficult because of the large input space and the ambiguities due to the above-mentioned object constancy problem. Clark and Thornton (1997) introduced the concept of type-2 problems to denote data sets for which the mapping from input to output cannot be

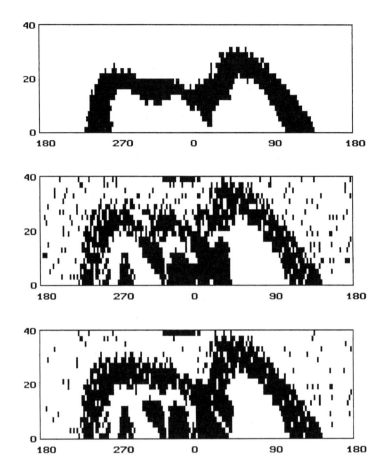

Figure 12.7 Distances (*y*-axis) and angles (*x*-axis) from which the back-propagation network is able to categorize the sensory patterns correctly. A black dot indicates correct categorization at a particular distance and angle. The top panel shows the results for the network without hidden units, the center and bottom panels for networks with a four-neuron and an eight-neuron hidden layer, respectively. (From Nolfi 1996, reprinted with permission.)

extracted by means of learning algorithms or statistical procedures. An example of a mapping that cannot be learned is Nolfi's experiment: Wherever the area in figure 12.7 is white, the mapping from sensory stimulation to category (cylinder or wall) cannot be learned, that is, category learning cannot be achieved. Whenever the mapping can be learned from the input data directly, the data are said to be of type 1. Often, type-2 problems can be transformed into type-1 problems.

An example is given in table 12.1. The first table (a) shows a mapping from input (x_1, x_2) to an output (y). The problem with the

Table 12.1 Illustration of type-1 and type-2 problems (after Clark and Thornton 1997).

a.

x1	x2		y
1	2	$\Longrightarrow$	1
2	2	$\Longrightarrow$	0
3	2	$\Longrightarrow$	1
3	1	$\Longrightarrow$	0
2	1	$\Longrightarrow$	1
1	1	$\Longrightarrow$	0

b.

x3		y
1	$\Longrightarrow$	1
0	$\Longrightarrow$	0
1	$\Longrightarrow$	1
2	$\Longrightarrow$	0
1	$\Longrightarrow$	1
0	$\Longrightarrow$	0

data set shown in the table is that the output cannot be predicted from the input and thus, there is nothing to be learned. For example, the conditional probability that $y = 1$ given that $x_1 = 1$ is 0.5 (in the first and the last row $x_1 = 1$ but y is 1 in the first row and 0 in the last). However, if we apply the following transformation, a simple subtraction to the data $x_3 = x_2 - x_1$, we find that all the conditional probabilities are 1. For example, if $x_3 = 0$ then $y = 0$, etc. In other words, after the transformation there is a well-defined mapping form input (e.g., x_3) to output (y), and thus this mapping can easily be learned. A type-2 problem (table 12.1a) has been transformed into a type-1 problem (table 12.1b). The difficulty is that in general the appropriate transformation is not known a priori but rather has to be found.

We can now reformulate the core problem of categorization as follows: The main problem in category learning of real-world objects is to turn type-2 problems into type-1 problems.

There are two main strategies for achieving this. First, the internal processing of the input can be improved. Clark and Thornton, for example, suggest that the appropriate transformation, that is, the one that transforms the data into a type-2 problem, might be achieved by what the organism has already learned—an attractive idea that will of course have to be elaborated in more detail.

The second approach for transforming type-2 into type-1 problems is directly derived from the basic tenets of embodied cognitive science and consists of exploiting processes of sensory-motor coordination. The idea is that through sensory-motor coordination a mobile agent can actively structure its own sensory input by manipulating the world. We show that this manipulation can serve to transform the former type-2 problem into a type-1 problem. Let us add a note on terminology. Assume that the robot approaches a cylinder. At every time step you can record its sensory data. Because the robot's distance and relative orientation to the object changes continuously, there will be a lot of variation in the sensory data recorded. However, because the sensory data originate from the same object, it should be possible to extract a common property or invariance in these patterns. Stated differently, an invariance is a property of the input data that remains constant as the data changes. If this invariance could be found by means of a learning mechanism or statistical procedure, the categorization problem could be solved. Alas, this would only be possible if the data were of type 1. Using this terminology, sensory-motor coordination serves the purpose of generating invariances.

12.2   The Sensory-Motor Coordination Approach

The concept of sensory-motor coordination is of fundamental importance in embodied cognitive science. We devote the rest of this chapter to summarizing the main ideas, approaches and results relating to this concept.

The Concept of Sensory-Motor Coordination

We have seen that the traditional way of approaching the categorization problem has had only limited success. We concluded our summary of the main reasons underlying this state of affairs with the suggestion that (a) the core challenge in category learning is transforming the input space such that categories can be learned (object constancy problem), and that (b) this problem can be approached through appropriate means of interacting with the environment, i.e. through sensory-motor coordination, and our goal in this section is to clarify what we mean by that term.

PERCEPTION, ACTION, AND THEIR INTERDEPENDENCY

The underlying idea behind sensory-motor coordination is best illustrated by a quote from American philosopher and psychologist John Dewey, who recognized the problem a long time ago and provided inspiration for our work.[1] Dewey first presents the standard view that starts from sensory stimulation, goes on to internal processing, and finally generates an action (i.e., what we have called the sense-think-act cycle). Here is the alternative he suggests: "We begin not with a sensory stimulus, but with a sensorimotor co-ordination.... In a certain sense it is the movement which is primary, and the sensation which is secondary, the movement of the body, head, and eye muscles determining the quality of what is experienced" (Dewey 1896/1981, pp. 127–128). Dewey's claim is that perception and action are tightly coupled, and he calls this coupling "sensory-motor coordination." This general idea of a close link between perception and action is at the core of the very influential theory of perception developed by Gibson (1966; see focus 12.1) and has recently gained increasing attention in a number of disciplines such as developmental psychology (e.g., Thelen and Smith 1994), cognitive psychology (e.g., Glenberg 1996), neurobiology (e.g., Edelman 1987) and neuropsychology (e.g., Milner and Goodale 1995). It is also supported by recent work on the primate visual system and the human visual system. For example, Douglas, Martin, and Nelson (1993) concluded in their review of recent findings on the primate visual system that vision should not be viewed as passive information processing but rather as an active integrated sensory-motor event. Milner and Goodale (1995) have also stressed the point that vision has evolved to subserve action in the real world and should be viewed as a process of sensory-motor coordination.

---

[1] We are grateful to Bill Clancey for drawing our attention to the work of John Dewey.

Focus 12.1: Gibson and Embodied Cognitive Science

The theory of direct perception (sometimes also called "ecological optics"), developed by American psychologist J. J. Gibson (1966), is still very influential and is considered by many (e.g., Gordon 1989) to be among the most interesting theoretical developments in perception research. According to this view, perception cannot be studied in isolation but rather the organism must be studied as it acts (perceives) in its natural environment. The same point is at the core of design principle 1, the three constituents principle. Moreover, perception is not a matter of a passive module processing information, rather, "Perceiving is an act, not a response, an act of attention, not a triggered impression, an achievement, not a reflex" (Gibson 1979, p. 68). Note the similarity to John Dewey's quote above. Similar to Dewey, Gibson's theory of direct perception stresses the fundamental importance of action in perception and criticizes the distinction between sensory and motor aspects of behavior. This is one core aspect of the concept of sensory-motor coordination. However, there is an important difference to Gibson's view. Gibson sees these invariances as being provided by the environment itself. For example, consider the following problem. How can an observer determine whether two objects of the same phyiscal size but at different distances from the observer are in fact the same size? It can be shown that there is an invariance that is directly perceivable from the environment (Gordon 1989). The ratio of an object's height to the distance between its base and the horizon is constant across all distances from the observer (see figure 12.8). Because this invariance is contained in the environment, it is directly reflected in the agent's sensory data. In conclusion, whereas some invariances may indeed be contained in the environment, in general, the agent must generate these invariances through processes of sensory-motor coordination.

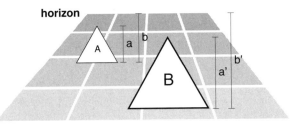

Figure 12.8 Solution of the size constancy problem based on invariants in the environment. If $a : b = a' : b'$, then A and B are the same size. (Adapted from Gordon 1989, p. 158.)

CHARACTERIZATION AND PURPOSE OF SENSORY-MOTOR
COORDINATION

Initially we pointed out that sensory-motor coordination is not
simply synonymous with behavior. For example, a robot turning
about its own axis is not engaged in a sensory-motor coordination
because the sensory patterns it generates through its behavior do
not guide its behavior in a way that leads to stable sensory-motor
patterns. The data from such behaviors are in general not very
interesting and useful, as a case study by Dedieu and Mazer (1992)
illustrates. Also, simply hitting an object is not an instance of
sensory-motor coordination—the sensory stimulation and the
robot's behavior do not lead to a stable sensory-motor pattern:
merely a reflex is triggered. Dedieu and Mazer (1992) developed
a robot that rotated at varying speeds around its own axis and
recorded the resulting input from its photosensors. They then analyzed the motor speeds and the sensory data recorded to find correlations between the two streams of data that would reduce the
dimensionality of the input space. This seems similar to the core
idea underlying the concept of sensory-motor coordination. The
authors noted that the results were disappointing and concluded by
suggesting that if the data had been preprocessed in appropriate
ways they might have found correlations. The problem is, however,
at a more fundamental level: Dedieu and Mazer's robot did not
really interact with its environment to fulfill some task (see
Hendriks-Jansen 1996, p.p. 172ff, for a similar conclusion). The
control of its actions is entirely within the agent itself. Recall that
the fundamental mechanism by which the Distributed Adaptive
Control robot introduced in chapter 5 learned about obstacles
was an association between activities of two modalities, collision
sensing and proximity sensing, by means of a Hebbian learning
rule. This worked because of the temporal correlation of these
activations due to a collision with the object. Note that unlike
Dedieu and Mazer's agent that merely turned around its own axis,
the sensory patterns in the DAC agent result from a coupling with
the environment, the collision. We will refer to this kind of simple
coupling as *direct* coupling.

In contrast to these examples, sensory-motor coordination
involves object-related actions used specifically to structure the
sensory space for the purpose of learning about an object. This is
an active process whereby the agent manipulates its own sensory
input to simplify the problem of category learning. For example,

human infants often explore objects by moving them in front of their faces at a fixed distance (Bushnell and Boudreau 1993), which automatically "normalizes" the size. This seems a really clever thing to do, because it drastically simplifies the object constancy problem: The object is always viewed from the same distance. Moreover, systematic rotations of the object generate additional correlations that the infant can exploit for learning. Another example is the circling behavior of the SMC I agent that we discuss below. SMC I agents learn about objects by circling around them, thereby generating correlations in their input space. This circling behavior is similar to object rotation at a fixed distance: the agent structures its own input by appropriate ways of coupling with the object. Other examples that we discuss in more detail below are the moving-back-and-forth behavior of the agent implemented by Beer (1996) and the contour-following behavior of Edelman's (1987) Darwin II agent.

There is one problem, however, that we have not addressed so far. By introspection, of our own perceptive processes, we understand that an agent does not have to execute an sensory-motor coordination with respect to an object for the agent to be able to reliably categorize that object. For instance, we can look at a bottle and immediately recognize it without having to interact physically with the bottle. While this phenomenon is not yet fully understood, there is a lot of evidence that sensory-motor coordination plays its main role in category learning (e.g. Thelen and Smith, 1994). This can be seen in infants' physical interactions with objects as their fundamental strategy for learning about objects. Even adults often resort to this type of interaction when confronted with objects they have never seen before.

Evolved Sensory-Motor Coordination

To reveal further details of the mechanisms underlying sensory-motor coordination, we now discuss a number of examples in more detail. So far we have argued that cognitive processes such as perception, categorization, or memory are best viewed from the perspective of sensory-motor coordination. An interesting way to further investigate the advantages or disadvantages of sensory-motor coordination for categorization is to employ the evolutionary approach described in chapter 8. Consider the generic robot introduced in chapter 5. Recall that this robot has a left-right symmetry, a number of proximity or distance sensors, and two wheels that can be individually driven. How can we enable a robot with such a simple sensory system to categorize objects in its environment? One approach is to hand-craft means of sensory-motor coordination, that is, appropriate ways of interacting with an object, and have the robot learn the resulting sensory patterns. This approach is adopted in the SMC agents presented below. Another way is to evolve the entire control architecture. Individuals that achieve a high percentage of correct categorization have a high fitness and are more likely to be included in the next generation. In this way, the following issue can be addressed: What strategy proves to be the fittest, that is, achieves the best categorization performance? Based on the arguments introduced above, we predict that whatever strategy emerges as the fittest must include mechanisms of sensory-motor coordination. An alternative hypothesis, derived from the information processing framework, is that the best strategy involves a mapping from sensory patterns to an internal representation of the categories.

These issues have been addressed in studies by Nolfi (1996) and Beer (1996). The surprising result of both studies is that the evolutionary process resulted in behaviors that exploited mechanisms of sensory-motor coordination to learn about the categories.

CASE STUDY I: LEARNING TO DISTINGUISH BETWEEN OBJECTS AND WALLS

Let us first look at the Nolfi study. We referred to one part of this study above. There the point was that a back-propagation network could not learn to distinguish between target objects (small cylinders) and walls. Here we summarize the alternative approach that Nolfi implemented to approach the problem of learning to distinguish between walls and objects. Nolfi used a genetic algorithm to evolve a neural controller able to perform the required categorization task. Individuals were evolved in simulation, using the same sensory data as in the experiments with the back-propagation networks; that is, real sensory data were used to drive a simulated robot. The evolved individuals were then downloaded onto the physical robot (a Khepera robot) to test their capability of operating in the real world. The process began with 100 randomly generated genotypes, each representing a network with a different set of randomly assigned connection weights from input to output layer. Each generation was allowed to operate for five epochs consisting of 500 actions each. At the beginning of each such epoch, the robot was randomly placed in the environment at some distance from the target object. After the fifth epoch, individuals were allowed to "reproduce" as follows. The networks of the 20 fittest individuals were copied five times, resulting in 100 (20 × 5) new individuals that constituted the next generation. Random mutations were introduced in this reproduction process. Overall, 100 generations were evolved. Fitness was computed by measuring the number of cycles an individual spent at a distance less than 8 cm from the target object. Three network architectures were used: networks without hidden units and those with four or eight hidden units. On average, networks without hidden units were found to be able to solve this task better than the ones with hidden units (Nolfi 1996). As Nolfi pointed out, this might relate to the fact that additional hidden neurons require longer genotypes and thus increase the genetic algorithm's search space. Let us summarize the behavior of the evolved robots. Individuals *never* stop once they are in front of the target. Rather, they start to move back and forth as well as slightly to the left- and right-hand side, thereby keeping a fixed range of angles and distances with respect to the target. In other words, the evolutionary process has produced a mechanism of sensory-motor coordination to solve the categorization (figure 12.9).

This study demonstrates not only how sensory-motor coordination can be used to enable a robot to categorize objects in its environment, but also how such a behavior actually evolves in robots faced with a categorization task. Using the terminology introduced above, we can describe the behavior of these agents as generating

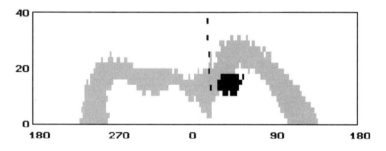

Figure 12.9 Categorization of sensory patterns after evolution. The gray area represents the sensory patterns which could be categorized correctly using the back-propagation networks (same data as shown in figure 12.7). The black area indicates the relative positions (angle and distance) that a typical evolved agent assumes when it reaches a target. Note that this area is very small and also contains regions where the back-propagation networks did not categorize correctly. (From Nolfi 1996, reprinted with permission.)

type-1 data. Had they not engaged in a sensory-motor coordination, the sensor data would have been of type 2 and they would not have made the distinction. This can also be seen in figure 12.9, which shows the relative positions a typical agent has assumed with respect to a target (the black area in the figure). Note that the agent has assumed only a small part of all possible positions, thus reducing the resulting sensor space significantly. Note that agents recognized objects from positions where the back-propagation networks failed, implying that the strategy of sensory-motor coordination—in this case moving back and forth, as well as moving to the left and to the right in front of the object—discovers regions in sensor space where the categorization is possible. This detection of regularities through active manipulation of the world is at the core of the concept of sensory-motor coordination: Through sensory-motor coordination, the agent generates "good" data, that is, data from which categories can be distinguished.

CASE STUDY II: LEARNING TO DISTINGUISH CIRCLES AND DIAMONDS

In another study, Beer (1996) obtained very similar results. Beer also evolved agents that had to solve a categorization task. More specifically, the agents had to discriminate between circles and diamonds, catching (moving close to) circles while avoiding the diamonds. The study was conducted in simulation; Figure 12.10 shows the experimental setup. The agents could move horizontally. Objects—diamonds and circles—were falling from above, from starting points with varying degrees of horizontal offset from the initial position of the agent. The neural network that controlled these agents was evolved using a genetic algorithm. (See Beer 1996, for details on this algorithm.) The network consisted of five fully interconnected neurons that received input from a number of distance sensors on the agent and were connected to two motor neurons (for operating the motors for moving left or right).

How did the agents solve the categorization task in these experiments? Figure 12.11 depicts the main results. They can be summarized as follows. The robot, when confronted with a circle or a diamond, first centered the object (first 20 time units). The robot then actively scanned the object until about 40 time units, and then either centered the object, in the case of circles, or avoided it, in the case of diamonds. This is another example of how sensory-motor coordination (centering, active scanning) can help simplify categorization. In this case, the agent reduces the sensor space by

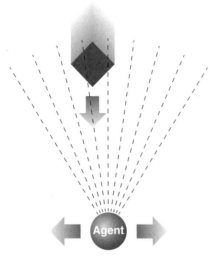

Figure 12.10 Setup of Beer's experiments. The agent is equipped with a number of rays (shown as dotted lines) with which it can measure distance from objects. Objects enter the environment from above and then move toward the agent. The agent can move horizontally left and right. The task of the robot is to discriminate between circles and diamonds. (Adapted from Beer 1996, p. 425.)

assuming a standard position with respect to the object it has to categorize. In other words, as Beer put it, "this agent is not merely centering and then statically pattern-matching an object. Rather, its strategy seems to be a dynamic one, with active scanning apparently playing an essential role" (1996, p. 426). Again, we suggest that sensory-motor coordination transforms the sensor space in such a way that regularities become apparent and objects can be learned. Based on this mechanism, all objects could be categorized correctly (Beer 1996). Note also that as in the case of the Nolfi study summarized above, this solution has not been hand crafted, but rather has emerged out of an evolutionary process.

In sum, the Nolfi and Beer experiments reveal that agents evolved to solve a category-learning problem employed mechanisms of sensory-motor coordination to solve the task and did not try to learn a mapping from input patterns to internal representations while standing still. The underlying reason is that in the latter case the problem is of type-2. However if the agents apply a "trick"—the one to which the evolutionary methods used in the experiments converged, that is, sensory-motor coordination—the problem is of type 1. We suspect that very similar processes were at work in natural evolution, leading to the types of sensory-motor

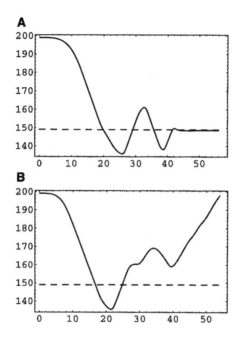

Figure 12.11 Results from Beer's categorization experiments (1996). The two figures represent plots of the horizontal positions (*y*-axis) over time (*x*-axis) of an evolved agent that could categorize circles and diamonds. The agent's path is indicated as a solid line, that of the object as a dashed line. (a) Path of the agent catching a circle. The agent categorized the object by staying close to it, as indicated by the overlap of the agent's and the object's path after about 43 time units. (b) Path of the agent avoiding a diamond (reprinted with permission).

coordination we can observe in animals and humans. We now look at two examples in which this idea can be further pursued.

The Darwin II Model

The Darwin series of models was developed by Edelman and his coworkers (see Reeke et al. 1989). We focus on Darwin II because it explicitly addresses categorization. Darwin II incorporates important aspects of the principle of sensory-motor coordination and of the redundancy principle as well. In chapter 14, we discuss its successor, Darwin III, as an example of the value principle and value-based learning.

CATEGORIZATION AND THE THEORY OF NEURONAL GROUP SELECTION

Before going into the details of Darwin II, we need to discuss Edelman's conceptualization of categorization, derived from his

Theory of Neuronal Group Selection (TNGS). The theory applies evolutionary thinking to development. It was formulated as an alternative to information processing models of mind. It tries to explain how perception, categorization, memory and learning can emerge from processes of system-environment interaction and how learning can occur without assuming that there is a homunculus in the brain or that the world presents itself in predefined categories. According to the theory, a selection mechanism is applied to assemblies of neurons, the neuronal groups, in the brain. The brain acquires its ability for mental capacities such as categorization as a result of this selection from a large population of structures resulting from the organisms's development. Note that the term "selection" is not used in the same way as in evolutionary theory. In the latter context, the timescale transcends the individual, whereas in the TNGS, the term applies to ontogenetic development. The term *somatic selection* is sometimes used to make this point explicit.

Three main claims underlie the TNGS:

1. *Developmental selection:* The neural structure is an epigenetic result of prenatal development. *Epigenetic* means that the phenomenon is not under genetic control. Because development is epigenetic, the connections among the cells cannot be precisely prespecified in the genes. Genetic activity only partly determines the diverse anatomical connectivity. This connectivity is the result of cell division, cell movement, and cell differentiation during embryonic development. By birth, cortical cells are arranged in a large number of highly diverse neuronal groups. This ensemble of neuronal groups is called the primary repertoire.

2. *Experiential selection:* After birth, the neural structure is basically "in place." During postnatal development the focus is on modifying the strengths of synaptic connections both within and between neuronal groups of the primary repertoire, a process that results in the so-called secondary repertoire. The strengthening and loosening of synaptic strengths depends upon the correlation of neuronal activities with sensory and motor signals.

3. *Reentrant mapping:* Connections must be established between those groups created in the secondary repertoire and those parts of the nervous system that make the "connection" to the outside world, namely the sensory and motor systems. The term "reentry" denotes the recurrent anatomical connections between sensory and motor areas. Recurrent connections are necessary to account for category learning.

The main goal of the TNGS is to understand the biological basis of categorization by studying how an organism can behave adaptively in an unlabeled world. The general framework that Edelman proposes overlaps significantly with the principle of sensory-motor coordination by suggesting that the results of motor activity are an integral part of categorization: "While sensation and perhaps certain aspects of perception can proceed without a contribution of the motor apparatus, perceptual categorization depends upon the interplay between local cortical sensory maps and local motor maps.... The strongest consequence of this assumption is that categorization cannot be a property of one small portion of the nervous system" (Edelman 1987, p. 210). Edelman suggests that categorization involves not only the brain but also the sensory-motor apparatus, a key implication of the principle of sensory-motor coordination. The essential mechanism of categorization in Edelman's theory is a parallel sampling of the environment by multiple sensory maps within the same modality and between different modalities. This sampling is a process of sensory-motor coordination in which various maps pick up different, but temporally correlated, signals from the environment. These correlations play a fundamental role in categorization. Thelen and Smith point out that "this perfect temporal association of multimodal information is perhaps the only perceptual invariant that spans all ages, contexts, and modalities. We believe, with Edelman, that this correlation is the primary link between the mind and the world" (1994, p. 149). This is very close to what we said earlier in our discussion of the concept of sensory-motor coordination: Sensory-motor coordination structures the high-dimensional sensor space by inducing regularities in that space. The temporal correlation of signals in many modalities, generated by interacting with an object, is the most basic example of such regularities.

Edelman views categorization as the most significant of mental activities. In the simplest case, categorization is a process of physically relating two functionally different neural maps by reentrant connections in so-called classification couples (figure 12.12). A feature detection system and a feature correlation system extract information about the environment. Whereas the feature correlation system responds to category properties of an input (e.g., characteristics of the letter "A"), the feature detector system responds to aspects of each individual stimulus (e.g., particular instances of the letter "A"). These networks respond to local properties of the

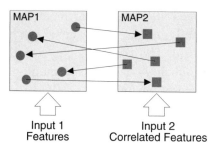

Input 1
Features

Input 2
Correlated Features

Figure 12.12 A classification couple linked through reentrant connections. The two feature maps (MAPI, MAP2) extract information about the environment in parallel. The feature detector system extracts basic features such as edges, lines, curves and orientations of objects. The feature correlation system responds to larger-scale correlations of features such as T-junctions by tracing the motion of objects with eyes or fingers. Because the two systems are linked through reentrant weights, individual and category properties of stimuli are linked.

stimulus only; that is, only parts of the input activate them. The feature correlation system responds to larger-scale correlations of features such as T-junctions by tracing objects by motion with eyes or fingers. The two systems are linked through reentrant weights, thus linking individual and category properties of stimuli. Thus the maps resulting from the two systems respond to different signals. However, they are connected via reentrant synapses in such a way that each map is also mapped to the other one, allowing the parallel simultaneous sampling of distinctive characteristics of a stimulus. These ideas are best exemplified with an example.

THE DARWIN II MODEL

Darwin II is a simulated agent equipped with a simple sensory system with which it can extract basic features of objects. In addition, it can trace objects with a simple effector system. Its task is to learn alphabetic letters. This task is not very illuminating from an autonomous agents perspective because the system does not really have to rely on or use the categories to solve a particular task, and therefore the categories are of no particular value for the system. It is, however, a good illustration of how letter categories can be learned based on sensory-motor coordination and principles of nonsupervised learning. Remember that the idea of explicit teaching of categories, that is, supervised learning, dominates connectionist categorization models. In contrast, categories Darwin II acquires are not explictely represented within its memory, and the

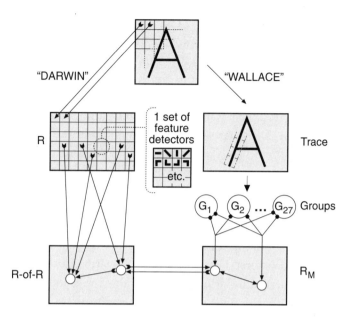

Figure 12.13 An overview of Darwin II.

system learns about the categories by interacting with them. Figure 12.13 offers an overview of Darwin II's architecture.

Darwin II's architecture is an instantiation of the general framework summarized above (figure 12.12). Darwin II consists of two systems, called "Darwin" and "Wallace," that comprise four neural networks in all. They are organized in two layers, and both receive their input from an input array, which Darwin and Wallace process simultaneously. In other words, they are redundant: they are separate and independent (one is not built out of the other), but they extract partially overlapping information about the input. Darwin II's real categorization power comes from coupling these two separate processes via modifiable weights that are adjusted based on the overlap or correlation between activity in Darwin and Wallace. Let us look at this in more detail.

The main purpose of Darwin is to extract features such as lines, orientations, and curves of incoming letters, which it accomplishes by means of two layers, R and R-of-R. The R layer consists of a number of identical-feature-analyzing networks, each of which extracts the same features (lines, orientations, line terminations, ect.) from different locations of the input pattern. These networks thus respond only to local properties of the stimulus. In other words, they are activated only by parts of the input, such as a line segment of the letter A. The R layer is connected to the R-of-R layer, whose purpose is to respond, by connecting each group of neurons in the R-of-R layer with numerous input connections from randomly selected neurons in R, to nonlocal combinations of the strictly local features the R layer extracts.

The Wallace pathway has the same two-layered structure as Darwin, but whereas Darwin maps the input letter to combinations of features, Wallace's main task is to map the input letter to the movement sequences of a continuous tracing of the letter. Wallace "interacts" with the letter by tracing its contours by hypothetical eye or arm movements. (Only the resulting activations but not the movements themselves are simulated.) Wallace works as a finger does in tracing an object's edges. The tracing is accomplished by Wallace's first layer, the Trace layer, implemented as a separate computer simulation that simulates the tracing. It does not consist of groups of neurons, but rather simulates the sensory input of a finger tracing objects. It responds to large-scale correlations of features, such as T-junctions. In other words, the tracing movements provide information about a letter's global shape and make Wallace's responses independent of translations and rotations of the stimulus. As a result of the tracing movement, a set of "virtual" groups ($G_1, \ldots, G_{27}$ in figure 12.13) is activated. (These groups are referred to as "virtual" because they are connected to the separate simulation system rather than other neuronal groups.) These virtual groups are connected to the next higher layer, called RM. RM responds to the activity in the Trace system in a similar way to that in which R-of-R responds to activity in the R layer. This makes RM even more independent of distortions of the stimulus. Put differently, RM responds to category properties of an input (e.g., characteristics of the letter "A"), whereas R-of-R responds to aspects of each individual stimulus (e.g., particular instances of the letter "A").

Let us now discuss how the different aspects of letters extracted by Darwin and Wallace become related. Reentrant connections between layers R-of-R and RM link the Darwin and Wallace pathways ("Reentrant" means simply that the connections go from R-of-R to RM as well as from RM to R-of-R.) We have seen that the two independent samplings by the Darwin and the Wallace pathway process qualitatively different aspects of the input: Darwin responds to characteristics of an individual stimulus, whereas Wallace responds to characteristics of the category to which a stimulus belongs. The activity of the two pathways is, however, correlated, because they process the same input in parallel. The resulting correlations are extracted by a simple Hebbian rule that strengthens the reentrant connections. If a particular group in R-of-R responds strongly, and at the same time a group in RM is strongly activated, these two groups are associated by Hebbian learning.

Darwin II is an example of how categorization can occur in a self-organized way by means of exploiting both sensory and motor processes. Notice the difference in comparison to the traditional models discussed earlier. There is no explicit category representation onto which sensory stimuli are mapped. Rather the system learns to categorize by interacting with the objects in appropriate ways. As Thelen and Smith (1994) pointed out, one prediction that can be derived from this system is that letter tracing should influence feature analysis. In other words, the letter categories should depend on the motor movements involved in tracing them, with the implication that if you wrote from right to left instead from left to right, you would accept different physical stimuli as instances of, say, the letter "A." Empirical data in fact supports this prediction. (See discussion in Thelen and Smith 1994.)

Darwin II is a simulation model. Let us now turn to a case study which used physical robots to study categorization from the perspective of sensory-motor coordination.

12.3 Case Study: The SMC Agents

We now present a series of agents that we call the SMC (for *sensory-motor coordination*) agents. These agents implement the concept of sensory-motor coordination on various levels. The task of these agents is to learn to collect some types of objects (e.g., small ones) while ignoring others (e.g., large ones). In order to solve their task, they have to be able to make distinctions between various types of objects; that is, they must be able to categorize the objects in their environment. The SMC I agent is a first attempt to equip a robot with the ability to categorize based on the notion of sensory-motor coordination. Extensive experimentation with these agents revealed that they have certain deficiencies. To illustrate the design process, we report these deficiencies here: The deficiencies are equal in importance to the achievements in terms of what we can learn from them. They also motivate the next agent, SMC II, which is implemented on a robot with a more complex sensory-motor setup, including a camera. Moreover, its categorization mechanisms are different from those used in the SMC I models. SMC I and SMC II will eventually lead to SMC III, a robot that can operate outdoors: It is a first step toward the overall goal of building a garbage-collecting robot. The main aim in this section is not so much to explain each and every detail of the individual agents but rather to illustrate the power of the metaphor of sensory-motor coordination in generating productive ideas that can be tested on autonomous agents or in experiments with natural agents.

SMC I: Basic Categorization

The SMC I agent was developed to investigate basic categorization behavior in the real world in a first attempt to study how autonomous agents can make sense of an unlabeled world on their own.

ECOLOGICAL NICHE AND TASK
Again we must first specify the agent's ecological niche and desired behaviors. The desired behavior in the case studies presented here was garbage collection, a task chosen because it involves all issues pertinent to the study of categorization from an embodied cognitive science perspective: In order to solve this task, the agent has to learn about the objects it has to collect and to distinguish these objects from others it should not collect. It has to learn this distinction based on its own interactions with the objects. The agent's ecological niche was a flat environment with a home base to which the robot had to bring the garbage it collected (figure 12.14). Instead

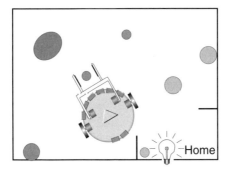

Figure 12.14   The ecological niche of the SMC I agents. The environment contains both small and large objects. The robot's task is to bring the small objects to a predefined location (Home) and to learn to avoid exploring the large objects.

of different types of garbage, the environment contained objects of different sizes constituting the categories the agent had to acquire. Two types of objects were used: small and large cylinders with a height of 3 cm and 2 cm and a diameter of 1.5 cm and 4 cm, respectively. The agent's task was to learn to bring the small objects to the home base while avoiding the large ones. In all experiments, fifteen objects of each category were randomly distributed over the whole arena.

LOW-LEVEL SPECIFICATION AND PLATFORM
The definition of the task environment largely determined the low-level specification of the SMC I agents. The generic agent was used because the ecological niche consisted of a flat, clean surface. The robot had to grasp objects in its environment and bring them to a home base. Thus, it needed means to pick up objects, which was provided by equipping the robot with the two-degrees-of-freedom arm-gripper system figure 12.15 shows. The arm of the gripper can move through any angle from vertical to horizontal, whereas the gripper can assume only an open or closed position. Position sensors coupled with the respective motors can sense arm and gripper positions. The arm position sensor takes on values from 0 (bottom back) to 255 (bottom forward); the gripper position sensor registers whether the gripper is open or closed. An optical barrier mounted on the gripper can detect objects inside the gripper. The optical barrier takes values from 0 (no object) to 255 (object presence).

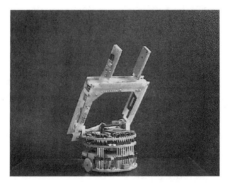

Figure 12.15 The arm-gripper system used in the SMC I experiments. The arm of the gripper can move through any angle from vertical to horizontal, whereas the gripper can assume only an open or closed position. Arm and gripper positions can be sensed via position sensors mounted in the respective motors. In addition, there is an optical barrier inside the gripper that can sense the presence of objects.

The SMC I agents used their IR sensors only to learn to categorize the objects in their environment. Their sensory system was deliberately kept simple to obtain an ecologically balanced design. The robot's effector system is relatively simple, consisting of two motors and the arm-gripper system just described. In the case of the SMC II agents, this arm-gripper system was controlled in relatively complex ways, and this increased complexity made it possible to achieve a balance with these agents' complex visual system (see below). In the SMC I agents, however, the arm-gripper system was controlled simply. Moreover, it was not used to explore the objects. Following the principle of ecological balance, we therefore opted to use simple IR sensors. Moreover, the fact that we used a very simple visual system forced us to actually exploit mechanisms of sensory-motor coordination and not rely on complex visual processing to extract properties of the objects.

We have now described the low-level specification of the robot's motors and sensor system. The next step in running agent experiments involves the design of a control architecture.

CONTROL ARCHITECTURE

We said in the previous chapter that a control architecture essentially specifies how the various parts of the low-level specifications should be connected to produce a desired behavior. The desired behavior here is garbage collection. One task in an autonomous agent model of categorization is to combine the general control architecture with the processes related to categorization: There is no special categorization module. This is an important issue. Most current models study categorization in isolation. Typically, the experiments stop when the network has converged on one out of a number of category nodes upon receiving some input. Such a modular approach implies that a separate categorization module would have to be implemented in the SMC agents. This approach, however, does not comply with the design principle of parallel, loosely coupled processes. From an autonomous agents perspective, categorization makes sense only with respect to the complete agent, as is summarized by the principle of sensory-motor coordination. This poses the problem of how categorization processes can be embedded in an agent's general control architecture. We used the EBA approach discussed in the previous chapter. Figure 12.16 illustrates the control architecture.

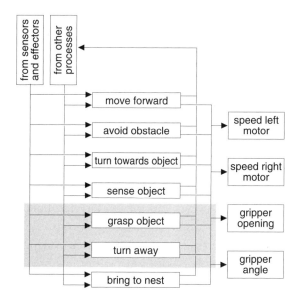

Figure 12.16 Architecture of SMC I agent. Seven EBA processes run in parallel. The shaded area—concerned with learning—is explained in detail in figure 12.25.

Remember that one of the EBA's fundamental characteristics is multiple processes functioning in parallel. Let us now have a closer look at the seven EBA processes used in the SMC I model: move-forward, avoid-obstacle, turn-toward-object, grasp-object, turn-away, and bring-to-nest. Each process is described in more detail below, we first need, however, to motivate the general ideas underlying this SMC I architecture. Recall that the task of this agent is to learn to distinguish between small and large objects. More specifically, it should learn to collect small objects and to avoid large ones using its sensors and its motor system. It has only two types of sensors: IR sensors and wheel encoders. Because it is moving around, it has to solve the object constancy problem. How should the agent learn about the categories? One way to achieve this is by imposing some constraints on the number of possible sensor states originating from the same object. This can be done by having the agent generate spatio-temporal correlations in the sensor space by interacting appropriately with the object. In other words, the strategy is for the agent to explore the object in such a way that the sensor readings are correlated in time and correlations exist among different sensors. This is the approach we have chosen for the SMC agents. In the case of the SMC I agents, the sensory-motor coordination leading to a reduction in sensor space is *circling.* Instead of having the robot approach the object from different angles and try to learn a mapping of the resulting sensor activation and some category node, we let the robot circle around the objects. This circling behavior induces high spatiotemporal correlations in the sensor patterns (see below). It is equivalent to the object rotation behavior found in human infants (Ruff 1984).

Before presenting results on the reduced sensor space, we need to introduce the mechanisms underlying the circling behavior. We mentioned that there is no simple one-to-one mapping between behavior (e.g., circling) and the underlying mechanisms. Thus, we do not want to design a "circling" module. Rather, we design simple EBA processes the joint dynamics of which result in circling behavior. The first behavior with which we have to equip the agent is the ability to move forward. Thus, there has to be a move-forward process. The activity of this process is extremely simple: A constant value is written to the motors, making the robot move forward at a fixed speed. We used the same process in the previous chapter in the case study of the self-sufficient garbage collector. In addition to the move-forward process, we need again to define a process by which the robot can avoid obstacles such as walls. This is the task of the avoid-obstacle process, which increases its influence on the speed variables as the robot approaches an obstacle. Its implementation is very similar to the one presented in the previous chapter.

In order to implement the circling behavior, the robot needs to somehow move along the objects. This can be achieved by introducing a turn-toward-object process that runs in parallel with the other two processes, move-forward and avoid-obstacle. This process was implemented as follows: Whenever there was lateral stimulation in a sensor, the agent turned slightly toward that object, the intuition being that objects are more interesting than open spaces. Such a reflex ensures that the agent has a tendency to be near objects, thus increasing the probability for an interaction of interest. This process is thus an instantiation of an implicit value. An agent with this architecture normally moves forward, move-forward process) and when it encounters an obstacle, avoids it by turning away (avoid-obstacle process). At the same time, if it senses stimulation in one of its lateral (left or right) sensors, it turns slightly toward the object turn-toward-object process).

a.

b.

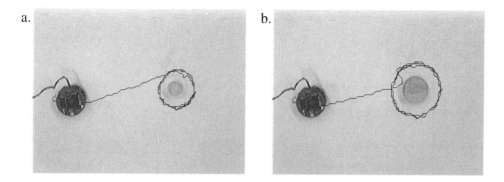

Figure 12.17 Adding the `turn-toward-object` process leads to circling behavior. (a) Agent circling around small object. (b) Agent circling around large object.

The interaction of these three processes leads to a behavior that we might call move-along-object, shown in figure 12.17. This behavior is a form of sensory-motor coordination: Sensors and motor actions are coupled via the basic processes. Note that there is no `move-along-object` process or module represented internally, as the contributions of the individual processes to the circling behavior shown in figure 12.17 illustrate. The contribution of the `move-forward` process is identical to that of the same process in the garbage collector of chapter 11: A constant value is continuously written onto the robot's motors. This makes the robot move forward at a constant speed. A more interesting pattern is evidenced in the contribution of the `avoid-obstacle` process shown in figure 12.18. The amplitude of the contribution is large in the case of large objects (figure 12.18b), because large objects activate the IR sensors, and in turn, the `avoid-obstacle` process more strongly. Figure 12.19 shows the contribution of the `turn-toward-object` process. The contribution of this process increases significantly as the robot encounters an object and remains large as long as the robot circles around the object. The contributions for small and large objects are almost identical because the robot reacts to the IR sensor on the side; its stimulation is the same in both cases. Together, the three processes just shown lead to the circling behavior illustrated in figure 12.17. Let us last look at the resulting motor speeds, which are essential for the category learning. They are shown in figure 12.20. The important point about these motor speeds is that they are different for the two types of objects. We can compute the robot's angular velocity by subtracting the motor speed of the left motor from the motor speed of

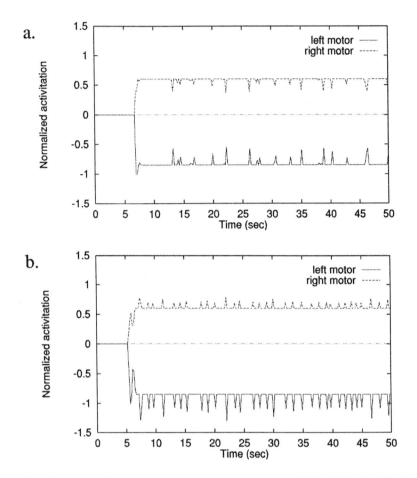

Figure 12.18 Contribution of the `avoid-obstacle` process to circling behavior. (a) Agent circling around small object. (b) Agent circling around large object. The amplitude of contributions is large in the case of the large objects; the robot is "wiggling" more than in the case of the small object.

the right. This is illustrated in the example of figure 12.21 where an agent was freely moving around in an arena cluttered with small and large objects: The robot first moved in the open plane for about 40 steps. It then started to circle around a small object for about 80 steps. After it had left the object, the robot first moved in the open plane again, then avoided a large object (indicated by large fluctuations around 150 and 170 steps), and finally started again to circle around a small object at around 180 steps. Note that the absolute value of the angular velocities is different for the two types of objects. This difference can be used for category learning. In addition, however, we want the learning to be based on the sensory readings. We said earlier that such learning is hard because of the

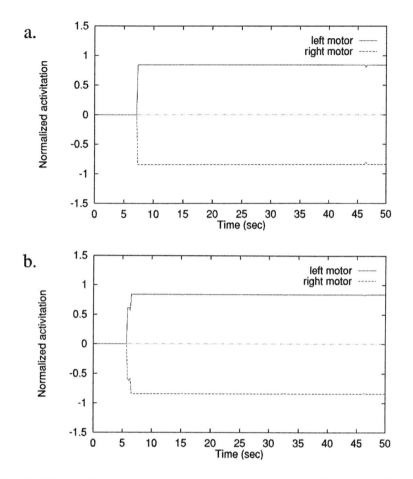

Figure 12.19 Contribution of the `turn-toward-object` process to circling behavior. (a) Agent circling around small object. (b) Agent circling around large object. The two are very similar.

high-dimensional state space. The circling behavior just described, an example of sensory-motor coordination, significantly reduces this space, as figures 12.22 and 12.23 show. Figure 12.22 shows the activation of the IR sensors as the robot circles around the objects.

The most important point to be noted is that the IR sensor activations vary very little because of the sensory-motor coordination behavior. In other words, the previously large state space has been significantly reduced. This can be computed explicitly as follows. We had the agent move across the open plane and then approach a large object. Figure 12.23 shows the resulting correlations among the 10-dimensional vectors consisting of the readings from the eight IR sensors and the two motor speeds. The correlations were calculated as follows. A "window" of 20 time steps (150 msec/step)

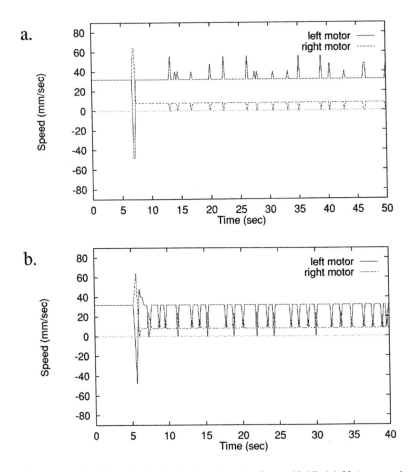

Figure 12.20 Motor speeds of the circling behavior shown in figure 12.17. (a) Motor speeds resulting from the agent's circling around small object. (b) Motor speeds resulting from the agent's circling around large object. On average, the differences in motor speeds in (a) are larger than the ones in (b).

was defined. For this window, the 20 × 20 correlation matrix of the 20 10-dimensional vectors (in other words, the correlation of the vectors at subsequent time steps) was computed. Finally, the average over all entries in the correlation matrix was taken to obtain a measure of how the vectors are correlated in time. High correlations indicate that subsequent vectors are very similar, which occurs when the robot is moving along an object, after it has established a sensory-motor coordination.

Figure 12.23 shows an intermediate level of coordination as the agent moves about in the open. Theoretically, this correlation should have a value of 1 because the IR sensors have a limited range, so that there would be no stimulation. Noise, however,

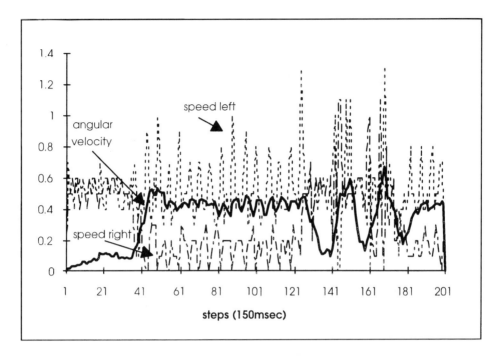

Figure 12.21   Motor speeds and resulting angular velocities of robot moving around in arena. The robot first moved in the open plane for about 40 steps. It then started to circle around a small object for about 80 steps. After it had left the object, the robot first moved in the open plane again, then avoided a large object (indicated by large fluctuations around 150 and 170 steps), and finally started again to circle around a small object at around 180 steps.

makes the correlations drop to roughly 0.5. The variation (the low correlation) is due to the fact that the activation levels are low, and small changes due to noise therefore have a large effect relative to the sensors' absolute level of activation. As the agent approaches an object, the correlation drops, because sensory activation is changing rapidly. Once the agent is near the object, the dynamics of the processes come into play and there is time-locked activity in the sensory-motor space spanned by the IR sensors and the motor speeds, as can be seen in the correlations, which rapidly jump to the maximum. Note that these correlations are induced by the agent's own movements, or in other words, by means of sensory-motor coordination.

LEARNING
We now have all the prerequisites for actually learning the differences between the two types of objects. After the agent had moved along an object for some time, i.e., after it has had continuous

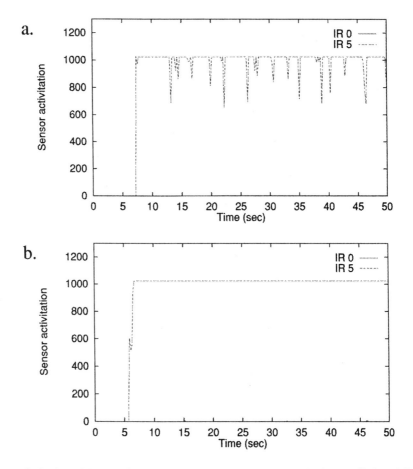

Figure 12.22 Activation of lateral IR sensors as the robot circles around objects. IR 0 and IR 1 denote sensors on the robot's left-hand side, and IR 4 and IR 5 denote sensors on its right-hand side. (a) Activation of lateral sensor IR 5 as the robot circles around a small object. (b) Activation of lateral sensor IR 5 as the agent circles around a large object. (c) Activation of lateral sensor IR 4 as the robot circles around small object. (d) Activation of lateral sensor IR 4 as the robot circles around large object.

stimulation of a lateral sensor, a reflex was triggered: This reflex, called sense-object process, enabled the agent to find out what it could do with the object. The process consisted of lowering the gripper over the object (figure 12.24). If the agent has successfully grasped an object (figure 12.24a), it brings the object to a home station by means of the bring-to-nest process. If the object is too heavy, it cannot be picked up, and the agent turns away from the object (figure 12.24b).

The robot in our experiment first tried to grasp all objects because of activity in the sense-object process. If the object was graspable and the agent could pick it up, a value signal was generated

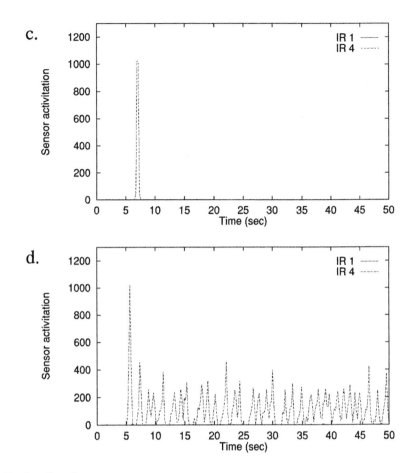

Figure 12.22 (continued)

that reinforced the association between the sensory-motor sequence in which the agent engaged right before grasping and the grasp process itself. Figure 12.25 depicts the part of the architecture responsible for learning.

To reinforce the connections between a particular sensory-motor coordination and the networks for the different processes, the readings from the IR sensors and the wheel encoders are projected onto a Kohonen map with leaky integrators for all the sensor variables. (Leaky integrators are nodes in neural networks that have a certain time constant for decaying their activation.) Leaky integrators provide a certain amount of information about the agent's recent sensory-motor past. The Kohonen map is connected to the grasp and the turn-away networks, which in turn write their outputs to the motors and the gripper. The gripper sensors provide input to the value system, which modulates the weight change in

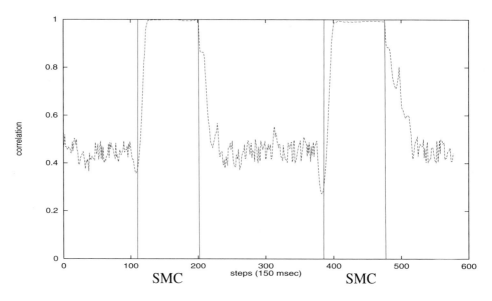

Figure 12.23 Change in correlations between subsequent input vectors as the agent approaches a large object. Vectors are 10-dimensional: eight IR sensors and two motor speeds. ("SMC" stands for "sensory-motor coordination.") There is a drop in correlation as the agent approaches an object.

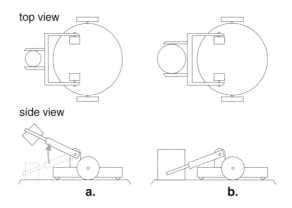

Figure 12.24 Different gripper positions leading to different behaviors. (a) If the object can be lifted, the robot brings it to the home base. (b) If the object is too heavy to be lifted, the robot turns away.

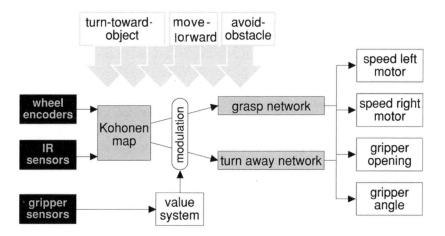

Figure 12.25 Learning in she SMC I agent. A Kohonen map receives input from the wheel encoders—measuring the speeds of the motors—and the IR sensors. The Kohonen map is connected to the `grasp` and the `turn-away` networks, which in turn write their outputs to the motors and the gripper. The gripper sensors provide input to the value system, which modulates the weight change in the connections between the Kohonen map and the two processes. The arrows pointing down from the `move-forward`, `avoid-obstacle` and `turn-toward-object` processes indicate that this learning is possible only through sensory-motor coordination by these processes.

the connections between the Kohonen map and the `grasp` and `turn-away` processes. When the robot in the experiment could lift an object, a value signal was triggered because of the input from the gripper sensors. Because in this case the `grasp` was active, the weights between the Kohonen map and this process were strengthened through Hebbian learning. If, on the other hand, the object was too heavy to be lifted, the `turn-away` process was triggered, and its activation resulted—again via Hebbian learning—in an increase of the weights from the Kohonen map. The learning rule is as follows:

$$\Delta w_{ij}^P = v^P[\eta \cdot a_j \cdot a_i^P - \varepsilon \cdot (a_j + a_i^P) \cdot w_{ij}^P], \tag{12.1}$$

where Δw_{ij}^P is the change of the weights from the Kohonen map to the process network p(`grasp-object`, `turn-away`), v^P is the value signal generated by the value system for process p, η is the learning rate, a_j the activation of node j in the Kohonen map, a_i^P is the respective activation in process network p, and ε is the forgetting rate.

This learning scheme implies that learning takes place when there is activation in the Kohonen map and one of the two networks and a value signal has been generated. Because the nodes are implemented as leaky integrators, the nodes associated with the sensory-motor sequence that led to the successful behavior are still active to some extent. Thus, sensory stimulation from the whole sensory-motor sequence is associated with the process network currently active.

If the environment does not change over time, it reaches an equilibrium, and the weights no longer change systematically; they change only slightly because of statistical fluctuations, as shown in figure 12.26.

The robot thus learns to distinguish between the two types of objects. Note that it perceives a difference between small objects seen from the left and small objects seen from the right (the same holds for large objects). This is because the sign of the motor speeds, which enter the learning process, changes as the direction changes. The important point, however, is that the Kohonen map can pick up the regularities induced by sensory-motor coordination. In this study, the robot's learning converged very rapidly, on average after the robot had encountered about 10 objects. Table 12.2 summarizes the results of our experiments. The numerical results show that the number of steps before the agent engaged in the right sort of behavior were significantly reduced after the agent had encountered 10 objects. Note that performance is only one possible way to evaluate an architecture. Chapter 17 discusses other means of evaluation, such as a model's predictive and heuristic value.

EXTENSIONS

The SMC I agent can learn, as we have shown, to distinguish between two types of objects. We now consider an extension of that learning to three categories by introducing a new object type, large rectangles, as well as a new agent capable of handling this more complex learning task. Before discussing the details of this new agent, however, we have to discuss a few theoretical points. Introducing a new category of object would seem to be a trivial thing. In connectionist models, this would amount merely to feeding the network with the data from the new category and having it adjust its weights accordingly. In the framework presented here, this is not as straightforward, mainly for two reasons. First, categories in this framework are not defined in terms of sensory patterns only; their definition crucially involves the agent's behavior with the

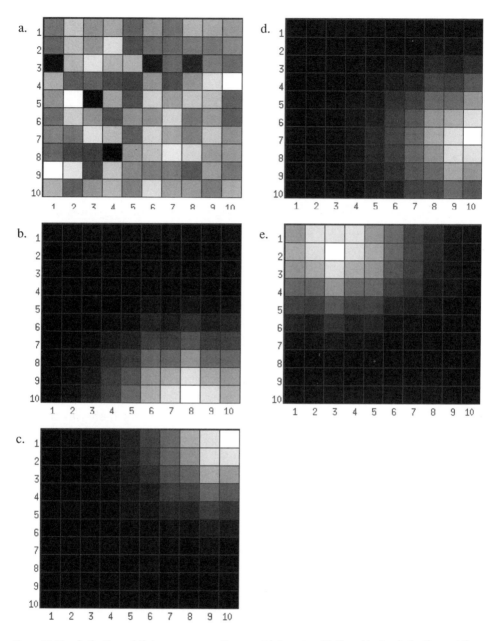

Figure 12.26 Activation of Kohonen map as the agent interacts with the objects. Activations at the beginning (panel a) are random; no learning has yet occurred. Panels (b) and (c) show activations later on, as the robot circles around a small object from the left (b) and the right (c). Panels (d) and (e) show the same data for a large object.

Table 12.2 Number of steps taken by robot along object before engaging in appropriate behavior (averaged over fifty trials)

SMC I	Initial	After 10 objects
Small	40.2 ± 1.44	14.2 ± 1.76
Large	41 ± 2.11	14.4 ± 2.08

category of object. When we introduce a new category, therefore, we also have to define a new behavior. This considerably increases the complexity of the required architecture, because now the agent must learn to engage in three different behaviors, depending on the object type. Second, we cannot, because of the notion of value, simply add new categories without asking what value these categories have for the agent. From an embodied cognitive science perspective, it makes sense to learn about categories only if they are of value for the agent. In other words, extending the basic SMC I scheme to include a third category also involves an extension of its value system. The agent now has to define value for three types of objects, instead of only two, and this again increases the complexity of the architecture required. Chapter 14 discusses the trade-off between very specific values, as used here, and more general ones that hold for different objects or situations.

In the extended version presented here, a `push` process was added to the already existing ones. The agent again used the `sense-object` process to explore the objects it encountered. This consisted of lowering the gripper as before. This time, however, in the case of rectangular objects, the robot could not lower the gripper at all, as figure 12.27 shows. The robot could not lower the gripper as before because the object was too large. Again, the resulting readings from the gripper triggered the value system.

Let us now examine the circling behavior of the extended SMC I agent. So far, the agent has encountered and circled only circular objects. The first question to be asked is whether the circling mechanism extends to rectangular objects as well. Figure 12.28 provides the answer. The agent successfully circles around the rectangular object; in other words, we can use the same sensory-motor coordination mechanism as we used in the prior experiments to generate the regularities needed for the category learning.

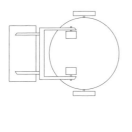

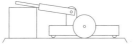

Figure 12.27 Gripper position when the robot tried to grasp a rectangular object. The robot could not lower the gripper, because the object was too large to fit within the gripper's handles.

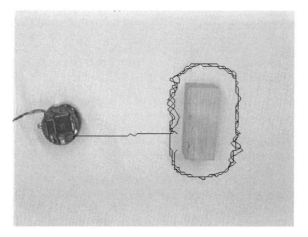

Figure 12.28 Trajectory of the extended SMC I agent as it "circles" around a rectangular object.

We can again isolate the contributions of the individual processes to this behavior, which are essentially the same as the ones shown above, except that the contribution of the avoid-obstacle process has a larger amplitude than in the case of the circular objects, because now the IR sensors are activated even more strongly. We again use the motor speeds resulting from the circling behavior, shown in figure 12.29, as a part of the input to learn the objects. These motor speeds are sufficiently different from the ones resulting from circling around the circular objects for the agent to learn this category of object as distinct from the prior two (see below). In addition to the motor speeds, the activation of the IR sensors, shown in figure 12.30, is also used for learning. Sensor IR 4 (figure

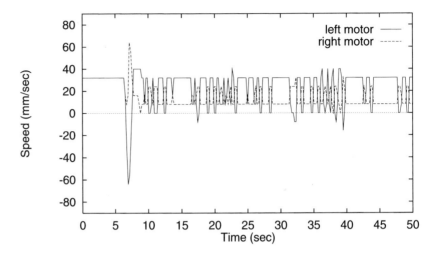

Figure 12.29 Motor speeds for the "circling" behavior shown in figure 12.28.

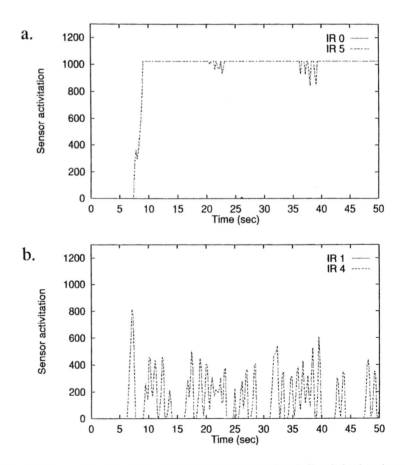

Figure 12.30 Activation of the lateral IR sensors resulting from the circling behavior shown in figure 12.28. (a) Activation of lateral sensor IR 5. (b) Activation of lateral sensor IR 4.

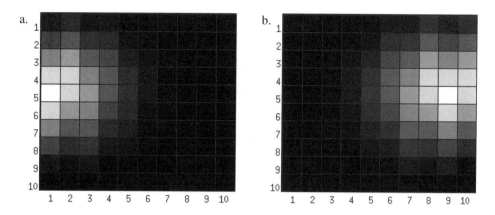

Figure 12.31 Activation of Kohonen map for rectangular objects. (a) Activation resulting from the robot's circling around the object from the left. (b) Activation resulting from the robot circling around the object from the right. The activations are sufficiently different from the ones obtained for the circular objects for the agent to associate a different behavior with rectangular objects.

12.30b) shows some variation in activation, but this variation is constrained to values within a limited range. IR sensor 5 (figure 12.30a) is again essentially constant. In other words, the sensory-motor coordination behavior again reduces the input space within which the agent has to learn. The variations are in fact important, as we argue in the next chapter, when we interpret sensory-motor coordination behavior from the perspective of information theory.

Let us finally look at how the extended SMC I agent learns about the rectangular objects. Figure 12.31 shows the Kohonen map activations resulting from this learning. The activations are sufficiently different for the robot to learn to associate a different behavior with rectangular objects. In summary, the SMC I models illustrate how the principle of sensory-motor coordination can be used to enable an agent to learn to distinguish reliably between different types of objects. Let us now consider the SMC II agent.

SMC II: Increasing the Complexity

SMC II (figure 12.32) is an extension of the SMC I agent. A comprehensive discussion of this architecture would be beyond the scope of this chapter, and the interested reader is referred to the original publications (Scheier and Lambrinos 1996a,b; Lambrinos and Scheier 1996; Pfeifer and Scheier 1997). The SMC II agent was again implemented on a standard robot (Khepera). As before, the

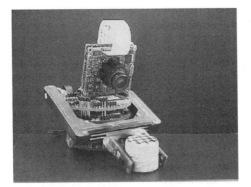

Figure 12.32 The SMC II agent. The basic platform is again the Khepera robot, but this time a camera and a gripper have been added.

robot's task was to collect certain objects and to bring them to a home base. In this case, the objects were cylindrical and all of the same size; additionally, they were either conductive or non-conductive. The conductive objects had a strongly textured surface, whereas the nonconductive ones had a white or only slightly textured surface. The robot's task was to collect the conductive objects. The control architecture of SMC II was again based on the EBA. In SMC II, two new processes replaced the various processes in SMC I that implemented object-related behavior (i.e., grasp-object, push-object, and turn-away): haptic and visual exploration. The focus in this architecture is how agents can learn about objects by exploring them visually and haptically, that is, by using their eyes and hands. To this end, the sensory-motor complexity of the SMC II agent was significantly augmented. Instead of IR sensors, a camera was used. The "ecological balance" principle states that if an agent's sensory complexity is increased, the complexity of the motor system and the neural substrate must be increased, too. Thus in addition to increasing the SMC's sensory complexity by adding a camera, the control of the arm-gripper system was been considerably improved. Moreover, a conductivity sensor was added. To enable the robot to do more than just passively scan the camera image, an artificial eye was implemented that actively moves a fovea to interesting parts (e.g., bright spots, texture, movement) of the image encountered. Once it has visually focused on an object, the robot moves up to it and starts exploring it using the arm-gripper system.

In SMC I, categorization was based on (a) learning a sensory-motor sequence and (b) associating this with the corresponding

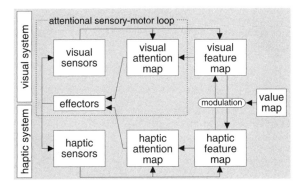

Figure 12.33 Parts of the architecture of the SMC II agent. The agent has a visual and a haptic system with similar structures: First, sensory networks receive input from the sensors on the robot. These sensory networks are connected to attention and feature maps. The sensory and the attention networks together with the effectors form an attentional sensory-motor loop. The feature maps are connected through reentrant weights; changes in these weights are modulated by a value map.

processes (grasping, pushing, turning away). Categorization in SMC II is achieved by learned reentrant connections between haptic and visual feature maps that are part of the haptic and visual systems of SMC II (figure 12.33). The fact that the agent can interact with its environment is exploited in two ways: First, in both the haptic and the visual system, an "attentional sensory-motor loop" is coupled to the arm, gripper, and wheel motors (i.e., the robot's effectors). As a result, the agent moves its body and the arm into a position from which it can explore an object it has encountered. Second, both haptic and visual data that result from the exploration process are used for learning and categorizing objects. As shown in figure 12.33, sensory maps in both systems are connected to feature maps. Feature maps are layers in a neural network that respond to properties of objects such as texture (visual) or conductivity (haptic). The interaction between the two modalities is implemented via reentrant weights between these feature maps. This part of the architecture is similar to the one used in Darwin II (figure 12.13). The correlation of signals of the haptic and the visual feature maps by these reentrant connections is part of the basic mechanism of categorization. A fundamental property of SMC II is that the feature maps are connected via modifiable feedback connections to the attention maps. The main idea is to link the correlated activity in the feature maps to the attentional sensory-motor loop. In essence, the result of learning is that relevant objects enhance activity in the attentional loop, but activity is not sustained in the case of unin-

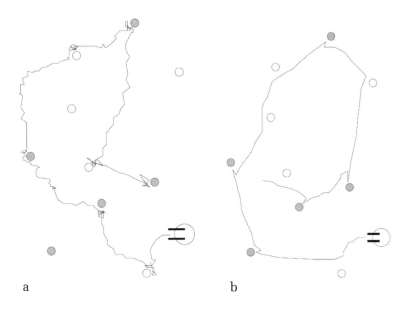

a   b

Figure 12.34   A typical trajectory of the SMC II agent (a) at the beginning of a trial and (b) after the agent had encountered 10 objects.

teresting objects (the object is ignored). Thus, no explicit avoidance or approach behavior is linked to the feature maps as was the case in SMC I. Instead, whether the agent approaches or avoids an object is the result of how the feature maps modulate the attentional sensory-motor loops depending on the kind of object encountered. Just as in SMC I, value signals modulate the learning process. The value map receives input form the conductivity sensor and the gripper sensors. The basic motivation behind these connections is that the robot should learn only when it explores an object. Activity in the value map is used as a reinforcement signal for the synaptic modifications among the feature maps. Thus, the value system triggers an explicit value signal.

Let us briefly look at the resulting behavior. Figure 12.34 shows the robot's behavior as it moves around in the environment and explores objects. Figure 12.34a shows a typical trajectory at the beginning of a trial. White and shaded circles indicate nonconductive/nontextured and conductive/textured objects, respectively. No distinct behavior for the two types of objects can be seen. Rather, the robot approaches all objects and explores them. Figure 12.34b shows a typical trajectory after the robot has encountered 10 objects of each type. Two main results can be taken from these trajectories. First, the robot has stopped exploring both types of objects because the dynamics of the coupled feature maps now govern its behavior. Second, the robot "ignores" nonconductive objects and grasps conductive ones (without first exploring them). We use the term "ignoring" instead of "avoiding" to indicate that there is no separate avoidance module. Rather, avoiding is achieved by not sustaining the activation in the attentional sensory-motor loop. Scheier and Lambrinos 1996a presents a detailed analysis of the internal dynamics underlying this learning process.

Finally, it is important to note that categorization in SMC II includes the agent as a whole; it is not a subsystem of some sort. Rather, the feature maps are tightly coupled to the attention maps, which in turn form sensory-motor loops via their connections to the motor system. Thus, categorization is distributed over all these areas and cannot be separated out of the system. In this respect, the term "classification couple," used by Edelman to designate the feature maps that are tightly coupled in both directions, is somewhat misleading.

12.4 Application: Active Vision

Active vision (also called "animate," "purposive," or "dynamic" vision) is the active control of all camera parameters. It has received increasing attention over the last decade as an alternative to the traditional machine vision approaches described at the beginning of this chapter. The main motivations underlying the active vision approach are as follows. Substantial work on vision within the traditional framework has resulted in the insight that "general vision does not seem to be feasible" (Fermüller and Aloimonos 1995, p. 726). We summarized the main problems of traditional computer vision earlier in this chapter. The active vision paradigm suggests, as an alternative, studying vision in conjunction with biology and the tasks that the system has to perform. Biological vision systems do not passively process their input but instead interact with the environment in an active and task-dependent way. This inspiration from biology is best illustrated with the following quote from Bajcsy (1988):

It should be axiomatic that perception is not passive, but active. Perceptual activity is exploratory, probing, searching; percepts do not simply fall onto sensors as rain falls onto ground. We do not just see, we look. And in the course, our pupils adjust to the level of illumination, our eyes bring the world into sharp focus, our eyes converge or diverge, we move our heads or change our position to get a better view of something, and sometimes we even put on spectacles. This adaptiveness is crucial for survival in an uncertain and generally unfriendly world. (p. 996)

Note that the idea that we do not just see, but look, is again an instantiation of the general idea that perception and action are closely linked. We have seen above that John Dewey had formulated this basic insight already more than 100 years ago. Active vision is concerned with how it can be implemented in artificial vision systems. We do not further elaborate on this idea here. We conclude by stating that active vision incorporates important aspects of sensory-motor coordination. We tried to demonstrate that the inclusion of active generation of sensory data can lead to additional simplifications for learning.

Issues to Think About

Issue 12.1: Dimensionality Reduction versus Generation of Diversity

We suspect most researchers would agree that dimensionality reduction is an important function of sensory-motor coordination. This phenomenon can be clearly demonstrated on robots and can also be argued theoretically. Reducing behavior to simpler concepts is one thing; generation of new behaviors is quite another. We said in chapter 1 that intelligence crucially involves generation of diversity. We must thus ask how new behaviors can come about despite these necessary reductions in dimensionality. The fact that complexity is reduced enables the organism to make cross-modal associations, that is, associations between different sensory channels. For example, in the SMC II agent, the fact that the agent viewed the objects from the same distance enabled it to learn through associations between its haptic and its visual system. If the dimensionality reduction did not take place, such correlations between different sensory modalities would neither exist nor could they be established. Such associations, however, may enlarge agents' behavioral repertoires. In other words, the initial reduction in complexity is a prerequisite for the eventual increase in complexity. For example, if a robot is able to form associations in the context of a visuo-haptic-motor coordination, it may be able to learn to home in from a distance on objects of interest from a haptic perspective. If the dimensionality were always low, there would be no reason for having high-dimensional motor spaces.

Issue 12.2: Where Is the Category?

We made a strong point of saying that the categories the robot acquires are, in fact, in the observer's head rather than the agent's. Categorization must therefore be defined in behavioral terms. This is a sensible thing to do, because to define the category, we do not need to refer to an internal mechanism. Note that we are not adopting a behavioristic framework. We want to know how a particular change in behavior comes about, and if the agent's behavior changes but the environment remains more or less the same, some change must have taken place within the agent. This change accounts for the acquisition of what the observer calls the category, but where is the change in the agent? Is it that sensory patterns get associated with a so-called grandmother cell? (A grandmother cell is another term for a particular neuron that stands for the category that is, a category node.) A belief in the existence of such a grandmother cell is actually quite prominent in the neural network community. From a cognitive science perspective, we do not think that the idea of the grandmother cell is a sensible one—at least not in general. The categories in our robots are represented in a distributed way in the weights of certain connections in the neural networks, and typically, many weights are involved in all systems: the haptic, the visual, the sensory-motor loops, and so forth. These weights make sense, though, only if they are embedded in a real-world physical agent. Take the same network and put it into different agents: The connections then mean something entirely different. If you take the same network initially and put it into a different agent, the new agent will acquire very different categories. Thus once more, we see that categorization is not what is done by a particular module, but is a property of the complete agent.

Points to Remember

- The principle of sensory-motor coordination states that all intelligent behavior (e.g., perception, categorization, memory) is to be conceived of as a sensory-motor coordination that structures input.

- This principle has two main aspects. First, whatever behavior we are analyzing, or whatever behavior we want to design a robot for, the principle suggests that we focus on how sensory and motor systems are coordinated. Second, embodied agents can structure their sensory input and thereby induce regularities that significantly simplify learning.
- In the information processing framework, categorization is defined in terms of mappings of sensory stimulation onto internal representations. In the ALCOVE model, this involves the mapping of an input pattern to a category node, and in machine vision, it involves the mapping of an image onto an internal object model.
- The object constancy problem denotes the problem of determining what parts of the sensory input belong to one and the same object. The problem is hard because the same object can lead to a very large number of different input patterns.
- Type-2 problems denote data sets from which no mapping from input to output can be extracted by means of learning or statistical procedures. In data sets of type 1 such a mapping can be extracted without much effort, because it is apparent in the raw input data.
- In the real world, sensory patterns are often of type-2. If an agent is to learn about categories in its environment, it needs type-1 data sets. Mechanisms of sensory-motor coordination can be used to generate type-1 data in the interaction with the environment.
- Sensory-motor coordination is not synonymous with behavior. Rather, it denotes object-related behaviors used specifically to generate structures in input space for the purpose of learning about objects.
- The SMC models instantiate the principle of sensory-motor coordination in mobile robots and are first steps toward the overall goal of understanding categorization.
- In addition to helping understand categorization, the SMC models are useful in working toward the goal of building a garbage-collecting robot that operates in outdoor environments.

Further Reading

Clark, A. and Thornton, C. (1997). Trading Spaces. *Behavioral and Brain Sciences*, 20, p. 57–90. (The original paper on the type-1 type-2 distinction.)

Thelen, E., and Smith, L. (1994). *A dynamic systems approach to the development of cognition and action.* Cambridge, MA: MIT Press (A Bradford book). (A nice application of the views presented in this chapter to the development of cognition. Shows the interdependence of sensory-motor abilities and intellectual development.)

13 The Principles of Cheap Design, Redundancy, and Ecological Balance

We are still in the process of elaborating the design principles of chapter 10. Previous chapters have discussed the principles of parallel, loosely coupled processes, and sensory-motor coordination. This chapter illustrates three additional principles: cheap design, redundancy, and ecological balance. All design principles are related to one another. But the notions of cheap design, ecological balance, and redundancy are so intimately related that they cannot be treated separately (figure 13.1). These principles also have a close alliance with the concept of the task environment. We illustrate all these relations with examples in the course of the chapter.

We start by discussing the principle of cheap design. We demonstrate how the physics of the system-environment interaction and the constraints of the ecological niche can be exploited to achieve a cheap design. We then introduce the "Zen of robot programming," the notion of parsimony, and the trade-off between cheapness and flexibility. Next, we take up the redundancy principle. In particular, we focus on the application of information theoretic considerations to agent design. Then we discuss the principle of ecological balance. We discuss how we might want to investigate ecological balance experimentally. We show that this requires the introduction of environmental pressures. We then briefly introduce a measure of brain complexity that attempts to quantify an agent's complexity.

13.1 The Principle of Cheap Design

The principle of cheap design states that good designs are "cheap." As we explained in chapter 10, we use the word "cheap" to mean essentially three things. First, it implies exploiting the physics of the system-environment interaction. Second, it means exploiting the constraints of the ecological niche. And third, it means parsimonious. We have already looked at some examples of cheap designs: insect walking, matched filters, and cheap vision for navigation purposes. To further support our intuition, let us look at a number of additional ones.

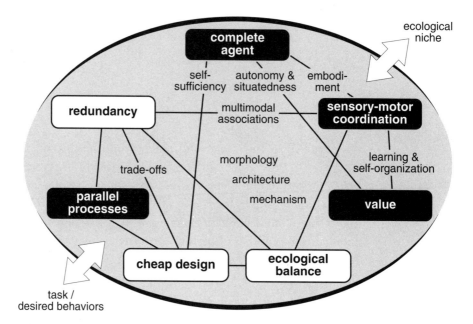

Figure 13.1 Overview of the design principles. This chapter discusses the principles of cheap design, redundancy, and ecological balance. These principles are strongly interdependent. Cheap implies ecologically balanced. The redundancy principle states how ecological balance can be achieved. The details of the interrelationship between these principles are discussed throughout this chapter.

Exploiting the Physics of the System-Environment Interaction

The goal of this case study is to show that implicit assumptions that are often made can substantially influence a control architecture's complexity. For example, if pixel arrays from a camera are used for navigation purposes, certain operations may be orders of magnitude more complex than if motion detectors are used. We show here how the "right" physics of the sensors automatically resolves certain difficult problems and leads to cheaper designs. Our presentation is inspired by work of Franceschini, Pichon, and Blanes (1992). These researchers were interested in building a model of housefly navigation. The housefly's impressive navigational skills are largely due to the fact that its visual system can detect optical flow. Franceschini, Pichon, and Blanes developed a robot that navigates based on principles derived from the housefly. The robot's neural system was largely built in hardware, and this massively parallel architecture led to excellent real-time performance. In what follows, we do not investigate the housefly itself; instead, we discuss a particular question relevant for robot navigation but often neglected.

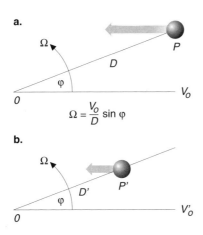

Figure 13.2 Navigation based on optical flow: (a) high speed, far away object, (b) low speed, nearby object. Allowing for certain idealizations, the angular speed Ω is the same in both situations if $(V_o/D) = (V_o'/D')$. So, if $D' < D$, then, if V_o' is proportionally smaller than V_o, the situation is identical to the agent. (Adapted from Franceschini, Pichon, and Blanes 1992.)

If dealing with a fast robot with inertia, we would want the following behavior: If the robot is moving fast, it should turn earlier to avoid obstacles than if moving slowly, in order to minimize the risk of hitting an obstacle. Intuitively one would think that this would require an assessment of the robot's speed and its distance from the obstacle, and a mechanism that adjusted the distance (and perhaps the angle) at which the agent should divert. This turns out to be unnecessary if motion detection is employed instead.

Figure 13.2 illustrates our simplified argument. Figure 13.2a shows the optical flow, as indicated by the angular speed Ω, induced by an object P at some distance D from the agent when moving at speed V_o. Figure 13.2b is the analog for a lower speed $V_{o'}$ and a proportionally less distant object P'. It is obvious from the figure that if $(V_o/D) = (V_{o'}/D')$, the angular speeds Ω and Ω' are the same. Let us assume that there is a hard-wired mechanism for obstacle avoidance that causes the agent to turn, given a certain Ω. It follows that whatever the agent's speed, it needs no internal adaptive mechanism to adjust for its speed—such an adjustment is taken care of by the mechanism determining motion relative to the environment. As an aside, we see here another instance of the frame-of-reference problem: Adaptivity is not purely a property of an agent, but rather of an agent's interaction with the environment. What we perceive as two different situations, figures 13.2a and 13.2b, is one and the same situation to the agent. This is, of course,

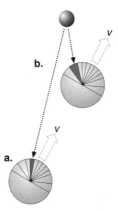

Figure 13.3 Exploiting motion parallax. (a) Point traveling across densely spaced vision segments in retina. (b) Point traveling across widely spaced vision segments in retina. If an object is moving through physical space at a constant speed, its image moves more slowly across the retina if it is near the front of the agent; it moves faster, if it is on the side. Because the vision segments are spaced more densely in the front of the retina than on the side, a point at a given distance from the agent requires the same amount of time to traverse one vision segment.

only strictly true in our idealization, that is, if the environment consists only of the objects shown in the figure.

Again we see that by taking the system-environment interaction into account, we can arrive at an effective and cheap mechanism for navigation that adjusts for speed without an information process or algorithm to instigate the adaptation. Moreover, the example demonstrates that adaptation is observer defined and does not necessarily require an adaptive mechanism inside the agent.

Figure 13.3 shows something called the principle of motion parallax. The eye of the fly has a nonuniform layout of its visual axes such that the resolution is finer toward the front than on the side. Figure 13.3a shows a point traveling across densely spaced vision segments in the retina, figure 13.3b a point traveling across widely spaced vision segments. If an object is traveling at a constant speed through physical space, its image moves more slowly across the retina if it is near the front of the agent; its image moves faster, if it is on the side. Everyone has experienced this phenomenon while riding in a train. Because the vision segments are spaced more densely in the front of the retina than on the side, an image at a given distance from the agent does require the same amount of time to traverse one vision segment. The speed at which a point traverses the visual field in fact follows a sine law: It is small at small angles (near the front), has maximum value at 90 degrees and then decreases again.

This unequal spacing of the vision segments in the retina, the *gradient*, compensates for the sine law inherent in the optic flow field. The introduction of the sine gradient allows the underlying motion detection system to be built uniformly by elements each displaying the same temporal properties as its neighbors. No neural circuitry is needed to compensate for the sine law. This illustrates two points. First, if we want to understand an agent's behavior, it is not sufficient to look at the control architecture; in this case, the control architecture—a uniform arrangement of identical motion detectors—suggests something linear and homogeneous, whereas motion parallax is in fact highly nonlinear. The advantages of having a sine gradient in the eye are so obvious that they may in retrospect contribute to explaining the gradient in resolution observed in the peripheral retina of so many creatures, including humans and flies (Franceschini, Pichon, and Blanes 1992). Second, the nonuniform physical arrangement of the visual segments, the *facets*, makes additional circuitry to compensate for the continuously changing angular speed unnecessary. Once again, a physical process is exploited, making the control architecture cheaper.

This example illustrates another important point: What seems most natural to at least some of us may often not be the most efficient. Although it seems natural to use pixel arrays in visual sensors, using flow sensors, as in the housefly, turns out to be much simpler for certain navigational tasks such as obstacle avoidance, and the related control architecture is much cheaper and more robust. What appears to require a lot of processing—the determination of optical flow—can be achieved cheaply because motion parallax has already been compensated for by the shape of the eye: by a homogeneous array of elementary motion detectors (EMDs; Franceschini, Pichon, and Blanes 1992). This example again illustrates that control algorithms make sense only with respect to the system-environment interaction and cannot be studied in isolation, as in the symbolic approach to cognition.

We see another, more general point here: The shape and the arrangement, that is, the morphology of the visual sensors is crucial to the navigation system's effective operation. If an appropriate morphology is chosen, neural processing may be reduced and simplified by orders of magnitude. Having the right morphology to exploit the system-environment interaction nicely illustrates the principle of cheap design. The general point is that often neural processing can be traded for morphology. The obvious advantages of morphology are speed and little required processing, the obvious disadvantage its lack of flexibility: Once the morphology is installed, it can no longer be changed, whereas neural processing offers much more flexibility. The same argument holds for robots in which computation replaces neural processing.

Exploiting the Constraints of the Ecological Niche

The second aspect of cheap design is exploitation of the constraints of the ecological niche. We have seen earlier that if the ecological niche is exploited appropriately, some behaviors can be achieved much more efficiently. Remember the "ground plane constraint" that Horswill's robot Polly took advantage of? It exploited the fact that office floors are flat and that the relevant objects were standing on the ground (see figure 10.3). Another example of a constraint that can be taken advantage of is, for example, the presence of walls. In the Distributed Adaptive Control agent, following walls is a good strategy, because the environment is closed. Thus the agent will eventually find anything deposited along the walls. Also, learning problems that are intractable if considered from a purely computational view often turn out to be benign, if the constraints of a particular ecological niche are taken into account. Normally in the real world, learning systems do not have to be universal. To illustrate this point assume that you want a learning machine, typically a neural network, to learn the XOR function based on examples. XOR is the exclusive "or" function: Its value is 1 if only one of the inputs is 1 but not the other; it is 0 if both are 1 or both are 0. Learning theory tells us that this is a hard problem: It is not linearly separable (e.g., Hertz, Krogh, and Palmer 1991). Thus, it requires powerful neural networks like multilayer perceptrons. Although XOR is an excellent case study for demonstrating the power of MLPs, it tells us relatively little about the real world, since fortunately, there is rarely a need to learn XOR in the real world: XOR is something unnatural. It has even been shown experimentally that natural systems (e.g., monkeys) perform poorly on XOR learning tasks (Thorpe and Imbert 1989), and it is hard to think of natural situations in which the ability to solve an XOR problem would confer an advantage: As Thorpe and Imbert put it, "In general, if two cues both signal that food is about to arrive, when the two are

present at the same time, the food is even more likely to appear!''
(1989, p. 85). As a consequence, much simpler neural networks
may almost always be used. This case provides an example in
which the environment gives the constraints. Often the environment does not give the constraints directly but they can be generated in its interaction with the agent through sensory-motor
coordination.

A Cheap, Self-Sufficient Robot

The self-sufficient robot introduced in chapter 11 is another illustration of the principle of cheap design. The only processes defined
on that robot were `move-forward`, `avoid-obstacle`, `go-to-
charging-station`, `recharge`, `home`, and `deposit`. Because of
the right dynamics, the robot actually "picks up" objects when
avoiding obstacles. "Picking up" in this case means getting the
objects into the wire loop on the robot's back. If the IR sensor in
that wire loop is activated, the `home` process gains strong influence
and quickly becomes dominant. If the robot is on its way to the
charging station, because of the different dynamics, it no longer
picks up objects when avoiding them, a very useful behavior
change, because when its battery is low, it should not waste energy
by carrying objects. As we pointed out, this behavior is emergent.
There are no internal links in the control architecture specifically
designed for this purpose. Emergent designs, in fact, often have the
additional advantage of being cheap. And we saw that emergent
designs can be produced by following the principle of parallel,
loosely coupled processes. The principle of complete agents is also
related to cheap design. Recall that when the agent in chapter 11
gets stuck along the wall, it frees itself after a while because its
battery level progressively decreases, and the robot eventually has
to go to the charging station: It is "pulled" in a different direction.
Again, no extra mechanism is designed into the robot to produce
this behavior. The fact that the agent must engage in a number of
different behaviors, not just a single one, takes care of the problem
of getting stuck.

The "Zen of Robot Programming": Control versus Exploitation

Consider now the well-known Puma arm. The Puma arm is an
industrial-strength robot arm used successfully in many industrial

and academic environments. The user can simply choose to program it with a particular trajectory, and if the trajectory is physically possible for the robot arm, it performs the desired movements. The user doesn't have to worry about the real world, about the physics, that is, friction, inertia, and the forces acting on the arm. The engineers who designed the arm have taken care of all of this. In a sense, the real world has already been taken care of: The user can focus on the geometry of the problem, where the hand has to move, what objects have to be picked up and manipulated. Within certain limits, he has complete control over the arm. And for industrial applications, this is what is required.

Let us consider the example of an arm that is not so well engineered, less precise, not so tightly controllable. In this case, the programmer has to concern himself much more about the physics of the process, about the arm's interacting with its environment. To speak metaphorically, he has to think about how the agent will "be" in the world. Such an arm would presumably have less use in industrial applications. However, on robots that have to interact with humans, it could be extremely useful. An arm of such a robot would need to have different properties than an arm on a robot designed for an industrial application. Rather than being precisely controllable, for example, it would have to be compliant. If the standard industrial robot arm meets resistance on its way to its target, it typically increases its force. By contrast, if an arm on a robot designed for human interaction touched a person, it would need to yield elastically instead of pushing harder. Chapter 16 offers an example of a compliant design: It concerns the control of the arm movements in the humanoid robot Cog. The Cog project employed a bottom-up design philosophy. The springlike properties of human muscles are simulated (e.g. Pratt and Williamson 1995). The arm has a natural resting position. If it is removed from the resting position, the arm swings back based purely on local processes at the joints of the arm, without central control. Control is achieved largely by changing the elastic properties of the (simulated) springs. The designer starts with minimal control circuitry and increases the complexity only if required. This resulting design is cheap and robust. Another impressive example of exploiting physics is the passive dynamic walker (see focus 13.1). More on the idea of exploiting physics can be found in Pfeifer 1995.

We suspect that this exploitation of environmental physics is the design philosophy Rodney Brooks had in mind when he used the

Focus 13.1:   A Passive Dynamic Walker

Figure 13.4 shows a so-called passive dynamic walker, which simulates human walking. It illustrates that something as complex as humanlike walking can be achieved without an internal controller. Most work on walking has focused on the neurobiology and on control and how "the brain does it." Often such models lead to overdesign: They make many assumptions about what simply *must* be included in terms of neural circuitry, what the design could not *possibly* work without. As we have now seen many times, if the system-environment interaction is properly taken into account, matters turn out to be much simpler, much cheaper. The passive dynamic walker project has focused on the interaction of gravity, inertia, and collision, rather than control. The passive dynamic walker can be thought of as a dynamical system being driven into a *limit cycle*, a steady periodic motion "inherent" to the mechanism. (Chapter 9 introduced the idea of limit cycles.) The resulting walking movement is surprisingly natural. The idea for the walker was introduced by Tad McGeer (1990a, 1990b). More details can be found in Garcia et al. in press.

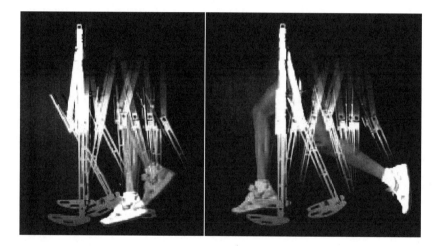

Figure 13.4   The passive dynamic walker built by the Department of Theoretical and Applied Mechanics at Cornell University. It walks down a shallow slope, driven solely by gravity. There is no electronic control whatsoever on the robot: the robot has no "brain." Still, its movements look very natural and humanlike, a beautiful example of the exploitation of dynamics.

term "Zen of robot programming." In general, we can conclude that incorporating considerations about the physics of the system-environment interaction typically leads to better and more robust designs. If an arm for a robot is not as well designed as the Puma arm, one has to include such considerations in the design process. Because a cheaper, not-so-well-designed arm forces the designer to consider these issues, it has been argued that working with cheap robots is a virtue and not a problem (Smithers 1994). But keep in mind the very different areas of application in which the different kinds of philosophies are applied.

So far we have illustrated exploitation of physics and constraints of the ecological niche in considering the various aspects of cheap design. Let us now turn to the last aspect, parsimony.

Parsimony

Parsimony is a general principle applied in modeling. As we briefly pointed out in chapter 10, it implies that the designer should aim for a kind of minimalist, simple agent or model in general. The search for parsimony is also referred to as Occam's razor in the philosophy of science. It is generally accepted that if there are a number of competing models, the more parsimonious ones are to be preferred. A model that can explain the clustering behavior of ants based on simple reflexes, for example, is to be preferred over one that postulates some sort of internal representation of clustering. In this sense, the Didabots are parsimonious models of ant behavior, irrespective of whether they are good models in other ways. A robot for obstacle avoidance that employs simple reflexes based on IR sensors is more parsimonious than one that does extensive visual analysis for the same purpose.

The concept of parsimony is not without its problems because there are no generally accepted quantitative measures for it. In the examples given above, it is intuitively clear which is more parsimonious; in others, however, it is not. For example, if we trade morphology for computation, for instance, an insect's eye with the visual segments spaced according to a sine law, is the overall solution more parsimonious than one based on computation? Is wheeled locomotion more parsimonious than walking? In spite of the fact that parsimony is only a qualitative term and not precisely defined, it still provides a heuristic on how to assess the quality of models or the quality of our designs. Other evaluation factors, however, are often more relevant. In the case of the housefly, the question is whether it can perform in real time, and for this purpose, it is a necessity to trade shape for computation. In other words, if the housefly were using a uniform visual sensor and doing the necessary processing for achieving the same kind of obstacle avoidance exclusively at the neural level, it would presumably not succeed: It could not possibly meet the real-time requirements.

Cheap versus Flexible

We have now seen a number of examples of how to exploit constraints to yield cheap designs. As always, however, there are trade-offs. Cheap designs exploit the specific characteristics of an ecological niche, which implies that whenever these constraints no longer hold, the system breaks down. The cheap vision system of our robot Polly works well as long as the floors are flat and as long as the objects to be avoided are standing on the ground. But what if there are stairs? Or what if the objects are standing on a table? With thin legs that would be hard to defect with a camera. The obstacle avoidance system ceases to function appropriately in that case, and if we want the agent to continue to function, we may have to drop the assumption that all objects to be avoided are standing on the ground. But the agent then needs additional capacities, better visual and perhaps more sophisticated motor control. Or take a person who all of a sudden finds himself in the dark. He can use, for example, his ears and his tactile system for orientation. But he may want not only to listen passively but also to explore the environment actively with a stick to generate the required information. In other words, he may need motor abilities to acquire the information he needs in the new situation. If an agent has only vision, as does Polly, it can no longer function once light is gone; it has to use a different strategy.

So, parsimony, cheapness, is not the only criterion in evaluating a design's merit. Remaining adaptive, allowing for behavioral diversity, is another. How can natural agents come up with new kinds of behaviors that help them adapt to new environments? Or synthetically speaking, how can we design agents to be able to adapt to new environments? We need to equip our agents with *redundancy*, which is what the redundancy principle addresses.

13.2   The Redundancy Principle

The redundancy principle concerns an agent's low-level specifications. It states that an agent has to incorporate redundancy. More specifically, in relation to the sensory system, the principle states that an agent's sensors have to be positioned on the agent in such a way that there is potential overlap in the information that can be acquired from the different sensory channels. As we pointed out in chapter 4, an agent's low-level specifications span a very large space incorporating a lot of redundancy. Introducing redundancy is a well-known engineering principle wherever mission-critical systems are concerned, that is, systems where security and reliability are crucial to success. An airplane is equipped with several computers for the same purpose, it has two pilots, and there are several braking systems working on the basis of different principles and mechanisms. Computer storage and network systems all incorporate considerable amounts of redundancy, from duplication of data sets, to parity bits, to more complex redundancy schemes for checking and potentially correcting erroneous transmissions. Although this aspect of redundancy is also relevant for agent design, we really mean something more specific when we speak of redundancy here.

In chapter 10, we pointed out that concept of redundancy stems from Shannon and Weaver's mathematical theory of communication, which is concerned with transmission of messages across noisy channels: The goal is to use redundancy to transmit messages error free over noisy channels. Redundancy takes several forms: (1) repetitive transmission of the same message over one channel, (2) duplication of channels, (3) restrictions on the use of characters transmitted across the channel, and (4) communicating something already known to its addressee. Forms (3) and (4) are closely related. If the addressee knows about the restrictions, something that he already (at least partially) knows is transmitted.

Before we can look at these points from an autonomous agents perspective, we have to specify what "communication channels" we are discussing in this context. For autonomous agents, communication channels are the signals generated by the sensory systems and then processed by the control architecture. As we know, situated agents have no other way of acquiring information about the environment. In contrast to communication channels, autonomous agents are active entities. Thus constraints are not only imposed by the information being transmitted over the channel but also gen-

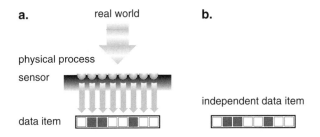

Figure 13.5 Redundancy from sensor data. (a) Data item (byte) connected to outside world via sensor. (b) Independent data item. In case of loss of data, the byte in figure (b) is lost; it is not backed up by any sort of redundancy. In (a), however, the data are redundant, because they are constrained by their connection to the real world via a physical process, i.e., via the system-environment interaction. On average, because a physical process is involved, the data item on the left does not change instantaneously but has a certain sluggishness, thus providing a temporal redundancy: the data can be repeatedly read into the storage location if need be.

erated by the agent's behavior. Let us now translate into the agent domain the four forms of redundancy we delineated above.

Repeated Messages

We start with form (1), the repetitive transmission of the same message over one channel. Assume that you have a certain storage location in computer memory. On the left (figure 13.5a), the data originate from a sensor; on the right, the origin (figure 13.5b) of the data is unknown. Because they translate a physical process into a signal that can be processed by the control architecture, sensors have a particular operating frequency, a rate at which they transform physical processes into internal signals. Since there is an actual physical process, and since the sensory stimulation and the objects in the real world normally don't change instantaneously, there is a high probability that two successive patterns will be similar. They will normally not be identical, however, because there is noise, and things do change, because the environment has its dynamics and the agent moves, too. Still, on average, two successive signals will be alike. This similarity constitutes temporal redundancy: It is like sending a message repeatedly over a communication channel. An engineer can exploit this redundancy: Because the redundancy is there, the sensor and the transmission channel between the sensor and the data storage location can be designed cheaply; that is, it does not have to be extremely reliable. Generally speaking, from the perspective of the control architecture, we see that the closer the data items are to the sensors from which they originate, the more there is redundancy contained in the interaction with the real world. The further away a data item is from the sensors, the less the real-world constraints exert their influence, and the more effort has to be expended to ensure that it is not distorted.

In chapter 10, we briefly pointed out redundancy's relation to sensory-motor coordination. Let us now look at this in more detail. Figure 12.23 shows the temporal correlations of the vectors of the 10-dimensional sensory space—the 8 IR sensors and the 2 motor speeds—of an agent approaching a large object. During the period when the sensory-motor coordination takes place, the sensory input is relatively stable. This temporal redundancy is required for learning to take place. If things change rapidly, beyond a certain rate of change, there is no sense in learning. The essential point here is that the robot's interaction with the environment in fact generates the prerequisites for learning in terms of redundancy. This further illustrates the information theoretic perspective on sensory-motor coordination. Note that this temporal redundancy does not come about if the focus is on the sensors only: The motor system has to be taken into account as well.

Duplication of Channels: Learning to Predict Sensory Inputs

Normally we are interested not only in repetition over one channel, but also in correlations among several channels. For example, we do not want an agent to know only the color of an object; we want the agent to associate the color with the object's shape and its texture. Moreover, we want to be able to associate information from different sensory modalities, like IR and haptic (touch), IR and vision, vision and haptic, or vision and audio. In terms of design, this implies that redundancy should be introduced with respect not only to one sensory modality but to several. Different sensory modalities are based on different physical processes. They should be designed in such a way that the information they deliver potentially overlaps. For example, vision sensors and IR sensors both yield spatial information. Depending on the environment's reflective properties, the physical characteristics of the sensors and their position on the agent, readings of the visual and the IR sensors show some correlation as the agent interacts with the environment.

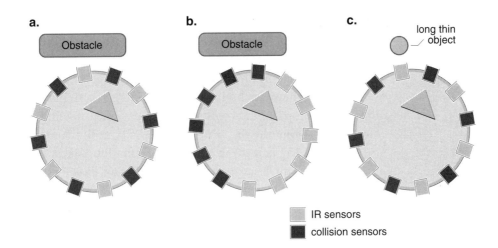

Figure 13.6 Spatial information overlap. (a) This generic agent (from chapter 5) has been designed to yield spatial information overlap. (b) All IR sensors are on one side of this robot, whereas all collision sensors are on the other. In this robot there is no spatial overlap in the information from different sensory channels by direct coupling. (c) There is no redundancy by direct coupling if there are only long thin objects in the environment.

Redundancy can occur in three cases. First, there can simply be temporal coincidence in the stimuli. To use an example by de Sa (1994), whenever you see a cow, there is a high probability that you will also hear a "moo" sound. Thus the environment alone lends a certain redundancy to the sensory stimuli. This redundancy can be picked up by unsupervised neural networks (e.g., Becker and Hinton 1992; de Sa 1994). Forming such associations as those between seeing a cow and hearing "moo" is an important aspect of concept development. In autonomous agents specifically, these associations can be formed only if the environment provides the opportunity. Moreover, this sort of associative learning requires that the "stimulus" cow has already been recognized—otherwise the association cannot be formed. Thus, we cannot rely on such a mechanism in general to ensure learning (for example, if the agent has not yet learned to recognize a cow or a "moo" sound).

Fortunately, because agents can interact with their environment, they do not have to wait passively for the right kinds of sensory signals to arrive. Through appropriate interaction, such signals can be generated, which leads us to the second case of how redundancy can occur: through spatial information overlap. Note the arrangement and the properties of the sensors in figure 13.6a. Collision sensors and proximity sensors are based on different physical processes: in the former case, it is actual touch (which can be implemented, for example, as a microswitch), in the latter, measurement of reflected intensity of infrared light. Whenever a collision occurs, there is high activation in the proximity sensors adjacent to the particular collision sensor. Thus, in a collision, the information from the IR sensors is largely redundant. In other words, the agent is getting similar information twice, once over each channel. This is an instance of direct coupling. It works only if the sensors are positioned appropriately, as can immediately be seen by inspecting the robot in figure 13.4b. If this robot hits an obstacle, the spatial information delivered by the two sensory channels does not overlap, because the two types of sensors are not collocated, and there is nothing to be learned. This robot has not been designed according to the redundancy principle. But it can still be used to pick up the correlations: It can behave in the real world. For example, it could simply continuously wiggle back and forth in such a way that both types of sensors are in the front of the robot alternately. Near an obstacle, the sensory signals from the different channels will then be correlated, just as for the properly designed robot in figure 13.4a. (An alternative would be to simply rotate the sensors, but that would be a somewhat different argument, and we do not discuss it here.) This is a more expensive solution, however, than designing the robot with its sensors inter mixed. Further, if the wiggling angle is preprogrammed, this is not a sensory-motor coordination, because the sensor signals do not influence the robot's wiggling behavior. But if the wiggling behavior depends on the sensory signals—and this is the third case of how redundancy can occur—we have the general phenomenon of sensory-motor coordination. It would be interesting to use artificial evolution to see whether such wiggling behavior would in fact be generated when we used as a fitness function the distance traveled, minus a reduction for the collisions.

What can we conclude from this case study? If the designers position different types of sensors appropriately in advance, correlations can be generated and learned through direct coupling—no sensory-motor coordination is required: a cheap solution. But even if the sensory channels are not a priori positioned to yield correlations, through its own behavior, through sensory-motor coordination, an agent can position itself so that correlations can be achieved which can then be picked up by a learning mechanism. This way, one sensory channel becomes a predictor for the other. To put it differently, the information from one sensory channel is partly contained in the other. We see that sensory-motor coordination provides flexibility in how the potential redundancy in the sensory signals of different channels can be exploited. So the design decision of where to put the sensors becomes highly involved: The potential overlaps in various types of sensory-motor coordinations have to be taken into account. The kinds of sensory-motor coordinations possible or necessary depend, in turn, on the environment. Imagine, for a moment, that the robot in figure 13.6a was operating in an environment with only narrow, vertical objects. The correlations necessary for learning could no longer be generated through direct coupling because the objects would not be large enough to stimulate both sensors simultaneously (figure 13.6c). The robot in figure 13.6c would have to engage in some kind of behavior to generate the appropriate redundancy required for learning.

There is currently no general solution to this problem of how to optimally design sensory systems with different channels and where to position the sensors. This is, once again, because the right choice strongly depends on the task environment. Thus a good bet is once again to draw inspiration from natural systems, hoping that evolution did in fact do a good designer's job.

Redundancy in the different sensory channels is a universal phenomenon. We have seen many examples from robots, and developmental studies provide abundant evidence for it. An entertaining illustration is provided by the so-called McGurk effect, which concerns the fact that visual and auditory channels are both used in speech perception. McGurk and McDonald (1976) took videotapes of people uttering certain sounds, then changed the sound so that the physical sound was not compatible with the sound suggested by the videotape. For example, when the tape showed /pa-pa/, the physical sound was /na-na/. Those watching the tape often reported hearing /ma-ma/. Another example was a /da/ on the video and a /ba/ as a physical sound, which was often reported as /va/ by those viewing the tape. Because there is redundancy in the two channels, the perceivers noted the incompatibility (not consciously). The result was a kind of compromise: They seemed to believe both channels to some extent.

Constraints—Communicating Information Already Known

Let us conclude this discussion by translating redundancy of types (3) and (4) to autonomous agents. Associations between sensory modalities exploit redundancy. The information from one modality (the visual one) reduces the uncertainty in the other (the IR sensors). In this sense, the information in the other (the IR sensors) is "communication" of information that the agent already has, at least partly. From the perspective of generating diversity, the information from the IR sensors is still necessary for the agent to remain adaptive: the situation may turn out to be a novel one, in which case the prediction is incorrect. For example, some black objects don't reflect IR radiation well, which leads the agent to predict that no object is nearby, whereas in fact one is. The visual system has to continue to do its job—it cannot fully rely on the IR system.

Accidental Redundancy

So far we have been talking about redundancy designed into the robots. But another type of redundancy is not designed but naturally incorporated in a particular physical substrate: It could be called *accidental redundancy*. Evolution (both natural and artificial) can exploit this accidental redundancy in interesting ways. For example, uses have evolved for various properties of waste products. The smell characteristics are used for informatory purposes: The smell of urine can be exploited to mark territory. Hormones seem to have sprung from waste products of cellular metabolism and later been employed as messengers to carry signals within the organism (e.g., Holenstein 1985).[1] When we say that evolution is exploiting redundancy, we are of course adopting an observer's perspective.

This phenomenon is also known from artificial evolution. Recall our discussion in chapter 8 of Adrian Thompson's experiments to evolve an electronic circuit that distinguishes between a high- and a low-frequency signal. In Thompson's experiments, evolution exploited the properties of the physical material, the silicon. In particular, it made use of subtle interactions between cells. The cells shaded in gray were not connected by wires to the rest of the circuit (figure 8.14b). Nevertheless, when clamped to a fixed value,

---

[1] The technical term used for these kinds of phenomena is *functionalization of epiphenomenal structure.*

the circuit ceased to function properly. So because some of the constraints were dropped, evolution was free to exploit all the rich dynamics of the silicon.

Information Theoretic Aspects

We now turn to a more formal discussion of redundancy and look at information theory. This section is slightly formal and may be skipped without losing the general thread of the argument.

What we have said about the redundancy principle can be described more formally in information theoretic terms. If X and Y are the variables representing the signals from two sensory modalities or channels (e.g., IR and touch), and $H(X)$ and $H(Y)$ are the respective entropies, we can define the mutual information

$$I(X, Y) = H(X) + H(Y) - H(X, Y). \tag{13.1}$$

Formally, entropy is defined as

$$H(Z) = -\sum_{i=1}^{N} p(z_i) \log(p(z_i)), \tag{13.2}$$

for a discrete variable z_i with probability distribution $p(z_i)$ and N possible states. We can assume that the sensory signals assume discrete values corresponding to the sensory states (e.g., 1,024 in a typical IR sensor). Intuitively, the entropy is a measure of disorder, of negative information. $H(x, y)$ is the joint entropy, which is defined as

$$H(X, Y) = -\sum_{x} \sum_{y} p(x, y) \log p(x, y), \tag{13.3}$$

where $p(x, y)$ is the joint probability distribution. If the signals in the two sensory channels are uncorrelated, $H(X, Y)$ is minimal: There is less disorder, more order. The more the two are correlated, the higher the mutual information will be. Note that mutual information is also high if the entropy in the individual channels is high. We return to this point shortly. The concept of mutual information is a special case of redundancy, namely, redundancy for two channels. These ideas can be generalized to more than two channels, for example, to an agent with an IR sensor, a sonar, and a vision sensor.

This standard information theoretic picture can be found in any textbook on information theory (e.g., Cover and Thomas 1991). We now want to apply these ideas to autonomous agents. Normally, H and I are properties of communication channels. In the case of an agent, we are interested in the entropies and in the mutual information as the agent is engaged in various behaviors. The entropies $H(X)$, $H(Y)$, and so forth, of the individual sensory channels, the joint entropy $H(X, Y, \ldots)$ and mutual information I are measured over a set of behaviors in a particular environment, preferably over the entire task environment. The individual entropies account for the variability in the sensory channels, the potential diversity of patterns of stimulation. The joint entropy is due to correlations, the redundancy contained in the sensory channels, for example, during sensory-motor coordination. If the sensory channels were always correlated, there would be no meaning in having two channels. Because of the different physical processes operating on different channels, the chance that the channels will always be correlated is very small. So we see that the mutual information reaches its maximum value when there is, at the same time, a lot of variation in the individual sensory channels and a lot of correlation among them.

Mutual information can also be viewed as a measure of complexity: the higher the mutual information, the higher the agent's complexity. We are clearly not talking about the complexity of a sensory channel here, nor the complexity of the entire agent, but about the complexity of an agent given a particular task environment: The entropies and the joint entropy depend on the probabilities of the sensory states, which in turn depend on the task environment. The more diverse the agent's behavior, the more variability there is in the various sensory channels, and if the behaviors involve sensory-motor coordination—leading to low joint redundancies—the higher the mutual information. This corresponds to our intuitions of complexity. A similar measure has been developed by Tononi, Sporns, and Edelman (1994, 1996) to measure brain complexity (see below). This measure also contains, indirectly, a characterization of the complexity of environments, not in isolation, but with respect to an agent's sensory system, which in turn is stimulated depending on the diversity of the agent's behavior.

So far we have been talking about the observer's perspective: We have analyzed the activation of different sensory channels. Now we turn to the agent's perspective. Let us assume that the agent encounters a new object. It explores the object, which leads to correlated activation, for example, in the visual and the haptic chan-

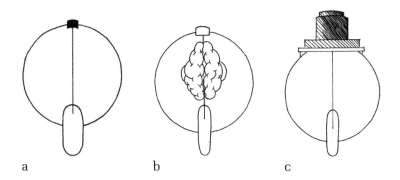

a   b   c

Figure 13.7 The principle of ecological balance. (a) Standard Braitenberg 1 vehicle. (b) Braitenberg 1 vehicle with augmented brain capacity. (c) Braitenberg 1 vehicle with high-resolution camera only. Vehicles (b) and (c) don't have any real advantage over (a). Only if all sensors, brain, and motor system are augmented will they have a true advantage over (a).

nel. Mutual information is high. Through Hebbian mechanisms, correlations are learned. Over time, the neural network has picked up some of the mutual information contained in the sensory signals during real-world interaction. After some time, it is no longer necessary for the agent to experience full sensory stimulation to recognize a particular object: It can exploit the mutual information now contained in the neural network.

13.3 The Principle of Ecological Balance

The principle of ecological balance brings together the ecological niche, the desired behaviors of an agent, and the agent itself. It states that the "complexity" of an agent has to match the complexity of its task environment. In particular, given a certain task environment, there has to be a match in the complexity of sensors, motor system, and neural substrate. It is best to illustrate the idea of ecological balance with a number of examples.

Augmenting a Braitenberg Vehicle

Let us conduct an amusing thought experiment. A particular Braitenberg type 1 vehicle, has one sensor, say for light intensity, and one motor (figure 13.7a). It is wired in such a way that the higher the light intensity, the faster the motor is driven. Its environment consists simply of varying light intensities. We have also looked at this vehicle's behavior: It seems to dislike brightly lit areas and prefers dim ones. Its "brain" consists of one neuron, so it's not much of a brain. Let's turn it into a more realistic brain, like an insect brain with 1 million neurons (figure 13.7b). What would the vehicle do with its enormous brain? It's hard to think of a good answer. In fact, such a brain would be pretty useless. Since ecological balance depends on the task environment, let's also increase the environment's complexity by introducing enemies. It is advantageous for the vehicle to recognize these enemies at a distance. Instead of a large brain let us now add a high-resolution camera to the vehicle (figure 13.7c). This would be equally useless, because the camera input could not be processed. So, let's now add the brain from vehicle (b) to this vehicle. Now it might be possible in principle for the vehicle to recognize the enemies (but note the difficulties with mapping a sensory stimulation onto an internal representation), but it couldn't really avoid them, because all it can do is go either faster or slower, though it might stop if it recognized an enemy far away. The best solution would seem to be to augment the capacity of all three systems, sensory, brain and motor. Then, the agent could actually change its behavior and exploit the augmented sensory and motor systems to meet the increased demands of its environment.

Further Illustrations of Ecological Balance

Let us elaborate the principle of ecological balance a bit further. People who, through some accident or illness, become blind start exploiting other resources to compensate for the loss of their sight: They start using their auditory, tactile, and proprioceptive (that is, their internal sensors) systems in novel ways. Prior to the loss of sight, they had not exploited the capacity of the auditory system because there was no need. The extra capacity—the part they had not tapped into prior to losing their sight—represents redundancy. As we stated above, it is always good design to have redundancy, especially if the additional—mostly unused—capacity is cheap. "Cheap" in this case means having low running costs (energy and processing power) and low reproductive costs (genetic transmission). The task environment for the people who have turned blind has now changed. They can no longer engage in a number of behaviors, for example driving a car, playing tennis, or watching a movie. Their reduced sensory capabilities have curtailed their behavioral repertoire; in particular, those behaviors requiring spatial information are now more taxing. But they can still engage in many behaviors, because spatial information, for example, can also be acquired from other sensory systems. While walking, the auditory system provides valuable spatial information. Note that the systems still intact can be better exploited by engaging in new behaviors, such as the exploration of the immediate surroundings with a stick, thus producing additional auditory, tactile, and proprioceptive feedback. Novel behaviors can generate sensory input that can—at least to some extent—replace the input from the visual one, as in the scanning of Braille script. Exploiting the previously unused capacity of sensory systems is possible only if there is sufficient neural plasticity, and fortunately, in humans, this is developed to a high degree. As the nervous system reorganizes to adjust to the loss of sight, the task environment gradually changes again. Through the better exploitation of the auditory system, walking becomes easier. But because the auditory system is now better exploited, music is heard differently and perhaps becomes more important. So we see that metaphorically speaking, some overall balance is maintained.

Another illustration of the principal of ecological balance comes from developmental studies. Bushnell and Boudreau (1993) suggested that there is a kind of coevolution of the sensory and the motor system in human infants. They investigated the motor components of haptic perception and those of visual depth perception. In both cases, they found a high correspondence between unfolding perceptual abilities and the acquisition of particular motor patterns. For example, children's performance on a task where they had to follow the gaze of the experimenter improved dramatically as soon as they started crawling (discussed in Thelen and Smith 1994, p. 201). These findings directly relate to the principle of sensory-motor coordination. Generating the "right" sensory stimulation requires the ability to generate the appropriate movements. At a more general level, the ecological balance principle describes the inseparability of perception and action.

A further illustration of the principle comes from the animal world: the phenomenon of rudimentary organs. Let us look at a few examples. The eyes of the European mole are very small but still functioning. By contrast, the North American mole is entirely blind. The bodies of the two species are very similar. It would be interesting to study in what ways the behavior of the two moles differs. Does the additional sensory capacity in the European mole imply a different behavioral repertoire, that is, can European moles exploit the additional sensory capacity? Another example is the family of proteidae. Normally, individuals belonging to this family live in dark caves under water. Below the skin of their head, they have the rudiments of eyes, however, as a rule they don't develop: They are blind. But if proteidae larvae are raised under red light, their eyes develop in ways similar to those of other kinds of newts. Again, the question would be whether the behavior repertoire is different in these newts. It would also be of interest to see to what extent this additional sensory ability changes the exploitation of other sensory abilities. These questions may be hard to investigate in natural systems, but we can study them using the synthetic methodology.

Experiments

One of the fundamental differences between natural agents and robots is that natural agents undergo a process of development during which their body, sensory, motor, and neural systems grow and change. It is currently not possible to reproduce these phenomena on real robots. But we can approximate the developmental process by building redundancy into the robot on the sensory and the motor side. For example, we can put a high-resolution camera on a simple two-wheeled robot, as well as a redundant manipulator (A redundant manipulator is one with many degrees of freedom, so that a particular task like picking up an object can be done in a number of different ways.) But we do not initially exploit the full capacity of the camera: We put a crude filter over it in such a way that the resolution is minimal, for example, yielding only, say, a 16×16 pixel image, to which only very simple processing is applied. The rest, that is, the additional capacity for higher resolution, is redundancy to be exploited whenever a more demanding task environment requires it. If we want to perform experiments to explore how redundancy can be exploited, we have to get the robot to actually do something, to make use of its setup. This necessitates a value system. Only if the agent gets additional value from better exploitation of its sensory-motor apparatus does it actually engage in related behaviors. When working with agents, this point immediately becomes obvious; we have generously glossed over it in our verbal descriptions of natural systems. In our experiments, then, we start with a simple task environment and make it successively more taxing.

An illustration of how this might be done can be found in the robot ecosystem developed by Steels and McFarland (Steels 1997) that we introduced in chapter 9. Recall that this ecosystem contained boxes with lamps consuming energy. The robots had to push against the boxes to dim their lights to reduce the energy consumption of the boxes. The darker the boxes, the more current there was in the charging station, which meant more energy available to the robots. The robots were equipped with various sensors that could be coupled to motivations. The point was that if the environment was made more taxing, for example, by increasing the number of energy-consuming boxes, the robots had to exploit these sensors to produce beneficial sensor-to-motor couplings. The primary source of value was energy level, for which there was a special sensor. The robots could get more value if they better exploited their sensors. At the start of the experiments, the sensors were not used; they constituted redundancy. An example of a sensor that was not exploited initially is the sensor for being in the charging station. As the environment was made more demanding, for example, by introducing more competitors or other robots, the robots had to exploit those additional sensors to learn the right couplings that would lead to more efficient exploitation of the resources. For example, by using the sensor for changing speed in the charging station, the robots could learn the appropriate couplings to the motors, that is, couplings that would slow them down as soon as they entered the charging station, which in turn would result in the robots' receiving more electricity. Note that this is a hard learning problem because of the delayed reinforcement (which the next chapter discusses). The robot ecosystem nicely demonstrates how environmental pressure can force agents to exploit their redundant sensory apparatus. So far, this has been done only on the ontogenetic scale. We could also imagine that the entire procedure was embedded into an evolutionary cycle. In this case, we would not explicitly have to define value (as the energy level) but could simply take as the fitness criterion how long an agent survived, that is, how long its energy level remained above 0. And then we could observe, for example, whether "something" evolved, whether the agents started exhibiting behavior, that we, as observers, might want to associate with a value system.

With this example, we wanted to illustrate how one might think about conducting experiments that relate to the principle of ecological balance. Because we deal with complete agents, we have to think about motivational issues, about value. So the task environment has to be designed in such a way that the agents can realize this value. If we want the agent to better exploit the capacity of its high-resolution camera, we have to produce an incentive for it to do so (for example, getting value from small objects, the manipulation of which requires exploiting the camera's additional capacity). This complicates matters considerably, but at the benefit of potentially producing more ecologically valid results. Instead of using real robots, we can opt to use a simulation task environment. We can also employ artificial evolution (which will eventually enable us to simulate actual growth of an organism; see Eggenberger's model of cell growth discussed in chapter 8). Artificial evolution can then be used to systematically explore the kind of balance that evolves in the agent's setup as a function of the task environment.

Another consideration in the choice of task environment relates to the frame problem. In chapter 3, we identified the frame problem not only as one of the fundamental problems of classical AI systems, but also as a problem inherent to any modeling approach: Keeping the model in tune with the environment. Intuitively, larger brains are only of advantage to an agent's adaptivity. They augment the potential for generating diversity. But there is also a danger in having large brains: The larger an agent's brain, the more information about the environment it can potentially acquire the more complex the models of the environment can be. If the environment is changing rapidly, the chance increases that this information becomes inaccurate, that the models do no longer correspond to reality and thus are no longer of value. Such information is only costly, consumes energy, and offers no benefit for behavior, for acquiring additional value. If the complex models in the brain have to be updated, this has to be achieved, in a situated agent, through its sensory system in the interaction with the real world. The amount of information that can be transmitted to the brain is therefore always limited and may not be sufficient to accurately update the world models. So eventually, systems with overly large brains run into trouble, although increasing brain size may, depending on the particular task environment, be beneficial to an agent. In particular, increased brain size may host redundancy that can be exploited for generating diversity. However, we can be certain that there is a limit beyond which further increasing the brain's size leads to a decrease in performance. This is because of the frame problem (the difficulty in keeping complex models in tune with the world) and the energy consumption at the brain. Building a brain the size of the moon is certainly not a very good idea, at least in those task environments that we can currently think of (see Issue 13.1).

Measuring Complexity

Let us now turn to a more formal treatment of ecological balance. Again, this section can be skipped without losing the thread of our argument.

If the principle of ecological balance is ever to achieve the status of an empirically testable hypothesis, we need to be more quantitative: we need a measure of complexity. This measure should take into account not only the agent's low-level specifications, but also the agent's task environment. We cannot look only at the states of the various sensory and motor channels in measuring complexity. Intuitively, we understand that an agent that exhibits a great variety of different behaviors is more complex that one always engaged in the same behavior. Behavioral diversity also requires diversity in sensory, motor, and internal states. As we noted above, the mutual information function $I(X, Y, \ldots)$ captures these intuitions in a formal way.

Tononi, Sporns, and Edelman (1994) have presented a measure for characterizing brain complexity similar to the mutual information function. They started from the well-known assumption that there is both functional segregation of brain areas that differ in their anatomy and physiology and global integration of these areas during perception and behavior; their measure of neural complexity captures these two aspects of brain organization. Functional segregation concerns the fact that different areas of the brain are devoted to the processing of different types of signals, say of visual, auditory, tactile, or motor signals. During perception and behavior, the processing of these areas has to be coordinated to achieve overall coherence, that is, to achieve global integration that leads to appropriate behavior. Functional segregation within a neural system is formally expressed as follows: The brain region is partitioned into small subsets, then the relative statistical independence of these subsets is determined. Functional integration is calculated in terms of deviations from statistical independence in large subsets. Tononi and colleagues obtained their measure of complexity, C_N, from estimates of the average deviation from statistical independence for subsets of increasing size. This measure is high when functional segregation coexists with integration and low when the components of a system are either completely independent (segregated) or completely dependent (integrated). Again, this is in line with our intuitions. If different areas are always integrated, it is not clear why different areas would need to exist in the first place: a single one would be sufficient. Conversely, if different areas are always segregated, no redundancy would exist to exploit for learning.

As we saw in our discussion of the principle of parallel, loosely coupled processes, correlations can come about not only through connections between various processes but also through interaction with the environment. The principle of sensory-motor coordination capitalizes on coordination through the environment. So we want to characterize not only brain complexity as such, but also the overall complexity of the agent in which the brain is embedded as it behaves in a particular task environment. Tononi, Sporns, and Edelman took a first step in this direction, extending their measure C_N to include sensory stimulation in a second measure called the *matching complexity* (C_M). It is calculated as follows:

$$C_M(X, S_i) = C_N^T(X) - C_N^I(X) - C_N^E(X), \tag{13.4}$$

where X is the neural system; S_i the sensory subsystem involved in processing the sensory stimulus i; $C_N^I(X)$ is defined as C_N above, that is, the complexity when the system is isolated from sensory stimulation, called the *intrinsic complexity*; $C_N^T(X)$, called the *total complexity*, is what we observe when the system processes a stimulus in subsystem S_i; and $C_N^E(X)$, the *extrinsic complexity*, is the complexity of the sensory stimulus itself, calculated by setting the neural connectivity in X to 0. To find the matching complexity, the brain complexity and stimulus complexity have to be subtracted from the total complexity. This brings us already closer to our intuitions: Matching complexity C_M takes into account an aspect of the task environment: sensory stimulation. In an agent context, this sensory stimulation has its origin largely in the agent's behavior. In a sense, this sensory stimulation reflects the agent's behavioral complexity: the more diverse the agent's behavior, the more variation in the sensory channels, and the higher the entropy in the individual channels. But C_M takes only the stimulus into account, not the fact that this stimulus may or may not be due to the agent's behavior. We are interested not only in complexity due to sensory stimulation, but also in complexity due to *self-generated* sensory stimulation. Equation (13.4) may therefore have to be extended to include aspects of the motor system's complexity.

Making this extension is a hard research task. As a first step, one could apply C_M to various agents in different task environments, which is difficult because we would have to assess the probability distributions of the different sensory channels. These distributions in turn depend on the task environment and the agent's motor abilities, in particular the agent's capacity for sensory-motor coordination. This in turn implies that we would have to take the low-level specifications into account, that is, where the sensory channels are positioned within the agent's morphology, as expressed in the redundancy principle. Exploratory empirical studies might provide us with some direction.

Issues to Think About

Issue 13.1:   Complexity and IQ

We have maintained that if we are to perform empirical tests on the design principles we have articulated, we need to be more quantitative about complexity. We examined some preliminary ideas on how such a measure might look. The measure has to capture our intuition that a system whose components are sometimes functioning independently and sometimes in a coordinated way is more complex than one in which all the components are always independent, or one in which they are always coordinated. We saw that coordination can come about through appropriate interaction with the environment, through sensory-motor coordination. Tononi, Sporns, and Edelman (1996) introduced a measure of brain complexity vis-à-vis a certain statistical distribution of sensory stimulation. In some sense, this distribution reflects the task environment, the agent-environment interaction: depending on an agent's behavior, this distribution looks different at different times. (We noted that this measure does not capture the origin of this sensory stimulation, the fact that the agent itself can move and generate sensory inputs.) Now think a moment about what we have just done: We have just mapped the complex agent-environment interaction onto one single number. Given our characterization of intelligence in chapter 1 in terms of diversity and compliance with the rules, we can ask ourselves if we now have a measure of intelligence in one number. This reminds us very strongly of the IQ discussion in chapter 1. The question then becomes what this single number tells us about the agent. Does it reveal interesting properties of an agent? In what sense can we use it to compare agents? In what sense do agents with similar complexity in fact seem similar to us under this measure? The advantage of the synthetic methodology here is that we can make systematic experiments to explore this issue. We can vary aspects of our agents and task environments by changing the agents themselves or by introducing more competitors into the ecological niche and compare the resulting complexities.

Issue 13.2: Walking: A Passive Dynamic Process?

Imagine that you are walking through Zurich. When you observe yourself, do you feel that you are a "passive dynamic walker" or that your brain is controlling the walking? Or do you think that the truth is somewhere in between (which is most likely what you think)? If you had the task to design a walking robot, how would you proceed in designing the control architecture? One way would be to start with a passive dynamic walker, then successively add small pieces of neural circuitry until the desired set of behaviors could be achieved. Another would be to analyze human walking by incorporating insights from neuroscience. Do you have other suggestions on how you might proceed?

Points to Remember

- The principle of cheap design states that good designs are "cheap." "Cheap" as used here means three things: First, it implies exploiting the physics of the system-environment interaction. Second, it means exploiting the constraints of the ecological niche. And third, it means parsimonious.
- The housefly achieves cheap navigation by exploiting the system-environment interaction, namely the phenomenon of motion parallax. Motion parallax refers to the phenomenon in which the speed at which an object's image travels across a visual field is low when the object is in front of the agent and high when it is on the side. More precisely, its speed follows a sine law. The facette eye of the fly has narrowly spaced visual segments in front and wider spaced ones on the side so that it can use identical neural circuits to detect motion for the entire eye.

- Examples of environmental constraints that can be exploited are closed environments, flat floors, and objects standing on the ground (ground plane constraint), as well as statistical properties of the particular environment (no XORs to be learned). Often the constraints are not provided by the environment but can be generated in the agent's interaction with the environment through sensory-motor coordination. By exploiting the constraints of the ecological niche, learning problems that at a purely computational level seem intractable can often be turned into benign ones.
- The passive dynamic walker is a robot that exploits physics in interesting ways. It illustrates that very natural walking can be achieved "without a brain."
- Emergent designs are typically cheap. If desired behaviors emerge, then normally fewer processes need to be designed. An example is the self-sufficient robot from chapter 11 that grasped pegs even though no special process had been designed for grasping.
- Cheap designs are parsimonious: The most parsimonious design is to be preferred among competing alternatives.
- The redundancy principle states that an agent has to incorporate redundancy; more specifically, in terms of sensory processes, the principle states that sensors have to be positioned on the agent in such a way that there is potential overlap in the information acquired from the different sensory channels.
- There are several forms of redundancy: (1) repetitive transmission of the same message over one channel, (2) duplication of channels, (3) restrictions on the use of characters transmitted across the channel, and (4) communicating something already known to its addressee. These can be translated into an agent context. Sensory channels can be interpreted in an agent context as "communication channels."
- Redundancy is either exploited by direct coupling or by sensory-motor coordination for learning. In the former case, the redundancies are given directly in the interaction: The agent does not have to do much (except for move around). The more general case is the second, in which the data are generated through a sensory-motor coordination.
- Entropy is a measure of disorder or diversity in a system, for example, in sensory channels. Entropy is high if there is a lot of variation in the sensory channels, otherwise it is low. Mutual information is defined as the sum of the entropies in the different sensory channels, minus the joint entropy. The joint entropy rep-

resents the correlations among the channels. Mutual information is high if the individual entropies are high and if the joint entropy (the correlations) is high: It is high if there is a lot of variation but also a lot of correlation.

- The principle of ecological balance states that the complexity of an agent has to match the complexity of its task environment. In particular, given a certain task environment, there has to be a match in the complexity of sensors, motor system, and neural substrate.

- Natural agents exploit redundancy in sensory systems if one of their existing sensory systems is damaged by an accident or by illness. Better exploitation of the sensory systems not damaged may also require novel behaviors.

- Developmental studies provide evidence for the principle of ecological balance. For example, it has been shown that there is a coevolution of perceptual and motor abilities in human infants.

- Experiments for investigating processes of exploiting redundancy for generation of diversity must provide a motivation for the agent to actually make use of the extra potential available. This motivation has to be related to value and environmental pressure. The robot ecosystem is an interesting illustration of how this might be achieved.

- There are complexity measures for the brain. They capture the fact that complexity should be low if there are no correlations among the different brain areas, but it should also be low if the activations are always correlated. Other measures include sensory stimulation, which indirectly includes the task environment. These measures must be augmented to include the idea of self-generated sensory stimulation. In other words, the agent's motor system has to be included as well.

Further Reading

Garcia, M., Chatterjee, A., Ruina, A., and Coleman, M. (in press). The simplest walking model: Stability, complexity, and scaling. *ASME Journal of Biomechanical Engineering*. (A very technical paper that demonstrates how a passive dynamic walker can be designed that walks down a shallow slope with no control. In other words, the researchers have developed a walking machine without a brain.)

Tononi, G., Sporns, O., and Edelman, G. M. (1996). A complexity measure for selective matching of signals by the brain. *Proc. Natl. Acad. Sci., USA, 93*, 3422–3427. (This paper develops a measure of complexity that takes the statistical distribution of the sensory inputs into account. We think that we will need this kind of formal measure of complexity to characterize more quantitatively the principles in this chapter.)

In this chapter we elaborate the value principle, which encompasses value systems, self-organization, and learning in autonomous agents. This principle states that the agent has to be equipped with a value system and with mechanisms for self-supervised, incremental learning employing principles of self-organization. It is related to the principle of sensory-motor coordination, and the complete-agent principle (figure 14.1).

Let us briefly introduce the three topics of this chapter. The notion of value is important for the following reason. If an agent is to be autonomous and situated, it has to have a means to "judge" what is good for it and what is not. A value system provides this means; it also modulates the learning process, either explicitly or implicitly. In an explicit value system, value signals that modulate learning are generated as consequences of behavior. In an implicit value system, modulation is achieved by mechanisms that select interactions with the environment for learning, leading to increased adaptivity. *Self-organization* has become a popular term that is used, often metaphorically, in a large number of scientific fields. It has been applied, for example, to thermodynamics, fluid dynamics, neurobiology, psychology, managment science, and sociology. (For an overview, see Dalenoort 1989.) There is no generally accepted definition of the term "self-organization." Rather, self-organization can be looked at in different ways, as certain ideologies and schools of thought conceptualize it. We cannot possibly review them all here; we focus instead on those aspects relevant to understanding self-organization in autonomous agents.

Learning is a phenomenon with which everyone is familiar. It has been studied extensively in many scientific fields, such as psychology, neurobiology, and artificial intelligence. Learning comes in a large number of forms and variations. One type that is of fundamental importance for any kind of agent, natural or artificial, is value-based learning. We will show that if we want to equip robots with self-organized learning mechanisms, we need value systems,

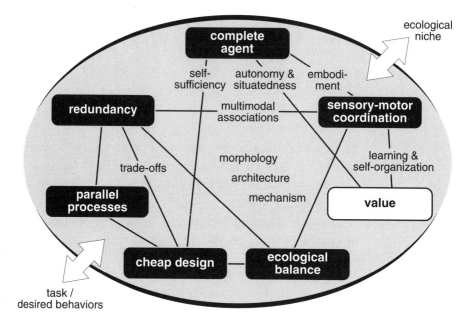

Figure 14.1 Overview of the design principles. The value principle (highlighted) relates directly to the principle of sensory-motor coordination and to the complete-agent principle. Moreover, the capacity for learning and self-organization (the links between the value principle and the sensory-motor coordination principle) depend on the ecological balance principle: Ecological balance is a prerequisite for learning and self-organization. The same holds for the redundancy principle.

because consequences of behavior must modulate the strengthening of synapses. Those self-organizational processes that lead to adaptive behavior should be reinforced. We introduced control architectures that employ value-based learning (the SMC agents) in chapter 12. Value, self-organization, and learning are important aspects of adaptive behavior. For an agent to be adaptive, there must be a very large number of possible states. These are given by the low-level specification and the control architecture (see chapter 4). What is then needed are mechanisms for generating candidate states for selection. Mechanisms of self-organization can be used to generate such states, and value systems ensure that states of value to the agent are being selected. Finally, learning—through structural changes in the system—increases the probability that states of value will reoccur. Before going into the details of value-based learning, we first discuss the general ideas of value systems and the foundations of self-organization theory as well as the basic concepts and paradigms of robot learning.

14.1 Value Systems

Autonomous agents face a continuously changing stream of input data. Extracting from all this input the data relevant for the current task is a difficult task for an agent. Learning cannot take place without some value placed on the various types of sensory-motor coordinations in which an agent can engage, without some mechanisms being better in a given context than others. Even more fundamentally, we have to ask why an agent should do anything in the first place: "Something has to start the process in the first place. Something has to motivate infants to look, to reach, to mouth, to seek out information about their worlds" (Thelen and Smith 1994, p. 313). This issue also arises in the case of autonomous agents. How should this motivational force be conceptualized? How or what drives agents to explore their environment and learn about it? The psychological literature addressed this issue by introducing the concept of instrinsic motivational forces such as "drives." Piaget (1952), for example, suggested that the driving force underlying infants' behaviors was the need to adapt to the environment. According to Piaget, this need is internal to the agent and a biological given. Similarily, Gibson (1988) suggested that a "baby is provided with an urge to use its perceptual system to explore the world" (p. 7). The essence of these proposals is that this internal driving force introduces *biases* into the agent. These biases make the agent prefer one behavior over another, given the current external and internal context. Biases implicitly or explicitly encode what "is good" for the organism; in other words, they encode what is of *value* for an agent (Reeke et al. 1989). Such values need not be complex internal structures. Rather, "simple, relatively low-level valences—for edges, for movement, for light, for sounds in the range of human voices, for warmth, for touch—can initiate the developmental process" (Thelen and Smith 1994, p. 315). An illustration of this idea is the attraction of young infants to faces, which begins with an initial reflex in newborns (Johnson and Morton 1991; cf. Thelen and Smith 1994) whose main result is an increased probability that the infant encounters high-contrast "blobs" corresponding to the eyes and the mouth. Given that infants often see such configurations in real faces close up during nursing, changing, and socializing, even a small initial bias toward such blobs leads to rapid learning of the mother's (or some other caretaker's) face. Similar biases have to be incorporated into autonomous agents. In the case of reaching, for example, an agent might incorporate a value scheme that treats the hand being in the proximity to the object as "good"; mechanisms similar to reinforcement learning (see below) would then reinforce those sensory-motor configurations underlying the behaviors that arrive at this favorable state.

Let us briefly look at the similarities and differences between value systems and reinforcement learning techniques. Value systems generate value signals that modulate Hebbian learning. More specifically, the activation of value systems—the value signals—enter the weight update rule in a multiplicative way. Recall from chapter 5 that basic Hebbian learning strengthens a weight between two neurons by multiplying their activations. In other words, the weight change is essentially.

$$\Delta w_{ij} = \eta \cdot a_i \cdot a_j, \tag{14.1}$$

where w_{ij} is the weight, η is the learning rate, and a_i and a_j are the activations of the neurons. (See equation (5.9) for a more elaborate version of this basic rule.) The hallmark of value-based learning, that is, learning modulated by the activity in value systems, is that the activity of the value system enters this update rule:

$$\Delta w_{ij} = V \cdot \eta \cdot \bar{a}_i \cdot \bar{a}_j, \tag{14.2}$$

where V is the summary term for the contribution of the value system and $\bar{a}_i$ and $\bar{a}_j$ are the time-averaged activations of the two neurons (i.e. the activations are averaged over a certain period of time). We discuss the reason for introducing time-averaged activations shortly. Let us first concentrate on the V term. If this term is large, then the weight increase between the neurons will be large, and vice versa. In other words, whenever the value system is strongly activated, the weights between the currently active neurons are strengthened. This implements the idea referred to above: Value systems should bias learning in a way that strengthens sensory-motor configurations resulting in favorable states (by setting V to same value > 0). We call such value systems that explicitly modulate the learning process by the multiplicative term V in equation (14.2) (or variants thereof) *explicit value systems*.

We discuss the specifics of value-based and reinforcement learning in more detail below. We want to make three important points here, however. First, in value-based learning, the modulation of learning happens a posteriori. Value systems are activated only after an agent has performed a behavior; they have an evaluative character. For example, the value system in the SMC I agent was activated only when the robot had grasped an object. When that behavior resulted in a sensory-motor configuration that was of value for the agent, for example, the agent could lift the object, the value system was activated. In a similar vein, Thelen and Smith suggest that infants learn through experiencing the consequences of their behaviors. We can now address the reason for taking time-averaged activations in update rule 14.2. Neurons whose connections are modulated by value signals have been activated before the behavior occurred. For example, the SMC agent's grasping was triggered by its circling around a small cylinder (see chapter 12). As it is grasping, the sensory stimulation that triggered the grasping is no longer present. The value signals, however, are triggered later, once the agent has successfully grasped the object. In other words, there is a delay between the start of the behavior, the activation in the respective neurons, and its evaluation by the value signal. To implement value-based learning in this situation, one needs a kind of "memory" of the recent history of the neuron activations responsible for the movement that triggered the value signal. The simplest such memory is time averaging of the neurons' activations, (see equation 14.2). The main result of time averaging is that these neurons are still sufficiently active when the value signal is triggered for value-based learning to work. We return to this issue in the last section of this chapter, in which we discuss value-based learning in more detail.

Second, value-based learning as shown in equation (14.2) differs from supervised learning schemes such as back-propagation in which the correct answer is given to the system and the weights are updated according to the difference between the system's answer and the correct answer. Here, the system is only "told" whether its behavior was good or bad. We return to this issue below.

Third and finally, value-based learning differs from reinforcement learning approaches as practiced by the machine learning community where the environment (somehow) gives the reinforcement signal. This latter philosophy is not compatible with the idea of a situated agent, since situated agents build up their experience through interaction with the environment from their very own perspective. So reinforcement has to be generated from within the agent rather than from the environment, unless the agent is capable of interpreting such a reinforcement signal with respect to its own value system. For example, if a mother tells her child that what he did was good, the child has to perceive what his mother said, understand it, and interpret it as a positive reinforcement signal. Despite this difference in focus between the two approaches, technically, value-based learning bears strong similarities to reinforcement learning approaches as we show below.

Let us now reconsider the issue raised at the beginning of this section: Why should agents do anything in the first place? And how does the notion of value systems address this problem? We have said that value systems act a posteriori, after the agent has moved in some way. This leaves open the problem of establishing the driving force that actually generates the movements that value systems can evaluate. A popular idea is to assume that infants (and robots) perform random movements that value systems can then evaluate. Such an approach has limitations, because the random exploration of favorable states is very time consuming. Technically speaking, such a learning process typically does not converge because not all states in a very large state space can be visited. The approach taken by most people to overcoming this limitation is to introduce biases into these random explorations or to present the agent with situations from which it can learn important aspects of the task (shaping). (We only discuss the former; for a review of shaping in autonomous agents, see Dorigo and Colombetti 1997). These biases most often take the form of *reflexes*. Viewed in this way, reflexes are mechanisms that select interactions with the environment for learning that lead to increased adaptivity or value; they increase an agent's probability of receiving explicit value for a particular action. For example, the EBA processes underlying the SMC I agent were reflexes that increased the agent's probability of entering favorable states. To express this idea informally, the agent somehow had to "like" collecting objects: Collecting objects was "good for" the agent. This was accomplished as follows: A value signal was generated whenever the agent successfully grasped an object. A basic reflex was added to increase the chances that the agent would successfully grasp something: Whenever the agent received lateral sensory stimulation for a period of time, it made a grasping movement. This reflex was part of the implicit value system of the SMC I agent and represented a bias analogous to the initial orienting bias in human infants. The main difference between the two is that in the infant's case, the bias is a result of evolution, and in the robot, it is introduced by the designer. The main purpose of the bias is to accelerate the learning and thus make the agent more fit for its particular ecological niche. Biasing the learning process by introducing such reflexes is also a technique in reinforcement learning (e.g., Kaelbling, Littman, and Moore 1996). The important point is that learning does not happen without these biases (Thelen and Smith 1994).

In summary, value systems—whether explicit or implicit—can be understood as basic evolutionary adaptations that define broad behavioral goals for an organism in terms of their recognizable consequences. In other words, they are very general biases that are the heritage of natural selection (in the case of natural agents) or are predefined by the designer (in the case of artificial agents) (Reeke et al. 1989). If we now try to apply these ideas to designing autonomous agents, we have to deal with the following hard problem: There is a trade-off between specificity and generality of value systems. If value systems are too specific, the system is not sufficiently flexible; that is, it is unable to generate diversity. On the other hand, if value systems are very general, they are of little selectional value and insufficiently constrain the very large space of possible movement patterns. A similar problem is encountered in artificial evolution, which has only a global value measure, the fitness function (see chapter 8). Indeed, Sporns and Edelman have indicated their belief that "the issue of value constraints and their number presents one of the greatest future challenges to selectional theories of brain function" (1993, p. 969). Work in embodied cognitive science will help to clarify this issue further by providing the possibility of testing a large number of different value systems, from specific to very general, in a variety of tasks.

Another fundamental issue underlying the above discussion is how we should conceptualize development. Should we view development as a process of selecting from among a great number of possible behaviors those that lead to value (selectionist development)? Or should we conceptualize development as a construction process in which new structures are built on top of already existing ones (constructionist development)? There is a hot debate in the neurosciences about which of the two should be preferred given the current evidence on brain growth (see, e.g., the discussion between Purves, White, and Riddle 1996, 1997, and Sporns 1997). Selectionist theories hold that "the organism spontaneously generates a multiplicity of internal variations and the interaction with the environment merely selects or "selectively stabilizes" some of these endogenous variations" (Changeux 1986). In this view, learning does not create novel connections, but rather contributes to either the strengthening or the elimination of preexisting ones. This is the core idea of "neural Darwinism": Development works analogously to natural selection. There is an immense redundancy (or degeneracy, as Edelman (1987) terms it) of synaptic connectivity from which only the fittest ones are selected, that is, those that result in value. The implication is that "when we think we are learning something, we are only discovering what has already been built into our brains" (Gazzaniga 1992, p. 68). The constructionist position, on the other hand, (e.g., Purves et al. 1996) holds that there is a gradual and ongoing elaboration of neuronal connectivity, suggesting "increasing, not decreasing, numbers of synapses during maturation" (Purves et al. 1996, p. 461). Learning consists, in the constructionist view, of adding new connections between neurons and not in eliminating existing ones.

The debate between selectionist and constructionist approaches is reflected in developmental psychology. For example, Thelen and Smith (1994) extensively argue for a selectionist view on development and support their argument with evidence about reaching behavior in infants, the development of which seems to be consistent with selectionist principles. On the other hand, Rutkowska's view on development "diverges from the selectionist approach by moving onto Piagetian territory, where the development of action is a process of construction not just selection" (1997, p. 294).

We pursue this issue no further, but instead point out that there is currently no decisive experiment to allow us to decide between the two views. Both have their merits and disadvantages, and both can be challenged or supported by empirical evidence. Moreover, both principles might well be jointly employed in development. Since learning and development are core issues in embodied cognitive science, we expect that many more experiments with autonomous agents need to be conducted in order to explore the selectionist versus constructionist debate. These explorations will help us elaborate those aspects of the two views that differ fundamentally and identify areas where the two might be complementary. Given our interest in value systems, redundancy, and self-organization, we focus on the selectionist aspects of development. Let us now turn to the second major topic of this chapter, self-organization.

14.2 Self-Organization

The phenomenon of self-organization can be looked at from (at least) two perspectives. In the first, processes of self-organization lead to structural changes in a system. In neural networks, for example, the learning process leads to changes in the connection weights, which amounts to a change in the structure of the network (e.g., a Kohonen map) brought about by self-organization. In the second self-organization involves no structural changes to the system and thus is not directly related to learning; rather, self-organization leads to a reversible formation of patterns. This distinction is important for understanding intelligence: Quite obviously individuals do change over time, in particular during ontogenetic development. Edelman and his coworkers demonstrated that the two forms in fact interact during development and that this interaction is important for the development of the nervous system (Tononi, Sporns, and Edelman 1992). (The German psychologist Norbert Bischof, capitalizing on this distinction, even coined special terms to differentiate the two: self-ordering (for self-organization without structural changes) and self-organization (for self-organization with structural changes). Although Bischof's terms do make the distinction explicit, we do not further use these terms because they are not widely employed). Let us look at a few examples to illustrate these concepts further.

Self-Organization without Structural Changes

In the autonomous agent domain, self-organization without structural changes is frequently found in collective phenomena, that is, phenomena involving many individuals.

THE DIDABOTS ARE CLEANING UP

Recall the robot experiment that we used in chapter 4 to illustrate the importance of embodiment (figure 4.10). The robot—the Didabot—pushed cubes when the sensors were placed appropriately, but did not push cubes when the sensors were moved to the front of the robot. In what follows we summarize experiments conducted by Maris and te Boekhorst (1996), who studied a collective heap-building process by a group of Didabots. Instead of predefining "high-level" capacities, they exploited the robots' physical structure and the self-organizing properties of group processes. The main idea behind the experiments was that seemingly complex

Figure 14.2 Didabots in their arena. The experiments by Maris and te Boekhorst (1996) involved an arena with a number of Didabots, typically three to five. The robots have the control architectures of simple Braitenberg vehicles with only one type of sensor, for proximity: All they can do is avoid obstacles.

patterns of behavior (such as heap building) can result from a limited set of simple rules that steer the interactions between entities (e.g., robots) and their environment. This idea has been successfully applied to explain, for example, the behavior of social insects (see below).

Figure 14.2 shows an arena with a number of Didabots. (The experiments by Maris and te Boekhorst typically employed three to five.) The Didabots are programmed as simple Braitenberg vehicles with only one type of sensor, for proximity. All they can do is avoid obstacles. In the sequence of pictures shown in figure 14.3, a number of cubes are initially randomly distributed. Over time, a number of clusters form, and by the end, there are only two clusters and a number of cubes along the walls of the arena. Maris and te Boekhorst performed these experiments many times: The result was very consistent—there were always a few clusters and generally a few cubes left along the walls. What would you say the robots are doing? "They are cleaning up"; "They are trying to get the cubes into clusters"; "They are making free space": These are answers that we often hear, and they are fine so long as we remain aware that they the represent an observer perspective. They describe the robots' behavior. The second also attributes an intention by using the word "trying." The designers can say very clearly what the robots were programmed exclusively to do: to avoid obstacles! (In fact, it would be more precise to say that they are programmed with the control rule: if sensory stimulation on left, turn right; if sensory stimulation on right, turn left.)

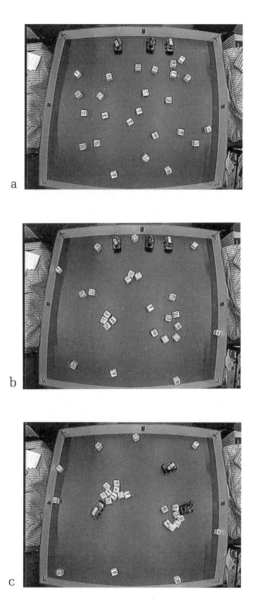

Figure 14.3 Heap building by Didabots. Initially the cubes are randomly distributed (a). Over time, a number of clusters form (b). At the end, there are only two clusters and a number of cubes along the walls of the arena (c).

The complexity of the robots' behavior with the cubes results from a process of self-organization of many simple elements: the Didabots, with their simple control rule. The Didabots use only the sensors on their front left and front right. Normally, they move forward. If they get near an obstacle within reach of one of the sensors (about 20 cm), they simply turn toward the other side. If they encounter a cube head on, neither the left nor the right sensor measures any reflection, and the Didabot simply continues to move forward. At the same time, it pushes the cube. (However, it pushes the cube because it does not "see" it, not because it was programmed to push it.) For how long does it push the cube? It will push it until it encounters another cube to the left or the right. It then turns away, thus leaving both cubes together. Now there are already two cubes together, increasing the chance that another cube will be deposited near them. Thus, the robots have changed their environment, which in turn influences their behavior. Although it is impossible to predict exactly where the Didabots will form the clusters, we can predict with high certainty that only a small number of clusters will be formed in environments with the geometrical proportions used in the experiment. We said in chapter 11 that collective approaches also instantiate the principle of parallel, loosely coupled processes. The Didabot experiment offers a further example of this point. Each robot can be seen as one such process. Coupling emerges through the interaction of each agent with the environment. This interaction, as we have seen, changes the environment, which in turn changes the other agents' behavior.

Principles similar to those observed in the Didabot experiments can also be found in natural agents. Let us look at an example from ant societies.

ANTS FIND THEIR WAY TO A FOOD SOURCE

In their experiments on ants, Deneubourg and Goss (1989) asked whether the complexity of social interactions may be attributed to individuals or to their interactions. For instance, colonies of certain species of ants appear able to select the nearest food source among several present at varying distances from the nest. Attributing the complexity of this phenomenon to the individual ants would imply that individual ants compare the distances to several food sources and on the basis of this knowledge choose the nearest food source. This would entail ample cognitive calculations. Instead, however, Deneubourg and Goss found a much simpler explanation, one based on self-organization. Ants mark their path with pheromones when they leave the nest to search for food as well as on their journey back to the nest. At crossings where several paths intersect, they choose the direction most heavily marked with these pheromones. Ants return sooner from nearer food sources, and as a consequence, shorter paths are marked more intensively than those leading to sources further away. Once a path is heavily marked, the probability that ants will follow it and add additional pheromones, is increased, thus leading to positive feedback. Such poitive feedback is a particular instantiation of self-organization. Such processes have been invoked to elucidate several other aspects of insect behavior as well, for example, the strict spatial distribution of honey, pollen, and youngsters observed in the combs of bees and the way a comb is built. In all cases, assuming processes of self-organization forms an alternative to the idea that patterns are controlled centrally by a blueprint or the high cognitive capacities of the individuals.

In summary, we have seen that the phenomena illustrated by the Didabots, and the ants, are examples of self-organization *without* structural changes in the system: The Didabots, for example, did not change during the heap-building process. If we started a new experiment with the blocks randomly distributed in the environment, the Didabots would behave in exactly the same way as in the previous trial: They would try to avoid obstacles.

Self-Organization with Structural Changes

We now turn to another type of self-organization: self-organization involving structural changes. In contrast to self-organization without structural changes, this type of self-organization leads to permanent changes in the system. For example, the Distributed Adaptive Control architecture, the SMC agents, and the Darwin models are systems that change their structures—the weights connecting the neurons—by means of self-organization. Let us look at an example in more detail.

HIERARCHIES EMERGE IN SOCIETIES OF ARTIFICIAL CHIMPS
Primates are known for their high cognitive capacities, which are thought to be especially manifest in their social behavior, particularly their coalition formation. Coalitions are a part of primates' dominance interactions. Dominance interactions consist of threats

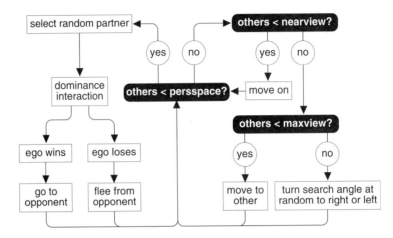

Figure 14.4 Flow chart of the behavioral rules for Hemelrijk's (1996a, 1996b, 1997) artificial chimps. The left side of the figure delineates dominance rules: After winning, ego approaches the opponent; after losing, it flees from it. The right side concerns aggregation rules: Creatures look for others at increasingly larger distances. If they see nobody at all, they turn at some point by a search angle to search for others.

and attacks that take place usually between two individuals only. Sometimes, however, a third individual intervenes by attacking one of the two, thereby supporting the other. This is called *coalition formation*. Primates are generally assumed to be highly strategic in their decisions when to form coalitions and with whom. For instance, they are thought to repay received support. To be able to do so, they are presumed to keep records of the frequency of support received from every partner. Yet in her individual-based computer simulations, Hemelrijk (1996a,b, 1997) made a first step toward showing how complex patterns of coalition formation may emerge in the absence of sophisticated cognitive reflections. Inspired by a simulation by Hogeweg (1988), Hemelrijk implemented a world in which creatures—artificial chimps—dwelled. These creatures were able to move and to see one another. Furthermore, if creatures perceived someone nearby, they engaged in dominance interactions; otherwise, they followed rules of moving and turning (figure 14.4) that kept them aggregated (because real primates live in groups). Interactions among these artificial chimps are triggered just by the proximity of others, not by record keeping or other strategic considerations. The creatures were not even endowed with rules to support others in fights. Yet support was recorded as an emergent event, occurring if creatures happened to attack others that appeared to be already involved in a dominance interaction with another

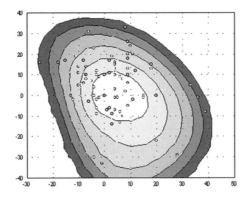

Figure 14.5 Emergent hierarchies in artificial chimps: spatial-social structure with concentric rings of entities of different rank categories. The *x*- and *y*-axis represent the position of the individuals in the two dimensional, simulated world. Gray-levels correspond to the rank of the individuals, the darker, the lower the rank.

creature. Dominance interactions in the model incorporated the so-called loser-winner effect established to exist in many animal species, such as insects, reptiles, birds, mammals, and humans. It implies that the effects of losing (and winning) are self-reinforcing, meaning that after losing a fight, an individual's chance of losing the next fight is larger (even if the opponent is weak). The winner effect is the converse.

This is another instance of a positive feedback loop that leads to the phenomenon of self-organization. In running the model, Hemelrijk noted several forms of emergent social behavior, as shown in figure 14.5. A dominance hierarchy arose, a social-spatial structure, with dominants in the center and subordinates at the periphery. Remarkably, exactly this same social-spatial structure has been described for several primate species. Furthermore, support in fights appeared to be repaid, despite the absence of a motivation to support or keep records of it. The support observed was a consequence of series of cooperation that consisted of two creatures alternatively supporting each other to chase away a third; these situations originated because by fleeing from the attack range of one opponent, the victim ended up in that of the other opponent. This typically ended when the spatial structure had changed so that one of both cooperators attacked the opponent. These series were particularly seen in loose groups, because chimps were less disturbed and distracted by others. Additionally, chimps that were more aggressive appeared to cooperate more because of their longer attack range.

Thus, Hemelrijk's model has shown how complex social interaction patterns may arise from local interactions only. It follows that this may also apply to real animals, and interaction patterns need not be genetically or cognitively predefined in the individuals. Furthermore, the model points to some new questions concerning real primates that would not be asked when approaching social behavior from a cognitive perspective only. For example, is cooperation (such as repayment of support) more generally found in loose than cohesive groups and more prevalent among strongly than mildly aggressive animals? Through lost or won dominance interactions, the internal dominance value of the individuals changes, which leads to different spatial distribution of the individuals in the environment (that is, the environment changes from the perspective of the individuals), which in turn influences the probabilities of interacting with other individuals, which again changes the internal dominance value. If an individual with a history is exposed to an environment like the initial one, it will, in constrast to the Didabots and the ants, react differently: there has been a structural change. Because the change has come about as a result of agents equipped with simple rules interacting with their environment (with no teacher or homunculus present), we also talk about self-organization with structural changes. In the context of neural networks such processes are often called unsupervised learning, but sometimes there is explicit mention of self-organization, for example, when one talks about self-organizing feature maps (Kohonen maps).

We now have covered the two main forms of self-organization important in embodied cognitive science. Let us now discuss how self-organization can be used in agent design.

Self-Organization in Agent Design

One argument often heard is that, in the real world, events, object shapes, and the like are unpredictable, which requires some form of unsupervised or reinforcement learning: Robots for such environments cannot be directly programmed. However, architectures like subsumption, in which often everything is preprogrammed, seem to prove the contrary, namely that reactive systems can be extremely robust. Thus, from an engineering perspective, focusing mainly on performance, learning may not be of great interest.

Brooks and Mataric, evaluating the progress in the area of robot learning, conclude that "there has been scant demonstration of robots being better off for having learning" (1993, p. 196). Although subsumption-based, preprogrammed systems are often very robust, they may be so precisely because the tasks for which they have been designed are typically not demanding in terms of categorization capacity. Thus, direct programming is in those instances indeed possible. The advantage of nonpreprogrammed categories becomes evident only as the complexity of the assigned tasks increases beyond the level considered by Brooks and Mataric. If we are interested in cognitive science, one of the widely agreed prerequisites for intelligent systems is that they have the capacity to learn. Thus, from a cognitive science perspective, we are interested in robot learning not primarily because a robot might perform better on a particular task, but because one core element of intelligence is the capacity to learn from experience. In addition to the fact that we are simply interested in learning, there are some important in-principle arguments why robots require learning, in particular learning involving processes of self-organization. We discuss each in some detail, because they are of significant theoretical relevance.

DESIGNER-DEFINED ONTOLOGIES

As discussed in chapter 4, ontological commitments must be made whenever designing a system of any kind. This holds for autonomous agents just as for computer systems like database or operating system. We saw that for classical systems, a high-level ontology or domain ontology has to be designed. In contrast, the designer commitments in agent design have to be low-level, concerned with the physical setup of the agent, its body, sensory, and motor systems. Whatever the agent learns about its environment should then emerge from the agent's interaction with the environment. We have called these designer commitments a low-level specification. The important point with respect to self-organization is that low-level specifications typically span a space that contains many more states than high-level ontologies. For example, a black-and-white camera with only two intensity levels (activation or no activation) and a 100×100 image yields roughly 10^{30} different states. The implication is that there is a lot of redundancy, leaving room for processes of self-organization to exploit the redundancy. Self-organization is thus necessary in autonomous agents because it is impossible to predefine meaningful configurations in this such a large state space. Through self-organizing processes some of these configurations are selected because they turn out to be useful to the agent, that is, the agent gets additional value. States that do not provide value will simply not be selected.

GENERATION OF DIVERSITY

The availability of a very large number of states is a prerequisite for generation of behavioral diversity: There must be many potential states of the sensory-motor system (i.e., there must be redundancy) on top of which selection by a value system can take place. One important mechanism by which this redundancy can be exploited to achieve behavioral diversity is learning. In the SMC II agent that we encountered in chapter 12, diversity was generated by means of cross modal associations. Through this association, the agent could link previously independent modalities and thereby establish a new behavior: It could avoid objects from a distance instead of having to approach them closely; moreover, it showed cross-modal transfer: When it perceived an object with its camera, it invoked the corresponding haptic "image." These new behaviors resulted from a self-organized learning process modulated by value. Moreover, as the world changes, and it is continuously changing, new categories may be required. Again, programming a new category into an agent might not be too difficult in simple worlds, but might be very hard for more complex ones. Moreover, the observer might not know when it is time to program a new category into the agent. Thus a learning mechanism is required by which the robot can incrementally learn categories. The important point here is that learning can generate behavioral diversity, that is, can lead to new solutions that make an agent more adaptive. In other words, learning is needed if we are to design truly intelligent agents.

SITUATEDNESS AND AUTONOMY

The issue of self-organization also relates to situatedness and autonomy. If the robot is to be autonomous, it has to be able to acquire its own history. It can acquire this history only through its own sensory system in interaction with the real world. Because it must be situated, it must "know" by itself what to learn, that is, what to incorporate into its own history and what to ignore. In other words, it needs a value system and a self-organizing learning scheme. Value-based learning is thus necessary for the design of autonomous, situated agents.

14.3 Learning in Autonomous Agents

Now that we have motivated the need for learning in autonomous agents, we can examine more closely the various approaches and paradigms suggested in the literature.

Learning in Natural Agents

Natural agents engage in many different types of learning. We do not discuss them in detail but instead focus on aspects relevant to autonomous agents. There are many excellent reviews on learning in animals and humans (e.g., Barker 1994; Hawkins, Kandel, and Siegelbaum 1993).

Learning phenomena can be divided into two broad classes, nonassociative and associative learning. In nonassociative learning, the subject learns about the properties of a single stimulus. The most important phenomena are habituation and sensitization. The term *habituation* is used if an agent shows a reduced intensity in its response to repeated stimulation. We talk about *sensitization* if an agent's response becomes more intensive each time the stimulus is presented. We do not further elaborate on this point, but focus on associative learning. Associative learning is the most common type of learning in natural and artifical agents: A subject learns about the relationship between two stimuli, or between a stimulus and a response. In psychology, the former is called *classical conditioning*, and the latter is referred to as *operant conditioning* or *reinforcement learning*. In classical conditioning, a neutral conditioned stimulus (CS) becomes associated with an unconditioned stimulus (UCS), which reflexively causes an unconditioned response (UCR). After learning has taken place, the CS comes to elicit a response of its own, the conditioned response (CR), which closely resembles the UCR or some part of it. For example, in the classical experiments by Petrowitsch Pawlow, a Nobel laureate in physiology who became famous for his experiments on classical conditioning, a dog is repeatedly presented with first the sound of a bell (the CS) and then its food (the UCS), which causes the dog to salivate (the UCR). Eventually, the sound of the bell alone causes salivation (the CR). The other important type of associative learning, operant conditioning or reinforcement learning, is described below. Let us first look at some more general issues related to robot learning.

The Robot Learning Problem

Although the engineering and cognitive science perspectives are different in many respects, they both have to deal with very similar problems when it comes to learning in the real world using real robots. It might be helpful to list some of the requirements for learning algorithms that have to function in the real world. We have argued throughout the book for the importance of taking real-world properties into account. Learning requires some additional considerations (e.g., Mahadevan and Connell 1992). Here are the most important requirements for a robot learning mechanism:

1. *Noise immunity:* This requirement holds for any system operating in the real world: it is one of the reasons for using robust, noise-tolerant neural networks.

2. *Fast convergence:* The algorithm should converge quickly, since actions are required to collect the experience—to get feedback about the success of these actions—and it takes too much time to execute a very large number of actions;

3. *On-line learning:* The algorithm should allow the robot to learn as it performs its task. Since the robot itself generates the "examples" through mechanisms of sensory-motor coordination, this enables the robot to explore its environment more quickly and generate better examples, because it continuously improves its performance.

4. *Incremental learning:* Learning must never stop. If the agent is to be adaptive, which is necessary in a changing world, it must always be ready to change. Since the data are not known beforehand, there can be no distinction between a learning and a performance phase as in the supervised learning paradigm. Incremental learning is at the core of the value principle.

5. *Tractability:* The learning algorithm should be computationally tractable; that is, every iteration should be capable of being performed in real time.

6. *Groundedness:* The technique should depend only on information that can actually be extracted from the sensors or information acquired by the robot over time. This is also the perspective of situatedness (design principle 2): Any learning should be based on the agent's view of the world, not that of the designer or observer. For example, Cartesian approaches to robot navigation that assume

location information in terms of x and y coordinates are of only limited value for real robots.

These constraints and requirements influence the design of learning algorithms. In what follows, we provide an overview of the main approaches to robot learning, showing their chief advantages and problems.

Robot Learning Paradigms

Robot learning is a relatively new field of research. Over the last few years, however, much pertinent work has been done. Since we are interested in autonomous agents, we focus on learning in mobile robots. There is currently no unifying theory or commonly accepted approach to robot learning. Rather, there are different approaches each with its own characteristics. Following the terminology introduced in the section on learning in natural agents, we can classify the field as follows. Most approaches to learning in robots study associative learning. The units and mechanisms of association, however, differ widely and range from models of classical conditioning to machine learning algorithms, symbolic as well as neural network based. Table 14.1 summarizes the learning paradigms discussed in the chapter. It is, of course, impossible to give an exhaustive account of the field. Those approaches relevant to understanding adaptive behavior are elaborated in detail. In the next section, we briefly summarize the others.

SUPERVISED LEARNING IN AUTONOMOUS AGENTS
Supervised learning was introduced in chapter 5, where we presented the NETTalk model. Recall that NETTalk learns to pronounce English text. The input consists of a widow of seven letters, the output of a phoneme encoding of the letter in the middle of the window. ALVINN (Autonomous Land Vehicle In a Neural Network) is a well-known application of supervised learning to robot control, or rather to the control of an autonomous car (Pomerleau 1993). The input layer of the neural network receives sensory input from a video camera and from a distance sensor (a scanning laser range finder); the output layer is a vector of units representing different steering responses ranging from a sharp left to a sharp right turn. The network receives as input an image of the road ahead and produces as output the steering command required to keep the car on the road. Recent versions of ALVINN perform with reasonable

Table 14.1 Overview of robot learning paradigms.

Robot learning paradigm	Description	Synonym	Learning Rules	Example	Location in text
Unsupervised learning	No explicit learning goal; learning based on correlations of input data	Classical conditioning	Hebb rule	Distributed Adaptive Control Darwin II	Chapters 5, 9, 12, 14
			Kohonen rule	Cairngorn Darwin II	Chapters 5, 12, 14
Self-supervised learning	Learning based on reward/punishment resulting from behavior	Operant conditioning			Chapter 14
(1) Reinforcement learning			Q-learning	Soccer-playing robot	Chapter 14
(2) Value-based learning			Variation of Hebb	SMC I, II Darwin III Nomad	Chapters 12, 14
Supervised learning	Learning based on direct comparison of output with known correct answers		Delta rule Back-propagation rule	ALVINN	Chapter 5 Chapters 5, 14

success on several types of roads (small, highway). Because of its supervised learning procedure, there is a learning and a performance phase: ALVINN is trained off-line using recorded camera images. Once it is performing in the real world, learning no longer takes place. Thus, ALVINN cannot incrementally adjust to changes in the environment. It is therefore not compatible with the value principle.

UNSUPERVISED LEARNING IN AUTONOMOUS AGENTS
To equip mobile robots with means of unsupervised learning, appropriate mechanisms have to be found. We said earlier that in natural agents, associative learning as expressed in conditioning phenomena is ubiquitous. One possibility for deriving mechanisms for conditioning phenomena is to exploit the Hebb rule (see equation (14.1)). Remember that the Hebb rule essentially states that when a cell A repeatedly and persistently takes part in firing another cell B, then A's efficiency in firing B is increased. This is a neural mechanism that leads to classical conditioning. Sutton and

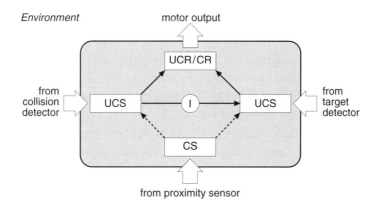

Figure 14.6   The Distributed Adaptive Control architecture, interpreted in terms of classical conditioning. The activations of the proximity sensors are the conditioned stimuli. The unconditioned stimuli are modeled as the activations of the collision or target (light) sensors. The motor responses are stored in the unconditioned response field. The CR and the UCR are identical.

Barto (1981), among others, proposed several models along this line. These models typically involve only a few neurons, called adaptive elements, that become associated with each other. In a more recent attempt to build neural mechanisms for classical conditioning by Verschure and Coolen (1991), these elements have been extended to adaptive fields with a large number of neurons. This model forms the basis for the Distributed Adaptive Control architecture, which we described in chapter 5. We can reinterpret what the Distributive Adaptive Control robot does in terms of classical conditioning, as shown in figure 14.6. Recall that the robot is equipped with proximity sensors and collision sensors. The conditioned stimuli (CS) are the activations of the proximity sensors. The unconditioned stimuli (UCS) are modeled as the activations of the collision and target (light) sensors. In addition, there is an unconditioned response (UCR) field in which the motor responses are stored. The UCS fields are connected to this UCR field. The conditioned response (CR), in this case, is not only similar to the UCR, but is in fact identical. As we described in more detail in chapter 5, each time the robot hits an obstacle, the corresponding node in the collision layer is turned on. This is the UCS, which causes the robot to turn away from the obstacle. Because now there is activation in a collision node and simultaneously in several proximity nodes—the CS field—the corresponding connections between the CS field and the UCS (i.e., the active collision node) are strengthened through Hebbian learning. This means that next time, more activation from the CS field will be propagated to the UCS field. Conditioning works as follows. Assume that the robot hits obstacles on the left several times. Each time it hits, the corresponding node in the UCS field becomes active; simultaneously, there is a pattern of activation in the CS field. The latter is similar whenever the robots hits an obstacle from the left. Thus, the same connections are reinforced each time. Nodes in the UCS field are binary threshold, so the activation originating from the CS field at some point becomes strong enough to raise the UCS node above threshold without a collision. When this happens, the robot has learned to avoid obstacles through principles of classical conditioning.

Another unsupervised learning paradigm is Kohonen maps (see table 14.1 and chapter 5), which are frequently used in autonomous agents, most often for categorization, (cognitive) map-building and motor control tasks. We present only a few examples. Cairngorn is a robot employing the Kohonen network for location recognition (Nehmzow et at. 1992). It learns to recognize a particular location based on information from motor signals. In particular, it measures the time between turn actions. It can build simple internal representations of its environment by a process of self-organization; there is no explicit world model. Another application of Kohonen maps has recently been developed by Ferrell (1996), who used the Cog robot (chapter 7) to study orientation behavior, that is, behavior in which the agent positions itself to get optimal sensory stimulation. A common example is turning head and eyes toward a source of noise. The ability to orient to multimodal stimuli—visual, auditory, or tactile—is an important skill for agents that interact with and explore the real world. In the nervous system of mammalian vertebrates, a brain structure called the superior colliculus is known to be specialized for integrating these multimodal stimuli. This integration is topographic, that is, there is a common coordinate system to register and align the multimodal stimuli. Ferrell has implemented such topographic maps in Cog by means of Kohonen maps. In contrast to Distributed Adaptive Control, learning in the Kohonen algorithm is not incremental. Although the agent can learn while it is performing its task, learning stops at some point. From there onward, the robot is no longer adaptive.

REINFORCEMENT LEARNING IN AUTONOMOUS AGENTS
The term "reinforcement learning" has been used in many approaches to denote different things. As with a number of other

terms widely used, there is no commonly accepted definition of reinforcement learning. The term is used in three important areas of research: First, in psychology it is equivalent to operant conditioning. Second, the machine learning community uses this term in a very specific and technical sense. Finally, the value-based approaches to robot learning again have their own notions of reinforcement. We do not further discuss operant conditioning here, but rather focus on the other two approaches to reinforcement learning in robots, namely reinforcement in machine learning and value-based learning.

Reinforcement in Machine Learning
Reinforcement learning in its technical sense refers to a subfield of machine learning (e.g., Kaelbling, Littman, and Moore 1996; Sutton and Barto 1998). This type of learning is very popular and is often used in robot learning architectures. In essence, learning in this view amounts to learning a mapping from perceived states to desired actions. Such a mapping is called a *policy*. The goal is to find a policy that maximizes the system's performance at the particular task assigned. For example, in a pole-balancing problem, the goal is to learn not to drop the pole. Most reinforcement learning algorithms try to infer a policy that optimizes a reward function. This policy, once learned, should enable the agent to perform optimal actions with respect to the reward function. The fundamental assumption underlying most reinforcement learning models is that agent-environment interactions can be modeled as a Markov decision process. According to this assumption, both the agent and its environment can be modeled as finite state machines acting in discrete time steps. The interaction dynamics are then modeled as follows (figure 14.7): First, the agent senses the state of the envi-

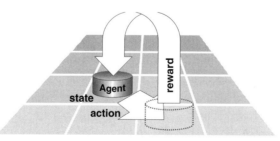

Figure 14.7 Reinforcement learning. The agent perceives the state of the world and executes an action. It then receives a reinforcement signal, the level and sign of which depends on how optimal the action has been with respect to the reward function.

ronment and uses this information to perform an action. Next, because of the agent's action, the environment changes to a new state. Finally, the agent receives a reinforcement signal from the environment, and the whole loop starts again.

Although this approach has been very successful for Markovian domains such as formal games like chess or backgammon (e.g., Tesauro 1991) or for simulated agents that operate in grid worlds (e.g., Whitehead, Karlsson, and Tenenberg 1993), there have been problems with its application to mobile robots that interact with the real world. Most of these problems are related to the Markovian assumption, which does not hold true in the real world. For example, it is not realistic to assume that the agent and the environment consist of discrete states with synchronized transitions. Rather, the environment has its own dynamics which are not discrete but continuous. Another problem is that these reinforcement learning algorithms converge only after thousands of trials, which makes them too slow for applications on a real robot. This sluggishness arises from the fact that reinforcement learning algorithms usually need to have "visited" every possible state in the environment, because only then is the policy function complete. Many reinforcement learning algorithms are not able to generalize. If a system employing a reinforcement learning algorithm has learned that in world state $(X1, Y1)$, it should perform action $A1$, it cannot generalize this information to state $(X2, Y2)$, which in a real robot could be the next sensor reading. Thus it cannot exploit correlations among successive sensor readings. Clearly, this severely constrains application in the real world.

Consider, for example, the simple IR sensors of Khepera. These eight IR sensors each have 1,024 states. It is easy to imagine that waiting until each of these states has been learned could take forever. Thus, reinforcement learning algorithms do not meet the requirements listed above.

A number of approaches have attempted to address the problems with reinforcement learning algorithms. Some have argued that one should not use these algorithms at all in real robots because of their unrealistic assumptions (e.g., Mataric 1994). Another approach has been to incorporate biases in the form of reflexes, as we argued earlier in our discussion of implicit value systems (see also Kaelbling, Littman, and Moore 1996). Others have tried to improve the algorithms to reduce their convergence time. For example, Mahadevan and Connell (1992) decomposed the learning problem into a collection of smaller ones: In their approach, a reinforcement signal is given for each behavior separately. More specifically, they separated a pushing task into three subtasks: "finding a box," "pushing a box," and "getting unwedged." They used Q-learning (see focus 14.1) to learn each of these subtasks separately. Finally, Asasda and his colleagues suggested a method they call "action-based state space construction" (e.g., Uchibe et al. 1996). They constructed the state space so that states that led to identical actions were merged into one single state. In other words, they simplified the learning problem by reducing the state space which enabled the agent to generalize. Action-based state space construction was first used to make a real robot learn to shoot a ball into a goal. In a subsequent step, a goalkeeper was added, and the robot had to learn to shoot the ball into the goal while avoiding this goalkeeper. This work is very promising, and it will be interesting to see how far action-based state space construction can be pushed.

Let us now look more closely at value-based learning.

VALUE-BASED LEARNING

The first section of this chapter introduced the concept of value systems. In brief, value systems can be understood as basic evolutionary adaptations that define broad behavioral goals for an organism in terms of their recognizable consequences (Reeke et al. 1989). For example, one general value implemented in the SMC I models is that it is good for the agent to grasp objects. Value systems are very general biases that are the heritage of natural selection. Value-based learning is learning modulated by activities of value systems (see figure 14.8).

Consider again equation (14.2), which illustrates the basic idea underlying value-based learning. Whenever the value system is activated, the weights between the currently active neurons are increased. An explicit value system biases learning in such a way that sensory-motor configurations resulting in favorable states are strengthened. This modulation occurs a posteriori: Value signals (and reinforcement signals) are generated after an agent has performed a particular behavior. Let us now look at two specific examples of value-based learning, Darwin III model and Nomad.

Darwin III

Darwin III is the third of a series of models built by Gerald Edelman and his group (e.g., Reeke et al. 1989; Edelman 1992). We discussed Darwin II in chapter 12. Recall that the goal of these studies is to

Focus 14.1: Basic Concepts of Reinforcement Learning

Reinforcement learning assumes that the robot's behavior can be specified by a control policy that describes which action to execute given the robot's current state. Formally, this policy is a function from states to actions ($f(x) : S \rightarrow A$), where $f(x)$ denotes the action the agent has to perform in state x. The robot's task is to learn a control policy that maximizes some measure of the total reinforcement or reward accumulated over time. Usually, a measure based on a discounted sum of the reward received over time is chosen. This sum is referred to as *return*:

$$return(t) = \sum_{n=0}^{\infty} \gamma^n r_{t+n},$$ (1)

where γ is called the temporal discount factor ($\gamma \in [0, 1]$), and r_{t+n} is the reinforcement received at time $t + n$. The value of γ^n decreases with increasing values of n. This can be interpreted in several ways. An intuitive way is that rewards far in the future (large values of n) are normally less trusted than the current one and the ones in the immediate future. It can also be seen the mathematical way, as a trick to bound the infinite sum. The goal of any reinforcement learning algorithm is to find a policy that maximizes this return (or the expected return, if the process is stochastic).

Q-learning, introduced by Watkins (1989), is one of the best-known reinforcement algorithms. We describe only the main ideas here. In Q-learning, the robot incrementally learns an action value function $Q(x, a)$, which it uses to evaluate the utility of performing action a in state x. That is, $Q(x, a)$ is defined as the return the robot expects to receive given that it starts in state x, applies action a next, and follows policy f thereafter. Initially, all Q values are set to some value, e.g., 0. Next, the robot's initial control policy, f, is established by assigning to $f(x)$ the action that locally (e.g., in the next step) maximizes the Q-value. In other words,

$$f(x) = a \quad \text{such that} \quad Q(x, a) = \max_{b \in A} Q(x, b),$$ (2)

where A is the set of possible actions in state x. The robot then enters a cycle of acting and updating Q-values and policy. First, the robot senses the current state, x. Next, it selects an action a to perform next. This action is specified most of the time by the robot's policy $f(x)$; occasionally, however, the robot is forced to chose an action at random. This is important because the robot needs to explore the entire environment, and choosing an action at random is one simple mechanism for achieving this. In the next step, the robot performs the selected action which leads to the next state of the environment, y, where it receives a reward r which is defined for each state of the environment. Then the Q-values are updated. Initially, the Q-values are not very accurate. If they have all been set to 0, for example, they do not contain any information about the environment yet. The agent has to visit states of the environment to learn about the environment's rewards. Through learning (i.e., by updating Q-values and policy), the agent successively accumulates knowledge about these rewards (which is reflected in the Q-values) so that the Q-values become more and more accurate estimates of the optimal Q-values. Learning is done as follows.

Focus 14.1   (continued)

$$Q^{new}(x, a) = (1 - \alpha)Q^{old}(x, a) + \alpha[r + \gamma U(x)],\qquad(3)$$

where

$$U(y) = \max_{b \in A} Q^{old}(y, b)$$

is the maximum estimated reward the agent can receive based on its current knowledge about the environment, which is reflected in $Q^{old}(y, b)$. y is the next state if action a is taken in state x. (Note that the Q-value itself does not tell us anything about which action should actually be taken, that is the task of the policy function f.) In the second term of (3) the value of $U(y)$ is multiplied by a discount factor γ that indicates how much weight is given to this estimate in relation to the immediate reward r. Similarly, α, the learning rate, indicates how much old Q-values are taken into account in the update cycle. If α is very high, say 1, then $(1 - \alpha)$ is 0, that is, the agent's prior knowledge, represented by $[Q^{old}(x, a)]$, is entirely ignored. If α is small, $(1 - \alpha)$ is large, meaning that a lot of weight is given to past experience. Finally, the new Q-values $Q^{new}(x, a)$ are used to update the policy function according to (2). If this procedure is repeated over time, the Q-values represent the true distribution of the rewards in the environment and the policy f yields maximum reward (for a mathe-matical proof, see, e.g., Watkins 1989).

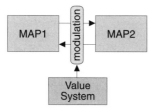

Figure 14.8   Value-based learning. Two maps of neurons (MAP1, MAP2) are connected to one another by reentrant weights. The activation in a value system modulates the update of these weights.

demonstrate that one can build automata that have some capabilities of animals (e.g., categorization) without having to use information processing algorithms. Like its predecessor, Darwin III is based on Edelman's theory of neuronal group selection (TNGS).

It is a simulated agent that has sensors for three modalities: vision, touch, and kinesthesia. Its nervous system consists of four neuronal subsystems: an oculomotor system, a reaching system, a tactile system, and a categorization system. Finally, Darwin III is equipped with an eye and an arm with which it can manipulate objects in the (simulated) environment. One of the skills Darwin III learns is to foveate on a particular object. Learning is achieved by first making random movements. If these random movements bring the object closer to the fovea, the respective movements are reinforced by changing the appropriate synaptic weights according to a value-based learning scheme. The details of this learning scheme are given in focus box 14.2. After some time, Darwin III is able to quickly foveate on an object that enters its visual field.

Let us now look at a final example of value-based learning. Verschure et al. (1995) compared three different learning rules in a robot, Nomad, that had to solve a block-sorting task. The environment presented red and blue blocks: The blue blocks were conductive, and the red ones were nonconductive. Nomad had to learn to collect the red blocks while avoiding the blue ones. It was equipped with a magnetic snout with which it could sense the conductivity of blocks and a color camera that served to extract the blocks' color. Basic, predefined reflexes made Nomad avoid conductive blocks and pick up nonconductive ones. The robot used learning to associate the color of the blocks with these basic reflexes. The three learning rules studied were:

(1) $\Delta w_{ij}(t) = \eta v(t)a_i(t)a_j(t) - \varepsilon v(t)a_i(t)w_{ij}(t),$

(2) $\Delta w_{ij}(t) = \eta a_i(t)a_j(t) - \varepsilon a_i(t)w_{ij}(t),$ and

(3) $\Delta w_{ij}(t) = \eta a_i(t)a_j(t) - \varepsilon w_{ij}(t),$

where η is the learning rate, $v(t)$ is the average activation of the value system, $a_i(t)$ is the activation of the postsynaptic neuron, $a_j(t)$ is the activation of the presynaptic neuron, and ε is the forgetting rate. Update rule (1) depends on a value signal; that is, it is an instantiation of value-based learning. It is a more elaborate version of the basic scheme introduced earlier in this chapter (equation 14.2). Update rule (2) is the same as (1), but is lacks a value signal. The last learning rule, update rule (3), implements classical Hebbian learning (with a forgetting term). Note that in all rules, the forgetting term includes the weight itself. This is a way of dynamically limiting the range over which the weight is allowed to vary. In essence, the presynaptic neurons were activated by the blocks' color, and the postsynaptic neurons by their conductivity characteristics, and the value signals were triggered by the activation in the magnetic snout. The main results were as follows. The value-based learning scheme (1) was found to be slower than the others (rules (2) and (3)), because learning occurs less frequently in (1) due to its dependence on the activation in the value system. The behavior resulting from (1), however, was more robust. Hebbian-based rules

Focus 14.2: Learning in Darwin III

Learning in Darwin III occurs through continuous changes in synaptic weights very much as in standard connectionist models. Darwin III implements the two main ideas of value-based learning: First, the weight changes depend on input from a value system that reflects the system's evaluation of its behavior. This input from the value system is functionally similar to an internal reinforcement signal. Second, because learning occurs a posteriori, that is, once an action has been executed by the system. Darwin III uses moving averages of past activations for Hebbian learning. Using moving averages allows the strengthening of connections between neurons that have been active just before the system effected a motor act. If, for example, Darwin III makes an eye movement that brings an object close to the fovea, the connections between neurons that led to this movement are strengthened.

The learning rule in Darwin III is a variation on value-based learning rule 14.2

$$w_{ij}(t+1) = w_{ij}(t) + \eta\phi(w_{ij})(\bar{s}_i - \theta_i)(m_{ij} - \theta_J)(v - \theta_v)R, \tag{1}$$

where

w_{ij}	is the connection strength between cell j and cell i,
η	is the learning rate,
$\phi(w_{ij})$	is the sigmoid function (see chapter 5)—It constrains the values of the connection strengths w_{ij} to be in the range $[0, 1]$,
$\bar{s}_i$	is the time-averaged activation of cell i,
θ_i	is the threshold of the postsynaptic cell,
m_{ij}	is the average concentration of a hypothetical postsynaptic "modifying substance" produced at a synapse made on cell i by cell j (see below),
θ_J	is the threshold of the presynaptic cell,
v	is the value signal,
θ_v	is the threshold for the value signal, and
R	is a so-called rule selector. R takes the values -1, 0 or 1.

There are several things to be noted about this learning rule: The increase of the connection strength (the second term in equation (1)) depends in a multiplicative way on the connection strength itself. The larger the connection already is, the larger the increase in connection strength. The sigmoid function ϕ is used to avoid an infinite increase in connection strengths. The rule selector R can be used to switch between learning ($R = 1$), no learning ($R = 0$) or unlearning/forgetting ($R = -1$). Typically, $R = 1$ when a value signal is present and both the presynaptic and postsynaptic cells are active (that is, exceed their threshold), and $R = -1$ when one cell is active and the other is not.

A large number of different learning rules can be implemented in this way. The "modifying substance" m_{ij} is simply the time-averaged activity of the presynaptic cell s_j. In the simplest variant of the learning rule, m_{ij} can be set equal to s_j, which then gives

$$w_{ij}(t+1) = w_{ij}(t) + \eta\phi(w_{ij})(\bar{s}_i - \theta_I)(s_j - \theta_J)(v - \theta_v). \tag{2}$$

The learning rule thus implements a Hebbian association mechanism between the presynaptic activity s_j and the time-averaged activity of the postsynaptic cell $\bar{s}_i$, if there is a value signal v that exceeds a certain threshold θ_v (negative values of v are not allowed and are set to 0). Thus, learning occurs only if there is activity in the value system. This is the basic scheme of value-based learning discussed previously (see equation 14.2). In the more general case (1) the increase in synaptic strength depends on the presynaptic cell's being active for one or more steps before the update occurs. (Presynaptic activity increases the modifying substance m_{ij}.) This can be seen as a form of stabilization: Transient short-term activations in the presynaptic cells do not lead to structural changes. In this way artificial activations (e.g., those caused by noise in the system) do not influence the learning process.

Given the learning rule (1), we can now summarize the learning process in Darwin III as follows: If there is activity in a presynaptic cell for some time (this time being specified by the decay rate of the modifying substance m_{ij}), activation in the postsynaptic cell for some time, and a value signal, the connection between the two cells is strengthened if $R = 1$ and weakened if $R = -1$. As mentioned in the main text, the value signal is triggered only when Darwin III performs a behavior that is in some way "good" according to the value system. The value signal then leads to a strengthening of connections between the sensory and the motor nodes that have actually caused this behavior. These cells have been active before the action occurred. This activity is reflected in the time-averaged activities of the presynaptic (m_{ij}) and the postsynaptic ($\bar{s}_i$) cell. It becomes clear that to implement value-based learning, one needs a kind of "memory"—a kind of working or short-term memory—of the recent history of the cell activations.

(2) and (3) led to learning that showed overgeneralization: Nomad learned even when the correlations in the activations of the pre- and postsynaptic neurons were due to noise. The value-based learning scheme was more robust because it constrained learning to occur only in relevant situations: In other words, augmenting Hebbian learning with the modulatory activitiy of a value system can make an agent's behavior more robust with respect to irrelevant signals originating from noise.

Issues to Think About

Issue 14.1:   Value and Evolution

We have looked at value in this chapter in terms of ontogentic development and learning. Value systems have an evaluative character: They evaluate consequences of behavior. On the phylogenetic time scale, the "evaluation" is achieved by natural selection. In artificial evolution, selection schemes are based on the evaluation of individuals with respect to the fitness function. Given our discussion of fitness functions in chapter 8 and value systems in this chapter, try to identify similarities and differences between these two types of value.

Issue 14.2: Teaching: Supervised Learning?

Supervised learning—in the technical sense of the word, that is, as error-directed learning—is a method popular in many connectionist models. Recall, for example, the NETTalk model from chapter 5 or the ALCOVE model from chapter 12. These networks are models of human learning behavior. The value principle states that methods of self-supervised learning employing principles of self-organization should be used. An often heard argument for the use of supervised learning is that it seems to resemble the way a mother teaches her child. In this view, the child can use the teaching signal from the mother to adjust its responses by means of a supervised learning scheme. Although this might be plausible at first sight, it becomes less so upon reflection. Such a scheme implies, that the feedback from the mother has to be translated into error signals. In other words, complex perceptual problems are implied. We do not want to continue our argument here, but rather encourage the reader to reflect upon his own learning experience. Does it make sense to conceptualize your learning behavior, for example, in school, in terms of supervised learning (in the technical sense of the word)? Or should different learning mechanisms be used to account for the influence of the mother on a child's learning processes?

Points to Remember

- If an agent is to be autonomous and situated, it has to have a means to "judge" what is good for it and what is not. This is achieved through the value system. Value systems are basic evolutionary adaptations that define broad behavioral goals for an organism in terms of their recognizable consequences. They modulate the learning process. This modulation can be explicit or implicit. In an explicit value system, value signals that modulate learning are generated as a consequence of behavior. Implicit modulation is achieved by mechanisms that select for learning interactions with the environment leading to increased adaptivity.

· In value-based learning, modulation of learning occurs a posteriori. Value systems are activated only after an agent has performed a behavior; they have an evaluative character.

· The term "self-organization" is used in a number of ways. From an agent perspective, it is important to distinguish between systems without structural changes and systems with structural changes. Examples of the former are collective systems such as the Didabots or ants; examples of the latter are unsupervised learning algorithms such as Kohonen map, or the artificial chimps of Hemelrijk.

· Self-organization is important in agent design because (a) agents need to be able to acquire their own experience over time (situatedness), (b) agents may have to form new categories because of changes in their environments (generation of diversity), and (c) the very large sensor space implied by the low-level specifications makes it impossible to predefine categories, which have to be formed on-line (domain ontologies): relevant configurations have to be selected using a value system.

· We have discussed three robot learning paradigms: supervised learning, unsupervised learning, and self-supervised learning. Value-based learning and reinforcement learning are examples of self-supervised learning.

· The term "reinforcement learning" has three different meanings: (a) as a synonym for operant conditioning in psychology, (b) in the technical sense of learning a policy in machine learning, and (c) for a particular kind of value-based learning in the autonomous agents community.

· In the machine learning sense, reinforcement learning reduces to learning a mapping—the policy—from perceived states to actions. The goal is to maximize some reward function that the environment provides. The optimal policy provides the best action for each perceived state. It is assumed that the agent-environment interaction can be modeled by a Markov process. This assumption does not hold for real-world environments.

· There have been several suggestions as to how to overcome the problems of traditional reinforcement learning. First, reflexes can be used to simplify the learning of the policy function. Second, the overall problem can be broken down into a number of subproblems, in each of which learning occurs autonomously. Third, the method of shaping can be used to speed up learning.

- Value-based learning is learning modulated by a value system. The value system provides a kind of basic motivation for the agent. It guides the process of self-organization.

Further Reading

Connell, J. H., and S. Mahadevan. (Eds.). (1993). *Robot learning*. Boston: Kluwer Academic Publishers. (A collection of papers illustrating various issues involved in robot learning. Examples include the credit assignment problem, reinforcement learning, and supervised-learning.)

Kaelbling, L. P., Littman, M. L., and Moore, A. W. (1996). Reinforcement learning: A survey. *Journal of Artificial Intelligence Research, 4,* 237–285. (An excellent overview of the field of reinforcement learning by one of the leading researchers in the field. Illustrates all major paradigms, and gives examples of specific applications to robotics.)

Sutton, R., and Barto, A. (1998). *Reinforcement learning*. Cambridge, MA: MIT Press. (A book by two of the leading researches in the field of machine learning. The only required mathematical background is familiarity with basic concepts of probability.)

We have almost completed our tour of the vast field of embodied cognitive science. All along the way, we have been arguing that autonomous agents provide a productive tool for studying various aspects of intelligence. In this chapter, we apply the insights gained so far to human memory. We show how insights from autonomous agents research can not only be applied to building better robots, but can also be transferred productively to issues in the psychology of memory.

We have already discussed memory a number of times in this book. The reason for this is obvious: Intelligence without something like memory is hard to imagine. Thus any truly intelligent creature, any autonomous agent, must incorporate something like memory. In chapter 2, we outlined the information-processing view on memory. We discussed Atkinson and Shiffrin's (1968) model. We also discussed the neural mechanisms that underlie memory formation: the modulation of synaptic strengths, both biological and artificial (chapter 5). In this chapter, we take a broader view and include a discussion of the traditional ideas concerning memory together with alternatives that have been suggested in the literature. We focus on how memory can be understood from the perspective of a complete agent interacting with its environment. This perspective leads to surprising ideas that go well beyond the standard view that memory is a place to store information. We start by looking at some definitions, then discuss some problems with the storage view of memory. In the subsequent section, we investigate memory from a complete agent's perspective, focusing in particular on the thorny frame-of-reference problem. We then present a number of alternatives and conclude by summarizing the main implications for the study of human memory that result.

15.1 Memory Defined

Definitions can be useful as starting points, although their value should not be overestimated. Let us examine a few of the various definitions of "memory" that have been advanced:

1. "Human memory is a system for storing and retrieving information, information that is, of course, acquired through our senses" (Baddeley 1997, p. 19).
2. "Consider memory to mean the mental processes of a acquiring and retaining information for later retrieval, and the mental storage system that enables these processes. Operationally, memory is demonstrated when the processes of retention and retrieval influence your behavior or performance in some way, even if you are unaware of the influence" (Ashcraft 1994, p. 11).
3. "Memory is an indexed encyclopedia; stimuli evoke the appropriate index entries, which point, in turn, to the relevant information" (Vera and Simon 1993, p. 10).
4. "[Memory] ... is a concept that the observer invokes to fill in the gap caused when part of the system is unobservable" (Ashby 1956, p. 117).
5. "Human memory is a capability to organize neurological processes into a configuration which relates perceptions to movements similar to how they have been coordinated in the past" (Clancey 1991b, p. 253).
6. "Memory is best viewed as a set of skills serving perception and action" (MacLeod 1997, p. 30).

Definitions (1), (2), and (3) clearly suggest the existence of a system in which certain processes are responsible for storing or retaining information for later use. These definitions make two main points: (a) Memory is concerned with information, and (b) The information is stored somewhere. So, they adhere, in essence, to an information-processing view of memory. The hallmark of this view is the "storehouse metaphor," (Koriat and Goldsmith 1996) according to which memory is a depository of input elements that can later be retrieved by a search process. Ashby's idea (definition 4) is more an operational definition that concerns an agent's unexplained behavior if part of the agent is unobservable. We will see that this definition departs in important ways from the storehouse view of memory. Finally, as Clancey indicates, memory might have something to do with sensory-motor coordination, with the ability to "relate perceptions to movements" in a way biased by previous experiences. Clancey's suggestion, although seemingly metaphorical and abstract, is made more specific below, in our discussion of the embodied cognitive science view on memory. Paul Broca, famous for this work on the neuropsychology of speech, suggested a similar view more than 100 years ago when he argued "not [for] a memory of words, but a memory for the movements necessary for articulating words" (Broca 1861, p. 20; cf. Clancey, 1991b, p. 407). Broca's conception is very similar to MacLeod's assertion (definition 6) that memory should be viewed as a set of skills, of which the skill to articulate words is just an example. Note the difference between this definition and the storehouse metaphor. The definition is *not* about storing and retrieving information, but rather about coordinating behavior in a way similar to past experiences.

The view of "memory as stored information" or "memory as stored structures (or representations)" (e.g., Clancey 1991b) is still very popular, and a significant number of psychologists, memory researchers, and nonscientists as well maintain this view. If one asked a layperson what memory was, more than likely his answer would be something like "a place in the brain where information is stored." In everyday language, we often describe mental processes as objects in an actual physical space. For example, we speak about storing something in memory, of searching through memory, or of holding ideas in our minds; like physical objects, memories may be lost or hard to find, and so forth. About 75% of the analogies used as models of memory assume storage and search (Roediger 1980), from Aristotle's famous notion of memory as a wax tablet on which experience writes, to James's (1890) analogy between remembering something and searching a house for a lost object. The storehouse view expressed in the computer analogy is yet another example: It clearly shows up in the first three of the six definitions listed earlier.

It should be noted that a closer look at the current literature does not reveal in all cases such an adherence to the storehouse metaphor. In their recent review of the various memory metaphors, Koriat and Goldsmith (1996) point out that "although perhaps no investigator today would endorse such an extreme version, it is important nonetheless to confront its implicit logic, which still pervades much contemporary research and thinking about memory" (p. 169). The storehouse metaphor comes so naturally that it is hard to see what other possibility there could be. There are, however, viable alternatives, and we discuss them in this chapter. The main motivation to look for such alternatives originates from the empirical and theoretical problems with the storehouse view that have been identified over the past decade.

15.2 Problems of Classical Notions of Memory

In the literature on memory there seems to be agreement that memory is not one homogeneous system but a complex, multifaceted entity. The evidence offered in this chapter has been taken mostly from several textbooks: Alan Baddeley's *Human Memory: Theory and Practice* (1997), Mark Ashcraft's *Human Memory and Cognition* (1994), and Don Norman's *Learning and Memory* (1982). This idea of memory as a multifaceted entity reminds us of our initial discussion on intelligence in chapter 1. There is an essential difference, however. Many people—except for the real cognitivistic hard-liners—agree that intelligence is not so much a component of thing, but rather a property of an organism that emerges from the interaction of a number of diverse subsystems (like perception, memory, planning, and so forth). Memory is considered to be much more of a system. It may consist of many subsystems that in turn are memory systems of their own, perhaps with differing characteristics, but they are all memory systems, and in all of them information is stored.

One of the fist things that attracts our attention when browsing through the classical memory literature is the large number of different terms, concepts, distinctions, and types of memories or memory systems that have been proposed (figure 15.1). One of the key distinctions among these systems can be made according to their temporal properties. For example, we encountered in the Atkinson-Shiffrin model a well-known distinction between short- and long-term memory. Instead of short-term memory the terms working memory and primary memory are used. Similarly, long-term memory is sometimes called secondary memory. Then there are memories for the various sensory modalities, again differentiated with respect to temporal properties. For example, in the visual modality, a distinction is made between iconic memory, short-term visual memory, long-term visual memory, and flashbulb memory. Iconic memory is a very short-term store for visual impressions, or icons. The retention period, that is, the period over which an image can be stored, is on the order of 100 ms. Short-term visual memory stores items over a few seconds, whereas long-term visual memory lasts from days to years. The term "flashbulb memory" is used to describe very vivid memories that may have happened a long time ago. A very famous example is people's ability to remember very precisely and report in great detail where they were in 1963 when they heard that John F. Kennedy had been

Figure 15.1 Researcher trying to make sense of all the different notions of memory. He is particularly puzzled by the large number of different memory conceptions.

assassinated. Distinctions similar to those for visual memory hold roughly for auditory memory, also called "echoic memory." There is also memory for smells (olfactory memory) and touch (haptic memory), although standard textbooks on memory often exclude them. Another modality of memory concerns sensory-motor skills, like playing tennis, juggling, or driving a car. Typically such sensory-motor skills are conceptualized as programs that can be "run" or activated if required. Within long-term memory, a number of additional distinctions, such as episodic memory and semantic memory, concern the kind of information stored or the form in which it is encoded. Episodic memory concerns an individual's experiences, whereas semantic memory includes general world knowledge and language. Autobiographical memory, related to episodic memory, deals with people's recollections of their earlier lives. Yet another distinction is the one between procedural and declarative memory, which is very similar to semantic memory. Procedural memory contains "know-how," programs on how to do things, whereas declarative memory contains facts. These varying types of memory are strongly intermixed. For example, a person's memory of the sight and sounds of Zurich's trams (sensory memory) is associated with the memory of that person's last visit to Zurich (episodic memory), and with the meaning of the term "tram" (semantic memory).

Encoding—the format in which the memories are stored—differs among the various types of memory. One of the issues in visual memory is whether the representation involved is propositional or pictorial in nature. (See the debate between Kosslyn and Pylyshyn, e.g., Block 1981). "Propositional" means "in the form of a logical expression or symbol structure." (Recall the physical symbol systems introduced in chapter 2). Another conception of memory, schema-based memory, maintains that memory is built out of certain types of schemas, like the restaurant script we encountered in chapter 2, or frames, which have become particularly popular in classical AI. In a sense, schemas epitomize the "memory as stored structures" metaphor. Most of the classical AI models employed schema-based memories in one way or other. Later, with the advent of connectionism, distributed memory, which is based on neural network models, became very popular. Still more distinctions can be found in the memory literature. For example, memory access is sometimes included in the memory concept. A pertinent distinction is the one between implicit and explicit memory. In the notion of implicit memory, prior experience affects long-term memory performance, but the individual may not be aware of this influence. Explicit memory, on the other hand, indicates that long-term memory performance requires deliberate recollection or awareness on the part of the individual. The literature makes a distinction between unconscious (or subconscious) and conscious memories in a way that relates to the distinction between implicit and explicit memories. One could go on in this vein for a considerable amount of time, but the point should be clear: An enormous number of different types of distinctions, concepts, and phenomena are involved. Conway (1996) suggests, instead of theory, certain fundamental assumptions are made that facilitate the generation of accounts of specific experimental findings. Such accounts are nearly always limited to the data they are intended to "explain". This is, of course, not very satisfactory and indicates that some fundamental problems may underlie the storehouse metaphor of memory. Although there is nothing intrinsically good or bad about having many different concepts in a research field, this extreme diversity makes one wonder if there might not be underlying problems. Let us look at some of them.

First, the metaphors employed in the literature on memory, in particular the storehouse metaphor, are sometimes taken too literally (Kolers and Roediger 1984). An example would be that the storehouse metaphor leads the researcher to actually search for a particular storage location and for the neural mechanisms underlying the storage and retrieval processes for the memory structures. Second, observations of behavior often seem to be mixed with hypotheses about mechanisms, a classical frame-of-reference issue. An example of this can be seen in definition 2 above, in which mechanisms ("processes of retention and retrieval") are used simultaneously with an operationalization of memory in terms of behavior ("processes influencing your behavior").

Third, research in the field has largely overlooked important issues and questions about memory. In his seminal paper "Memory: What Are The Important questions?" Neisser argued that "the orthodox psychology of memory has very little to show for a hundred years of effort, perhaps because it has always avoided the interesting issues" (1978, p. 3). Neisser went on to suggest that these "interesting" issues could be found only in an ecological, naturalistic approach to memory in which the everyday use of memory is studied. We discuss the ecological approach to memory, initiated by Neisser's (1978) paper, below (see also Neisser 1982). It is one of the important alternatives to the traditional approach.

Fourth, a number of phenomena are difficult to explain using the classical idea of "memory as stored structures." Consider Rosenfield's questions: "When we speak of a stored mental image of a friend, *which* image or images are we referring to? The friend doing what, when and where?" (1988, p. 163; italics in original). How can we explain, in a stored-structures conception of memory, the fact that, for example, in tennis every stroke is different from previous strokes, that every stroke is unique? Let us illustrate this with a quote from Bartlett's, famous book "Remembering":

It is with remembering as it is with the stroke in a skilled game. We may fancy that we are repeating a series of movements learned a long time before from a text-book or from a teacher. But motion study shows that in fact we build up the stroke afresh on the basis of the immediately preceding balance of postures and the momentary needs of the game. Every time we make it, it has its own characteristics. (Bartlett 1932, p. 204)

Indeed, it is difficult to explain this phenomenon on the basis of a memory with stored structures, as programs that are run. This notion could not explain the diversity of tennis strokes. Let us look at other examples. If a piece of music is represented in memory as a stored structure, how can a different rendition of the piece be recognized as the same piece (Bursen 1980)? This point has a lot of similarity to that concerning the memory for tennis strokes: Each time, the sequence is new, different from all previous ones, but we can still recognize it with no problems whatsoever. Let us look at a final example. We usually remember names, telephone numbers, or passwords without great effort. Although we certainly remember a phone number, we do so in a particular context: "Phone numbers and log-on passwords are not retrieved, but are speaking or typing or dialing behaviors that occur in the context of other perceptual and motor processes. You can establish this context by sitting in front of the keyboard, by visualizing a phone, etc." (Clancey 1991b, p. 256). How the original event corresponds to the way it is being remembered and the influence of context on recall are issues at the core of the ecological approach to memory (see below).

Fifth, there is the homunculus problem: Recall from chapter 3 that the homunculus problem refers to a kind of circularity of psychological explanations. Postulating a memory consisting of stored

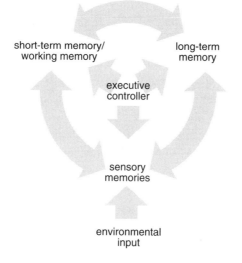

Figure 15.2 Flowchart model of memory. The model includes sensory memories that register environmental input, a short-term/working memory, and a long-term memory. An executive controller manages the information flow among these memory systems. (Redrawn from Ashcraft 1994, p. 68.)

structures implies postulating an agent, a homunculus, that is going to process and interpret these structures. In other words, the homunculus is used to explain the memory processes the model was intended to explain in the first place. Often the metaphor of an executive controller that coordinates the processing activities to interpret the memory structures is invoked (figure 15.2). This executive controller is like a homunculus, an internal executive that directs and controls the activity in memory. Bursen (1980) has illustrated this problem effectively on philosophical grounds.

Finally, flowchart "models" are often presented to describe human memory. We saw one classic example, proposed by Atkinson and Shiffrin (1968), in chapter 2. Figure 15.2 shows another, more recent example. Whereas such models are useful to highlight the main concepts involved and their relations, they do not indicate the mechanism underlying memory.

Having discussed some of the problems with the storehouse metaphor, we now examine carefully some of the implications of the frame-of-reference problem.

15.3   The Frame-of-Reference Problem in Memory Research

We have already encountered an instance of the frame-of-reference problem: Behavior and mechanism, as we noted, are often confounded. In this section, we look at the issues involved in the frame-of-reference problem in more detail. Before doing that, let us briefly look at the nature of metaphors, because we are concerned with the problems of the storehouse metaphor.

Metaphors are cognitive vehicles that help us focus on the crucial aspects of a natural phenomenon, such as memory, and organize our thoughts about them. The main role of metaphors is to serve the development of concrete and testable models and theories. They are neither right nor wrong; rather, they are more or less productive. The main problem with the storehouse metaphor, and its instantiations in various theories and models, is that it has turned out not to be useful in accounting for a significant number of memory phenomena, in particular those concerning real-world situations outside the laboratory (Neisser 1988). In fact, as we try to show in the remainder of this chapter, the storehouse metaphor not only is problematic on empirical and theoretical grounds, but it may in fact even be unnecessary altogether.

The following quote is taken from Ashby's excellent book *An Introduction to Cybernetics*:

Thus, suppose I am in a friend's house and, as a car goes past outside, his dog rushes to a corner of the room and cringes. To me the behaviour is causeless and inexplicable. Then my friend says, "He was run over by a car six months ago." The behavior is now accounted for by reference to an event of six months ago. If we say that the dog shows "memory" we refer to much the same fact—that his behavior can be explained, not by reference to his state now but to what his state was six moths ago. If one is not careful one says that the dog "has" memory, and then thinks of the dog as having something, as he might have a patch of black hair. One may then be tempted to start looking for the thing; and one may discover that this "thing" has some very curious properties.

Clearly, "memory" is not an objective something that a system either does or does not posses; it is a concept that the observer invokes to fill in the gap caused when part of the system is unobservable. (1956, p. 117; see figure 15.3)

So the issue of memory, for Ashby, is linked to the observability of a system. This is quite an unusual way of looking at memory. Ashby's operational definition of memory implies that memory might be more a property of the relation between the observer and the observed subject (in Ashby's case, the dog who had been hit by a car), rather than a property of the subject itself.

a   b

Figure 15.3 Ashby's concept of memory. (a) A dog is hit by a car. (b) After a while, it still runs
away at the noise of cars. An observer attributes memory to the dog. In this view,
memory is a concept that the observer invokes to fill in the gap caused when part of
the system—e.g., the dog's car accident—is unobservable in the present context.

Let us elaborate on this idea a little using a classical psychological experiment on list learning. A subject is shown a list of words
to remember, and later asked to reproduce the words on the list.
As the experiment is performed, certain regularities in subjects'
behavior in the second half of the experiment can be observed:
Depending on what words were induced on the lists with which
they were presented, they utter, when asked to reproduce the list,
certain words and not others (at least not many others). These
words are typically words from the list (with errors, of course). We
explain these regularities by referring to the theoretical construct
of a memory. Obviously, some change has taken place within the
individuals so that they display a behavior that can be well predicted by proposing a memory or a system of memories. Note that
when Ashby refers to memory as being a theoretical construct, he is
not addressing the issue of underlying mechanisms. There is no
doubt that behavioral change over time, behavior that we associate
with memory, is ultimately achieved by mechanisms of neural
plasticity. Again, it would be a category error to confound a concept used to describe behavior with mechanism (and vice versa).

We said that the subjects in the experiment were able to reproduce the list of words later on because of some kind of memory.
This behavioral characterization of memory is perfectly satisfactory; a problem arises only if, from these descriptions, it is inferred
that there is a storage mechanism in memory that also works on the
basis of lists, that is, if we say that the words on the list are stored

in memory, implying that there is a storage area, as in a computer where the lists are stored for later retrieval. By analogy, the storage view of memory is like modeling a camera's mechanisms by describing the photographs it produces. (Clancey 1991b). In other words, there is a frame-of-reference problem. More specifically, Clancey refers to the perspectives issue of the frame-of-reference problem. Whose perspective are we talking about? We said in chapter 4 that adopting inappropriate perspectives leads to category errors. In particular, we pointed out that descriptions of behavior must not be taken as the internal mechanisms. With respect to memory, the issue is that although we can describe a certain behavior as recall or retrieval, we should not take this description as the basis for our model of the mechanism underlying that same behavior.

If we think about the problem for a moment, we realize that the empirical evidence we have for memory is one situation in which the subjects study the lists and a different situation in which subjects reproduce the items on the initially presented list either by speaking, by writing, or by pressing keys on a keyboard. But we have no idea whatsoever what is going on inside the person, at least not from this kind of empirical evidence. And then we have to be careful with the choice of our words. We said "inside" the person, but much of the person's response is happening not "inside," but in the interaction with the outside world. As a simple example, consider that in calling a friend on the telephone, we quite frequently can remember the phone number only while sitting in front of the phone and actually punching in the number.

If we look at it this way, we can see that memory may not be something really located within the individual, but rather something that manifests itself in the individual's interaction with the environment. As research has shown many times, the kinds of materials subjects produce differ enormously depending on the setting in which recall takes place and on what happened between when they encountered the original stimulus and when they were asked to recall it. This has led to a new approach in memory research, called the *accuracy-oriented* approach to memory (Koriat and Goldsmith 1994). The focus in the accuracy-oriented approach is on the faithfulness of memory, on the correspondence between what is remembered and what actually occurred. Typical areas of research are autobiographical memory and eyewitness testimony. Studies involving this approach have revealed that memory is crucially context dependent. For example, the accuracy of a witness's response to a question is extremely sensitive to the witness's choice of whether or not to volunteer a response, and how precisely the response must be reported (Fisher 1996). Therefore, "any explanation of the behavior and performance of the memory system must account for the pragmatics of the situation, that is, the task itself, the particulars of the task environment, the dependence of memory on context, and the historic nature of the task" (Alterman 1996, p. 189). In other words, memory depends very much on the interaction with the environment; it cannot be considered and studied as an internal entity in isolation.

The simple fact that something an observer describes as a list of words (which is presented to the subjects) is later reproduced (by the same subjects) in some form that we also describe as a list of words is not sufficient to postulate some kind of a storage entity with roughly the same characteristics as our description (as experimenters, or observers). Memory is an abstract concept, and therefore certain assumptions have to be made when trying to account for a behavior by means of the concept. The most popular assumption, as we have pointed out, is that memory is a storage place from which items can be retrieved by a search process. But where is the evidence? All we know for certain is the behavior and the behavioral changes over time that we want to explain. Note that we are not adopting a behaviorist position. Rather, our point is that we have to reconsider the empirical evidence that has been taken as evidence for the storehouse view, because storehouse accounts for a given data set—recordings of the behavior of a subject in an experiment—are interpretations based on certain assumptions. These assumptions are problematic, and the data in favor of the storehouse model must therefore be reinterpreted.

Another significant reason why the classical notion of memory is problematic is that memory is viewed in information processing terms, as suggested by classical cognitivistic thinking. We do not have to repeat the arguments (see chapter 3)—they can be applied one to one to the study of memory.

If all of this is true, and the classical notion of memory as storage is indeed problematic, what alternative is available for conceptualizing memory? There are indeed viable alternatives; however, they are harder to understand, they are more difficult to describe and communicate, and they cannot be easily represented graphically. Koriat and Goldsmith (1996) point out that there is no single concrete metaphor (like the storehouse) that alone can provide the essential features for an alternative conception of memory. One of the main reasons why the notion of memory as storage has had such a great influence in science and in everyday thinking is that it seems so plausible, and that it can be described in a straightforward way. The alternative views described next cannot (yet) be cast in similarly neat concepts, but that does not imply that they are less valid. Representing structures is just simpler than representing dynamics. There are, however, commonalities among the various alternative approaches. These commonalities provide the starting point for an alternative, equally principled and specific approach to memory that focuses on system-environment interaction instead of storage. A number of models, supported by recent experiments, incorporate this alternative view. Perhaps the most important point is that these alternative notions require a different kind of thinking. This thinking also strongly influences the particular methods used in empirical research. This is an important point: When we change the focus from storage to embodiment and system-environment interaction, we also change the type of studies we conduct, the methods we use, and the kinds of questions we ask. For example, instead of asking how many items a subject can remember, people now study how memory is used in such natural tasks as dishwashing, driving, or even walking (Karn and Zelinsky 1996). Here the alternatives to the storehouse metaphor have their strongest impact: They trigger new experiments, new models, and new ways of thinking about memory. Let us now look at these alternative approaches.

15.4 Alternatives

Let us briefly review some of the proposals in the literature, then draw some conclusions.

The hallmark of the alternative approaches discussed here is a focus on how memory relates to embodiment and system-environment interaction. For example, the *ecological approach* to memory as introduced by Neisser (1978) investigates how humans "use" memory in their everyday activities, in particular contexts and situations. We put the term "use" between quotation marks to indicate that in most of the alternative views, memory is not a box inside an agent and thus cannot be "used" in the standard sense of the word. The approach of *memory* as *recategorization* views

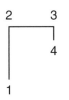

Figure 15.4 Embodied memory: the four-point path.

memory as emergent from processes of sensory-motor coordination involving the agent as a whole. The approach put forward by Freeman (1991) and his coworkers has its origins in the theory of dynamical systems (see chapter 9). It revolves around the metaphor of chaotic attractors as a means of conceptualizing memory phenomena. Such chaotic dynamics, so Freeman's argument goes, enable a system to react rapidly to incoming stimuli. In other words, theoretically speaking, chaos enables an agent to interact with the environment in real time. Because of this focus on the dynamics of memory, we briefly discuss Freeman's work later in the chapter. The other alternatives discussed focus more on embodiment, which is, of course, at center stage in embodied cognitive science. They conceive of memory not as a place where information is stored, but rather as emergent from a set of underlying mechanisms that enable the agent to interact with its environment in real time and to remain adaptive over extended periods of time. Given this perspective, memory can clearly be understood only from the perspective of embodiment. There is, in fact, evidence demonstrating the interrelationship between embodiment and performance on memory tasks.

As an example, consider figure 15.4. The figure shows a four point path. If you study the figure for a few seconds, then try to perform the following actions without looking at the figure:

1. Without rotating your body, point to 1 as if standing at 3 facing 4.
2. After rotating your body 180 degrees, point to 4 as if standing at 2 facing 1.

You will find that the first judgment is hard, the second is (relatively) easy. Why? Bodily movement helps remembering. In a similar experiment by Montello and Presson (1993), subjects were asked to memorize locations of objects in a room. The subjects were then blindfolded and asked to point to the objects. In this setup, pointing was fast and accurate. In a subsequent step, half the subjects were asked to imagine rotating 90 degrees and to point to the objects again. This resulted in a dramatic decrease of pointing accuracy and speed. The other subjects, while blindfolded, where asked to actually rotate 90 degrees and to point to the objects. These subjects were as fast and accurate as when pointing originally. Thus, embodiment strongly affects even a task like mentally keeping track of the locations of objects, typically believed to be a purely cognitive problem.

Glenberg (1997) has recently argued for an embodied view of memory according to which memory works in the service of perception and action. We discuss his approach below. The point we want to make here relates to the peer commentary on Glenberg's paper, in which several authors have argued that, although it is an important step beyond simple storehouse views on memory, the embodied approach cannot capture several aspects of human memory. Most of these criticisms, however, relate to aspects of human memory involving conscious recall, for example, our ability to reexamine our past. We agree with Karn and Zelinsky (1996) that these conscious operations, though interesting in themselves, are relatively infrequent compared to the unconscious use of memory in natural tasks. Similarly, Kolers and Roediger (1984) argue that conscious recollecting may be of only limited importance to many activities in our daily lives. Moreover, it is generally believed, in embodied cognitive science, that we can learn a lot about human intelligence by studying how animals solve the tasks they encounter. It is thus not a good idea to couple memory a priori with consciousness, which is itself an ill-defined concept. In traditional cognitive science, the umbrella term for the unconscious use of memory is *implicit memory*. As mentioned above, implicit memory denotes those experiences that never seem to enter conscious awareness, or that cannot be explicitly remembered later on, but nonetheless can have important effects on performance. For example, Jacoby and Dallas (1981) found that regardless of whether subjects could recognize a particular passage as one they had read before, they read passages that they had previously encountered more rapidly the second time. Thus, irrespective of whether people are consciously aware of their influences, these memory processes help people be adaptive. Although the notion of implicit memory suggests something passive, there is always an active component to adaptive behavior, as we argued in chapter 1. This is the main idea underlying alternative conceptions of memory. Let us now look at some of these alternative notions.

The Ecological Approach

The ecological approach to memory is discussed here because its fundamental concerns, the study of memory in naturalistic contexts with a focus on how a complete agent operates in the real world, are very similar to those of embodied cognitive science. The approach has its origins in early work by, among others, Bartlett (1932), who studied several aspects of memory in natural contexts. The most influential contribution to the ecological approach to memory was, however, Neisser's (1978) influential paper that we referred to above. Neisser presented his paper at the first Conference on Practical Aspects of Memory. This talk was a milestone in the psychology of memory.

In our discussion of the ecological approach, we do not examine methodological details such as the problem of how to conduct controlled studies outside the laboratory (see Cohen 1996 and Koriat and Goldsmith 1996 for such a discussion), but rather describe the conceptual advances in this field that are compatible, often identical, to those of embodied cognitive science. Our point is to illustrate how memory researchers have, based on empirical research, reached conclusions about the nature of memory similar to those of researchers in embodied cognitive science, based on agent experiments.

The main idea underlying the ecological approach is nicely summarized in the following quote by Neisser: "Rather than beginning with the hypothetical models of mental functioning, ecological psychologists start with the real environment and the individual's adaptation to the environment" (1988, p. 153). Similarly, Karn and Zelinsky have concluded that "memory, like perception, can be more fully understood in the context of action" (1996, p. 198). Two main points should be taken from these statements. First, focus has shifted away from mechanisms of internal processing (e.g., storage, retrieval) to mechanisms of system-environment interaction, implying, in turn that one has to study how a complete, embodied agent uses memory. Remember that expressions like "using memory," or "memory use" should not be taken to imply that there is a box inside the head that can be "used." Rather they designate the experience of an individual that has been described in terms of memory, that is, how past experiences influence his actual behavior. Instead of studying how people remember isolated items in a list, memory researchers have begun to focus on how memory is used in such natural tasks as driving, walking, grasping, speaking, or dishwashing, Consider, for example, the task of driving along a familiar road. Although this seems to be an almost automatic routine, Karn and Zelinsky (1996) point out that this task involves memory for motor sequences (e.g., hand movements to shift gears), for decisions as to which direction to turn, and for direct interactions with the environment (e.g., stopping for lights). Researchers have often ignored this type of memory use, but we agree with Karn and Zelinsky that humans apply precisely this type of memory use most often (compared to, for example, conscious recall of the past), and thus this is what should be studied. We show below that even simple robots, such as the SMC agents discussed in chapter 2, demonstrate behaviors that can be described by invoking the concept of memory. Second, focus has also shifted to what purpose memory serves in an agent that interacts with its environment, that is, what memory is for. Glenberg (1997) addressed this question in a paper, entitled "What Memory is For." He suggests that rather than for the purpose of memorizing, memory evolved in service of behavior in a three-dimensional environment, and that memory is embodied to facilitate interaction with the environment. Just as in the case of memory use, when asking about the function of memory, one has to be careful not to postulate that there *is* such a thing inside an agent, that there exists a box or other entity that we might label "memory." Rather, and this is what we think Glenberg really meant, we should ask what the neuronal plasticity is for, why neural mechanisms exist that allow an agent to use past experiences in its current situation. Interpreted in this way, Glenberg's idea of an embodied memory that serves an agent in behaving within its environment is, of course, an instantiation of how embodied cognitive science conceptualizes memory and its function for behavior (see below).

In the ecological approach, memory is conceptualized in terms of global changes in behavior: "Clearly something in the system must change as a result of experience, but the changes may be diffuse and widespread modifications of the whole cognitive system so that the system now interacts with aspects of the environment in a different way, rather than events being recorded specifically and discretely like events on a video recorder" (Craik 1983, p. 356; cf. Koriat and Goldsmith 1996). This is an important idea: Memory might not be some location inside an agent but rather manifests itself in global changes in the entire system, leading to different interactions with the environment, interactions that we, as observers, might describe by invoking the memory concept. This is precisely what Ashby meant when he suggested that memory is a theoretical construct invoked to explain behavior by referring to events that happened in the past.

Because of the distributed nature of memory stressed here, we are reminded of connectionist models of memory (e.g., Rumelhart and McClelland 1986; Hintzman 1990). We saw in chapter 5 that neural networks store their information in a distributed way, not in a particular location; rather, the whole system changes over time, and learning is distributed across the entire system. It is therefore not surprising that many memory researchers interested in alternative approaches to the storehouse view look to connectionist models as a promising vehicle for developing ecological memory models. We have pointed out several times throughout this book that connectionist models deliver on this promise only if these models are embedded in an agent that interacts with its environment. For example, we pointed out in chapter 5 that the classification learned by NETTalk has to be interpreted by a human. Moreover, the network's output has no effect whatsoever on the behavior of the network itself. Because the human designer is still mediating the system's interaction with the environment, connectionist models per se do not lend themselves to a truly ecological and embodied conception of memory. (See chapters 5 and 12 for a similar argument in the context of connectionist categorization models.) Nevertheless, connectionist models are a starting point toward models of memory that go beyond simple storehouse ideas.

In summary, the ecological approach stresses the importance of viewing memory from a complete-agent perspective, in which the focus is on not how much information an agent can store, but rather how it adapts to its environment and how context influences memory performance. From an embodied cognitive science perspective, the ecological approach's main value is that it provides empirical evidence for the embodied view of memory. As an empirical approach, however, the ecological approach is less concerned with the particular mechanisms that underlie the behaviors investigated. In the remainder of this section, we discuss a number of approaches that show how such mechanisms might look, that is, how the notion of embodied memory might actually be implemented in agent models. One core idea underlying the embodied cognitive science approach is that embodied agents can exploit ways of interacting with the environment to simplify problems such as learning, categorization, and memory. In chapter 12, we showed how this basic idea can be used to enable agents to learn about categories in their environment. Here we discuss how embodied agents can employ this same idea to simplify what they have to remember about the environment.

Memory as Recategorization

Psychological research makes a clear distinction between categorization and memory. Categorization pertains to terms like prototypes and exemplar-based models, whereas memory relates to concepts like short and long-term memory and so forth. But recent research, mainly within the ecological approach introduced earlier, has shown that the two cannot be separated. Moreover, as we show in this and the following section, both are closely related to sensory and motor processes. This view is supported by recent evidence from neuroscience that suggests that the same cortical areas that serve us to perceive and move in the world serve us to remember (Fuster 1997). The following quote by Rosenfield summarizes these issues:

The hypothesis of a fixed record [the storehouse hypothesis] may have been formulated prematurely, before sufficient attention could be paid to the means by which we recognize objects and events. We are probably much better at recognition than we are at recollection. We recognize people despite changes wrought by aging, and we recognize personal items we have misplaced and photographs of places we have visited. We can recognize paintings of Picasso as well as adept imitations of Picasso. When we recognize a painting we have never seen as a Picasso or as an imitation, we are doing more than recalling earlier impressions. We are categorizing: Picasso and fakes. Our recognition of paintings or of people is the recognition of a category, not of a specific item. People are never exactly what they were moments before, and objects are never seen in exactly the same way. (1988, p. 163)

Rosenfield's quote offers several key insights. First, in saying that people are never exactly what they were before, Rosenfield dismisses the idea of an ideal recording device that stores information for later retrieval, implying instead that remembering is always a coordination between what has been experienced in the past and

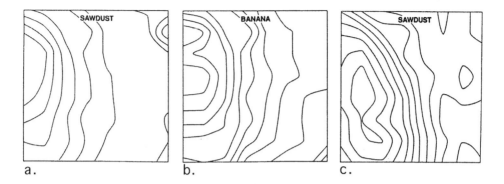

Figure 15.5 EEG patterns recorded from a rabbit's olfactory bulb during a classification task. (a) Pattern for sawdust at initial presentation. (b) Pattern for banana, presented between the two presentations of sawdust. (c) Pattern for sawdust at second presentation. The striking result is that the patterns for (a) and (c) are completely different (reprinted with permission).

the current context (see definition 5 above). Second, he suggests that remembering is a form of categorization, but since our categories change continuously, it is actually a recategorization. For example, assume you meet a friend you have not seen for a while. Remembering him means that you can recognize him. The point is that you are not retrieving a picture of your friend from an internal store but rather categorizing him using your past experiences with him and the current situation. Since you have changed since you last saw your friend, your categories have changed, too. Therefore, your remembering is a recategorization (see also Fuster 1997). Let us pursue this issue a little further, because it involves two fundamental points about memory.

Freeman and his colleagues have aptly illustrated how categories —and thus, memory—change with experience (e.g., Freeman 1991). Freeman has investigated the cooperative behavior of millions of neurons spread throughout the rabbit's brain. The patterns shown in figure 15.5 were obtained by recording electroencephalograms (EEGs) simultaneously from 60 to 64 sites covering a large part of the surface of the rabbit's olfactory bulb, the part of its brain responsible for smell. The recordings from each EEG site reflected the excitation of pools of thousands of neurons just below the EEG electrode. The rabbit was trained to recognize different odorants. An important result was that a reexposure to a certain category led to the emergence of a different spatial pattern than when the category was first presented. More specifically, the EEG pattern shown in figure 15.5a was recorded from a rabbit that had been condi-

tioned to associate the scent of sawdust with a particular reinforcement. The animal was then presented with the smell of
banana, leading to the spatial pattern shown in figure 15.5b. After
reexposure to sawdust, a new spatial pattern for sawdust emerged
(figure 15.5c), different from the one originally observed. In other
words, the activation of the olfactory bulb for the category "sawdust" changed as the animal learned to respond to a different category, "banana." Because the animal showed the same response in
the situations that lead to the EEG patterns in figures 15.5a and
15.5c, we can conclude that the animal had remembered the scent
of sawdust, but the category was represented by a different pattern
of activation in the respective neurons. This dynamical change due
to experience is what Rosenfield referred to when he said that
people are never exactly what they were moments before.

This example yields two main points, both fundamental when
thinking about memory. The first is that brain representations are
dynamic processes and not fixed structures, as the storehouse
metaphor would have it. So, rather than looking for representations
in terms of actual structures within the agent, we have to look at
dynamics, which leads to the second point. It relates to the question already raised in chapter 12: Where are the invariances that
reveal categorical knowledge despite all these changes in brain
representations? Figure 15.5c suggests that these invariances cannot
be found at the level of EEG patterns. More generally, the invariances cannot be found at the level of internal dynamics only. In
chapter 12, we defined categorization with respect to invariances in
behavior (i.e., a system-environment interaction). For example, we
said that the agent has learned the categories "small object" and
"large object" if it consistently picked up small objects and ignored
large ones. We strongly suspect that the rabbit's behavior at both
presentations of sawdust was roughly the same. The invariances we
are seeking are, so goes our suggestion, not to be found at the level
of EEG patterns, or—to use the terminology of embodied cognitive
science—at the level of internal mechanisms only, but rather in the
behavioral response of the complete agent. (See our discussion of
the frame-of-reference problem in chapter 4.) Edelman (e.g., 1987)
uses the term "recategorization" to refer to the continuously
changing pattern of activation in the brain.

Rosenfield's notion of a recategorizing memory is based on
Edelman's framework, in which perception, memory, and categorization are closely interrelated. Edelman views memory as an

ability to organize the world into categories: "Memory is the enhanced ability to categorize or generalize associatively, not the storage of features or attributes of objects as a list" (Edelman 1987, p. 241). Note that this is a behavioral characterization and does not imply specific mechanisms. Moreover, memory is not viewed as a static storage place but rather as an activity. It is therefore more correct to talk about "remembering," instead of "memory" or "retrieving."

Edelman views remembering similarly to the ecological approach, as a property of a complete system. The results of motor processes are considered to be an integral part of categorization and recategorization. There is no linear chain from sensors to cortical areas to motor activity. Recategorization depends crucially upon the interplay between sensory maps and motor maps, which interact to to enable categorization. As a consequence, remembering and categorizing are not properties of one small portion of the nervous system, but rather a property of the whole system. Or, as Edelman put it: "It is the entire sensory-motor system and its repetitive activity and responses coordinated with the function of classification couples in global mappings ... that leads to memorial response" (1987, p. 266). The emphasis here is on the complete agent involved in memory responses. Recall that the principle of sensory-motor coordination states that perception, categorization, and memory involve the complete agent, that is, the sensors, motor system, and neural substrate. Remembering, like categorizing, thus is not the activity of a module inside the brain, but rather involves the agent as a whole.

Fuster (1997), a brain researcher, has presented a memory model—called *network memory*—derived from neuroscientific evidence on various aspects of memory that strongly supports the view of memory as recategorization. Fuster starts from the observation that memories are networks of interconnected neurons— with the connections formed by association—that contain our experience in their connectivity. On the neuronal level, the acquisition of memory basically consists of the modulation of synaptic weights between neurons (see chapter 5), as shown in figure 15.6. The figure shows how the neural substrate of memory is formed by simple Hebbian-type learning processes. Two inputs that arrive at the same time increase the strength of the respective synapses. To use our terminology from chapter 5, the weights are increased. In the absence of input, this increased strength might be seen as pas-

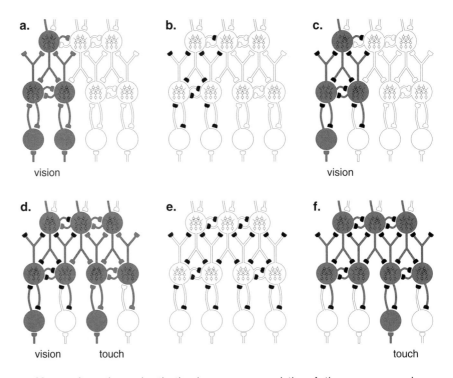

Figure 15.6 Memory formation and activation by sensory association. Active neurons are shown in black. (a) Two visual inputs arrive at the same time; through Hebbian learning the synaptic strengths between the simultaneously active nodes are increased. (Note that the same holds for other modalities such as smell, audition, or touch.) (b) Passive long-term memory resulting from the learning process; endpoints with a black marker indicate synapses with increased strengths. (c) Because of this increased strength one of the inputs from (a) can now activate neurons previously activated only by the other visual input. (d) A visual and a tactile input arrive at the same time. (e) Again, endpoints with a black marker indicate synapses with increased strength; there is now a bimodal (vision and touch) network of long-term memory. (f) Touching an object alone is now sufficient to activate the associated visual image of the object (after Fuster 1997).

sive long-term memory. The inputs can originate from any sensory modality. In figure 15.6d, a visual and a tactile input arrive at the same time (for example, the agent has touched an object at which it was looking). Thus the connections between the nodes representing visual input and those representing touch are strengthened. This scheme, suggested by Fuster (1997), is nearly identical to parts of the architecture of the SMC II agent we encountered in chapter 12. This equivalence between Fuster's notion of memory formation and the category learning process in the SMC II agent supports our earlier claim that categorization and memory cannot be separated, since memory constitutes a process of recategorization.

We can now also discuss the relation of memory formation to sensory-motor coordination and value-based learning. The process of sensory-motor coordination, that is, the active manipulation of the world, generates the temporally correlated input to the memory networks and thus makes Hebbian learning work. Moreover, a value system is needed that modulates this learning process. As Fuster has pointed out, the neural substrate of such a memory-related value system might be found in a particular area of the brain, the temporal lobe.

We stress again that this neuronal processing and adaptation must be embedded in a sensory-motor system, for this embedding enables such processes to occur in the first place. The implication is, as Edelman has pointed out, that memory encompasses the complete agent and is not found at the level of synaptic strenghts only. This line of thinking is compatible with Ashby's memory definition. After having interacted with its environment for a while, the SMC II (and SMC I) agent showed an increased ability to categorize. As it encountered an object, it recognized very quickly whether the object was graspable or not. It showed a behavior it did not show before. Following Ashby, we attribute memory to the agent, saying that its current behavior can be explained only by reference to events that happened some time ago. The "events" in this case are the "encounters" with objects of various categories.

Another important issue brought up by Fuster's framework is that there is no distinction between different types of memory processes, say for episodic or semantic memory (nor for any of the other types of memory introduced at the beginning of this chapter). This suggests a view of memory that does not involve separate storage systems coordinated by a central executive, but rather focuses the distributed, self-organizing nature of memory formation in a complete, embodied agent that interacts with its environment. At the basis of this alternative approach is the neural plasticity that enables associations to be built up between different brain areas. This association process, in turn, relies on mechanisms of sensory-motor coordination that provide the neural substrate with appropriate, spatially and temporally correlated input, enabling Hebbian learning. An important issue in such a view is how these processes can work in real time, as the agent interacts with the environment. The problem of how the brain is able to deal with the complexity of the world in real time is the focus of the final alternative memory approach on our list, dynamical systems.

Attractors and Memory

One reason for studying autonomous agents that move around is that we are faced with real time issues. As we pointed out earlier, these are fundamental issues, not merely issues pertaining to lack of computational power. Memory, if it is to be of any use at all in a real-time context such as car driving, skiing, or dancing, must be fast. We argued earlier that we are interested in memory performance in precisely such real-time contexts, that is, in activities in everyday life. The crucial issue then becomes, What mechanisms underlie memory performance in real time?

Freeman addresses, from a neurobiological perspective, precisely this problem, namely the speed at which animals and humans perceive, classify, and memorize, even when the stimuli are complex and the context in which they arise varies (Freeman 1991). Freeman, like others (e.g., Kelso 1995; Thelen and Smith 1994), considers the brain to be a dynamical system (see chapter 9 for some basic dynamical systems concepts). He proposes that the brain's ability to process complex stimuli in real time is based on a global chaotic attractor. A chaotic attractor is formed by repeated episodes of learning under reinforcement. Recall that a chaotic attractor is a region in phase space that is bounded but whose trajectory cannot be predicted. During each of these learning episodes, synaptic change leads to the emergence of novel neural activity patterns, in turn implying that new states become possible. According to this model, chaotic dynamics provide an essential interface between the environment's infinite complexity and the brain's finite capacity. Freeman has speculated that "chaos underlies the ability of the brain to respond flexibly to the outside world and to generate novel activity patterns" (1991, p. 34). More specifically, Freeman observed that in the rabbit's olfactory bulb, chaos results when large collections of neurons—analogous to Edelman's neural groups—shift instantaneously and simultaneously from one activation pattern to another in response to the smallest changes in incoming signals.

Recurrent connections link neuronal groups in the rabbit's cortex to the olfactory bulb. Excitatory input to one part of a neuronal group when the rabbit sniffs excites other parts via synaptic connections. Next, those parts reexcite the first, and so forth, so that the input—a sniff—rapidly leads to an "explosion" of neuronal activity in the group. The activation of the group then spreads to the entire bulb, which leads to the macroscopic chaotic activation —a chaotic attractor—observed in EEGs of rabbits trained to remember certain odors (see figure 15.5). For each odor the organism can discriminate, there is a chaotic attractor. In Freeman's model of the olfactory bulb, remembering is achieved by jumping between different chaotic attractors (i.e., one for sawdust, one for banana, and so forth). Each attractor is the behavior the system settles into when it is presented with a particular input, that is, an odor it has learned to recognize. Categorization, in this view, consists of a transition from one chaotic attractor to another. Whenever a new odor becomes meaningful to the system, another attractor is added, and all the others undergo slight changes. An odor becomes "meaningful" whenever several sensory and motor activities are somehow integrated in response to the odor. Thus, what is meaningful to an agent is, in essence, a sensory-motor coordination. Whereas Edelman provides detailed descriptions of the mechanisms by which such a coordination might occur, Freeman focuses on the internal dynamics of the processes.

In Freeman's model, remembering and categorization are again intrinsically related and dynamical. There is no such thing as storage or retrieval. Rather, remembering is "a step in a trajectory by which brains grow, reorganize themselves and reach into their environment to change to their own advantage" (Freeman 1991, p. 85). Note that Freeman talks about *re*organizing, which reminds us of Edelman's idea of *re*categorization. Moreover, remembering "reaches into" the environment, that is, is not internal processing only, but crucially includes processes of system-environment interaction. Freeman's model can be seen as an instance of the general class of *attractor neural networks* (see Amit 1989 and Hertz 1995, for a reviews), in which remembering is modeled as transitions between attractors. The model summarizes 30 years of empirical research on the rabbit's olfactory system. It represents an attractive alternative to the storehouse metaphor of memory. To assess its real power and its capabilities for dealing with the interaction with the real world, the model will have to be embedded into a complete agent.

This concludes our discussion of alternative views on memory. It is now time to tie together the various ideas presented in the previous sections, which is the task of the following section.

15.5 Implications for Memory Research

We started this chapter arguing that one of the most influential ideas in cognitive science, the view of memory as a storehouse, should be revised because it involves considerable theoretical and empirical problems. What, if not a place where we store our experiences, could memory be? In what follows, we extract from the various ideas represented in the approaches just discussed what we think are the main ingredients in a new view on memory, a view fundamentally rooted in the core metaphor of embodied cognitive science: a complete agent interacting with its world to solve a number of tasks.

The most radical idea presented in this chapter is Ashby's (1956) claim that memory is not something inside an agent's brain, but rather a construct evoked by an observer to account for an agent's behavior in terms of events that have occurred in the past. Memory, in this view, is a property of the relation between an observer and the observed agent, in Ashby's example the dog that had been hit by a car. In the embodied cognitive science framework, the frame-of-reference problem addresses the relation between observer and observed agent. We said that with respect to memory, the issue in the frame-of-reference problem is that although we can describe a certain behavior as recall or retrieval, we should not take this description as the basis for our model of the mechanism underlying that same behavior. Doing so would be, to use Clancey's (1991b) analogy again, like describing a camera's workings by the photographs it produces. So a particular memory construct, although useful to describe a large number of phenomena, should not be taken as a starting point when thinking about the mechanisms underlying those phenomena. As we have extensively argued, this holds particularly for the memory construct used in the computational, information processing framework.

You might argue that there must be certain internal processes that lead to the behavior we describe by invoking the memory construct. Yes and no. Yes, because there certainly are internal processes in the brain that relate to remembering (see figure 15.6). No, because these changes cannot be seen in isolation: Behavior we describe as showing memory effects is, like all behavior, emergent from the agent's interaction with the environment and cannot be reduced to internal processing only. As such, it is not sufficient to reduce memory to synaptic changes in a neural network, whether synthetic or biological. Rather, as stated in design principle 2—

the complete-agent principle—we must consider the complete, embodied agent in its interaction with the environment. The principle of sensory-motor coordination suggests that memory, like perception or categorization, involves the whole agent, including sensory and motor systems. This is reflected in the claim put forward by both the ecological approach and Edelman's theory, according to which changes in memory affect the complete system, and thus its interactions with the world. Recall Craik's (1983) claim that these changes may be diffuse and widespread modifications of the whole cognitive system. Their main consequence is that the system interacts with aspects of the environment in a different way. This is not an argument for a holistic conceptualization of memory. Rather, the deeper underlying reason why this view should be seriously considered is that the invariances underlying memory performance cannot, so our argument goes, be found on the level of internal mechanisms only. Freeman's EEG data, shown in figure 15.5, exemplify this idea. Recall that because of the brain's enormous plasticity, the rabbit's representation of the category "sawdust," as measured by EEG recordings, changed as the animal learned to respond to a different category, "banana." This is illustrated by the different patterns for sawdust (figures 15.5a and 15.5c). The conclusion we have drawn from this astonishing phenomenon is that if we are ever going to find the invariances underlying memory performance, we must find them at a different level, one that takes the behavior of the organism and thus embodiment into account. From this perspective, it would be of great interest to record neural activity from multiple locations in the brain, while the animal was behaving in the real world, so that behavior and mechanism could be related to one another. But we realize the enormous technological problems involved in such an experiment.

Although there have been dramatic and impressive methodological and conceptual improvements in the neurosciences, there are currently still strong methodological limitations when it comes to recording from multiple sites in a behaving animal (Dudai 1994). Only such analyses, however, would reveal how brain activity relates to behavior and where we can find the invariances that correlate with memory performance. There is, however, a way to study such processes: Autonomous agents provide us with a tool to investigate, simultaneously, neuronal dynamics, synaptic changes, and the behavior of an agent solving a task. We expect that this framework will yield valuable insights as to where one might find invariances in such a complex system, and what these invariances will look like. Some examples of how this might be done are discussed in chapter 12.

This concludes our case study. The overview we have presented is still speculative and will need much more empirical and synthetic work to support its basic claims. Moreover, although we have tried our best to bring the various ideas together, the alternative framework presented here still lacks the conceptual clarity of its counterpart, the storehouse view. We nevertheless think that these alternative views should be pursued further, for they represent the starting point for a new, embodied theory of memory, a memory that consists of cross-modal associations formed during sensory-motor coordination and modulated by value systems.

Issues to Think About

Issue 15.1:   How Many Memory Systems?

We have seen that the literature on memory has suggested a large number of memory systems. Recall our example of a person's memory of the sight and sounds of Zurich's trams (sensory memory) that is associated with the memory of that person's last visit to Zurich (episodic memory), with the meaning of the term "tram" (semantic memory), and with the concept of public transportation (conceptual memory). Think about your own memory. How many memory systems can you identify? Do you think that these memories are really different, or might there be an underlying common denominator?

Issue 15.2:   Embodied Cognitive Science and Common Sense

This chapter has summarized alternatives to the storehouse approach to memory. These alternative approaches suggest a number of mechanisms (recategorization, attractors) that lead to behavior that can be described by invoking the concept of memory. There is a discrepancy between the suggestion that only a few mechanisms underlie the behavior that we describe by resorting to the memory construct, and the claims for multiple memory systems. One of the great challenges facing the embodied cognitive science view of memory discussed in this chapter is to test whether these mechanisms are sufficient to produce behavior that an observer would describe by resorting to the various types of memory constructs described in this chapter. Additional mechanisms might well be needed.

Points to Remember

- Most definitions of memory focus on information processing aspects. Moreover, they often do not make clear distinctions between behavior and mechanism.
- Definitions of memory at the behavioral level are given by Ashby (memory as a theoretical construct evoked to explain behavior of an incompletely observable system by reference to an event in the past), Clancey (memory as a capability to relate perceptions to movements similar to how they have been coordinated in the past), MacLeod (memory as a set of skills serving perception and action), and Edelman (memory as the enhanced ability to categorize).
- Most theories or models of modern cognitive psychology, artificial intelligence, and cognitive science endorse, explicitly or implicitly, a view of "memory as stored structures."
- The information processing view of memory presents a number of problems. First, there are very many memory topics in this view. Statements about behavior and mechanism are often intermixed. And many memory phenomena have no proper explanations in terms of the storehouse metaphor. Finally, a homunculus is required to interpret the memory structures.
- One of the main problems with information processing theories of memory relates to the perspectives issue of the frame-of-reference problem. It is exemplified by Ashby's definition of memory.
- The ecological approach, the notion of memory as recategorization, and the idea of attractors underlying memory provide viable alternatives to the information processing view. The latter two provide mechanisms for memory.
- Neurobiological evidence supports the view of memory as recategorization. This evidence is summarized in the network memory model of Fuster.
- Memory encompasses the complete agent. Memory-related regularities that we observe, for example, in Ashby's dog or in the SMC agents are not solely located in the corresponding neuronal activity or connectivity patterns.

- We should not treat perception, categorization, and memory as separate systems, but rather focus on their common underlying mechanisms.
- In spite of the enormous differences between humans and today's autonomous robots, the latter provide an excellent metaphor for shedding new light on issues in memory research. For example, they prevent the researcher from focusing on the information processing aspects only: the robot's entire behaving system must be taken into account.

Further Reading

Ashcraft, M. H. (1994). *Human memory and cognition* (2nd ed.). New York: HarperCollins College Publishers. (Comprehensive textbook on human memory. Endorses an information processing perspective.)

Baddeley, A. (1997). *Human memory: Theory and practice* (Revised edition). Hove, UK: Psychology Press (an imprint of Erlbaum (UK) Taylor and Francis). (The classical textbook on human memory. Based, in essence, on information processing approach.)

Clancey, W. J. (1997). *Situated cognition: On human knowledge and computer representations*. New York: Cambridge University Press. (Part I of this book is about criticisms of the "stored-structures" view of memory. Alternatives to this view are discussed as well.)

Fuster, J. M. (1997). Network memory. *Trends in Neurosciences, 20*, 451–459. (Fuster presents neurobiological evidence supporting the view of memory as recategorization. Nice summary of some of the main issues in memory research.)

Rosenfield. I. (1992). *The invention of memory: A new view of the brain* (2nd. ed.) New York: Basic Books. (This excellent and easy-to-read book argues strongly against the notion of "memory as stored representations." Rosenfield reinterprets a host of empirical data and shows that much of the literature either misinterprets the data or fails to take all of it into account.)

V Design and Evaluation

In part II we laid the foundations for a framework for design. In part IV, we complemented this framework with a set of design principles, formulated at a relatively abstract level, that specifically characterize intelligent agents. Now we need to discuss in more concrete terms how to actually go about designing an agent to investigate a particular issue. One of the surprising insights, to us, is the extent, the vastness, and the variety of considerations that need to be taken into account, ranging from basic scientific reflections, the search for a goal for investigation, the consideration of the research environment with all its resources including funding, and the availability of expertise, all the way to the selection of particular sensors and motors. The way of proceeding we advocate is by no means linear, step by step, but rather chaotic and highly intertwined.

Once we have designed our agent, we need to ask the question of how good it is. Does it fulfill its purpose? If it was designed to investigate a natural agent (e.g., an ant or a human infant), does the agent appropriately mimic the natural system's behavior? At what level do we want to make the comparison? How can we compare, for example, a robot's behavior to that of an ant if the robot is a hundred times larger than the ant? Similarly, how can the behavior of a robot with a simple gripper be compared to that of a human infant? We can also ask if the agent is well designed, that is, if it complies with the design principles of autonomous agents. We also want to find out what will need to be changed in the agent's design in the future. And most importantly, we have to ask what we have learned by building this particular agent. Proper evaluation is important: If embodied cognitive science is to become a proper science, we have to go beyond the early standard, under which simply saying "it works" was sufficient.

Chapter 16 discusses the issues involved in agent design. Although the focus is on agent design, the discussion has been embedded into the general design literature, because a great deal of pertinent know-how is already available in many areas. Design is not only about the agent's physical setup (its low-level specification), but also about its internal mechanisms, which include control architectures and formalisms. Pertinent design considerations are also included here. Chapter 17 tackles evaluation. Again, it is important to point out that evaluation is not a one-dimensional task but includes many levels and facets.

We have now worked our way through a number of approaches and theoretical considerations as well as technical and conceptual details: It's time to get our hands dirty and run some experiments. But even if you don't intend to run experiments, to engineer actual robots, or even if you do not want to build simulated agents, you might still find interest in reading this chapter. The complete-agent principle tells us that agents have to be embodied: There have to be sensors, otherwise the robot cannot acquire any information about its environment. If there is no energy source and no motors, the agent does not move, nor does it move if it lacks means of locomotion: wheels, legs, fins, or wings. If it has no gripper, no arm, no other means of manipulating objects, it is unable to pick up anything.

This chapter has two main goals. First it is intended to give you a feel for what we are glossing over easily when we talk lightly about a complete agent. Everybody is aware of the enormous complexity of a human being. If we look at something comparatively simple like a robot, we may be surprised how complicated it is, all the topics and issues one has to think about, design, and build before anything moves. At that point, we start appreciating the complete-agent principle and the kinds of abstractions, simplifications, and omissions we make when designing our models, be they computer or robot models. Second, this chapter is intended to provide some intuition about all the considerations involved in designing an agent. Design is not a straightforward activity, but rather highly involved and hard to capture precisely. In chapter 4 we laid the groundwork for designing agents. There, we introduced (high-level) domain ontologies and low-level specifications. We argued that we want to design the low-level specifications of our autonomous agents rather than the high-level ones, because we are interested in emergence. High-level ontologies require a designer-based pre-classification of the world and leave no room for emergence. We then looked at many examples of particular designs, such as Braitenberg vehicles, subsumption-based robots, agents designed by artificial evolution, designs based on microeconomic considerations, and so forth. In chapter 10, we summarized the design principles underlying embodied cognitive science, which are relatively abstract. As we show in this chapter, these principles can strongly inform even something very practical like the selection of sensors. We also show in this chapter how these principles can be mapped onto concrete steps in agent design when conducting agent experiments.

All our discussions in the chapter are conceptual: They are not recipes on how to actually build robots. For example, we do not discuss the issues involved in engineering basic motor control, such as the design of H-bridges (which is a particular type of electronic circuit frequently used for this purpose). That is the task of other textbooks (e.g., Jones and Flynn 1993). Fortunately, commercial robot platforms often include libraries of basic sensor and motor functions, so you do not need to engineer everything down to the very low level yourself. As mentioned before, we have added a set of programming examples. We have provided some pseudo-code. You can download the full code from our Internet page, which should enable you to create and conduct experiments on your own. For those who want to dig into robot building or heavy programming, for example, the Internet page also provides references to the technical literature, and pointers to Internet pages that in turn contain a wealth of materials. But since this is not a technical book about robot building and agent programming, you need to refer to additional specialized literature if you want to do either of those things.

We start with some general comments about design, then turn to agent design in particular. We delineate the steps in designing agent experiments, giving some practical advice on how to go about choosing the desired behaviors and ecological niche and designing an agent for them. We demonstrate that the design principles of autonomous agents have a direct impact on practical decisions such as choice of sensors. We then turn to a discussion of design issues for the motor system: Most of the topics that need to be discussed are research issues to be resolved, which is why most agent experiments are conducted with relatively simple motor systems. Next we discuss choice of control architecture and formalism. We conclude by pointing out a fundamental design issue concerning digital microcontrollers for mimicking intelligent systems.

Before we start our discussion, a note on the role of artificial evolution in design is in order. In chapter 8 we pointed out that in evolutionary circles sometimes the slogan "Design is out—evolution is in" is used to argue that artificial evolution can be employed to overcome biases of the human designer. We argued that the real question is what to design and how to design, not whether to design. So the distinction between evolutionary and "hand design" approaches is not that in the former no design is required whereas in the latter a lot of design is involved, but rather where the designer commitments are made. Surely the kinds of considerations for evolutionary systems will be different. But we expect that just as many underlying implicit assumptions would come to the fore if the kind of analysis suggested in this chapter were applied to evolutionary approaches. Because evolution is not the central focus of this book, we do not discuss those explicitly here, but rather focus on design considerations in general, and the ones related to "hand design" of autonomous agents in particular.

16.1 Preliminary Design Considerations

In chapter 10 we defined the design problem for an agent informally as follows: Given the intended ecological niche and the desired behaviors, how do we design the agent? But this does not yet say anything about how to actually design the agent. Let us look at a definition by one of the leading industrial designers of our times, Nam M. Suh of MIT: "Design may be formally defined as the creation of synthesized solutions in the form of products, processes or systems that satisfy the perceived needs through the mapping between the functional requirements in the functional domain and the design parameters in the physical domain, through the proper selection of the design parameters that satisfy the functional requirements" (Suh 1990, p. 27). Functional in this context refers to the functions the device is to perform, that is, the specifications of the device. Physical means the actual realization of the specified functionality as a physical system, the product to be designed. Design, in Suh's terms, consists of a continuous interaction between the functional and the physical spaces. Thus we have to define the functional requirements, devise the solution, analyze whether the solution is consistent with the problem definition, and finally check whether the solution is really what was wanted in the first place. This definition applies, of course, also to agent design. Although the needs of industrial design are quite obviously different from those of cognitive science, these steps are generally valid for both. Our "steps in running agent experiments" fit in well with Suh's concept.

General Issues in Design

Design is an almost universal activity. Engineers design cars, airplanes, and computers, but also simpler things like tables, soda cans, pens, tea bags, shoestrings and paper clips. Architects design buildings. Fashion designers design clothes. Scientists design experiments. Artists design logos, Internet home pages, and magazine title pages. Computer programmers design software. Teachers design materials to be used in their classes. And last but not least, researchers in our field of embodied cognitive science design physical and simulated agents. Virtually every object we use in our lives has been designed at some point: our watches, T-shirts, shoes, cameras, bicycles, glasses, combs, stoves, coffee cups, note pads, telephones, flower pots, bus tickets, knapsacks, key rings, and pillow cases. As might be expected, an enormous wealth of design knowledge has been accumulated in many areas.

To demonstrate the complex considerations that go into engineering design, we briefly describe some of the criteria. In our treatment, we draw inspiration from Henry Petroski's thoughtful and entertaining book *Invention by Design* (1996). Petroski uses examples from paper clips to modern passenger airplanes to large buildings. Whereas Suh focuses on industrial design, Petroski's interests are somewhat more general. We present the following list of factors usually taken into account in a design process, without commenting on it in detail—that would require another book—to demonstrate the broadness and variety of considerations that go into design: mechanics, energy-related issues (production, running, disposal), visibility of function, naturalness of mapping of controls to function, availability of raw or recycled materials, ease of manufacturing, markets, cost (production, running, disposal), safety, potential manipulation errors and failures, smoothness and ease of use, corporate policy, prospects for patent application, psychological (emotional), esthetic, environmental, ethical, cultural. From this impressive list of considerations it is obvious that design is not something simple, something that can be formalized easily. As prominent psychologist Don Norman, author of the enjoyable book *The Design of Everyday Things* (1988), put it: "Engineering design is a very human activity, with social and cultural factors playing as much a role as science and mechanics" (quoted on cover jacket of Petroski 1996).

The design process can be formalized, but only for relatively restricted, well-defined domains. This typically includes individual components of more complex objects or systems. Well-formalized are the designs of shapes of cogs for transmission boxes, turbine blades, bearings, pistons, rotor blades, fuel ducts, and so forth. Logic circuit design is especially well formalized, most likely because it is typically very clear what function the circuit should achieve, and the components to be used are usually given. Such individual components, in particular logic circuits, can thus be designed mostly in a top-down manner. The top-down way of proceeding implies a design philosophy in which the complex final product to be designed is decomposed into individual components that are designed separately and finally put together. The underlying assumption here is that the components only interact via well-defined interfaces or that they do not interact, (or at least that the interaction can be neglected). It is well known that such interactions can often be the source of problems. But it is certainly plausible to assume that the hands of a watch do not significantly interact with the battery. However, they do interact with the glass that covers the watch: depending on the shape of the glass, the hands may be seen as enlarged or distorted. Headlights on a car usually don't interact with the tires: These two components can safely be assumed to be decomposable and separately designable. At some level, of course, all components of an artifact interact. Because of the tires' limited capacity for adhesion, it takes some time to brake. This limitation in turn necessitates a certain range of vision that leaves the driver enough time to brake, which in turn implies that the headlights must have a certain range. Of course, the situation is more complicated, because these processes are mediated through the driver's sensory-motor systems and the car's braking system. But for all practical purposes headlights and tires can be considered independent. Simon (1969) has used the expression "near decomposability." We know that all components or subsystems interact, but we assume that most, at least, are largely independent, a necessary assumption because we cannot analyze and design a complex system all at once.

Decomposition is normally driven by the philosophy "one function–one module." It leads to modular designs. Recall that this is also the approach of traditional AI. We have called it the modularity principle (chapter 2). Headlights have the function of providing the basis for vision at night, tires of keeping contact between the wheels and the ground while absorbing potential shocks from uneven ground. From an engineering perspective, such a philosophy has enormous advantages. Separate development teams can work on separate components. Fault diagnosis is reduced to the comparatively simple task of identifying the malfunctioning module. Repair consists simply of replacing this module. In software engineering, modularization is one of the essential virtues. Modules can be tested independently of one another and combined in larger programs in arbitrary ways. Agent design, however, is somewhat different.

Issues in Agent Design

Agent design presents a significant conflict. On the one hand, an agent is a product of engineering that has to function properly. As such, its construction should follow the principles of engineering design, such as modularity. On the other, the functions in natural systems are often shared: One component serves several purposes, particularly in the neural system. Arms, for example, are used for object manipulation, for maintaining balance in walking, for protection, and for communication. They can also be applied for locomotion (crawling). This kind of resource sharing has to be kept in mind when designing agents.

We also have to take into account the principles delineated in chapter 10. Principles of this overall nature do not apply to engineering design in general—for example, that sensor, motor, and neural systems depend on one another, that they must be "balanced" with respect to a particular task environment. Although there is some general notion of "balance" in industrial design, most products lack sensory and motor systems. A robot for industrial purposes, say a manufacturing robot, has to meet very different criteria. For example, it has no need for self-sufficiency: We simply attach the robot to a power cable. And we don't want autonomy: We want the robot to perform exactly the tasks it is supposed to. The major differences between the two design philosophies are, of course, due to the different goals.

16.2 Agent Design

Let us now turn to the steps in designing agents for the purpose of investigating issues in intelligence. Well-established disciplines like cognitive psychology or experimental biology have standard ways of proceeding. However, in the field of embodied cognitive science, such a consensus does not (yet) exist. Our suggestions are meant to be a start in turning this field into a discipline with scientific standards as they are known from other fields without sacrificing its creative potential and its playful, synthetic character. We go through the steps outlined in chapter 4 (table 4.5) in more detail and focus on design issues. We delay the discussion of the more methodological questions until the next chapter. We restrict our discussion here to the design of individual robots; to design groups of robots involves yet other considerations (e.g., Mataric 1995).

Research Goals

Before we start designing anything we have to be clear about our research goals. What scientific questions do we want to answer? Do we want to study how babies learn to make distinctions in the environment? Or are we interested in ants' navigational system? Do we want to know more about why and under what conditions animals eat, sleep, or forage? Or are we interested in how people learn and forget? Or do we want to build a robot for data collection on Mars? Often this very general kind of decision is easy: It is given by the current research environment. Then the really hard part starts. We have to define the agent's ecological niche and the desired behaviors, and then we have to design the agent. This is the classical design problem. In chapter 10, we mentioned that there are alternative ways of proceeding. We can also start with an agent and a particular ecological niche and ask what behaviors will emerge. This was the approach taken in chapter 6 when discussing the Braitenberg vehicles. Alternatively, we can start with an agent and a set of desired behaviors and ask in what kinds of environments the agent will exhibit the desired behaviors. This perspective might be adopted by a robot manufacturer, who wants to design a robot that assembles a motor from parts on a conveyer belt. In this chapter, we focus on the classical design problem. There is an overall goal to be pursued in agent design. We would like the desired behaviors of the agent to be emergent; i.e., we want to design for emergence (as Luc Steels called it). Earlier we elaborated in detail that agent designs must be emergent, because we cannot design behaviors into the system (chapter 10). The idea is that once we have a good understanding of emergence, we can define a design methodology that starts from desired behaviors.

Currently such a methodology does not exist. Given a certain task or set of desired behaviors, for example, to mow the grass of a very large soccer field, how do we design robots so that the appropriate mowing behaviors will be emergent? This is a basic research issue. But the situation is not as bad as it sounds. Although there is no *general* methodology, in particular cases determining what processes are required to achieve a particular behavior is often straightforward. For example, to generate circling or wall-following behavior, we need three processes: move forward, turn toward, and turn away. The interaction of these three processes as the agent is near an object results in the desired behavior (chapter 12). If we want the agent to engage in categorization behavior, it needs processes to get near the object and processes to explore and manipulate the object. If exploration is to be in the form of circling, we can plug in the processes just described for circling. This is the same evolutionary philosophy that we described for the subsumption architecture in chapter 7. And then, we have the design principles, which impose constraints and provide guidance. Upon reflection, it is no surprise that there is no top-down methodology for designing autonomous agents. Assume that there were such a methodology. Designing agents would no longer be interesting from a scientific perspective: We could simply build them. For the time being, designing for emergence in general is an unresolved issue; it requires creativity and ingenuity.

Task Environment

Once we are clear about our research goals, we have to define the task environment, that is, the tasks, desired behaviors, and ecological niche. This is the equivalent of determining functional requirements. We have been careful to talk about desired behaviors, rather than internal modules, to be clear about the frame-of-reference issue. This use of terminology also stresses the point that the agent must actually behave. Say we want to study perception. The question is what the desired behaviors are. What is the context? We will see that the interesting behaviors from the perspective of embodied cognitive science differ considerably from those in more classical approaches.

Perception is a popular and important research topic. Broadly speaking, it involves "those processes that give coherence and unity to sensory input" (Reber 1985, p. 549). So to study perception, we first have to find a behavioral context. For example, in foraging, the agent (e.g., ant) moves toward a food item and picks it up, then brings it back to the nest, which in turn requires navigational behaviors. Navigation may require that the agent recognize —"perceive"—the food items, certain landmarks, and the nest. The question now is how these behaviors are to be achieved. This includes many issues that relate to perception.

Another example is a human infant learning to sort objects into different piles. He can be said to "perceive" the objects, but all we as observers see is whether he does the sorting correctly. The internal mechanisms for these two kinds of "perception," one in the foraging agent and other in the infant sorting objects, are likely quite different. It is always important to have a clearly defined behavioral context, because the processes involved strongly depend on the overall behavior. Milner and Goodale (1995) have made this point for visual perception. So we see that navigation and sorting provide a good behavioral context for studying issues in perception, which is one of the reasons why these behaviors are so popular in the field. They are also suitable for studying learning and memory.

Learning and memory involve how behavior changes over time. Learning is not something to be looked at in isolation but again in a behavioral context. The following task requires learning: The agent has to collect objects in an unknown environment. It has to learn about its environment, it has to find out where the objects to be collected are located, it has to find its way to a charging station, and it has to find its way back to the home base where it has to bring the objects. Moreover, it has to learn to make distinctions between the objects to be collected and those to be left alone. Recall the SMC agent that had to learn the distinction between small and large objects, a typical learning task. The desired behaviors were as follows: Initially, the agent should treat all objects the same. By interacting with the environment, it should change its behavior, gradually treating different types of objects differently, so that it picks up only the small ones while leaving the large ones alone. Learning long lists of words or numbers would not be a suitable task for a robot: there is no relevant behavioral part to the task. The same holds for problem solving, reasoning, and logical-inferencing tasks, which are unbalanced tasks because they mostly require central processing. Tasks requiring balanced designs are potentially more interesting to study.

Intelligence is also associated with social behavior, with communication and cooperation. We may choose to employ groups of agents rather than individuals, in which case we have to be particularly careful that we leave room for emergence, that we do not predefine too much. The clustering behavior of ants inspired the desired behaviors in the Didabot example (chapter 14). The clustering behavior in the Didabots was emergent from processes related to obstacle avoidance. More complex behaviors are required, for example, when agents have to play soccer. This task environment requires many competences: recognizing the direction and speed of the ball and the opponent's goal; manipulating the ball; fast and precise locomotion; anticipating the behaviors of others, opponent and team mate alike; cooperating; passing; and so forth. All of these competences can be studied from the perspective of learning. This is the idea underlying the RoboCup, which we discuss in chapter 18.

Desired behaviors can be defined only with respect to a particular ecological niche. Behavior, by definition, is the result of a system-environment interaction. For example, we have to decide what kinds of objects have to be sorted: little pegs on a table, or garbage in the real world. Or we have to say where the navigation behavior is to take place: in an environment specifically built for the robots, in an office setting, in a less-structured outdoor environment such as a university campus, the Sahara desert or in the sewage system of a large city. And this leads to an important design consideration: Depending on the choice of desired behaviors and environments, significant engineering problems will arise that must be mastered first, before the scientific issues can really be tackled. If we are to study navigation behavior in sewage systems, we first have to develop a robot that can move about in this environment consisting of slippery, wet, cluttered pipes of very different sizes. For other kinds of behaviors, like object manipulation, robots with suitable motor capabilities can be bought off the shelf.

The choice of tasks, desired behaviors, and ecological niche strongly influences the robot's design. If a garbage-collecting robot has to operate only in the streets, it can be equipped with wheels, and wheeled locomotion is much easier to design than walking (see below). However, if it has to collect garbage deposited in people's backyards, it might need the ability to walk. If we are interested in investigating the navigation behavior of the desert ant *Cataglyphis*, we know that its ecological niche, a salt pan in the Sahara desert, is very flat, very hot, and very windy. We also know that any agent designed to study its behavior should exploit the polarization pattern of the sky, as *Cataglyphis* itself does (e.g., Wehner 1994). From chapter 4 we know that we have to make good abstractions. Exploiting the polarization pattern requires sunlight and a partially open sky. Indoors, there is no partially open sky and not much sunlight. Thus, the experiments will have to be conducted outdoors. In Zurich or Boston, there is often no sunlight, or not enough to get a good polarization pattern. Quite in contrast, in the desert there is virtually always sunshine. So perhaps the experiments should be conducted in the desert itself. But that would be impractical: We would have to travel there, there are no well-equipped workshops, and it is very hot and dusty. Moreover, the desert has a particular surface. Is the particular surface relevant for the navigation behavior? Would there be sufficiently many sunny days in Zurich that the experiments could be run there? Do the differences in the polarization patterns between Zurich and the desert matter? Does the ecological niche require walking or wheels? Should a real robot be used or should a simulation be developed? How hard would it be to model the polarization pattern of the sunlight? As we see, many issues are involved in the choice of the ecological niche to run the experiments.

Once these issues have been settled and the ecological niche has been chosen, we have to decide on the behaviors desired of the agent. Here thoughts about evaluation already creep into our deliberations. Should the agent perform the full spectrum of navigation behaviors—leaving the nest, foraging, going back to the nest in a straight line, using landmark navigation near the nest? Should we start with one part only? What does it mean for the robot to "find food"? How are we going to compare the agent's behavior with that of the ant? How do we account for the potential differences in size? If the robot is 100 times the size of the ant, does it have to travel 100 times further than the ant? That would mean between 20 and 30 kilometers which is unrealistic. So we probably want to decide that these size relationships are irrelevant. But would that be a good decision? Note that if the robot had to travel 20 km energy would suddenly turn out to be an essential factor, and we have stressed the importance of self-sufficiency for intelligent behavior. Undoubtedly, we will still decide to use shorter distances, but we have to be aware that this is again a simplification. It is not feasible to list all these possible points systematically. They very closely depend on the particular area of investigation. The idea has been merely to illustrate the relatively disorderly types of thoughts involved.

If we are to study category learning in human infants, the situation is entirely different. In that case, we need various types of objects to be manipulated in the ecological niche. Presumably the required experiments can be run indoors, which is, of course, always the most convenient solution: We can structure our environment and tailor it to our needs more closely there. One idea might be to approximate the experimental settings of the psychological experiment: It depends on how closely we want to reproduce the experiment. Should the agent manipulate exactly the same types of objects as the human infant? Would that make sense, given that it has a very different sensory-motor system from the infant? Is it necessary to actually reproduce psychological experiments, or can we generally run category learning experiments on the robot and still say something relevant about humans? Again, the answers to these questions influence the choice of tasks and experimental setting (i.e., the ecological niche). We pick up this issue again in chapter 17 in the context of evaluation.

Low-Level Designer Specification and Choice of Platform

All the considerations above have direct implications for the low-level specification, that is, the basic designer commitments, which in turn influence choice of platform and control architecture. Once again, we see that although all the steps specified for designing agent experiments are required, there is no neat sequence in reality (even though in theory this might seem possible). Remember that the low-level specification represents an abstract definition of the physical agent's setup as well as basic interconnections of its components.

Once we have the agent's specification we have to choose a platform. This implies searching for the appropriate hardware and software, or if we are using simulated agents, searching for a simulation platform or developing our own. Now things get really messy, because the considerations are no longer of a purely scientific nature. We have to take into account practicality, available skills (Is the know-how and manpower available?), financial considerations and the state of the art in technology (Can we afford to buy the latest technology?), as well as aesthetic issues (Does the robot have to look "cool"?), ecological issues (Can we use rechargeable batteries?), temporal issues (Can we build the robot in a very short period of time?), and ergonomic issues (Can the people who need to do the experiments actually work with this kind of agent?). Moreover, the choices made here may in fact have an influence retroactively on the low-level specifications. For example, certain parts may turn out be unavailable or to have delivery times so long that you do not want to wait. So you may have to change the goals of your experiments, at least somewhat.

The number of potential design considerations is virtually unlimited. Let us look at a few examples. The Mars Sojourner has to be able to navigate on the surface of Mars. This implies, among other things, that it has to be able to detect obstacles and target objects, mainly rocks, and to navigate around them, or move up to them. Thus its low-level specification has to include means of perceiving rocks and perhaps other kinds of objects (such as the home base). Many different types of sensors could be used for this purpose. The designers of the Sojourner opted for vision sensors (cameras), bumper sensors, and proximity sensors. Moreover, its body had to be built in such a way that it could overcome obstacles of significant height. We mentioned in focus 4.2 that this is why the Sojourner has been equipped with six instead of four wheels: Six-wheeled robots can overcome obstacles three times larger than four-wheeled ones. Of course, the Sojourner's designers knew that they would be designing their robot from scratch. Therefore, they had the liberty of choosing any sensors they pleased. Normally, however, the situation is quite different.

Assume that a researcher has tentatively decided to use a real robot for his experiments, but perhaps he is not really sure yet. One of the decisions to be made is whether he should buy a robot off the shelf, or whether he should build his own. Say he is a psychologist planning to run experiments on category learning. Most likely, then, he will not have an engineering laboratory, circuit designers, mechanical workshops, and robot specialists at his immediate disposal. If expertise, workshops, circuit board designers, and mechanical engineers are lacking, designing a robot from scratch is out of the question. Then the question becomes whether it is really necessary to use a real robot, or if a simulation can be used as well. He might want to consult table 4.2, which compares robotic and simulated agents. If he should decide that a real robot is needed, he may want to purchase one. There are many good alternatives on the market. Here, practical considerations about space, price, and again available skill are important. Some platforms, like the Nomad 200 or the Khepera, require only a little knowledge of hardware: Programming skills are enough to operate them. But then, they are not cheap. There is a third alternative, namely getting a robot construction kit. The reader might consult our Internet page for pointers to pertinent information.

Imagine now that he has convinced your psychology department to buy a Khepera robot. He is certainly not going to follow the steps as outlined. Rather, he knows that he will be using Khepera for your experiments. Thus, the low-level specification—and, of course, its implementation, the Khepera robot itself—is largely given. However, if he has a flexible robot platform and the skill to add to, remove from, and modify it, he is less constrained in thinking about the low-level specification.

Choice of Sensors

One choice that always has to be made is the kinds of sensors to employ, irrespective of whether simulation or real robots are used. Let us now take a list of criteria for choosing sensors from the literature (Everett 1995), go through it, and show how the design principles we outlined in chapter 10 strongly influence the answers to the questions raised by the criteria. Before we do that, however, a more general comment is necessary. Principle 2, the complete-agent principle, states that we must always take the complete agent into account. Combined with the principle of ecological balance, this tells us that we should not choose sensors or motor setup in isolation, but that they have to be chosen together and with the task environment in mind. Let us now look at the list of criteria we mentioned, which is found in table 16.1.

The first entry in the table concerns field of view. This is a typical issue for vision sensors. First, the required field of vision depends on the agent's motor capabilities: If the agent has sufficient mechanical capacities, specifically sufficient flexibility to move the field of vision in a particular direction, the field of vision can be reduced. This is important, for example, in active vision. The field of vision depends also on the task environment. The issue of field of view is coupled with points 2 (range capability), 3 (accuracy and

Table 16.1 Overview of design considerations for sensors. (Adapted and extended from Everett 1995.)

	Design criterion	Comment (design principles involved)	Examples of sensors
1.	Field of view	Opening should be wide enough with sufficient depth of field; equally, opening should be restricted to limit processing; depends on tasks but also on motor capabilities (ecological balance)	Camera opening normally restricted Sahabot II uses 360° camera horizontally, vertical view is restricted between −15° and +15° with respect to the horizon; active vision dynamically adjusts camera parameters such as field of view
2.	Range capability	Minimum and maximum range of detection; must be balanced with speed and other motor capabilities (ecological balance)	Touch sensors have a range of 0; cheap sonars: typical range .4 m to 10 m (inaccurate); IR sensors on Khepera up to 4 cm
3.	Accuracy and resolution	Both must be in keeping with the needs of the given tasks; should be balanced with accuracy of motor system (ecological balance; redundancy; sensory-motor coordination)	Cheap sonars and IRs are inaccurate but may suffice for a given task; they are often sufficient for navigation and obstacle avoidance
4.	Ability to detect all objects in environment	Objects can absorb emitted energy; target surfaces can be specular as opposed to diffuse reflectors; ambient conditions and noise can interfere with the sensing process (point 7, redundancy, below)	IR radiation is absorbed by matte black surfaces; use a camera in addition
5.	Real-time operation	Update frequency must provide rapid, real-time data at a rate commensurate with the platform's speed of advance; this consideration trades off with point 3, accuracy, and resolution (ecological balance; parallel, loosely coupled processes)	In particular cheap frame-grabbers for CCD cameras often have low frame-rates (depending on the resolution of the image); be careful: high frame-rates may require lot of processing
6.	Concise, easy-to-interpret data	Output format should be realistic from the standpoint of processing requirements; too much data can be as meaningless as not enough; some degree of preprocessing and analysis may be required to provide appropriate sensory output (cheap design; sensory-motor coordination)	Often a high-resolution camera is given, but for a particular task only low resolution is required (cheap vision); low resolution can be achieved through preprocessing
7.	Redundancy	System should provide graceful degradation and not become incapacitated because of the loss of a sensing element; multimodal capability would be desirable to ensure detection of all targets, as well as to increase confidence level of output (redundancy)	IRs are often used in addition to a camera for obstacle avoidance; in contrast to normal cameras IRs also function in the dark; redundancy in sensors is also important for learning

Table 16.1 (continued)

	Design criterion	Comment (design principles involved)	Examples of sensors
8.	Simplicity	System should be low cost and modular to allow for easy maintenance and evolutionary upgrades, not hardware-specific (cheap design; parallel, loosely coupled processes)	Simple and cheap sensors like sonars or IRs are often entirely sufficient; they can be used in parallel and relatively independently
9.	Power consumption	Power requirements should be minimal in keeping with the limited resources on board a mobile vehicle; (important for self-sufficiency considerations)	Often there is an accuracy-power consumption trade-off: high-precision laser scanners consume a lot of energy
10.	Size	Physical size and weight of system should be practical with regard to intended vehicle (ecological balance; self-sufficiency)	Often high-resolution devices are larger, e.g. high-resolution cameras; small high-resolution cameras are more expensive

resolution), and 5 (real-time operation). If the task requires the robot to move fast, it needs sufficient range capabilities to minimize risk of hitting. Vision sensors are well-suited for this purpose. If the vision sensors have high resolution, a lot of processing is required, and we may not be able to meet the real-time demands. This is where the principle of parallel, loosely coupled processes comes in. To meet real-time demands, we have to organize the architecture in terms of parallel, largely peripheral processes. If internal processing is minimal, there is a good chance that the sensory data can be processed fast enough. It may be a good idea to have a number of specialized distance sensors that operate in parallel, or a very simple, low-resolution visual sensor, with just enough resolution to achieve the task of moving fast while avoiding obstacles. Remember Ian Horswill's robot Polly which used low-resolution vision for navigation? By looking at the y-axis only, Polly could measure relative distance very quickly (assuming that the obstacles stood on the ground). As a result, it could move really fast, much faster than other, more sophisticated robots. If obstacle avoidance is the only task, cheap sonars or IR sensors might be sufficient. A low-resolution visual sensor can also be contrived by having a high-resolution camera but processing only parts of the image it transmits, for example, by using a horizontal one-dimensional array, by processing only 1 out of 25 pixels, or by taking an average over a square area. The closer to the periphery this can be done, the better criterion 5, real-time operation, can be fulfilled. For reasons of flexibility, this kind of filtering can also be done in software. An interesting solution to this trade-off between resolution and processing requirements is to use *space-variant* vision sensors (e.g., Ferrari, Nielsen, and Sandini 1995), that is, sensors with high resolution in the center and low resolution toward the periphery. This design that is found in the retinas of many animals has the advantage that due to the low resolution at the periphery, processing is significantly reduced. Because the periphery is only used for motion detection, low resolution is sufficient.

So far we have been talking about constraints originating from the task environment. If we are interested in modeling natural agents, the system we model imposes additional constraints. For example, ants, the desert ant *Cataglyphis* in particular, have a compound eye with almost 360-degree vision. The Sahabot, used to model the navigation behavior of *Cataglyphis*, had a camera with 360-degree vision and a vertical opening that varied somewhat between +15 degrees (above the horizon) and −15 degrees (below the horizon). As an aside, 360-degree vision, or omnidirectional vision, can be achieved cheaply by having a camera face a conic, hyperbolic, or spherical mirror from below. Figure 16.1b shows such a camera. The compound eye of an ant has individual facettes, the ommatidia, all of which have a particular opening angle that is given and that might have to be reproduced more or less precisely.

An example in which adjustment of resolution and accuracy through software might be useful is infant development. As pointed out earlier, the acuity of an infant's visual distinctions increases over time (and is coupled to an increase in precision of motor movements). The design strategy would be to use a camera with enough resolution for those stages requiring the highest resolution. Initially, a filter placed over the camera would simply prevent it from being exploited to its full capacity; such a filter is typically generated via software. This is another case of redundancy being employed: The camera provides redundant signals that are not exploited initially but may be exploited later if required by the needs of the motor system. This in turn is a consequence of the principle of sensory-motor coordination.

Consider now point 4, the ability to detect all objects in the environment. A robot that has to operate at night cannot use visual

Figure 16.1 The Sahabot II robot, developed to investigate the navigation behavior of the desert ant *Cataglyphis*, in particular to study landmark navigation. (a) The robot with its exchangeable wheels. (b) The omnidirectional camera, based on a conical mirror. To imitate the ant's visual input, an unprocessed stripe (c) was extracted from the direct camera image.

sensors exclusively but will have to incorporate active sensors, in addition, such as IRs or sonars (ultrasound). A robot equipped only with IR sensors for obstacle avoidance has problems, for example, with black matte surfaces that absorb IR radiation. It must therefore be equipped with additional sensors, for example, visual ones. Note that we have just introduced a certain amount of redundancy into our agent.

Point 6 tells us that we should aim for just the right amount of data: Too much is just as bad as too little. This exemplifies the principle of cheap design. We should add that appropriate motor action may signifantly reduce the amount of data required. Through appropriate sensory-motor coordination, a problem seemingly requiring a lot of data, like recognizing an object, may be turned into a much simpler one, as the principle of sensory-motor coordination states.

Point 7, an explicit reference to redundancy, adds an interesting twist to these considerations. On the one hand, having multimodal capabilities can increase reliability of recognition. Moreover, it permits graceful degradation: If one sensory modality ceases to function, others can, at least partially, compensate for this loss. An IR sensor can partly take over from a vision sensor, though possibly only at short range. Note that optimal redundancy is achieved if the sensors are positioned so that there is a potential information overlap, as the redundancy principle states. If the sensors function based on different physical properties, that increases adaptivity. On the other hand, multimodal associations enable category learning. Thus, if learning experiments are planned, this has a direct influence on the choice and the positioning of the sensors.

Point 8 states that the sensors should be low cost and modular, which refers to the principle of cheap design. Often, if the constraints of the niche are exploited, really cheap sensors can be used. The idea of modular sensors also relates to the principle of parallel, loosely coupled processes: If we rely on parallel processes, additional sensors can be added and only minimal modifications to the existing sensors and architecture have to made. Ecological balance must also be taken into account: Depending on the task environment, primitive motor systems often require only primitive sensors.

Point 9 relates to self-sufficiency and to the fact that some sensors, especially high-precision ones, may require a lot of energy. But high precision may simply not be required by the task involved.

Finally, point 10 states that the sensors' size should be practical: if too large, they will not fit or be too heavy; if too small, they might be difficult to handle. Again, the idea of ecological balance is involved here.

We are still not quite done. We do not simply want to build robots, we also want to run experiments and evaluate our robots' behavior. Step 7 in agent design (table 4.5) tells us that we have to think about the data that we plan to collect about the agent in an experiment. This potentially implies additional sensors. For example, we might want to register deviations in direction. A magnetic compass could make this possible in the Sahabot. We might want to include means that make it easy for the agent to record its position, for example, by using GPS-based devices. GPS, the Global Positioning System, can be used to record position anywhere on earth.

So far we have proceeded only to the specification of the sensors. Similar considerations would arise in choosing other system components. We hope that we have demonstrated, however, that agent design is not a straightforward, linear activity. Rather, it requires a lot of creativity. It requires thinking about many issues and constraints simultaneously. And the considerations are not only of a technical or scientific nature. Software designer Morten Kyng coined the term "situated design" (Greenbaum and Kyng 1991). He describes design as a dynamic process in which the designer continuously interacts with the evolving artifact and with other members of the design team. This implies that even if the design decision just discussed has been made, as the process of building the agent starts, there will be an iterative process, implying potential revisions of previous decisions.

The choice of sensors is an important part of working out the low-level specifications. But alas, it is only one among many: We also have to devise the motor system, the body and the potential connections, and ultimately the processors and the power supply. Defining motor systems and building controllers for the sensor and motor systems are also nontrivial and involved problems. We do not, however, outline our approach to making the required choices in the same detail as we did for sensors.

Choice of Motor System and Mechanical Parts

Sensors cannot be chosen in isolation—the intended task and the motor system must also be taken into account. We have been considering aspects of the motor system already as we pondered our choices for sensors. Let us now pick out for closer examination two of the most prominent components of motor systems, namely those for locomotion and for object manipulation. Other components of motor systems are concerned with body movement, facial expression (see also the "face robot" in chapter 19), movement, of the neck, the eyes, the vocal cords, and so forth. Because we are interested only in illustrating some design considerations, we omit from our deliberations some forms of locomotion, such as swimming or flying. The choice of motor components is closely tied to the control architecture, which is why this section already discusses many aspects of control architecture.

FOR LOCOMOTION

Locomotion is clearly one of the most elementary capacities of a mobile agent: If it can't move, it's not mobile. The means we choose for locomotion depend, of course, on the agent's desired behaviors. Let's again take the example of the Sahabot. Since it was designed to mimic the desert ant *Cataglyphis*, does its locomotion have be legged? Or can we abstract from the type of locomotion and use a wheeled robot? Wheels are very common in robots that move on solid ground. Robots equipped with wheels have many advantages over legged ones: They are easy to build and control, they are in general cheaper than legged robots, they have fewer joints than legged ones, they can carry more weight, they are robust, they can—to some extent—be used in rough territory, they move backward easily, they are fast, and they can vary their speed continuously. The designers of the Sahabot decided that navigation mechanisms are independent of a particular way of locomotion, so they used wheels rather than legs. But their reflections were not entirely "pure": They were not driven exclusively by scientific biological considerations only. The Sahabot's designers knew that they would want an onboard PC, batteries with at least half an hour of operating time, a polarization sensor module of considerable weight, an adjustable 360-degree camera, and several fans to keep the agent cool in the heat of the desert. Moreover, they knew that in the desert's dusty, salty, and sandy environment, wheeled locomotion would be easier to engineer. So, the choice to use wheels was made quickly. An additional requirement was easy maneuverability, in particular, turning on the spot. The solution can be seen in figure 16.1a.

The other main means of locomotion for agents on solid ground, besides wheels, is walking. Walking has definite advantages for

Figure 16.2 A special walking robot being designed and built by Peter Dilworth at the MIT Leg Lab. The robot is modeled after the dinosaur Troodon. It has legs with many degrees of freedom. At some point it should be able to stand up, walk, run, walk, and sit down again with smooth transitions. It will have its power supply and controller on board (reprinted with permission).

locomotion over rough terrain and stairs. Walking's disadvantages are that it is harder to control, it requires limbs that may be quite complex, in nature it occurs at only a few speeds (the various gaits), and the speed at which it can occur has an upper limit. Moreover, as pointed out above, walking robots can carry less weight. It is also more difficult to make them really small. When researchers develop walking robots, most of the time, walking itself is their research area. For example, the MIT Leg Lab has legged locomotion as its main research area. A great deal of engineering expertise is required to design and build walking robots. Figure 16.2 illustrates this point. It shows a dinosaur designed by Peter Dilworth at the MIT Leg Lab. Its legs have many degrees of freedom, thus making it an especially hard problem to generate its walking behavior. It has specifically been designed with the goal of investigating control architectures for complex walking behaviors. In design environments, where expertise in agents exhibiting walking behaviors is lacking in most cases designers are better off using wheeled locomotion for their agents. For those whose research interest is not in walking per se, the effort involved in employing a walking agent might be very high compared to the additional insights gained.

FOR OBJECT MANIPULATION
Another major function of the motor system is object manipulation. Humans and animals manipulate objects in their environment with great ease. A variety of devices for object manipulation exist from

which to choose. Figure 16.3 shows a number of them with varying degrees of freedom, including wire loops, grippers, hands with several fingers, and robot arms and shoulders. Some are available commercially; others have been developed in research labs. The point, however is not only the manipulation device as such, but its control. The fundamental problem is the control of a large number of degrees of freedom. We do not go into the details here—that would be beyond our scope and competence. This topic in itself constitutes a vast research field in engineering and in neuroscience. From the perspective of autonomous agents, it is important that the problem not be viewed as a computational one, but as one where dynamics play an essential role as well (as stated in the principle of cheap design). A promising approach in this respect has been developed by Matt Williamson (1996) of the MIT AI Lab, who built controllers for Cog's arm. Williamson was specifically interested in modeling humanlike behavior in Cog's arm. The arm needed also to be safe for people to interact with: It needed to be compliant. For example, it needed, when it touched a person, to yield elastically rather than push harder, as numerous existing robotic arms would do. To achieve this compliance, Williamson has mimicked, using electric motors, the springlike properties of human arm muscles. This leads to a distributed system: The (simulated) springs work continuously and independently of what happens elsewhere in the system, embodying the principle of parallel, loosely coupled processes. Cog can manipulate certain kinds of objects: It can swing a pendulum or turn a crank.

From the perspective of autonomous agents, Williamson's research is highly relevant. But Cog's capabilities need to be extended to more complex kinds of manipulations if it is to be used to study category learning based on sensory-motor coordination. In particular, sensors, most importantly tactile sensors, must be mixed in with the motor systems (as stated in the redundancy principle). Another big "problem" with Cog is that it is not commercially available, and even if it were, it would be—at least at the moment —too expensive for most research labs to afford.

MOTOR SYSTEMS: A CHALLENGE

Some sensor systems are well developed. They seem to be much easier to deal with than motor systems. Researchers in the field of autonomous agents work with IR sensors, sonars, laser scanners, standard cameras, omnidirectional cameras, specialized sensors

a
b

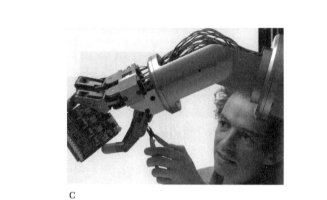

c

d

Figure 16.3 Devices for object manipulation: (a) wire loop, (b) gripper, (c) Salisbury hand, (d) Cog's arms. As the number of degrees of freedom increases, it becomes more difficult to control the manipulator (c and d reprinted with permission).

(like polarization sensors), tilt sensors, and accelerometers, to name the most common ones. But most employ robot platforms that have comparatively simple motor systems. The robots with which they work are wheeled, have simple manipulators, and have a camera with perhaps two degrees of freedom. Many even lack facilities for object manipulation. This sparsity of motor equipment on most robots reflects the fact that motor systems, in particular sophisticated motor systems, are very hard to synthesize. As we have seen, investigating motor systems is a research issue in the neurosciences and in engineering. We have argued all along that motor systems are of crucial importance, that we should not consider the sensory side in isolation. So how should we proceed, given this difficulty: Should we employ only agents with simple motor systems? There is no clear answer. If we want to develop agents with more complex sensory-motor coordination, we need more complex motor systems. But such motor systems are not readily usable off the shelf. This represents a challenge for the current research in the field. Some of the current problems with motor systems may be due to the materials employed (e.g., electrical motors instead of muscles), others due to issues concerning the control architecture. If we want to develop autonomous agents, the application of the synthetic methodology using embodied systems may eventually provide new perspectives on issues in motor control, as illustrated by Cog's arm. But currently, the lack of better motor control systems indeed represents an obstacle. However, experience shows that by working even with simple motor components like grippers, a great deal of progress can already be made.

Other Considerations

Choosing a motor system involves many additional considerations. To conclude our discussion, let us mention just two more: choice of processors and energy supply. The choice of processors for the agent depends again on many factors, such as processing requirements from the sensory and motor systems, including number and type of ports (for input-output operations); availability of programming environments and public domain software; visualization tools; and available expertise; but weight, power requirements, and robustness also have to be taken into account. One decision that must be made is whether onboard computing is to be used, as is desirable if the agent is to be autonomous. That decision has consequences in terms of the agent's weight, size, and power supply. For flexibility and easy of use, PCs are convenient, but they require a great deal of space and power. The latter is a problem only if the power supply is to be onboard, in which case the robot has to be equipped with batteries, and batteries are very heavy; this in turn creates a problem in particular for walking robots. Using an off-board power supply, on the other hand, makes it necessary to connect the robot to its power supply via a cable or in some other way that limits its mobility. Concerning the choice of processors, instead of having one powerful central processor, one might also think of having many small processors that run independently, as would be desirable from the point of view of parallel, loosely coupled processes. This is the approach taken in Cog. In an off-the-shelf platform, the designers have mostly already made these decisions and there is no need not worry about them. If building robots per se is not the focus of the research, given the many considerations that we have outlined, there is something to be said for off-the-shelf solutions.

If simulation instead of a physical agent is used, many issues concerning the hardware don't have to be considered. But then there are the problems outlined in chapter 4, namely that it is hard to simulate the dynamics of a physical robot and of an environment realistically, especially if the simulated agents have many degrees of freedom, whereas in the real world the dynamics are simply given. A definite advantage of simulation, on the other hand, is that since most of the hardware considerations can be omitted, there is more time to focus on the conceptual issues of agent design.

16.3 Putting It All Together: Control Architectures

We saw in chapter 11 that control architectures are the means for putting together the sensory and motor systems to achieve the desired behavior: They make it all work. In that chapter, we presented an overview of the different architectures in the field of embodied cognitive science. We showed there that the hallmark of these architectures is that they employ a number of parallel, loosely coupled processes, each of which is directly connected to the robot's sensory-motor apparatus. Agents designed in this particular manner have the potential for emergence, so the goal is to employ architectures that support emergence. We also mentioned in chapter 11 that one important issue in designing an architecture is the formalism selected to implement these processes. In this section, we discuss some of the considerations involved in selecting the agent's architecture and formalism.

Choice of Architecture

We have introduced a number of architectures throughout the book, for example, Distributed Adaptive Control (chapter 5), Braitenberg architectures (chapter 6), and Extended Braitenberg Architectures (chapters 6 and 11), subsumption (chapter 7), schema-based architectures (chapter 9), Process Description Language (chapter 11), and action selection dynamics (chapter 11). Given a particular low-level specification and a set of desired behaviors, how should we decide which one to choose? Unfortunately, it is the same story again: There is no recipe, no top-down procedure for making such a decision. As we have already pointed out a number of times, the low-level specifications are never worked out in isolation. But we normally have an idea about the architecture in mind before we start. Then we simply make it work. The architectures we have discussed are not formally specified. Thus, there is a lot of freedom in how they are to be interpreted (which has obvious advantages and disadvantages). Given what we have discussed in this book, the important choice is not a particular architecture. What does matter is that certain principles of embodied cognitive science are observed and that there is room for emergence. The choice of an architecture does not free us, however, from the fundamental design problem: Given a particular task environment, how do I design the agent?

One frequently asked question in this context is whether we should choose an architecture that includes learning or adopt an evolutionary approach. This question is especially relevant, since so far, learning agents have not shown significantly better performance on most tasks than hand-designed robots (e.g., Brooks and Mataric 1993). If you are interested in the study of intelligence, it is always a good idea to include learning of some sort (see also chapter 14, concerning the value principle). Similar considerations apply to artificial evolution. This brings us to the next topic, the choice of formalism.

Formalisms for Agent Design

If you want to implement an architecture, you have to choose a formalism: There is no way around it. Verbal descriptions simply don't run on computers. Several formalisms have already been discussed as we introduced the various approaches, including neural networks of various kinds (chapters 5, 6, 11, 12, 14), finite state machines and augmented finite state machines (chapter 7), evolutionary algorithms (chapter 8), differential equations (chapter 9), immune system formalisms (chapter 11), and Q-learning (chapter 14). Of course, there are many more in existence, like classifier systems, control theory, fuzzy logic, and Markov models, but the ones we have discussed are among the most frequently used in the field of embodied cognitive science. Let us briefly go through each and inspect the design decisions involved (see table 16.2 for an overview).

But before we start, a note on terminology is in place. The term "formalism," with its etymological connection to the word "form"—often used in opposition to "content"—suggests something essentially free of content or at least not dependent on it, something that can be used to represent a theory formally. Differential equations very much have this content-free character, but the other formalisms presented here do not. They are not really theories, but they imply a significant amount of content about the subject matter they describe: Neural networks relate to real biological neurons (perhaps only remotely, but still they do), evolutionary algorithms endorse the idea of artificial evolution, Q-learning implies that learning of this particular kind is basically a good thing, and immune system algorithms capitalize on (abstractions of) mechanisms found in natural organisms. In our discussion of the formalisms we therefore sometimes make reference to cognitive science, even though if we were talking about pure formalism, this would be inappropriate. Some of these formalisms—neural networks, classifier systems, immune system formalisms, and dynamical systems—have been shown actually to be equivalent (Farmer 1990). This is, however, a purely mathematical equivalence. From a cognitive science perspective, it still makes a great deal of sense to distinguish between the different formalisms: One can get very different kinds of inspiration from each of them.

Neural networks

By far the most popular formalism is neural network. Let us recall the reasons for their popularity: They are fault and noise tolerant, they are intrinsically learning systems, and they can generalize, i.e., they are robust. Moreover, because they are inspired by natural

Table 16.2 Overview of formalisms used for autonomous agents.

Formalism	Comments	Pros	Cons
Neural networks	Extremely popular in autonomous agents field; come in many variations (spiked, nonspiked, synchronized, asynchronous, feedforward, recurrent)	Large number of parameters available; for certain types of networks, parallel implementation possible; well-suited for adaptive behavior; capture nonlinear phenomena; integrated learning; intrinsic robustness; many simulation tools available	Many types not appropriate for adaptive behavior (e.g., MLPs with back-propagation); large number of parameters to adjust (weights, learning parameters, temporal characteristics)
Differential equations	Universal tool used in all sciences	Well-established formalisms; focus on dynamics; global characteristics can be extracted; attractive metaphors (attractors, chaos)	Integration computationally expensive; systems of differential equations get complicated for complex systems; nonlinearities prevent analytic solution; finding appropriate operationalization (i.e., choice of variables and parameters) may be hard; use for synthetic purposes not clear
Finite state machines and augmented finite state machines	Used in the context of the subsumption architecture; finite state machines too limited for real world—augmented finite states machines must be used	Simple, straightforward to implement; programming language available (Behavioral Language); encourages architectures with only little internal state	Learning not included; prespecification of priorities required (inhibition and supression links)
Evolutionary algorithms	Popular in ALife and autonomous agents	Well-suited for generation of diversity and emergence; intrinsically robust	Computationally expensive; design of fitness function not straightforward; restricted to simulation if applied to complete agents
Immune system formalisms	Popular in ALife community; currently not widely used in the field of autonomous agents	Well-suited for generation of diversity and emergence; massively parallel	Computationally expensive; understanding dynamics can be difficult
Q-learning	Popular in machine learning community	Mathematically clean formalism with optimality properties	Mostly grid-based simulations requiring constraining assumptions; not easily interpretable in terms of natural intelligence
Classifier systems	Mostly used in ALife community; not widely used for real robots	Lend themselves to parallel implementation; integrated learning	Computationally expensive

brains, it is relatively straightforward to implement in neural networks ideas from neurobiology. One of these ideas is the parallel nature of neural systems. Parallelism is required for adaptive real-time behavior. Moreover, neural networks can be embedded in physical robots in natural ways.

Neural networks are widely used in many fields and their basic principles are well understood. Because of their parallel nature, they lend themselves to parallel implementation, especially adaptive networks. (Some neural network learning algorithms require global control, like back-propagation, and the parallel implementation of global control is not straightforward.) Because of their many free parameters, in particular the weights, they incorporate a sufficient amount of redundancy for adapting to novel situations. Of course, there are also trade-offs, but they are minor ones compared to their advantages. The many parameters of neural networks must be adjusted. In addition to the weights, there are learning rates, thresholds, time constants, and forgetting rates. Moreover, because of their many free parameters, they can be computationally expensive and—especially for large networks—their dynamics is not always easy to follow.

Examples of neural networks we have seen are the Distributed Adaptive Control architecture, the SMC agents, Beer's walking insect, and Sims' virtual creatures. Neural networks are often used in combination with evolutionary algorithms.

When designing a neural network, the type of network to be employed has to be decided: one using activation levels or one using spiked neurons. Whenever temporal characteristics play a crucial role, spiked neurons may have to be used. We also have to decide on the network architecture. (Be careful here: network architecture is not the same as control architecture.) The appropriate network architecture always has to be determined in the context of a particular task. If possible simple forms of learning should be used exclusively, like Hebbian learning, which is entirely local, that is, it requires the activation levels only of those nodes to which it is directly connected. As a general heuristic, if the data are such that you need powerful learning mechanisms, there may be something fundamentally wrong with your design.

Finite state machines and augmented finite state machines
Finite state machines are used to implement the subsumption architecture. In chapter 7, we used the example of a turnstile to illustrate the basic idea. Finite state machines are characterized

by states and transitions. As such, they are relatively limited. For example, they do not incorporate a time component. Often we want the robot to do a particular action for a certain amount of time, such as turning or moving backwards. Finite state machines have therefore been augmented to make them usable in robots (see chapter 7). As in the case of neural networks, the formalism of augmented finite state machines imposes a bias on how control architectures are designed. For example, it makes designers think about problems in terms of states and state transitions, which is natural for many robot problems: The robot is in a particular state, such as moving fast, and given a certain input, such as a sensory stimulation pattern indicating an obstacle, the robot changes to a state with motor speed low.

Finite state machines are simple entities that run asynchronously. Moreover, because augmented finite state machines are simple and run asynchronously, they—implicitly—encourage the designer to apply the principle of parallel, loosely coupled processes. The last point to mention is that the formalism of augmented finite state machines is not really essential to the subsumption architecture. Many robot designers who in principle adhere to the subsumption architecture, employ general purpose programming modules instead (typically in a language like C). The latter has the additional advantage that subsumption-like architectures can easily be augmented with neural networks.

Evolutionary algorithms
Evolutionary algorithms, which we discussed in chapter 8, are very popular formalisms in the field of embodied cognitive science and artificial life. As pointed it out in the introduction, the design decisions that have to be made when applying evolutionary algorithms are different from the ones made in the other formalisms. Still, they can be used to design, or rather to evolve, control architectures. Some of the difficult design decision in this case are: What information should be encoded in the genome and how should it be represented? What is the fitness function to be applied to the agent? Further design challenges (evolving physical robots, simulation vs. hardware, coevolution of morphology and control architecture, and so forth) are discussed in chapter 8.

Differential equations
Differential equations are universal mathematical tools used in all sciences. Whenever temporal evolution is primary, differential

equations are well suited for the task. Any dynamical system, an (artificial) neural network, or a physical system can be described by a set of differential (or difference) equations. We encountered these equations in chapter 9 when discussing the dynamical systems approach. We pointed out in that chapter the temptation offered by metaphors such as attractors, chaos, fractality, and sensitivity to initial conditions. Nevertheless, this formalism has not been widely employed in the autonomous agents community, one main reason being that it is a descriptive rather than a synthetic tool. Also, the concrete description of complex systems like robots in this formalism turns out to be highly involved. One of the few attempts to use this tool to actually synthesize behavior was made by Steinhage and Schöner (1997; see chapter 9).

Immune system formalisms

Immune system formalisms are highly promising, especially because of their ability to evolve novel behaviors. Thus in the context of generating diversity, they are certainly tools to be taken into account. Moreover, because they are entirely distributed, they can be implemented on parallel architectures. But potential users should beware of their heavy computational cost. To date, immune system approaches have become fairly prominent in artificial life, but they have not been widely used in the embodied cognitive science community. An exception is the work of Ishiguro and his colleagues, which we discussed in chapter 11.

Q-Learning

Q-learning has become very popular in recent years in the machine learning community because of its mathematically clean representation and its optimality properties. The goal of *Q*-learning was to make reinforcement learning more efficient. It was not intended to provide a model of learning in natural systems, which is why it is not widely applied in the cognitive science community in spite of its mathematical rigor. Moreover, although there have been certain attempts to do so, it has not been extensively used on real robots. For a detailed discussion of this issue, see Mataric 1995.

Classifier systems

The last formalism that we want to discuss is classifier systems, which have been around for a long time and have been used both in classical artificial intelligence (e.g., Holland et al. 1986), and in the field of autonomous agents (e.g., Colombetti and Dorigo 1993). Classifier systems are attractive because they combine evolution and learning and because they are highly distributed. Interestingly, they are nevertheless only used by a relatively small group of researchers, presumably because similar results can be achieved with a combination of evolutionary algorithms and neural networks. And the latter two are, at least at present, the clear leaders in the field. We do not discuss classifier systems any further here, other than to note that a simplified version of classifier systems can be shown to be equivalent to Q-learning.

We have not given a very comprehensive answer here to the question of how to go about choosing a formalism. We have merely presented a review of some common existing formalisms and raised some issues you might consider when choosing a formalism. As with architectures, what specific choice you make is not essential as long as you observe the design principles. And last but not least: Let's be honest. What formalism will a psychologist or biologist choose? Presumably one in which expertise is available in his lab or his surroundings, and one that is already used and enjoys a certain popularity. He might even take into account what formalisms look good to a funding agency. Again, this is not quite a scientific perspective, but reality in design. This observation connects to some of the points made in general about the rather chaotic nature of design.

16.4 Summary and a Fundamental Issue

We have shown in a rather practical way how the design principles of autonomous agents in fact exert a direct influence on the design of agents. Thus, the design principles not only are general overall standards or beliefs, but also provide guidance for design. Although they do offer guidance, they are not precise step-by-step recipes. Trying to devise such recipes is neither desirable nor possible: We do not want merely to build something that works for a particular purpose. We want to build agents to explore issues in the study of intelligence. This requires innovation and ingenuity, not rigid prescriptions and top-down methods.

One of the crucial questions in agent design is the choice of task environment. The success—whether you gain interesting insights —crucially depends on a good choice of task environment. Here, the principle of ecological balance is particularly relevant. For example, it helps us avoid studying tasks that are too computational or tasks that are beyond the current technology (with respect to sensory-motor complexity; neural complexity is, given today's microprocessor technology, not a problem). The appropriate behavioral context is also central (complete-agent principle and three constituents principle, see chapter 10).

The space of possible designs, or to put it more bluntly, the number of possible agents is obviously unlimited. Even if the purpose of a product to be designed is precisely given, such as in the case of a paper clip, an enormous number of considerations still go into its design, as Petroski (1996) has shown us very convincingly. Except for those designed for specific applications, the exact purpose of an autonomous agent is in general not given beforehand. Thus, the number of considerations and possibilities is even larger. Then, the complexity is considerable, given that there are sensors, motor systems, power supply systems, computers, communication lines, and so forth. In other words, there is absolutely no hope that we can ever achieve a neat top-down methodology for designing autonomous agents.

Actually building a robot draws attention to the enormous complexity of behaving systems. It also shows us very clearly all the assumptions we are making, all the processes that we are leaving out when we focus only on internal "high-level" processing, as in the cognitivistic paradigm. So, a psychologist, a neurobiologist, or an ethologist who never wants to build actual robots may have been surprised at all that is required to build a complete robot. And one can imagine that even more is involved in natural systems with their higher degree of sophistication.

We have argued throughout this book that building agents leads to important insights. But a fundamental problem remains. All our robots have used some kind of digital microprocessors. The signals from the sensors are converted to digital signals, to data; they are transmitted across a data bus to a processor. The data are processed, a motor signal is calculated, transmitted across a bus, and converted to a voltage that can be applied to control the motor system. If we look at natural systems, matters seem to work very differently. There are no data buses, and brains don't simply run programs. So ultimately, we may want robots functioning on a different, more natural principle, a principle that does not rely on processors and programs.

A first step in this direction has been made in the field of *neuromorphic engineering*, that is, the designing and building of chips

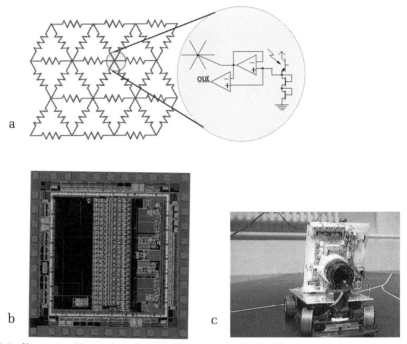

Figure 16.4 Neuromorphic engineering. (a) The basic functionality of a retina chip, represented schematically. (b) A sensory-motor chip. (c) The robot Morpho, equipped with the sensory-motor chip. The retina chip was developed by Carver Mead and Misha Mahowald at the California Institute of Technology, the sensory-motor chip and Morpho by Marinus Maris at the University of Zurich.

that mimic certain brain structures. Carver Mead and his colleagues (e.g., Mahowald and Mead 1991; Mead 1989) at the California Institute of Technology in Pasadena, California, initiated the field. The technology used is analog VLSI. In contrast to digital circuits, analog circuits directly exploit physical processes, rather than transforming the physical process into a "digital" one. They also consume orders of magnitude less energy than digital circuits.

The most prominent piece of neuromorphic engineering developed so far is the artificial retina (e.g., Douglas, Mahowald, and Mead 1995; Mahowald and Mead 1991), an example of which is shown in figure 16.4a. Retinas, in contrast to standard sensors (such as standard cameras), perform a great deal of processing at the periphery. This is an especially important consideration when fast real-time response is required. Some features can be extracted directly by the retina at the very periphery. Examples are detectors for direction, edges, or motion. Retinas are extremely useful, and natural systems are almost universally equipped with some kind of retina. Recall that the principle of sensory-motor coordination tells us that we should not focus exclusively on the sensory or the input side, but rather include sensory-motor processes in our consideration. For this reason, some researchers have started to build neuromorphic sensory-motor chips, which contain not only light-sensitive cells and feature extraction mechanisms, but also the necessary circuitry to generate a motor signal. Figure 16.4b shows a sensory-motor chip designed by Marinus Maris and Misha Mahowald at the University of Zurich in Switzerland. Such a chip, this one specifically for line following, was tested on a robot called Morpho, which is shown in figure 16.4c. As always, there are trade-offs. Morpho demonstrates the in-principle feasibility of having direct sensory-motor loops without an intervening digital processor, an idea with great potential, and one that is highly appealing if we are interested in studying natural systems. However, analog VLSI chips have so far been developed only for relatively simple tasks. Analog VLSI is also very hard to design, and once it is built, it cannot be changed. It therefore lacks flexibility, and flexibility accounts for the success of today's information technology. Thus unless neuromorphic engineering happens to be your research area, you are better off, given today's technology, with the more traditional microprocessor solution. But we should closely watch the developments in neuromorphic engineering.

Issues to Think About

Issue 16.1:   Making Design Considerations Explicit

Choose a problem from your own research environment that you have been working on recently. Now look at it from the perspective of what we have said in this chapter. As you will immediately recognize, there are many design issues involved. This is of course true if you have been working with autonomous agents already. But it is also the case if you are, for example, designing psychological experiments. Try to make all the design decision explicit. We suspect that you will be surprised first at how many decisions were actually involved and second at how many assumptions you have made. Moreover, your examination will reveal that design is neither step by step nor top-down: It is very chaotic. But the result is well-structured.

Issue 16.2: Simulation and Real Robots

Take again a problem from your own research. If you are a psychologist, for example, this might be related to category learning or if you are a biologist to ant navigation. Imagine that you are going to investigate certain issues using the autonomous agents approach. Think of how you would go about designing a simulation study. What would the design considerations be? What would they be if you were to employ a real robot for this problem?

Points to Remember

- Design can be formally defined as the creation of synthesized solutions in the form of products, processes, or systems that satisfy perceived needs through the mapping between the functional requirements (what the product is for) in the functional domain and the design parameters in the physical domain (how the product is realized).
- If design is performed by means of artificial evolution, the designer commitments have to be made at a different level. Two essential design decisions concern the encoding in the genome and the fitness function.
- Design is a highly complex process that involves considerations that go way beyond the technical problems involved. They include safety, social, cultural, environmental, esthetic, psychological, market, corporate policy, practicality, and legal considerations. Thus, the design process can be formalized only for restricted, well-defined domains, examples of which are shapes of mechanical parts and logic circuits.
- It is good engineering practice to modularize functions. Although modularization is present to some extent natural systems, a great deal of resource sharing also occurs. If we are interested in understanding natural intelligence, we have to consider the potential for resource sharing.
- As we have argued throughout the book, we should design for emergence. We have to answer the following general design question: Given the functional requirements, the task environment in the case of an agent, how should the agent be designed? Although there is currently no general methodology for design, it is in many cases clear how to proceed. If we had such a methodology, building agents would no longer be of scientific interest: We could simply build them.

- Research questions always have to be translated into task environments. The choice of the task environment strongly influences the low-level design specifications for the agent and the platform (robot hardware or simulation) to be used. The task environment is in turn influenced by considerations concerning evaluation, that is, how the agent will be evaluated later on.

- The choice of platform not only depends on the low-level specifications for the agent but also on considerations about available skills and other resources, costs, ergonomics, and perhaps even esthetic and political concerns. Such considerations may in turn force you to change your task environment and the experiments you had in mind.

- Not only are the design principles we have articulated general guidelines, but they also have a direct influence on choice of sensor and motor systems. When choosing sensors, one has to think about the motor system and evaluation, since these last two may require additional sensors.

- The main types of locomotion on solid ground are driving (wheeled) and walking (legged). Legged locomotion is hard to design properly and still subject to basic research. Wheeled locomotion is much easier to achieve. Unless walking is your research area, you are normally better off using a wheeled agent, always assuming, of course, that you can justify that what you are investigating does not crucially depend on the kind of locomotion.

- Object manipulation is also the subject of current research, especially in embodied cognitive science. The ideal complex manipulators for many of our experiments are currently only available in research labs. Although complex manipulators are desirable to comply with the principle of sensory-motor coordination and ecological balance, even a simple manipulator is helpful: It changes the design focus from sensor-processing to sensory-motor processes.

- Simulation has an advantage over physical agents in that the hardware-related issues of developing an agent can largely be neglected, and all that is needed is a computer to conduct experiments. The trade-off, that is, the disadvantage, is that it is hard to simulate the dynamics of systems with many degrees of freedom realistically.

- The crucial point in choosing an architecture is compliance with the principle of parallel, loosely coupled processes.

- Although formalisms are in principle "neutral," the choice of one influences the kind of system built. Formalisms "suggest" particular ways of proceeding.

- Studying design of autonomous agents directs our attention to the potential complexity of behaving systems and the kinds of abstractions we are making when we simulate only internal, high-level processing (as in the cognitivistic paradigm).
- Neuromorphic engineering proceeds by reproducing functions of the nervous system in analog VLSI. This technology leads to more natural designs that eliminate data buses and digital processors.

Further Reading

Greenbaum, J., and Kyng, M. (Eds.) (1991). *Design at work: Cooperative design of computer systems*. Hillsdale, NJ: Erlbaum Associates. (A collection of papers outlining software design as an interactive process. The principles outlined are of general validity and apply to autonomous agents design as well.)

Jones, J. L., and Flynn, A. M. (1993). *Mobile robots: Inspiration to implementation*. Wellesley, MA: A. K. Peters, Ltd. (This book belongs in any mobile robot laboratory's library. Among other things, it provides a short, compact description of the subsumption architecture.)

Norman, D. A. (1988). *The design of everyday things*. New York: Doubleday. (Previously published as *The psychology of everyday things*.) (Norman argues that the products around us are often poorly designed and introduces the notion of user-centered designs. The book contains many amusing examples and reads easily.)

Petroski, H. (1996). *Invention by design: How engineers get from thought to thing*. Cambridge, MA: Harvard University Press. (Recommended for anyone interested in more than just the technical and physical aspects of the design process. Using case studies from the very simple, like paper clips, to the very complex, like airplanes and buildings, Petroski demonstrates in an entertaining way all the considerations that go into designs, ranging from the very technical, to those of the manufacturing process, to aesthetic, ecological, and cultural ones.)

In this chapter, we address the problem of evaluation. What do we exactly mean by evaluation? When we read papers in the field of autonomous agents, we often encounter phrases like "it works." Although this kind of "gestalt" assessment is certainly valuable and an important part of the research process, it is, scientifically speaking, not quite appropriate. It constitutes a kind of evaluation, but it is not what we are looking for. In contrast to many other scientific fields, such as experimental psychology or biology, there is no generally accepted way to evaluate work in cognitive science. We speculate on the underlying reasons for this situation below. How, then, should an agent's behavior be assessed? How can we tell a good design from a bad one? This chapter addresses that question.

In the last chapter, we saw that some of the major decisions to be made in agent design involve the agent's desired behaviors, its low-level specifications, and the platform on which it will operate. In our discussion, we pointed out that issues of evaluation show up as early as the beginning of the design process, when we have to specify the desired behaviors our agents should exhibit. Evaluation is closely related to the problem of running agent experiments: For these experiments to be useful, we have to know how we want to evaluate an agent's behavior. Evaluation considerations strongly influence how we set up our experiments and the particular experimental factors we want to manipulate. Because of this close relationship between evaluation and agent experiments, this chapter includes a discussion of issues involved in robot experiments.

Evaluation is always conducted with respect to something. There is no "absolute" evaluation; it depends very much on the goals we have in mind. We have pointed out that we can pursue three basic goals with the autonomous agents approach:

1. building a robot for a particular task or a set of tasks
2. studying general principles of intelligence
3. modeling certain aspects of natural systems, that is, humans or animals

In our discussion here, we focus on (2) and (3), because these are the main goals we are pursuing in embodied cognitive science.

We proceed as follows. First, we discuss general considerations in the evaluation of autonomous agents. We then summarize the main characteristics of agent experiments. Next, we examine issues involved in measuring behavior. followed by a look at some additional considerations in the evaluation of agents.

17.1   The Basics of Agent Evaluation

Typically, the autonomous agents that we develop are complex artifacts, and we can expect that their evaluation criteria depend on the goals we have when building them. Even though the goals pursued cannot always be neatly identified and are often mixed, the discussion is structured with respect to the goals of modeling natural systems and using agents to explore general principles of intelligence. The most important criteria for agent evaluation are:

1. Task performance
2. Comparison with natural agents
3. Compliance with design principles
4. Heuristic value
5. Cost-benefit as compared to other approaches

Depending on the particular goals, these criteria are more or less relevant. For example, when developing an agent for a particular task, say garbage collection, we are not interested in whether it mimics a human or an ant. We are interested in its performance on the task: It should do the task better than humans or other machines; it should be cheap, reliable, ecological (in terms of pollution, noise, etc.). Also, compliance with the design principles of autonomous agents is not an issue in this case, whereas when exploring general principles of intelligence or modeling a natural agent, compliance with these principles is crucial. We will take these criteria into account as required in our discussion.

Before we start, a short note is necessary. In this chapter we frequently make reference to the SMC agents introduced in chapter 12. For the purposes of this chapter, it is not necessary to be familiar with the details. We briefly summarize the essential points here. The SMC agents (for sensory-motor coordination) are based on the generic architecture introduced in chapter 5: they have a ring of IR sensors and a gripper for picking up objects. Their task is to learn the distinction between small and large cylinders. Large objects are too heavy to be picked up, only small ones can be lifted. Every time the SMC agent successfully picks up an object, its behavior is reinforced by means of a value signal. It identifies the objects (small or large) by circling around the objects. Initially, it tries to pick up all objects (small and large). Over time, because picking up is successful only for small objects, it learns to ignore the large ones. Moreover, the circling time, the time to identify the type of object, is significantly reduced.

Agent Models of Natural Systems: Synthetic Modeling

CHARACTERIZATION
In previous chapters, we have encountered various examples of how autonomous agents can be used for synthetic modeling, that is, for building models of natural agents. We have discussed, among others, Barbara Webb's robot cricket (chapters 1 and 4), Rodney Brooks's Cog robot (chapter 7), Randy Beer's simulated insect (chapters 8 and 9), Demetri Terzopoulos's artificial fish (chapters 4 and 8), and the Sahabot robot (chapters 4 and 16). In this section, we distill the main characteristics underlying these projects. First and foremost, all are models of natural agents. Models play a fundamental role in science. There is hardly any science that doesn't use models. Models can be formulated in a number of ways, from verbal descriptions to mathematical formalisms. Here we focus on models that have been implemented in an autonomous agent, that is, in a mobile robot. There are some similarities, but also important differences, between agent-based models and more traditional models (e.g., connectionist models) implemented in a computer. Let us first look at some characteristics of models in general.

In essence, models are a particular way of describing, predicting, and explaining behavior, of capturing the essential features of the behavior of interest in a compact way. Models are not just simplifications: They assert that certain aspects are important and others are not. For example, the Sahabot robot—a model of the navigation behavior of the desert ant *Cataglyphis* that we discussed in chapters 4 and 16—implicitly assumes that legs are not crucial to capture the essence of the ant's navigational system: It uses wheels to navigate. In the last chapter, we discussed in some detail why and how such decisions are made. In particular, we saw that both scientific and pragmatic considerations enter the decision process. The important point to be noted here is that a model always abstracts from the system it models, otherwise it would not be a model, but rather an exact duplicate.

Implementing a model in a computer program has several important advantages over natural language or flowchart models. The key advantages are

1. the precision of the model,
2. the claritiy of the underlying assumptions,
3. the ease of judging the model's internal validity, and
4. the relatively unambiguous communication among scientists using the same formal language.

(For a more complete overview, see Taber and Timpone 1996.) The last point holds particularly for agent models: Autonomous agents are, as we hope we have shown in this book, a cognitive vehicle for discussing a large number of concepts concisely and precisely. For example, we can look at the behavior of a Braitenberg vehicle that seems to be attracted to light sources. It looks as though the vehicle "likes" light. Would you call this behavior "emotional"? If so, why? If not, why not? We can look at certain behavioral patterns or at internal states and reason about their relation to what we would call attraction. We can speculate about the minimum requirements such a vehicle must have for us to attribute emotions to it.

We said above that models play a fundamental role in science. In chapter 4, we contrasted classical, computer-based models with agent models. The core difference between these two approaches, we argued, is that in contrast to agent simulations, a computer-based model has no interaction with its environment. For example, it lacks embodiment and situatedness, autonomy and self-sufficiency. Agent models can be thought of as extensions of such computer-based models. Currently the most popular computer-based modeling approach in traditional cognitive science is connectionism. We have presented several instantiations throughout the book, in particular, in chapters 5 and 12. Connectionist models have been formulated for a large number of cognitive phenomena, from pattern recognition to memory. (See, e.g., Quinlan 1991 for a review.) These models are important in that they specify mechanisms underlying these cognitive phenomena. From an embodied cognitive science perspective, it is important that they are embedded in an agent by connecting their input to sensors and their output to the motor system: In other words, they have to have an interface to the world which is provided by embodiment. We have shown that embodiment can be exploited in several ways to reduce the complexity of internal processing.

Agent models do have a potential drawback, however. In contrast to more traditional modeling tools such as mathematical formalisms or connectionist models, agent models typically require a full specification of all the model's parts. For example, we have to decide which type of sensor and motor component to use, even when the model's focus is on something entirely different, say mechanisms of leg coordination. We cannot abstract from the sensory-motor interface. Suppose you want to model how infants perform a sorting task. In an agent model of sorting, we would have to specify the visual processes, the neural mechanisms, and the reaching behavior involved. We would have to decide which type of sensor to use, its resolution, how many degrees of freedom the arm should have, and so forth. But what from among all this is relevant for the observed regularities? What if the model does not produce the desired behavior: Which parts should we change? Consider an alternative model based on a simulated robot model. In a simulation, we can neglect certain aspects that we have to consider when using a real robot. For example, we can simplify the input to the model by using abstract representations of the objects to be sorted, rather than the input from a camera. The problem with the latter approach, however, is that it easily biases thinking: In more abstract models, we tend to neglect the influence of embodiment. An example is the neglect of realistic amounts of noise. One of the main results of the Sahabot project was a new interpretation of how the neurons in the ant's brain exploit sensory signals for navigation. Previous models had only been employed in simulations. Their input consisted of signals generated by a mathematical function that the designer had chosen to mimic the real sensory input. When running experiments with the robot in the ant's actual habitat, the Tunisian desert, it became clear that the signals from the real sensors were not sufficient to control the robot with the required precision using for the mechanisms previously proposed. Upon inspection of these sensory data it further became clear that a different mechanism, based on additional neurons that had so far not been considered to be relevant, had to be at work in the ant. This was referred to as the "triple-unit solution." The authors point out that "if there had been smooth signals available, like those obtained in computer simulations, we would probably not have considered a possible triple-unit solution" (Lambrinos et al. 1997).

The Sahabot project highlights another important advantage of agent models: We can, in principle, test such models in the same environment or experimental setup as the natural agent. This ability is not restricted to insect modeling. For example, we can envision robot models in the psychophysical domain, for example, models of perceptual or attentional processes, that can be tested with the same stimuli presented to the human subjects. (Egner and Scheier 1997 offers an example.) This also simplifies the evaluation of these models, because in addition to the two having the same experimental setup, the same or similar methods can be used to evaluate the model and the natural system. Let us pursue the issue of evaluating agent models a bit further.

EVALUATION

The core question in evaluation is how to tell a good agent model from a bad one. It is generally believed that the most important goal for any scientific statement is that it be true. In practice, this means that we have to assess the correctness or accuracy of our models. The following dimensions of accuracy are usually considered in making such assessments: outcome validity, process validity, internal validity, and reliability (e.g., Taber and Timpone 1996). Let us start with reliability. In essence, reliability means consistency over multiple runs of the model that is, if we run several experiments, the model produces the same or similar behavior each time. Reliability has to be assessed whenever a model is not deterministic that is when different runs of the experiment do not lead to exactly the same behavior, as is the case in agent models: Autonomous agents interact with the real world, which has its own dynamics; their sensors and actuators are subject to a considerable amount of noise, and most fundamentally, their behavior is emergent from their interaction with the world. These aspects of agent models are the main reason why we have to run systematic experiments to evaluate them. We return to these issues in the section on robot experiments below.

A model is *internally valid* if it faithfully represents the theory from which it has been derived. Internal validity relates to a model's intrinsic quality. In embodied cognitive science, the most important way of assessing a model's intrinsic quality is to compare it to the design principles from chapter 10, in particular those concerned with morphology, architecture, and mechanisms. Another aspect of internal validity is the consistency of the model—it should not contain logical errors and contradictions.

One example is the requirement, derived from the design principles, that the agent be cheap. It is not easy to define clearly what cheap means; we made some effort to clarify the term in chapter 13. In modeling jargon, the term "parsimonious" is used: Cheap designs are more "parsimonious" than others. We related this idea to Occam's razor, a generally accepted principle in the philosophy of science. Occam's razor is generally accepted in spite of the fact that parsimony cannot be directly quantified. Another example of a design principle that can be used to assess a robot model's internal validity is the following: We would say that we prefer designs based on value systems, self-organization, and learning to those in which everything is preprogrammed (design principle 3 in chapter 10). We would say this even though in terms of performance, a robot without learning mechanisms might be just as good or even better. We consider agents that embody these design principles to have good designs because we believe, as we stated in chapter 10, that designs based on these principles lead to behaviors we call intelligent. However, this line of argument has a whopper of a problem: It is circular. We have simultaneously argued that designs based on our principles are good because they lead to intelligent behavior by agents and that such agents demonstrate intelligent behavior because our design principles are good. If we apply these design principles to build agents, obviously they will incorporate these principles. Most models, however, do not incorporate all the principles at once. The design principles help to identify those parts of the model that, from an embodied cognitive science perspective, are compatible with our assumptions concerning intelligent behavior. Models that violate a significant number of the design principles, for example, models that employ supervised rather than nonsupervised learning methods, that are based on hierarchical processing or explicit representations of actions rather than parallel, loosely coupled processes, can be said to be less internally valid—from an embodied cognitive science perspective —than others that incorporate these principles.

Another method of assessing a model's internal validity (in particular its consistency is *sensitivity analysis*. When implementing a model, the designer has to make specific choices: He has to choose the parameter values, define the number of neurons, initialize the weights at certain (often random) values, and so forth. In sensitivity analysis, the values of the parameters or other model components (e.g., number of neurons or connectivity in a neural network) are systematically changed to see how the change affects the model's behavior. A good model should be robust with respect to small changes in its parameter values. If we are employing robotic agents, sensitivity analysis is less readily performed, because now the positions of the sensors and the properties of the motor system are also subject to variation. This can make it time consuming to perform sensitivity analysis, but the folklore says that variation at the hardware level is often the reason why robot models do not yield the expected behavior. Thus, special attention must be given to robustness with respect to variations at the hardware level.

After a model's internal validity has been established, we can assess its process and outcome validity. *Process validity* denotes the correspondence between a model's mechanisms and those of the behavior of interest. It is very hard to test directly for process validity; it can usually only be approximated. One approach is to have experts in the field judge the plausibility of the model's processes. Do they seem reasonable to experts in the field? Ideally, one could use a Turing test (see chapter 1): If a model's performance cannot be distinguished from that of the real system by independent human evaluators, the model is considered process valid. Further, something may already be known about the mechanisms that generate the behavior in the real system. In the case of ant navigation (see chapter 4), a lot of pertinent knowledge is actually available (Wehner, Michel, and Antonsen 1996). Remember that the ant uses polarization sensors to derive compass information. We can use this as a constraint on our model by specifying that the model, in some sense, should reflect this mechanism.

Finally, we can assess a model's *outcome validity*. Outcome validity concerns the degree of correspondence between a model's predictions and the behavior of the real agent. Ideally, the model should not only account for data from experiments that have already been conducted (from which its outcomes are in fact not real predictions), but also predict how the system will behave in a number of different conditions. The model's most interesting predictions concern situations in which the natural agent has not been tested. This seems very natural and straightforward: When the model's behavior is close enough to the real behavior, the model is outcome valid. There is a problem, however: Many different models can predict the same kinds of behavior. This fact is also known as Moore's Law (Moore 1956). It implies that pure behavioral performance measures are not sufficient for assessing the quality of a model. A similar conclusion has been put forward by Oreskes, Shrader-Frechette, and Belitz in their important paper on how to evaluate models:

If we compare a result predicted by a model with observational data and the comparison is unfavorable, then we know that something is wrong, and we may or may not be able to determine what it is. Typically, we continue to work on the model until we achieve a fit. But if a match between the model result and observational data is obtained, then we have, ironically, a worse dilemma. More than one model construction can produce the same output. This situation is referred to by philosophers as underdetermination. Model results are always underdetermined by the available data. Two or more constructions that produce the same results may be said to be empirically equivalent. If two theories (or model realizations) are empirically equivalent, then there is no way to choose between them other than invoke extraevidential considerations like symmetry, simplicity, and elegance, or personal, political, or metaphysical preference. (1994, p. 642)

The problem of undertermination is inherent in all modeling efforts. Thus, as Oreskes and colleagues suggest, additional criteria have to be applied. We have already mentioned some of the most important ones: reliability, internal validity, cost-benefit compared to other modeling approaches, and compliance with design principles. Below we discuss another: the heuristic value of models; that is, one important value of models is that they help generate new ideas on the behavior and mechanisms of natural agents.

Studying General Principles of Intelligence

So far, we have been discussing the characteristics of agent-based modeling. In cognitive science, and particularly in AI, one often thinks of a model's behavior not only in terms of specific empirical phenomena, but also as a phenomenon in its own right.

CHARACTERISTICS
We can study on autonomous agent's behavior without relating that behavior to some particular empirical phenomenon, although, in

general, we always try at least to relate its behavior to what is known about related phenomena in the empirical sciences. For example, the SMC agents presented in chapter 12 are not models in the strict sense of the term; that is, they do not try to account for a certain set of data from particular categorization experiments. Rather, they capture our hypotheses about categorization in general. We can study the SMC agents as psychologists study infants: We can ask specific questions about their behavior, we can test their performance on a number of tasks, we can test their limitations by presenting them with difficult tasks, and so on. Such agents are actually categorizing their world; they are not just modeling categorization. The mechanisms we provide are the only means these agents can use to perform their tasks. We are not interested, however, in just any mechanism leading to categorization behavior. Rather, we focus on those mechanisms that can also be observed in natural agents. For example, we can look at the literature in developmental psychology and try to incoporate into our system those aspects that have been shown to be crucial in infant categorization. In some respects a real robot faces problems similar to those of an infant: It is faced with a continuously changing stream of input from a three-dimensional world that has its own dynamics. When thinking about mechanisms by which the agent could confront this task, we have often realized that our ideas turned out to be similar, if not identical, to the principles discovered in, for example, developmental psychology.

EVALUATION

How should we evaluate agents that model general principles of intelligence? We have said that their main value is to illustrate a way of thinking about and tackling a particular problem. In other words, we mainly evaluate these agents by assessing their heuristic value. Do they further our understanding of a particular problem? Do they lead to new ways of thinking about a problem? Do they inspire others to implement similar solutions? Do they inspire psychologists or biologists to think differently about their data? We judge the quality of designs, then, by estimating the insights we have gained from implementing them. We hope we have shown throughout the book that autonomous agents have enormous potential in this respect. They make us ask questions that other approaches have not addressed. A fundamental question that emerged in the studies involving the SMC agents was how categories are linked with actual behavior: How should we represent sensory and motor processes so that they lead to categorization behavior? Where are categories represented in such a system? Where are the invariances that underlie these agents' categorization behavior? Standard connectionist models do not have to address these questions, because their output does not result in actual behavior. Categories are represented in the output layer, and categorization terminates when a node is activated corresponding to the category to which the input is known to belong. We could go on for a long time with examples of questions that are unique to agent implementations, but instead we stress again the impressive heuristic value of autonomous agents for cognitive science research.

In addition to assessing the heuristic value of an agent implementation we have to consider the cost and benefit compared to those of other approaches, in particular simulations. Does it make sense to use a real robot in our research, or can the same insights be gained with a simulation? We addressed this question in chapter 4, where we listed the advantages and disadvantages of using real and simulated robots. We said, for example, that a problem in using simulated robots is that many aspects of the real world are very hard to simulate.

Consider, for example, the humanoid robot Cog. Imagine the effort involved in building even a moderately realistic simulation of this robot! We also argued, however, that despite these difficulties, simulations are important in various respects. Now that we have seen additional examples of simulated agents, let us briefly pick up again our discussion of chapter 4 weighing the advantages and disadvantages of real versus simulated agents. Recall, for example, the case studies of Beer (1996) and Nolfi (1996) that we presented in chapter 12, which showed that simulated evolutionary processes can result in categorization mechanisms very similar to the ones we have identified in our experiments with real robots. Moreover, in simulation we can test very rapidly a large number of different morphologies and their influence on the resulting categorization behavior. When running experiments on real robots, on the other hand, we are constrained by the available hardware. Since we are interested in embodiment, it is of value to explore in simulation how categorization behavior results when different shapes, for example, of a rectangular, circular, or asymmetric shape, are used. Moreover, we can freely position the sensors and motor components on a simulated agent and explore how this affects the resulting sensory-motor coordination. All this does not, of course, diminish the role of real robots in embodied cognitive science. As the type of robots in which we are interested become more complex, it grows progressively harder to write realistic simulators for them. In conclusion, whether one uses a real or a simulated robot to study general principles of intelligence largely depends on the particular research issues, and practical aspects such as the availablity of a hardware platform.

Independent of the particular platform one chooses and the particular goal one pursues when building an agent, at some point one has to actually run experiments. In what follows, we introduce some important issues that have to be considered when performing agent experiments.

17.2 Performing Agent Experiments

We have said that the type of evaluation one conducts depends on the goal one pursues when building an agent. Irrespective of whether one studies general principles of intelligence, formulates a model of a natural agent, or designs an agent for a particular application, certain general aspects of evaluation need to be taken seriously. In particular, in all three approaches to agent design we must run experiments with our agents to assess their value. This section summarizes the main issues that emerge when performing experiments with agents (simulated or physical). The first issue addressed is why we should run experiments in the first place. We then describe different types of experiments one can conduct. Finally, we look more closely at the various ways behavior can be measured.

Why Systematic Agent Experiments?

Looking at the literature in embodied cognitive science reveals that for the most part, research papers focus on a particular approach or implementation thereof but rarely present data from more than one run, if at all. Papers that evaluate a particular agent architecture by means of statistical analyses are the exception. This situation is not specific to embodied cognitive science, of course. In his survey of 150 papers in the *Proceedings of the Eighth National Conference on Artificial Intelligence* (1990), Cohen (1995) discovered that only 42 percent of the papers suggested a program had been run on more than one example; only 30 percent assessed performance in some way; and just 21 percent formulated hypotheses or made predictions. This situation is in sharp contrast to that in empirical sciences such as biology and psychology, where most papers present extensive statistical analyses in support of their hypotheses. What is the underlying reason for this lack of evaluation in the synthetic approaches? Consider Newell and Simon's perspective:

Each new program that is built is an experiment. It poses a question on nature, and its behavior offers clues to an answer. Neither machines nor programs are black boxes; they are artifacts that have been designed, both hardware and software; and we can open them up and look inside. We can relate their structure to their behavior and draw many lessons from a single experiment. We don't have to build 100 copies of, say, a theorem prover, to demonstrate statistically that it has not overcome the combinatorial explosion of search in the way hoped for. Inspection of the program in the light of a few runs reveals the flaw and lets us proceed to the next attempt. (1976, p. 114).

To a large extent this point also holds for agent experiments: A lot can be learned from a very few runs performed on a robot. If a flaw is detected (e.g., the robot keeps running into walls), there is no need to carry out additional experiments with the same agent; we know that something must be changed. However, in contrast to classical AI, there is still a need to perform systematic experiments: First, as has been stressed repeatedly throughout this book, behavior cannot be reduced to internal mechanism. In other words, by looking at the source code of even the simplest Braitenberg vehicle, we cannot predict in a deterministic way how the system will behave in different environmental situations. The implication is that we have to resort to statistical methods to characterize an agent's behavior, for a number of reasons: Realistic environments have their own dynamics, making an agent's behavior a complex function of the underlying mechanism, the current environmental situation, and their coupling. Second, sensors and motor system are always subject to noise. Third, as our models grow more complicated, it becomes harder to predict how they will behave in a given environment, in particular when learning is involved. Moreover, a significant number of parameters are typically involved, and we can usually only guess how a particular parameter configuration affects an agent's behavior. For example, the choice of the learning and decay rates in a neural network-based architecture dramatically affects the resulting perfomance, and most of these effects are not fully predictable.

On the other hand, an agent's behavior must show *some* regularities, otherwise the agent would be useless in the first place. Except in trivial cases, though, behavior cannot be characterized deterministically, but rather has to be assessed in a probabilistic way. Because of this nondeterministic nature of behavior, we have to rely on statistical methods to measure an agent's performance on a given task. An architecture must be tested by performing multiple runs in a number of different environmental settings, parameter configurations, and tasks, which implies that studying a synthetic agent's behavior is similar to studying that of natural agents. Therefore, we can and should take advantage of the sophisticated methodological tools developed in the empirical sciences to measure behavior. Both natural and artificial agents share the important property that their behavior can only be described probabilistically. Accepting these similarities does not deny the differences between empirical and synthetic studies, however. As we show below, in contrast to what is possible in most studies in the empirical sciences, we can simultaneously look at and record both the internal dynamics of a synthetic agent (e.g., neural network activations, evolution of weight patterns) and its behavior. In this way, autonomous agents offer an important advantage: They allow us to investigate the relationship between internal dynamics and external behavior.

Once one accepts that behavior must be measured in systematic ways, one can begin to ask how such measurements should be made. What strategies should one adopt? What types of measures should be considered? How can these measures be assessed statistically? In what follows, we look at each of these issues in turn.

Types of Experiments

There are two broad classes of experiments: exploratory and confirmatory. The term "exploratory" is used in two rather different ways. In the autonomous agent context, the term is often used informally to designate the rapid development and testing of agents. In statistics, it has a technical meaning that we elaborate on in this section. Cohen (1995) compares exploratory experiments to a test kitchen and confirmatory experiments to recipes in cook books. Typically, one starts with exploratory experiments before more precise questions can be addressed by means of confirmatory studies. The goal of exploratory studies, then, is to identify specific features of the architecture (or model in general) by collecting, visualizing, and analyzing large sets of data from different experimental conditions. Such studies typically analyze the resulting data in a number of different ways to find relevant invariances. Exploratory data analysis does not simply consist of applying statistical methods, but instead crucially involves conceptual work that guides the quantitative analysis: What variables should be considered? How should they be measured? At what level of resolution? How should they be analyzed? These questions have no general answers. Rather, one has to try out a number of different measurements and different ways of looking at the data before satisfactory results can be found. An important part of this process are *pilot experiments*, which explore different parameter settings in an informal way. Before actually collecting massive amounts of data and investing a lot time in analyzing them, it is often useful to run the system, sometimes in a simplified version, a number of times to get a feel for its behavior in different parameter settings and environmental situations. This is a highly interactive process whereby an agent is tested, refined, tested again, and so forth until a solution is found that seems worth exploring and analyzing in more detail. To be sure, even when such a solution has been found, the process is not linear. Rather, one usually refines the architecture on the fly, incorporating new parts or throwing away parts that have been found to be either wrong or superfluous. We saw in chapter 16 that this iterative process is characteristic of agent design in general.

Let us now look at confirmatory studies, the kind of studies most often conducted in the empirical sciences. We summarize only the main ideas here. In contrast to the paucity of literature on exploratory experiments, a large number of textbooks exist on how to perform confirmatory experiments: what methods to choose, their requirements and assumptions, and so on. Cohen (1995, chapters 4 and 5) offers a nice review of the most important techniques, including more recent ones such as bootstrap methods, as well as their applications to examples from (traditional) AI.

In essence, confirmatory studies test precise hypotheses about the effects of certain factors on specific results. Assume, for example, that you have built two agents, A and B, that play soccer against each other. Agent A wins ten and loses three out of fifteen games, the remaining two games being undecided. One statistic that characterizes this situation is the sample proportion of games A has won, $p = .67$. The fundamental question in statistical terms is whether this result is representative for agent A's general capability to win over B, or whether this result has occurred by chance. In other words, we want to know whether agent A is *in general* a better soccer player than agent B. To answer this question definitely, we would have to have the two agent's play a very large number of soccer games, which would be very time consuming. A better way would be to estimate how well the result obtained in a small number of experiments, 15 in the example above, approximates the "true" result, that is, the result obtained from a very large number of experiments. Let us denote by the symbol T the "true" proportion of games A would win in a very large number of games. We can now ask specific questions about the performance of our agents based on our much smaller sample of games. For example, we can test the hypothesis that one agent is a better soccer player than the other as follows. First, we assume that they are actually equally good, that is, that T equals .5: Both agents have the same chance of winning. We have already run 15 experiments and observed that the proportion of games A won was $p = .67$. We can now assess the probability that this result occurs, given $T = .5$. If this probability is very small—if it is very unlikely that A would win two-thirds of the games against B if they are equal in soccer ability—we can reject our assumption that $T = .5$ and that the two agents play soccer equally well. Much more could be said about hypothesis testing (see any textbook in statistics, or consult Cohen 1995), but for our purposes it suffices to stress the point that only by testing results statistically can we really judge the value of these results. For example, assume that you read a paper describing two soccer-playing agents and presenting as the main result the observed proportion of games won by A, say $p = .67$. How could you assess whether this result was due to chance or whether it represented a significant difference in the two agents' soccer-playing capabilities? Without more information, you couldn't: The result could have been obtained on the basis of as few as three games, with one agent winning two out of the three.

17.3 Measuring Behavior

We have now discussed various aspects that have to be considered when running experiments with agents. There is one important issue that we have not addressed: how to actually measure behavior.

Preliminaries

Measuring behavior is a nontrivial task. What constitutes behavior? Which aspects should be measured to assess an architecture's or an entire agent's quality? Consider again the Sahabot project. Should the agent involved perform the full spectrum of navigation behaviors: leaving the nest, foraging, going back to the nest in a straight line, using landmark navigation near the nest? Should we start with one part only, say foraging? We have already touched on these issues in chapter 16. There we asked how we should compare the agent's behavior with that of the ant. For example, how should we account for the potential differences in size? If we build an agent to model certain aspects of a human infant's reaching behavior, should the agent manipulate exactly the same types of objects as the infant? Would that make sense, given that it has a very different sensory-motor system than the human infant? Is it necessary to actually reproduce psychological experiments, or can we generally run category learning experiments on the robot and still say something relevant about humans?

These issues have no straightforward solution. Note, however, that such considerations are already part of the research process. The better we understand what the important factors are in the behavior of the agent we want to study, the better we know what parts of that behavior the agent model should reproduce and what parts of the resulting behavior should be measured. For example, if we knew that the type of object is irrelevant for the reaching behavior in human infants, it would then be safe to assume that we could choose any type of object in our agent experiments. A very important advantage of building agent models is that we are forced to ask such questions in the first place. The questions we ask when we are trying to build an agent model can themselves be valuable for the experimentalists, because they are derived from a different, synthetic perspective.

In sum, then, building an agent model and measuring its behavior involve asking fundamental questions about the nature of the task and agent being modeled. In the following discussion, we

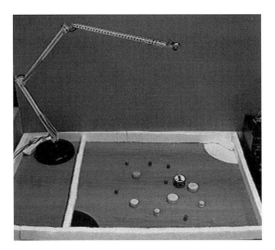

Figure 17.1 Robot movement tracking system using a wide-angle lens. A video camera is mounted on a stand, facing down over the desk. The robot has to be marked to facilitate its tracking.

assume that these questions have somehow been answered and that we are in a position to measure the behavior of a complete agent built either to study aspects of a natural agent or to study general principles of intelligence. The first issue then becomes: What tools can we use to measure behavior?

Tools

Measuring the behavior of an autonomous agent involves two aspects, in rough terms: recording the trajectories of the agent, or aspects thereof (e.g., heading directions, distance traveled, arm movement), and recording the internal dynamics (e.g., process activations, network activations, weight patterns, energy levels, sensor activations, motor speeds, joint angles, forces on limbs). Let us first look at how trajectories can be recorded.

Recording the details of an agent's trajectories involves taking a "bird's eye" view of its behavior. A simple tracking system such as the one illustrated in figure 17.1 can accomplish this. In this particular setup, which is by no means the best solution to the problem, a video camera is mounted on a stand or the ceiling and faces down on the desk. The camera is focused on the agent's current position. Two approaches for tracking the agent's trajectories can be used. First, a camera with a wide-angle lens can be employed to capture the entire environment. In that case, the robot is always in the camera's field of view. Second, an active vision system (see chapter 12) can be used that follows the robot. From the resulting gaze angles of the camera, the trajectory of the robot can be reconstructed.

Making a tracking device operate reliably thus involves some effort, but once the selected algorithms work, we have an excellent opportunity of measuring all aspects of an agent's behavior. The next step is to process the raw image data using a program that extracts the agent's trajectory, that is, the sequence of (x, y) coordinates, or in the case of flying or underwater vehicles, the sequence of (x, y, z) coordinates. The resulting data can then be used to check whether the robot indeed does what it is supposed to do. Figure 17.2c shows an example of such a trajectory.

Once the data have been recorded, they are open for any kind of analysis. We discuss some of the more common types below. In addition to behavioral data, we can and should record values of internal variables. In principle, and this is an important difference from empirical studies of natural agents, we can store every single internal state of the robot, from motor speeds to activations in a neural network. One important practical issue is that the recording of the internal variables has to be synchronized with the trajectory data. This involves marking the data with time stamps indicating at what time step a particular portion of the trajectory and the corresponding internal variables were recorded. Trajectories are usually recorded by camera, as just described. Images of the camera are "grabbed" with a so-called frame grabber. Frames have to be grabbed at a certain frequency, for example, 30 frames per second. Two issues have to be considered with respect to this frequency. First, it should be matched with the robot's speed. If the robot is fast, we have to grab frames at a higher frequency. Some robots, such as Khepera, move at a relatively low speed, in which case lower frequencies suffice. We want to grab frames fast enough to record all relevant changes in the robot's behavior, but we do not want to do it too fast, because then we "oversample" the behavior, resulting in unnecessary storage of identical frames. Second, a problem arises when the agent's internal variables change more frequently than we can sample images with the frame grabber. In this case, we cannot really synchronize the internal variables with a particular point in the robot's trajectory. The frequency with which the frame grabber operates therefore constitutes an upper bound for the temporal resolution at which we can compare

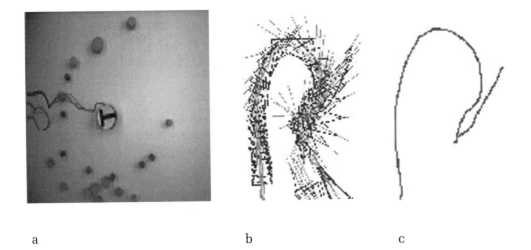

a   b   c

Figure 17.2 Recording robot behavior: (a) raw camera picture; (b) trajectory with direction of robot; (c) plain trajectory.

internal data to behavioral data. In such cases, we usually interpolate the high-frequency variables between different frames. It should be noted, however, that in most applications, in particular those involving large neural networks, frames grabbed at a reasonable frequency, say 30 frames per second, are sufficient, because the internal processing itself is time consuming. In general, the trajectory-recording device has to be tuned so as to yield sensible results, the main constraints being the speed of the internal processing and the resulting behavior. Let us now look in more detail at the issues involved in measuring behavior.

Measures of Behavior

Storing all possible data generated by the agent can lead to data files of significant size. We emphasized, in our discussion of the steps involved in running agent experiments (table 4.5), that it is important to formulate predictions (hypotheses) before the experiments are run. Deciding what types of variables to record is like looking at an agent's behavior through various lenses: Sometimes, we are interested only in global variables such as distance traveled or number of objects collected; at other times our focus might be more on the underlying internal dynamics, in which case we can focus on the particular weight patterns that have evolved in a neural network or examine the time series of a network's activations.

Ideally, we should consider all aspects involved in explaining the behavior being studied. Recall that there are three different time perspectives that can be applied to explain a given behavior (see chapter 4): short-term, ontogenetic, and phylogenetic. With respect to measuring behavior, the implication is that the particular perspective we adopt and the specific variables we measure crucially depend on our research goal, and on the particular theoretical position we prefer. The following discussion is therefore meant only to highlight the most common measures and by no means provides a comprehensive list of possible measures of behavior.

The core question in assessing an agent's performance is whether it works. Several aspects have to be addressed in answering this question. For example, an agent might learn just about everything in its environment, but it might take it days to do so, whereas another agent might learn only certain specific aspects and consume about half the time to solve its task. Which one should be preferred? The more accurate one or the faster one? Again, there is no straightforward answer, because it depends on one's aims with the robot, not how one measures its performance. The most frequent questions asked to assess the performance of an agent are how fast, how accurate, and how efficient the agent is in solving its task. The answers to these questions are only the first step in a true evaluation of an agent's behavior. The next steps, then, involve correlating internal and sensory-motor states with behavioral data (the trajectories) in order to generate explanations of the behavior. This can be done in the short term, or over extended periods of time, as required in learning experiments.

Recall that the latter involves relating the agent's actual behavior to events that have happened in the past. Since the data about the agent's past, internal and behavioral, have all been recorded, such explanations can now be generated.

The simplest and most often used assessments of performance are *descriptive statistics*. The most common examples are simple visualization techniques such as frequency histograms (counting how often a certain value occurred) and scatterplots (plotting several variables against each other). Another approach, equally simple, is to compute the mean, standard deviation, and variance over a number of experiments. For example, we can compute the mean number of times an agent has reached a target location in, say, 50 runs of 3 minutes each. Or we can calculate an agent's mean categorization accuracy. Assume, for example, that we have established a particular agent's mean accuracy to be 85 percent; that is, it categorized 85 percent of the objects it encountered correctly. We still cannot tell whether this result is better than one achieved by a different agent without applying the statistical inference process discussed above. Nevertheless, such descriptive statistics allow us to assess the robustness or reliability of an agent's behavior provided we compute, in addition to the mean, the standard deviation over all runs. If the standard deviation is very large (e.g., as large as the mean itself), we know that the robot behaved very differently in the different runs. Thus, its behavior is not reliable in the statistical sense.

Take our SMC I agent introduced in chapter 12. It had to learn how to distinguish between objects of different sizes. To quantify this learning process, we used the following performance measures: We measured the time the agent spent circling around the different types of objects before engaging in the appropriate behavior. Measurements were taken at the beginning of a trial and after the agent had encountered 10 objects. Our hypothesis was that once the categories were acquired, that is, the agent could distinguish between small and large objects, the agent would need significantly less time to categorize the objects. To assess the reliability of the agent's behavior, measures were taken over 50 runs. In essence, our hypothesis was confirmed: The number of steps the agent circled around objects decreased after learning had taken place. But was this decrease significant in the statistical sense? More specifically, were the two means significantly different? Again, we can tell only by applying statistical tests. Note that these results do not tell us why the robot solved the problem. Rather, they indicate that its behavior was robust; that is, the results were similar in the 50 runs (indicated by the small standard deviations we calculated). Moreover, the results do not allow us to judge whether this particular agent was better or worse than an agent with a different architecture. To determine that, we would need to compare this particular agent with other agents that solve the same problem, i.e., perform an analysis similar to the one concerning the two (hypothetical) soccer-playing robots discussed earlier.

Another important evaluation step is comparing a robot's behavior to some external standard. In most agents used to study general principles of intelligence, such external standard is not available. In some cases, we have two different implementations to achieve the same task which we can compare. In the case of agent models, however, we can use the natural agent's behavior as an external standard to which we can compare the robot's behavior. In other words, we can assess the agent's outcome validity. We have already pointed out that this is particularly interesting in the context of agent models because we can test the model and the natural agent in the same environment, and in addition use the same methods and tools to measure their behavior. This was done, for example, in the Sahabot project and in Barbara Webb's experiments on cricket phonotaxis that we discussed in chapter 4.

Finally, let us address some other ways to measuring an agent's behavior. Given our focus on system-environment interaction, it would be interesting to know something about the relation between a robot's internal mechanisms and its behavior. Smithers (1995) viewed the agent-environment system as a dynamical system in the sense of the mathematical theory (see chapter 9). He suggested taking the amount of time (in milliseconds) the agent spent with motors in forward mode (rather than in turn or reverse mode) as an "interaction variable." Though it is an internal variable, it is a characteristic of the interaction. If the environment offers no obstacles, this variable is much larger than if it has a lot of obstacles and impasses, forcing the motors to stop or to go into reverse mode. Although potentially interesting, it is not obvious from Smithers' research where this kind of analysis will go and what it actually tells us.

Although perhaps limited at the moment, Smithers' analysis opens an interesting new direction for methods of evaluation. A large number of methods are being developed in the dynamical systems community (e.g., Scheier and Tschacher 1996). At least some may well prove useful in investigating the dynamical structure of autonomous agents' behavior. Let us look at another example in which dynamical systems theory is used in a different way for evaluation, namely for a qualitative characterization of behavior. In chapter 9, we discussed Beer's analysis of evolved leg controllers. Beer suggested employing concepts like point attractors and limit cycles to describe the behavior. The advantage of this kind of qualitative assessment is that it does not rely on strong assumptions and is based directly on the behavioral data. Its disadvantage is that for reasons of visualization, we can work with only a very few dimensions. Since problems are often of high dimensionality, by looking only at a few dimensions, we may miss important aspects of the dynamics.

One of the essential goals of any method of evaluation is to test the limitations of a particular design. This can be accomplished by systematically varying the environment, for example the density of obstacles or the size of the objects to be collected, then listing the cases in which the desired behaviors are clearly present and when they cease to be displayed. Although this kind of analysis is important, it is limited to situations the agent has encountered in the experiments. But there are ways in which certain predictions can be made not only on the basis of the empirical evidence, but also on the basis of theoretical reflection. Given a spherical object, if the opening of the agent's gripper is smaller than the diameter of the sphere, it is not able to grasp the sphere: We do not need to conduct the experiment to determine this.

In conclusion, evaluation is not a simple matter in which a fixed scheme can be followed, but a complex task. It is hard, and it requires a lot of creativity and thinking, as well as a combination of quantitative and qualitative methods.

Issues to Think About

Issue 17.1: Total Turing Test

In chapter 1 we introduced the idea of the Turing test. Harnad (1995), who elaborated the symbol-grounding problem that we discussed in chapter 3, suggested an extension of the Turing test for autonomous agents. He suggests that an agent "should be able to discriminate, manipulate, categorize, name, describe and discourse about the real-world objects, events, and state of affairs that its symbols[1] are about; it should be able to do so Turing indistinguishably from the way we do." (p. 280). Harnad called this test the Total Turing Test, and he suggests it can be used to evaluate an agent's intelligence. What do you think such a test would have to look like? What precisely would an agent have to do to pass this test? Is it a sensible test in the first place?

Issue 17.2: Explanation of Behavior

We have discussed a considerable number of ways to evaluate an agent's behavior. One of the important goals of the methods dis-

---

[1] Note that Harnad does not dismiss the idea of symbols, but rather suggests that they should be grounded in an agent's interaction with the world. We have argued that the symbol-grounding problem is really an artifact of symbolic systems and "disappears" if a different approach is used.

cussed is to improve the understanding of the behavior and ultimately to explain it. For example, when we conduct sensitivity
analysis, we systematically explore in what ways the agent's behavior changes if we change a parameter, for example, the learning
rate of its neural network. Alternatively, we can systematically vary
the agent's ecological niche, for example, by varying the changes
and shapes of the objects an agent has to sort. More generally, scientists conduct experiments to explain behavior. What would you
accept as a good explanation of behavior? What would it have to
include? And most fundamentally, what constitutes an explanation
of behavior in the first place? Does it have to include the type of
evaluation suggested in this chapter or are additional ingredients
needed? If so, what are they?

Points to Remember

- The most important criteria for agent evaluation are: Performance
  on a task, comparison with natural agents, compliance with design
  principles, heuristic value, and cost-benefit as compared with other
  approaches.
- Models, agent or otherwise, are a certain way of describing, predicting, and explaining the behavior of a natural agent, of capturing
  the essential features of the behavior of interest in a compact way.
  Models are not just simplifications: They assert that certain aspects
  are important and others are not.
- Key advantages of computer program models over verbal descriptions or flowchart models are (1) the model's precision, (2) the
  clarity of its underlying assumptions, (3) the ease with which
  the model's internal validity can be judged, and (4) the relatively
  unambiguous communication it makes possible among scientists
  using the same formal language.
- The main difference between agent models and computer-based
  models is that the latter have no means of interacting with the
  environment because they lack embodiment. By contrast, in agent
  models all parts have to be fully specified, and abstractions are
  harder to make than in computer-based models.
- One aspect of a model's evaluation involves the assessment of its
  accuracy. The most important dimensions of accuracy are outcome
  validity, process validity, internal validity, and reliability. Outcome
  validity refers to the correspondence between a model's behavior
  (its outcome) and the behavior of the system it is intended to

model. Process validity is established when a model's mechanism corresponds to the real system's mechanism. Internal validity is high if the model faithfully represents the theory from which it has been derived. (This includes the internal, logical consistency of the model). Reliability means consistency over multiple runs of the model.

- One fundamental problem in establishing a model's outcome validity is underdetermination, that is, the fact that two or more models can sometimes produce the same results. If the models are empirically equivalent, then additional criteria such as parsimony, reliability, internal validity, cost-benefit ratio compared to other approaches, and compliance with the design principles have to be applied.

- We evaluate agents designed to explore general principles of intelligence mainly by assessing their heuristic value and cost-benefit as compared to other approaches. In addition, however, we have to assess an agent's performance, that is, how well it can actually perform its task.

- Because of behavior's nondeterminism, we have to rely on statistical methods to measure an agent's performance in a given task, implying that studying the behavior of a synthetic agent is similar to studying that of natural agents. We can and should take advantage of the sophisticated methods developed in the empirical sciences to measure behavior.

- There are exploratory and confirmatory experiments. Exploratory studies identify specific features of the model by collecting, visualizing, and analyzing large sets of data from different experimental conditions. An important part of this process is pilot experiments, in which different parameter settings are explored in an informal way. Confirmatory studies test precise hypotheses about the effect of certain factors on specific results.

- Measuring the behavior of an autonomous agent involves two main aspects: (1) recording the trajectories of the agent or aspects thereof and (2) recording the internal dynamics. Recording the details of an agent's trajectories involves taking a bird's-eye view of its behavior by means of a tracking system. These data must be synchronized with the data about internal dynamics.

- The most frequent questions asked to assess the performance of an agent are how fast, how accurate, and how efficient the agent is at performing its task. The simplest and most often used assessments of performance are descriptive statistics. The most common examples are simple visualization techniques such as frequency histograms and scatterplots.

- An important evaluation step is to compare a robot's behavior to some external standard. In the case of agent models, we can use the natural agent's behavior when exploring general principles of intelligence, such a standard is normally not available.

Further Reading

Cohen, P. R. (1995). *Empirical methods for artificial intelligence.* Cambridge, MA: MIT Press. (An excellent overview of the most important statistical methods using examples from (traditional) artificial intelligence.)

Oreskes, N., Shrader-Frechette, K., and Belitz, K. (1994). Verification, validation, and confirmation of numerical models in the earth sciences. *Science, 263,* 641–646. (Definition and critical review of various concepts in relation to evaluating the quality of models.)

Taber, C. S., and Timpone, R. J. (1996). *Computational Modeling.* Sage Thousand Oakes, CA: Sage University Papers. (A review of the main issues involved in evaluating computational models.)

VI Future Directions

Having covered a lot of rough and messy territory, having studied many examples, approaches, principles, and theoretical concepts, we attempt, in this last part of the book, to bring the large variety of topics and issues together, to point the way toward future developments, and to examine how our view of intelligence has changed since the beginning of the book. Initially, we outlined various intuitive notions of intelligence, we gave a number of definitions, and we characterized the commonalities of the various concepts. The issue that we want to explore here is what we see differently now, what questions we would ask in another way or what new questions would we ask now, and what kinds of explanations we are looking for now. Where do we feel that the most pressing research topics are, and where are the most crucial technological problems that must be resolved, so that progress can be made? For example, we know that fast computer hardware is not the major factor: Since we now know about the importance of embodiment, other aspects are more important, like the development of affordable robots with sophisticated sensory-motor systems. The development of applications is also a concern here. If we can in fact build intelligent machines in the form of autonomous agents, we should also be able to develop sophisticated applications, and indeed the potential for novel types of applications seems almost unlimited. These kinds of applications may have a major impact on society. But it is not only in applications where we see an impact. We also feel that embodied cognitive science may change the way we think not only about intelligence, but about human nature in general. For this change in thinking to take place, these ideas need to be spread, need to be made available to a wide audience.

Research directions, necessary theoretical and technological developments, and applications of strategic importance are discussed in chapter 18. Chapter 19 outlines the first steps toward a theory of intelligence and the ramifications of such a theory in society, today and tomorrow.

In this chapter we outline some research directions in which we think the field of embodied cognitive science should go. We also discuss a number of applications and projects that suggest ways autonomous agents might become part of our society. How the field will evolve largely depends on certain developments. First, existing limitations have to be overcome, and the hard problems in the field have to be addressed, including basic research involving both theoretical and technological advances. If theoretical advances are to be made, the appropriate tools have to be available, which necessitates technological progress. Second, the framework and methodology of embodied cognitive science needs to be made accessible to a broad audience. This again requires both theoretical and technological advances. A number of books have recently been or are currently being published that make the field attainable to a wide audience beyond the researchers actively involved in the field. Examples include Franklin 1995; O' Nuallain 1995; Hendriks-Jansen 1996; Arkin 1998; Brooks and Breazeal in press; and, of course, this book. In terms of technology, flexible, cheap, and easy to handle robot platforms are needed. By analogy to Bill Gates's slogan "computers for the masses," we think that "agents for the masses" are required that enable a large number of people to work with real robots to study principles of intelligence.

We begin with a discussion of some of the hard research problems that need to be resolved if the field is to make significant progress. Then we consider the interaction between theory development and technology. We then move on to describing applications that have great potential.

18.1 Hard Problems

Before we start, a disclaimer is in order. The following hard problems represent those that the authors consider, from a larger selection of hard problems, to be of general importance to the field of embodied cognitive science. Moreover, although we have tried to make a coherent argument, the hard problems we discuss are at various levels of abstraction, from the very detailed to the much more abstract. We nevertheless hope that the following discussion provides some inspiration for productive research topics. This section contains material mostly of interest to active researchers and may be skipped without losing the thread of the argument.

Embodied cognitive science capitalizes on building autonomous agents as its main methodology. Throughout the book, but specifically in the previous chapter, we tried to sketch how agent experiments can be conducted in productive and systematic ways. We hope we have shown that the methodology is indeed productive and powerful, but it needs to be further developed. For example, how can neurobiologists use autonomous agents to explore brain function in a behavior context? How can psychologists design new types of synthetic experiments to complement existing empirical research? What is needed to embed currently existing models into autonomous agents? From a model-theoretic perspective, it will be interesting to see how these models can be used to generate actual behavior. Many models are suggestions of mechanisms for various types of behaviors, but often they are tested only in simulated worlds. Autonomous agents are the methodology for providing these models with an interface to the real world. In addition, it is necessary to develop appropriate metrics to compare such extended models to empirical data. Let us now turn to some hard problems that emerged in our discussion of the design principles.

In our discussion of cheap designs in chapter 13 we mentioned that often shape—morphology—can be traded for computation (or neural processing): If the appropriate shapes are used (e.g., of an eye), computation may be reduced by orders of magnitude. The trade-off is less flexibility. In fact, there are two fundamental issues here. First, there is a question as to when it makes sense in general for an agent to embody more capabilities in the morphology and when flexibility is required. Second, the morphology does not have to be fixed once and for all. Living beings can change their shape, and depending on the shape, they can perform different functions. A hand that is first open and then closed can be used for grasping, a fist is good for hitting, or a slightly bent hand can be used for typing. The question now becomes where to have rigid structure, where to have changing shapes, and where flexibility at the neural level is required. We can actively explore these issues in experimental studies. For example, we can ask, given a particular task environment, what is the optimal mix of fixed morphology, flexible morphology, and flexible neural processing?. But how would we explore this? We would need a way to evolve entire agents, to coevolve morphology and sensory, motor, and neural systems. Currently, we have a good idea of how to evolve controllers for existing agents, and we have some ideas on how to evolve shapes. Karl Sims has demonstrated that entire agents can indeed be evolved. In his experiments, Sims showed that morphology, sensory-motor systems, and neural substrate can be coevolved. However, his developmental processes were preprogrammed. Developmental processes are also the focus of Eggenberger's model of cell growth. A combination of both is needed: We need to be able to grow shapes and neural substrate and to model cell differentiation vis-à-vis a particular task environment.

To achieve all this, we need to have a good understanding of (artificial) evolution and ontogenetic development. If we had this we could also investigate the information-theoretic issues in sensory-motor coordination: Where do we have to position the sensors to get interesting kinds of cross-modal association? Again, if the agent's shape is not given, this question has an enormous number of degrees of freedom. Studies of this nature would reveal a lot about the question of "ecological balance" as well. One could explore the relation of the complexity of the sensory, motor, and neural system given a particular task environment.

In chapter 11, we saw that one of the hard problems when working with multiple, parallel processes concerns their coordination. We called this the coordination problem. The two main coordination mechanisms proposed in the literature are competitive and cooperative coordination. In the former, only one process is allowed to write its outputs to the motors, while the other processes are deactivated or inhibited. In the latter, the output of two or more processes that involve the same effector are combined into a single output that is then sent to the effector. The most popular cooperative coordination scheme is linear summation. We saw that with this relatively simple mechanism, surprisingly sophisticated behaviors can be generated. It is important, however, to go beyond summation and devise more sophisticated means of cooperative coordination. Of particular interest are approaches that include learning. Currently, most coordination schemes are fixed a priori. In the subsumption approach, for example, the relations between the different layers of competence are prewired; in the EBA approach, the designer defines the weights connecting the processes to the motors. It would be desirable to have agents learn the coordination themselves as they interact with their environment. This would have to include value systems that incorporated certain basic biases that the agent could exploit to learn the coordination. Moreover, we have to better understand the role of the environment in coordinating processes. We have pointed out that coordination should not be seen as an internal problem only, but rather one that crucially involves the environment. We currently have no systematic ways to exploit the environment for coordination, however. Exploiting the environment for the coordination problem implies a better understanding of ecological niches. In chapters 4 and 13, we pointed out the need for a characterization of niches. Although such a characterization is important and would be very helpful, it has so far resisted explication. The main problem that we have identified is that such characterizations must be done not in isolation but with respect to the agent's capabilities. Another issue along this line concerns the definition of the basic processes. Again, in most approaches the designer defines the basic processes needed to achieve a desired behavior. It would be interesting, however, to have agents learn the required processes themselves. To this end, one could, for example, equip the agent with a largely unstructured neural network and have it learn the processes needed to solve a task by inducing structures in that network.

A more general issue concerns the relation between the agent's behavior and the functional modules used in the traditional approaches. We saw in chapter 11 that traditional approaches to behavior control decompose behaviors into modules such as perception, memory, planning, and action. Often, these modules are arranged hierarchically. We contrasted this view with that of parallel, loosely coupled processes. We need, however, a better understanding of how the two approaches relate. In particular, it is important to understand better what basic processes produce behavior that we would describe by resorting to functional modules. Ultimately, we would like to show that the functional modules the traditional approaches describe can emerge from the joint processing of parallel processes. We made one such attempt in chapter 12: The SMC agents learned categories without having an explicitly represented categorization module. We saw that these agents learned about objects by means of sensory-motor coordination, rather than by mapping stimuli onto an internal representation of the categories. We stressed that categorization is a property of the complete agent. The problem that has emerged is the identification of the invariances underlying categorization behavior. If we dismiss the idea of an internal categorization module and postulate that categorization is instead an emergent phenomenon, we have the hard problem of identifying where the invariances are located that make the agent categorize its environment. We cannot simply point to some internal representation such as an output node in a back-propagation network. Of course, there are regularities: They are to be found in the agent's behavior. For example, whenever the SMC I agent encountered small objects, it consistently picked them up while it avoided large objects. This raises two important issues: First, where are the invariances underlying this consistent behavior? Second, how can the behavioral regularities be exploited? Let us start with the first issue. Because there is no one-to-one mapping of the behavioral regularity onto some internal module, we can find the underlying invariances only if we take multiple levels into account, including the weights, the activations of the neural networks, the morphology of the agent, its interaction with the environment, and the structure of the particular niche in which the agent is operating. Future work needs to address what the important levels are and come up with characterizations of the invariances.

Let us now turn to the second issue: The exploitation of behavioral regularities. Patterns and regularities, though emergent, are objectively measurable. Recall, for example, that we computed the regularities—the correlations in the sensory data—generated by the SMC I agent. These regularities can be potentially observed and used by the agent itself. This, in fact, might form the basis on which the agent could eventually develop a sense of "self"[1] that would be grounded in physical interactions rather than an abstract entity living in the agent's head. It would enable the agent to develop knowledge about its own sensory-motor setup and its relations to the world. Eventually, the agent might employ such a self to increase its adaptivity. We should note, however, that such developments would have to be embedded in appropriate task environments. It makes sense for an agent to use the self-generated regularities only if the task environment imposes a need to do so. It might well turn out, for example, that such a need is only present

---

[1] We owe this idea to Yasuo Kuniyoshi of ETL in Tsukuba, Japan.

in social environments, where the agent has to be able to communicate about his own needs or capabilities. These ideas are still rather speculative, but we can easily envision their concrete experimental operationalizations. As soon as the agent generates emergent regularities, and any truly intelligent agent should be able to do so, we can start to think about how the agent can extract, learn and use them in various ways. This is an exciting line of future research that should eventually shed light on such important concepts as "self," empathy, and more generally, social intelligence.

One of the most frequently asked questions in this fledgling field of embodied cognitive science is whether the approach will eventually scale to human levels of intelligence. This question is certainly justified: We want to use the synthetic methodology to understand human intelligence. Can we build robots that have the complexity of humans? We suggest that a distinction should be made here. Are we trying to understand human intelligence, or are we trying to build an enormously complex robot, comparable in complexity to a human? If the goal is the former, we have shown that even the relatively simple agents we have used can be employed to study issues in human intelligence (e.g., category learning). In this case, we are talking about a model, whose purpose is not so much to perform a task as to help us understand something else, that is, humans. So, the point is not so much one of scale, but one of how to employ models in the scientific process. Whenever we build models, we have to make abstractions and simplifications. Extracting the essence of a phenomenon is what models are for. And models are always to be seen in a theoretical context. Building a model is not the only goal. We are just as much interested in the theoretical understanding that informs the model-building process. Let us now look at the other case, in which building a highly complex robot is the issue. This is indeed the real scaling issue. Concerning this issue, we feel that currently we have not found any in-principle reasons why the approach should cease to work at some level of complexity. But whether it will work remains to be seen.

18.2 Theory and Technology

To investigate the problems we raised in the last section, progress in theory as well as technology is needed. This section identifies some of the directions in which we think the field should move.

Basic Research

One obvious development to be expected concerns more complex and more flexible robot platforms. Looking back on the agents we have encountered in this book, we find that the better part are relatively simple in terms of their sensory-motor systems, in particular when compared to a robot like Cog or other humanoids (e.g., Kuniyoshi and Nagakubo 1997). Because of this simplicity, we have been able to work out some of the fundamental principles of agents. We deliberately decided to discuss simple agents first to develop a basic understanding of principles of intelligence. Now that we have a deeper understanding, we can move on to more complex task environments and agents. Before augmenting the complexity of the agent, careful consideration should be given to the question of how much additional complexity is really required to investigate a particular issue. For many scientific questions, it is neither necessary nor desirable to have the complexity of a humanoid robot. Modeling human behavior, for example, does not necessarily require a humanoid robot. Having said that, we can now speculate on what is required to conduct more complex experiments.

Let us look at an example. We have argued that category learning crucially depends on the agent's being able to perform appropriate kinds of sensory-motor coordinations, directly implying that the complexity of the categories an agent can acquire depends on the complexity of its sensory-motor apparatus. In other words, if we want an agent's categories to evolve beyond simple objects such as the wooden cylinders used in the SMC agent experiments, we need more sophisticated sensors and more degrees of freedom in the motor system. More specifically, we need to be able to integrate the sensory systems flexibly with the motor systems. For example, manipulators need to be equipped with skin sensors that can provide feedback from the object exploration process. This requires both theoretical and technological advances. Theoretically, the challenge is to apply the principle of parallel, loosely coupled processes: We do not want to control a manipulator by means of a complex, internal control policy but prefer instead solutions that are largely peripheral. In the object exploration example, this requires the control to be located largely in the hand itself. In terms of technology, this indicates that manipulators need to be dextrous, have some processing capacity (e.g., very small microcontrollers) at the periphery, and be covered with skin sensors. If we take the current technology as a starting point, making such modifications would increase significantly their weight and size, which is obviously undesirable. It is not obvious that the current technology with electrical motors is the way to proceed. For example, artificial muscles may turn out to be necessary to achieve this level of performance, like the McKibben pneumatic artificial muscles used in systems that mimic characteristics of human arms (e.g., Chou and Hannaford 1997). More generally, new materials may be required alltogether. Given our focus on embodiment, it would be interesting to experiment with such materials, particularly in combination with new types of sensors. New types of bodies may well lead to unexpected intelligent behavior. Having new kinds of materials also significantly changes the problem of how to control the limbs: The inherent material properties like stiffness and sluggishness may turn a very hard control problem into a much simpler one. The passive dynamic walker illustrates how the control problem can be simplified by exploiting the physics; specific materials impose different constraints that can potentially be exploited. The study of such properties and how they can be exploited to achieve sophisticated behaviors is an essential research topic. Another research area likely to play an important role along these lines is the rapidly developing field of nanotechnology. Within this field, very small sensors, processors, motor components, and energy supply systems are developed (e.g., Drexler 1992; Ishihara, Arai, and Fukuda 1996). Such small devices may enable us to build relatively complex robots of very small size and weight.

In addition to increasing agents' complexity, we need to increase that of the task environments. We can envisage two main lines of developments. First, we can study more elaborate processes of natural agents. For example, in the Sahabot project, first the navigation with polarized light was investigated. Later, the complexity of the task environment was increased by adding landmark navigation. The next step in the SMC agents project will be the study of more realistic object exploration processes. There is no limitation on the possibilities for mimicking ever more complex behaviors observed in natural agents. Eventually, this might require the use of humanoid robots. Kuniyoshi and his colleagues at the Electrotechnical Laboratory in Tsukuba (Japan), for example, use a humanoid robot to study not only sensory-motor processes but also social interaction, an important research area because so far the extent to which social interaction relates to sensory-motor devel-

Table 18.1 Comparison of chess and RoboCup. (Adapted from Kitano et al. 1997.)

Game characteristic	Chess	RoboCup
Environment states	Static Discrete	Dynamic No states; continuous
Operators	Finite set of possible moves	Indefinite number of possible moves
Information accessibility	Complete	Incomplete
Communication with environment	High-level ontology	Low-level specification
Behavior control	Hierarchical	Parallel, distributed

opment has not been systematically investigated. More generally, the social context of intelligence needs to be better included in our modeling efforts.

The other approach to increasing the complexity of the task environment focuses more on general principles of intelligence. It is exemplified by the Robot World Cup Initiative[2] (Kitano et al. 1997), an attempt to foster cognitive science research by providing (a) a landmark project comparable to the Apollo space program, which had the goal of "landing a man on the moon and returning him safely to earth" (Kennedy 1961; cf. Kitano et al. 1997), and (b) a standard problem whereby a wide range of approaches, architectures, algorithms, and technologies can be integrated and evaluated. The standard problem in traditional artificial intelligence has been chess. The RoboCup can be considered the equivalent for embodied cognitive science. Table 18.1 compares the two problems, largely summarizing the comparison between virtual and real worlds discussed in chapter 3. We do not repeat the arguments here but simply point out that from an embodied cognitive science perspective, the RoboCup problem encompasses all major issues of interest because it involves complete agents that have to solve a number of tasks in real time. RoboCup consists of three competition tracks: (a) a real robot league involving physical robots playing soccer games (figure 18.1), (b) a software robot or simulator league involving software agents playing soccer games on an offi-

[2] The first RoboCup competition was held at the Fifteenth International Joint Conference on Artificial Intelligence in Nagoya, Japan, in 1997.

Figure 18.1   RoboCup competition (reprinted by permission of Eurelios, Paris).

cial soccer server over a network, and (c) an expert robot competition for robots that have special skills—such as shooting a ball into a goal in particular ways—but are not able to play an entire game. For example, they might not be able to detect and approach the ball from a distance and pass it on to a teammate; they have only this one particular skill. The simulator league not only enables a wider range of researchers to participate but also fosters research on network-based multiagent interactions, computer graphics, physically realistic animations, and new technologies to exploit the Internet. More generally, future research will have to increase the complexity not only of hardware platforms, but also of simulators. We pointed out in chapter 4 that simulators play an important role in embodied cognitive science, but their complexity needs to be significantly increased if we are to investigate more complex skills such as playing soccer or basketball.

The ultimate goal in a RoboCup player is "a humanoid type that can run and kick or pass a ball with its legs and feet, can throw a ball with its arms and hands, and can do a heading with its head" (Kitano et al. 1997, p. 76). This comes very close to our own vision about the far future of embodied cognitive science illustrated in figure 19.4. Such ambitious long-term goals create subgoals that can be achieved first. In the case of RoboCup, the first subgoal is to build physical and software robot soccer teams that play reasonably well (Kitano et al. 1997).

RoboCup is a challenging task environment in terms of both theory and technology for a number of reasons. First, it requires sophisticated sensory-motor skills such as shooting balls or avoiding dynamic opponents. A RoboCup player has to engage in multiple desired behaviors such as shooting, dribbling or pushing, passing, heading, throwing a ball, and avoiding opponents. The principle of parallel, loosely coupled processes and the approaches derived from it can be applied to—and thus tested in—the design of the processes the player needs to produce these desired behaviors. Second, the agents have to categorize the ball, the goal, the opponents, and the members of their own team while moving about with high speed. We predict that for the players to be really robust in their interactions with the ball, for example, they will have to first be given some time to explore and learn about it by employing mechanisms of sensory-motor coordination. Otherwise the category "ball" will not be grounded, and problems related to the symbol-grounding problem will come to the fore. Third, "because of the uncertainties in sensory data processing and action execution, it is infeasible to program the robot behaviors to consider all situations; thus robot-learning methods seem promising" (Kitano et al. 1997, p. 77). Here we can use the value principle to devise value systems and appropriate self-supervised learning mechanisms. It will be interesting to see, for example, what type of value system is needed to make a robot play soccer. And forth, the agents have to be cooperative, i.e., possess social skills. Clearly there is virtually no limit as to the complexity of this task environment.

We said in the introduction to the chapter that in addition to addressing these problems in basic research we have just outlined, the field of embodied cognitive science must be made accessible to a broad audience. Let us now look at this in more detail.

"Agents for the Masses"

The framework of embodied cognitive science outlined in this and the other books mentioned in the introduction to this chapter can be applied to the study of intelligence in a number of ways. Some may prefer to take the framework and use it to theorize about various aspects of intelligence, from insect navigation to memory or language. Others may want to actually use the synthetic methodology presented here to build models of various kinds and complexity. A first step might be to download the source code from the Web page associated with this book and start playing with the various architectures or even embark on a new research project. Appropriate tools are needed, of course, to do either of these things, in essence agent simulators and physical agents. We have also included a number of pointers to agent simulators on our Web page. All of the experiments suggested in this book can be replicated with these simulators. If one's goal is to use a physical robot to conduct these (or other) experiments, the situation is a bit more involved; we discussed the various considerations in chapter 16. Nevertheless, there is a strong need for more flexible, cheaper, easier-to-handle robot platforms. We envision robot kits that can be assembled easily without sophisticated engineering skills. Such kits should enable the user to immediately start experimenting, without having to solder various parts or program low-level routines: they should have the "plug-and-play" character of modern software programs. Only then can we expect a large number of people actually to use physical robots to study intelligence. The very best scenario would be if this platform were built on top of an already widespread technology like Lego. There are indeed efforts underway to equip Technic Lego kits with robotic capacities by adding sensors, motor systems, and computing power. With the number of people interested in this field increasing, such agents should become economically viable in the very near future. Just as the information age really took off with the advent of cheap personal computers for the masses, a similar development—on a smaller scale—is needed to boost the use of autonomous agents and embodied thinking in research, education, and applications.

18.3 Applications

In principle, the framework presented in this book can be applied to every area of mobile robotics that requires intelligent behavior. In this section, we present a few such applications that we consider to be of particular interest.

Agents for Hazardous and Difficult Environments

One particularly useful area of application of mobile agents is in hazardous environments. Demining robots have recently received increasing attention (e.g., Nicoud 1996). Currently about 100 million mines remain in the ground in 62 countries. Demining these mines is a dangerous business, with one death per 5,000 mines cleared. Cleaning only the mines in Afghanistan, for example, with the currently existing methods would take more than 4,000 years. These statistics are daunting and call for alternative approaches. Robots are clearly an interesting potential solution. A demining robot has the task of finding all mines within a given area and destroying or deactivating them. Of course, military motives for demining differ from humanitarian ones. The military's goal in demining is to quickly make a breach in a minefield to allow troops to progress without delays. Typically, a tank pushes a mechanical demining system, and the troops follow. Speed is a primary consideration, and mine finding or destruction rates of about 80 percent are considered acceptable. For humanitarian mine clearing this is clearly not sufficient; for humanitarian purposes, accuracy is the paramount consideration: demining systems must have a detection rate approaching 100 percent (United Nations specifications require more than 99.8%). This is, of course, a very rigorous requirement, and the task is made even harder by the necessity of vegetation clearance: Up to 50 percent of a deminer's time is spent in removing trees and shrubs under 20mm. Burning, though in general a very quick way of clearing vegetation, is not acceptable in this case because burnt plastic and unexploded TNT can pollute the soil. Demining is thus a very challenging task environment for mobile robots.

Let us look at a few demining robots. Pemex is a lightweight prototype robot (16kg) developed at the Laboratoire de Microinformatique, École Polytechnique Fédérale de Lausanne, Switzerland (figure 18.2) that is supposed to detect mines but not trigger them. The robot is equipped with two bicycle wheels with which it can move 2 meters per second. When searching for mines, Pemex's head oscillates right and left, covering a path one meter wide. Another example is Ariel (figure 18.3), a crab robot developed by IS Robotics, a spin-off company of the MIT AI Lab. Ariel is an autonomous legged underwater vehicle designed for mine countermeasures in the surf zone. These vehicles operate together to clear the craft landing zone for naval operations. They are deployed in numbers based on the expected mine density and collectively search a craft landing zone for mines. The idea is that each robot, secures itself next to a mine it has found; upon a control signal from the command center, all the robots detonate, destroying all mines simultaneously. Ariel has six legs and onboard

Figure 18.2 The robot Pemex. It is a prototype for a demining robot, built at the LAMI-EPFL in Lausanne, Switzerland (reprinted with permission).

Figure 18.3 The robot Ariel. This crab robot was built by IS Robotics. It is an autonomous legged underwater vehicle designed for mine countermeasures in the surf zone. It walks sideways and continues to walk if it is overturned (reprinted with permission).

power and sensors and is waterproof to a considerable depth. To better understand the issues involved in locomotion in a surf zone, the designers have studied the locomotion of real crabs. Ariel walks sideways just as real crabs do, but in contrast to real crabs it continues to walk if it is turned upside down, which can happen frequently in the presence of strong dynamic ocean currents. Ariel is controlled by a distributed, subsumption-like architecture.

From an embodied cognitive science perspective, the task environment of demining is not as appropriate as, for example, that in the RoboCup competition discussed earlier. The perfect detection rate this environment demands typically requires strategies that are not relevant from a cognitive science point of view, such as the use of a global positioning system (GPS) that yields global information about the environment or of predefined navigation strategies (e.g., systematic search patterns). However, it does comprise certain issues that are of high interest for embodied cognitive science. For example, no currently existing sensor technology achieves good detection rates in all types of soil, with all types of mines and false targets. Redundant sensory systems that provide potential information overlap might help achieve these goals. The design and integration of redundant sensory systems is a problem of great interest for cognitive science, and some of the research in this area might well lead to practical solutions that can be used in demining robots.

Another interesting application in this context are robots for cleaning up radioactive wastes. A recent example is the project to clean up the Chernobyl plant, situated near Kiev in the Ukraine. Tecnomatix Technologies Ltd., an Israeli software company, has developed a three-dimensional graphic simulation of this plant. The program allows for the design of a three-dimensional sarcophagus into which simulated robots are then moved to clean up the Chernobyl plant. The main advantage of this simulator is that robot designers can test whether specifically designed robots are capable of doing the needed work before they are actually built. As in the case of the Mars Sojourner, it is crucial to test a large number of designs in simulation before actually building the physical robots. The software is also indispensable because one cannot bring anything living inside the Chernobyl plant: the high doses of radioactivity would kill it.

Let us look at a final example: sewage. Sewage systems are among the largest infrastructural investments of mankind. For example, in Germany alone, the total length of the sewage system is estimated to be almost one million kilometers. As documented in a number of studies, the overall system is not in good condition. Sewers may be blocked, and sewage may leak out, possibly polluting soil and ground water. In consequence, much effort must be devoted to inspecting, maintaining and repairing the sewage pipes. A large part of the public sewage system consists of circular pipes with inner diameters of 30–60 cm. They are obviously not accessible for humans. The current state of the art for maintaining such pipes uses teleoperated camera platforms that are connected to the operator by a cord. However, such tethered platforms have severe limitations in terms of mobility and radius of action. One idea to tackle these issues is to employ teams of mobile robots that can undertake sewer inspection autonomously over long periods of time, in order to support sewers. This task involves a wealth of

Figure 18.4 A prototype of a multi-segment sewage system robot built at the GMD in Bonn (Germany) (reprinted with permission).

challenges for research and development in robot hardware and control. In addition to their narrow dimensions, sewage pipes are slippery, dirty, and wet. They can involve all levels of water from none to complete flooding. They consist of very different kinds of materials. Moreover, this ecological niche is very uneven: It contains steps in the connections between pipes of different diameters and may contain clogs, sediments, cracks, holes, or roots grown into the pipes through cracks or leaking joints. The research group of Thomas Christaller at GMD, the German National Research Center for Information Technology in Bonn (Germany), in cooperation with various universities and industrial companies, has developed several prototypes of mobile robots capable of navigating in this challenging ecological niche. One of them, a snakelike multisegment robot capable of negotiating the difficult intersections of pipes with different diameters, is shown in figure 18.4.

Agents for Service

One of the big challenges of the twenty-first century is the aging of the population. How can the life of the elderly be made as agreeable as possible? How can they be supported in a way that maintains their independence and autonomy even if their physical systems start to deteriorate. One suggestion pursued with great force, especially in countries like Japan with a very high life expectancy, is service agents. To be sure, service agents are meant to alleviate problems, not to replace human caretakers. Their purpose is to complement care provided by humans. The potential of service agents to be helpful is enormous. Especially in hospitals and homes for the elderly, but also for delivery and for carrying heavy things, such agents might be employed to great advantage. Takashi Gomi, chairman of Applied AI Systems in Canada, among other projects oversees research, development, and marketing of products related to autonomous agents. He suggested developing robots that simply follow people. Such robots can be used to carry goods that people buy, for example, in grocery stores. Gomi is also pursuing the development of an autonomous or, rather, semiautonomous wheelchair, aimed largely at elderly as potential users. Let us look at this example a bit more closely.

The first question that comes to mind is why a wheelchair would ever need any degree of autonomy. Why should it not be controlled only by a joystick or some other steering device? Gomi, who has studied the situation in detail, especially in Japan, argues as follows: Many homes for the elderly are not in the centers of the cities, but at the periphery. Going to town may take a long time, say on the order of an hour. The physically challenged may—depending on the seriousness of their impairment—not be able to control a steering device over extended periods of time. Even handling a joystick for more than a few minutes might require too much effort. Thus, autonomous wheelchairs that can, for example, navigate safely and autonomously in the streets of a city, can help. Figure 18.5 shows a prototype of a semiautonomous wheelchair.

The wheelchair problem is interesting not only because it represents an application that may turn out to be a great boon for society, but also for scientific reasons. Gomi has adopted the strategy of equipping all his agents, his robots, with subsumption-like architectures, because he strongly believes that this is the best way to equip the agents with reliable, cheap real-time behavior. From the perspective of this book, of embodied cognitive science, it will be very interesting to see how the approaches advocated by this field will be able to compete with those offered by the more traditional ones, especially since traditional approaches currently still dominate the field of mobile robotics.

Yet another tough research issue is involved, the problem of communication between humans and machines, more specifically between humans and artificial agents, or robots. We give this issue separate treatment in chapter 19. For now, let us just point out that there must be a smooth interplay between an agent's autonomy and

Figure 18.5 A semiautonomous wheelchair robot developed by Applied AI Systems in Ottawa, Canada (reprinted with permission).

a human user's control, that is, when should the human get control and when should the agent take over? Some of these problems are known from the airline industry, where these issues have been addressed in the context of safety. Some of the insights gained might translate to the agents domain.

Agents for Entertainment

In addition to service and safety, agents can be used for entertainment. Entertainment is one of the largest existing industries, and enormous growth is yet predicted. The only constraint on the applicability of autonomous agents to entertainment is creativity. For example, agents are used in the movie industry to mimic dinosaurs and other creatures that have sprung from people's fantasies.

Another example is Craig Reynolds's flocking algorithm, which has been used as the basis for animations in movies like *Star Trek*, *Lion King*, and *Batman Returns*. They are also used as pets, as digital pets in cyberspace, or as dolls displaying facial expression and emotional reactions.

The most famous example of these is Tamagotchi. Tamagotchi is a simple virtual creature invented in Japan. *Tamago* is the Japanese word for *egg*; *Tamagotchi* is a verbal combination of *egg* and *watch*. Tamagotchi hatch from tiny eggs after traveling millions of light-years through cyberspace. With proper care and feeding, performed by pushing buttons on the egg, Tamagotchi grow into a virtual reality pet. Tamagotchi have very crude graphics; the screen is barely capable of displaying a primitive line drawing of a chicken. One observes with astonishment how something as primitive as Tamagotchi has managed to fascinate the masses. Almost in the entire industrialized world, they immediately sold out. We can only speculate about the success of Tamagotchi. Using our framework, we strongly suspect that one of the reasons relates to autonomy. Tamagotchi has a certain degree of autonomy, a very simple kind of autonomy, but it is there. For example, as mentioned above, if the virtual creature is to grow, it has to be taken care of. The caretaker is forced, for example, to perform certain actions periodically like feeding or playing with the pet. If it does not receive a sufficient amount of care and attention, the pet will not develop properly and may even "die." This is an implementation of a certain environmental pressure that real agents always experience in their econiches. The caretaker, that is, the child or adult (and there are many adults playing with Tamagotchi), experiences dynamics in the environment that are independent of the "moves" of the caretaker: Tamagotchi has its own, independent behavior. Thus, we have a situation that is very different from chess, in which the world only changes if one of the players makes a move. The autonomy of Tamagotchi, together with this pressure that forces the caretaker to act, seems to be evoking a considerable amount of emotions (empathy, pity, anger), and it also triggers attributions of various types. (Children attribute feelings to Tamagotchi, for example, sadness or disappointment if they have neglected their pet.) It will be interesting to explore further the idea of digital pets or more generally agent pets with higher degrees of autonomy.

Another example of an agent that entertains people is Silas T. Dog, developed by Bruce Blumberg and his research group at the

Figure 18.6 The virtual creature Silas T. Dog developed at the MIT Media Lab. Silas can interact with humans in cyberspace and is equipped with an ethologically inspired control architecture (reprinted with permission).

MIT Media Lab to explore ways in which people can interact with creatures in cyberspace (e.g., Blumberg, Todd, and Maes 1996). In particular, Blumberg's research focuses on developing ethologically inspired architectures for building autonomous animated creatures that live in virtual 3-D environments. The creatures have a certain level of autonomy in that at every instant they decide, within a given set of actions that they can perform, what to do, based on what they can sense of the world and their internal state (motivations, "goals," etc.). Silas, an example of such a creature, navigates in its world by using his nose and simulated vision, and it has a dozen or so goals, for example, goals related to eating, drinking, and playing with a ball, which it tries to satisfy. Silas is a fully situated agent: It experiences the world exclusively through its own sensors and acts on it via its motor system. It is a virtual reality creature that has at least some of the properties of a complete, embodied agent and thus bears the potential for intelligence.

Blumberg's experimental setup is as follows. There is a very large screen, large enough that adults can be visualized on it in full size. There is a camera that captures the person interacting with Silas. Silas itself is shown on the large screen in cyberspace and so is the human. The image and the position of the human are extracted from the camera image and transferred into cyberspace, where the human and Silas can be seen on the screen and can now interact. For example, the human can throw a ball for Silas to play with. The human can always see himself, together with the dog, in cyberspace and can determine his actions based on what he sees. Figure 18.6 shows a picture of Silas with his teacher, Dr. J. T. Puppet.

Puppet and Silas can interact through various scenarios. The human can control Puppet through the camera that monitors the movement of the human. The only difference between this and the previous setup mentioned is that instead of the human interacting directly with Silas in cyberspace, the human controls Puppet; Puppet simply performs the same movements as the human. Blumberg is also experimenting with emotions. He is interested in the extent to which emotions will be important in human-agent interaction. We return to this issue in the next chapter.

Issues to Think About

Issue 18.1: Artificial Brains

We have shown throughout the book that to understand intelligence, it is not sufficient to understand the brain only. The embodied perspective tells us that we have to take the organism in its entirety into account. But the view that the brain is the sole factor responsible for intelligence is hard to eradicate. In science, but also in the society at large, the idea of enormously powerful computers, of superbrains that will at some point exceed human intelligence by far, is still common. While for some this vision represents the ultimate nightmare, building large brains has been a dream of a considerable number of scientists. Hugo de Garis, a researcher in the field of ALife who calls himself a "brain builder" (see de Garis (1994) for a review of an artificial brain project), has set out to build a brain "the size of the moon." Assume for a moment that de Garis were actually to succeed and that at some point in the future we had such a superbrain. Would we really have to be afraid of it? In what ways could the brain be harmful to us? First of all, it would have to have some means of acquiring knowledge about the world. We have seen that agents cannot simply be programmed with knowledge, since that would imply a designer-based high-level ontology that would in turn lead to an ungrounded system, a system that would not be situated and thus not be capable of interacting efficiently with the world on its own. The latter capability would be required for an autonomous system, and autonomy would be necessary for true intelligence to emerge. From our discussion of embodiment we know that the brain would have to be appropriately embedded in a sensory-motor system. The idea of a superbrain seems to be based on a misunderstanding of the nature of intelligence. Information processing is very powerful in virtual worlds like chess, but it is not sufficient to make sense of the real world. But there is an alternative way for an artificial brain to acquire information, the Internet. Think about such a brain "sitting" in the Internet, where it has access to enormous amounts of information. Would that change the situation fundamentally, that is, would we really have to be scared of such a brain?

Issue 18.2: Your Own Soccer Player

We have introduced the RoboCup initiative. Now that we have covered the essentials of embodied cognitive science, we would like you to think about the following task: How would you design your own soccer player? What would be its desired behaviors? What morphology and what sensors would you use, and where would you position them on the robot? What would be the mechanisms with which you equipped the agent for kicking the ball? How would you design the learning mechanisms and the value system? What scheme of behavior control would you use? Would you want to simply define the task of "winning the game" and apply artificial evolution to evolve an entire soccer-playing agent and then observe the kinds of behaviors that emerge? What would be the pros and cons of employing this approach? Would you use simulation or hardware or both? Again, what would be the pros and cons?

Points to Remember

- A number of hard problems need to be resolved if the field of embodied cognitive science is to make significant progress. They include the questions of morphology, that is, trading shape for computation; of positioning sensors to yield potential information overlap; of how morphology and interaction with the environment can be exploited to generate correlated data; of evolving entire agents through artificial evolution; of coordination schemes between processes; of value systems; and of identifying the appropriate levels at which invariances can be identified.
- An issue of special interest concerns the question of how an agent can acquire a sense of "self." It has been suggested that this will have to be achieved by picking up the—objectively measurable—correlations generated as the agent is engaged in a system-

environment interaction. The mechanisms by which this might be accomplished are to date unknown.

- When we ask whether the approach of embodied cognitive science will scale to human levels of intelligence, a distinction must be made between a modeling approach and one of robot building. If agents are used as models, we can, already make statements about human intelligence. If the goal is to build sophisticated, highly complex robots, we are faced with an empirical question: We have to try and actually build such robots before we know; we cannot decide how far we can get on purely theoretical grounds.

- Technological advances must be made if the theory behind embodied cognitive science is to advance. The most obvious technologies required are more-complex sensory-motor systems. In particular, manipulators must become more flexible, cheaper, and especially smaller which will involve the use of new materials. Moreover, they must have a certain amount of processing capacity at the very periphery. Technological advances also need to occur in the form of a better mix of sensors from different channels, so that there can potentially be information overlap.

- Increasing the agent's sensory-motor complexity alone is not sufficient; the task environment must be augmented at the same time. A particularly interesting and taxing task environment is that of the Robot World Cup initiative, which provides a great test bed for virtually all issues in embodied cognitive science.

- If ideas concerning complete agents, concerning embodiment, are to spread, we need "agents for the masses": cheap and flexible platforms, robot-building kits that do not require a lot of in-depth knowledge of robot hardware.

- Applications of autonomous agents can be envisaged in almost any area that requires intelligence. Examples are demining robots of various sorts (even though in this field, intelligence is often not the main criterion, rather 100 percent security), robots for cleaning up radioactive wastes, those for monitoring sewage systems, service agents, and agents for the entertainment industry.

Further Reading

Kitano, H., Asada, M., Kuniyoshi, Y., Noda, I., Osawa, E., and Matsubara, H. (1997). RoboCup: A challenge problem for AI. *AI Magazine*, Spring, 1997. American Association for Artificial Intelligence, 73–85. (Paper describing the RoboCup and illustrating its main ideas and scientific issues.)

We have worked our way through a lot of difficult territory, broached a host of topics, and raised many issues. For example, we have talked about theoretical issues like symbol grounding and frame of reference, about low-level specifications, emergence, behavior control, robot hardware, control architectures, neural networks, artificial evolution, simulated fish, design principles of autonomous agents, value systems, learning algorithms, self-organization, complexity, evaluation, and memory, to mention but a few. This enormous range of topics is unavoidable—it reflects the nature of intelligence. Intelligence is not something neat and clean that can be studied and tested in isolation from the real world. But the minute you do get to the real world, matters become messy. Just think of all the unsystematic considerations involved in designing an agent for the real world. In spite of this seemingly chaotic situation, it is possible to find some underlying structure. Making this structure explicit is the task we have set ourselves for this final chapter: It constitutes the first steps toward a theory of or a theoretical framework for intelligence. From this theoretical framework, ideas on future developments of theory, and of applications, as well as implications for society can be derived. We have looked at applications in the previous chapters. Here we focus on theory and implications for society. We begin by outlining the theoretical framework and conclude with some comments on agents in society.

19.1   Elements of a Theory of Intelligence

Figure 19.1 provides an overview of a theoretical framework. It can be seen as a first step toward a theory of intelligence. In the center of figure 19.1 is the complete agent whose behavior emerges as it interacts with its ecological niche. This center is surrounded by a number of principles that inform the design process. The methodology of embodied cognitive science is synthetic, its goal is understanding by building.

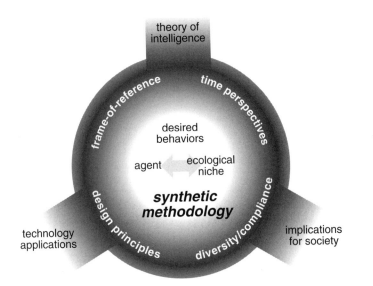

Figure 19.1 The theoretical framework. In the center is the agent and its task environment. On the periphery are the various elements of the theory. From this framework, we can derive implications for society, for applications, and for the further development of the theory.

We expect from a theory of intelligence an answer to the following question: Given an agent, an animal or a human, that exhibits certain behaviors, what are the underlying mechanisms? Human infants behave in certain ways on category learning tasks; the desert ant *Cataglyphis* shows particular navigation behaviors. In a synthetic methodology this question is translated into a design issue: How can we design an agent so that it will exhibit the desired behaviors? The Sahabot and the SMC agents, for example, are the result of such a design effort. There are a number of variations on this question. Once we have designed and built an agent, we can ask how it will perform if we change its environmental conditions; that is, we can try to predict an agent's behavior in different environments. How will the agent adapt to these changes? What kinds of novel behaviors will it display? This question is of central importance for the study of intelligence: It pertains to diversity-compliance considerations that we identified in chapter 1 as being a core characteristic of intelligence. Diversity-compliance refers to a trade-off that any intelligent agent must resolve, a trade-off between a conservative aspect that exploits the givens, and one that is responsible for generating the diversity required to remain adaptive. The diversity-compliance trade-off tells us what to look out for: Intelligent agents solve it in interesting, nontrivial ways. Before going on to discuss the implications of our new view of intelligence, let us briefly mention the other elements of the theory that inform the design process: frame-of-reference, time perspectives, and design principles of autonomous agents. Considerations concerning the frame-of-reference problem, such as the clear distinction of the various perspectives—designer, agent, observer—of the separation of behavior and mechanism, are fundamental to any investigation of intelligence, as we have stressed throughout the book. The time perspectives principle on the right of the figure reminds us that our reflections always include different timescales, the short, the intermediate (ontogenetic learning), and the long term (evolutionary). Finally, the design principles of autonomous agents explicate characteristics of intelligent agents. They inform us about physical setup, control architecture, learning mechanisms, and how to design agent-environment interaction. Let us now look at some implications of this view.

The starting point is a complete agent—autonomous, embodied, situated, self-sufficient agents are what interests us. This follows from one of the design principles, the three-constituents principle. Although this idea may look very natural and innocuous, it has far-reaching consequences. The first thing to note is that because we have a complete agent, we are dealing with the real world. Intelligence is not something that can be understood in the abstract: We must understand how an agent interacts with its environment. Because the agents of interest are complete, we must analyze them in their entirety. But we are not postulating some kind of holistic, ill-defined doctrine. Rather, we have established a concrete methodology of how the entire agent can be taken into account: the synthetic methodology. Any time we have a complete agent, we have an object that is of interest for the study of principles of intelligence. From this perspective, we can learn important principles from the desert ant *Cataglyphis* and from human infants—two examples of very different agents. Seen from this perspective, there are no clear distinctions between high and low levels of intelligence—we always have to consider agent, niche, and behavior.

A key implication of having a complete agent is that it has to interact with its environment on its own. Thus, the hard problems of categorization, of rapidly changing sensory stimulation, of behaving sensibly in dynamic environments, have to be resolved.

This perspective forces us always to consider a behavioral context. If we want to study perception, for example, we have to define a task environment first, and we have to do it in such a way that the behaviors we find interesting, that is, the behaviors to which we would apply the term "perception," occur naturally. Recall our case studies of category learning (the SMC agents). Categorization was defined with respect to regular behavioral patterns (e.g., picking up small objects, ignoring large ones), not through internal representations. Likewise, perception should be investigated from the point of view of finding regularities in behavior rather than mapping sensory stimulation onto an internal representation. This leads to a new perspective not only for synthetic investigation, but also for empirical work: Experimental designs should incorporate an appropriately defined task environment. We realize that this is not always easy to accomplish. Many experimental methods investigating perception in psychology and neurobiology have a focus on the input side: there is no behavioral context. Through the agent perspective, through embodiment, it becomes clear that perception's motor aspects are equally important and cannot be separated. Adopting this perspective often leads to surprising insights. Remember our self-sufficient agent discussed in chapter 11? It had to collect pegs and bring them to a home base. In a sense, through its behavior, it was categorizing the world: It would collect only small pegs, those that fit into its wire loop. The "grasping" was achieved by an obstacle avoidance process. Although simple, this example makes the following point vividly: Categorization in this case is clearly not a decision process but is emergent from the dynamics of the entire agent's behavior.

Let us now look at potential ways in which the embodied cognitive science perspective could influence empirical work. Most empirical experiments in cognitive psychology and neuroscience are conducted within an information processing framework; motor and sensory-motor processes—embodiment—therefore are usually neglected in learning, perception, categorization, or memory experiments. Adopting an embodied cognitive science framework implies a shift in focus from information processing to embodiment and sensory-motor coordination, which in turn leads to new perspectives on how to design experiments. Let us look at an example. Vision is still being viewed by many as a process that is independent of embodiment. Consider the following quote by Milner and Goodale (1995):

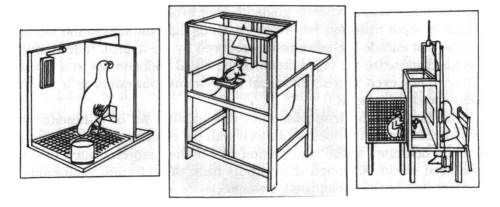

Figure 19.2 Typical experimental setups used to study discrimination learning in animals. Independent of the type of animal tested, it is assumed that the motor output (e.g. grasping, pecking, or jumping) is irrelevant, since only the choice behavior of the animal matters. (From Milner and Goodale 1995, p. 12, reprinted with permission.)

Almost all studies of vision in mammals (including humans) have approached the problem [of vision] in perceptual and cognitive terms and have largely ignored the visual control of motor output. Indeed, a theoretical commitment to vision qua perception has shaped the methodology used to study vision and the visual system of animals in most laboratories throughout this century. Instead of examining the relationship between motor outputs and visual inputs ... investigators working with mammals have typically looked at the performance of their subjects on some form of visual discrimination task.... For most investigators, the study of vision is seen as an enterprise that can be conducted without any reference whatsoever to the relationship between visual inputs and motor outputs. (p. 12)

The questions that are typically addressed in vision research concern issues in information processing. Consequently, in pertinent experiments, various aspects of the stimuli presented to the animal are manipulated to study how the animal encodes, stores, or retrieves this input (figure 19.2). Moreover, explanations focus on the relation between the type of stimulus presented and the choice the animal makes. The animal's actual motor output is considered irrelevant. For example, whether a monkey grasps for the object, a pigeon pecks on a light, or at rat jumps or presses a lever is considered irrelevant: All that matters is the decision the animal makes when presented with some visual stimuli. Note that the same approach characterizes the majority of studies in human vision, learning, categorization, and memory. Categorization studies, for example, typically require subjects to indicate which stimulus belongs to which category. Let us recall an experiment from chapter 15, the four-point task (figure 15.4): The subjects had to point in the direction of the other "points" on the four-point path. In one condition, the subjects had to sit in the same position whereas in the other they were allowed to physically rotate. As we learned, those that were allowed to physically turn performed much better. This experiment is an instance of the more general class of mental rotation tasks. Many view mental rotation as the epitome of a high-level cognitive task. In a recent paper, Wexler (1997) presented empirical evidence that questions this view, that is, the view that mental rotation pertains to information processing only. The paper's title, "Is rotation of visual mental images a motor act?" makes that point very clear. Subjects had to mentally rotate an object while at the same time moving a joystick, that is, they had to mentally *and* physically rotate. In essence, they showed that physical rotation with a joystick significantly interacts with mental rotation processes. For example, the speed of the mental rotation echoed the speed of the physical rotation: the faster the physical rotation, the faster the mental rotation. In addition, mental rotation performance was found to be disrupted if the joystick was moved in the opposite direction. More generally, these experiments demonstrate how embodiment can lead to new perspectives on what has been called high-level cognition. They show how embodiment can be taken into account in the design of experiments, thus complementing experiments within an information processing framework. We strongly hope that the embodied view will foster a wealth of new experiments geared toward explicating the influence of embodiment on cognitive tasks.

To close this section, let us reconsider a few issues we raised in chapter 1. We said in our discussion of the computer Deep Blue that although it is certainly a milestone in the history of artificial intelligence, more is required before we can attribute true intelligence to such a system. Now that we have worked out the essentials of the embodied cognitive science framework, we can specify more concretely what the missing ingredients are. In essence, Deep Blue is a disembodied system that works only in the formal world of chess. True intelligence, however, requires a body and means of interacting with the real world. An intelligent system needs to be able to acquire knowledge on its own, using sensors and actuators. Thus, from our perspective, it would be more sensible to employ our systems in tasks like RoboCup to really test their intelligence: Rather than having people play chess against a computer, we would prefer them to play soccer with our agents. Another interesting way to assess our agents' intelligence would be to have them interact with primates or young infants. This is currently being tried at Waseda University in Tokyo in experiments where a humanoid robot has to interact with a chimpanzee. The idea is to see how the monkey reacts and interacts with the robot. These experiments can be seen as a kind of Turing test: If the monkey's behavior toward the robotic agent is indistinguishable from its behavior vis-à-vis humans, the robot will have passed—in a sense —the Turing test. Similar experiments could be conducted with human infants and, ultimatly, with human adults. In any case, the truly hard tests to intelligence are not to be found in formal worlds, but rather involve a complete agent interacting with the real world in a given task environment.

In chapter 1 we also said that people often do not consider perceptual and motor abilities essential for intelligence. We have argued in complete contrast throughout this book that they are prerequisites for intelligence: Without a body to perceive and interact with the world, true intelligence cannot develop. From the embodied cognitive science perspective, processes like thinking or intuition emerge from and are grounded in the interplay between sensory and motor systems. (see Thelen and Smith 1994 for a detailed discussion). It is thus necessary first to understand the basics of embodied intelligence before we can tackle these so-called high-level phenomena. The claim that embodiment is a prerequisite for intelligence also pertains to intelligence testing, another issue we raised in chapter 1. We have repeatedly stressed in this book that in general, it does not make sense to reduce intelligence to a single number such as the IQ. On the other hand, such numbers may be of value in comparing agents and predicting their behavior in certain task environments. We outlined the first steps towards a measure of what we might want to call an "embodied IQ" in chapter 13: the complexity measure first introduced by Tononi, Sporns, and Edelman (1996). If this measure is extended to include the motor system, we can start to compare the complexity of different agents in a number of task environments. This characterization might eventually help predict an agent's behavior in a given task environment. How such a measure could be extended to measure aspects of human intelligence is currently an open issue. In any case, intelligence tests should include all three constituents of design principle 1: the agent, the tasks and desired behaviors, and the ecological niche. Although it is certainly somewhat vague, this line of thinking might eventually lead to new tests, tests that capitalize on embodiment and system-environment interaction rather than abstract thinking and logical reasoning.

19.2 Implications for Society

In this final section, we point out some implications of the embodied view of intelligence for society at large. Our discussion is by no means exhaustive, and many of the ideas we present are still rather speculative. Our goal is to highlight some important conclusions we can draw from the embodied cognitive science perspective, together with pragmatic suggestions of how to communicate and perhaps implement some of them.

We spend an increasing amount of time in cyberspace. When we read or send electronic mail, when we order pizza or an airline ticket over the World Wide Web, or when we surf the Net to find background information about an opera, theater, or movie, or to look for job opportunities, we are in cyberspace. Schools and universities are getting connected to the Internet, and an increasing number of classes are being taught on the Web. The integration of the Internet into classwork opens new and fascinating possibilities for teaching, in particular when the world of multimedia is exploited. Web pages can use three-dimensional graphics and audio and video snippets to improve the presentation of lecture notes, and by providing appropriate links, they can take the student to other relevant pages. More generally, cyberspace opens new possibilities for the society at large. We can converse with people from around the world, we can exchange ideas and feelings with people we have never met, and we can assume identities of our own creation and imagination.

This new "culture of simulation" (Turkle 1995), where the boundaries between real and virtual are beginning to erode, is making its way into our everyday lives and will have profound influences on our society. Turkle has pointed out some of the fascinating and far-reaching implications and possibilities of this "life on the screen." One is that the more time we explore and navigate cyberspace, the less time we spend in the real world. Although we can only speculate about the influence of "life in cyberspace" on our intellectual development, it is clear that there will be significant differences between the concepts we acquire there and those that we acquire through interaction with the physical world. Throughout the book, we have stressed the importance of embodiment, of an agent's—animal, human, robot—physical interactions with the world. We have pointed out, for example, that an agent's categories are grounded only if they are acquired by the agent itself through its interactions with the physical objects involved. In the real world, this interaction leads to the activation of several modalities, each of which provides separate but overlapping information about the object. When we experience an apple, for example, the experience is visual, but it also involves the smell of the apple, its taste, its feel, its heft, and a number of sensations and movements associated with various actions upon the apple such as slicing it, eating it, making applesauce, and so on. These signals which are temporally correlated constitute the basis for the acquisition of concepts such as "apple."

Now imagine that you have never experienced an apple and the first time you learn about apples is in cyberspace. Again, your experience will be visual—maybe even three-dimensional—but your other modalities will not be stimulated: You will not smell the apple, you will not be able to taste or feel it, nor will you be able to eat or slice it by using your own body. The sensory input will contain significantly less redundancy. Your sensory experience with the apple will be mainly visual, and a computer mouse, with which you might be able to click on the apple, view it from different perspectives, maybe even "walk" through it or change its shape, will mediate your physical interactions with it. Your actions will be restricted to moving your hand and using your fingers to click on the mouse.

How this will change your knowledge about apples, and how this knowledge will differ from that acquired through real-world interactions, we do not know. But from the embodied cognitive science framework, it follows that we should compensate for the increasing amount of time we spend interacting with virtual objects with appropriate experiences with the real world, since we know that the sensory-motor link is crucial to concept acquisition. This is particularly important in education. As schools and universities are being connected to the Internet and our children spend a significant number of hours in cyber- rather than in physical space, it will be necessary to think about and implement appropriate compensatory actions. Instead of teaching mathematics with a computer only, for example, we might use physical representations—objects they can grasp and assemble—with which children can learn basic ideas by means of physical interaction. Such tools are important because they enable children to experience the world by means of all their sensory modalities and behavioral possibilities, an experience of fundamental importance for intellectual development that cannot be replaced by even the most sophisticated virtual animation. Note that we are not arguing against cyberspace in general, nor are we questioning the role of computers and the Internet for education. Quite to the contrary: As our society moves toward a culture of simulation, it will be of critical importance to be able to understand and use cyberspace. The virtual reality of cyberspace is being increasingly accepted as a reality in its own right: "We come to question simple distinctions between real and artificial" (Turkle 1995, p. 23). The desktop on our computer screen has become as real to (many of) us as one mounted on four legs; this shows that we can learn about and use virtual objects. Such knowledge is indispensable if we are to take part in modern society. We should not forget, however, that it is different from the knowledge we acquire by direct physical interaction with real world objects.

Let us now turn to a final point with potentially enormous implications: communication between agents and humans. In the previous chapter, we introduced a number of applications, demining robots, sewage system robots, service agents, and agents for entertainment. Just as we interact and communicate with our computers and with other machines, we will communicate with agents in certain ways. We also briefly mentioned in the last chapter the subtle problem of controlling a semiautonomous wheelchair. We can now ask generally the question of what form communication with agents should take. One obvious form is talking. As long as we realize that an agent's understanding of what we are saying is restricted because of its limited and very different sensory-motor setup, this poses no problem. However, since we know how readily people attribute intelligence and even emotions to agents, we

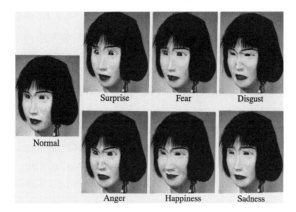

Figure 19.3 Facial expressions displayed by Kobayashi's face robot. On the left is a neutral face. The other emotions expressed are surprise, fear, disgust, anger, happiness, and sadness (reprinted with permission).

have to be careful to avoid misunderstandings, to attribute understanding to an agent and draw inappropriate conclusions about its potential behavior. For example, if we give an order to an agent, and it replies by OK, we must not infer that it has adopted the responsibility for the task, as we would expect from a human; it is simply registering that it has heard what was said. As agents get more autonomous, they are harder to control. It then ceases to be a question of interface only, but instead becomes one of getting an intelligent agent to do something for us. In humans, a good means of assessing another person's state is to look at his face to try to identify his emotions. Although we cannot infer emotions unequivocally from facial expression, it does tell us a great deal about a person's inner state. Also, faces are extremely important in human-to-human communication in general. Just imagine the different nature of a conversation as you are talking on the phone. But what about human-robot communication? Would it make sense to equip our robots with faces and exploit facial expressions in the service of communication?

Hiroshi Kobayashi of the Science University of Tokyo is exploring facial expressions in robot-human communication. Together with Fumio Hara, a professor of mechanical engineering, Kobayashi built a robot capable of displaying humanlike facial expressions. In particular, it can display a number of basic emotions like surprise, fear, disgust, anger, happiness, and sadness, as shown in figure 19.3. Through its eyes, which are equipped with cameras, it can also identify facial expressions in humans. In one experiment, the face robot mimics the facial expressions of a human observer. It is an empirical question to test the extent to which robots with facial expression will be smooth and agreeable for humans to communicate with.

The "face robot" can serve as a tool to make progress on this question, which is especially relevant for our purposes because we identified emotion as a central component of intelligence. Recall our discussion in chapter 1 in which Goleman suggested emotional intelligence—recognizing, using, understanding, and regulating emotions—as an additional key factor in human intelligence. One might even ask the provocative question whether robots will in fact need to have emotions, similar to the way humans have emotions. Without going into detail, what we can say at first consideration is that because of their different sensory-motor and physical setup, robots will have emotions of a completely different nature than human emotions. The communicational skills a robot with such emotions could be evaluated in a Turing test—like situation such as the one used to assess how a monkey would interact with a robot.

Using facial expression for purposes of communication is an instance of a more general means of nonverbal communication. Earlier, we discussed the RoboCup initiative and mentioned that the most sophisticated skills including skills for communication can be tested by having the agents play soccer. Nonverbal communication, using the body, gestures, and playing the ball in particular ways, can all be exploited for communication purposes during a game. Communication is also a crucial factor in cooperation. If team members are to cooperate quickly and efficiently, they need to employ all communication channels possible. As pointed out in the previous chapter, this requires truly intelligent agents. In our embodied perspective, such agents will have passed the ultimate test for intelligence when the agent team wins a basketball game against the human team (figure 19.4).

Points to Remember

- A theory of intelligence should answer the following question: given an agent, an animal or a human, that exhibits certain behaviors, what are the underlying mechanisms?
- The elements of a new theory of embodied intelligence are (a) the three constituents: complete agent, desired behaviors and task, and

Figure 19.4 A team of robotic agents playing basketball against a team of humans. In contrast to figure 1.1, in which a human plays against a computer that runs a chess program in a virtual world, the humans in this figure are playing against embodied agents. (Only one player of each team is shown.)

ecological niche, (b) diversity-compliance trade-off, (c) frame-of-reference, (d) time perspectives, and (e) the design principles of autonomous agents.

- The embodied cognitive science framework implies a shift in focus from information processing to embodiment and sensory-motor coordination. This in turn opens up new perspectives on how to design experiments, for example, on mental rotation.

- Perceptual and motor abilities are prerequisites for intelligence: without a body to perceive and interact with the world, true intelligence cannot develop. Processes like thinking or intuition emerge from and are grounded in the interplay between perceptual and motor systems. The implication for intelligence testing is that new measures that take the system-environment interaction into account have to be developed.

- The increasing amount of time we spend interacting with virtual objects on the Internet should be compensated by appropriate experiences with the real world. This is particularly important in education. As schools and universities are being connected to the

Internet, and our children spend a significant number of hours in cyber space rather than in physical space, it will be necessary to think about and implement appropriate compensatory actions.

- From an embodied cognitive science perspective autonomous agents will have passed the ultimate test for intelligence if a team of artificial agents team wins a basketball game against a human team.

Further Reading

Turkle, S. (1995). *Life on the screen: Identity in the age of the Internet.* New York: Simon & Schuster. (A discussion of the influence of the Internet on the society at large with a focus on how it changes our identities.)

Glossary

action: This term has several meanings: (1) In many disciplines, the term "action" denotes the output of the perception-action system. (2) In psychology, an action is always related to an anticipated result—a goal—and to an intention to reach this goal. In other words, the term "action" always refers to a *goal-oriented* action. (3) In autonomous agents research, "action" is used in two ways, (a) as a synomym of "behavior," and (b) to denote internal modules, typically in the context of the "action selection." (4) In machine learning, an action is an operator that changes the state of the environment; a reinforcement signal communicates the value of this state transition to the agent. In this book, the sense in which the term is used is always explicitly given.

action selection: The process of selecting a particular action for execution from a given set of possible actions, depending on the current situation and context, as well as the internal state of an autonomous agent.

active forgetting: A process by which forgetting takes place only if the agent learns something new at the same time. In the absense of any interaction with the real world, the agent does not forget.

active sensor: A sensor that acts upon the environment in order to receive a signal. Contrasts with *passive sensors*. Typical example: an Infrared sensor.

actuator: A mechanical device for moving or controlling objects such as limbs, wheels, and body parts.

adaptation: Maintaining a given structure under varying environmental circumstances. In biology, four types are usually distinguished: (1) evolutionary, (2) physiological, (3) sensory, and (4) adaptation by learning. In the context of evolution, adaptivity refers to the change of a trait due to mutation and favored by natural selection.

agent: The term is used in many ways. (1) As an umbrella term if no distinction between humans, animals, and robots is intended. (2) To designate an animated creature in cyberspace. (3) To distinguish a certain type of simulation model (agent simulations) from others. In agent simulations, agent and environment are modeled separately and have independent dynamics. Agents acquire information about the environment only through their (simulated) sensory systems. (4) In the context of the Internet, to describe programs (software agents) that perform a certain service for a user, typically information retrieval.

algorithm: A step-by-step procedure for solving a problem, especially a formal problem. In this book, we are interested in algorithms that can be implemented as computer programs.

alleles: Alternative expressions of one and the same gene. For instance, a gene for eye color has the alleles "brown," "blue," "black," etc.

analytic approach: An approach, ubiquitous in all sciences, in which the object of investigation is separated into component parts that are then—in the empirical sciences—investigated experimentally. The term is used here to contrast with the synthetic approach (*see synthetic methodology*).

artificial intelligence: Discipline that seeks to understand natural intelligence and to build intelligent systems.

artificial life: The study of man-made systems that exhibit behavior characteristic of natural living systems. It locates life-as-we-know-it within the larger picture of life-as-it-could-be. (cf. Langton 1989, p. 1)

augmented finite state machine: A finite state machine with delay elements determining how long the machine resides in each state. Augmented finite state machines are used in the *subsumption* architecture.

artificial neural network: Abstract computational model inspired by the architecture of the brain.

associative learning: A type of learning in which the agent learns about the relationship between two stimuli or between a stimulus and a response. Associative learning includes most forms of learning used in the field of autonomous agents. It includes *value-based learning*.

attractor: A configuration in state space that is stable under the given dynamics. The most important types are point attractors, limit cycles, and chaotic attractors.

autonomy: Highly involved; no generally accepted definition available. Roughly, freedom from external control; the concept must be viewed relative to an external "controller."

autonomous agent: An *agent* that has a certain independence of external control.

back-propagation: A supervised learning procedure for multilayer feedforward networks Minimizes error between desired and actual output using a gradient method.

behavior: What an autonomous agent is observed doing. Always the result of an interaction of an agent with its environment.

behavior control: Set of mechanisms that determine the behavior in which an agent will engage.

behavioral economics: The study of the behavior of autonomous agents by assuming that they obey the principles of macroeconomics. An agent's behavior is determined on the basis of consequences of actions in terms of utility or costs implied by taking the action.

behavior-based robotics: The term has a narrow and a broad use: (1) *Narrow*: approaches to robotics employing variations of the *subsumption* architecture. (2) *Broad*: designates the whole field embodied cognitive science, or New AI (in contrast to traditional AI).

behaviorism: Important orientation in psychology during the first half of this century that explains behavior in terms of stimulus-response relationships. The most famous example is Pavlov's dog, which initially salivated only at the presentation of food; it was conditioned to salivate at the sound of a bell.

binary threshold: Designates a particular type of node in an artificial neural network. If the summed input exceeds a certain threshold, the neuron becomes active (activation level 1), otherwise its activation level is 0.

Braitenberg vehicles: A series of vehicles of increasing degrees of complexity illustrating fundamental principles of behavior. Originally invented as thought experiments by the neurobiologist Valentino Braitenberg, who used them, among other things, to illustrate how simple systems can lure observers into attributing cognitive and emotional capacities to mindless machines.

bus: An electronic device for transmitting data shared between the various components of an information processing system.

category error: In the agent context, the attempt to reduce behavior to internal mechanism only.

central pattern generator: A neural circuit that produces rhythmic behavior in the absence of sensory feedback.

Chinese Room: A thought experiment by Searle. He argues that it is possible to build a system which shows plausible input-output behavior, answering to questions in Chinese without any understanding whatsoever. There has been a great deal of argument in the literature as to whether the Chinese Room argument is sound.

chromosome: A structure contained in every cell of the organism that holds strings of DNA, a macromolecule that serves as a "blueprint" for the buildup and functioning of an organism. A chromosome can be conceptually divided into *genes.*

circadian cycles: Periodic changes of environmental conditions that recur once per day. Typical examples are changes in temperature and lighting conditions over a period of one day.

classical conditioning: An experimental procedure in which a conditioned stimulus (CS), which is, at the outset, neutral with respect to the unconditioned response (UR) is paired with an unconditioned stimulus (US) that reliably elicits the unconditioned response. After a number of pairings the CS will elicit, by itself, a conditioned response (CR) which is very much like UR. In Pavlov's classic experiments, the neutral CS (a bell) was paired with a US (food) that reliably produced UR (salivation). After some trials the bell was sufficient to produce salivation (the CR).

cognitive science: The interdisciplinary study of the mind. Disciplines involved in classical cognitive science are computer science/artificial intelligence, psychology, neuroscience, philosophy, and linguistics. In embodied cognitive science, biology in general and engineering also play an important role.

cognition: Various definitions of this term exist in the literature. The most widespread use is as a descriptive term for the large class of so-called higher-level processes, that is, processes not directly driven by the sensory and motor systems.

cognitivistic paradigm: Paradigm that claims that the mind can be studied at the level of algorithms, without any need to study its physical realization.

complete agent: An *agent* that is *autonomous, self-sufficient, embodied,* and *situated.*

compliance: There are two meanings of this term: (1) Conforming to requirements (e.g., physical laws). This is the meaning intended in the *diversity-compliance trade-off.* (2) The ability of an object—often a limb of a robot—to yield elastically when a force is applied. This is the meaning intended, for example, when talking about a compliant arm.

computational neuroethology: See *neuroethology.*

connectionism: A research paradigm that uses *neural networks* to model phenomena from the field of cognitive science. The main underlying belief in connectionism is that intelligent behavior is based on massively parallel control architechtures.

contralateral: Term used by biologists to designate "on the opposite side."

control architecture: Structure that determines the agent-environment coupling, that is how the sensory and motor signals are processed to produce behavior. In natural agents, control architectures often refer to the structure of the neural substrate; in artificial agents, specifically designed artificial neural networks are often used for this purpose.

cross-modal association: Association of sensory signals from different sensory modalities.

crossover: The main operator used in artificial evolution for generating offspring from two parents. It works through choosing an insertion point and exchanging the string on one side with the corresponding string of the other parent.

degrees of freedom: Number of components that can be independently moved. A robot with two independently driven wheels has two degrees of freedom. If a gripper is added that independently controls the elevation and the opening of the hand, the robot has four degrees of freedom, two from the wheels and two from the gripper, which controls two different movements.

dendrite: Fine extension of the cell body of the neuron through which the neuron receives signals from other neurons.

dexterity: Skill and ease in flexibly using the hands. Applies also to body movements in general.

dimensionality (reduction of): Refers to the number of variables, the "dimensions," that make up a system. There is a reduction of dimensionality when correlations are present in the data. Dimensionality reduction can, for example, be achieved by *sensory-motor coordination.*

diversity-compliance trade-off: Generation of diversity while complying with the givens of the system. Represents a compromise between, on the one hand, generating new behavior, and on the other, conforming to existing conditions. Similar trade-offs are exploration-exploitation (in the evolutionary algorithms literature), and stability-flexibility (in the neural networks literature).

domain ontology: A systematic list—a vocabulary if you will—of the fundamental categories, relations, and operators that can be used in the design of a system.

dynamical system: Generally speaking, a system that changes over time. mathematically speaking, a set of differential equations that describe the change of state variables as a function of themselves. Formally, a dynamical system can thus be represented as $dx_i/dt = f(x_i)$.

dynamics: Three usages are common: (a) Anything that changes over time. (b) A mathematical discipline that studies a certain class of differential equations that include time. (c) Term used by roboticists to distinguish geometric problems from those involving physics (such as forces, gravity, inertia, friction, and stiffness of the springs or muscles), the latter being the type that would be said to involve "dynamics."

ecological niche: The ecological niche for an animal is the range in each variable in its environment, such as temperature, humidity, and food items, within which a species can exist and reproduce. In the case of autonomous robots, the term "reproduce" has to be replaced by "survive in the market." Niche occupancy usually implies competition (when animals of different species use the same resources).

EBA: See *Extended Braitenberg Architecture.*

ecological balance: Balance in complexity among an agent's task environment and sensory, motor, and neural systems.

effector: In the context of this book, typically a muscle or motor controlled by the (artificial or natural) nervous system.

embodiment: A term used to refer to the fact that intelligence cannot merely exist in the form of an abstract algorithm but requires a physical instantiation, a body. In artificial systems, the term refers to the fact that a particular agent is realized as a physical robot or as a simulated agent.

embodied cognitive science: What this book is all about: The relatively diverse interdisciplinary field of research that aims at explaining the mechanisms underlying intelligent behavior. There are three main goals of embodied cognitive science: (1) building an agent for a particular task or a set of tasks, (2) studying general principles of intelligence, and (3) modeling certain aspects of natural systems, i.e., humans or animals.

emergence: As used in the fields of embodied cognitive science and artificial life, the term typically has a positive connotation. (a) A surprising property of a system that is not fully understood. (b) A property of a system not contained in any one of its parts. Requires many compoments whose behavior is based on local rules. This is the typical usage in the field of artificial life, dynamical systems, and neural networks. (c) Behavior that arises from the agent-environment interaction. The term is normally used whenever several, independent processes interact to produce a particular behavior and the environment plays a significant role. Contrasts with pre-planned behaviors, like a trajectory of a hand that has been precalculated by a planner.

EQ test: Test for "emotional intelligence." Includes the following areas: Recognizing emotions, using emotions, understanding emotions, and regulating emotions.

evolutionary algorithm: An umbrella term that includes various types of algorithms that are, in one way or another, inspired by natural evolution. It includes genetic algorithms, evolutionary strategies, and evolutionary programming.

evolutionary robotics: Branch of robotics in which methods from artificial evolution are used in design.

exploration-exploitation trade-off: Net benefit or loss resulting from the combined advantages and disadvantages of exploration on the one hand and exploitation on the other. Used in the context of search procedures in general and in the field of artificial evolution in particular. Designates the idea that a solution that seems worthwhile to pursue in a particular situation may turn out to be globally suboptimal. Thus it is important to preserve diversity in the search procedure; however, if too much diversity is maintained, convergence to stable behavior will be slow or will not be achieved at all.

expert system: Problem-solving system based on classical AI techniques. The view underlying expert systems is that knowledge can be extracted from humans and stored in a computer, that is, an expert system.

Extended Braitenberg Architecture (EBA): Architecture that instantiates the principle of parallel, loosely coupled processes.

fitness: In biology: (a) The probability that the organism will live to reproduce (viability); (b) a function of the number of offspring the organism has (fertility). In artificial evolution: The value of the *fitness function* for a particular individual.

fitness function: In artificial evolution, a function that evaluates the performance of a phenotype. Used as an optimiziation criterion. Individuals with high fitness have a high probability of being selected for reproduction.

foraging: Behavior associated with the harvesting of food. It includes searching, recognizing, handling, and consuming.

foveal vision: Vision taking place in or affected by the fovea, that is, the center of the retina. Typically high-resolution vision. The term is used in opposition to "peripheral vision," in which the resolution is lower but motion detection is better.

FPGA (field programmable gate array): A device used to configure logic circuits within a fraction of a second. Rather than only simulating it, the FPGA physically constitutes the circuit.

frame-of-reference problem: Conceptualizing the relationship between the participants in the design process, namely the subject to be observed, the observer, the designer, the artifact (i.e., the computer program or the robot), and the environment.

frame problem: Roughly speaking, the frame problem refers to the issue of how, in a continuously changing environment, the model can be kept in tune with the real world.

Fungus Eater: A complete, embodied, autonomous, self-sufficient, situated agent. The term "Fungus Eater" was coined by Masanao Toda (1982). In his story, Fungus Eaters were sent to a distant planet to collect uranium ore, necessitating that they had to be autonomous and self-sufficient (since they would be well beyond the direct control of humans).

functionalism: As used in this book, this view endorses, in essence, a distinction between hardware (or wetware, in the case of a brain) and software. Take care, however: This term is used very differently in different scientific disciplines.

gene: Parts of the DNA molecule that direct the synthesis of particular proteins, which in turn are essential in the building up and functioning of an organism. Certain end results of such processes are recognizable as traits (for instance, eye color).

genetic algorithm: A special class of evolutionary algorithms originally proposed by Holland.

Genome: The entire collection of genetic materials; the totality of the genes possessed by an organism. The genome consists of one or more *chromosomes* that contain the individual *genes*.

genotype: Refers to the particular set of *genes* contained in a *genome*, that is, an individual's genetic constitution.

grandmother cell: Hypothetical neuronal cell that becomes active if an object or person, for example, "my grandmother," is recognized.

goal: In the context of classical artificial intelligence and folk psychology, a symbolic representation of a desirable state of affairs that differs from the state that is currently accessible through the sensory system. In embodied cognitive science, a set values or region of values the agent tries to achieve.

habitat constraint: Term introduced by Horsewill to designate constraints that hold in a particular environment. For example, office floors are flat, and most objects stand on the ground; this is the "ground plane constraint." In this book such constraints are referred to as constraints of the ecological niche.

haptic: Relating to touch.

Hebb rule, Hebbian learning: In the area of artificial neural networks, a rule stating that if two neurons are simultaneously active, the connection between them is reinforced.

Homunculus: Literally: Little man. A term whose main use is to criticize circular accounts of psychological processes that ascribe to some internal mechanism (the homunculus) the very psychological properties which were being investigated in the first place. For example, a theory of vision which says that there is within the brain a mechanism that scans, views, or inspects images on the retina refers to a homunculus.

Hopfield net: Fully interconnected neural network, typically with symmetric connectivity. Many variations on the basic network exist.

information processing metaphor: A position that views intelligence as being the result of information processing: An input is somehow processed, generating an output. Classical AI and cognitive science, in particular cognitive psychology, endorse an information processing perspective.

infrared (IR) sensor: Active sensor that sends out a signal (infrared light) and measures the intensity of the reflected signal.

intelligence: No generally accepted definition exists. The term is used to describe *complete agents* (agents that are autonomous, self-sufficient, embodied, and situated) that resolve *the diversity-compliance trade-off* in interesting ways. Intelligence must always be seen with respect to a *particular ecological niche*.

ipsilateral: Term used by biologists to designate "on the same side."

IQ test: General intelligence test, originally invented to see whether certain children would be better off in a special school. Was later turned into a general intelligence test, claiming to measure a general intelligence factor "g". Controversial because many people now believe that something as complex as intelligence cannot be reduced to a single number, the IQ. Another source of controversy concerns the extent to which the IQ is genetically predetermined or changeable by education.

IR sensor: See *infrared sensor.*

kinesthetic sensors: An umbrella term encompassing the sensors providing signals from muscles, tendons, and joints (forces, angles).

knowledge-based approach: Relates to the cognitivistic paradigm. The knowledge-based approach assumes that knowledge can be formalized and stored in a computer program. It is exemplified by the *physical symbol systems hypothesis.*

Kohonen map: Large class of nonsupervised neural networks that map a high-dimensional space onto a low-dimensional one while preserving the topology (i.e. neighboring points of the first space are mapped onto neighboring points in the second). Often the term self-organizing map, or self-organizing feature map, in used to indicate that no a priori knowledge of the categories is required.

Lamarckism: Evolutionary hypothesis that proposes the inheritence of acquired traits.

lateral: Term used by biologists to designate "on the side." See *ipsilateral, contralateral.*

leaky integrator: An artificial neuron whose activation does not instantaneously decay but decays at a particular rate. It thus contains a certain amount of information about the past.

linear threshold unit: A type of model neuron that becomes active if the sum of its inputs exceeds a given threshold value.

low-level specification: Designer commitments concerned with the physical setup of the agent, its body, sensory, and motor systems.

map (neural): A number of connected neurons that have the same or a similar functionality.

Markov (decision) process: Process in which the current state of a system depends solely on the immediately preceding state of the system. This implies that given the present state, the future of a system is independent of its past.

matched filter: Biological term for sensory systems that react only to a small portion of a possibly complex physical stimulation (e.g., they react only to selected frequencies), rather than "analyzing" the complete stimulation and then selecting the part to which they will react.

means-ends analysis: A process by which an operator or action is chosen on the basis of how much it reduces the distance to the desired goal. Used for goal-oriented systems.

MIT: Massachusetts Insitute of Technology. A famous university in Cambridge, Massachusetts, with a strong focus on science and engineering.

morphology: Form and structure of an agent. Includes the positioning of the sensors on the agent.

neural network: Networks composed of either natural or artificial neurons —"brain cells." Natural neural networks correspond to the network of connected neurons in animals, whereas artificial ones are simplified formal models thereof. Artificial neural networks are widely employed in the field of cognitive science and also applied in physics, optimization, control, time series analysis, signal processing, and pattern recognition.

neuroethology: Studies the neurobiological mechanisms underlying behavior. Computational neuroethology develops computational models for these mechanisms.

neuromorphic engineering: The scientific discipline that is modeling neural systems using analog VLSI technology. Rather than just simulating neural processing, this techology uses the actual physical processes on the chip to represent the neural signals.

noise (noisy channel): Broadly, any disturbance interfering with the operation of a device or system. Also, irrelevant or meaningless data transmitted along with the desired signals.

nonassociative learning: In nonassociative learning, the subject learns about the properties of a single stimulus. Its most important phenomena are habituation and sensitization.

nonparametric (statistics): Branch of statistics dedicated to the development of tests that hold no assumptions about the frequency distribution of the data. Also called "distribution-free" statistics.

nonsupervised learning: A class of learning algorithms that require no prior knowledge of the functions to be learned.

object invariance (object constancy): General term used for the tendency that objects can be recognized under wide variations in viewing conditions (such as color, brightness, distance, size, and form).

Occam's razor: A generally accepted principle in the philosophy of science. It states that the most *parsimonious* model/explanation is the best.

olfactory: Relating to smell.

ontology: See *domain ontology.*

operant conditioning: A type of conditioning in which the reinforcement is given only if the organism is emitting the desired response (like pressing a lever). Contrasts with *classical conditioning*, in which the "reinforcement" (the UCS) is given irrespective of the organism's response.

optical flow: The apparent motion of brightness patterns as a camera or an eye moves.

orienting response: Behavior in which the agent positions itself to get optimal sensory stimulation. A common example is turning head and eyes toward a source of noise.

paradigm: A particular set of explicit or implicit assumptions within which research is conducted.

parametric (statistics): Statistical tests and models that depend on the specific probability distribution of the variables considered. Such distributions are described by parameters such as mean, variance, and covariance.

parsimonious: Used in the philosophy of science to characterized explanations and models that employ a minimum number of assumptions and concepts. The most parsimonious explanation is typically favored in scientific explanations and models. This principle is also known as *Occam's razor.*

passive sensor: A sensor that receives signals from its environment without acting upon is. Typical example: Standard camera.

PDL (Process Description Language): A programming language that implements the idea of parallel, loosely coupled processes.

perception: Awareness of the elements of the environment through physical sensation. This is the standard definition. It involves the problematic notion of awareness, which implies the *homunculus* problem.

phase space: See *state space*.

phenotype: Actual physical appearance of an organism as a result of a process of development during which the *genotype* interacts with its environment.

plan: A sequence of operations that will get an agent from an initial state to a goal state (Newell and Simon 1972). Similarly, Miller, Galanter, and Pribram (1960) use the term to refer to hierarchical processes in the organism that can control the order in which a sequence of operations is to be performed.

Physical Symbol Systems Hypothesis (PSSH): Empirical hypothesis established by Newell and Simon (1976) that states that a physical symbol system is a necessary and sufficient condition for general intelligent action. Examples of physical symbol systems are rule-based systems (popular in the early days of AI), or more generally, computer programming languages like Pascal or C.

principle of rationality: See *rationality (principle of)*.

propagation rule: A rule characterizing the way activation in a neural network propagates through the net, including temporal characteristics (how long does it take for the activation to travel across a link, or a synapse; how much activation is lost along the way and across a synapse). Typically, a synchronized regime is assumed, in which it takes exactly one time step to traverse a link.

propositional representation: Representation consisting of a set of logical propositions like ON(CUP, TABLE), which represents the fact that the cup stands on the table. Most representations used in classical AI are of the propositional type.

proprioception: A general term used to cover all those sensory systems that provide information about the body itself (from *kinesthetic sensors* or from the inner ear).

proximity: "nearness" to an object. Proximity is the opposite of distance: if something is said to have high proximity to something else, this means that the two objects are very near one another.

proximity sensor: A sensor measuring proximity, that is, "nearness" to an object. Equivalent to a distance sensor.

Q-learning: One of the most widely used variants of *reinforcement learning*. In Q-learning the agent incrementally learns an action-value function $Q(s, a)$ that it uses to evaluate the utility of performing action a in state s. Q-learning leads to optimal behavior, i.e., behavior that maximizes the overall utility for the agent in this particular task environment.

range sensor: A sensor of measuring distance.

rational behavior: Behavior fulfilling the following four basic requirements: incompatibility of activities (activities are mutually exclusive), common currency, consistency, and transitivity of choice.

rational thought: Thought that obeys the *principle of rationality*.

rationality (principle of): If an agent has a goal and the knowledge that a particular action will get him closer to the goal, under the principle of rationality, it will choose that action.

recategorization: Categories continuously change; they are dynamic. It is therefore more useful to talk about recategorization rather than categorization (which would suggest static categories).

recurrent network: A neural network with loops, that is, connections that are not exclusively feed-forward. Recurrent networks retain a certain amount of information about their past.

redundancy: Generally, whatever can be omitted without significant loss of functionality is said to be redundant. Applied to the transmission of messages across information channels, it designates that part of a message that can be eliminated without loss of information. Redundancy is a prerequisite to achieve robust, adaptive behavior.

reentrant connections: Used in particular by Edelman to designate massively recurrent connections in a—biological or artificial—neural network (cf. *recurrent network*). To be distinguished from feedback loops, where error correction is the main purpose.

reinforcement learning: Generally, learning processes based on receiving a reinforcement signal if a behavior sequence has been successful. In machine learning, the reinforcement signal is typically given by the environment; in value-based learning, by the agent's *value system*.

retention period: Term used in the literature on memory to designate a period over which an item can be stored in a particular memory type (such as an iconic buffer, short-term memory, long-term memory).

scaling problem: The term "scaling" is used in different ways, leading to a number of different interpretations of the term "scaling problem." The most common are (1) the fact that the sensory stimulation from a particular object varies greatly, depending on orientation, distance, and lighting conditions, but the visual system is capable of identifying images registered through this variety as being one and the same object (see also: *object constancy*); (2) the question of whether a phenomenon that has been demonstrated in a simple system also applies to larger, more complex ones; (3) (similar to point 2) the question of whether something that has been shown in a simple robot or simple animal also applies to human-level intelligence; (4) the issue of whether something that has been demonstrated in simulation will work on real robots.

schema: Used in many different, typically relatively vague ways. Examples: (1) A memory structure in classical AI and cognitive science. (2) In Bartlett's view, an active organisation of past reactions, or of past experiences, which must always be supposed to be operating in any well-adapted organic response (Bartlett 1932) (3) More specifically, a motor schema is the basic unit of motor behavior from which complex actions can be constructed (Arkin 1993).

self-organization: A process by which patterns are formed in systems containing a large number of elements. A distinction is made between self-organization without structural changes the standard use of the term, and self-organization with structural changes. Self-organization without structural changes is completely reversible: given the same conditions, the system will always show the same patterns. This is in contrast to self-organization with structural changes. The latter is of special importance in the study of intelligence.

self-organizing (feature) map: See *Kohonen map*.

self-sufficiency: An agent is said to be self-sufficient if it is capable of sustaining itself over extended periods of time.

sensory-motor coordination: Coordination of sensory and motor systems to perform a particular task. Coordination implies that the motor system is influenced by the sensory stimulation: Merely turning on the spot or hitting an obstacle is not a sensory-motor coordination. Sensory-motor coordination leads to structured inputs that can be exploited for learning.

sigmoid (logistic) function: In the neural network literature, a frequently used activation function, similar to a threshold function, but "rounded off" at the corners. For values far below threshold, it is 0; for values far above threshold, 1. It rapidly changes near the threshold value.

situated agent: An agent is said to be situated if it acquires information about its environment solely through its sensors in interaction with the environment. A situated agent interacts with the world on its own, without an intervening human. It has the potential to acquire its own history, if equipped with appropriate learning mechanisms.

situatedness: A term used to characterize the essential quality possessed by a *situated agent*.

SMC models: Models used specifically to investigate the concept of sensory-motor coordination.

state space: In dynamical systems, the mathematical space with each dimension representing a variable needed to specify the system's state.

subject: A person or animal studied in an experiment.

subsumption architecture: As used here, a particular type of architecture for autonomous agents, championed by Rodney Brooks, based on the idea of a large number of parallel, loosely coupled processes connecting sensors to actuators with relatively little internal processing. Not to be confounded with the term "subsumption" as used in logic.

supervised learning: A large class of learning algorithms, especially in the neural network literature. During supervised learning, the network is given predefined input-output pairs where the output represents the category onto which the input is to be mapped (the desired output). Thus a priori knowledge of the categories to be learned is required. Learning is achieved by comparing the actual output of the network to the desired output.

symbol-grounding problem: The problem of how symbols acquire meaning and of how they are grounded in an agent's experience.

synthetic methodology: A methodology that seeks to understand by building. It is typically applied in a bottom-up way: First simple systems are built and explored, then their complexity is successively augmented if required to achieve the desired behaviors.

systems theory: Approach that seeks to understand a system's behavior by considering the mutual effects that the variables exert on each other.

task: As used in a design context, the designer's perspective on what the agent should accomplish. A task is accomplished by a set of behaviors.

task environment: Term used to designate an autonomous agent's task and desired behaviors as well as its ecological niche.

TNGS (Theory of Neuronal Group Selection): A theory concerning the development of brain structures that applies principles of evolutionary theory (selection) to ontogenetic development. The term somatic selection is also used.

tit-for-tat strategy: A game theoretical strategy in which individuals keep track of passed interactions and pay back services (in return) only to those from whom they have received favors.

top-down approach: Approach that decomposes the system under investigation into parts, which are then studied separately.

transitive closure: The set of all states generated by applying all possible rules to all possible states.

Turing test: An empirical test for intelligence. Roughly, the test's goal is to find out whether a computer program whose intelligence is to be assessed can be distinguished from a human. The interaction is mediated via a computer connection to exclude visual and auditory information that might help in the distinction.

unsupervised learning: See *nonsupervised learning*.

value-based learning: A form of learning in which the agent, via a so-called *value system*, provides its own reinforcement. We view this as a kind of *self-organization* with structural changes.

value system: Value systems are assumed to be basic evolutionary adaptations that define broad behavioral goals in terms of their consequences. In other words, they are very general biases that are supposed to be the heritage of natural selection. More concretely, value systems modulate learning. This modulation can be explicit or implicit. *Explicit value system:* Based on the consequences of behavior, signals (e.g. neural, hormonal) that modulate learning are generated. In neural network–based architectures, the modulation concerns change in synaptic strength. *Implicit value system:* Mechanisms that select interactions with the environment for learning that lead to increased adaptivity. Reflexes are examples of implicit value: They increase the probability of obtaining explicit value.

visuomotor loops: Direct couplings between visual and motor processes. A primary example is eye movements.

VLSI (Very Large Scale Integration) technology: Standard technology used in today's digital computers. Analog variants are used in *neuromorphic engineering*.

von Neumann machine: Two main ideas underly the von Neumann machine: storing the program together with the data in main memory, and sequential execution of instructions. Today, most computers are, in essence, still von Neumann machines, though even in regular PCs there is a certain level of parallelism.

wheel encoders: Sensors measuring the angle how much a wheel has turned. This measurement can be used to measure distance traveled (given that the radius of the wheels is known) and the speed of the turning wheel, if used with a clock. Wheel encoders are often implemented simply by optical means.

XOR problem: Exclusive OR: a logical function of a and b. The function is true if a or b, but not both, are true. It is false if either both are true or both are false. XOR is harder for an agent to learn than the normal logical OR (because it is not linearly separable).

References

Alterman, R. (1996). Everyday memory and activity. *Behavioral and Brain Sciences, 19,* 189–190.

Amit, D. J. (1989). *Modeling brain function: The world of attractor neural networks.* New York: Cambridge University Press.

Anderson, J. A. (1995). *An introduction to neural networks.* Cambridge, MA: MIT Press (A Bradford Book).

Arbib, M. A. (1981). Perceptual structures and distributed motor control. In V. B. Brooks (ed.) *Handbook of physiology: The nervous system, II* (Chap. 33, pp. 1449–1480). Oxford, UK: Oxford University Press.

Arbib, M. A. (1992). Schema theory. In S. C. Shapiro (Ed.), *Encyclopedia of artificial intelligence* (2nd ed., pp. 1427–1443.) New York: John Wiley.

Arbib, M. A. (1995). Schema theory. In M. A. Arbib (Ed.), *Handbook of brain theory and neural networks* (pp. 830–833). Cambridge, MA: MIT Press (A Bradford Book)

Arkin, R. C. (1989). Motor schema based mobile robot navigation. *International Journal of Robotics Research, 8,* 92–112.

Arkin, R. C. (1993). Modeling neural function at the schema level: Implications and results for robotic control. In R. D. Beer, R. E. Ritzmann, and T. Mckenna (Eds.) *Biological neural networks in invertebrate neuroethology and robotics* (Chap. 17, pp. 383–410). Boston: Academic Press.

Arkin, R. C. (1998). *Behavior-based robotics.* Cambridge, MA: MIT Press.

Arrowsmith, D. K., and Place, C. M. (1990). *An introduction to dynamical systems.* Cambridge, UK: Cambridge University Press.

Ashby, W. R. (1956). *An introduction to cybernetics.* London: Chapman and Hall.

Ashby, W. R. (1960). *Design for a brain.* London: Chapman and Hall.

Ashcraft, M. H. (1994). *Human memory and cognition.* (2nd ed). New York: HarperCollins College Publishers.

Atkinson, R. C., and Shiffrin, R. M. (1968). Human memory: A proposed system and its control processes. In K. W. Spence (Ed.), *The psychology of learning and motivation: Advances in research and theory* (Vol. 2, pp. 89–195). New York: Academic Press.

Bäck, T. B., and Schwefel, H.-P. (1993). An overview of evolutionary algorithms for parameter optimization. *Evolutionary Computation, 1,* 1–23.

Baddeley, A. (1997). *Human memory: Theory and practice* (Revised edition). Hove, UK: Psychology Press (an imprint of Erlbaum (UK) Taylor and Francis).

Bajcsy, R. (1988). Active perception. *Proceedings of the IEEE. Special Issue on Computer Vision, 76,* 996–1005.

Baker, G. L., and Gollup, J. P. (1990). *Chaotic dynamics: An introduction.* Cambridge, UK: Cambridge University Press.

Baldwin, J. M. (1896). A new factor in evolution. *American Naturalist, 30,* 441–451, 536–553.

Ballard, D. H. (1991). Animate vision. *Artificial Intelligence, 48,* 57–86.

Barker, L. M. (1994). *Learning and behavior: A psychological perspective.* New York: Macmillan College Publishing.

Barsalou, L. W. (1992). *Cognitive psychology: An overview for cognitive scientists.* Hillsdale, NJ: Lawrence Erlbaum.

Bartlett, F. C. (1932). *Remembering.* Cambridge, UK: Cambridge University Press.

Basri, R. (1996). Recognition by prototypes. *International Journal of Computer Vision, 19,* 147–167.

Becker, S., and Hinton G. E. (1992). Self-organizating neural network that discovers surfaces in random-dot stereograms. *Nature, 35,* 161–163.

Beer, R. D. (1990). *Intelligence as adaptive behavior: An experiment in computational neuroethology.* San Diego, CA: Academic Press.

Beer, R. D. (1995). A dynamical systems prespective on autonomous agents. *Artificial Intelligence, 72,* 173–215.

Beer, R. D. (1996). Toward the evolution of dynamical neural networks for minimally cognitive behavior. In P. Maes, M. Mataric, J.-A. Meyer, J. Pollack, and S. W. Wilson (Eds.), *From animals to animats: Proceedings of the 4th International Conference on Simulation of Adaptive Behavior* (pp. 421–429). Cambridge, MA: MIT Press.

Beer, R. D. (1997). The dynamics of adaptive behavior: A research program. Practice and future of autonomous agents [Special issue, R. Pfeifer and R. Brooks (Eds.)]. *Robotics and Autonomous Systems, 20,* 257–289.

Bicho, E., and Schöner, G. (1997). The dynamic approach to autonomous robotics demonstrated on a low-level vehicle platform. *Robotics and Autonomous Systems, 21,* 23–35.

Bischof, N. (1990). *Ordnung und Organisation als Heurisitken des Reduktiven Denkens.* Acta Psychologica, *60,* p. 1–32 [Order and organization as heuristics of reductionist thinking]

Block, N. (Ed.). (1981) *Imagery.* Cambridge, MA: MIT Press (A Bradford Book).

Blumberg, B. M., Todd, P. M., and Maes, P. (1996). No bad dogs: Ethological lessons for learning in Hamsterdam. In P. Maes, M. Mataric, J.-A. Meyer, J. Pollack, and S. W. Wilson (Eds.), *From animals to animats: Proceedings of the fourth International Conference on Simulation of Adaptive Behavior* (pp. 295–304). Cambridge, MA: MIT Press (A Bradford Book).

Boden, M. (1977). *Artificial intelligence and natural man* (2nd ed.). Cambridge, MA: MIT Press.

Boden, M. (1996). *The creative mind: Myths and Mechanisms.* London: Weidenfeld and Nicolson.

Braitenberg, V. (1984). Vehicles: Experiments in synthetic psychology. Cambridge, MA: MIT Press.

Bridgeman, B. (1990). Intention itself will disappear when its mechanisms are known. *Behavioral and Brain Sciences, 13,* 598.

Broadbent, D. E. (1957). A mechanical model for human attention and immediate memory. *Psychological Review, 63,* 205–215.

Brooks, R. A. (1986). A robust layered control system for a mobile robot. *IEEE Journal of Robotics and Automation.* RA-2, 14–23. (Also published as *MIT AI Memo 864,* September 1985.)

Brooks, R. A. (1989). A robot that walks: Emergent behaviors from a carefully evolved network. *Neural Computation, 1,* 153–162.

Brooks, R. A. (1990a). Elephants don't play chess. *Robotics and Autonomous Systems, 6,* 3–15.

Brooks, R. A. (1990b). The Behavioral Language user's guide. Memo 1227, MIT Artificial Intelligence Laboratory, Cambridge, MA.

Brooks, R. A. (1991a). Intelligence without representation. *Artificial Intelligence, 47,* 139–160.

Brooks, R. A. (1991b). Intelligence without reason. *Proceedings Internadtional Joint Conference on Artificial Intelligence-91,* 569–595.

Brooks, R. A. (1994). Coherent behavior from many adaptive processes. In D. Cliff, P. Husbands, J.-A. Meyer, and S. W. Wilson (Eds.), *From animals to animats: Proceedings of the third International Conference on Simulation of Adaptive Behavior* (pp. 421–430). Cambridge, MA: MIT Press (A Bradford Book).

Brooks, R. A. (1997). From earwigs to humans. Practice and future of autonomous agents [Special issue, R. Pfeifer and R. Brooks (Eds.)]. *Robotics and Autonomous Systems, 20,* 291–304.

Brooks, R. A., and Breazeal, C. (in press). *Embodied intelligence.* Cambridge, MA: MIT Press.

Brooks, R. A., and Mataric, M. J. (1993). Real robots, real learning problems. In J. H. Connell and S. Mahadevan (Eds.), *Robot learning*. Boston: Kluwer, pp. 142–168.

Brooks, R. A., and Stein, L. A. (1993). Building brains for bodies. Memo 1439, Artificial Intelligence Lab, Massachusetts Institute of Technology, Cambridge MA.

Bursen, H. A. (1980). *Dismantling the memory machine: A philosophical investigation of machine theories of memory*. Dordrecht, the Netherlands: D. Reidel Publishing.

Bushnell, E. M. and Boudreau, J. P. (1993). Motor development in the mind: The potential role of motor abilities as a determinant of aspects of perceptual development. *Child Development, 64,* 1005–1021.

Carpenter, G. A., and Grossberg, S. (1988, March). The ART of adaptive pattern recognition by a self-organizing network. *Computer, 77–88.*

Carroll, J. B. (1993). *Human cognitive abilities: A survey of factor-analytic studies.* Cambridge, UK: Cambridge University Press.

Cartright, B. A., and Collett, R. S. (1983). Landmark navigation in bees. *Journal of Comparative Physiology, 151,* 521–543.

Changeux, J-P. (1986). Coexistence of neuronal messengers and molecular selection. *Progress in Brain Research, 68,* 383–403.

Chapman, D. (1987). Planning for conjunctive goals. *Artificial Intelligence, 32,* 333–337.

Chomsky, N. (1959). A review of Skinner's *Verbal Behavior. Language, 35,* 26–58.

Chou, C. P., and Hannaford, B. (1997). Study of human forearm posture maintenance with a physiologically based robotic arm and spinal level neural controller. *Biological Cybernetics, 76,* 285–298.

Churchland, P. S., and Sejnowski, T. J. (1992). *The computational brain.* Cambridge, MA: MIT Press (A Bradford Book).

Clancey, W. J. (1991a). The frame of reference problem in the design of intelligent machines. In K. van Lehn (Ed.), *Architectures for intelligence* (pp. 357–423). Hillsdale, NJ: Erlbaum.

Clancey, W. J. (1991b). The invention of memory (by Israel Rosenfield). [Book review]. *Artificial Intelligence, 50,* 241–284.

Clancey, W. J. (1997). *Situated cognition: On human knowledge and computer representations.* New York: Cambridge University Press.

Clark, A., and Thornton C. (1997). Trading spaces. *Behavioral and Brain Sciences 20,* pp. 57–90.

Cohen, G. (1996). *Memory in the real world.* Hillsdale, NJ: Erlbaum.

Cohen, P. R. (1995). *Empirical methods for artificial intelligence.* Cambridge, MA: MIT Press.

Colombetti, M., and Dorigo, M. (1993). Learning to control an autonomous robot by distributed genetic algorithms. In J.-A. Meyer, H. L. Roitblat, and S. W. Wilson (Eds.), *From animals to animats: Proceedings of the second International Conference on Simulation of Adaptive Behavior* (pp. 305–312). Cambridge, MA: MIT Press (A Bradford Book).

Connell, J. H. (1990). *Minimalist mobile robotics: A colony-style architecture for an artificial creature.* San Diego, CA: Academic Press.

Connell, J. H., and Mahadevan, S. (Eds.). (1993). *Robot learning.* Boston: Kluwer Academic Publishers.

Conway, M. A. (1996). What do memories correspond to? *Behavioral and Brain Sciences, 19,* 195–196.

Cover, T. M., and Thomas, J. A. (1991). *Elements of information theory.* New York: John Wiley.

Crockett, L. J. (1994). *The Turing test and the frame problem: AI's mistaken understanding of intelligence.* Norwood, NJ: Ablex Publishing.

Cruse, H. (1991). Coordination of leg movement in walking animals. In J.-A. Meyer and S. W. Wilson (Eds.), *From animals to animats: Proceedings of the First International Conference on Simulation of Adaptive Behavior* (pp. 105–119). Cambridge, MA: MIT Press (A Bradford Book).

Cruse, H., Bartling, C., Dean, J., Kindermann, T., Schmitz, J., Schumm, M., and Wagner, H. (1996). Coordination in a six-legged walking system: Simple solutions to complex problems by exploitation of physical properties. In P. Maes, M. Mataric, J.-A. Meyer, J. Pollack, and S. W. Wilson (Eds.): *From animals to animats: Proceedings of the fourth International Conference on Simulation of Adaptive Behavior* (pp. 84–93). Cambridge MA: MIT Press (A Bradford Book).

Dalenoort, S. J. (Ed.). (1989). *The paradigm of self-organization.* London: Gordon and Breach.

Dawkins, R. (1976). Hierarchical organisation: A candidate principle for ethology. In P. P. G. Bateson and R. A. Hinde (Eds.), *Growing points in ethology* pp. 7–45. Cambridge, UK: Cambridge University Press.

Dawkins, R. (1988). *The blind watchmaker.* London: Penguin Books. (Original work published 1986, Longman).

de Garis, H. (1994). An artificial brain: ATR's CAM-brain project aims to build/evolve an artificial brain with a million neural net modules inside a trillion cell cellular automata machine. *New Generation Computing Journal, 12,* 215.

Dedien, E. and Mazer, E. (1992). An approach to sensorimotor relevance. In F. Varela, and P. Bourgine (Eds.). *Toward a practice of autonomous agents. Proceedings of the First European Conference on Artificial life.* Cambridge, MA: MIT Press 88–96.

De Jong, K. A. (1975). An analysis of the beahvior of a class of genetic adaptive systems. Ph.D. dissertation, University of Michigan, Ann Arbor.

Deneubourg, J. L. and Goss, S. (1989). Collective patterns and decision-making. *Ethology, Ecology, and Evolution, 1,* 295–311.

Deneubourg, J.-L., Goss, S., Franks, N., Sendova-Franks, A., Detrain, C., and Chrétien, L. (1991). The dynamics of collective sorting: Robot-like ants and ant-like robots. In J.-A. Meyer and S. W. Wilson (Eds.), *From animals to animats: Proceedings of the First International Conference on Simulation of Adaptive Behavior* (pp. 356–363) Cambridge, MA: MIT Press (A Bradford Book).

Deneubourg, J.-L., Theraulaz, G., and Beckers, R. (1992). Swarm-made architectures. In F. J. Varela and P. Bourgine (Eds.), *Toward a practice of autonomous systems: Proceedings of the First European Conference on Artificial Life* (pp. 123–133). Cambridge, MA: MIT Press.

Dennett, D. C. (1987). Cognitive wheels: The frame problem of AI. In C. Hookway (Ed.), *Minds, machines, and evolution: Philosophical Studies (1984)* (pp. 129–51). Bantain, US: Baen Books.

Dennett, D. C. (1997). Cog as a thought experiment [Special issue, R. Pfeifer and R. Brooks (Eds.)]. *Robotics and Autonomous Systems, 20,* 251–256.

de Sa, V R. (1994). *Unsupervised classification of learning from cross-modal environment structure.* PhD dissertation, Department of Computer Science, University of Rochester, NY.

Dewey, J. (1981). The reflex arc in psychology. *Psychological Review, 3,* 357–370. (Reprinted in J. J. McDermott (Ed.), *The Philosophy of John Dewey* (pp. 136–148). Chicago: University of Chicago Press. (Original work published 1896)

Dorigo, M., and Colombetti, M. (1997). *Robot Shaping. An Experiment in behavior engineering.* Cambridge, MA: MIT Press.

Douglas, R., Mahowald, M., and Mead, C (1995). Neuromorphic analogue VLSI. *Annual Review of Neuroscience, 18,* 255–281.

Douglas, R. J., Martin, K. A. C. and Nelson, J. C. (1993). The neurobiology of primate vision. *Baillière's Clinical Neurology, 2,* 191–225.

Drexler, K. E. (1992). *Nanosystems: Molecular machinery, manufacturing and computation.* New York: John Wiley.

Dreyfus, H. L. (1979). *What computers can't do: A critique of artificial reason.* Cambridge, MA: MIT Press.

Dreyfus, H. L. (1992). *What computers still can't do: A critique of artificial reason.* Cambridge, MA: MIT Press.

Dudai, Y. (1994). *The neurobiology of memory.* Oxford, UK: Oxford University Press.

Edelman, G. E. (1987). *Neural Darwinism: The theory of neuronal group selection.* New York: Basic Books.

Edelman, G. E. (1992). *Bright air, brilliant fire: On the matter of the mind.* New York: Basic Books.

Eggenberger, P. (1996). Cell interactions as a control tool of developmental processes for evolutionary robotics. In P. Maes, M. Mataric, J.-A. Meyer, J. Pollack, and S. W. Wilson (Eds.), *From animals to animats: Proceedings of the Fourth International Conference on Simulation of Adaptive Behavior* (pp. 440–448). Cambridge, MA: MIT Press (A Bradford Book).

Eggenberger, P. (1997). Evolving morphologies of simulated 3-D organisms based on differential gene expression. In P. Husbands and I. Harvey (Eds.), *Fourth European Conference on Artificial Life* (pp. 205–213). Cambridge MA: MIT Press.

Egner, S., and Scheier, C. (1997). Feature binding through temporally correlated neural activity in a robot model of visual perception. In W. Gerstner, A. Germond, M. Hasler, and J.-D. Nicoud (Eds.). *Artificial Neural Networks—ICANN'97* (International Conference on Artificial Neural Networks) (pp. 703–709). Berlin: Springer.

Elman, J. L., Bates, E. A., Johnson, H. A., Karmiloff-Smith, A., Parisi, D., and Plunkett, K. (1996). *Rethinking innateness: A connectionist perspective on development.* Cambridge, MA: MIT Press (A Bradford Book).

Epstein, J. M., and Axtell, R. (1996). *Growing artificial societies: Social science from the bottom-up.* Washington, DC: Brookings Cambridge, MA: MIT Press.

Epstein, R. (1992). The quest for the thinking computer. *AI Magazine, 13,* 81–95.

Everett, H. R. (1995). *Sensors for mobile robots: Theory and application.* MA: A. K. Peters Ltd.

Farmer, J. D. (1990). A Rosetta Stone to connectionism. *Physica D, 42,* 153–187.

Feigenbaum, E. A., and Feldman, J. (Eds.) (1963). *Computers and thought.* New York: McGraw-Hill.

Fermuller, C., and Aloimonos, Y. (1995). Vision and action. *Image and Vision Computing, 13,* 725–744.

Ferrari, F., Nielsen, P. Q. J., and Sandini, G. (1995). Space variant imaging. *Sensor Review, 15,* 17–20.

Ferrell, C. (1994). Robust adaptive locomotion of an autonomous hexapod. In P. Gaussier and J.-D. Nicoud (Eds.), *Proceedings: From Perception to Action Conference* (pp. 66–77). Los Alamitos, CA: IEEE Computer Society Press.

Ferrell, C. (1996). Orientation behavior using registered topographic maps. In Maes, P., Mataric, M., Meyer, J.-A., Pollach, J. and Wilson, S. W. (Eds.) *From Animals to Animats 4.* Cambridge, MA: MIT Press, 94–104.

Fikes, R. E., and Nilsson, N. J. (1971). STRIPS: A new approach to the application of theorem proving and problem solving. *Artificial Intelligence, 2,* 189–208.

Fikes, R. E., and Nilsson, N. J. (1993). STRIPS: Retrospective. *Artificial Intelligence, 59,* 227–232.

Fisher, R. P. (1996). Implications of output-bound measures for laboratory and field research in memory. *Behavioral and Brain Sciences, 19,* 197.

Floreano, D., and Mondada, F. (1994). Automatic creation of an autonomous agent: Genetic evolution of a neural-network driven robot. In D. Cliff, P. Husbands, J.-A. Meyer, and S. W. Wilson (Eds.), *From animals to animats: Proceedings of the Third International Conference on Simulation of Adaptive Behavior* (pp. 421–430). Cambridge, MA: MIT Press (A Bradford Book).

Fodor, J. A. (1975). *The language of thought.* New York: Thomas Y. Crowell. (Reprinted in 1980 by Harvard University Press, Cambridge, MA.)

Fodor, J. A. (1983). *The modularity of mind.* Cambridge, MA: MIT Press.

Fogel, D. B. (1995). Computer simulation of natural evolution. In *Evolutionary computation: Toward a new philosophy of machine intelligence.* In D. B. Fogel (Ed.) (pp. 67–119). Piscataway, NJ: IEEE Press.

Fogel L. J. (1962) Autonomous automata *Industrial Research 4,* 14–19.

Franceschini, N., Pichon, J. M., and Blanes, C. (1992). From insect vision to robot vision. *Philosophical Transactions of the Royal Society, London B, 337,* 283–294.

Franklin, S. (1995). *Artificial minds.* Cambridge, MA: MIT Press (A Bradford Book).

Freeman, W. J. (1991). The physiology of perception. *Scientific American, 264,* 78–85.

Fuster, J. M. (1997). Network memory. *Trends in Neurosciences, 20,* 451–459.

Garcia, M., Chatterjee, A., Ruina, A., and Coleman, M. (in press). The simplest walking model: Stability, complexity, and scaling. *ASME Journal of Biomechanical Engineering.*

Gardner, H. (1985). *Frames of mind: The theory of multiple intelligences.* New York: Basic Books.

Gardner, H. (1987). *The mind's new science: A history of the cognitive revolution.* New York: Basic Books. (Original work published 1985.)

Gat, E., Rajiv, D., Ivlev, R., Loch, L., and Miller, D. P. (1994). Behavior control for exploration of planetary surfaces. *IEEE Transactions on Robotics and Automation, 10,* 78–95.

Gazzaniga, M. S. (1992). *Nature's mind: The biological roots of thinking, emotions, sexuality, language, and intelligence.* New York: Basic Books.

Gibson, E. J. (1988). Exploratory behavior in the development of perceiving, acting, and the acquiring of knowledge. *Annual Review of Psychology, 39,* 1–41.

Gibson, J. J. (1966). *The senses considered as perceptual systems.* Boston: Houghton Mifflin.

Gibson, J. J. (1979). *The ecological approach to visual perception.* Boston: Houghton Mifflin.

Glenberg, A. M. (1997). What memory is for. *Behavioral and Brain Sciences, 20,* 1–56.

Gluck, M. A., and Bower, G. H. (1988). From conditioning to category learning: An adaptive network model. *Journal of Experimental Psychology: General, 117,* 227–247.

Goldberg, D. E. (1989). *Genetic algorithms in search, optimization and machine learning.* Reading, MA: Addison-Wesley.

Goleman, D. (1995). *Emotional intelligence.* New York: Bantam Books.

Gordon, I. E. (1989). *Theories of visual perception.* Chichester, UK: John Wiley.

Goss, S., and Deneubourg, J. L. (1992). Harvesting by a group of robots. In F. J. Varela and P. Bourgine (Eds.), *Toward a practice of autonomous systems: Proceedings of the First European Conference on Artificial Life* (pp. 195–204). Cambridge, MA: MIT Press.

Gould, S. J. (1996). *The mismeasure of man.* New York: W.W. Norton. (Paperback edition, 1996)

Greenbaum, J., and Kyng, M. (1991) (Eds.). *Design at work: Cooperative design of computer systems.* Hillsdale, NJ: Erlbaum Associates.

Gregory, R. L. (1987). *The Oxford companion to the mind.* Oxford, UK: Oxford University Press.

Harnad, S. (1990). The symbol grounding problem. *Physica D, 42,* 335–346.

Harnad, S. (1995). Grounding symbolic capacity in robotic capacity. In L. Steels and R. Brooks (Eds.), The artificial life route to artificial intelligence: Building embodied, situated agents (pp. 277–286). Hillsdale, NJ: Laurence Erlbaum.

Harvey, I., Husbands, P., and Cliff, D. (1994). Seeing the light: Artificial evolution, real vision. In D. Cliff, P. Husbands, J.-A. Meyer, and S. W. Wilson (Eds.), *From animals to animats. Proceedings of the Third International Conference on Simulation of Adaptive Behavior* (pp. 392–401). Cambridge, MA: MIT Press (A Bradford Book).

Harvey, I., Husbands, P., Cliff, D., Thompson, A., and Jakobi, N. (1997). Evolutionary robotics: The Sussex approach. Practice and future of autonomous Agents [Special issue, R. Pfeifer and R. Brooks (Eds.)]. *Robotics and Autonomous Systems, 20,* 205–224.

Hasemann, J.-M. (1995). Robot control architectures: Application requirements, approaches, and technologies. In *Proceedings of the SPIE Intelligent Robots and Computer Vision XIV: Algorithms, Techniques, Active Vision, Material Handling.* Philadelphia, PA, pp. 22–36.

Haugeland, J. (1985). *Artificial Intelligence: The very idea.* Cambridge, MA: MIT Press (A Bradford Book).

Hawkins, R. D., Kandel, E. R., and Siegelbaum, S. A. (1993). Learning to modulate transmitter release: Themes and variations in synaptic plasticity. *Annual Review of Neuroscience, 16,* 625–665.

Hebb, D. O. (1949). *The organization of behavior.* New York: John Wiley.

Heckhausen, H., and Kuhl, J. (1985). From wishes to action: The dead ends and short cuts on the long way to action. In M. Frese and J. Sabini (Eds.), *Goal directed behavior.* Hillsdale, NJ: Erlbaum, pp. 78–94.

Hemelrijk, C. K. (1996a). Reciprocation in apes: From complex cognition to self-structuring. In W. C. McGrew, L. F. Marchant, and T. Nishida (Eds.), *Great ape societies* (pp. 185–195). Cambridge, UK: Cambridge University Press.

Hemelrijk, C. K. (1996b). Dominance interactions, spatial dynamics and emergent reciprocity in a virtual world. In P. Maes, M. Mataric, J.-A. Meyer, J. Pollack, and S. W. Wilson (Eds.), *From animals to animats: Proceedings of the Forth International Conference on Simulation of Adaptive Behavior* (pp. 545–552). Cambridge, MA: MIT Press (A Bradford Book).

Hemelrijk, C. K. (1997). Co-operation without games, genes or cognition. In P. Husbands and I. Harvey (Eds.), *Fourth European Conference on Artificial Life* (pp. 511–520). Cambridge, MA: MIT Press.

Hendriks-Jansen, H. (1996). *Catching ourselves in the act: Situated activity, interactive emergence, evolution, and human thought.* Cambridge, MA: MIT Press (A Bradford Book).

Herrnstein, R. J., and Murray, C. (1994). *The bell curve. Intelligence and class structure in American life.* New York: Free Press.

Hertz, J. (1995). Computing with attractors. In M. A. Arbib (Ed.), *Handbook of brain theory and neural networks* (pp. 157–159). Cambridge, MA: MIT Press (A Bradford Book).

Hertz, J., Krogh, A., and Palmer, R. G. (1991). *Introduction to the theory of neural computation.* Redwood City, CA: Addison-Wesley.

Hintzman, D. L. (1990). Human learning and memory: Connections and dissociations. *Annual Review of Psychology, 41,* 109–139.

Hogeweg, P. (1988). MIRROR beyond MIRROR, Puddles of LIFE. *In Artificial life: SFI studies in the sciences of complexity* (pp. 297–316). Redwood City, CA: Addisson-Wesley.

Hogg, D. W., Martin, F., and Resnik, M. (1991). Braitenberg creatures [On-line: MIT Media Laboratory]. Available: http://lcs.www.media.mit.edu/people/fredm/papers/vehicles/

Holenstein, E. (1985). Natural and artificial intelligence. In D. Ihde and H. J. Silverman (Eds.), *Descriptions* (pp. 162–174). Albany: State of New York University Press.

Holland, J. H. (1975). *Adaptation in natural and artificial systems.* Ann Arbor: University of Michigan Press. (Second edition: Cambridge, MA: MIT Press, 1992.)

Horn, B. K. P. (1986). *Robot vision.* Cambridge, MA: MIT Press.

Hornik, K., Stinchcombe, M., and White, H. (1989). Multi-layer feedforward networks are universal approximators. *Neural Networks, 2,* 359–366.

Horswill, I. (1992). Characterizing adaptation by constraint. In F. J. Varela and P. Bourgine (Eds.), *Toward a practice of autonomous systems: Proceedings of the First European Conference on Artificial Life* (pp. 58–64). Cambridge, MA: MIT Press.

Horswill, I. (1993). A simple, cheap, and robust visual navigation system. In J.-A. Meyer, H. L. Roitblat, and S. W. Wilson (Eds.), *From animals to animats: Proceedings of the Second International Conference on Simulation of Adaptive Behavior.* Cambridge, MA: MIT Press (A Bradford Book).

Huxley, J. S. (1942). *Evolution, the modern synthesis.* London: Allen and Unwin.

Ishiguro, A., Shirai, Y., Watanabe, Y. and Uchikawa, Y. (1997). Emergent construction of Immune networks for autonomous mobile robots through the metadynamics function. In P. Husbands and I. Harvey (Eds.) *Proceedings of the Fourth European Conference on Artificial Life* (pp. 318–326). Cambridge, MA: MIT Press.

Ishihara, H., Arai, F., and Fikuda, T. (1996). Micro mechatronics and micro actuators. *IEE/ASME Transactions on Mechatronics, 1,* 68–79.

Jackson, E. A. (1991). *Perspectives on non-linear dynamics.* Cambridge, UK: Cambridge University Press.

Jacoby, L. L., and Dallas, M. (1981). On the relationship between autobiographical memory an perceptual learning. *Journal of Experimental Psychology: General, 110,* 306–340.

Jakobi, N. (in press). Evolutionary robotics and the radical envelope of noise hypothesis. *Adaptive Behavior.*

James, W. (1890). *Principles of psychology* (Vol. 1). New York: Holt.

Janlert, L. E. (1987). Modeling change: The frame problem. In Z. W. Pylyshyn (Ed.), *The robot's dilemma: The frame problem in artificial intelligence* (pp. 1–40). Norwood, NJ: Ablex.

Jeannerod, M. (1997). *The cognitive neuroscience of action*. Oxford, UK: Blackwell.

Johnson, M. H. and Morton, J. (1991). *Biology and cognitive development: The case of face recognition*. Oxford: Blackwell.

Johnson-Laird, P. N. (1988). *The computer and the mind: An introduction to cognitive science*. Cambridge, MA: Harvard University Press.

Jones, J. L., and Flynn, A. M. (1993). *Mobile robots: Inspiration to implementation*. Wellesley, MA: A. K. Peters, Ltd.

Journal of Educational Psychology, 1921, Vol. 12, pp. 123–147, 195–216, Intelligence and its measurement: A symposium.

Kaelbling, L. P., Littman, M. L., and Moore, A. W. (1996). Reinforcement learning: A survey. *Journal of Artificial Intelligence Research, 4*, 237–285.

Kalawsky, R. S. (1993). *The science of virtual reality and virtual environments*. Reading, MA: Addison-Wesley.

Kandell, E. R. Schwartz, J. H., and Jessell, T. M. (1991). *Principles of neural science* (3rd ed.). Norwalk, CT: Appelton & Lange.

Karn, K. S. and Zelinsky, G. J. (1996). Driving and dish washing: Failure of the correspondence metaphor for memory. *Behavioral and Brain Sciences, 19*, 198.

Kelso, J. A. S. (1995). *Dynamic patterns: The self-organization of brain and behavior*. Cambridge, MA: MIT Press (A Bradford Book).

Kennedy, J. F. (1961). Urgent national needs. Speech to a Joint Session of Congress, 25 May 1961. Congressional Record—House, 8276.

Kien, J., and Altman, J. S. (1992). *Neuroethology of action selection*. Cambridge, MA: MIT Press.

Kirsh, D. (1991). Today the earwig, tomorrow man? *Artificial Intelligence, 47*, 161–184.

Kitano, H., Asada, M., Kuniyoshi, Y., Noda, I., Osawa, E., and Matsubara, H. (1997). RoboCup: A challenge problem for AI. *AI Magazine*, Spring, 1997. American Association for Artificial Intelligence, 73–85.

Kodjabachian, J., and Meyer, J. A. (1995). Evolution and development of control architectures in animats. *Robotics and Autonomous Systems, 16*, 161–182.

Kohonen, T. (1988a). *Self-organization and associative memory*. Berlin: Springer.

Kohonen, T. (1988b). The "neural" phonetic typewriter. *IEEE Computer, 3*, 11–22.

Kolers, P. A. and Roediger, H. L., III (1984). Procedures of mind. *Journal of Verbal Learning and Verbal Behavior, 23*, 425–49.

Koriat, A., and Goldsmith, M. (1994). Memory in naturalistic and laboratory contexts: Distinguishing the accuracy-oriented and quantity-oriented approaches to memory assessment. *Journal of Experimental Psychology: General, 123*, 297–316.

Koriat, A., and Goldsmith, M. (1996). Memory metaphors and the laboratory/*real-life* controversy: Correspondence versus storehouse views of memory. *Behavioral and Brain Sciences, 19*, 175–227.

Kruschke, J. K. (1992). ALCOVE: An exemplar-based connectionist model of category learning. *Psychological Review, 99*, 22–44.

Kuniyoshi, Y., and Nagakubo, A. (1997). Humanoids as a research vehicle into flexible complex interaction. In *Proceedings of the IEEE/RSJ International Conference on Intelligent Robots and Systems* (IROS, pp. 811–819). C. Langier (Ed.) Piscataway, NJ: IEEE Service Center.

Kurzweil, R. (1990). *The age of intelligent machines*. Cambridge, MA: MIT Press.

Lachman, R., Lachman, J. L., and Butterfield, E. C. (1979). *Cognitive psychology and information processing*. Hillsdale, NJ: Erlbaum.

Lakoff, G. (1987). *Women, fire, and dangerous things: What categories reveal about the mind*. Chicago: University of Chicago Press.

Lambrinos, D. and Scheier, C. (1995). Extended Braitenberg Architectures. *AILab Technical Report* No. 95-10, University of Zurich, Switzerland. F. Fogelman-Soulié, J-L. Rault, P. Gallinari and G. Dreyfus (Eds.) Paris: EC2 and Cie.

Lambrinos, D., and Scheier, C. (1996). Building complete autonomous agents: A case study on categorization. In *Proceedings of the 1996 IEEE/RSJ International Conference on Intelligent Robots and Systems* (pp. 170–177). Piscataway, NJ: Institute of Electrical and Electronics Engineers, Inc.

Lambrinos, D., Maris, M., Kobayashi, H., Labhart, T., Pfeifer, R., and Wehner, R. (1997). An autonomous agent navigating with a polarized light compass. *Adaptive Behavior, 6,* 175–206.

Langton, C. (1989). Artificial life. In C. Langton (Ed.), *The proceedings of an interdisciplinary workshop on the synthesis and simulation of living systems.* Redwood City, CA: Addison-Wesley, pp. 1–18.

Langton, C. (Ed.). (1995). *Artificial life: An overview.* Cambridge, MA: MIT Press: (A Bradford Book).

Leahey, T. H. (1994). *A history of modern psychology.* Englewood Cliffs, NJ: Prentice-Hall, Inc.

Levy, S. (1992). *Artificial life: A report from the frontier where computers meet biology.* New York: Vintage Books.

Lorenz, K. (1981). *Foundations of ethology.* Berlin: Springer-Verlag.

MacLeod, C. M. (1997). Is memory caught in the mesh? *Behavioral and Brain Sciences, 20,* 30 (Peer Commentary on Glenberg, A. M. (1997). What memory is for. *Behavioral and Brain Sciences*, 1997, *20,* 1–55.)

Maes, P. (1991). A bottom-up mechanism for behaviour selection in an artificial creature. In: J.-A. Meyer and S. W. Wilson (Eds.), From animals to animats: *Proceedings of the First International Conference on Simulation of Adaptive Behaviour.* Cambridge, MA: MIT Press, 238–247.

Maes, P. (1993). Behavior-based artificial intelligence. In J.-A. Meyer, H. L. Roitblat, and S. W. Wilson (Eds.), *From animals to animates: Proceedings of the Second International Conference on Simulation of Adaptive Behavior* (pp. 2–10). Cambridge, MA: MIT Press (A Bradford Book).

Mahadevan, S., and Connell, J. (1992). Automatic programming of behavior-based robots using reinforcement learning. *Artificial Intelligence, 55,* 311–365.

Mahowald, M., and Mead, C. A. (1991, May). The silicon retina. *Scientific American,* 40–46.

Maris, M., and te Boekhorst, R. (1996). Exploiting physical constraints: Heap formation through behavioral error in a group of robots. In: M. Asada (Ed.) *Proceedings of IROS'96: IEEE/RSJ International Conference on Intelligent Robots and Systems,* pp. 1655–1660.

Marjanovic, M., Scassellati, B., and Williamson, M. (1996). Self-taught visually-guided pointing for a humanoid robot. In P. Maes, M. Mataric, J.-A. Meyer, J. Pollack, and S. W. Wilson (Eds.), *From animals to animats: Proceedings of the Fourth International Conference on Simulation of Adaptive Behavior* (pp. 35–44). Cambridge, MA: MIT Press (A Bradford Book).

Marr, D. (1982). *Vision: A computation investigation into the human representation and processing of visual information.* San Francisco: W.H. Freeman.

Martin, P., and Bateson, P. (1993). *Measuring behavior: An introductory guide* (2nd ed.). Cambridge, UK: Cambridge University Press.

Mataric, M. (1991). Navigating with a rat brain: A neurobiologically-inspired model for robot spatial representation. In J.-A. Meyer and S. W. Wilson (Eds.), *From animals to animats: Proceedings of the First International Conference on Simulation of Adaptive Behavior* (pp. 169–175). Cambridge, MA: MIT Press (A Bradford Book).

Mataric, M. (1993). Designing emergent behaviors: From local interactions to collective intelligence. In J.-A. Meyer, H. L. Roitblat, and S. W. Wilson (Eds.), *From animals to animats: Proceedings of the Second International Conference on Simulation of Adaptive Behavior* (pp. 432–441). Cambridge, MA: MIT Press (A Bradford Book).

Mataric, M. (1994). Learning to behave socially. In D. Cliff, P. Husbands, J.-A. Meyer, and S. W. Wilson (Eds.), *From animals to animats: Proceedings of the Third International Conference on Simulation of Adaptive Behavior* (pp. 453–462). Cambridge, MA: MIT Press (A Bradford Book).

Mataric, M. (1995). Designing and understanding adaptive group behavior. *Adaptive Behavior, 4,* 51–80.

Mataric, M. (1997). Learning social behaviors. Practice and Future of Autonomous Agents [Special issue, R. Pfeifer and R. Brooks (Eds.)]. *Robotics and Autonomous Systems, 20,* 191–204.

Mataric, M., and Cliff, D. (1996). Challenges in evolving controllers for physical robots. *Robotics and Autonomous Systems, 19(1),* 67–83.

Matijevic, J. (1996). Mars Pathfinder Microrover: Implementing a low cost planetary mission experiment. In *Proceedings of the Second IAA International Conference on Low-Cost Planetary Missions,* http://robotics.jpl.nasa.gov/tasks/mfex_cns/papers/IAA96_jake.ps.

McCarthy, J. (1980). Circumscription: A form of non-monotonic reasoning. *Artificial Intelligence, 13,* 27–39.

McCarthy, J., and Hayes, P. J. (1969). Some philosophical problems from the standpoint of artificial intelligence. *Machine Intelligence, 4,* 463–502.

McClelland, J. L., Rumelhart, D. E., and the PDP Research Group. (1986). *Parallel distributed processing: Explorations in the microstructure of cognition* (Vol. 2. Cambridge, MA: MIT Press (A Bradford Book).

McCorduck, P. (1979). *Machines who think: A personal inquiry into the history and prospects of artificial intelligence.* San Francisco: W.H. Freeman.

McFarland, D. (1989). The teleological imperative. In A. Montefiori and D. Noble (Eds.), *Goals, no goals, and own goals.* London: Unwin Hyman, pp. 39–58.

McFarland, D. (1991). What it means for robot behavior to be adaptive. In J.-A. Meyer and S. W. Wilson (Eds.), *From animals to animats: Proceedings of the First International Conference on Simulation of Adaptive Behavior* (pp. 22–28). Cambridge, MA: MIT Press (A Bradford Book).

McFarland, D. (1995). Autonomy and self-sufficiency in robots. In L. Steels and R. Brooks (Eds.), *The artificial life route to artificial intelligence: Building embodied, situated agents* (pp. 287–309). Hillsdale, NJ: Lawrence Erlbaum.

McFarland, D. (1994). Towards robot cooperation. In D. Cliff, P. Husbands, J. A. Meyer, and S. W. Wilson (Eds.), *From animals to animats: Proceedings of the Third International Conference on Simulation of Adaptive Behavior* (pp. 440–444). Cambridge, MA: MIT Press (A Bradford Book).

McFarland, D., and Bösser, M. (1993). *Intelligent behavior in animals and robots.* Cambridge, MA: MIT Press.

McGeer, T. (1990a). Passive dynamic walking. *International Journal of Robotics Research, 9,* 62–82.

McGeer, T. (1990b). Passive walking with knees. *Proceedings of the IEEE Conference on Robotics and Automation, 2,* 1640–1645.

McGurk, H., and McDonald, J. (1976). Hearing lips and seeing voices. *Nature, 264,* 746–748.

Mead, C. A. (1989). *Analog VLSI and neural systems.* Reading, MA: Addison-Wesley.

Meinhardt, H. (1995). *The algorithmic beauty of sea shells.* Berlin: Springer.

Meyer, J.-A., and Guillot, A. (1991). Simulation of adaptive behavior in animats: Review and prospect. In J.-A. Meyer and S. W. Wilson (Eds.), *From animals to animats: Proceedings of the First International Conference on Simulation of Adaptive Behavior* (pp. 2–14). Cambridge, MA: MIT Press (A Bradford Book).

Miller, G. A. (1956). The magical number seven plus or minus two: Some limits on our capacity for processing information. *Psychological Review, 63,* 81–97.

Miller, G. A., Galanter, E., and Pribram, K. (1960). *Plans and the structure of behavior.* New York: Holt, Rinehart and Winston.

Milner, A. D., and Goodale, M. A. (1995). *The visual brain in action.* Oxford, UK: Oxford University Press.

Minsky, M. (1975). A framework for representing knowledge. In P. Winston (Ed.), *The psychology of computer vision.* New York: McGraw-Hill.

Minsky, M., and Papert, S. (1969). *Perceptrons.* Cambridge, MA: MIT Press.

Mitchell, M. (1997). *An introduction to genetic algorithms.* Cambridge, MA: MIT Press (A Bradford Book).

Montefiore, A., and Noble, D. (1989) (Eds.). *Goals, no goals, and own goals: A debate on goal-directed and intentional behaviour.* London, UK: Unwin Hyman Ltd.

Montello, D. R., and Presson, C. C. (1993). Movement and orientation in surrounding and imaginal spaces. Manuscript in preparation.

Moore, E. F. (1956). Gedanken-experiments on sequential machines. In C. E. Shannon and J. McCarthy (Eds.), *Automata Studies* (pp. 129–153). Princeton, NJ: Princeton University Press.

Moses, Y., Adini, Y. and Ullman, S. (1994). Face recognition: the problem of compensating for illumination changes. *Proceedings of the European Conference on Computer Vision, 286–296.*

Nehmzow, U. and Smithers, T. (1992). Using motor actions for location recognition. In Varela, F. and Bourgine, P. (Eds.) *Toward a practice of autonomous systems.* Cambridge, MA: MIT Press, pp. 96–104.

Neisser, U. (1978). Memory: What are the important questions? In M. M. Gruneberg, P. E. Morris, and R. N. Sykes (Eds.), *Practical aspects of memory.* London: Academic Press.

Neisser, U. (1982). *Memory observed: Remembering in natural contexts.* San Francisco, CA: W. H. Freeman.

Neisser, U. (1988). The ecological approach to perception and memory. *New Trends in Experimental and Clinical Psychiatry, 4, 153–166.*

Neisser, U. (1996). Remembering as doing. *Behavioral and Brain Sciences, 19, 203–204.*

Neisser, U., Boodoo, G., Bouchard, T. J. Jr., Boykin, A. W., Brody, N., Ceci, S. J., Halpern, D. F., Loehlin, J. C., Perloff, R., Sternberg, R. J., and Urbina, S. (1996). Intelligence: Knowns and unknowns. *American Psychologist, 51, 77–101.*

Nelson, J. I. (1995). Binding in the visual system. In M. A. Arbib (Ed.), *Handbook of brain theory and neural networks* (pp. 157–159). Cambridge, MA: MIT Press (A Bradford Book).

Newell, A. (1982). The knowledge level. *Artificial Intelligence, 18, 87–127.*

Newell, A. (1990). *Unified theories of cognition.* Cambridge, MA: Harvard University Press.

Newell, A., and Simon, H. A. (1956). The logic theory machine. *IRE Transactions of Information Theory,* IT-2,3,61–79.

Newell, A., and Simon, H. A. (1963). GPS, a program that simulates human thought. In E. A. Feigenbaum, and J. Feldman (Eds.). *Computers and Thought.* New York: McGraw-Hill, pp. 279–293.

Newell, A., and Simon, H. A. (1972). *Human problem solving.* Englewood Cliffs, NJ: Prentice-Hall.

Newell, A., and Simon, H. A. (1976). Computer science as empirical inquiry: Symbols and search. *Communications of the ACM* (Association for Computing Machinery), *19,* 113–126.

Nicoud, J. D. (1996). Mine clearance: Not only a problem for the military any more. In Y. Bandoin (Ed.) *Proceedings of the 6th International Symposium on Measurement and Control in Robotics,* (ISMCR'96). pp. 6–10. Groat-Bijgaarden, Belgium: Technipress.

Nolfi S. (1996). Adaptation as a more powerful tool than decomposition and integration In: T. Fogarty and G. Venturini (Eds.), *Proceedings of the Workshop on Evolutionary Computing and Machine Learning, 13th International Conference on Machine Learning,* University of Bari, Italy. (available at http://kant.irmkant.rm.cnr.it/ nolfipub.html)

Nolfi, S., and Parisi, D. (1995). Evolving non-trivial behaviors on real robots: An autonomous robot that picks up objects. In M. Gori and E. Soda (Eds.) *Proceedings of the Fourth Congress of the Italian Association for Artificial Intelligence.* Berlin: Springer. pp. 661–669.

Norman, D. A. (1980). Twelve issues for cognitive science. *Cognitive Science, 4, 33–46.*

Norman, D. A. (1982). *Learning and memory.* San Francisco: W. H. Freeman and Company.

Norman, D. A. (1988). *The design of everyday things.* New York: Basic Books.

O'Nuallain, S. (1995). *The search for mind: A new foundation for cognitive science.* Norwood, NJ: Ablex.

Oreskes, N., Shrader-Frechette, K., and Belitz, K. (1994). Verification, validation, and confirmation of numerical models in the earth sciences. *Science, 263,* 641–646.

Penrose, R. (1989). *The emperor's new mind: Concerning computers, minds, and the laws of physics.* Oxford, UK: Oxford University Press.

Petroski, H. (1996). *Invention by design: How engineers get from thought to thing.* Cambridge, MA: Harvard University Press.

Pfeifer, R. (1994). The "Fungus Eater Approach" to emotion: A view from artifical intelligence. *Cognitive Studies, 1,* 42–57 (in Japanese). English version: Technical report NO. IFI-AI-95.04, AI Lab, Computer Science Department, University of Zurich, Switzerland.

Pfeifer, R. (1995). Cognition: Perspectives from autonomous agents. *Robotics and Autonomous Systems, 15,* 47–70.

Pfeifer, R. (1996a). Symbols, patterns, and behavior: Beyond the information processing metaphor. In A. Kent and J. G. Williams (Eds.), *Encyclopaedia of Microcomputers.* New York: Marcel Decker, pp. 253–275.

Pfeifer, R. (1996b). Building "Fungus Eaters": Design principles of autonomous agents. In P. Maes, M. Mataric, J.-A. Meyer, J. Pollack, and S. W. Wilson (Eds.), *From animals to animats: Proceedings of the Fourth International Conference on Simulation of Adaptive Behavior* (pp. 3–12). Cambridge, MA: MIT Press (A Bradford Book).

Pfeifer, R., and Leuzinger-Bohlerber, M. (1986). Cognitive science and psychoanalysis: A case study and some theory. *International Review of Psycho-Analysis, 13,* 221–224.

Pfeifer, R., and Scheier, C. (1997). Sensory-motor coordination: The metaphor and beyond. Practice and future of autonomous agents [Special issue, R. Pfeifer and R. Brooks (Eds.)]. *Robotics and Autonomous Systems, 20,* 157–178.

Pfeifer, R., and Verschure, P. F. M. J. (1992). Distributed adaptive control: A paradigm for designing autonomous agents. In F. J. Varela and P. Bourgine (Eds.), *Toward a practice of autonomous systems: Proceedings of the First European Conference on Artificial Life* (pp. 21–30). Cambridge, MA: MIT Press.

Piaget, J. (1952). *The origins of intelligence in children.* New York: International University Press.

Pinker, S. (1994). *The language instinct: How the mind creates language.* New York: William Morrow.

Poggio, T., and Girosi, F. (1990). Regularization algorithms for learning that are equivalent to multilayer networks. *Science, 247,* 978–982.

Pomerleau, D. A. (1993). *Neural network perception for mobile robot guidance.* Dordrecht, The Netherlands: Kluwer Academic Publishers.

Pratt, G. A., and Williamson, M. M. (1995). Series elastic actuators. In *Proceedings of the IEEE/RSJ International Conference on Intelligent Robots and Systems* (*IROS,* Vol. 1, pp. 399–406). Los Alamitos, CA: IEEE Computer Society Press.

Purves, D., White, L. E., and Riddle, D. R. (1996). Is neural development Darwinian? *Trends in Neuroscience, 19,* 460–464.

Purves, D., White, L. E., and Riddle, D. R. (1997). Reply to Sporns. *Trends in Neuroscience, 21,* 293.

Putnam, H. (1975). Philosophy and our mental life. In H. Putnam (Ed.), *Mind, language and reality: Philosophical papers* (Vol. 2). Cambridge, UK: Cambridge University Press, pp. 48–73.

Pylyshyn, Z. W. (1984). *Computation and cognition: Toward a foundation for cognitive science.* Cambridge, MA: MIT Press.

Pylyshyn, Z. W. (Ed.). (1987). *The robot's dilemma: The frame problem in artificial intelligence.* Norwood, NJ: Ablex.

Quillian, R. (1968). Semantic memory. In M. Minsky (Ed.), *Semantic information processing.* Cambridge, MA: MIT Press, pp. 18–29.

Quinlan, P. (1991). *Connectionism and psychology: A psychological perspective on new connectionist research*. Chicago: University of Chicago Press.

Raphael, B. (1976). *The thinking computer: Mind inside matter*. San Francisco: W. H. Freeman.

Reber, A. S. (1995). *Dictionary of psychology*. London: Penguin Books.

Rechenberg, I. (1973). *Evolutionsstrategie: Optimierung Technischer Systeme nach Prinzipien der Biologischen Evolution [Evolutionary strategies: optimization of technical systems with principles from biological evolution]*. Stuttgart, Germany: Frommann-Holzboog.

Reeke, G. N. Jr., Finkel, L. H., Sporns, O., and Edelman, G. A. (1989). Synthetic neural modeling: A multilevel approach to the analysis of brain complexity. In G. M. Edelman, W. E. Gall, and W. M. Cowan (Eds.), *Signal and sense: Local and global order in perceptual maps*. New York: John Wiley, pp. 282–324.

Reynolds, C. W. (1987). Flocks, herds, and schools: A distributed behavioral model. *Computer Graphics, 21*, 25–34.

Rieke, F., Warlaud, D., de Ruyter van Steveninck, R., and Bialek, W. (1997). *Spikes: Exploiting the neural code*. Cambridge, MA: MIT Press.

Riecken, D. (Ed.). (1994). Intelligent agents [Special issue]. *Communications of the ACM, 7(7)*.

Ritz, R., Gerstner, W., and van Hemmen, J. L. (1994). Associative binding and segregation in a networks of spiking neurons. In E. Domany, J. L. van Hemmen, and K. Schulten (Eds.), *Models of neural networks* (Vol. 2). New York: Springer, pp. 34–48.

Roediger, H. L. (1980). Memory metaphors in cognitive psychology. *Memory and Cognition, 8*, 231–246.

Rosch, E. (1973). On the internal structure of perceptual and semantic categories. In T. E. Moore (Ed.), *Cognitive development and the acquisition of language*. New York: Academic Press, pp. 178–194.

Rosch, E. (1975). Cognitive representations of semantic categories. *Journal of Experimental Psychology: General, 104*, 192–233.

Rosenblatt, F. (1958). The perceptron: A probabilistic model for information storage and organization in the brain. *Psychological Review, 65*, 386–408.

Rosenblueth, A., Wiener, N., and Bigelow, J. (1943). Behavior, purpose, and teleology. *Philosophy of Science, 10*, 18–24.

Rosenfield, I. (1988). *The invention of memory: A new view of the brain*. New York: Basic Books.

Rosenfield, I. (1992). *The strange, familiar, and forgotten: An anatomy of consciousness*. New York: Alfred A. Knopf. (Paperpack edition: New York: Vintage Books, 1993).

Ruff, H. A. (1984). Infants' manipulative exploration of objects: Effects of age and object characteristics. *Developmental Psychology, 20*, 9–20.

Rumelhart, D. E., and McClelland, J. L. (1986). *Parallel distributed processing: Explorations in the microstructure of cognition* (Vol. 1: Foundations). Cambridge, MA: MIT Press (A Bradford Book).

Russell, S. J., and Norvig, P. (1995). *Artificial intelligence: A modern approach*. Upper Saddle River, NJ: Prentice Hall.

Rutkowska, J. C. (1997) "What's value worth? Constraints on unsupervised behaviour acquisition." In: P. Husbands and I. Harvey (eds.), *Proceedings of the Fourth European Conference on Artificial Life*. Cambrdige, Mass.: MIT Press, 45–56.

Sacerdoti, E. D. (1974). Planning in a hierarchy of abstraction spaces. *Artificial Intelligence, 5*, 115–135.

Salomon, R. (1996). Increasing adaptivity through evolution strategies. In P. Maes, M. Mataric, J.-A. Meyer, J. Pollack, and S. W. Wilson (Eds.), *From animals to animats: Proceedings of the Fourth International Conference on Simulation of Adaptive Behavior* (pp. 411–420). Cambridge, MA: MIT Press.

Salovey, P., and Mayer, J. D. (1990). Emotional intelligence. *Imagination, Cognition and Personality, 9*, 185–211.

Schank, R. C., and Abelson, R. P. (1977). *Scripts, plans, goals and understanding: An inquiry into human knowledge structures*. Hillsdale, NJ: Erlbaum.

Scheier, C., and Lambrinos, D. (1996a). Categorization in a real-world agent using haptic exploration and active perception. In P. Maes, M. Mataric, J.-A. Meyer, J. Pollack, and S. W. Wilson (Eds.), *From animals to animats: Proceedings of the Fourth International Conference on Simulation of Adaptive Behavior* (pp. 65–75). Cambridge, MA: MIT Press (A Bradford Book).

Scheier, C., and Lambrinos, D. (1996b). Adaptive classification in autonomous agents. In *Proceedings of the European Meeting on Cybernetics and Systems Research (EMCSR '96)* (pp. 1011–1023). R. Trappl (Ed.) Vienna: Austrian Society for Cybernetic Studies.

Scheier, C., and Pfeifer, R. (1995). Classification as sensory-motor coordination. In F. Moráu, A. Moreno, J. J. Merelo and P. Chacón (Eds.) *Advances in Artificial Life.* Third European Conference on Artificial life. Berlin: Springer. (pp. 656–667).

Scheier, C., and Tschacher, W. (1996). Appropriate algorithms for nonlinear timeseries analysis in psychology. In W. Sulis and A. Combs (Eds.), *Nonlinear dynamics in human behavior* (pp. 27–44). Singapore: World Scientific.

Schöner, G., Dose, M., and Engels, C. (1995). Dynamics of behavior: Theory and applications for autonomous robot architectures. *Robotics and Autonomous Systems, 16,* 213–245.

Schwefel, H.-P. (1977). *Numerische Optimierung von Computer-Modellen mittels der Evolutionsstrategie* [Numerical optimization of computer models with evolutionary strategies]. Basel, Switzerland: Birkhäuser.

Searle, J. R. (1980). Minds, brains, and programs. *Behavioral and Brain Sciences, 3,* 417–424. (Reprinted in J. Haugeland 1981 (Ed.), *Mind design.* Montgomery, VT: Bradford Books.)

Sejnowski, T. J., and Rosenberg, C. R. (1987). Parallel networks that learn to pronounce English text. *Complex Systems, 1,* 145–168.

Shannon, C. E., and Weaver, W. W. (1948). *The mathematical theory of communication.* Urbana: University of Illinois Press.

Simon, H. A. (1969). *The sciences of the artificial* (2nd ed.). Cambridge, MA: MIT Press.

Sims, K. (1994a). Evolving virtual creatures. *Computer Graphics, 28,* 15–34.

Sims, K. (1994b). Evolving 3D morphology and behavior by competition. In R. Brooks and P. Maes (Eds.), *Artificial Life IV Proceedings* (pp. 28–39). Cambridge, MA: MIT Press.

Smith, L. B., and Thelen, E. (Eds.). (1993). *A dynamic systems approach to development: Applications.* Cambridge, MA: MIT Press (A Bradford Book).

Smithers, T. (1994). On why better robots make it harder. In D. Cliff, P. Husbands, J. A. Meyer, and S. W. Wilson (Eds.), *From animals to animats: Proceedings of the Third International Conference on Simulation of Adaptive Behavior* (pp. 64–72). Cambridge, MA: MIT Press (A Bradford Book).

Smithers, T. (1995). On quantitative performance measures of robot behaviour. The Biology and Technology of Intelligent Autonomous Systems, [Special issue, L. Steels (Ed.)]. *Robotics and Autonomous Systems, 15,* 107–135.

Spearman, C. (1904). "General intelligence" objectively determined and measured. *American Journal of Psychology, 15,* 201–293.

Spelke, E. S. (1994). Initial knowledge: Six suggestions. *Cognition, 50,* 431–445.

Sporns, O. (1997). Variation and selection in neural function. *Neuroscience, 20,* 291–293.

Sporns, O., and Edelman, G. M. (1993). Solving Bernstein's problem: A proposal for the development of coordinated movement by selection. *Child Development, 64,* 960–981.

Srinivas, M., and Patnaik, L. M. (1994). Genetic algorithms: A survey. *IEEE Computer, 27,* 17–26.

Steels, L. (1991). Towards a theory of emergent functionality. In J.-A. Meyer and S. W. Wilson (Eds.), *From animals to animats: Proceedings of the First International Conference on Simulation of Adaptive Behavior* (pp. 451–461). Cambridge, MA: MIT Press (A Bradford Book).

Steels, L. (1992). The PDL reference manual. VUB AI Lab, Memo 92-5. Brussels, Belgium.

Steels L. (1997). A selectionist mechanism for autonomous behavior acquisition. Practice and future of autonomous agents [Special issue, R. Pfeifer and R. Brooks (Eds.)]. *Robotics and Autonomous Systems, 20,* 117–132.

Steels, L., and Brooks, R. (Eds.). (1995). *The artificial life route to artificial intelligence: Building embodied, situated agents.* Hillsdale, NJ: Lawrence Erlbaum.

Steinhage, A., and Schöner, G. (1997). Self-calibration based on invariant view recognition: Dynamic approach to navigation. Practice and future of autonomous agents [Special issue, R. Pfeifer and R. Brooks (Eds.)]. *Robotics and Autonomous Agents, 20,* 133–156.

Stone, H. W. (1996). Mars Pathfinder Microrover: A low-cost, low-power spacecraft. In *Proceedings of the 1996 AIAA Forum on Advanced Developments in Space Robotics.* http://robotics.jpl.nasa.gov/tasks/mfex_cns/papers/AIAA96.ps

Suchman, L. A. (1987). *Plans and situated actions: The problem of human-machine communication.* Cambridge, UK: Cambridge University Press.

Suh, N. P. (1990). *The principles of design.* New York: Oxford University Press.

Sutton, R. S., and Barto, A. G. (1981). Toward a modern theory of adaptive networks: Expectation and prediction. *Psychological Review, 88,* 135–170.

Sutton, R., and Barto, A. (1998). *Reinforcement learning.* Cambridge, MA: MIT Press.

Taber, C. S. and Timpone, R. J. (1996). *Computational Modeling.* Sage Thousand Oaks, CA: Sage University Papers.

te Boekhorst, I. J. A., and Hogeweg, P. (1994). Effects of tree size on travel band formation in orangutans: Data analysis suggested by model study. In R. Brooks and P. Maes (Eds.), *Artificial Life IV Proceedings* (pp. 119–129). Cambridge, MA: MIT Press.

Terzopoulos, D., Tu, X., and Grzeszczuk, R. (1994). Artificial fishes: Autonomous locomotion, perception, behavior, and learning in a simulated physical world. *Artificial Life, 1,* 327–351.

Tesauro, G. J. (1991). *Practical issues in temporal difference learning.* RC 17223(76307). IBM T. J. Watson Research Center, Yorktown Heights, NY.

Thelen, E., and Smith, L. (1994). *A dynamic systems approach to the development of cognition and action.* Cambridge, MA: MIT Press, (A Bradford Book).

Thompson, A. (1995). Evolving electronic robot controllers that exploit hardware resources, In F. Moran, A. Moreno, J. J. Merelo, and P. Chacon (Eds.), *Advances in artificial life: Proceedings of the Third International Conference on Artificial Life* (pp. 640–656). Berlin: Springer.

Thompson, A. (1996). Silicon evolution. In J. R. Koza et al., (Eds.), *Genetic Programming 1996: Proceedings of the First Annual Conference (GP96)* (pp. 444–452). Cambridge, MA: MIT Press.

Thompson, A. (1997). Artificial Evolution in the Physical World. In T. Gomi (Ed.), *Evolutionary robotics: From intelligent robots to artificial life (ER'97)* (pp. 101–125). AAI Books. Tokyo.

Thorpe, S. J. and Imbert, M. (1989). Biological constraints on connectionist modelling. In R. Pfeifer, Z. Schreter, F. Fogelman-Soulié, and L. Steels (Eds.) *Connectionism in Perspective,* Amsterdam: North-Holland, 63–92.

Tinbergen, N. (1951). *The study of instinct.* Clarendon Press.

Tinbergen, N. (1963). On aims and methods of ethology. *Zeitschrift Tierpsychologie, 20,* 410–433.

Tistarelli, M. (1995). Active space-variant object recognition. *Image and Vision Computing, 13,* 215–226.

Toda, M. (1982). *Man, robot, and society.* The Hague, The Netherlands: Nijhoff.

Tononi, G., Sporns, O., and Edelman, G. M. (1992). Reentry and the problem of integrating multiple cortical areas: Simulation of dynamic integration in the visual system. *Cerebral Cortex, 2,* 310–335.

Tononi, G., Sporns, O., and Edelman, G. M. (1994). A measure for brain complexity: Relating functional segregation and integration in the nervous system. *Proceedings of the National Academy of Science, (USA), 91,* 5033–5037.

Tononi, G., Sporns, O., and Edelman, G. M. (1996). A complexity measure for selective matching of signals by the brain. *Proceedings of the National Academy of Science, (USA), 93,* 3422–3427.

Turing, A. M. (1936). On computable numbers, with an application to the *Entscheidungsproblem. Proceedings of the London Mathematical Society, Series 2, 42,* 230–265, and *43,* 544–546.

Turing, A. M. (1950). Computing machinery and intelligence. *Mind, 59,* 433–460. (Reprinted in E. A. Feigenbaum and J. Feldman (Eds.), *Computers and thought.* New York: McGraw-Hill, 1963.)

Turkle, S. (1995). *Life on the Screen: Identity in the Age of the Internet.* Simon and Schuster.

Turvey, M. T., and Carello, C. (1986). The ecological approach to perceiving-acting: A pictorial essay. *Acta Psychologica, 63,* 133–155.

Tyrell, T. (1993). *Computational mechanisms for action selection.* Unpublished doctoral dissertation, University of Edinburgh, Scotland.

Uchibe, E., Asada, M., Noda, S., Takahashi, Y., and Hosoda, K. (1996). Vision-based reinforcement learning for RoboCup: Towards real robot competition. *Proceedings of IROS '96: Workshop on RoboCup* (pp. 16–24).

Ullman, S. (1996). *High-level vision. Object recognition and visual cognition.* Cambridge, MA: MIT Press.

UniMagazin. (1995). *Intelligence.* Zurich, Switzerland: University of Zurich Press.

van Gelder, T. (1998). The dynamical hypothesis in cognitive science. *Behavioral and Brain Sciences, 21,* 615–624.

Varela, F. J., Thompson, E., and Rosch, E. (1991). *The embodied mind: Cognitive science and human experience.* Cambridge, MA: MIT Press.

Vera, A., and Simon, H. A. (1993). Situation action: A symbolic interpretation. *Cognitive Science, 17,* 7–48.

Verschure, P. F. M. J. (1992). Taking connectionism seriously: The vague promise of sub-symbolism and an alternative. In *Proceedings of the Fourteenth Annual Conference of The Cognitive Science Society.* Hillsdate, N.J: Glbaum, 653–658.

Verschure, P. F. M. J., and Coolen, A. (1991). Adaptive fields: Distributed representations of classically conditioned associations. *Network, 2,* 189–206.

Verschure, P. F. M. J., Kröse, B. J. A., and Pfeifer, R. (1992). Distributed adaptive control: The self-organization of structured behavior. *Robotics and Autonomous Systems, 9,* 181–196.

Verschure, P. F. M. J., Wray, J., Sporns, O., Tononi, G., and Edelman G. M. (1995). Multi-level analysis of classical conditioning in a behaving real world artifact, *Robotics and Autonomous Systems, 16,* 247–265.

Watanabe, Y., Ishiguro, A., Shirai, Y., and Uchikawa, Y. (1998). Emergent construction of behavior-arbitration mechanism based on the immune system. In *Proceedings of the 1998 IEEE World Congress on Computational Intelligence,* (pp. 481–486). Los Alamitos, CA: IEEE Computer Society Press.

Watkins, C. J. (1989). *Learning from delayed rewards.* Unpublished doctoral dissertation, King's College, Cambridge University, Cambridge, UK.

Webb, B. (1993). *Perception in real and artificial insects: A robotic investigation of cricket phonotaxis.* Unpublished doctoral dissertation, University of Edinburgh, Scotland.

Webb, B. (1994). Robotic experiments in cricket phonotaxis. In D. Cliff, P. Husbands, J.-A. Meyer, and S. W. Wilson (Eds.), *From animals to animats: Proceedings of the Third International Conference on Simulation of Adaptive Behavior.* (pp. 45–54). Cambridge, MA: MIT Press (A Bradford Book).

Wechsler, H. (1990). *Computational vision.* San Diego, CA: Academic Press.

Wehner, R. (1994). The polarization-vision project: Championing organismic biology. In K. Schildberger and N. Elsner (Eds.). *Neural basis of behavioural adaptations* (pp. 103–143). Stuttgart: Gustav Fischer Verlag.

Wehner, R., Michel, B., and Antonsen, P. (1996). Visual navigation in insects: Coupling of egocentric and geocentric information. *Journal of Experimental Biology, 199,* 129–140.

Wexler, M. (1997). Is rotation of visual mental images a motor act? In K. Donner (Ed.). *Proceedings of the 20th European Conference on Visual Perception ECUP'97.* London, UK: Pion Ltd.

Whitehead, S. D., Karlsson, J., and Tenenberg, J. (1993). Learning multiple goal behavior via task decomposition and dynamic policy merging. In J. H. Connell and S. Mahadevan (Eds.), *Robot learning* (pp. 45–78). Boston: Kluwer Academic Publishers.

Williamson, M. M. (1996). Postural primitives in a robot arm. In P. Maes, M. Mataric, J.-A. Meyer, J. Pollack, and S. W. Wilson (Eds.), *From animals to animats: Proceedings of the Fourth International Conference on Simulation of Adaptive Behavior* (pp. 65–75). Cambridge, MA: MIT Press (A Bradford Book).

Wilson, E. O. (1975). *Sociobiology* (Abridged ed.). Cambridge, MA: The Belknap Press of Harvard University Press.

Wilson, S. W. (1991). The animat path to AI. In J.-A. Meyer and S. W. Wilson (Eds.), *From animals to animats: Proceedings of the First International Conference on Simulation of Adaptive Behavior* (pp. 15–21). Cambridge, MA: MIT Press (A Bradford Book).

Winograd, T., and Flores, F. (1986). *Understanding computers and cognition.* Reading, MA: Addison-Wesley.

Wolfe, W. J., and Chun, W. H. (1992). Robot architectures and design paradigms. In M. A., W. J. Wolfe, and W. H. Chun (Eds.), *Proceedings of SPIE: Mobile Robots* (pp. 18–20). VII, Vol 1831.

Wynn, K. (1992). Addition and subtraction by human infants. *Nature, 358,* 749–750.

Author Index

Subject Index

Page numbers in italics indicate pages with figures or tables.